HISTORY

OF THE

STATE OF NEW YORK.

BY

JOHN ROMEYN BRODHEAD.

SECOND VOLUME.

FIRST EDITION.

NEW YORK:
HARPER & BROTHERS, PUBLISHERS,
FRANKLIN SQUARE.
1871.

PREFACE

TO VOLUME SECOND.

When this volume was begun, it was my purpose to bring its contents down to the accession of Queen Anne of England, and the chapters embracing the years between 1691 and 1702 are ready for the printer. But, by the affluence of original authorities, and the temptation to use them, perhaps, too liberally, this book, in spite of laborious condensation, may have grown unfashionably large; and these chapters must be reserved for another volume—should the public manifest a desire to learn more of early New York, down to the inauguration of Washington.

Descended from an English officer who helped his king to conquer Dutch New Netherland, as well as from a colonial Hollander who stood up manfully for his Republican Fatherland, I feel no partiality in telling the history of the greatest European plantation in America. My object has been to exhibit the truth honestly and minutely. In doing this, I have long and carefully studied the received authorities relating to the colonial annals of our country, and also all that I have seen, recently brought to light. If I have missed my aim, let my failure be imputed to incapacity rather than to lack of industry or candor.

John Romeyn Brodhead.

New York, February, 1871.

CONTENTS.

CHAPTER I.

1664.

CHAPTER II.

1664–1665.

CHAPTER III.

1666–1668.

CHAPTER IV.

1668–1673.

CHAPTER V.

1673–1674.

CHAPTER VI.

1674–1678.

CHAPTER VII.

1678–1683.

CHAPTER VIII.

1683–1685.

CHAPTER IX.

1685–1688.

CHAPTER X.

1688–1689.

CHAPTER XI.

1688–1689.

CHAPTER XII.

1689-1691.

APPENDIX.

HISTORY

OF THE

STATE OF NEW YORK.

CHAPTER I.

1664.

THE year sixteen hundred and sixty-four found the strongest powers of Europe on the brink of a fierce war. That war determined the fate of New York.

CHAP. I. 1664. War at hand.

In France, Louis the Fourteenth was pushing up to its pinnacle the idea of absolute monarchy. The king was himself the state. Laborious and untiring, Louis had the rare faculty of choosing well his subordinates. Colbert became his minister of finance; Lionne, of foreign affairs; Louvois, of war. Condé, Luxembourg, and Turenne, his victorious generals, earned him bloody renown. The French king was a devout son of the Roman Church. But, above all other characteristics, he had the instinct of grandeur and the thirst for glory. "There is stuff enough in him," said Mazarin, "to make four kings and an honest man." If Louis was not the greatest sovereign, he was "the best actor of majesty that ever filled a throne." More than any other monarch, he had "the marvellous art of reigning." Supreme in France, he wished to sway all Europe, and to that end he directed his subtile diplomacy. He soon established a control over the half French king of England. With the United Netherlands he made a treaty of alliance. But the system of bribery by which Louis succeeded almost every where else, failed when it was used against the chief servants of the Dutch Republic.

France and Louis the Fourteenth.

After the death of the second William of Orange, in

CHAP. I. 1664.

November, 1650, the dignity of stadtholder had remained in abeyance, and the Dutch executive authority had been administered by statesmen whose political opinions were opposed to those of the deceased prince. One of these opinions was that the almost royal power which the stadtholderate gave to the house of Orange was dangerous to the republic. A few days after the death of William, his widow, who was the daughter of Charles the First of England, gave birth to a son, whom she desired to name Charles, but who was baptized William Henry, in the great Dutch Church at the Hague. He succeeded his father as William, the Third Prince of Orange. This event roused the apprehensions of the Louvestein, or aristocratic party, at the head of which was the young John De Witt, a disciple of Descartes, already conspicuous for his ability, firmness, and integrity. So highly were his talents and prudence esteemed, that he was frequently called "The wisdom of Holland." His mind was well compared with that of Richelieu. In 1653, De Witt was made Grand Pensionary of Holland, and thenceforward he became the real chief magistrate of the republic. To gratify Cromwell, he procured an act of the States excluding the Prince of Orange from the office of stadtholder. Upon the restoration of Charles the Second to the throne of England, this act, so insulting to his nephew, was repealed. De Witt, nevertheless, remained at the head of Dutch affairs, which he directed with consummate skill and nearly regal authority. His country had reached the zenith of its prosperity and glory. Domestic trade and manufactures maintained a growing population in content and abundance; while foreign commerce, searching every shore of the globe, poured continual riches into the warehouses of Holland and Zealand. An alliance had secured the friendship of France. A similar treaty promised peace with England; and Charles, solemnly professing gratitude and affection toward the Dutch people, confided to the States of Holland the guardianship of his infant nephew, William of Orange. With the king apparently so well disposed, it seemed as if enduring friendship was established between the two great Protestant nations of Europe—continental Holland and insular England.

The Dutch Republic and William the Third.

John De Witt.

CHAP. I.

1664.

It was an interesting circumstance that the royal family of Great Britain was connected with the King of France and the Prince of Orange in a nearly equal degree. Toward Louis and William, Royalist Englishmen felt much more kindly than did the men of the Commonwealth. But Englishmen generally hated both Frenchmen and Hollanders with strong national antipathies. The court poets praised the frivolous French, whose fashions were imitated at Whitehall, while they lampooned the honester Dutch, whose national virtues were a reproach to their king and to themselves. Even the most accomplished English scholars were superciliously ignorant of the literature of Holland, then so rich in varied learning. Yet, with all their affectation of contempt, the English were intensely jealous of the Dutch, whose enterprise, outrunning their own, had established a profitable commerce in Asia and Africa. The Navigation Act of the Commonwealth, devised to cripple the foreign trade of the Netherlands, was made more vindictive just after the Restoration. Dryden but uttered the envy of his countrymen when he wrote of the Hollanders—

England and her national antipathies.

"As Cato fruits of Afric did display,
Let us before our eyes their Indies lay;
All loyal English will like him conclude,
Let Cæsar live, and Carthage be subdued."*

Nevertheless, there was no cause of war between England and Holland. The British sovereign ostentatiously professed his own good feeling toward the nation which he allowed his courtiers to abuse. But there was no faith in the frivolous King of England. Of all her monarchs, Charles the Second was the meanest and most insincere. If Louis of France was the best actor of majesty, Charles of England was the greatest dissembler that ever sat on a throne. He did not lack talent, nor education, nor the training of adversity, but he did lack conscience, a sense of shame, and an honest heart. His early years had been passed in his father's palace, whence he had been driven into strange lands. During the period of the Commonwealth he had wandered among princes and peoples, enduring vicissitudes of fortune which few royal personages

Charles the Second.

* Satire on the Dutch, 1662.

CHAP. I.

1664.

ever had the advantage of enjoying, but profiting nothing from an experience which should have made him one of the greatest of kings. At the age of thirty years he was recalled to England and crowned its sovereign. But Charles brought back with him from his exile no proper sense of his kingly office. Like a prodigal heir, who possessed an estate after long nursing by a prudent guardian, he came home to Whitehall, eager to expend a splendid inheritance. His selfish heart, and easy temper, and glib tongue enabled him calmly to put by every embarrassing question of public concern, while he submitted himself to the most degrading influences. It followed that the reign of Charles the Second was the most execrable of any in the annals of England.

James, Duke of York.

Charles had a brother, three years younger than himself, James, Duke of York and Albany. As the king had no legitimate offspring, the duke was heir presumptive to the British throne. Although married to a daughter of his brother's chief minister, James was a cold-blooded libertine; and, while he professed to be a Protestant, was gradually becoming a Roman Catholic. His temper was harsh and obstinate, his understanding slow, and his views narrow; but his word was sacred. He loved the details of business as much as the king detested them, and with all the method of a conscientious clerk, he seemed to work for work's sake. To aid in supporting his dignity, the revenues of the post-office, estimated at about twenty thousand pounds a year, were settled on the duke by an obsequious Parliament. One of the first acts of the king was to appoint his brother lord high admiral of England. In executing the duties of this office, which involved all the administration of the navy, James was assisted by a Board of Admiralty, of which John Lord Berkeley, of Stratton, and Admiral Sir William Penn, were commissioners, Sir George Carteret treasurer, and Samuel Pepys clerk. The duke's own private affairs were managed by three commissioners, Sir William Coventry, who also acted as his secretary, Henry Brouncker, and Thomas Povey, who was likewise his treasurer and receiver general.

The duke's commissioners.

There was at this time, properly speaking, no ministry to conduct the public affairs of England. The privy coun-

CHAP. I.

1664.

cil were the nominal advisers of the sovereign. Each department of the government was directed by a counselor responsible for his own acts, but not for those of his associates, as is the modern British cabinet minister. The most important, and by far the most able of the king's servants, was the lord chancellor, Edward Hyde, Earl of Clarendon, and father-in-law of the Duke of York. The secretaries of state were Sir William Morrice and Sir Henry Bennet, afterward Earl of Arlington. Sir Anthony Ashley Cooper, Lord Ashley, and afterward Earl of Shaftesbury, was president of the council, and Thomas, Earl of Southampton, lord high treasurer. These five chief ministers were collectively called "The Cabal," or cabinet. The affairs of the colonies and foreign plantations of England were managed by a council appointed by the king, consisting of the chief officers of state and others, among whom were Lord Say and Sele, John Lord Berkeley, Sir George Carteret, Denzil Hollis, Robert Boyle, Sir William Coventry, and the poet, Edmund Waller. They were specially instructed to acquaint themselves with the condition of each colony, correspond with the governors, cause the Act of Navigation to be strictly executed, provide for the settlement and maintenance of "learned and orthodox ministers," and endeavor to bring the several colonies into more certain uniformity of government, and render "those dominions useful to England, and England helpful to them."*

Ministers of Charles the Second.

The English "Cabal."

Plantation council.

Of all the servants of Charles the Second, the one whose influence was at this moment most pernicious was Sir George Downing, his envoy to the United Provinces. Downing was a nephew of the elder John Winthrop, and was one of the earliest, ablest, and basest graduates of Harvard College in Massachusetts. He was sent by Cromwell ambassador to Holland, where he insulted his exiled king; but as he was "capable of managing a bad design," he was forgiven and taken into the favor of Charles at the Restoration. Those who knew Downing best described him as "a crafty, fawning man," a "perfidious rogue," a "most ungrateful villain," and "a false man who betrayed

Downing.

* Pepys's Diary (Bohn's ed.), ii., 312; iii., 167, 328, 331; Letters of D'Estrades, ii., 487; Rapin, ii., 635; Lingard, xii., 266; Macaulay, i., 211, 212, 273; iv., 435; New York Colonial Documents, iii., 32–36; Sainsbury's Calendar of State Papers, i., 492, 493, 494; *ante*, vol. i., p. 686.

CHAP. I. 1664. his trust." The renegade certainly seems to have merited his damaging portrait. "If we may believe history, he was a scoundrel." He was "keen, bold, subtile, active, and observant, but imperious and unscrupulous; naturally preferring menace to persuasion; reckless of the means employed and the risk incurred in the pursuit of a proposed object; disliking and distrusting De Witt and the Dutch, and forearmed with a fierce determination not to be foiled or overreached."*

Downing's evil influence.

Downing lost no opportunity to inflame English jealousy of the Hollanders. His correspondence with Lord Chancellor Clarendon, who seems to have as much to do with the foreign department as the secretaries Morrice and Bennet themselves, exhibits a constant desire to provoke the king into a war with the United Provinces. Pretexts were not wanting. The Dutch East and West India Companies were charged with colonial aggressions. Charles, however, disliked hostilities, although he hated De Witt, whom he considered the chief obstacle to the advancement of his nephew, William of Orange. The Duke of York, on the other hand, absolutely detested the Zealanders, who had punished, less promptly than he wished, the authors of some libels against himself. Besides, said Clarendon, "having been, even from his childhood, in the command of armies, and in his nature inclined to the most difficult and dangerous enterprises, he was already weary of having so little to do, and too impatiently longed for any war in which he knew he could not but have the chief command." Moreover, James was the governor of the new Royal African Company, which, besides selling their negro slaves "at the Barbados, and other the king's plantations, at their own prices," imported into England from the coast of Guinea "such store of gold that administered the first occasion for the coinage of those pieces which from thence had the denomination of *guineas*." The Dutch West India Company were accused of injuring the duke's African interests; but

English negro slaves.

Origin of "guineas."

* Hutchinson's Massachusetts, i., 111, 510; Savage's Winthrop, ii., 240-243; Mass. Hist. Soc. Coll., xxxvi., 536-544; Palfrey's New England, ii., 431; John Adams's Works, x., 329; Pepys, i., 264, 265; Evelyn, ii., 8; Burnet, i., 798; Lister's Life of Clarendon, ii., 231; D'Estrade's Letters, ii., 363, 364; N. Y. Col. Doc., ii., 416-418 note; *ante*, vol. i., p. 700. There is a curious narrative of an interview between Charles the Second and Downing at the Hague, while the latter was Cromwell's ambassador, in the Antiquarian Repertory, and in the Universal Magazine for November, 1779, vol. lxv., p. 245.

even Downing could not make out a fair case against them. Nevertheless, Sir Robert Holmes was secretly dispatched with a squadron to the coast of Guinea, where he seized the Dutch fort of Cabo Corso, and committed other acts of aggression, which Lord Clarendon afterward admitted were "without any shadow of justice."*

1664. February.

Another motive influenced the mind of James, and eventually governed the action of Charles. This arose out of the condition of affairs in North America. There, for nearly half a century, England, France, and Holland had each, with various success, endeavored to appropriate territory and plant and rear dependent colonies. France, the pioneer, had first pushed her adventurous way through the valley of the Saint Lawrence, and had set up the emblem of her national faith beside the banner of her king among the savage tribes which inhabited its borders. Thus arose her dominion over New France, or Canada and Acadia. Farther south, England had clung to the sea-coast, the clear waters of which were alive with the finest fish, and where commodious harbors invited her emigrants to linger near those crystal waves which could roll unbroken to Land's End. Yet England had not explored nor occupied the whole of that more southern coast. Midway between Virginia and New England—in a region, the most of which no European eye had seen before—colonists from Holland, following the track of the Half Moon of Amsterdam, planted themselves, without question, among the native Americans, from whom they bought the soil, and thus added a NEW NETHERLAND to the Dutch Republic.

European colonies in North America.

Canada.

Virginia and New England.

New Netherland.

The progress of the various enterprises by which these several territories were first colonized has already been minutely traced. Each has its own peculiar history, eventful, romantic, and instructive. Of none of them were the motives of the projectors or the views of the promoters exactly alike. Canada was peopled by Europeans, speaking the French tongue, and professing the Roman faith. New

* Pepys, ii., 68, 128; Clarendon's Life, ii., 232–234; Lister's Clarendon, ii., 241, 251, 258–262; iii., 288, 290, 301, 302, 347; Basnage, i., 711; Aitzema, iv., 579; D'Estrades, ii, 364, 435; Lingard, xii., 165–168; Rapin, ii., 636; Davies's Holland, iii., 19, 20, 25; Anderson's Colonial Church, ii., 279, 280; Cobbett's Parliamentary History, iv., 292, 293; *ante*, vol. i., p. 735. Anderson, in his Origin of Commerce, ii., 473, 526, seems to think that guineas were first coined in 1673. But Pepys, ii., 483; iv., 26, alludes to them, in 1666 and 1668, as already at a premium in London.

CHAP. I. 1664. Motives of colonization.

Netherland was colonized by Protestant emigrants from a fatherland which had conquered in the most glorious strife for civil and religious liberty that the world has ever witnessed. Virginia was occupied by loyal Englishmen who admired the hierarchy; New England chiefly by Puritans who abhorred prelacy; Maryland by larger-minded Roman Catholics. But all these were Britons, who spoke the tongue of Shakspeare and Milton; who, much as they differed among themselves respecting creeds or fashions, were the subjects of one common sovereign; and who, arrogant and exclusive by nature, looked upon other races as their inferiors, and willingly combined against them as national foes. Their hereditary hatred of foreigners accompanied the English emigrants across the Atlantic, and even burned more brightly in some parts of the wilderness. There was a constant tendency on their part, and especially among the New England Puritans, to quarrel with and overbear both their neighbors, the Roman Catholic French of Canada, and the Protestant Dutch of New Netherland. This tendency had already resulted in the conquest of Acadia, or Nova Scotia, from the French, by order of Cromwell, in 1654. That acquisition the Protector declined to restore, and made it a British province. His design to reduce the Dutch possessions, which were the more coveted because they were so advantageously situated, was abandoned in his treaty with De Witt, by which England virtually conceded New Netherland to Holland.*

English insolence.

Cromwell's recognition of New Netherland.

The Dutch province was indeed the most admirably situated region in North America. Its original limits included all the Atlantic coast between Cape Henlopen and Montauk Point, and all the inland territory bounded by the Connecticut Valley on the east, the Saint Lawrence and Lake Ontario on the north, and the affluents of the Ohio, the Susquehanna, and the Delaware on the west and south. Within those bounds is the only spot on all the continent whence issue divergent streams which find their outlets in the Gulf of Saint Lawrence, the Atlantic Ocean, and the Gulf of Mexico. Diagonally across its surface runs a

Admirable situation of New Netherland.

* Charlevoix, ii., 199–204; Chalmers's Political Annals, i., 187; Pepys, iii., 126, 344; Williamson's Maine, i., 361; Palfrey's New England, ii., 372; Proud, i., 281; Grahame (ed. 1848), i., 406; Smith, i., 387; *ante*, vol. i., p. 586.

CHAP. I.

1664.

Its physical characteristics.

chain of the Alleghanies, through which, in two remarkable chasms, the waters of the Delaware and the Hudson flow southward to the sea. At the head of its tides, the Hudson, which its explorers appropriately named "The Great River of the Mountains," receives the current of the Mohawk rushing in from the west. Through the valleys of these rivers, and across the neighboring lakes, the savage natives of the country tracked those pathways of travel and commerce which civilized science only adopted and improved. Along their banks grew up flourishing villages, all contributing to the prosperity of the chief town, which, with unerring judgment, had been planted on the ocean-washed island of Manhattan. In addition to these superb geographical peculiarities, every variety of soil, abundant mineral wealth, nature teeming with animal and vegetable life, and a climate as healthful as it is delicious, made New Netherland the most alluring of all the European colonies in America. From the first, it was always the chosen seat of empire.*

Influence of its Dutch founders.

It was an admirable decree of Providence which ordained that this magnificent region should first be occupied by the Batavian race. If originally as homogeneous as the English, that race had certainly become less selfish and exclusive. The well-considered policy of Holland attracted to her shores many of whom their own lands were not worthy. This magnanimity was rewarded by almost unexampled national prosperity. After achieving their own independence and establishing a republic on the basis of religious toleration, the Dutch colonized the American province which they had discovered, and at the same time invited strangers of all races to come and find homes along with themselves in its temperate and attractive territory. The Batavian emigrants brought with them the liberal maxims of their fatherland. Soon, eighteen different languages were spoken in New Amsterdam.† Thus, by degrees, grew up the germ of a mighty cosmopolitan state. In spite of the stunting mismanagement of the West India Company, to which its government had been unwisely intrusted, New Netherland gave early promise of coming

* Lecture on the "Topography and History of New York," by Governor Horatio Seymour, Utica, 1856; also Colden, in Col. Doc., vi., 122; Doc. Hist., iv., 112.

† *Ante*, vol. i., p. 374.

CHAP. I. 1664.

grandeur. The fatherland scarcely appreciated the trans-Atlantic dominion which its emigrants had founded. But the growing greatness of that dominion, which had long excited the jealousy of its New England neighbors, at length moved both the pride and the cupidity of the English court to seize it as a royal prize.

To estimate properly the course which Charles the Second now pursued, we must consider the irreconcilable views of title to American territory which the English and the Dutch severally maintained. They may be stated thus: As Columbus had discovered the New World, which should have borne his name, in the service of Spain, the Pope granted it to the Spanish sovereigns. A few years afterward the Cabots, under commissions of Henry the Seventh of England, discovered Newfoundland, and sailed at a distance along the North American continent as far south as the latitude of Gibraltar. By virtue of these discoveries, the English sovereigns claimed dominion over all that part of North America along the coast of which the Cabots had sailed. But, as the previous sweeping title of Spain was in the way of the English claim, Queen Elizabeth, in 1580, announced the principle that "prescription without possession is of no avail;" or, in other words, that actual occupation must follow discovery in order to confer a valid right. Accordingly, England did not question the title of France to Canada and Acadia. But, as the discoveries of Verazzano and of Gomez, farther to the south, did not lead to French or Spanish colonization, James the First granted a patent in 1606, under which the English asserted an exclusive right to colonize all the Atlantic coast between Cape Fear and Acadia not "actually possessed by any Christian prince or people." Under this patent no English mariner had searched the shore between Buzzard's Bay and the Chesapeake, when Henry Hudson, in 1609, in the service of the Dutch East India Company, explored "the great River of the Mountains." This gave the Hollanders an unquestionable title by discovery, which they soon fortified by farther visitation and actual occupation. In 1614, the States General granted a trading charter which recognized "New Netherland" as a Dutch territory. Six years afterward, James the First granted, in 1620, a second patent for "New

The territorial question in North America.

England in America," which included all the region between the fortieth and the forty-eighth degrees of latitude, and from the Atlantic to the Pacific. But his patent expressly provided that no territory was intended to be granted which was "actually possessed or inhabited by any other Christian prince or estate." This proviso clearly excepted New France and New Netherland. Nevertheless, from the time of the landing of the first Puritan emigrants on new Plymouth beach, the English pertinaciously insisted on styling the Dutch occupants of New Netherland "intruders" into New England. With inconsistent logic but characteristic assurance, they maintained their own title under the patent of James, while they denied that of the Hollanders, which was recognized in its proviso. This they continued to do, although the House of Commons in 1621 confirmed Queen Elizabeth's doctrine, and insisted that "occupancy confers a good title by the law of nations and nature." In 1635, the grantees of the New England patent conveyed to the Earl of Stirling the territory of Pemaquid, between the Saint Croix and the Kennebeck in Maine, and the island of Matowack, or Long Island. The Dutch, however, utterly denied the English claim to any part of Long Island, and expelled Lord Stirling's agents. At length Peter Stuyvesant, the director of New Netherland, by a treaty made at Hartford in 1650, surrendered to the English all the territory south of Oyster Bay on Long Island, and east of Greenwich on the continent. This treaty was ratified by the States General in 1656, but no reciprocal action was taken by the British government. Cromwell, however, after directing an expedition to take New Netherland, recognized the Dutch title by the treaty of 1654; and no demonstration was afterward made against what New England men pertly considered "a thorn in the side."*

Canada and New Netherland not in the New England Patent.

Conflicting Dutch and English claims.

Thus stood the question when Charles the Second was restored to the throne. The antipathy of the Puritan colonists of New England against their Dutch neighbors in New Netherland, which to some extent seems to have moved the

* *Ante*, vol. i., pages 4, 11, 36, 63, 64, 96, 139, 250, 262, 519, 582, 583, 586, 621, 625, 643, 653, 685; Thurloe's State Papers, i., 564, 721, 722; ii., 419; Mass. H. S. Coll., xxxii., 230–232; Sainsbury's Calendar, i., 204; Chalmers's Political Annals, i., 6, 82, 83; Kennett's England, ii., 480; Parliam. Debates, i., 250, 251; Smith, i., 387; Proud, i., 281; Palfrey, ii., 371, 372. Smith, i., 7, errs in attributing to Richard Cromwell the instructions given by Oliver in February, 1654; and Grahame, i., 409, follows Smith; see *ante*, vol. i., p. 583.

CHAP. I. 1664. Policy of Charles the Second. Protector, had no similar influence on the king. Charles had no sympathy with the likes or the dislikes of his New England subjects. His restoration had been a sore disappointment to them. They had received the tidings with "scrupulous incredulity." They had acknowledged him as king with a very grim austerity. Constant complaints were preferred against them at Whitehall. In the summer of 1661, Henry, the fourth Earl of Stirling, complained to the king of the "intrusion" of the Dutch upon Long Island, and petitioned that they might be subdued or expelled. Lord Stirling's petition was referred to the Council of Plantations, at the head of which was Clarendon. But before any action was taken, the king granted to John Winthrop a charter for Connecticut, which appeared to cover a large part of New Netherland, together with "the islands thereunto adjoining." The charter, however, was violently opposed; and it finally passed the great seal in April, 1662, with the understanding that the king would "send Commissioners into those parts, who upon the place should settle all differences and pretences upon the bounds of each colony." In the following September, Clarendon declared in the Plantation Committee that the king would dispatch commissioners, and the Duke of York was requested "to consider of the choice of fit men." Charles himself, in April, 1663, announced to the Privy Council that he intended to send commissioners speedily to New England, "to see how the charter is maintained on their part, and to reconcile the differences at present among them."*

The English Navigation Act. There was another subject which was now pressed upon the king's attention. The Navigation Act of 1660 had been openly disregarded or clandestinely evaded in the British American plantations. One of the chief obstacles to its execution was charged to be the existence of the Dutch province. The trade carried on between New Netherland and New England on the one side, and Maryland and Virginia on the other, was alleged to be "very much to the prejudice of England, and to the loss of his majesty, in re-

* Chalmers's Pol. Ann., i., 249, 250, 253, 256, 257, 293, 386, 432; Col. Doc., ii., 389; iii., 32, 42, 43, 55; vii., 431; Mass. H. S. Coll., xxxii., 284; Duer's Life of Stirling, 31; Trumbull's Connecticut, i., 523; Col. Rec. Conn., i., 581; ii., 3–11; Palfrey, ii., 540–545, 574, 575; *ante*, vol. i., p. 189, 702, 720; N. Y. H. S. Coll. (1869), 1–57.

CHAP. I.

1664.

spect to customs, many thousand pounds yearly." Lord Baltimore, the Proprietary of Maryland, promised to "do his best to prevent" this trade; and Sir William Berkeley, the royal governor of Virginia, was ordered to enforce the law. Still, the intercolonial traffic was continued. Parliament accordingly enacted a new law in 1663, which prohibited the importation of European commodities into the English plantations, except in English vessels from England. In June of the same year, the Privy Council ordered all the American governors to enforce this act, which the king was determined to have "very strictly observed, in regard it much concerneth the trade of this kingdom." At last, in December, 1663, the farmers of the customs, who were paying the king nearly four hundred thousand pounds a year for their monopoly, demanded redress for the "great abuses committed and done as well by the inhabitants and planters on, as by the masters, mariners, and traders to, Virginia, New England, Maryland, Long Island, etc., who, under pretence of furnishing some of those plantations and other his majesty's dominions, do both, by land and water, carry and convey great quantities of tobacco to the Dutch, whose plantations are contiguous, the custom whereof would amount to ten thousand pounds per annum or upward, thereby eluding the late Act of Navigation and defrauding his majesty." This brought the question to a crisis. The Navigation Law, meant to cripple the commerce of the Dutch and foster that of the English, must be maintained. It could be enforced, and it was enforced in England. It was evaded, and it could not be enforced in America as long as New Netherland existed as a Dutch plantation. New Netherland, therefore, must no longer exist.*

New navigation law.

This convenient and characteristic logic was exactly adapted to the situation of Charles the Second. The readiest way to sustain it was to insist that New Netherland was "the true and undoubted inheritance of his majesty," and to subject it accordingly to English rule. It so happened that three persons had just before this time come

England resolves to seize New Netherland.

* D'Estrades, ii., 312; Chalmers's Pol. Ann., i., 242, 260, 261; Holmes, i., 330; Anderson on Commerce, ii., 475; New Haven Rec., ii., 510–512; Col. Doc., iii., 40, 44, 50, 209, 210; Lister's Clarendon, ii., 458; iii., 308; Statute 15 Ch. II., cap. xvii.; Grahame, i., 92; Bancroft, ii., 43; Palfrey, ii., 566; *ante*, vol. i., 685, 702, 725, 735; N. Y. H. S. Coll. (1869), 1–57.

Chap. I.

1664.

Scott, Baxter, and Maverick testify.

over to London, who were admirably qualified to stimulate English animosity against the Dutch colonists in America. These persons were John Scott and George Baxter, who cherished no "good opinion of the law" under which they had smarted in New Netherland, and Samuel Maverick, a zealous Episcopalian who had formerly lived in tribulation in Massachusetts. All the three made universal professions of loyalty. Scott, especially, was clamorous for a royal grant to him of the government of Long Island, nearly the third part of which he pretended to have purchased. But Lord Stirling's claim, which had not yet been acted on by the Council for Plantations, stood in his way. The three American witnesses, however, were called before the board, and ordered to draw up a statement of "the title of his majesty to the premises; of the Dutch intrusion; of their deportment since and management of that possession, and of their strength, trade, and government there; and of the means to make them acknowledge and submit to his majesty's government, or by force to compel them thereunto or expulse them." The result of these witnesses' labors and of Downing's arguments from the Hague was to satisfy Lord Clarendon that New Netherland belonged to the king, and that it had been "only usurped" by the Dutch, who had "no colour of right to pretend to" its possession. The chancellor's opinion, although it was utterly inconsistent with truth and reason, was conclusive. The difficult point was that the Dutch were, and for half a century had been, in uninterrupted possession of the Valley of the Hudson and its neighborhood. How the English could best gain possession became the question.*

Clarendon's opinion.

It was certain that the government at the Hague would not acknowledge any English pretension of right to Dutch New Netherland. The States General had, indeed, just directed their ambassador at London to insist on "the determination of the boundary line" between the English and Dutch possessions in North America. They also requested the king to issue orders "for the immediate restoration of the towns and places in New Netherland invaded by his subjects within the aforesaid limits, and for the cessation

13/23 Jan'ry. The Dutch maintain their rights.

* Col. Doc., iii., 46, 48, 105; Lister's Clarendon, iii., 276, 347; Hutchinson's Massachusetts, i., 147; Collection, 380, 381; Palfrey, ii., 564–567, 583; Aspinwall, in Mass. H. S. Proceedings, 1862, 66–72, *note;* N. Y. H. S. Coll. (1869), 19–67; *ante*, vol. i., 579, 620, 671, 725.

of all further usurpations." Of this action Clarendon was promptly informed by Downing, to whom De Witt had also spoken about the "encroaching" of the English upon the Dutch in New Netherland. "It would be good, I think," was the crafty envoy's advice to the chancellor, "after three or four months' delay, to give them for answer that his majesty will write into those parts, to be informed of the truth of the matter of fact and right on both sides." The next month, referring to the complaints of the West India Company against the aggressions of the English, he suggested "if his majesty think fit to leave that matter to me, I shall deal well enough with them."*

15 January.

12 February.

Yet Charles and his ministers were for some time perplexed whether they should view the Dutch "intruders" as subjects or as aliens. At length the king's course was determined. In spite of treaties, at the risk of war, it was resolved that the principle announced by Queen Elizabeth and affirmed by Parliament in 1621 should be repudiated and reversed. New Netherland must be seized at all hazard, and the English claim by "prescription" must be maintained against the Dutch title by actual discovery and continuous occupation. An expedition "against the Dutch in New England" was ordered. But this was kept profoundly secret, lest the States should send a squadron to aid the weak garrison at Manhattan. A quiet grant to the king's own brother would be both the readiest assertion of title and the best apology for any consequences. This, indeed, had been decided upon before Scott returned to America with the royal orders to enforce the navigation laws. Its execution was perhaps hastened by his report to Under Secretary Williamson of the condition of affairs at the western end of Long Island.†

English expedition ordered.

29 February.

Lord Stirling's interest was accordingly purchased by Clarendon for his son-in-law, who promised to pay for it three thousand five hundred pounds. Long Island, of which the greater portion was already subject to the crown, being thus secured to the Duke of York by a color of title,

The Duke of York's patent.

* Col. Doc., ii., 224–229; Aitzema, v., 64, 65; Holl. Merc., 1664, 13–15; Lister's Clarendon, iii., 276, 277, 278; *ante*, vol. i., 730.

† Ogilby's America, 169; Chalmers's Rev. Col., i., 116; Col. Doc., ii., 302, 324, 325, 332, 379, 380, 400, 507; iii., 47, 48; New Haven Rec., ii., 510, 515; *ante*, vol. i., 725, 726. On the 29th of February, 1664, a warrant for £4000 was issued on account of the expedition against New Netherland: Am. and W. I. (S. P. O.), 372.

CHAP. I. 1664. the rest of New Netherland was added by the mere word of the king. The Connecticut charter was entirely disregarded. A patent to James was prepared, to which his father-in-law hastened to affix the great seal. The description of the premises conveyed was framed in part from Lord Stirling's original grant, which Clarendon borrowed

12 March. for the purpose. By his patent, Charles the Second granted to his brother, and to his heirs and assigns, the territory of Pemaquid, in Maine, between the Saint Croix and the Kennebeck, "and also all that island or islands commonly called by the several name or names of Matowacks or Long Island, situate, lying, and being towards the west of Cape Cod and the Narrow Higansetts, abutting upon the main land between the two rivers there called or known by the several names of Connecticut and Hudson's River; together, also, with the said river called Hudson's River, and all the land from the west side of Connecticut to the east side of Delaware Bay, and also all those several islands called or known by the names of Martin's Vinyard, and Nantukes,

Territorial extent of the Duke's patent. otherwise Nantuckett." The inland boundary most consistent with this description was "a line from the head of Connecticut River to the source of Hudson's River, thence to the head of the Mohawk branch of Hudson's River, and thence to the east side of Delaware Bay." The grant "was intended to include all the lands which the Dutch held there." These territories were to be held of the king in free and common soccage, and under the yearly rent of forty beaver-skins, when demanded. The patent invested the Duke of York and his heirs, deputies, and assigns with "full and absolute power and authority to correct, punish, pardon, govern, and rule" all British subjects inhabiting the territory, according to such laws as he might establish, and

The duke's powers of government. in cases of necessity according to the "good discretions" of his deputies, provided that such laws should be, not contrary, but agreeable to the statutes of England. It granted him authority to appoint and discharge all officers, execute martial law, regulate trade and the tenure of lands, send out emigrants "not prohibited or under restraint," expel all persons living under his government without his license; and it declared that, notwithstanding any uncertainty or imperfection, or any former grants to any other persons, or any statute to the contrary, this patent to the Duke of York should be "good and effectual in the law, to all intents and purposes whatsoever." This instrument, clearly defective in many material points, was much less cumbersome than those which the kings of England had previously sealed to American proprietaries. It was the most impudent ever recorded in the colonial archives of England. But its crisp clauses warranted all that a despot could desire.*

The duke's parchment title now appeared to be complete. The next step was to give it validity by obtaining possession. James was informed that his newly-patented territory might yield him thirty thousand pounds a year, and he was anxious to enjoy his anticipated revenues, peaceably or by force. To this end, it was necessary that the person to secure and govern the prize should be well selected. The duke was singularly fortunate in the choice he made. There was at this time in his household Colonel Richard Nicolls, a gentleman whom he had long known, and in whom he justly felt great confidence. Nicolls was born in 1624, at Ampthill, in Bedfordshire, where his ancestors had lived in great esteem. His father was a barrister of the Middle Temple, and his mother a daughter of Sir George Bruce, ancestor of the Earl of Elgin. At the University he distinguished himself as a scholar; but on the breaking out of the civil war in 1643, he left his college and joined the royal forces, in which he obtained the command of a troop of horse. Nicolls adhered faithfully to the royal cause, and shared its fortunes. Attaching himself in Paris to the Duke of York, he served with him in the French army under Turenne, and afterward on the other side under Don John of Austria and the Prince of Condé. At the Restoration Nicolls returned to England, and was made a groom of the bedchamber to the duke. His sincerity, courage, capacity, and prudence recommended him for the most important trust which his patron could now confer. Nicolls was accordingly commissioned by the

Colonel Richard Nicolls.

2 April.

* Patents, i., 109; Duer's Life of Stirling, 37, 38; D'Estrades, iii., 334; Chalmers's Ann., i., 573, 580; Col. Doc., ii., 295–298, 400, 507; iii., 47, 48, 215, 225, 240, 260, 606, 607, 796; v., 330, 596; vi., 508; vii., 431, 564, 596, 597; viii., 107, 436, 440; Maine H. S. Coll., v., 2–6; Leaming and Spicer's Grants and Concessions, 3–8; Smith's N. Y., i., 15; Thompson, ii., 308-311; Wood, 6, *note;* Palfrey, ii., 580; *ante*, vol. i., 725, 726. The original patent, beautifully engrossed, is in the State Library at Albany; a copy is in Appendix, Note A.

CHAP. I. 1664. Appointed Deputy Governor.

Duke of York to be his deputy governor during pleasure, within his American proprietorship, to execute all the powers granted by the patent, and obey such orders as he might receive. A set of instructions from the duke was also given to Nicolls for his general guidance.*

The king now determined to send commissioners to New England, as he had announced his purpose of doing a year before. They appear to have been selected by the Duke of York. The first was Colonel Richard Nicolls, whom he had just commissioned to be the deputy governor of his yet unpossessed transatlantic territory. The second was Sir Robert Carr, a needy Royalist knight, of loose principles, avaricious, and supercilious, and a "rank papist," who had already been talked of as governor general of New England. The third was Colonel George Cartwright, of Nottinghamshire, "naturally morose, saturnine, and suspicious," but clear-sighted and energetic. These three were officers in the royal army. The fourth commissioner was Samuel Maverick, an ardent Episcopalian, who had lived from his youth in Massachusetts, of which he was the avowed and well-informed enemy, and who, with Scott and Baxter, had just before advised the Council of Plantations respecting the best means of subduing New Netherland. To these four persons a royal commission was issued, directing them, or any three or two of them (of whom Nicolls was always to be one), to visit the several New England colonies, and "examine and determine all complaints and appeals in all cases and matters, as well military as criminal and civil, and proceed in all things for the providing for and settling the peace and security of the said country, according to their good and sound discretion, and to such instructions as they, or the survivors of them, have, or shall from time to time receive."†

Royal Commissioners to New England.

25 April.

* Col. Doc., ii., 234, 400, 507; iii., 133, 154; Thompson's Long Island, ii., 325; Clarke's James II., i., 54; Chalmers's Pol. Ann., i., 573; Lyson's Magna Britt., i., 38; Lister's Clarendon, i., 368; ii., 259; N. Y. H. S. Proc., 1844, App., 116–118; Notes and Queries (2d series), iii., 214–216; Nichols's Topographer and Genealogist, iii., 539–544; Leaming and Spicer, 665–667; Patents, i., 146; *ante*, vol. i., 727, 736. A copy of Nicolls's Seal is in Hist. Mag., ix., 177. A copy of Nicolls's Commission is in Appendix, Note B. His Instructions from the Duke, which were exhibited at Hempstead in March, 1665, are not on record at Albany, nor did I find them in the State Paper Office at London. Perhaps they were lent to Evelyn in 1671, and he may not have returned them: Pepys, iv., 221, 222; Evelyn, iii., 241, 240; *post*, p. 422, *note*.

† Hutch. Mass., i., 225, 230, 250, 535; Evelyn, ii., 65; Chalmers, i., 386, 432; Winthrop,

It was the duty of the secretary of state to prepare instructions for the commissioners. But the lord chancellor had given minute attention to the affairs of the New England colonies, and, in the plan which he drew up for their visitation, had considered them as "already well-nigh ripened to a commonwealth." To Clarendon, therefore, appears to have been assigned the task of drafting the commissioners' instructions, of which there were different sets relating to the several colonies. In those for their private direction they were thus instructed: "You may inform all men that a great end of your design is the possessing Long Island, and reducing that people to an entire submission and obedience to us and our government, now vested by our grant and commission in our brother the Duke of York, and by raising forts or any other way you shall judge most convenient or necessary, so to secure that whole trade to our subjects, that the Dutch may no longer engross and exercise that trade which they have wrongfully possessed themselves of; that whole territory being in our possession before they, as private persons, and without any authority from their superiors, and against the law of nations and the good intelligence and alliance between us and their superiors, invaded, and have since wrongfully obtained the same, to the prejudice of our crown and dignity, and therefore ought in justice to be resumed by us, except they will entirely submit to our government, and live there as our good subjects under it; and in that case you shall let them know, both by private significations and treaties, or by any public declaration set out by you in our name, that we will take them into our protection, and that they shall continue to enjoy all their possessions (forts only excepted), and the same freedom in trade with our other good subjects in those parts." It would be difficult to find in any official document of any government a more impudent falsehood than the one in this clause, that the "whole territory" of New Netherland had been in the "possession" of the En-

23 April. Instructions of the commissioners.

i., 27; Mass. H. S. Coll., xxxii., 284; Maine H. S. Coll., i., 301; Barry's Mass., i., 390; Col. Doc., iii., 64, 92, 94; Patents, i., 148–150; Hazard, ii., 638; Trumbull's Conn., i., 522; *ante*, vol. i., 736. Palfrey, ii., 580, *note*, errs in confounding Sir Robert Carr, Knight, the commissioner (who died at Bristol, 2d June, 1667; Col. Doc., iii., 161; Morton's Memorial, 315, *note*; Smith, i., 33, *note*), with Sir Robert Carr, Baronet, of Sleeford, in Lincolnshire, who married a sister of Secretary Bennet, and certainly was alive in 1668: compare Collins's Peerage, iv., 312, 330; Evelyn, i., 401; Pepys, iii., 206, 427.

CHAP. I. 1664.

glish crown before the Dutch "wrongfully obtained the same." Several other particular directions were given to the commissioners, who, when in New England, were to avoid giving any offense in matters of religion, and even to frequent the Puritan churches, while their own Episcopalian chaplain was not to wear his surplice, "which, having never been seen in those countries, may conveniently be forborne at this time." The main object of the king, however, was to obtain such alterations in the charters of the New England colonies as would give him the appointment of their governor and of the commander of their militia. "We should look upon it as a good omen," said Charles, "if they might be so wrought upon at the General Assembly as that Colonel Nicolls might be chosen by themselves for their present governour, and Colonel Cartwright for their major general."

23 April. Royal letters.

Royal letters were also addressed to the several colonies. The reasons for the visit of the commissioners were explained in soothing language; the motives for subduing the Dutch, and "the benefit and advantage which, with God's blessing, must accrue" to New England from the reduction of New Netherland, were seductively exhibited, and a full compliance with all the king's desires was required. "For the glory of the matter," these letters were dated on Saint George's day.*

The English expedition against New Netherland.

The Duke of York, who, as lord high admiral, directed the fleet, now borrowed several men-of-war from the king. They were the Guinea, of thirty-six guns, Captain Hugh Hyde; the Elias, of thirty, Captain William Hill; the Martin, of sixteen, Captain Edward Grove; and a chartered transport, the William and Nicholas, of ten, Captain Morley. About four hundred and fifty of the king's veteran soldiers, forming three full companies, which were commanded by Colonels Nicolls, Carr, and Cartwright, were embarked on the squadron. Nicolls was commander-in-chief of the expedition. Among the commissioned officers serving under him were Captains Matthias Nicolls, Daniel Brodhead, Robert Needham, Harry Norwood, and Ensign Sylvester Salisbury, of the British army, some of whom,

* Col. Doc., ii., 237; iii., 51–63; Oldmixon, i., 238; Trumbull, i., 523; Holmes, i., 333, *note;* Hazard, ii., 364; Palfrey, i., 193, *note;* ii., 560, 578, 579, 582–586; iii., 238.

CHAP. I.

1664.

intending to settle themselves permanently in the Dutch province after its reduction, were accompanied by their families. The forces were "exceedingly well fitted with all necessaries for warre, with such ingineers and other expedients for the forcing the strongest fortifications." Nicolls and Cartwright went on board the Guinea, while Carr and Maverick embarked in the Martin. The expedition set sail from Portsmouth, with orders to assemble in Gardiner's Bay, at the eastern end of Long Island.* ($\frac{15}{25}$ May.)

Intelligence of these preparations soon reached the Hague. Stuyvesant had already warned the West India Company of the intended grant of Charles to the Duke of York, and that not only Long Island, but the whole of New Netherland, would be lost, unless speedily re-enforced from Holland. (29 February.) But the company, now on the brink of bankruptcy, wrote back, with marvelous infatuation, that the king, "being inclined to reduce all his kingdoms under one form of government in Church and State, hath taken care that commissioners are ready in England to repair to New England to install bishops there, the same as in Old England; therefore we believe that the English of the North, who mostly left England for the aforesaid causes, will not give us henceforth so much trouble, and will prefer to live under us with freedom of conscience, rather than risk that in order to be rid of our authority, and then again to fall under a government from which they formerly fled." (21 April. Infatuation in Holland.) Never was the Puritan sentiment in New England more thoroughly misapprehended than by the Dutch West India Company. Scarcely had this absurd letter been dispatched before the real purpose of Nicolls's expedition was better understood. In great concern, De Witt sought from Downing some explanation of the report of the English "sending to take New Netherland." The British envoy replied, "I know of no such country but only in the maps;" and he boldly insisted that "the English had the first pattern of first possession of those parts." The Dutch govern- ($\frac{6}{16}$ May.)

* Col. Doc., ii., 243, 372, 410, 423, 445, 501; iii., 65, 66; Mass. H. S. Coll., xxxvi., 527; Smith, i., 16; Clarke's James II., i., 400; Pepys, iv., 353; N. Y. General Entries, i., 2, 3, 22, 27, 28; Valentine's Manual, 1860, 592; Wood, 144; *ante*, vol. i., 736, 744, *note*. Of the English officers who accompanied Nicolls, the family of Captain Matthias Nicolls settled on Long Island, and those of Captain Daniel Brodhead and Ensign Sylvester Salisbury in Ulster County, in the province of New York. Numerous descendants now bear these ancestral names. See also N. Y. H. S. Coll. (1869), 57.

CHAP. I. 1664. ment was now sufficiently warned of the danger which menaced New Netherland. But a purblind confidence in the honor of Charles, and an unjust estimate of the importance of its American province to the fatherland, clouded the judgment of De Witt. Prompt orders to De Ruyter, who was now on his way to the Mediterranean, might have hurried his squadron to Manhattan in time to assist Stuyvesant, and give the Duke of York's expedition a memorable repulse. But, unhappily, the Dutch province was under the immediate government of a commercial monopoly which had but little popular sympathy. "What!" cried the commonalty at the Hague, "must we have a war for the East and West India Companies? We will rather pull them by the ears."* And so the fatherland abandoned New Netherland to her fate.

Nicolls's squadron worked slowly to the westward. It was nearly ten weeks before the first of his ships reached New England. In the mean time, Appleboom, the Swedish minister at the Hague, awakened from its sleep of eight

17/27 June. Swedish complaints. years the complaint of his king against the proceedings of Stuyvesant on the Delaware in 1655. In a well-written memorial to the States General, he demanded that the West India Company should be ordered to restore the "wrested lands" to the Swedish Company and pay all damages. This should be speedily done, because it was reported that the Dutch Company "were themselves now questioned by

5/15 August. others in those parts." Two months afterward, the Amsterdam chamber submitted a full justification of their proceedings against the Swedes; and here the question, which

29 Sept./9 October. had been revived "for form's sake," was ended.†

Appleboom's suggestion was almost a prophetic sneer. The Dutch were, indeed, effectually "questioned by others" in New Netherland. In alarm at the now certain destination of Nicolls's squadron, the West India Company de-

28 June/8 July. manded assistance from the city of Amsterdam, and asked the States General for "three hundred soldiers as a re-enforcement for New Netherland, and a ship of war to op-

* Lister's Clarendon, iii., 307, 310, 318, 320, 322; Kennett's England, iii., 251, 253; D'Estrades, ii., 435; Col. Doc., ii., 230–237, 367, 400, 408, 421, 431, 432, 492, 493, 505, 507; Letter of W. I. Co. to S. G., 20 June, 1664, MS., N. Y. Historical Society; Mass. Rec., iv. (ii.), 101–110; Palfrey, ii., 576, 586, 587.

† Col. Doc., i., 615; ii., 240–242, 246, 247, 258–260; Aitzema, v., 247–249; Holl. Merc., 1664, 135–137; Lister's Clarendon, iii., 359; *ante*, vol. i., 622.

pose the English designs there." But Van Gogh, the ambassador at London, reported that the king constantly protested that "he would not in any way violate his alliance with the Dutch;" and the States General, wishing to give no umbrage to England, refused the company's request for assistance. Early in the autumn, Van Gogh wrote that it was rumored that the English had taken Long Island, and intended to reduce New Amsterdam and the rest of New Netherland. Soon afterward the West India Company notified the States General that Stuyvesant's dispatches announced that the Duke of York had already reduced Long Island, and was about to attack New Amsterdam, the capital, "and thereby to erase the name of New Netherland from the map, and cause a loss of millions to the company." The same week intelligence reached London that the Dutch had been "beat out" of Guinea and New Netherland, "without public knowledge or reason," according to the honest notion of Pepys, the clerk of the Admiralty. The king did "joy mightily at it." The mask need no longer be worn. "But," said Charles to his vice-chamberlain Carteret, laughing, "how shall I do to answer this to the ambassador when he comes?"*

CHAP. I. 1664. 30 June / 10 July. The States General refuse to defend New Netherland. 2/12 Sept. 26 Sept. / 6 October. 29 Sept. / 9 October.

Meanwhile Nicolls and Cartwright, with part of the squadron, had reached Boston after a tedious voyage, and had dispatched a letter to Winthrop requiring the assistance of Connecticut. This was very readily given. At the suggestion of the commissioners, the Massachusetts authorities, with evident unwillingness, ordered two hundred volunteers to be called out to aid in reducing New Netherland. The West India Company, as we have seen, had cherished the absurd belief that the Puritan colonists would not assist the royal forces in overthrowing the government of New Netherland, in which "freedom of conscience" was so fully recognized. But the English jealousy of the Dutch, which New England fostered, together with a curious notion of loyalty to the king, prevailed over Puritan dread of episcopacy. Nevertheless, the backwardness of Massachusetts

23 July. Nicolls at Boston. 3 August.

* Col. Doc., ii., 243–246, 253, 255, 256; Lingard, xii., 168; Davies, iii., 25; Rapin, ii., 637, 638; Parliamentary History, iv., 298–302; D'Estrades, ii., 459, 460, 494; Lett. of De Witt, iv., 306, 342; Pepys, ii., 171. It is another instance of the ignorance which English scholars so constantly display in regard to American history, that the editor of Bohn's recent edition of Pepys repeats the erroneous statement of Hume, vi., 383, and others, that the expedition sent against New Netherland was commanded by Sir Robert Holmes.

CHAP. I. 1664. 29 July. gave Nicolls and Cartwright an opportunity to complain to Secretary Bennet. As soon as the rest of the English ships reached Boston, Nicolls wrote again to Winthrop at Hartford, and also to Captain Thomas Willett at Plymouth, desiring them to meet the commissioners at the west end of Long Island, whither the expedition soon afterward sailed. The squadron, piloted by New England mariners, anchored at Nyack or New Utrecht Bay, just inside of Coney Island. Here the royal commissioners were joined by Winthrop and his son Fitz John, with Willys and several other Connecticut magistrates. Willett also appeared on behalf of the new Plymouth colony, and "greatly recommended himself to the commissioners by his activity and intelligence." Scott was likewise at hand, with men from New Haven, "pressed by authority," to go with him to Long Island. A number of militia, summoned from Southold and the other towns at the eastern end of the island, soon appeared in arms under the command of Captain John Younge. Thomas Clarke and John Pynchon also came from Boston with a report of its military arrangements. But, as there was already an overpowering force collected, the services of the Massachusetts troops were found to be unnecessary.*

18/28 August. The squadron at Nyack.

Connecticut, Plymouth, and Massachusetts delegates.

18/28 August. New Amsterdam blockaded.

All the approaches to New Amsterdam by land and water were immediately blockaded, and communication between the city and Long Island, Bergen, and Achter Cul was cut off. The block-house on Staten Island, opposite the squadron, was occupied. Several coasting vessels, on their way to the South River, were captured. The Long Island farmers were forbidden to furnish any supplies to the capital, on pain of destruction of their property. At the same time a proclamation was issued by the commissioners on board the Guinea, copies of which were "scattered broadcast" among the Dutch towns, and soon found their way to the burghers of the metropolis. "Forasmuch," were its words, "as his majesty hath sent us, by commission under his great seal, among other things to expel or to re-

20/30 August.

Proclamation of the Royal Commissioners.

* General Entries, i., 2–7; Col. Doc., ii., 235, 236, 372, 409, 410, 438, 444; iii., 65, 66, 84; Chalmers, Ann., i., 386, 387, 573; Mass. Rec., iv. (ii.), 117–128, 141, 149, 157–168; Mass. H. S. Coll., xviii., 92–94; xxxvi., 527, 528; Hutch. Mass., i., 230, 231; Barry, i., 390, 391; Palfrey, ii., 578, 586, 591; iii., 236, 238; Morton's Mem., 311, *note;* New Haven Rec., ii., 550; Trumbull, i., 267; Smith, i., 17, 18; Wood, 27; Thompson, i., 127; *ante*, vol. i., 737.

duce under his majesty's obedience all such foreigners as have without his majesty's leave or consent seated themselves amongst any of his dominions in America, to the prejudice of his majesty's subjects and the diminution of his royal dignity, WE, his Majesty's Commissioners, declare and promise that whosoever, of what nation soever, will, upon knowledge of this proclamation, acknowledge and testify themselves to submit to this his majesty's government, as his good subjects ought to do, shall be protected by his majesty's laws and justice, and peaceably enjoy whatsoever God's blessing and their own honest industry have furnished them with, and all other privileges with his majesty's English subjects. We have caused this to be published that we might prevent all inconveniences to others, if it were possible; however, to clear ourselves from the charge of all those miseries that may any way befall such as live here and will not acknowledge his majesty for their sovereign—whom God preserve." The inhabitants of the several towns on Long Island were also specially summoned to meet the commissioners at Gravesend on the following Thursday.*

In the mean time, Stuyvesant, on receiving the letter which the West India directors had written to him in April, was somewhat relieved from fear of an attack by the English, although he could not refrain from writing to the company that the design of the royal commissioners was rather against New Netherland than for the "imagined reform of New England." Willett, of Plymouth, who had originally warned him of the danger, now contradicted his previous statements, and the director incautiously went up to Fort Orange to repress some disorders among the Indians in its neighborhood. Upon learning the approach of the English expedition he hurried back to New Amsterdam, which he reached only the day before the Guinea anchored in Nyack Bay. According to the rule "in such critical circumstances," the burgomasters were called into council, and every thing possible was done for the fortification and defense of the city. But its condition was

25 July / 4 August.

27 July / 6 August. Stuyvesant at Fort Orange.

Returns to New Amsterdam.

15/25 August. The city magistrates called into council.

* Col. Doc., ii., 372, 410, 411, 434, 438, 443, 444, 476; General Entries, i., 7, 8; Colonial Manuscripts, x. (iii.), 299–303; Albany Rec., xxii., 307, 385; Smith, i., 387, 388; S. Smith's New Jersey, 36, 37; Oyster Bay Rec., A., 19; O'Call., ii., 521, 522; Thompson, i., 124, 125; *ante*, vol. i., 738; N. Y. H. S. Coll. (1869), 58, 68.

1664.

hopeless from the first. No aid could be obtained from Long Island. The regular soldiers in the garrison did not exceed one hundred and fifty; and the burghers—of whom only two hundred and fifty were able to bear arms—thought more of protecting their own property than of defending the open town. The whole city force, placed man by man four rods apart, could not guard its breastwork.

Defenseless condition of the metropolis.

Fort Amsterdam itself was untenable against a regular beleaguering, having been originally built to resist an attack of the savages rather than an assault by European arms. Houses were clustered around its low earthen walls, which in some places were not over ten feet high, and were commanded, within pistol-shot on the north, by much higher ground on the "Heere-weg," or Broadway. Its six hundred pounds of serviceable powder were not sufficient for more than a few hours' firing. Long before its extremity, Stuyvesant had given his military opinion, which modern judgment has only confirmed, that "whoever by water is

The river its master.

master of the river will be in a short time master by land of the feeble fortress." The contingency he dreaded had now happened, and the English squadron was in full command of the harbor. Nevertheless, the director resolved to hold out to the last. At the request of the burgomasters, and to ascertain the condition of affairs on Long Island, he sent four commissioners, representing the council

$\frac{19}{29}$ August. Stuyvesant sends to Nicolls, who replies.

and the city, down to the English commanders, with a letter inquiring the object of their coming, and why they remained at Nyack without giving notice to him. Nicolls answered them that he had come to reduce the country to the obedience of the King of England, whose commission he exhibited; that he would not argue about his majesty's right, which he would leave to be vindicated by the king himself; and that, the next day, he would send a letter to New Amsterdam "over the ferry."*

Colonel Cartwright, Captain Needham, Captain Grove, and Mr. Thomas Delavall accordingly came up to the city

$\frac{20}{30}$ August.

on Saturday morning with a letter from Nicolls to Stuy-

* Alb. Rec., xviii., 276–297, 311, 312; Colonial MSS., x. (iii.), 251, 299; xv., 140; Mass. Rec., iv. (ii.), 101–106; Palfrey, ii., 576; New Amsterdam Rec., v., 552–554, 567–570; Val. Man., 1860, 592; 1861, 603–605; Col. Doc., ii., 235, 248, 367, 368, 371, 372, 376, 377, 408–411, 421, 431–434, 438, 440, 441, 443, 446, 469, 474, 475, 494, 499, 505, 508; Gen. Ent., i., 8, 9; Smith, i., 18; S. Smith, 37, 38; Hazard's Reg. Penn., iv., 30, 31; Letter of Drisius, 15 Sept., 1664; *ante*, vol. i., 737, 738, 741.

vesant, asserting the "unquestionable right" of the English king "to these parts of America," and requiring the surrender of the "town situate upon the island commonly known by the name of Manhatoes, with all the forts thereunto belonging," at the same time assuring him "and every respective inhabitant of the Dutch nation that his majesty, being tender of the effusion of Christian blood, doth by these presents confirm and secure to every man his estate, life, and liberty, who shall readily submit to his government, and all those who shall oppose his majesty's gracious intentions must expect all the miseries of a war which they bring upon themselves." A copy of the proclamation of the royal commissioners was also sent. Fond of parade, and determined to "keep up state" to the last, the Dutch director received the English delegates with a salute of artillery which expended a large proportion of his slender stock of powder. As Nicolls had omitted to sign his summons, it was returned to the delegates, and a delay was thus gained. Stuyvesant, on his part, showed them his commission as Director General of New Netherland, and the grant of the States General to the West India Company in 1621, which, he insisted, gave as much power and authority as the King of England had given or could give to any colony in America. The municipal authorities, with some of the burghers, now assembled at the City Hall, and agreed that the city should be so fortified as to prevent a surprise, that thus "good terms and conditions" might be obtained from the enemy. But, as protracted resistance was out of the question, a copy of the English communication was to be demanded from the director.

CHAP. I. 1664. Nicolls demands the surrender of Manhattan. Terms offered. Stuyvesant procrastinates.

On the following Monday morning, Nicolls, having signed his summons, sent it back with a note of apology by Captains Hill, Needham, and Matthias Nicolls. Another salute was fired, and on the departure of the English deputies the burgomasters asked Stuyvesant for a copy of the summons, to be shown to the citizens. But the director, fearing that its easy terms might lead them to capitulate at once, refused. The burgomasters endeavored to explain the purport of the summons, but the citizens insisted upon seeing for themselves. Stuyvesant then went in person to their meeting, hoping to dissuade them from their purpose.

22 August. 1 Septem. Nicolls's second summons.

CHAP. I. 1664. "Such a course," he said, "would be disapproved of in the fatherland: it would discourage the people, and he would be held answerable for the surrender." At last, finding it useless to resist the popular will, the director furnished the required copy, with a protest that he should not be held responsible for "the calamitous consequences."*

Communicated to the people.

With a sorrowful heart Stuyvesant now drew up a dispatch to the West India Directors, informing them of his "perilous and very alarming" situation. "Long Island is gone and lost." The capital, threatened by Old and New England forces, could not hold out long. "The company is scolded and cursed by the inhabitants, in regard that notwithstanding the so often renewed and successive warnings and remonstrances from time to time, no attention has been paid, and none of the solicited succor obtained. Yea, it is loudly and openly proclaimed, to the contempt and shame of your faithful servants, that your honors by premeditation abandoned the inhabitants, if you did not intend to expose them for sale, and endeavored to devote them to slaughter." This dispatch was intended to be sent by the recently arrived ship Gideon, which was to pass that night "in silence through Hellgate." But, upon consideration, Stuyvesant refused to let the vessel sail, and Gelde, her master, could only protest against his detention.†

22 August. / 1 Septem.

Stuyvesant's letter to the W. I. Company.

By this time Nicolls had become better informed of the state of affairs in New Amsterdam through Willett, who was "more acquainted with the manners and customs of the Dutch than any Englishman in the country." Winthrop had also explained to him how easily the citizens might be induced to compel Stuyvesant to surrender, if they were assured that their intercourse with Holland would not be interrupted. Nicolls accordingly wrote to Winthrop, "As to those particulars you spoke to me, I do assure you that if the Manhadoes be delivered up to his majesty, I shall not hinder, but any people from the Netherlands may freely come and plant there, or thereabouts; and such vessels of their owne country may freely come

Willett and Winthrop.

22 August. / 1 Septem.

Nicolls's promises to Winthrop.

* General Entries, i., 9–11; Alb. Rec., xviii., 311–317; xxii., 314, 315; Col. MSS., x. (iii.), 309, 311; xv., 143, 144; Col. Doc., ii., 441, 443, 469, 498; Hazard's Reg. Penn., iv., 31, 41; Smith, i., 18–21; S. Smith, 38, 39; Thompson, i., 128; Bancroft, ii., 314; O'Call., ii., 522, 523; *ante*, vol. i., 738, 739.

† Alb. Rec., xviii., 302–304; xxii., 318–321; Col. MSS., x. (iii.), 313; xv., 141; Thompson, i., 128, 129; General Entries, i., 34, 141; Col. Doc., ii., 222, 430, 469, 744.

thither, and any of them may as freely returne home in vessels of their owne country; and this and much more is contained in the privilege of his majesty's English subjects; and thus much you may, by what means you please, assure the governor." In thus promising the people of New Netherland a free intercourse with Holland, in violation of the English Navigation Acts, Nicolls exceeded his instructions from the king, which authorized him to assure the Dutch colonists only "the same freedom in trade with our other good subjects in those parts;" and he even assumed more power than his own sovereign possessed, who "could not dispense with the laws by permitting a commerce which they had prohibited."*

CHAP. I. — 1664.

Having, nevertheless, gained his point, Winthrop addressed a friendly letter to Stuyvesant and his council, urging them to "speedily accept his majesty's gracious tender," and adding that "otherwise you may be assured that both the Massachusett colony and Connecticutt, and all the rest, are obliged and ready to attend his majestie's service; and if you should, by wilfull protraction, occasion a generall rising of the English colonies, I should be sorry to see the ill consequences which you will bring upon your people thereby, of which I hope and persuade, in reall compassion, that you will not run so great an hazard to occasion a needless warre, with all the evills and miseries that may accompany the same, when nothing but peace, and liberties, and protection is tendered. I have, I hope, obtained of their honors this farther addition to their former free tenders for the good of yourselves, your friends, and allies, that any of your friends in Holland that will come over hither shall have free liberty to inhabite and plant in these parts, under his majestie's subjection, and to transport themselves in theire owne country ships, which (if you consider well) gives you such a settlement in your present condition, that you will find little alteration but your submission to and acknowledgment of his majestie's empire (for the most apparent future good of all your people), who hath imployed such persons of honor and worth that your people may be happy under their government." To this

22 August. / 1 Septem.

Winthrop's letter to Stuyvesant.

* Gen. Ent., i., 12; Morton's Memorial, 311, *note;* Col. Doc., iii., 57, 165; Chalmers, i., 574, 596; O'Call., ii., 523; *ante*, p. 19; vol. i., 739.

CHAP. I. 1664.

letter Nicolls, Carr, and Cartwright added their autograph approval and assent "that it be sent to the governor of the Manhadoes."*

Winthrop, with his son Fitz John, and Willys of Connecticut, accompanied by Willett of Plymouth, and Clarke and Pynchon of Massachusetts, came up the next day with this letter from Gravesend "in a row-boat with a white flag," to the city wharf, whence they were "immediately conducted to the nearest tavern." Another salute was fired as they landed, and Stuyvesant went with his council and the two burgomasters to greet them. The English delegates declared that they had come to offer "all the inhabitants, in the king's name, fair conditions, and, in case these were not accepted, to excuse themselves for any mischief that might follow—it being their business, as they had been ordered by England's majesty, and were therefore obliged to assist General Nicolls." Many "speeches and answers" passed at the long conference. On taking leave, Winthrop handed his own sealed letter to Stuyvesant, who, when he returned to the fort, opened and read it before the council and the burgomasters. Its effect was immediate. In a short time the burgomasters came back to the council chamber, and demanded a copy of Winthrop's letter to be communicated to the city authorities. This Stuyvesant declined to allow, thinking it "rather disadvantageous than favorable to communicate such letters to the inhabitants." The burgomasters insisted that the director "ought to communicate to the commonalty all that had any relation to the public welfare." Stuyvesant explained the disastrous consequences of so doing; but the burgomasters persisted, and as they went away, "greatly disgusted and dissatisfied," the director, against their protest, tore the letter in pieces, "in order thereby to prevent its communication." Shortly afterward, most of the burghers assembled at the City Hall; the work on the palisades suddenly stopped; and three of the principal citizens, "not belonging to the government," came to the council chamber and peremptorily demanded a copy of the letter. The fragments were shown to them, but no reasoning would satisfy; and Stuyvesant

23 August. 2 Septem. Winthrop at New Amsterdam.

Stuyvesant tears up Winthrop's letter.

* This letter was published for the first time in 1863, from Winthrop's original draft, in Mass. H. S. Coll., xxxvi., 527-529; N. Y. H. S. Coll. (1869), 58.

1664.

was obliged to hasten to the City Hall, "to encourage and appease the burghers, and bring them back to work." In vain did he try to pacify them; complaints against the company's shameful neglect of the people's representations were uttered on all sides; and a prolonged defense of the city, without hope of relief, was declared to be impossible, "seeing that to resist so many was nothing else than to gape before an oven." In vain did the director again refuse a copy of the letter, because "it did not concern the commonalty, but the government," and, moreover, it had been torn up. "The letter! the letter!" was the only reply. Fearing a mutiny, Stuyvesant returned to the council chamber; and Bayard, the clerk, having made a copy of Winthrop's mutilated writing, gave it to the timorous burgomasters.*

A copy given to the citizens.

23 August. / 2 Septem. Stuyvesant's justification of the Dutch title.

Meanwhile Stuyvesant had been preparing a reply to the summons of Nicolls. It was an overwhelming argument, tracing the history of New Netherland, denying the English pretension, and maintaining the Dutch title by first discovery, uninterrupted possession, purchase of land from the native owners, and the recognition of the sovereignty of the States General by the articles of peace with England. For these reasons, the unsoundness of the English claim was "as manifest and palpable as the brightness of the sun at noonday." At the same time, the director proposed to renew the agreement with Scott in the previous March, that the question of boundaries on Long Island should be amicably determined by the king and the States General, "in order to prevent bloodshed here and further trouble in Europe," which must follow any hostile aggressions.

23 August. / 2 Septem. Nicolls declines discussion.

This letter was conveyed by four of Stuyvesant's ablest advisers, two from the council and two from the city, who were instructed to "argue the matter" with the English commander. But Nicolls, declining discussion, told them that the question of right did not concern him; it was to be considered by the king and the States General. He must and should take the place; and if the reasonable terms he

* Col. Doc., ii., 368, 369, 444, 445, 469, 476; iii., 165; Alb. Rec., xxii., 316; Col. MSS., x. (iii.), 311, 313; Smith, i., 20; Trumbull, i., 268; Bancroft, ii., 314; O'Call., ii., 523, 524; Mass. H. S. Coll., xxxvi., 528, 529; *ante*, vol. i., 739. According to Smith, Trumbull, and others, Stuyvesant tore Winthrop's letter "in a fit of anger;" according to his own account, in Alb. Rec., xxii., 316, and Col. Doc., ii., 445, "to prevent its communication" to the people.

CHAP. I.

1664.

had offered were not accepted, he would attack the city, for which purpose, at the end of forty-eight hours, he would bring his forces up nearer. "On Thursday, the fourth," he added, "I will speak with you at the Manhattans." The Dutch deputies replied, "Friends will be welcome if they come in a friendly manner." "I shall come with my ships and soldiers," said Nicolls, "and he will be a bold messenger, indeed, who shall then dare to come on board and solicit terms." To their demand, "What, then, is to be done?" He answered, "Hoist the white flag of peace at the fort, and then I may take something into consideration." With this imperious message the Dutch delegates returned sadly to New Amsterdam.*

Nicolls's imperious reply.

Seeing that Stuyvesant was disposed to hold out, Nicolls directed Hyde, of the Guinea, "to prosecute, with the advice of the captains under his command, his majesties' claim and interest by all ways and means as they shall think most expedient for the speedy reducing of the Dutch under his majesties' obedience." The transport ship William and Nicholas was also "pressed" for active service, and an agreement was signed with Morley, her captain, to indemnify her owners in case she should be damaged.†

24 August. / 3 Septem. An attack ordered.

At the appointed day, a great number of the inhabitants of Long Island assembled to meet the royal commissioners at Gravesend. Winthrop and the other Connecticut magistrates were present. Nicolls, in their presence, published the king's patent to the Duke of York, with his own commission, and demanded the submission of Long Island to his authority. On the part of the inhabitants living east of the Dutch towns there was no doubt respecting allegiance. They were already British subjects, and under the jurisdiction of Connecticut. The only question was about coming under the Duke of York's government. Winthrop, on behalf of Connecticut, declared that as the king's pleasure was now fully signified by his letters patent, the jurisdiction which that colony had claimed and exercised over Long Island "ceased and became null." Nicolls, on the part of the duke, replied that he would not displace any of

25 August. / 4 Septem. Nicolls at Gravesend.

* Col. Doc., ii., 406, 411-414; Gen. Ent., i., 15-20; Alb. Rec., xviii., 319, 320; xxii., 317; Col MSS., x. (iii.), 313; xv., 144; Hazard's Reg. Penn., iv., 41, 42; Val. Man., 1860, 592; Smith, i., 20-26; Bancroft, ii, 314; O'Call., ii., 526; *ante*, vol. i., 728, 740.

† Gen. Ent., i., 21, 22, 27, 28; Smith, i., 27; S. Smith, 40; Hazard, Reg. Penn., iv., 42, 4[illegible].

CHAP. I.

1664.

the civil officers appointed by Connecticut, but would confirm them to act under him "until a convenient season served to convene deputies from all the towns on the island, when and where laws were to be enacted and civil officers established." This assurance seemed to explain the vague promise in the proclamation of the commissioners, that all persons submitting to the royal government should enjoy "all other privileges with his majesty's English subjects." It was, at all events, considered satisfactory. Long Island, chiefly inhabited by Englishmen already subject to the crown, submitted at once to the authority of the Duke of York; and the volunteer forces from its eastern towns, joined by those of New England, marched from Amersfoort and Midwout toward Brooklyn, to assist in reducing the Dutch capital.*

Submission of Long Island to the Duke of York.

Observing the approach of the English forces, Stuyvesant wrote once more to Nicolls, that although by his orders he was "obliged to defend our place," yet, to prevent the shedding of innocent blood, he proposed that commissioners should be appointed on both sides to treat about "a good accommodation," and that in the mean time all hostilities should cease. The English commander replied from Gravesend that he would willingly appoint commissioners "to treat upon articles of surrender." At the desire of Stuyvesant's delegates, orders were given to Commodore Hyde not to fire first on the city. But Nicolls refused their request that the troops should not be brought nearer. "To-day I shall arrive at the ferry," he added: "to-morrow we can agree with one another."†

25 August. / 4 Septem. Stuyvesant proposes an accommodation.

25 August. / 4 Septem.

The regular soldiers, consisting of three full companies, eager for booty, were then landed at Gravesend, whence they marched up to the ferry at Brooklyn, where the auxiliaries from Long Island and New England were already stationed. Two of the ships moved up near Nooten, or Governor's Island. The other two frigates came on with full sail, and guns ready to open broadsides, and, passing in front of Fort Amsterdam, anchored in the East River. Watching them from the parapet as they sailed along, Stuyvesant

The English forces at Brooklyn.

New Amsterdam beleaguered.

* Deeds, ii., 43, 44; Wood, 27, 28, 87, 173, 177; Thompson, i., 126, 127; ii., 323, 328; Col. Doc., ii., 407, 408, 414, 445, 501; Col. Rec. Conn., i. 424, 427, 429; *ante*, vol. i., 733, 734.

† Gen. Ent., i., 13, 14, 15; Alb. Rec., xviii., 321; Col. MSS., xv., 144; Col. Doc., ii., 414; Hazard, Reg. Penn., iv., 31; Smith, i., 27; S. Smith, 41, 42; *ante*, vol. i., 740.

CHAP. I. 1664.

was about to order his gunner to fire, when the two Domines Megapolensis led him away between them, imploring him not to begin hostilities. Leaving fifty men in the fort, under the command of Fiscal de Sille, the director, at the head of one hundred of the garrison, marched into the city, in order to prevent the English from landing "here and there."*

Panic in the metropolis.

By this time the Dutch regular soldiers themselves had become more disposed to plunder than to defend. They openly talked of "where booty is to be got, and where the young women live who wear chains of gold." Warnings had come from Long Island that the New England auxiliaries of Nicolls declared "that their business was not only with New Netherland, but with the booty and plunder, and for these they were called out and enrolled." The "cursing and talking" of these Eastern adventurers forced the citizens of New Amsterdam to look upon them as their "deadly enemies, who expected nothing else than pillage, plunder, and bloodshed." The whole population on Manhattan Island was about fifteen hundred, of whom only two hundred and fifty were able to bear arms. Opposed to these were more than a thousand effective soldiers and sailors in the English squadron, besides the re-enforcements from New England and Long Island. Moreover, it was understood that six hundred Northern savages and one hundred and fifty French rovers, with English commissions, had offered their services against the Dutch. Seeing themselves thus "encircled round about," with no means of deliverance, and considering "the notorious and palpable impossibility of being able to defend and hold the place," the city authorities, clergy, and officers of the burgher guard, at the suggestion of the elder Domine Megapolensis, adopted a remonstrance to the director and his council, imploring them to accept the conditions offered by the English commander. His threats, it stated, "would not have been at all regarded, could your honors, or we, your petitioners, expect the smallest aid or succour. But God help us! whether we turn for assistance to the north or to the south, to the east or to the west, it is all in vain." Ninety-three of the principal citizens, including all the municipal

26 August. / 5 September.

Remonstrance to Stuyvesant.

* Col. Doc., ii., 414, 422, 444, 445, 501, 502, 503, 508, 509; Val. Man., 1860, 592; Drisius to Classis of Amsterdam, 15 Sept., 1664; *ante*, vol. i., 740.

CHAP. I. 1664.

officers, and Stuyvesant's eldest son, signed the paper. The threatening answer of Nicolls to the Dutch commissioners had meanwhile been spread among the people, and many of them, with their wives and children crying and praying, besought the director to parley. To all their supplications he sturdily replied, "I had much rather be carried out dead!" But now he was obliged to yield to inevitable necessity, and prevent the mischiefs about to overtake, "evidently and assuredly, the honest inhabitants."*

Stuyvesant yields.

The lesson in Saint Luke's Gospel taught Stuyvesant how vain it was, with ten thousand men, to resist him that came with twenty thousand. Yet there was one balm for the director's wounded spirit. Nicolls had voluntarily proposed "to redeliver the fort and city of Amsterdam, in New Netherland, in case the difference of the limits of this province be agreed upon betwixt His Majesty of England and the High and Mighty States General." A full power to agree upon articles with the English commander or his deputies was accordingly given by the Dutch director and his council to Counselor John De Decker, Commissary Nicholas Varlett, and Doctor Samuel Megapolensis, representing the provincial government, and Burgomaster Cornelis Steenwyck, old burgomaster Oloff Stevensen van Cortlandt, and old schepen James Cousseau, representing the city. Nicolls was now encamped at the Brooklyn ferry, "before the Manhatans," with the royal "beleaguering" forces. On his part, he promptly named his two colleagues, Sir Robert Carr and Colonel George Cartwright, with John Winthrop and Samuel Willys of Connecticut, and Thomas Clarke and John Pynchon of Massachusetts, as his commissioners. "The reason why those of Boston and Connecticut were joined in the treaty," Nicolls afterward explained to Arlington, "was because those two colonies should hold themselves the more engaged with us if the Dutch had been over-confident of their strength."†

26 August. / 5 Septem.

Dutch commissioners appointed.

English commissioners named.

27 August. / 6 Septem.

The next morning, which was Saturday, the plenipoten-

* Alb. Rec., xviii., 320, 321; Col. MSS., xv., 144; Col. Doc., ii., 248–250, 369, 423, 444, 446, 476, 503; Drisius's Letter; Val. Man., 1860, 592, 593; *ante*, vol. i., 741.

† Col. Doc., ii., 414, 440; iii., 103; Gen. Ent., i., 30–33; Alb. Rec., xviii., 322, 323; Col. MSS., xv., 144, 145; Hazard's Ann. Penn., iv., 44; O'Call., ii., 531; Saint Luke's Gospel, xiv., 31; *ante*, vol. i., 741, 742. Smith, i., 27, inaccurately says that Stuyvesant agreed to surrender "on condition the English and Dutch limits in America were settled by the crown and the States General."

CHAP. I. 1664.

tiaries on both sides met by agreement at Stuyvesant's "Bouwery," or farm. Their only dispute was about the Dutch garrison, whom, as the English refused to do it, the city deputies agreed to convey back to Holland. The proclamation of the royal commissioners and the reiterated promises of Nicolls formed the basis of the twenty-four articles of capitulation. These declared all the inhabitants of New Netherland to be "free denizens," and secured to them their property. Any persons might come from Holland "and plant in this country," while Dutch vessels might "freely come hither, and any of the Dutch may freely return home, or send any sort of merchandise home, in vessels of their own country." For the next six months, intercourse with Holland was to continue as before the coming of the English. The Dutch inhabitants were to "enjoy the liberty of their consciences in divine worship and Church discipline," as well as "their own customs concerning their inheritances." All public buildings were to continue in their existing uses, and all public records to be respected. All inferior civil officers were to remain as they were until the customary time for new elections; and the town of Manhattan might choose deputies with "free voices in all public affairs." Owners of houses in Fort Orange were to enjoy their property "as all people do where there is no fort." The articles of capitulation were to be consented to by Nicolls, and delivered to Stuyvesant, together with copies of the king's patent and the Duke of York's commission, by eight o'clock the next Monday morning, "at the old mill."* Within two hours afterward, the fort and town "called New Amsterdam, upon the isle of Manhattoes," were to be surrendered, and the military officers and soldiers to "march out with their arms, drums beating and colors flying, and lighted matches."†

Articles of capitulation agreed upon.

28 August. 7 Septem.

These very advantageous and conciliatory terms were explained to the burgher authorities at the City Hall on

* This "old mill," which was the nearest point on Manhattan to "the ferry" at Brooklyn, was on the shore of the East River, near what is now the foot of Roosevelt Street, but then at the outlet of a brook running out of the "Kolck," afterward vulgarly called "the Collect:" see Valentine's Manual, 1859, 551, and 1863, 621, and the maps appended; *ante*, vol. i., p. 167, note. We owe the recovery of these maps to the research and care of George H. Moore, the present librarian of the New York Historical Society.

† Gen. Ent., i., 23–26, 33; Col. Doc., ii., 250–253, 414; Smith, i., 27–32; S. Smith, 43–46; Hazard's Reg. Penn., iv., 43; Holl. Merc., 1664, 153, 154; Alb. Rec., xviii., 325; Col. MSS., xv., 145; Chalmers's Ann., i., 574; O'Call., i., 532–535; *ante*, vol. i., 742, 762.

Chap. I. 1664.

Sunday afternoon, "after the second sermon." It was the last religious service that was expected to be celebrated under the Dutch flag in Kieft's old church in Fort Amsterdam. The next morning Stuyvesant and his council, having ratified the articles of capitulation, exchanged them with Nicolls, who, on his part, delivered the stipulated documents; and thereupon New Amsterdam was surrendered, and "the English, without any contest or claim being before put forth by any person to it, took possession of a fort built and continually garrisoned about forty years at the expense of the West India Company."*

Terms explained to the people. 29 August. 8 Septem. Articles ratified. New Amsterdam surrendered.

The story of the reduction of Long Island and New Amsterdam has now been minutely told: the unexpected blockade of the port by the English; the overwhelming force of the invaders; the weakness of Fort Amsterdam and its garrison; the almost solitary heroism and loyalty of Stuyvesant; the natural resentment of the city burghers against the authorities in Holland, who had left them unprotected against surprise; their common prudence, which preferred the easy terms offered by the English commander to the consequences of an unavailing resistance and a capture by storm; their reasonable dread of being plundered by the English colonial volunteers from the east; the inevitable capitulation of the metropolis, and the consequent surrender of the whole Dutch province. There was, indeed—as Stuyvesant reluctantly confessed—"an absolute impossibility of defending the fort, much less the city of New Amsterdam, and still less the country."†

The Dutch province defenseless.

On the part of England this conquest of New Netherland was an act of peculiar national baseness. It was a scandalous outrage. It was planned in secret, and was accomplished with deliberate deceit toward a friendly government. None but Englishmen had the impudence to do so vile a wrong. Its true motive was carefully concealed

The conquest a scandalous outrage.

* Col. Doc., ii, 414, 415; Alb. Rec., xviii., 323, 324, 326; Col. MSS., xv., 145; Gen. Ent., i., 31, 32; *ante*, vol. i., 763. Smith, i., 32, errs in stating that Stuyvesant refused, for two days, to ratify the articles, because they were "very disagreeable" to him. The true reason was that a Sunday intervened, and the articles themselves provided for their due execution on Monday.

† Col. Doc., ii., 366. The first dispatches which Nicolls sent home, containing an account of his transactions with the New England colonies and the surrender of New Netherland, were lost at sea in the Elias frigate, as will be stated hereafter: see Col. Doc., iii., 68, 92, 103; Pepys, ii., 185; *post*, p. 50, *note*.

CHAP. I. 1664. in all the diplomatic statements which attempted to justify the deed. The navigation laws of England, which were chiefly meant to cripple the commerce of her great maritime rival, could not be enforced in America as long as that rival possessed so important a province there. The intensely selfish spirit of those laws eagerly employed the most unjustifiable means to maintain them. Because England coveted New Netherland, and not because she had any rightful claim, she treacherously seized it as a prize. The whole transaction was eminently characteristic of an insolent and overbearing nation. On no other principle than that which frequently afterward governed the predatory aggressions of England in India and elsewhere can her conquest of the Dutch province be defended.

Nevertheless, unjustifiable as was the deed, the temptation to commit it was irresistible. Its actual execution was probably only a question of time. The event itself could hardly have been avoided by the Dutch government, unless all their previous policy had been reversed, and the holding of New Netherland at all hazards against any enemies been made an indispensable obligation. But this could not have been expected. Neither the West India Company—now on the brink of bankruptcy—nor the States General adequately valued their American province. It was not until toward the end of their rule that the importance of New Netherland and the necessity of securing it seriously engaged the attention of the authorities in Holland. Even then their apparent indifference encouraged the mousing designs of England. Charles the Second decreed that the United Netherlands should no longer have a foothold in North America. The decree was executed; and the Dutch province became the easy prey of undeclared enemies, who sneaked, in time of peace, into her chief harbor. New York replaced New Netherland on the map of the world. Although wars in Europe followed, the result in America was the same. Holland retired from the unequal strife, leaving France and Spain to contend for a season with England for ultimate supremacy in North America.

The event inevitable.

What England gained.

By the conquest of New Netherland England became the mistress of all the Atlantic coast between Acadia and Florida. On the north and west her colonies were now

CHAP. I. 1664.

bounded by the French possessions, on the south by those of Spain, on the east by the ocean. Yet, although the British American dominions thus became geographically united, they were neither homogeneous in character nor sympathetic in feeling. The Puritan colonies, while they rejoiced in the subjection of their "noxious neighbors" to the crown of England, had themselves no respect for their own ungodly sovereign. The aid which they had given to the royal commissioners was a fatal political mistake, if any purpose of independence was really cherished. They thus lost the best opportunity they ever had of securing their local governments, because the king was now master of the most advantageous position on the continent, from which he could, if necessary, direct military and naval operations for their reduction in case of revolt. Maryland, equally removed from Puritan severity and Cavalier license, was content that its territorial dispute should at all events be adjourned. Virginia, perhaps, felt less interest in the event, although the prompt loyalty of her people, who had hastened to proclaim their restored sovereign, was naturally gratified at the extension of his dominion over all the neighboring coast between Cape Henlopen and Montauk Point.

Prevailing influence of New York.

In the progress of years, a common allegiance and common dangers produced greater sympathy among the Anglo-American plantations. Nevertheless, although incorporated into the British colonial empire, New York never lost her social and political identity and her salutary moral influence. It was her lot to sustain fiercer trials, and gain a more varied experience, than any other American state. It was equally her destiny to temper the narrow characteristics of her English sister colonies with the larger ideas which she had herself derived from Holland. Midway between New England and Virginia, she stood for nearly a century guarding her long frontier against the attacks of Canada; and at length she became the PIVOT PROVINCE, on which hinged the most important movements of that sublime revolt against the oppression of England, the only parallel to which was the successful struggle that the forefathers of her first settlers maintained against the gigantic despotism of Spain.

CHAP. I.

1664.

Liberal policy of the Duke of York.

The terms of capitulation offered by Nicolls and accepted by Stuyvesant were, perhaps, the most favorable ever granted by a conqueror. In theory, the king only resumed his rightful authority over a province which had been intrusively occupied and improved by the Dutch. Once reduced under his own proprietary rule, the Duke of York hoped that it would become not only profitable to himself, but a valuable accession to the colonial dominions of the crown, to which he was the presumptive heir. His policy, therefore, was to obtain peaceful possession of the territory, and at the same time induce its Dutch inhabitants to remain there and become loyal English subjects. Indeed, the duke's patent authorized him to govern British subjects only. The most liberal inducements were accordingly offered to the people of New Netherland, with ostentatious benevolence. On the other hand, the Dutch colonists, chagrined at the imbecility and seeming indifference of the authorities in the fatherland, and having many causes of complaint against their own provincial government, accepted the change of rulers calmly and hopefully, if not with positive satisfaction.

The people gain nothing by the change.

Yet, by becoming British subjects, the Dutch inhabitants of New Netherland did not gain political freedom. Fresh names and laws, they found, did not secure fresh liberties. Amsterdam was changed to York, and Orange to Albany. But these changes only commemorated the titles of a conqueror. It was nearly twenty years before that conqueror allowed for a brief period to the people of New York even that faint degree of representative government which they had enjoyed when the three-colored ensign of Holland was hauled down from the flag-staff of Fort Amsterdam. New Netherland exchanged Stuyvesant, and the West India Company, and a republican sovereignty, for Nicolls, and a royal proprietor, and a hereditary king. The province was not represented in Parliament; nor could the voice of its people reach the chapel of Saint Stephen at Westminster as readily as it had reached the chambers of the Binnenhof at the Hague.

Loyalty of the Dutch.

Nevertheless, to all the changes which befell them, the Dutch colonists of New York submitted with characteristic good faith. No more loyal subjects than they were ever brought under the British crown. Yet it was not pleasant for them to watch the red cross of England waving where the emblems of the Netherlands had floated for fifty years. To Holland they felt a deep, unalterable, hereditary attachment. Nor have the vicissitudes of time extinguished that sentiment in their descendants. Two centuries have scarcely weakened the veneration which citizens of New York of Dutch lineage proudly cherish toward the fatherland of their ancestors. Year by year the glorious and the genial memories of Holland are renewed by those whom long generations have separated from the country of their forefathers. But colonists usually retain more affection toward their fatherland than those who remain at home ever feel toward the emigrants who leave its shores. As years roll on, the contrast becomes more marked. Two centuries have almost wiped out of the recollection of Holland the once familiar name of New Netherland. A few of the more curious of her scholars and her statesmen may sometimes, by careful search, discover the meagre paragraphs in which her ponderous histories dismiss the story of her ancient trans-Atlantic province. But the people of the Low Countries scarcely know that New York was once their own New Netherland, or that they have any right to the glory of having laid the foundations of the mightiest state in the American Union, and the metropolis of the Western World.

Holland forgets New Netherland.

CHAPTER II.

1664–1665.

CHAP. II.

1664. 29 August. 8 Septem.

The Dutch march out of Fort Amsterdam.

On Monday morning, the twenty-ninth of August, sixteen hundred and sixty-four, Peter Stuyvesant, having performed his last official act as Director General of New Netherland by ratifying the articles of capitulation, placed himself at the head of his garrison, and marched out of Fort Amsterdam with arms fixed, colors flying, drums beating, and matches lighted. Wheeling to the left, the veteran led his sullen troops down the Beaver Street to the North River. From there they were hurried on board the West India Company's ship Gideon, which was preparing to sail for Holland. This was so arranged because the Dutch soldiers were enraged at not being allowed to strike a blow, and the British infantry were prudently kept out of sight until they were safely embarked. In the mean time the English regulars had taken post near the old mill. The Long Island and New England auxiliaries, by previous agreement between Stuyvesant and Nicolls, were kept together on the Brooklyn side of the river, and were not allowed to enter the city, because the burghers "were more apprehensive of being plundered by them than by the others." As the Dutch garrison marched out, the ensign of the United Provinces was hauled down, and an English corporal's guard took possession of the fort and hoisted the British flag, which Nicolls had borrowed from the frigate Guinea. Leaving Colonel Cartwright with his company, which was stationed at the ferry, to occupy the city gates and the City Hall, Nicolls advanced at the head of his own and Sir Robert Carr's companies, and, accompanied by the burgomasters, marched into the fort. After being formally inducted by the civic authorities, who "gave him a welcome reception," the English governor performed his first

The English flag hoisted.

CHAP. II.

1664.

official act by directing that the city of New Amsterdam should thenceforth be called "New York," and Fort Amsterdam "Fort James."*

New York and Fort James named.

The surrender being thus accomplished without bloodshed, Nicolls at once dismissed the Long Island and New England volunteers. The Massachusetts delegates were sent back, with the thanks of the royal commissioners to her General Court. The governor also addressed a letter to Captain John Younge, of Southold, who commanded the Long Island militia, desiring him to make out a list of those who had taken up arms "for their king and country," so that they might be suitably rewarded, and promising that deputies from the several towns should, "in convenient time and place, be summoned, to propose and give their advice in all matters tending to the peace and benefit of Long Island."†

29 August. Long Island and New England volunteers dismissed.

The new provincial government was now organized. The governor's subordinate, Captain Matthias Nicolls, of Islip, in Northamptonshire, who had accompanied him from England, and was a lawyer, was appointed secretary of the province. Captains Robert Needham and Thomas Delavall, also from England, together with Secretary Nicolls, Thomas Topping, of Southampton, and William Wells, of Southold, were named counselors. On extraordinary occasions, Stuyvesant's late secretary, Cornelis van Ruyven, and Schepen Johannes van Brugh, were sometimes called on to assist. Delavall was also appointed collector and receiver general of New York and its neighborhood.‡

Nicolls's new government.

The Dutch municipal officers were continued in their places by virtue of the articles of capitulation. The day after the surrender, the Court of Burgomasters and Schepens of the city of New York assembled to transact their ordinary business, and proceeded to administer justice as if

30 August.
9 Septem.

* Alb. Rec., xviii., 326; Col. MSS., xv., 145; Gen. Ent., i., 32, 55; Hazard's Reg. Penn., iv., 56; New Amst. Rec., v., 567–570; Val. Man., 1860, 592, 593; Col. Doc., ii., 250–253, 415, 422, 440, 445, 446, 501, 502, 509, 744; Bushwick Rec.; Thompson, ii., 165; *ante*, vol. i., 742, 743, 763. As the old style was used in England, it was now introduced into New York. I shall therefore follow that supputation, adding, whenever necessary, the corresponding date in the new style in a line under the old. The historical, and not the English legal year, will, however, be used between 1 January and 25 March.

† Gen. Ent., i., 29, 30; Thompson, i., 127; Smith, i., 32.

‡ Patents, i., 3; Deeds, ii., 24; S. Wood, 144; Thompson, ii., 390; Val. Man., 1847, 351, 360; 1852, 381; 1853, 380, 383.

CHAP. II. 1664.

6/16 Septem. City officers continued.

nothing unusual had occurred. A few days afterward they wrote to the West India Company, by the ship Gideon, which, with a pass from Nicolls, took home the late garrison, under the command of Ensign Nyssen, describing the surrender, and adding that, "since we have no longer to depend upon your honor's promises or protection, we, with all the poor, sorrowing, and abandoned commonalty here, must fly for refuge to the Almighty God, not doubting but He will stand by us in this sorely afflicting conjuncture." By the same vessel Stuyvesant and his late coun-

6/16 Septem. Letters to Holland.

cil also sent the company an official account of the capitulation, and declared "that they would prefer to suffer shipwreck in the empty praise and esteem of the world, than, waiting to the last moment without hope of relief, subject every thing to bloodshed, or at least to the danger of being plundered."* Domine Samuel Drisius, one of the collegi-

15 Septem.

ate ministers of the Dutch Church, also wrote an interesting letter to the Classis of Amsterdam, detailing the circumstances of the surrender.†

English and Dutch Church service.

For the first time, the English Episcopal service was now celebrated in New York. The articles of capitulation expressly declared that all public buildings should continue in their previous uses, and that the Dutch should enjoy their accustomed divine worship and church disci-

11 October.

pline. Provision was accordingly made by the burgomasters and schepens for the due support of the Domines Megapolensis and Drisius, until the governor should make farther arrangements. The chaplain of the English forces had, however, no proper place in which to celebrate divine service, except in the Dutch Church in the fort. It was very cordially arranged that after the Dutch had ended their own morning worship in their church, the British chaplain should read the Church of England service there to the governor and the garrison. This was all the footing that the English Episcopal Church had in New York for more than thirty years.‡

* Gen. Ent., i., 34, 35, 141; New Amst. Rec., v., 555, 560–570; Val. Man., 1860, 592, 593; Col. Doc., ii., 422, 504, 744; Mass. Hist. Soc., Trumbull Pap., xx., 73; Col. MSS., x. (iii.), 323.

† A translation of this letter, which gives several details heretofore unknown, was published for the first time in the Appendix to Brodhead's Oration on the Conquest of New Netherland, delivered before the New York Historical Society on 12 October, 1864.

‡ Doc. Hist. N. Y., iii., 265; Col. Doc., iii., 262, 415; iv., 325, 526; New Amst. Rec., v., 599; Hist. Mag., i. (ii.), 322; Benson's Mem., ii. N. Y. H. S. Coll. (ii.), 103; Humphreys's

1664.

9/19 Septem.

Meanwhile, Fort Orange and Esopus, although included in the capitulation, remained to be reduced under the duke's authority. Accordingly, as soon as the Gideon had sailed for Holland with the Dutch garrison, and the safety of the capital was thus assured, Nicolls commissioned his colleague, Colonel Cartwright, to go up the river with his company and occupy those places. The authorities and inhabitants of Fort Orange were required to aid him in obtaining quiet possession, and to obey him according to the governor's instructions, especially "in case the Mohawks or other Indians shall attempt any thing against the lives, goods, or chattels of those who are now under the protection of his majesty of Great Britain." Van Rensselaer was also directed to bring the title papers respecting Rensselaerswyck down to New York for the governor's inspection, and, in the mean time, to obey Cartwright's orders. In order to secure the transfer to the English of the friendship which the Iroquois had cherished toward the Dutch, Nicolls requested some persons who had experience in dealing with the savages to accompany the military officers of the expedition. One of these was Willett, of Plymouth, and the other was Captain Thomas Breedon, of Boston, formerly governor of Nova Scotia, who had visited Fort Orange in 1662. Cartwright's chief military subordinates were Captain John Manning and Captain Daniel Brodhead. Manning seems to have formerly commanded a trading vessel between New Haven and Manhattan, but was now in the regular service. Brodhead was a zealous Royalist, of Yorkshire, England, where his family had lived "in the credit and reputation of gentlemen," and who, having a captain's commission from the king, embarked with his household for America in the expedition of Nicolls.*

10/20 Septem. Expedition to Fort Orange.

September.

When Cartwright reached Fort Orange, he found that De Decker, one of Stuyvesant's late plenipotentiaries at the capitulation, had hurried up thither from New York,

Hist. Acc., 201; Thompson, ii., 205; Christian Journal, quoted in Dr. Berrian's sketch of Trinity Church, 11. The names of the earliest chaplains of the English forces in New York are not known. The first that has come down to us is that of the Rev. Charles Wolley, a graduate of Cambridge, who officiated from Aug., 1678, to July, 1680: Hist. Mag., v., 153, 189.

* Gen. Ent., i., 34, 35, 141; Renss. MSS.; Col. Doc., i., 496; ii., 422, 502; iii., 39–41, 65, 83, 149, 270; ix., 75; Munsell's Ann., vii., 97; Morton's Mem., 311, *note;* Hutch. Mass., i., 215, 220, 224, 225; Mass. Rec., iv. (ii.), 69, 75; Hazard, ii., 462, 463; Palfrey, i., 163; ii., 495, 525, 575; New Haven Rec., ii., 68–75; Josselyn's Voyages, 153; ii. N. Y. H. S. Coll., i., 384; (1869), 16, 37, 57, 337, *ante*, vol. i., 519, 525, 579, 585, 704, 736, 743.

CHAP. II. 1664.

and was endeavoring "to alienate the minds of his majesties' Dutch subjects from that happy reconcilement without bloodshed upon articles so lately made." But the counselor's efforts were vain. La Montagne and the magistrates had no disposition to resist. Little change was made except in the name of the place, which was thenceforth to be called "Albany," after the Scotch title of the Duke of York. All the inferior officers and civil magistrates were continued in their places. An English garrison occupied the little fortress, which was named "Fort Albany," and placed in charge of Captain Manning. Soon afterward, several Mohawk and Seneca sachems appeared at the fort, and signed with Cartwright the first treaty between the Iroquois and the English. It was covenanted that the Indians should have all the commodities from the English which they formerly had from the Dutch; that offenses should be reciprocally punished; and that the River Indians, and those below Manhattan, should be included in the treaty. The next day it was farther agreed that the English should not assist the hostile Eastern tribes, that they should make peace for the Iroquois with the nations down the river, that the Iroquois should have free trade, and "be lodged in houses" as formerly, and that, if they should be beaten by the Eastern tribes, they should "receive accommodation" from the English. The friendship thus established continued to be maintained with remarkable fidelity on both sides for more than a century, until the American Revolutionary War.

Fort Orange submits. Named Albany. Manning commander. 24 Septem. First English treaty with the Iroquois. 25 Septem.

On his return from Albany Cartwright landed at Esopus. As at Albany, care was taken to conciliate the inhabitants. William Beekman was retained in his place as schout, or sheriff, while Thomas Chambers remained commissary, and Matthys Capito secretary of the village of Wildwyck. A garrison of regular soldiers occupied the fort, under the command of Captain Brodhead. The only opposition which Cartwright experienced during his expedition was from De Decker, at Albany; and Nicolls, on learning his conduct, ordered the too patriotic Hollander to leave the government within ten days. The deputies who accompanied Cartwright from Albany agreed to written articles with Nicolls that the inhabitants there "should en-

Brodhead in command at Esopus. 30 Septem. 10 October.

1664.

joy all the articles of surrender" made at New York, and that former local arrangements were generally to remain in force. Jeremias van Rensselaer was also confirmed in his authority, on condition that a new patent should be obtained from the duke, and the inhabitants of Rensselaerwyck should take the oath of allegiance.* 18 October. Rensselaerwyck.

By the articles of capitulation, the Dutch, who were three fourths of the inhabitants, were at liberty to sell their lands, and remove with their families and personal effects to Holland. But Nicolls, from the first, had been anxious to retain them all in their present homes, and induce them to become British subjects. He therefore went to the meeting of the metropolitan burgomasters and schepens, and having sent for Stuyvesant, Van Ruyven, and the Dutch ministers, invited them to take an oath to be true subjects of the King of Great Britain, and to obey all commands from his majesty, the Duke of York, or his governors and officers, while they lived in any of his majesty's territories. This obligation did not involve any permanent renunciation of allegiance to the Dutch government. Nevertheless, great reluctance to take it was shown, as the articles of surrender, while they declared that "all people shall still continue free denizens," did not provide for their swearing to a new allegiance. After much debate, "all the meeting roundly declared" that they could not take such an oath unless the governor should add to it "conformable to the articles concluded on the surrender of this place." Their reason for insisting was that otherwise they might "nullify or render void the articles." Domine Megapolensis and Secretary Van Ruyven, however, "saw no impediment" to taking the proposed oath. 14 October. Oath of allegiance required.

A few days afterward the burgomasters called upon Nicolls, with whom, in the presence of Cartwright and Willett, the matter of swearing was again discussed. To put an end to the "false and injurious aspersion" regarding it by which the minds of the inhabitants were by this time distracted, Nicolls declared in writing "that the articles of surrender are not in the least broken, or intended to be broken, by any words or expressions in the said oath." This 18 October. 20 October.

* Gen. Ent., i., 36–50; Col. Doc., iii., 67, 68, 94; Colden (ed. 1755), i., 34; Smith, i., 33; ii. N. Y. H. S. Coll., i., 384; Munsell, vii., 97, 98; Val. Man., 1847, p. 370; Esopus Records; O'Call., ii., 305, 431, 552; *ante*, vol. i., 714, 729, 732, 744, 761.

CHAP. II. 1664. 21 October to 26 October. Allegiance sworn by the Dutch.

answer satisfied all. Tonneman, the schout, although intending to return to Holland in the next ship, did not refuse to take the obligation. In the course of the next five days, upward of two hundred and fifty of the Dutch inhabitants, including Stuyvesant, Van Ruyven, the Domines Megapolensis and Drisius, Beekman, Van Rensselaer, and others from New York, Esopus, and Albany, swore allegiance to Charles the Second and the Duke of York.*

The governor's statesmanship was quickly vindicated. The "Vroedschap," or great council of the city, having been called together to elect a successor to Tonneman, chose Allard Anthony; and Nicolls, confirming their choice, gave the new sheriff a commission and instructions for his guidance. As the soldiers had already become unruly, Nicolls appointed Anthony Wharton to be provost-marshal, to keep them from interfering with the citizens, and to punish offenders. The city authorities testified their good will in a letter to the Duke of York, drawn up by Burgomaster Steenwyck, praising Nicolls as a "gentle, wise, and intelligent" governor, under whose wings they hoped to "bloom and grow like the cedar on Lebanon." To this end they prayed that the city of New York might have the same commercial privileges as the king's subjects in England, or even be as free from burdens as Boston; in which case, in a few years, the duke would derive great revenues from a province which would be "then peopled with thousands of families, and having great trade by sea with New England, and other places in Europe, Africa, and America."†

22 Novem. 12 Decem. 21 Novem. 22 Novem. City's letter to the Duke of York.

Thus was an imperial territory added to the dominions of England. Specific names were now given to the acquisition, so as to "comprehend all the titles" of the Duke of York. The province itself was called "New York." Long Island was designated as "Yorkshire." The region between the Hudson and the Delaware, of which little was known beyond the few hamlets near Manhattan, was named "Albania."

Yorkshire and Albania.

Of all the territory of New York, Albania offered the greatest attractions to emigrants. It was considered the

* Gen. Ent., i., 49, 50; New Amsterdam Rec., v., 614–618; Val. Man., 1861, 605–607; Col. Doc., iii., 74–77; H. B. Dawson's "Sons of Liberty in New York," 14–16.

† New Amst. Rec., v., 643–646; Patents, i., 151–155; Val. Man., 1861, 607, 608; Valentine's City of New York, 161–163.

most "improveable part" of the province "in respect not CHAP. II.
only to the quantity of the land, but to the sea-coast and
Delaware River, the fertility of the soil, the neighborhood 1664.
to Hudson's River, and, lastly, the fair hopes of rich mines."
Communipaw, Bergen, and Staten Island, already settled Settlements in Albania.
by the Dutch, were now to gain new neighbors. John
Bailey, Daniel Denton, and others, of Jamaica, on Long Isl-
and, asked leave to buy and settle a tract of land on the 26 Sept.
After Cull River,* which they had formerly intended to
do, but had been "obstructed by the then ruling Dutch."
Nicolls, wishing to give the Long Island people some "reward for their fidelity" previous to the surrender, cheerfully assented, and promised the petitioners "all due en- 30 Sept.
couragement in so good a work." Bailey and Denton,
with their associates, soon bought from the savages the 28 October.
land between the Raritan River and Newark Bay, which
had been purchased thirteen years before by Augustine
Heermans. The English purchase, however, was confirmed 2 Dec.
by Nicolls to Captain John Baker and John Ogden, who
had bought out Denton's interest, and to Bailey and their
associates, upon condition of their "doing and performing
such acts and things as shall be appointed by his royal
highness the Duke of York or his deputy." Before long,
four families from Jamaica began the settlement of what
was soon afterward known as Elizabethtown.†

The military and naval officers who accompanied Nicolls
from England also became large landholders. Captain
James Bollen, the commissary of ammunition at Fort Grants of land.
James, and others, received a grant on Staten Island. A 24 Dec.
tract at Hackensack was granted to Captain Edward Grove, 3 October.
of the Martin. To Captain William Hill, Lieutenant Hum-
phrey Fox, and Master Coleman, of the Elias, were severally allotted parcels of land on Staten Island. The naval
grantees, however, had scarcely time to take possession of
their domains; for their ships, being no longer required for
service at New York, were sent back to England with dis-

* This was an English corruption of the Dutch name "Achter Cul" (now called Newark Bay), which was given because it was *achter*, or "behind" the bay of New York. The passage leading to this cul was called the "Kil van Cul," and is now known as "the Kills." See *ante*, vol. i., 313, *note*.

† Col. Doc., iii., 105; Chalmers, i., 615, 624, 625; Patents, i., 20; Elizabethtown Bill in Chancery (1747), 25–28; Leaming and Spicer, 668–673; Smith's N. Jersey, 62; Gordon, 27; Whitehead's E. J., 19, 36–39; Index N. J. Col. Doc., 47; Thompson's L. I., ii., 103; Denton's N. Y., 13, 15; *ante*, vol. i., 537, 707, 708, 724.

CHAP. II.

1664.

patches from Nicolls announcing the success of the expedition, and the establishment of the duke's government in what was lately New Netherland.*

The Delaware Territory.

An important question had been meanwhile presented for the action of the royal commissioners. The Duke of York's patent included only the territory lying east of the Delaware, and the authority of Nicolls as governor extended no farther. Yet the commissioners were instructed by the king to reduce to his obedience the Dutch wherever seated within his claimed dominions in North America. Nicolls soon learned that the Maryland people were "in some sort overawed" by the city of Amsterdam, to which the Delaware settlements belonged, and that, unless those possessions were acquired, the gaining of New York would be "of small advantage to his majesty." Without regarding Lord Baltimore's pretensions, the commissioners determined "to reduce the Delaware, thereby to assure this place for his royal highness."

3/13 Sept. Expedition to reduce the Dutch on the Delaware.

Five days after the capitulation of New Amsterdam, Nicolls, with Cartwright and Maverick, accordingly commissioned their colleague, Sir Robert Carr, to go with the Guinea, Captain Hyde, and the William and Nicholas, Captain Morley, and "all the soldiers which are not in the fort," and reduce the Delaware settlements. Carr was instructed to promise the Dutch the possession of all their property and all their present privileges, "only that they change their masters." To the Swedes he was to "remonstrate their happy return under a monarchical government, and his majesty's good inclination to that nation." To Lord Baltimore's officers in Maryland he was to declare that their proprietor's pretended right to the Delaware being "a doubtful case," possession would be kept for the king "till his majesty is informed and satisfied otherwise."†

Carr's expedition sailed from New York just before Cart-

* Patents, i., 5, 7–9, 22; Col. Doc., ii., 470; iii., 68, 92, 103. The Elias was wrecked near the Lizard, and all the letters in her sent by Nicolls were lost. For this reason, among others, the early records relating to New York in the State Paper Office are so defective. Captain Hill and a few men were saved. Hill afterward obtained another ship, was at the battle of Lowestoffe the next June, then at Barbadoes, and in the autumn of 1667 returned to England from France, where he had been a prisoner. Captain Grove arrived safely with the Martin, and behaved like a coward at Lowestoffe. He was "reckoned a prating coxcomb and of no courage," and was certainly an adept in the business of bribing for office: Pepys, i., 401, 402; iii., 294; Mass. H. S. Coll., xxxvii., 190.

† Gen. Ent., i., 53, 58, 59; Hazard's Reg. Penn., 36, 37; Col. Doc., ii., 296; iii., 52, 57, 63, 69, 70; Col. MSS., xx., 1.

wright's went up to Fort Orange. After a tedious voyage, prolonged by the ignorance of the pilots and the shoaliness of the Delaware, the ships anchored above New Amstel. The Swedes were soon made friends. But the Dutch at first were obstinate for a defense. After a long parley, Fob Oothout and five others, on behalf of the burghers, signed articles of capitulation as favorable as those which had been agreed to by Stuyvesant. But Hinnoyossa, the city's governor, with less than fifty soldiers, resolved to defend the fort. The next Sunday morning the ships dropped down, and fired two broadsides each, while a company of foot, under the command of Lieutenant John Carr, a son of Sir Robert, with Ensign Arthur Stock, stormed the works. The Dutch fired three volleys of musketry, but none of their ordnance, on their assailants, who did not lose a man; while three of the garrison were killed and ten wounded. Carr now landed from the Guinea, and claimed the pillage for himself as "won by the sword." Assuming an authority independent of Nicolls, he claimed to be "sole and chief commander and disposer" of all affairs on the Delaware. With quick rapacity, he appropriated Hinnoyossa's farm to himself, Schout Van Sweringen's to his son John, and Peter Alricks's to Ensign Stock. To Captains Hyde and Morley he granted a tract of land in the upper part of the river, called by the Indians "Chipussen," which he erected into a manor by the name of "Grimstead." The Dutch soldiers were sent into Virginia to be sold as slaves. The property of the city of Amsterdam, as well as that of the inhabitants about New Amstel, was remorselessly seized. To complete the work of Carr—in such disgraceful contrast to that of Nicolls at Manhattan—a boat was sent down to the Hoarkill, where all the city's effects were plundered, and even the inoffensive Mennonists, who formed "the Quaking Society of Plockhoy," were stripped "to a very naile."

Chap. II.

1664.
30 Sept.
10 October.

$\frac{1}{11}$ Oct.

$\frac{2}{12}$ Oct.

Conquest of the Delaware.

Rapacity of Carr.

$\frac{10}{20}$ Oct.

The ships were quickly sent back to New York with a report from Carr of his proceedings, and of the hostile attitude of the Susquehanna Indians, who were then at war with the Iroquois Senecas. But Carr himself, instead of returning to assist in executing the royal commission, would not leave the Delaware. His colleagues thought his conduct there presumptuous and disgraceful. They

$\frac{13}{23}$ Oct.

Carr rebuked.

CHAP. II. 1664. 24 Oct./3 Novem. peremptorily required him to return to New York; and Cartwright and Maverick commissioned Nicolls to proceed to Delaware Bay, "there to take special care for the good government of the said place, and to depute such officer or officers therein as he shall think fit, for the management of his majestie's affairs, both civil and military, until his majestie's pleasure be further known." In writing to Secretary Bennet, Nicolls rebuked Carr's conduct, and added that because of his absence, "his majestie's commission can not be pursued in the several colonies of New England unless I should leave New York, and thereby put to hazard the security of all at once, contrary to the opinions of Colonel Cartwright, Mr. Maverick, and all the reason which God hath given me. For we do concur that we came to serve his majesty and not our own ends." Nicolls farther urged that merchandise for the Indian trade and the necessities of the inhabitants should be promptly sent out. By the loss of the former Dutch trade, thousands in Virginia, Maryland, and New England were deprived of their accustomed necessaries, and would not know how to live "without speedy care be taken from England." If Lord Baltimore should solicit the grant of Delaware to himself, the king ought to look upon his patent as forfeited, for trading with the Dutch contrary to the Navigation Act. Nicolls also submitted that if the Dutch should attempt to recover either New York or Delaware, the king should "enjoin all his colonies, none excepted, under severe penalties, to resist and expel all such foreigners out of these his majesty's territories." With these dispatches the Guinea was ordered to follow the Elias and the Martin to England. But her departure was delayed by a mutiny which broke out among the soldiers in the garrison of Fort James, and she did not sail until nearly a month afterward. Captain Harry Norwood, whom Nicolls not long afterward recommended as his own successor, returned in her to England.

26 Oct./5 Novem.

Nicolls's report to Secretary Bennet.

26 Oct.

22 Novem.

In pursuance of the commission of his two colleagues, Nicolls visited the Delaware, accompanied by Captain Robert Needham, whom he proposed to leave there as his deputy in command. Carr was severely rebuked, and obliged to give up much of his ill-gotten spoil. Nevertheless, he could not be persuaded to leave the place for some time.

Nicolls goes to the Delaware.

The name of New Amstel was now changed to New Castle, and an infantry garrison established there. As Needham's presence at Fort James, to act as first counselor, was desirable, Captain John Carr was appointed commander of the Delaware, in subordination to the government of New York, to which it was annexed "as an appendage;" and thus affairs remained for several years.*

Upon the return of Nicolls to New York, the royal commissioners proceeded to execute a very delicate duty. The Connecticut Charter of 1662 covered not only the entire territory of New Haven, but also a large part of New Netherland. The Dutch rejected the claims of the Hartford Court, and New Haven stoutly refused to yield to Connecticut, because her charter had been surreptitiously obtained "contrary to righteousness, amity, and peace." The Duke of York's patent, however, not only comprehended Long Island and other neighboring islands, but the whole of New Haven, and the greater part of Connecticut, including Hartford itself. When this became known, both the wrangling Puritan colonies were seriously troubled at a specimen of majestic usurpation which outdid their own encroachments on the Dutch territory. Yet Connecticut was in no condition to oppose so powerful an antagonist as the presumptive heir to the crown. New Haven was still more helpless. Her only alternative was submission to Connecticut, or annexation to New York. After a sorrowful debate, her General Court determined to submit to Connecticut; yet final action was postponed until it could no longer be avoided.

Boundary with Connecticut.

11 August. 14 Septem.

In this dilemma it was important to conciliate the royal commissioners. At their first meeting after the surrender of New Netherland, the Connecticut Court voted a present of five hundred bushels of corn to Nicolls and his colleagues. They also appointed Mathew Allyn, Nathan Gold, James Richards, and Captain John Winthrop to go with Governor Winthrop to New York and congratulate the commissioners, "and, if an opportunity offer itself, that they can issue the bounds between the duke's patent and

13 October.

Agents sent to New York.

* Gen. Ent., i., 53, 55, 56, 57, 60, 61, 62, 67; Coll. MSS., xx., 1; Col. Doc., ii., 369, 411, 421, 434, 438; iii., 68-74, 83, 103, 104, 109, 113, 115, 345, 346; Mass. H. S. Coll., xxxvii., 309-311; Chalmers, i., 634; Hazard's Reg. Penn., i., 37; iv., 56; Ann. Penn., 355-369; S. Smith's N. J., 46-50; Proud, i., 122-124; N. Y. H. S. Coll. (1869), 81; *ante*, vol. i., 717, 744.

CHAP. II. 1664. ours (so as in their judgments may be to the satisfaction of the court), they are impowered to attend the same." John Howell and Captain John Younge, of Long Island, were desired "to attend the same service." Horses were likewise presented by Winthrop to the royal commissioners.*

The Connecticut delegates accordingly visited New York, where they were received by Nicolls, Cartwright, and Maverick. 30 Novem. Both patents were produced, and all that could be said on each side was fully considered. The question about Long Island was soon decided. The duke's patent expressly included it by name; that of Connecticut did not. Moreover, Governor Winthrop, at Gravesend, a few days before the surrender, had declared that the jurisdiction formerly exercised by Connecticut over Long Island "ceased and became null." The commissioners, therefore, at once determined that the southern boundary of Connecticut should be the Sound, and that Long Island should be under the government of the Duke of York, "as is so expressed by plain words in the said patents respectively." Long Island adjudged to New York.

But Connecticut claimed that, under her charter, her territory extended across the continent to the Pacific Ocean. On the other hand, the Duke of York's patent covered all her territory west of the Connecticut River, and left her only the narrow strip between the east side of that river and Rhode Island. Moreover, she had not yet obtained possession of New Haven. Her charter had been granted only upon Winthrop's promise of submission "to any alteration" in her boundaries which might be made by the king's commissioners. Their authority to declare Hartford itself within the jurisdiction of New York, as it had once been within the jurisdiction of New Netherland, could not be disputed. The original Indian deed of 8 June, 1633, to Commissary Van Curler, of the land around Hartford, was appealed to in proof. But the commissioners were supplicated not to enforce the duke's patent to its full extent, which would deprive Connecticut of her "very bowels and principal parts." In the judgment of Nicolls, such a decision would "cast dishonor upon his majesty,"

* Col. Rec. Conn., i., 415, 427, 433, 435; iii., 480; New Haven Rec., ii., 467–483, 491-548; Mass. H. S. Coll., xxxvii., 311; Col. Doc., iii., 184; Chalmers, i., 293–296; Doc. Hist. N. Y., i., 504; Trumbull, i., 249–272, 515–521; Palfrey, ii., 545–556, 592–595; iii., 236; *ante*, vol. i., 519, 702, 733.

and be "to the utter ruin of that colony, and a manifest breach of their late patent." Besides, in the delicate relations in which the commissioners were placed respecting all the New England colonies, it was important this should be made "a leading case of equal justice." They therefore determined that five towns, which "had been purchased, possessed, or gained" by Hartford, or by New Haven, should be "relinquished to Connecticut by virtue of their precedent grant from his majesty." Such a settlement, they "were assured, would be an acceptable service" to the Duke of York, although to the diminution of his patented bounds.

CHAP. II.

1664.

Five towns yielded to Connecticut.

At the same time, it was distinctly understood on both sides that the dividing line should run "about twenty miles from any part of Hudson's River." An agreement to this effect was drawn up between Nicolls and Winthrop and his colleagues. To define the starting-point and the compass direction of this boundary, an amendment was inserted, describing it as running from the head of Mamaroneck Creek to the north-north-west, until it reaches the Massachusetts line. The amendment seems to have been proposed by the Connecticut delegates, who assured Nicolls that the boundary thus described would be "twenty miles every where from Hudson's River."

30 Novem.

Boundary-line on the main land.

Upon this basis the royal commissioners the next day signed an instrument, in which, after declaring Long Island to be under the government of the Duke of York, they ordered "that the creek or river called Mamaroneck, which is reported to be about thirteen miles to the east of West-chester, and a line drawn from the east point or side, where the fresh water falls into the salt at high-water-mark, north-north-west to the line of the Massachusetts, be the western bounds of the said colony of Connecticut; and all plantations lying westward of that creek and line so drawn to be under his royal highness's government; and all plantations lying eastward of that creek and line to be under the government of Connecticut." Winthrop and his colleagues at the same time gave their "consent to the limit and bounds above mentioned."*

1 Decem.

Boundaries established.

* Gen. Ent., i., 70, 71; N. Y. Col. MSS., xxii., 5; lxix., 1-6; N. Y. Senate Doc., 1857, No. 165, p. 7, 39, 41, 42, 100-104; Col. Doc., ii., 139, 140; iii., 55, 106, 238; vii., 564, 597; Col.

CHAP. II. 1664. 13 Decem.

For the moment, this settlement of the dispute seemed to be satisfactory to both parties. The submission of New Haven to Connecticut was soon completed. But Nicolls and his colleagues were strangers, and ignorant of the geography of the country. They supposed that they had adopted substantially the same boundary agreed to by the Dutch and English colonies in 1650. Unfortunately, they "relied upon" the assurances of the Connecticut delegates, and were deceived by "wrong information" which no honest or intelligent adviser could have given. The line assented to and intended by Nicolls—twenty miles every where from the Hudson River—instead of starting at Mamaroneck, should have started several miles farther to the east, near Stamford; and, instead of running north-north-west, it should have run due north. But the duped commissioners established a line, the starting-point of which was about ten miles from the Hudson, and which, crossing that river near Peekskill, intersected the prolonged southern boundary of Massachusetts near the north-west corner of the present New York county of Ulster. All the territory north and east of this line was thus apparently assigned to Connecticut and Massachusetts. The absurd error was soon detected, and the boundary was never ratified by the Duke of York or by the crown. But the pertinacity with which Connecticut clung to what looked very much like a mean deception on her part was afterward the cause of great controversy.*

Trickery of Connecticut.

Long Island being now settled under the Duke of York's authority, Nicolls, to conciliate its inhabitants, addressed a letter to Howell and Younge, who acted as their representatives at New York. Referring to his promise when he dismissed the troops in August, after the surrender, he informed all persons that Long Island was declared to be under the duke's government; that, as it was now winter, he would not trouble the inhabitants to send deputies to an Assembly in relation to the affairs of the island; but that,

Long Island affairs. 1 Decem.

Rec. Conn., ii., 341, 570–573; iii., 330; New Haven Rec., ii., 555, 556; Smith, i., 36–38, 297; ii., 305, 306; Trumbull, i., 273, 523, 525; Wood's Long Island, 28, 170, 173; Thompson, i., 126; ii., 323; Dunlap, ii., App. ccvi.; *ante*, vol. i., 96, 189, 234, 235, 519.

* Col. Rec. Conn., i., 441; ii., 341, 572, 573; iii., 330; New Haven Rec., ii., 551–557; Col. Doc., iii., 94, 230, 231, 235, 238, 247, 257, 333, 356, 406, 761; iv., 625; v., 698; vi., 125, 776, 885; vii., 563, 564, 596, 597; viii., 345; Hutch. Coll., 412; Smith, i., 38; Chalmers, i., 296, 576; Trumbull, i., 274; N. Y. H. S. Coll. (1869), 76.

CHAP. II. 1664.

as soon as the weather should permit, he would notify them of the time and place of meeting. In the mean time, the existing magistrates should remain in their places under the duke's government. No new taxes had yet been thought of; those laid by Connecticut should continue for a time; but the people might "assure themselves of equal (if not greater) freedoms and immunities than any of his majesty's colonies in New England." Upon the return of Howell and Younge, a town meeting was held at East Hampton, at which, "understanding that we are off from Connecticut, and the magistrates not willing to act further on that account, that we may not be without laws and government, it is agreed the former laws shall stand in force till we have further order from New York."* (21 Decem.)

In the mean time, the West India Company had informed the States General of the English conquest of New Netherland, by which the republic had "lost a province, the appearance whereof was wonderful to behold." The States at once directed Van Gogh, their ambassador at London, to expostulate with the king, and demand "prompt restitution and reparation." Van Gogh, in an audience with Charles, denounced the capture as "an erroneous proceeding, opposed to all right and reason, contrary to mutual correspondence and good neighborhood, and a notorious infraction of the treaty lately concluded." Finding that he could no longer dissimulate, the king replied with the audacious falsehood that his "dependency" New Netherland "had been settled and occupied before this by the English, who only permitted the Dutch nation at the outset to settle there, without any authority having been thereby conferred upon the Dutch West India Company." The next day Clarendon wrote to Downing that the Dutch need not expect the king to restore his conquests; "for they have no color of right to pretend to New Netherland, nor is our possessing that the least violation of the treaty." Downing accordingly told De Witt that the king was not accountable to the Dutch government for what he had done in America, "no more than he should think himself obliged to let them know his mind, or to have their consent, in case

(14/24 Oct.) (21/31 Oct.) (27 October / 6 Novem.) (The Dutch government denounce the conquest of New Netherland and demand its restitution.) (28 October / 7 Novem.) (4/14 Novem.)

* Gen. Ent., i., 29, 65, 66; Thompson's L. I., i., 127, 311, 382, 383; ii., 323, 324, 327; Wood, 177; Dunlap, ii., App. xxxvii.; Col. Doc., iii., 86; Doc. Hist., i., 462; *ante*, p. 43.

CHAP. II.

1664.

he should think fit to proceed against any Dutch that live in the fens in England, or in any other part of his dominions." Without stopping to demonstrate the transparent absurdity of this comparison, the Grand Pensionary peremptorily replied that New Netherland "must be restored."*

25 Novem. / 5 Decem.

Not long afterward Downing presented an insolent memorial to the States General, in which any reference to New Netherland was avoided. It was now clear that no redress was to be expected from England. Secret orders

2/12 Decem. Orders to De Ruyter.

were therefore sent to De Ruyter, who commanded the Dutch squadron on the coast of Africa, to reduce the English possessions there, after which he was to proceed on his voyage home, "and inflict, by way of reprisal, as much damage and injury as possible on said nation, either at Barbadoes, New Netherland, Newfoundland, or other islands and places under their obedience."

24 Novem. / 4 Decem.

At the opening of Parliament, the king laid great stress upon the proceedings of the Dutch in Africa and the East Indies, but did not allude to his own treacherous conquest

6/16 Decem.

of New York. A few days afterward Van Gogh had unsatisfactory interviews with the king and the Duke of York, both of whom were evidently disposed to hostilities. With his report, the ambassador communicated to the States General, for the first time, a copy of the king's grant of New Netherland to the Duke of York.

16/26 Decem.

It was not long before Downing informed the British government of the secret orders which the States General had sent to De Ruyter. Bennet and Coventry warmly urged hostilities against the Dutch. The Privy Council

Hostilities begun by England.

immediately directed letters of reprisal to be issued against "the ships, goods, and servants" of the United Provinces. According to British custom, without any formal declaration of war, one hundred and thirty Dutch merchant vessels were seized in the English ports.†

* Col. Doc., ii., 272–285; iii., 77–81; Aitzema, v., 193; Sec. Res. Holl., ii., 445; De Witt, iv., 386, 387, 390, 391, 393; Holl. Merc., 1664, 178; D'Estrades, ii., 530, 538; Lister's Clarendon, ii., 269; iii., 346–351; Hume, vi., 385.

† Col. Doc., ii., 285–298; iii., 85; Parl. Hist., iv., 296–303; Clarke's James II., i., 401–404; Aitzema, v., 93, 94; De Witt, iv., 413; Sec. Res. Holl., ii., 459; Holl. Merc., 1664, 185, 186; Lister, ii., 270; iii., 352–355; Basnage, i., 714; Davies, iii., 27, 28; Pepys, ii., 186, 192; Martin, i., 269. Downing stopped at nothing to gain his objects. He told Pepys "that he had so good spies that he hath had the keys taken out of De Witt's pocket when he was a-bed, and his closet opened, and papers brought to him and left in his hands for an hour;" and "that he hath always had their most private debates that have been but between two or

Intelligence of the threatening aspect of affairs in Europe had meanwhile reached Nicolls by way of Boston. As a measure of precaution, he ordered all the estate of the West India Company in the hands of Stuyvesant and Van Ruyven to be put under arrest. A few days afterward all persons were directed to report what they knew about the property thus sequestrated to the benefit of the Duke of York.*

CHAP. II. 1664. 13 Decem. 24 Decem. 27 Decem. Action of Nicolls.

The West India Directors, on their part, felt the loss of New Netherland very keenly. Stuyvesant's official report was unsatisfactory. The "licentious prating" of the soldiers who had returned in the Gideon from New York only increased their annoyance. They determined to "disavow all the articles and capitulations" made with the English by the governor and council, and endeavor to regain New Netherland. Accordingly, they sent one of their ships to New York, with a dispatch to Stuyvesant, requiring him to come home and give "by word of mouth more comfort" than his letters had afforded. They also desired Van Ruyven to save what he could of their property.

18/28 Novem. The West India Company recall Stuyvesant.

When these letters were received at New York, Nicolls, anxious for news, required Stuyvesant and Van Ruyven to bring them to him. As the West India Company appeared determined to annul the capitulation and retake the province, he felt himself "obliged so far to abide their displeasure as to seize upon their effects, and to remit the decision to his majesty, whether, after such a letter, they ought to claim any benefit by articles which in so contemptuous a manner they have disavowed."

1665. 15/25 Feb. 23 Feb./5 March. Nicolls seizes the company's estate.

Stuyvesant, however, could not avoid going to Holland to defend his action; and Nicolls granted him a passport to go and return, with his son and his servants. Considering the need of supplies to New York, Nicolls also licensed the West India Company's ship "Crossed Heart" to go to and return from Holland with merchandise. By her Van Ruyven wrote to the Amsterdam directors that it was "impossible to keep" New Netherland against the "vast, overwhelming force of the assailants;" and that, if their

21 April/1 May. 29 April/9 May.

three of the chief of them brought to him in an hour after, and an hour after that hath sent word thereof to the king."—Pepys, iv., 72, 73; see also Temple's Works, i., 307.

* Col. Doc., iii., 84; Gen. Ent., i., 76, 78, 79; Col. MSS., xxii., 1; Smith, i., 38.

CHAP. II. 1665.

honors had been personally present, they would, "without doubt, have considered it better and more Christian-like to agree to some conditions, than be obliged to look upon the ruin of the place and the murder of the poor people, women and children, without being able to do any thing to prevent it." A few days afterward Stuyvesant appeared, for the last time, in the Court of Burgomasters and Schepens, to take his leave, and asked of them a certificate of his deportment while their governor. The city authorities declared "that his honor hath, during eighteen years' administration, conducted and demeaned himself not only as a director general, as according to the best of our knowledge he ought to do, on all occasions for the best interest of the West India Company, but besides as an honest proprietor and patriot of this province, and as a supporter of the Reformed religion."*

2/12 May. Stuyvesant returns to Holland.

Notwithstanding all the changes which had occurred in the province, the city magistrates of whom Stuyvesant thus took leave still exercised the same powers which he had himself conferred on them twelve years before. When their term of service expired, the burgomasters and schepens named their successors, as they had done under the Dutch government. This they did on the usual day, and in pursuance of the sixteenth article of the capitulation. The new officers were confirmed by Nicolls, and announced to the commonalty after the usual ringing of the bell. They were Cornelis Steenwyck and Oloff Stevensen van Cortlandt, burgomasters; Timotheus Gabry, Johannes van Brugh, Johannes De Peyster, Jacob Kip, and Jacques Cousseau, schepens; and Allard Anthony, schout. An oath, drawn up by Nicolls, was taken by them, to do right and justice to all persons, and demean themselves in their places "according to the good and wholesome laws which are or shall be ordained by virtue of his majesty's commission to his Royal Highness the Duke of York, within this government and city of New York." A controversy soon arose between the provincial and the city authorities.

2 Feb'ry. New city officers. 6 Feb'ry.

* Col. Doc., ii., 361, 365, 369, 377, 420, 470, 744; iii., 164; Trumbull Papers, Mass. Hist. Soc., xx., 73; Hutch. Mass., i., 231, *note;* Gen. Ent., i., 168, 169, 170; New Amst. Rec., v., 755; Val. Man., 1861, 620, 621. Stuyvesant, accompanied by Ægidius Luyck, the late principal of the grammar-school at New Amsterdam (who now returned to study theology in Holland), landed from the "Crossed Heart" at Bergen, in Norway. From there they proceeded to Amsterdam, in July, 1665, in the company's yacht the Musch.

By the capitulation, the burgomasters were bound to provide quarters for the soldiers who could not be lodged in the fort. Nicolls therefore proposed that one hundred of them should be quartered among the inhabitants, who were to be compensated; and that, in consideration of this, the city should have, in addition to the great excise, the income of the scales and of the ferry. The municipal authorities endeavored to comply with the governor's requisition; but they were so unsuccessful that he accused them, apparently without justice, of sloth. The English soldiers were quarrelsome and insolent, and the Dutch burghers were unwilling to receive them into their houses. Most of the citizens preferred to pay an assessment in money; and the matter was finally arranged in this way, to the satisfaction of all parties, under the supervision of Captains Delavall and Salisbury.*

CHAP. II. 1665. 28 March. Soldiers quartered. 6 April. 19 April.

The provincial revenue had, up to this time, been left unsettled. Two months after the surrender, Nicolls had directed that the customs rates, "according to English law," should be paid to Delavall, the collector. He now enacted that, until farther order, imported liquors should be taxed ten per cent., Indian goods ten, other goods eight, and English manufactures five per cent. These duties were to be paid in beavers, at eight guilders, or thirteen shillings and four pence each. Export duties were also laid on beaver and tobacco.†

Provincial revenue. 27 Feb'ry.

Nicolls, however, was a friend of colonial enterprise. Paulus Richards, one of the burghers at New York, intending to establish a vineyard at the "Little Fief" on Long Island, and manufacture wine, the governor granted him several special privileges. All the produce of Richards's vines, if sold in gross, was to be forever free from any imposts; if sold in retail by him in any one house in New York, his wines were to be free for thirty years; and

Vineyards. 10 Jan'ry.

* N. Y. City Rec., v., 680, 682, 718-725, 737-743; vi., 86, 87; Gen. Ent., i., 83, 84; Col. Doc., iii., 117; Val. Man., 1848, 125; 1850, 196; 1861, 608-620; *ante*, vol. i., 548, 578, 613, 640, 674, 762. Among the burghers thus assessed, Jeronimus Ebbinck, Frederick Phillipse, Peter Stuyvesant, Cornelis van Ruyven, Paulus Leendertsen van der Grist, Johannes van Brugh, and Oloff Stevensen van Cortlandt paid four guilders a week; Allard Anthony, Johannes de Peyster, Jacob Kip, Simon Jansen Romeyn, and Carel van Brugh, three guilders; Jan Evertsen Bout, Evert Duyckinck, Johannes De Witt, Hans Kierstede, Jacob Leisler, and Paulus Richards, two guilders; Isaac Bedlow, Augustine Heermans, Ægidius Luyck, and many others, one guilder. The Dutch domines were not assessed.

† Gen. Ent., i., 68, 112, 113; Thompson, i., 144.

CHAP. II.

1665.

any person who, during that time, should plant vines in any part of the province, should pay five shillings for each acre so planted to Richards, "as an acknowledgment of his being the first undertaker and planter of vines in these parts."*

January. Royal commissioners in New England.

Soon after the arrangement of the Connecticut boundary, Cartwright and Maverick went to Boston to prosecute their duties as royal commissioners. But they could do nothing without the presence of Nicolls or Carr. The governor of New York was too much occupied to leave his post. Carr could not be persuaded, for some time, to quit the Delaware and follow the king's commission. At

4 Feb'ry.

length he came to New York, and went on to join his colleagues at Boston. The commissioners, finding much opposition there, determined to visit the other colonies, and wait until the next April before opening their business with Massachusetts, when they hoped that Nicolls would be able to join them. They were not deceived. Connecticut answered their inquiries with prudent facility. Their stumbling-block was to be Massachusetts.†

Policy of Nicolls.

Meanwhile, the details of the system upon which he was to administer his government in New York had seriously occupied the attention of Nicolls. The policy of the Duke of York was to win the Dutch, who were three quarters of the population, to become contented English subjects. To this end, as little alteration as possible was to be made in the form of administration to which they had been accustomed. The director general and his council had been the executive authority in New Netherland. The deputy governor of the proprietary and his council were now the executive authority of New York. Nicolls accordingly "copied," or rather "continued," with some modification, "what had been already established by the Dutch." He erected

Court of Assizes.

a "Court of Assizes," which, like its New Netherland prototype, was the supreme tribunal of the province, having both common law and equity, as well as original and appellate

* Deeds, ii., 87; Hist. Mag., vii., 30. New Netherland was famous for its native wines before 1650: Col. Doc., i., 277. Lord Bellomont, in 1700, wrote enthusiastically about the "fair clusters of grapes" which he saw about Albany: Col. Doc., iv., 787. Denton, 14, speaks of "grapes great and small" as natural to Long Island.

† Col. Doc., iii., 64, 83, 84, 87–89, 93; Mass. H. S. Coll., xxxvi., 532; Mass. Rec., iv. (ii.), 141; Plymouth Rec., iv., 85; R. I. Rec., ii, 60, 86–89, 91, 93; Palfrey, ii., 597–606; Barry, i., 396; Arnold's Rhode Island, i., 314.

jurisdiction. In this court, the governor and his counselors possessed the same powers that had formerly been exercised by the Dutch director and his counselors. But the peculiar condition of New York required that other members should be added to the Court of Assizes. Yorkshire, or Long Island, peopled chiefly by Englishmen, with Westchester and Staten Island, was erected into a shire, and, like its English namesake, was divided into three districts or ridings. What is now Suffolk County formed the East Riding; Staten Island, King's County, and the town of Newtown, in Queen's, the West Riding; and the remainder of Queen's County, with Westchester, the North Riding. The governor and council were to appoint a high-sheriff every year over the whole of Yorkshire, and also justices of the peace, who were to continue in office during the governor's pleasure in each of the ridings. These justices were to hold a "Court of Sessions" in each riding three times a year, in which the governor or any counselor might preside. Besides their local duties, the high sheriff and the justices were to sit with the governor and his council in the Court of Assizes, which was to meet at New York once a year, on the last Thursday in September. This court was invested with "the supreme power of making, altering, and abolishing any laws" in the government of New York.*

Ridings of Yorkshire.

High-sheriff and justices.

Court of Sessions.

The Court of Assizes thus established by Nicolls was no advance toward democracy. It was not, in any popular sense, a Legislature. It had not even the representative character enjoyed by Stuyvesant's "Landt-dag," or Assembly. Its members were wholly dependent on the governor's will, and they were expected to perform their legislative function with the usual docility of a French "bed of justice." The governor and his council remained the real law-makers, as well as the interpreters of the laws they made. Before long, it is true, the Court of Assizes delib-

The Court of Assizes not an Assembly.

* Chalmers's Pol. Ann., i., 575, 596; Rev. Col., i., 117; Col. Doc., iii., 188; N. Y. H. S. Coll., i., 321, 336, 342, 359, 374, 385, 391; *ante*, vol. i., 163, 247, 276, 277, 327, 405, 414, 431, 467, 540, 548, 570-575, 720. Chalmers, in Pol. Ann., i., 575, says that Nicolls "erected," and in Rev. Col., i., 117, that he "continued," the Court of Assizes, one of "the prior customs of the Dutch." The erroneous statements of Smith, i., 41, 47, on this point, are corrected by Chalmers, Pol. Ann., i., 596, and by Wood, 90, *note*. I can not doubt that the Court of Assizes was established, if it was not completely organized, before March, 1665, the period stated by Wood; compare H. B. Dawson, and N. Y. H. S. Coll. (1869), 76.

CHAP. II. 1665.

erated with closed doors upon the general concerns of the province, and made such changes in the laws as were thought proper. But the Duke of York, who, by his patent, had "full and absolute power," disapproved of legislative assemblies as inconsistent with the form of government which he had established in his province. Yet he supposed that no harm and much good might result from the justices being allowed once a year to meet with the governor and his council, and make desirable changes in the laws, which, after all, were subject to his own approval. These justices, he complacently assumed, would be chosen by the people themselves as "their representatives, if another constitution were allowed." Moreover, the Court of Assizes was the most convenient place for the publication of any new laws, or of any business of general concern. In establishing that court, the duke's deputy did not concede any political privileges to the people. All its officers were his own subordinates; none of them his colleagues. Nicolls was, and he continued to be, a provincial autocrat, who exercised, indeed, his delegated powers with the prudence and moderation which belonged to his character, but who, in adroitly allowing his official dependents apparently to share with himself the responsibility of legislation, did not in the least curtail his own vast authority.*

Purpose of the Court of Assizes.

The governor and his council, who at present were the only members of the Court of Assizes, were early called upon to frame a body of laws for the province. Its condition was more anomalous than that of any other American plantation. It had no charter like the New England colonies. It was not a royal province like Virginia. As a proprietary government, it resembled Maryland in some respects; yet Lord Baltimore's charter was very different from the despotic patent of the Duke of York. When Charles the Second granted New Netherland to his brother, he affected to consider it a resumption of British territory, the possession of which England had never enjoyed, and Holland had maintained for half a century. In reality, he obtained possession only by a conquest from the Dutch, and upon articles of capitulation. Excepting Aca-

Legal effect of the English conquest.

* Col. Doc., ii., 296; iii., 230; Chalmers's Ann., i., 581, 600; Court of Assizes, ii., 320, 325, 414; Wood, 90, 91; Thompson, i., 141, 142; *post*, p. 293.

dia and Jamaica, New York was the first colony which the English arms ever gained. The rights which the king thus acquired over the Dutch territory were those of a conqueror, limited, however, by the terms agreed upon at the surrender. This principle did not affect that part of Long Island which was actually British territory before the capitulation, and where, of course, the English law prevailed. But with respect to the Dutch possessions, the right of conquest governed; which was, that where a country was conquered by or ceded to England, the sovereign might establish such government and laws as he should think proper, but that the ancient laws of such conquered or ceded country were to remain in force, if not contrary to the law of God, until the king should change them. Accordingly, Charles authorized the Duke of York "to make, ordain, and establish all manner of orders, laws, directions, instructions, forms and ceremonies of government and magistracy fit and necessary for and concerning the government of the territories and islands aforesaid, so always as the same be not contrary to the laws and statutes of this our realm of England, but as near as may be agreeable thereunto, and the same at all times hereafter to put in execution, or abrogate, revoke, or change, not only within the precincts of the said territories or islands, but also upon the seas in going and coming to and from the same." The duke thereupon commissioned Nicolls as his deputy, "to perform and execute all and every the powers which are by the said letters patent granted." But, before he could obtain peaceable possession of New Netherland, Nicolls was obliged to concede special privileges to its inhabitants, which placed them in many respects upon a better footing than the king's own English subjects on Long Island. Among other things, the Dutch were to enjoy their own church discipline and customs concerning inheritances. Besides these guaranteed rights, they were, as a conquered people, entitled to be governed according to their ancient laws, which were to remain in force until changed by the actual authorities in the province.*

The Duke of York's power to make laws.

* Chalmers's Pol. Ann., i., 574; Rev. Col., i., 116, 117; Calvin's Case, 7 Coke's Rep., 17; Show. Parl. C., 31; Cowper, 204; Blackstone's Comm.; Jacob, v., 159; Col. Doc., ii., 296; Leaming and Spicer, 666; *ante*, vol. i., p. 762; *post*, App. A and B. I venture, with much deference, to express my opinion that Mr. Barnard, in his sketch of Rensselaerwyck, 136, and

CHAP. II. 1665.

It was nevertheless generally understood that "English lawes" were to be established in New York at the end of six months after the surrender. In writing from Boston, Cartwright advised Nicolls that the Dutch "will rather take that for oppression which shall be imposed on them afterward, than for the present acknowledge your indulgence in letting them for a while longer use their own lawes." But, if the governor hesitated at following his colleagues' advice with respect to the Dutch portion of the province, he had no doubt in regard to Yorkshire. Before the surrender, in explaining at Gravesend the phrase of the proclamation that all persons submitting to the royal government were to enjoy "all other privileges with his majesty's English subjects," he had promised the people of Long Island that at a convention of delegates from their towns, "laws were to be enacted and civil officers established." A few days afterward, he told them that they should be summoned "to propose and give their advice in all matters tending to the peace and benefit" of the island. Again he assured them "of equal (if not greater) freedoms and immunities than any of his majestie's colonies in New England." These expressions appear to have been differently understood by Nicolls and by the Long Island people. The latter supposed that the New England system was to be transplanted into New York, with all the machinery of royal corporations to perpetuate their benefits or abuses. The governor, on the other hand, was the deputy of a proprietor who centred in himself all the delegated authority of the king possessed by any of the New England oligarchies. It was his function under a royal patent, as it was theirs under royal charters, to make laws. Nicolls, however, was desirous to adopt in New York all that he might find good or expedient in the several codes of the New England colonies. For this purpose he appears to have obtained copies of those of Massachusetts and of New Haven, the latter of which had been printed at London in 1656. He also applied to Winthrop for a copy of that of Connecticut, which existed only in manuscript; but a transcript

4 Feb.

English laws to be established.

Power of Nicolls to make laws.

Chancellor Walworth, in 17 Wendell, 587, and Mr. Butler in ii. N. Y. H. S. Coll., ii., 43, have not accurately stated the condition of the law in New York immediately after the surrender. Certainly Long Island was differently situated from the rest of the province.

could not be made for him in time to be of use. With the assistance of members of the Court of Assizes, he made it his "whole business to prepare a body of lawes" to be submitted to the general meeting proposed to be held on Long Island. These laws were largely borrowed from those "in practice in his majesty's other colonies in New England," but with a relaxation of their severity against those who differed "in matters of conscience and religion."*

CHAP. II. 1665. Code prepared by Nicolls.

To fulfill his promises, Nicolls addressed a letter to each of the towns on Long Island, announcing that in discharge of his "trust and duty to settle good and known lawes within this government for the future," and receive their "best advice and information in a general meeting," he had appointed such a meeting to be held at Hempstead on the last day of February, to which he invited each town to send two deputies chosen by a majority of the tax-payers. These deputies were to be "the most sober, able, and discreet persons;" and were to produce at the meeting the documents showing the boundaries of their respective towns, notify the Indian sachems whose presence there might be necessary, and bring with them certificates of their due election, "with full powers to conclude any cause or matter relating to their several towns." A similar letter was sent to Westchester. But no deputies were summoned from New York, Esopus, Bergen, or any other town in the province.†

8 Feb. Meeting called at Hempstead.

At the appointed day the Convention met at Hempstead. It consisted of thirty-four delegates—two from each of the English and Dutch towns on Long Island, and two from Westchester. Some of them had been members of Stuyvesant's last General Assembly of New Netherland a year before. New Utrecht sent Jacques Cortelyou and Younger Fosse; Gravesend, James Hubbard and John Bowne; Flatlands, Elbert Elbertsen and Roeloff Martense; Flatbush, John Stryker and Hendrick Jorassen; Bushwick, John Stealman and Guisbert Teunis; Brooklyn, Frederick Lubbertsen and John Evertsen; Newtown, Richard Betts and

28 Feb. Delegates.

* Gen. Ent., i., 23, 29, 66; Deeds, ii., 43; Col. Doc., ii., 251; iii., 86, 88, 114; iv., 1154; Thompson, i., 126, 127, 382; ii., 323, 324, 327; Dunlap, ii., App. xxxvii.; Smith, i., 388; Hist. Mag., viii., 211; Trumbull MSS., xx., 74; *ante*, p. 25, 33, 43, 57.

† Gen. Ent., i., 93–95; Wood, 87, 88; Thompson, i., 131, 132; Bolton, ii., 180; Journ. Leg. Council of N. Y., i., Int., iv.

CHAP. II.

1665.

John Coe; Flushing, Elias Doughty and Richard Cornhill; Jamaica, Daniel Denton and Thomas Benedict; Hempstead, John Hicks and Robert Jackson; Oyster Bay, John Underhill and Matthias Harvey; Huntington, Jonas Wood and John Ketcham; Setalcott (or Brookhaven), Daniel Lane and Roger Barton; Southold, William Wells and John Younge; Southampton, Thomas Topping and John Howell; Easthampton, Thomas Baker and John Stratton; and Westchester, Edward Jessop and John Quinby.*

28 Feb.

The governor opened the meeting by reading the duke's patent and his own commission; and told the delegates that their first business should be to decide some of their local differences about boundaries, which were afloat before he came to the government; but that "he had prepared a body of general laws hereafter to be observed." These were delivered to the delegates, who, upon perusal, found them to be chiefly compiled from the laws then in force in New England, "with abatement of the severity against such as differ in matters of conscience and religion." The delegates, however, were not satisfied. Most of them represented towns which had recently been under the jurisdiction of Connecticut; and they supposed that in promising them "equal, if not greater freedoms and immunities than any of his majestie's colonies in New England," Nicolls meant to establish in New York a government resembling those of his Puritan neighbors. The inhabitants of Southold especially had signified their desire that all civil officers should be annually elected by the freemen, that all military officers should be chosen by the soldiers, that no magistrate should have "any yearly maintenance," and that taxes should be levied only by consent of a majority of the deputies at a General Court. But the code prepared by the governor recognized none of these points. The delegates therefore objected against some of its clauses, and proposed others. Several of their amendments were accepted by Nicolls, who moreover promised that when any reasonable alterations should be afterward offered by any town to the

Nicolls's code proposed.

Objected to.

* Gen. Ent., i., 96; Journ. N. Y. Leg. Council, Int., v. It will be observed that the names of several of these towns are different from those which they had borne under the Dutch authority. Flatlands was formerly Amersfoort; Flatbush, Midwout; Bushwick, Boswyck; Brooklyn, Breuckelen; Newtown, Middleburgh or Hastings; Flushing, Vlissingen or Newarke; Jamaica, Rustdorp or Crafford; and Oyster Bay, Folestone: see *ante*, vol. i., 619, 723, 729.

Sessions, the justices should tender them at the next Assizes, "and receive satisfaction therein." He further declared that "he expected no benefit for his labours out of the purses of the inhabitants," but that it was absolutely necessary to establish a system of county rates to support the public charges. The delegates accordingly "pitched upon the form and rule" then observed in Connecticut, with which most of them were familiar. But when they asked to be allowed, "according to the custom of the other colonies," to choose their own magistrates, Nicolls exhibited his instructions from the Duke of York, "wherein the choice of all the officers of justice was solely to be made by the governor." Upon this point the delegates were pacified by the consideration "that a Parliament of England can neither make a judge nor justice of the peace." To stop further debate, Nicolls told them that they had seen and read his commission and instructions, and that if they would have a greater share in the government than he could allow, they "must go to the king for it." This was decisive. The delegates found that instead of being popular representatives to make laws, they were merely agents to accept those already prepared for them. Nicolls's code, as amended, was now formally promulgated at the "General Meeting." During its session, which lasted ten days, several orders were made respecting the boundaries of some of the towns. The only act which the delegates really performed was to adopt a loyal address to the Duke of York, in which, after acknowledging their dependence, they declared their "cheerful submission to all such laws, statutes, and ordinances which are or shall be made by virtue of authority from" his royal highness; whose rights under the king's patent they would forever maintain, and whom they besought "to accept of this address, as the first-fruits of this General Meeting, for a memorial and record against us, our heirs and successors, when we or any of them shall fail in our duties."*

1 March. Nicolls's code promulgated.

1 March. Address to the Duke of York.

The New York code thus promulgated at the Hemp-

* Deeds, ii., 1–15, 43, 48; Col. Doc., iii., 91, 260; N. Y. H. S. Coll., i., 307; ii. (ii.), 32; Journ. Leg. Council of N. Y., i., Int., v.; Thompson, i., 132, 136, 382; ii., 324, 325, 327; Wood, 87, 88, 171–175; Dunlap, ii., App. xxxvi.; Bolton, ii., 180; Smith, i., 41; Chalmers, i., 577, 578, 598. The duke's instructions, which Nicolls exhibited at Hempstead, were not recorded in the New York provincial archives, as was his commission: *ante*, p. 18, *note*.

CHAP. II. stead meeting is generally known as "THE DUKE'S LAWS." It was arranged in an alphabetical order of subjects, like

1665. "The Duke's Laws." the New England codes. A very general analysis of its provisions is all that can now be attempted.

The Court of Assizes—as an existing institution—was to meet in the city of New York once a year, on the last

Courts. Thursday in September. But, in pressing capital cases, the governor and council might issue commissions of Oyer and Terminer. Inferior courts of Sessions, composed of the justices of the peace, and in which any counselor might preside, were to be held three times a year in each rid-

Jurymen. ing of Yorkshire. Trials by jurymen, who were not to exceed seven, except in capital cases, were provided for. Arbitrators might be appointed in small causes between neighbors. Whenever the law was silent in any case, the Sessions were to remit it to the next Assizes, where matters of equity were to be decided and punishments awarded "according to the discretion of the bench, and not contrary to the known laws of England."

Each town had a local court for the trial of small causes under five pounds, which was to be held by the constable and six overseers, and from which there was an appeal to the Sessions. Eight "men of good fame and life" were to

Overseers. be chosen as overseers for each town by a majority of the freeholders. Four of these overseers retired at the end of

Constable. each year, and from them a constable was to be annually chosen, on the first or second of April, by the freeholders, who was to be confirmed by the justices at the next sessions. The constable and overseers had power to make local ordinances in the several towns.

Sheriffs. A high-sheriff over Yorkshire was to be annually appointed by the governor from each riding in rotation, and also an under-sheriff or high-constable in each riding. Justices of the peace were to continue in office during the governor's pleasure. But the governor and council might, by special warrant, displace any officer within the government "for neglecting of his office, or other notorious misdemeanor and misbehavior."

Rates. Each inhabitant was to contribute to public charges in Church and State according to his estate. Assessments were to be made every year, after the first of June, by the officers in each town. Provision was made for the enforcement of the rates imposed; and all the plantations within the government were "fully comprehended in this law."

The tenure of lands was to be from the Duke of York. All persons were required to bring in their old grants and take out new patents from the governor, upon the sealing of which a fee was to be paid. After the first of March, 1665, no purchase of lands from the Indians was to be valid unless the governor's leave was obtained, and the savage owner acknowledged satisfaction before him, upon which a grant was to be made by the governor and recorded in the secretary's office. All conveyances in the several ridings were also to be recorded in New York. Lands.

No barter with the savages in ammunition, fire-arms, strong liquors, or furs, was allowed without the governor's license. All harm done by the English to them, or their cattle, or corn-lands, was to be promptly and justly satisfied, as fully "as if the case had been betwixt Christian and Christian." But no Indian was to "be suffered to Powow, or perform outward worship to the devil, in any town within this government." Indians.

There was no particular Protestant denomination more favored than any other in the province. The English Episcopal Church was not established. The Reformed Dutch Church, by the articles of capitulation, preserved its ancient ecclesiastical system. But in every parish a church was required to be built, the expense of which, and of the maintenance of its minister, was to be provided for by the church-wardens, appointed yearly by the overseers and constables. No minister was to officiate within the government but such as should produce testimonials to the governor of his having "received ordination, either from some Protestant bishop or minister within some part of his majesty's dominions, or the dominions of any foreign prince of the Reformed religion." Thereupon the governor was to induct such minister "into the parish that shall make presentation of him as duly elected by the major part of the inhabitants householders." Each minister was to preach every Sunday; and on the fifth of November, the anniversary of the gunpowder treason; on the thirtieth of Religion. Churches. Ministers. Sundays and holidays.

CHAP. II. 1665.

January, when King Charles the First was beheaded; and on the twenty-ninth of May, when King Charles the Second was born and restored to the throne. He was also to pray for the king, queen, Duke of York, and the royal family, baptize the children of Christian parents, and marry persons "after legal publication or sufficient license." No congregations were to be disturbed during divine service; "nor shall any person be molested, fined, or imprisoned for differing in judgment in matters of religion who profess Christianity."

Freedom of religion.

Negro Slavery.

Negro slavery was recognized; but servants were protected from tyranny and abuse. No Christians were to be kept in bond slavery except those sentenced thereto by authority, "or such as willingly have sold or shall sell themselves." All servants were prohibited from trading or trucking "any commodity whatsoever." If servants ran away, justices and constables were authorized to press men, horses, and boats, at the public charge, and bring them back by force.

Militia.

All males above sixteen years old, except certain exempt persons, were subject to military duty. Enrollments, the supply of arms, the appointment of officers, and the punishment of offenders were provided for. In each town there were to be four days of training every year; and in each riding a general training of all the towns once a year. Once in every two years there was to be general training of all the soldiers within the province. No person was obliged to bear arms beyond the limits of the government; but volunteers might be raised by beat of drum to assist the neighboring English colonies. All defensive or vindictive wars against the Indians were to be maintained by a general assessment on each town.

Capital offenses.

In many respects the duke's capital laws followed those of the New England colonies. Denying the true God, murder, treason, kidnapping, the striking of parents, and some other offenses, were punishable with death. But witchcraft and blasphemy were not included. There were numerous regulations respecting the administration of estates, boundaries of towns, brewers, births and burials, conveyances of lands, surgeons and midwives, children and servants, marriages, laborers, orphans, pipe-staves and casks,

Other regulations.

sailors, weights and measures, the destruction of wolves on Long Island, and wrecks and whales. Inn-keepers were not allowed to charge "above eight pence a meal, with small beer," and were always to have a supply of "strong and wholesome" malted liquor. No mares were to be carried out of the government to other plantations without special license. Cattle and horses were to be marked with a letter which distinguished each town on Long Island and Westchester. Every town was to provide a pair of stocks and a pound; and a pillory was to be erected in each place where the Courts of Sessions were held.

Operation of the code.

The code was intended to be ultimately the law of the whole province, and several of its provisions went into general operation at once; but many of them were evidently applicable only to Long Island and its neighborhood. The inhabitants of the Valley of the Hudson, most of whom were Dutch, hardly understood the yet strange English tongue. Only by degrees could the institutions which they derived from Holland, and under which they had lived so long, be safely altered. Nicolls, therefore, prudently abstained from enforcing the new code in New York, Esopus, Albany, and Schenectady. From the original manuscript deposited in the office of the Provincial Secretary at Fort James, copies and translations were made for the several towns on Long Island and Westchester. It was not until more than a century after the "Duke's Laws" had become obsolete that they were first printed as historical curiosities.*

Upon the adjournment of the Hempstead meeting, Counselor William Wells, of Southold, in the East Riding, was commissioned by the governor to be high-sheriff of Yorkshire. Captain John Underhill, of Oyster Bay, who had been so prominent in the affairs of New Netherland, was appointed high-constable and under-sheriff of the North Riding; and similar appointments were made for the oth-

11 March. Officers appointed. 18 March.

* Col. Doc., iii., 104, 188, 230; Chalmers, i., 596; Wood, 88–90; Thompson, i., 138–150; Butler, in ii. N. Y. H. S. Coll., ii., 33; Daly's Introduction, 21–25; Dankers's and Sluyter's Journal, 166. The Duke's Laws, copied from the transcript in the Easthampton town-clerk's office, deposited there on 24 June, 1665, are printed in the first volume of N. Y. Hist. Soc. Coll., 305–428, published in 1811. There is a copy in the Secretary of State's office at Albany, approved by the Duke of York, and certified by his secretary, Matthew Wren, which was probably brought over by Governor Lovelace in 1668. A much-needed compilation of all the laws of New York previous to 1691 has been, for several years, promised by Mr. George H. Moore.

CHAP. II. 1665. er ridings. Daniel Denton, of Jamaica; John Hicks, of Hempstead; Jonas Wood, of Huntington; and James Hubbard, of Gravesend, were appointed justices. Underhill 22 April. was also made surveyor general of Long Island. All these appointees had been delegates to the Hempstead meeting, and, by thus promptly favoring them, the governor expected to silence their murmurs.*

Nicolls's visit to Hempstead was the immediate cause of the establishment of a race-course on Long Island. To improve the provincial Dutch or Flemish breed, which was better adapted to slow labor than to fleetness or display, the governor directed that a plate should be run for every year. The ground selected for the course was in the town of Hempstead, on a part of the great plain, about sixteen miles long and four broad, which was covered with fine grass like the English downs, and where could be found "neither stick nor stone to hinder the horse heels, or endanger them in their races." For many years this remarkable tract was known as "Salisbury Plains." The race-course itself was named "Newmarket," after the famous English sporting ground, and it long continued to be the favorite annual resort of the governors of New York and the farmers of Long Island.†

May. Race-course at Hempstead.

Captain John Manning, the commander of the garrison at Albany, was now commissioned as schout, with instructions similar to those of the schout of New York. Notwithstanding the Duke's Laws, the municipal affairs of Albany continued to be managed as they had been under the Dutch, by commissaries elected by the people, and confirmed by the governor. Excepting some differences between the townspeople and the soldiers there and at Esopus, there was little to disturb their tranquillity.‡

6 April. Albany affairs.

Thus occupied in arranging his government, Nicolls had been unable to act as a fourth commissioner to the New England colonies. His colleague, Cartwright—while conceding that the duke's deputy had work enough at New York, where "the bare hearing of impertinences, without

13 April.

* Deeds, ii., 16, 17, 19, 20; Gen. Ent., i., 115; Dunlap, ii., App. xxxv.; Wood, 150; Thompson, i., 130; ii., 157, 359; Riker's Newtown, 70; Bolton, ii., 170, 180; *ante*, vol. i., 556, 671, 728; N. Y. H. S. Coll. (1869), 76.

† Thompson, i., 271, 272; ii., 63; Dunlap, i., 119; Prime's L. I., 71; Denton's New York (Gowan's ed.), 6, 34, 35; Burnaby, in Pinkerton, xiii., 739; Oldmixon, i., 275.

‡ Patents, i., 155; Col. Doc., iii., 94, 117, 143.

the framing of laws, the ordering of the soldiers, the gaining of the Dutch, the governing of the English, the regulating of the trade, and the providing of necessaries, is more than enough to trie one"—urged that the chief business of the commissioners was now at Boston, where, "though they should refuse us all three, having a prejudice against us, you, whom they respect and honor, might be prevalent with them, because acceptable to them." Finding that his presence was indispensable at Boston, Nicolls appointed Captain Robert Needham to command in New York during his absence. (20 April. Nicolls at Boston.) As the new code had just gone into operation, Captain Topping, High-sheriff Wells, and Secretary Nicolls, all members of the Court of Assizes, were appointed to sit with the justices of the East, (21 April.) North, and West Ridings of Yorkshire at their approaching sessions, and explain the laws to them.*

The visit of Nicolls to Boston was unavailing. (May. The royal commissioners repelled.) Massachusetts, "presumptuous and refractory," repelled the royal commissioners, who "could obtain nothing that might be satisfactory to his majesty's desires." Finding that their time and labor were lost upon men "misled by the spirit of independency," Carr, Cartwright, and Maverick went eastward to Maine, and Nicolls hastened back to New York, (26 May.) at any rate with a better reputation for prudence and discretion than was accorded to either of his colleagues.†

The first care of the governor, after his return, was, in obedience to the duke's instruction, to make the city government, (City government of New York changed.) which had remained unaltered for nearly ten months since the capitulation, "conformable to the custom of England." To do this in the most conciliatory manner, he selected, as the first mayor of New York, Captain Thomas Willett, of Plymouth, who, while he was an Englishman, was highly esteemed by the Dutch. He had been one of Stuyvesant's negotiators at Hartford in 1650, and had acted with discreet friendship at the surrender. So much did his prudence on the Albany expedition impress Cartwright, that he wrote to Nicolls from Boston, (4 Feb.) "I believe him both a

* Deeds, ii., 23, 24; Gen. Ent., i., 116-119; Dunlap, ii., App. xxxvi.; Col. Doc., iii., 93, 94; Val. Man., 1861, 613; N. Y. H. S. Coll. (1869), 75.

† Col. Doc., iii., 95-103; Mass. Rec., iv. (ii.), 141, 143, 177-215; Hutch. Mass., i., 234-250; Coll., 417-422; Chalmers's Ann., i., 388, 389, 502-504; Rev. Col., i., 114; Bancroft, ii., 84-86; Barry, i., 398-400; Palfrey, ii., 607-618; Williamson, i., 411.

CHAP. II. 1665. very honest and an able gentleman, and that he will serve you both for a mayor and a counsellor." At Nicolls's request, Carr, while on his way to Boston, visited Willett at Rehoboth, and obtained for him from Governor Prence leave of absence from Plymouth, to assist in remodeling the city government in New York, as he was "more acquainted with the manners and customs of the Dutch than any Englishman in the country, and his conversation was very acceptable to them." No better choice could have been made.*

12 June. Nicolls, by a proclamation, now revoked "the form and ceremony of government of this his majesty's town of New York, under the name of Schout, Burgomasters, and Schepens," and declared that its future government should be administered by persons who should be known by "the name and style of Mayor, Aldermen, and Sheriff, according to the custom of England in other his majesty's corporations."† By a separate instrument of the same date, he ordained that "the inhabitants of New York, New Harlem, with all other his majesty's subjects, inhabitants upon this island commonly called and known by the name of the Manhattan's Island, are and shall be forever accounted, nominated, and established as one body politic and corporate, under the government of a mayor, aldermen, and sheriff;" and he appointed Thomas Willett to be mayor; Thomas Delavall, Oloff Stevensen van Cortlandt, Johannes van Brugh, Cornelis van Ruyven, and John Lawrence, to be aldermen, and Allard Anthony to be sheriff. These officers were to hold their places for a year, and any four of them, of whom the mayor or his deputy was always to be one, were to have full authority to govern the city according to the general laws, "and such peculiar laws as are or shall be thought convenient and necessary." Of the new corporate

Mayor, aldermen, and sheriff.

12 June.

Willett mayor.

* Col. Doc., iii., 68, 87, 94; Morton's Memorial, 251, 304, 311; Mass. H. S. Coll., xiv., 100, 293; xxxvi., 532; Arnold's Rhode Island, i., 314; Deane's Bradford's Plymouth, 260; Savage's Winthrop, i., 322; Palfrey, i., 163; Thompson, i., 130; Val. Man., 1853, 379, 380; *ante*, vol. i., 519, 525, 585, 736, 743. After serving as mayor of New York in 1665 and 1667, Willett remained there acting as a counselor until the Dutch conquest, when he returned to his farm at Rehoboth, in Seekonk, Bristol county, Massachusetts, where he died on the 4th of August, 1674. A rough stone with an inscription still marks the place of his burial. His son Thomas remained in New York, where he became prominent; and his great-great-grandson, Colonel Marinus Willett, was mayor of the city in 1807.—Munsell, iv., 22; Col. Doc., ii., 617, 647; Val. Man., 1861, 553; Val. Hist. City of N. Y., 246, 247.

† Ogilby, in his America, 169, remarks that in New England the only municipal officer retaining his Old-country name was "constable."

authorities three were Englishmen—Willett, Delavall, and Lawrence; and four were Hollanders—Van Cortlandt, Van Brugh, Van Ruyven, and Anthony. The latter had been prominent in the late government, and eminently represented the Dutch element; while Anthony, the old schout, only assumed a new title when he became sheriff.

Nevertheless there was much dissatisfaction shown when the governor appeared in the Court of Burgomasters and Schepens to install the new officers. Burgomaster Van Cortlandt, who had been selected to be alderman, objected that the new charter violated the sixteenth article of the capitulation; but Nicolls quietly showed him that the old officers had been continued, and new ones elected in February, who had been retained until now. Yet "divers debates occurred," because the magistrates wished the Dutch system to be retained, under which they nominated their own successors, while under that established by the English governor they were to be chosen by himself without any restraint. Nicolls, however, told them that he had received letters from the Duke of York "to make the government of this city conformable to the custom of England," and that, while he acknowledged the good conduct of the former magistrates, he had qualified some Englishmen for office, "on purpose that parties may be better aided on both sides, as well English as Dutch, who go to law, and the better to strengthen the peace and quiet of the inhabitants of this place." The new magistrates were then sworn and installed, and were proclaimed to the commonalty after "the customary ringing of the bell three times."

14 June. The Dutch dissatisfied.

The new city officers installed.

Thus were inaugurated the first mayor and aldermen of the city of New York. The new court was organized the next day, and Johannes Nevius was retained as secretary, assisted by Nicholas Bayard to translate his Dutch minutes. Soon afterward Nevius resigned, and Bayard was appointed secretary in his place. Little change was made in the mode of judicial proceedings, except the substitution of the English tongue for the Dutch. Jury trials, as provided for in the code, were ordered to be held on the first Tuesday of each month. But suitors generally preferred to have their causes disposed of in the summary manner to which they had been accustomed; and many forms peculiar to

Mayor's Court.

15 June.

18 July.

CHAP. II. 1665.

the Dutch jurisprudence continued for half a century to be recognized in "The Mayor's Court of the City of New York."*

1664. 8/18 Decem. Holland appeals to France against England.

Meanwhile important events had happened in Europe. The States General represented to the King of France the wrong which the King of England had done them in capturing New Netherland, and asked for the aid guaranteed by the treaty of 1662. This appeal embarrassed Louis, whom Charles had tried to persuade that he was the aggrieved instead of the aggressor. D'Estrades, writing from

13/23 Decem.

the Hague, urged his sovereign "to prefer England to the States," because he could thereby "procure the restitution of Acadia from Penobscot to Cape Breton, being eighty leagues of coast, where there are fine harbors, and oblige the King of England, by the same treaty, to declare war against the Iroquois, whom the Hollanders, who have their plantations adjoining, have always assisted with arms and munitions against us. By this means your majesty would free Canada from the only enemies which she has in that country; and by attacking them on the Canada side, and on that which the English occupy, they would all be destroyed in a year." Finding that the designs of Louis on

1665. 8 January. The restoration of New Netherland demanded.

the Spanish Netherlands controlled his action, the States General informed him that they were ready to adjust their differences with King Charles, by restoring every thing they had taken from him, if he would "bind himself to restore New Netherland," and other prizes.†

1664. 20/30 Decem. Downing's memorial.

In reply to the Dutch statements, Downing insisted that New Netherland was within the New England patent; that the treaty of 1654 had not cut off the English claim; and even if it did, that the New England colonies had "*jura belli* within themselves, without appealing first into Eu-

1665. 9 Febr'y.

rope." A committee of the States General soon published a "demolition" of Downing's memorial. "The English," it was conclusively argued, "have no other title to the pos-

* Gen. Ent., i., 120–124; N. Y. City Rec., v., 780–784; vi., 3, 47; Col. Doc., ii., 373, 407, 445, 473; Doc. Hist., i., 389, 390; Val. Man., 1852, 381, 383, 389, 391, 395, 473, 476, 492; 1853, 380, 383, 389; 1860, 601, 602, 608; Thompson, ii., 363; Daly's Introductory Sketch, 14, 25, 26; Hoffman's Treatise, i., 19; ii., 3–5; *ante*, vol. i., 388, 410, 548, 640, 689, 703, 720, 728, 738.

† Col. Doc., ii., 286–291, 305, 306; De Witt, ii., 2, 4, 14–17; D'Estrades, ii., 550, 555–564, 567, 568, 570, 575–577; iii., 5, 10, 11, 13; Rapin, ii., 639; Aitzema, v., 93, 288–294; Lister's Clarendon, iii., 352; Basnage, i., 718, 719, 737; Martin, i., 269; *ante*, vol. i., 586.

session of what they hold, namely, New England, than those of this nation have to New Netherland, to wit, the right of occupation; because all those countries being desert, uninhabited, and waste, as if belonging to nobody, became the property of those who have been the first occupants of them. It is thus the English have occupied, and this is the title by which they possess New England, as those of this nation New Netherland. The right which the English found on the letters patent wherein their king grants such a vast extent to the limits of the English, so as to include also all the possessions of this nation, is as ridiculous as if your high mightinesses bethought yourselves of including all New England in the patent you would grant to the West India Company; therefore a continued possession for such a long series of years must confer on this nation a title which can not be questioned with any appearance of reason."*

CHAP. II. 1665. The States defend their right.

Affairs now approached a crisis. The West India Company was authorized "to attack, conquer, and ruin the English every where, both in and out of Europe, on land and water." The East India Company equipped twenty ships. The herring and whale fisheries were suspended, in order to man the war vessels of the nation. Fourteen millions of guilders were voted for the fleet and the fortifications. The Dutch, who lived by commerce, resolved that they must fight to deliver themselves from the English yoke; and all the cities broke out in cries of joy at the hope of triumph. As De Ruyter was far away in the West Indies, Wassenaar of Opdam was made admiral, with the younger Tromp and other renowned commanders under him.†

6 Febr'y. The Dutch equip a fleet.

The English Parliament granted two millions and a half of pounds sterling; and Holmes was sent to the Tower, so that if the Dutch should be successful, he might be made "a sacrifice, as Sir Walter Raleigh was." The Duke of York prepared to take command of the fleet. At length the king, without the concurrence of Clarendon or Southampton, issued a declaration of war, full of bitterness against the Dutch.‡

English preparations. 22 Febr'y. 4 March. War declared.

* Col. Doc., ii., 298–304, 307–331; Aitzema, v., 356–368.

† Col. Doc., ii., 306, 307; D'Estrades, iii., 32, 42, 63; Aitzema, v., 413–443; Basnage, i., 736; Davies, iii., 29, 30; Pepys, ii., 205; Lister, iii., 361.

‡ Pepys, ii., 187, 196, 199, 215; Kennett, iii., 252; Lister, ii., 271–276; Aitzema, v., 368;

Chap. II.

1665.
28 Jan'y.
7 Feb'y.
Orders to the colonies.

Charles also wrote to Nicolls and his colleagues, informing them of De Ruyter's expedition, and enjoining them "to use all possible diligence for their security." They were, moreover, directed to observe all orders from the Duke of York, whom the king had authorized to grant letters of marque against Dutch ships, and condemn them in Admiralty. Clarendon likewise warned Nicolls that he "must expect all the mischief the Dutch can do him." 11/21 Febr'y. The Duke of York directed that his province should be put "into a posture of defense against the Dutch." He 28 Febr'y. also appointed Nicolls and Captain Philip Carteret sub-commissioners in Admiralty, to dispose of all prizes in any of the ports or harbors of New England.*

These dispatches were brought by Carteret to Virginia, and forwarded thence to New York. As soon as he re- 22 June. Action of Nicolls. ceived them, Nicolls issued a proclamation for the confiscation of the West India Company's estate, which had al- 24 June. ready been attached. Letters were also sent to the several New England governments inclosing copies of the king's orders, and instructing them how to treat Dutch prizes in any of their ports. The inhabitants of Long Island were 30 June. especially warned to be ready against Dutch invasion. The 28 June. commonalty of New York were called together to consult about fortifying the city on the river side. The governor offered to contribute palisades and wampum, and promised "not to constrain any inhabitant to fight against his own nation." Steenwyck, the deposed burgomaster, declared Feeling in New York. that he would always be a faithful subject. But the burghers generally were not zealous to prepare defenses against an expedition which might restore the authority of their fatherland. "Some of the people answering said that the town was sufficient enough; others that they could not work before they had their arms restored to them again; and many other excuses; but no categorical answer was given."†

Basnage, i., 736; Lingard, xii., 170; Davies, iii., 30; Rapin, ii., 638, 639; Parl. Hist., iv., 303–309. There is an interesting account of the origin of this war in Temple's Works, i., 307–310.

* Col. Doc., iii., 85, 86, 92, 104; Val. Man., 1847, 353; N. Y. Surrogate's Rec. Wills, i., 9.

† Col. Doc., iii., 67, 92, 103; N. Y. City Rec., vi., 19, 29; Col. MSS., xxii., 1; Val. Man., 1852, 480, 484; 1853, 381; Gen. Ent., i., 76, 125–132; Ord. Warr. and Lett., ii., 2; Col. Rec. Conn., ii., 21; Mass. H. S. Coll., xxx., 52; Trumbull, i., 278; Thompson, i., 140; Smith, i., 38, 41. De Ruyter was actually on his way from the West Indies to Newfoundland in May, 1665. If he had visited New York, as he intended, he would easily have reconquered the prov-

1665. 31 July. Condition of the metropolis.

The condition of the metropolis was told in a letter from Nicolls to Lord Arlington: "We have had no ship or the least supplies directly out of England since the surrender, which hath brought the soldiers and planters into very great wants of meane necessaries, though I will still have hopes that a place of this importance will fall into due consideration with his majesty and royal highness." The colonies had less cause to apprehend De Ruyter than the privateers, "and this place doth not apprehend either or both; for we have no ships to lose, no goods to plunder, but a ragged sort of a fort, put into the best posture of defence possible, well fitted with cannon, no want of ammunition for the present, and as many soldiers as will not lose his majestie's interest but with their own lives." Fort James, indeed, with its low ramparts, greatly needed strengthening. But Cartwright thought that it could not be kept "two hours by having its walls raised higher," and advised that "a battery upon the point would be of greater advantage, and more considerable than the fort itself, if ever the town be fortified."*

While Nicolls was thus securing his government, annoying orders came to him from England. The Duke of York had dismembered his province, and had laid the foundation of another American state. James was fond of naval affairs, and a degree of intimacy existed between him and his assistants in the Admiralty Board. One of them, John, Lord Berkeley of Stratton, a brother of the Governor of Virginia, had been the duke's own governor in his youth, and afterward was made treasurer of his household. At the request of James, the king, two years before his restoration, had raised Berkeley to the peerage. Berkeley was a "bold and insolent" man, weak, popishly inclined, "not incorrupt," and very arbitrary. The Treasurer of the Admiralty, Sir George Carteret, "the most passionate man in the world," had been Governor of the Channel Island of Jersey, where he received Charles while Prince of Wales, and which he afterward gallantly defended against Crom-

Berkeley.

Carteret.

ince. But, being short of provisions, he was obliged to hasten homeward. See Aitzema, v., 469, 477; Le Clerc, iii., 79, 80; Basnage, i., 744, 745; Davies, iii., 83; Kennett, iii., 253, 257; Col. Doc., ii., 289, 422; Mass. Rec., iv. (ii.), 154, 276, 280; N.Y. H. S. Coll. (1869), 74, 75.

* Col. Doc., iii., 87, 101, 103; Val. Man., 1859, 548–552, and the map of 1661 appended, showing the situation of the fort.

CHAP. II. 1665. well's forces. At the Restoration, Carteret rode with the king triumphantly into London, and was made chamberlain of his household. Both Berkeley and Carteret were members of the Council for Plantations, and in the spring of 1663 had, with Clarendon, Albemarle, Ashley, and other courtiers, obtained a grant of Carolina.*

The two royal favorites early prevailed on the Duke of York to convey to them a part of his splendid American domain. They seem to have been prompted by Captain John Scott, "who was born to work mischief, as far as he is credited or his parts serve him." Disappointed in his own aim to get a part of New Netherland, and well knowing its geography, which the duke did not, Scott contrived to make Berkeley and Carteret the instruments of his malice by inducing them to procure from its proprietor the cession of one of the most valuable parts of his province. James, not yet in possession, was easily cajoled. Nicolls's expedition was yet on the Atlantic, when the duke, by deeds of lease and release, in consideration of "a competent sum of money," conveyed to Berkeley and Carteret, and their heirs and assigns, the portion of his territory which he described as "that tract of land adjacent to New England, and lying and being to the westward of Long Island and Manhitas Island, and bounded on the east, part by the main sea and part by Hudson's River, and hath upon the west Delaware Bay or River, and extendeth southward to the main ocean as far as Cape May, at the mouth of Delaware Bay, and to the northward as far as the northermost branch of the said Bay or River of Delaware, which is forty-one degrees and forty minutes of latitude, and crosseth over thence in a strait line to Hudson's River in forty-one degrees of latitude." In memory of Carteret's gallant defense of the island of Jersey, this "tract of land" was "hereafter to be called by the name or names of New Cæsarea or New Jersey." Thus the name of New Jersey was given in London to a part of New Netherland before it had been conquered from the Dutch.

1664. 23 June. 24 June. The duke conveys a part of New York to Berkeley and Carteret.

Called "New Jersey."

The Duke of York's release of New Jersey was in the

* Pepys, i., 31, 88; ii., 271; Clarke's James II., i., 54; Burnet's Hist., i., 267, 618, 619; Chalmers, i., 517; Lister's Clarendon, i., 296, 307, 341, 368, 372; iii., 7, 419; Whitehead's East Jersey, 30, 31; Col. Doc., ii., 410, 599; Collins's Peerage, iv., 167, 212.

1664. Effect of the Duke of York's conveyance.

ordinary form of conveyances of land. It merely confirmed to his grantees a part of his province, which he described as "that tract of land" between the Hudson and the Delaware, and the "royalties" and "hereditaments" belonging to the same, with their "appurtenances." This land and its appurtenances was conveyed "in as full and ample manner as the same is granted to the said Duke of York" in his patent from the king. By that patent the king granted New Netherland to his brother in free and common socage, subject to the yearly rent of forty beaver-skins. In the same "full and ample manner" James now released to Berkeley and Carteret a "tract" of this territory, subject to the rent of twenty nobles a year. This was the legal scope of the instrument, which, in words usual in deeds of real estate, conveyed a tract of land and its appurtenances to Berkeley and Carteret as amply as the same had been granted to the Duke of York by the king; namely, in socage, subject to an annual rent. The king, however, besides his gift of territory, had intrusted to his brother and his assigns "full and absolute" authority to govern all English subjects inhabiting within the same. This jurisdiction the duke did not convey. Nevertheless, as he did not reserve it, his grantees assumed that he had transferred to them "every right, every royalty, and all the powers of government which he himself possessed." It was not until many years afterward that this interesting question was settled.*

Powers of government not conveyed.

As soon as news of the reduction of New Netherland reached England, Berkeley and Carteret hastened to avail themselves of their grant, by procuring from James a letter to Nicolls, "signifying the same to him, and requiring him and all others therein concerned to yield their best assistance in the quiet possession and enjoyment of the premises to all such persons as my said grantees should at any time appoint and authorize to negotiate their affairs in those parts." Soon afterward they signed and published an instrument which, under the title of "The Concessions and Agreement of the Lords Proprietors of the Province of

28 Novem. The duke's letter to Nicolls.

1665. 10 Febr'y. New Jersey "Concessions."

* Col. Doc., ii., 243; iii., 46, 48, 105, 229, 240, 285; Pepys, ii., 103; Leaming and Spicer, 8–11; S. Smith's New Jersey, 60, 61, 567–570; Gordon, 20, 23, 24, 42, 43; Chalmers, i., 613, 614, 624, 625; Grahame, i., 462, 463; Bancroft, ii., 315; Whitehead, 31, 32; *ante*, vol. i., 725, 736; ii., 14, 21.

CHAP. II. 1665. Philip Carteret governor.

New Cæsarea or New Jersey," formed its liberal constitution. At the same time, Captain Philip Carteret, a cousin of Sir George, was commissioned as governor, and received his instructions from the Proprietors.*

With about thirty emigrants, several of whom were Frenchmen skilled in making salt—which was apparently intended to be the staple of New Jersey—Carteret sailed for New York in the ship Philip, belonging to Sir George. The vessel was driven into the Chesapeake, and anchored at Newport News. From there Carteret transmitted to Nicolls some of the dispatches intrusted to his care. He also forwarded several letters to Captain James Bollen, the commissary at Fort James, among which was one from Berkeley and Carteret, containing a copy of the duke's grant of New Jersey. As soon as he received them, Bollen showed these interesting documents to his chief.†

Carteret in Virginia. 13 June.

22 June.

This was the first intimation to Nicolls of the dismemberment of his government of New York. The duke's own dispatch to him had not yet been delivered by Carteret; but he could not doubt the news which Bollen communicated. His surprise was grievous. For ten months he had exercised dominion, as the deputy of James, over ancient New Netherland. Only a few weeks before, he had confirmed to Goulding, Bowne, and others, from Long Island, the lands between Sandy Hook and the mouth of the Raritan, upon which the towns of Middletown and Shrewsbury were afterward settled. He had looked upon "Albania," within which three new towns were already begun, as the most "improveable part" of the province of New York. And now the mortified governor was warned to give up

Surprise of Nicolls.

8 April.

* Elizabethtown Bill in Chancery (1747), 12–16, 35; Leaming and Spicer, 12–31; Smith's N. J., 512–521; Collins's Peerage, iv., 208; Whitehead's East Jersey, 32–36; Gordon, 24–27; Bancroft, ii., 315–316; Chalmers's Ann., i., 614, 615; N. J. H. S. Proc., i. (ii.), 23, 30, 31; Mass. H. S. Coll., xxxvii., 319. The New Jersey "Concessions," among other things, provided that the inhabitants should every year elect representatives to a General Assembly, and that there was to be imposed no "tax, custom, subsidy, tallage, assessment, or any other duty whatsoever, upon any colour or pretence, upon the said province and inhabitants thereof, other than what shall be imposed by the authority and consent of the said General Assembly, and then only in manner as aforesaid." These memorable words—which were borrowed from the Petition of Right assented to by Charles the First in 1628, and recognized by him in his charter of Maryland in 1632—were adopted by the Assembly of New York in 1683 and 1691, and by that of Massachusetts in 1692. See Chalmers, i., 204, 205; Rapin, ii., 270, 271; Kennett, iii., 42; Lingard, ix., 317–321; Gordon's American Revolution, i., 47, 66, 97, 99.

† Mass. H. S. Coll., xxx., 49–53; Elizabethtown Bill in Chancery, 28; Smith's New Jersey, 67; Whitehead's East Jersey, 36; Col. Doc., ii., 470; iii., 103, 105; Rhode Island Rec., ii., 80.

CHAP. II. 1665. July.

that desirable region. Thenceforth "New Jersey" was to take the place of "Albania" on the map of America. Too good an officer to disobey, Nicolls could not refrain from a manly remonstrance against his master's improvident grant, "to the utter discouragement" of any that might desire to live under his protection. "For my boldness," he added, "I can at last but beg pardon. Neither can I suppose that my Lord Berkeley or Sir George Carteret knew how prejudicial such a grant would prove to your royal highness; but I must charge it upon Captain Scott, who was born to work mischief as far as he is credited or his parts serve him."* Hoping that he might yet induce the duke and his grantees to make other arrangements, Nicolls urged that the latter should give up New Jersey, and receive "a better and a more entire tract of land, worthy of great consideration to my Lord Berkeley and Sir George Carteret, which is that part of Delaware River which is reduced from the Dutch, if it is not already disposed; if so, then that my Lord Berkeley and Sir George Carteret may have a hundred thousand acres all along the sea-coast, which is a most noble tract of land, but it will cost them twenty thousand pounds before it will yield a penny, and their children's children may reap the profit."†

Nicolls remonstrates to the duke.

This letter may have caused the duke to repent his precipitate grant; but it reached him too late. Toward the end of July, Carteret arrived at New York. After exhibiting his authority to Nicolls—with whom he had been joined as a sub-commissioner in Admiralty—he received from him, according to the duke's orders, quiet possession of New Jersey, whither he proceeded with his ship. Early in August, Philip Carteret landed at the head of his followers, carrying a hoe on his shoulder, "thereby intimating his intention of becoming a planter with them." He chose for the seat of his government a spot on the north bank of

29 July. Carteret at New York.

August. Carteret lands in New Jersey.

* Nicolls, on his return to London in 1668, told the king, the queen, and the duke enough about Scott to make the latter "forsake Whitehall:" see Mass. H. S. Coll., xxxvii., 315, 316.

† Col. MSS., xxiv., 1; Hist. Mag., ii., 293; Leaming and Spicer, 661–663; Smith's N. J., 62–67; Whitehead, 39, 40, 57, 180; N. J. H. S. Proc., i., 165; Col. Doc., iii., 105, 174. Chalmers, i., 614, 615, 624, 625, erroneously states the date of this letter of Nicolls—of which only a fragment exists in the State Paper Office—as *November*, 1665. It was evidently written before Carteret arrived at New York from Virginia (on 29 July, Col. Doc., iii., 103), and about ten days after Bollen showed the governor the letter he had received from the proprietaries of New Jersey, which was on the 20th or 22d of June (Mass. H. S. Coll., xxx., 52; Col. Doc., iii., 105); N. Y. H. S. Coll. (1869), 74. Its date, therefore, must have been about the beginning of July, 1665.

CHAP. II. 1665. "the Kills," where four families had already been settled under the authority of Nicolls, but which, in compliment to Sir George's wife, he named "Elizabethtown." Captain James Bollen, who seems to have been a favorite of the proprietaries, was soon afterward appointed secretary of New Jersey; the annals of which, from this time forward, assume a distinct place in American history.*

The Delaware territory. The Delaware territory, which Nicolls had proposed should be taken by Berkeley and Carteret in exchange for New Jersey, had meanwhile been governed as an appendage to New York, but without any special orders from England. In consideration of the good service of Captain
20 June. John Carr, its commander, a grant was made to him of the confiscated estate of the former Schout Van Sweringen, who emigrated to Maryland. Hinoyossa having also gone there, his property was given to Sir Robert Carr, and Alricks's to Ensign Arthur Stock. But the trade of the place languished for want of supplies; and Nicolls besought Arlington to send him orders at once, as the garrison there was now maintained at his own private cost.†

After their failure at Boston, the three royal commissioners visited the other New England colonies, leaving Nicolls at New York "to attend De Ruyter's attempt." At their colleague's request, they organized a government
Pemaquid. within the duke's territory of Pemaquid, the few colonists of which, chiefly fishermen, appeared to be "the worst of men." Cartwright, weary of his unprofitable labors, and suffering from the gout, now determined to return to England. The command of his company of foot at New
26 June. York was accordingly assigned by Nicolls to Captain Robert Needham. With full dispatches prepared by the com-
August. Cartwright. missioners, Cartwright sailed from Boston, intending to explain in person to the home government the condition of affairs in New England; but he was captured at sea by a Dutch privateer, who took all his papers and carried him to Spain. Massachusetts was well pleased at the mishap which delayed injurious reports from reaching the king. Carr and Maverick, however, before returning to New

* Col. Doc., ii., 607; iii., 103; Smith's N. J., 67; Whitehead, 36, 84, 85; Val. Man., 1852, 483, 492, 495; Elizabethtown Bill in Chancery, p. 28; *ante*, p. 49.

† Col. Doc., iii., 82, 103, 109, 113, 115, 346; Patents, i., 15; S. Hazard's Reg. Penn., iv., 74; Ann., 369; Davis's "Day Star," 79.

York, wrote to the secretary of state, inclosing fresh documents, among which was a "narrative" of the condition of the several New England colonies. Strong prejudice was shown against Massachusetts, where some dared to say, "Who knows what the event of this Dutch war will be?" Carr also urged Secretary Morrice and Lord Lauderdale to have Delaware, Rhode Island, and all the territory as far west as the Connecticut River annexed to the Narraganset country or the "King's Province," and then make him governor over the whole, where he promised to serve his majesty "as faithfully as any he shall set over them."*

CHAP. II. — 1665. 20 Novem. Feeling in New England. 5 Decem.

The war with the Dutch obliged Nicolls to erect a prize court at New York. He accordingly appointed Captains Needham, Willett, and Topping, with Secretary Nicolls and Alderman Lawrence, to be Commissioners of Admiralty for the province, and R. Charlton to be clerk of the court. The organization of this tribunal was, however, several times altered; and the Mayor's Court of New York frequently acted as a Court of Admiralty.†

23 August. Admiralty Court in New York.

Fresh troubles had meanwhile broken out between the Mohawks and Mahicans, and some of the Dutch near Albany were killed. Two of the savages were arrested and imprisoned for the murder. Willett, the new mayor of New York, was sent thither to advise; and, on his return, the Albany magistrates were directed to hang one of the Indians, and send the other in chains to Fort James. Winthrop was also asked to aid in making peace between the Mahicans and the Mohawks. Having taken precautions for the safety of New York during his absence, Nicolls went up to Albany. Manning, who was needed at Fort James, was relieved; and the command of Fort Albany, with its nine cannon, and its garrison of sixty men, was given to Captain John Baker, who was commissioned to be "chief military officer" of the place. Baker was instructed to keep constant guard and good discipline, and to avoid all disputes with the inhabitants, with whom he

4 July. 27 July. 2 August. Nicolls visits Albany. 23 August. 25 Septem. Baker made commander at Albany.

* Col. Doc., iii., 101–113, 160; Patents, i., 156; Morton's Mem., 315, *note;* Hutch., i., 250; Coll., 412–425; Chalmers, i., 277, 296, 389, 483, 504; Maine H. S. Coll., i., 110–116; v., 232, 236; Williamson, i., 415–425; Rhode Island Rec., ii., 93–95, 102, 110–114, 118, 127, 132–138, 157, 257; Mass. H. S. Proc., 1858–1860, 274; Palfrey, ii., 619–624.

† Court of Assizes, ii., 345, 346; N. Y. Surrogate's Rec. Wills, i., 5–10, 35–47; Val. Man., 1847, 352, 353, 362–367; Col. Doc., ii., 296, 297; iii., 67, 239, 260, 268; Daly's Sketch, 30, 51; *post, notes* A and B. Nicolls's Admiralty power in New York came from the duke.

CHAP. II. 1665. was to live "as brothers together." In capital cases or treaties with the Indians he was to sit in the fort, with the schout and commissioners of Albany; but he was to have no concern with the ordinary civil courts. He was also to act as deputy collector, and send the entries of goods by each sloop to Van Ruyven, the collector at New York.
12 October. John Shutte, one of Baker's soldiers, was also licensed to be the "only English school-master at Albany," upon condition that he should not "demand any more wages from each scholar than is given by the Dutch to their Dutch school-masters."*

Nicolls at Esopus. Nicolls also visited Esopus, where troubles had occurred during the previous winter between the soldiers and the townsmen. Beekman and the other officers of Wildwyck
14 Septem. were continued, and Chambers was appointed captain of the local militia company. As it was necessary that the commander of the regular soldiers who formed the garrison should have general military authority, Captain Daniel
14 Septem. Brodhead commander at Esopus. Brodhead was commissioned to be "chief officer of the militia in the Esopes," and all inferior officers and soldiers were required to obey him as such. Like Baker at Albany, Brodhead was instructed to keep constant guard,
23 October. cause the village authorities to be respected, and prevent his soldiers from abusing the Indians or quarreling with the burghers. In general, he was to use his best discretion, but to "avoid harshness of words and heat of passion on all occasions; seeking rather to reconcile differences than to be head of a party. Preserve yourself," said the prudent governor, "single and indifferent as to justice between
Nicolls's instructions to Brodhead. soldiers and burghers. Give not too easy an ear to private whisperers and insinuators, which may overrule your judgment and beget a prejudice in your mind against the Dutch. For, though I am not apt to believe they have a natural affection to the English, yet, without ill usage, I do not find them so malicious as some will seek to persuade you they are."†

One of Nicolls's chief objects in his visit to Esopus was

* Patents, i., 20, 155, 157, 158, 161–164; Orders, Warrants, etc., ii., 3–5, 9, 17, 229; Col. Doc., iii., 104, 117, 119, 143; Chalmers, i., 576; Munsell's Ann. Alb., iii., 327; iv., 16; vii., 98–101; Val. Man., 1847, 354, 356, 357; 1852, 484, 490; Mass. H. S. Coll., xxx., 54, 55; MSS. Trumbull Papers, xxii., 74; *ante*, vol. i., 530, 533, 535, 733.

† Patents, i., 158, 159, 167–169; Col. Doc., iii., 94; Esopus Records; Ulster H. S. Coll., i., 49, 52–54, 98.

to purchase from the savages fresh lands on which to settle colonists. This was the more important since the separation of New Jersey from his government. A treaty was accordingly executed at Fort James between Nicolls and the Esopus sachems, by which a large tract of land to the west and southwest of the "Kahanksen" Creek, in the present towns of Rochester and Wawarsing, was conveyed to the Duke of York. All past injuries were buried on both sides, and the sachems engaged "to come once every year and bring some of their young people to acknowledge every part of this agreement in the Sopes, to the end that it may be kept in perpetual memory."*

CHAP. II.

1665.

7 October. Purchase of Esopus lands.

This treaty with the Esopus Indians enabled Nicolls to offer new inducements to planters, of which the province was in great need. While at Boston in the previous May, he had caused to be printed by Samuel Green, at the Cambridge press—then the only printing-press in the British American colonies—on a half sheet of foolscap paper, "The conditions for new planters in the territories of his Royal Highness the Duke of York." In this document the terms upon which lands could be purchased and held were stated, in conformity to the "Duke's Laws," which had just been promulgated at Hempstead. "Liberty of conscience" was prominently allowed. "The lands which I intend shall be first planted," said Nicolls, "are those upon the west side of Hudson's River, at or adjoining to the Sopes." In this form numbers of copies had been distributed. As soon as he had made the treaty, Nicolls added, in his own handwriting, to the copies not yet issued, "The governor hath purchased all the Sopes land, which is now ready for planters to put the plough into, it being clear ground."†

New offers to planters.

* Col. MSS., xxii., 4; Deeds, iii., 7-10; Esopus Records; Ulster H. S. Coll., i., 59-62, 97; Denton's N. Y., 14; *ante*, vol. i., 675, 678. This purchase of Nicolls was beyond the "new village," now known as Hurley, which Stuyvesant had caused to be laid out after his treaty with the Esopus sachems in 1660: *ante*, vol. i., 678, 690, 710-714; Ulster H. S. Coll., i., 71, 72.

† Thomas's History of Printing, i., 226, 258; ii., 89; Ulster H. S. Coll., i., 97, 98. An original of these "conditions" is in the library of the N. Y. Hist. Society; and there is a reprint of them in Leaming and Spicer, 667, 668. Another original, with Nicolls's manuscript addition (formerly belonging to Ebenezer Hazard), is in the Force Library at Washington; and one of these amended copies Smith reprinted in his revised edition (1830), i., 39, 40.

It is interesting to note that a censorship of the press was established by Massachusetts on 8 October, 1662, and repealed on 27 May, 1663. But when the royal commissioners, on 24 May, 1665, desired that certain papers should be printed, the General Court, three days afterward, to prevent "abuse to the authority of this country by the printing-presse," again ordered "that there shall be no printing-presse allowed in any towne within this jurisdiction but in Cambridge, nor shall any person or persons presume to print any copie but

CHAP. II. 1665. 28 Septem. to 4 October. Court of Assizes.

According to the requirements of the code, the Court of Assizes was now held at New York. It was attended by the governor, his counselors, and the justices of Yorkshire. Several amendments to the laws were adopted and promulgated. Among other things, all wills were required to be deposited in the Record Office at New York, and all land patents to be recorded there. To enforce the provision in the code, it was ordered that "all persons whatsoever who have any grants or patents of townships, lands or houses within this government, shall bring in the said grants or patents to the governor, and shall have them renewed by authority from his Royal Highness the Duke of York, before the beginning of the next Court of Assizes."*

3 October. Long Island affairs. 5 October.

At this court some of the sachems of the Long Island Indians appeared before the governor, and agreed to submit to his authority. A few days afterward Nicolls issued a patent to David Gardiner, confirming to him the grant of the Isle of Wight, or Gardiner's Island, which had been originally made to his father in 1640, by Farrett, as agent of the Earl of Stirling. This was the promptest compliance of any considerable landowner with the requirement of the code.†

2 October. Case of witchcraft.

An interesting criminal case was also decided at Nicolls's first Court of Assizes. Ralph Hall and his wife Mary having been presented by the authorities of Brookhaven for practicing "some detestable and wicked arts, commonly called witchcraft and sorcery," which, it was alleged, had caused two deaths, were arraigned before the Court of Assizes. As the New England penalties against that delusion had been left out of the New York code, the prisoners were indicted, not for witchcraft, but for murder by means of witchcraft. Twelve jurymen, one of whom was Jacob Leisler, afterward so prominent in provincial affairs, tried the case. They found that there were "some suspicions by the evidence of what the woman is charged with, but

by the allowance first had and obtained under the hands of such as this court shall from time to time impower." Mass. Rec., iv. (ii.), 62, 73, 141, 211; Hutch. Mass., i., 248. Thomas, Hist. Print., i., 247, gives the date of this order erroneously as of 19 October, 1664, instead of 27 May, 1665.

* N. Y. H. S. Coll., i., 402–411; Col. MSS., xxii., 7, 107; Wood, 90; Hoffman's Treatise, i., 96, 97.

† Deeds, ii., 127; Patents, i., 80; Thompson, i., 311; Doc. Hist., i., 463; Dunlap, ii., App. cxix.; *ante*, vol. i., 297, 298.

nothing considerable of value to take away her life." As to the man, there was "nothing considerable to charge him with." The court thereupon sentenced Hall to give a recognizance for his wife's appearance from Sessions to Sessions, and be of good behavior while they remained within the government.*

CHAP. II. 1665.

In consequence of the war between the United Provinces and England, Nicolls now ordered in council that all the lands and property within the territories of the Duke of York, belonging to Dutch subjects who had not taken the oath of allegiance to the king, should be confiscated to his majesty's use. This decree was entered on the records; yet while, "for reasons and considerations" satisfactory to the governor, it was not made public, it was to stand as firm and effectual "as if the same had been publicly declared and manifested."†

10 October. Property of Dutch subjects confiscated.

Nicolls, however, did not dislike the Dutch. When it was found that the salary of their ministers at New York had fallen into arrear, the governor directed the mayor and aldermen to enforce a contribution of twelve hundred guilders for their support. As Megapolensis and Drisius also preached in some of the parishes on Long Island, the people of Bushwick were directed to raise a proportion of the sum.‡

26 Decem. 27 Decem. Church affairs.

To the duke Nicolls modestly reported: "My endeavors have not been wanting to put the whole government into one frame and policy, and now the most refractory Republicans can not but acknowledge themselves fully satisfied with the method and way they are in. * * * I have been

November.

* Court of Assizes, ii., 39-42; Doc. Hist. N. Y., iv., 85, 86; Yates's note to Smith, ed. 1814; Wood, 24; N. Y. H. S. Coll., i., 326; Col. Rec. Conn., i., 77; New Haven Col. Rec., ii., 576. One of the last acts of Governor Nicolls, just before he left New York, was to release Hall and his wife from their bonds, on 21 August, 1668: Ord., Warr., etc., ii., 216, 217; Doc. Hist., iv., 86. By the statutes of England (33 Hen. VIII., cap. 8, and 1 Jac. I., cap. 12), witchcraft, sorcery, and the invocation of evil spirits were felony, without benefit of clergy. These English laws were not repealed until 1736. It is worthy of remark, that on the 10th of March, 1665, a few months before Hall and his wife were acquitted in New York, "two wrinkled old women" were convicted of bewitching, before Sir Matthew Hale, chief baron of the English Court of Exchequer, at Bury Saint Edmonds, and were hung, protesting their innocence: Howell's State Trials, vi., 647-702; Campbell's Chief Justices, i., 562-566.

† New York Surrogate's Rec. Wills, i., 1, 2; Val. Man., 1847, 351. By virtue of this decree, Hog Island in Hellgate, afterward called Manning's, and Blackwell's Island, was, among other property, confiscated: Patents, i., 120. The earlier volumes of records in the New York Surrogate's Office are full of documents of general interest to the state, copies of which, at all events, ought to be preserved in the Secretary's Office at Albany.

‡ Ord., Warr., and Lett., ii., 24; Dunlap, i., 120; N. Y. City Rec., vi., 73, 105; Thompson, ii., 158, 159; Hist. Mag., i. (ii.), 322.

CHAP. II. 1665. more industrious than in all the other actions of my life to this day; and what I have done towards the settlement of laws in the government, Mr. Coventry will show to your royal highness." At the same time the governor sent over "a copy of the laws as they now stand, with the alterations made at the last General Assizes, which," he added, if the duke should "be pleased to confirm, and cause them to be printed at London, the whole country will be infinitely obliged."

Laws submitted to the duke.

Condition of New York.

The condition of the metropolis Nicolls told in feeling terms. Its whole trade, "both inwards and outwards, is lost for want of shipping." The people of Long Island were very poor, and labored only to get bread and clothing. From the city of New York alone "is the great hopes of all the benefit which can arise to your royal highness; and, if my former proposals of encouragement meet with a good answer, I may, without boasting, assure your royal highness that within five years the staple of America will be drawn hither, of which the brethren of Boston are very sensible."

This prophetic remark was made by Nicolls after he had visited the capital of Massachusetts in the previous spring. Yet New York, at that day, sadly wanted those comforts to which even English private soldiers were accustomed. "Such is the mean condition of this town, which I am sure is the best of all his majesty's towns in America, that not one soldier hath to this day, since I brought them out of England, been in a pair of sheets, or upon any sort of bed but canvass and straw." Owing to the want of supplies, the whole charge of four garrisons had fallen upon the governor, which had nearly ruined his private fortune. Cartwright's capture was very unlucky, because, among other things, it had prevented the duke from receiving a full detail of the condition of his province. Oppressed by these considerations, Nicolls asked to be relieved from his government, and proposed as his successor "Harry Norwood," who had returned to England in the Guinea, after the conquest, and "whose temper would be acceptable both to the soldiers and country."*

Want of supplies.

* Col. Doc., iii., 104, 106; Chalmers, i., 575, 576, 597, 599; Gen. Ent., i., 62; N. Y. City Rec., vi., 86, 87. Norwood appears to have been governor of Dunkirk and deputy governor

CHAP. II. 1665.

Yet gloom was relieved by news that the English had gained a great naval victory over the Dutch in the North Sea, and that the Duke of York, "to whose wisdom and courage" the result was attributed, had escaped unhurt. This event was celebrated in New York with "a general joy and thanksgiving;" and Nicolls assured his chief that "it hath revived our spirits, and is antidote both against hunger and cold, until such time as your royal highness shall think us worthy of a nearer consideration."*

Thanksgiving.

Before war opened between England and the United Provinces, De Witt and D'Estrades had many conferences about the interference of France. The States General, while insisting upon a reciprocal restitution of conquests, were willing to adopt the French suggestion that hostilities should be confined to New Netherland in America and Guinea in Africa, without affecting Europe. Charles having accepted the mediation of Louis, the French king proposed that New Netherland should be exchanged for Poleron, one of the Banda or Nutmeg Islands, which the Hollanders had retaken from the English. But this was declined by the Dutch, who maintained that if conquests were mutually restored, they would only receive back what had been "ravished from them in full peace," and which the English "could not appropriate by any just title, nor retain under any probable pretext."†

Affairs in Europe. 24 April. 26 May. 27 May.

Hostilities now began vigorously. Off Lowestoffe, on the coast of Suffolk, the Duke of York, with a large English fleet, fought the Dutch under Admiral Opdam, whose ship blew up. After an obstinate combat the Dutch retired to their ports, and the English remained, for a short time, masters of the sea. James returned in triumph to London. An English medal was struck bearing the words "Quatuor maria vindico"—*I claim the four seas.* But the bonfires in London which celebrated the victory glared over a doomed city. The plague broke out. The appalled court fled from Whitehall. During the next five months the metropolis was almost a desert. Thoroughfares were over-

3/13 June. Battle between the Dutch and English at Lowestoffe. November. Plague in London.

of Tangier, and in 1671 to have been granted the quit-rents of Virginia: Pepys, i., 46, 355; iv., 67, 91, 130; Chalmers, i., 328; Evelyn, ii., 87; Campbell, 215, 272; *ante*, p. 52.

* Col. Doc., iii., 104.

† Col. Doc., ii., 336–339; iii., 104; D'Estrades, iii., 81, 85, 89, 92, 93, 164, 168, 179, 188–192; Aitzema, v., 373–376; Rapin, ii., 639; De Witt, ii., 68, 70, 93; iv., 463; Basnage, i., 737–740, 806; Anderson on Commerce, ii., 426, 482, 493; Pinkerton, viii., 457; xi., 198; *ante*, p. 78.

CHAP. II. 1665.

grown with grass, and the awful silence was broken only by the nightly round of the pest-cart.*

23 July. New Netherland and Poleron. 16 August. 20 August.

In Holland, naval defeat almost produced a revolution. The people began to murmur against De Witt, and all anxiously looked for the return of De Ruyter from America. Louis, annoyed at the growing haughtiness of Charles, pressed De Witt to exchange New Netherland for Poleron; and the Pensionary, avowing that the sacrifice would be great, agreed that the French king might, "as of his own accord," propose it to the King of England. This step was kept secret from the States General, for both Louis and De Witt feared that the people might declare for the young Prince of Orange. The French ambassadors at London were directed to make the proposed offer "as from themselves," and Louis promised to break with Charles if it was not accepted. The States General were urged to sustain De Witt's secret agreement; but they only directed the East and West India Companies, which were chiefly interested, to give their opinions upon the proposition.†

August. Haughty English claims.

The English answer to the French overture was, that the Dutch had usurped New Netherland, to which they had no right, and that the king was surprised at a proposal to cede Poleron "in compensation for a country already his own." With headstrong subserviency, Clarendon reiterated the falsehood that King James had granted the country, "afterwards named New Netherland," to Lord Stirling; that "the Scotch had begun to cultivate it a long time before the Hollanders were received there;" and that, as the Duke of York had bought the rights of Stirling's heirs, the Dutch province legitimately belonged to the English. Yet the chancellor well knew that Lord Stirling's claim affected Long Island only, and not the rest of New Netherland.

* Aitzema, v., 377–384, 443–460; Basnage, i., 741–743; Pepys, ii., 243–330; Evelyn, i., 417–422; Kennett, iii., 255, 256; Burnet, i., 218, 219; Rapin, ii., 639, 640; Clarke's James II., i., 405–422; Lister's Clarendon, ii., 333–335; iii., 380–384; Courtenay's Temple, i., 80; Martin, i., 270. The Guinea and the Martin, two of the ships which had assisted in the reduction of New Netherland, were in the British fleet in the battle of June, 1665, but under other commanders. Three of the captains who returned from New York were also in that battle with other ships. Hyde, of the Guinea, commanded the Jersey, 48; Grove, of the Martin, the Success, 30; and Hill, of the Elias, which foundered on her voyage home, the Coventry, 22.—Allen's Battles of the British Navy, i., 46; Aitzema, v., 444, 445; Pepys, ii., 185, 249; iii., 249; *ante*, p. 50, *note*.

† D'Estrades, iii., 197, 215, 219, 221, 242, 249, 250, 262, 265, 278, 295–301, 318; Aitzema, v., 348–388, 393; Col. Doc., ii., 341–353; Basnage, i., 743, 750–754; Lister, iii., 381, 387, 388, 393; Lambrechtsen, 78, *note*.

1665.

The Hollanders, he argued, had only been tolerated there as they would have been had they established themselves in England or elsewhere, where they would not, for that reason, acquire any right of sovereignty for their republic. The ambassadors of Louis answered this burlesque of reasoning by showing its utter want of analogy. But they saw that "the interest of the Duke of York prevailed," and that Clarendon did not believe that the Dutch would break off on the point of New Netherland, especially as the King of France himself had offered to cede it for Poleron.

Answer of the French.

This answer of Charles was justly considered by Louis as rather "hard, dry, and haughty." He wrote at once to D'Estrades, at the Hague, "I will say to you that, having examined what the English and the Hollanders have written upon the subject of New Netherland, it appears to me that the right of the Hollanders is the best founded; for it is a species of mockery to make believe that those who have built and peopled a city without any one saying a word to hinder them would have been tolerated as strangers in France or in England; and habitation, joined to a long possession, are, in my judgment, two sufficiently good titles to destroy all the reasons of the English." At the same time, Louis thought, that as the Dutch had already lost their American province, they should be willing to abandon it for the sake of peace.*

18/28 August. Louis declares the right of the Dutch to New Netherland.

But the States of Holland were too much interested in the preservation of New Netherland to consent to its surrender. The city of Amsterdam likewise insisted upon recovering what had cost it so much. The States General would not treat with England unless Charles receded from his position; and De Witt's private agreement with Louis was repudiated. The French mediators—who thought that while the Duke of York would not give up New Netherland, the Dutch made its restitution rather "a point of honor"—made farther propositions to the English government. Charles haughtily replied that they were "not adapted to secure a firm peace." The West India Company, not yet satisfied with Stuyvesant's behavior, resolved that their own province in America should not be exchanged for Poleron, because they had "no partnership"

3 Septem.

17/27 Septem.

25 October.

27 October. The W. I. Co. will not give up New Netherland.

* D'Estrades, iii., 324, 330–354; Aitzema, v., 393; Col. Doc., ii., 354, 355; Basnage, i., 754.

CHAP. II. with the East India Company, which had an entire monopoly in the Eastern seas, while not only were private persons largely concerned in New Netherland, but also great public interests were involved which would be ruined by its loss.*

1665.

Meanwhile Downing had left Holland, after having sent to the States General a reply to their answer of the ninth of February, in which he insisted upon the English title to New Netherland, and mendaciously affirmed that it had not been "taken by any order" of the king. This having been published in London, the Dutch government ordered their rejoinder to be printed. The absurdity of the English claim was demonstrated; because, while James the First might insert in a patent such clauses as he chose, he could not thereby prejudice the rights of others; and, moreover, he had expressly excepted territory in the possession of other states. The "imaginary subterfuge" that Charles had not directed the capture of New Netherland was exposed by quoting his own orders to Nicolls of the 23d April, 1664. Full appendices completed this able state paper, which fitly closed the long correspondence between Holland and England about the conquest of New Netherland.†

7/17 April. 10 Septem. 31 Decem. The States maintain their right to New Netherland.

The answer of Charles to the propositions of Louis ended any hopes of a peaceable adjustment. All the cities of Holland thanked God that he had not accepted them. They determined to bear increased taxation for war rather than submit to dishonorable terms of peace. Van Gogh was recalled from London by a letter, in which the States General set forth their offers of reciprocal restitution, and the British haughty repulse of them. Charles, on his part, insisted that the Provincial States of Holland were "the real authors" of a war which seemed to "prejudice the Protestant religion."‡ And as this eventful year closed, the two great champions of the Reformation prepared for a fiercer struggle.

3 Decem. Fiercer war at hand. 11 Decem. 16 Decem.

* D'Estrades, iii., 360, 365, 371, 382, 395, 435, 444, 472; Aitzema, v., 395; Basnage, i., 755; Col. Doc., ii., 357, 358, 361, 417–419; Courtenay's Temple, i., 75; MSS. N. Y. H. Soc., communicated by M. F. A. G. Campbell, of the Hague.

† D'Estrades, iii., 363; Aitzema, v., 394; Col. Doc., ii., 331-335, 379–415; *ante*, p. 19.

‡ Aitzema, v., 394, 396, 397; D'Estrades, iii., 565, 566, 577, 581; Basnage, i., 756.

CHAPTER III.

1666–1668.

A FRESH element now entered into the history of New York. Louis, reluctantly fulfilling his engagement to assist Holland against England, issued a declaration of war against Charles the Second. It was very moderate in its tone; for the French king secretly sympathized with his English brother, and was really hostile to the Republic of heretics and merchants. "This is a great step I have taken," wrote Louis to D'Estrades at the Hague, "for the sole interest of the States, and in almost every thing contrary to my own." The next month England declared war against France. Charles immediately directed his American colonies to be on their guard against the enemy, and to reduce "all islands and plantations in those parts belonging to the French or Dutch nation, and especially that of Canada." These orders, however, did not reach New York until the following summer. But they foreshadowed an aggressive colonial policy, which, culminating in the conquest of New France by England a century afterward, prepared the way for the American Revolution.*

CHAP. III. 1666. 29 Jan. France declares war against England. $\frac{9}{19}$ Feb. 22 Feb. English colonial orders.

Interesting events had meanwhile happened on the northern frontier of New York. The treaty which Nicolls had so promptly caused to be made with the native Indians at Albany, and his subsequent behavior toward them, were meant to make them firm friends of the English, as they had been of the Dutch. The territory of the Mohawks and Oneidas was within the Duke of York's patent; and even at that early day the time was perhaps anticipated when the five confederated nations, instead of

* Aitzema, v., 693, 695, 912; D'Estrades, iv., 47, 65, 76; Kennett, iii., 258; Rapin, ii., 641, 642; Basnage, i., 770; Lavallée, iii., 212; Martin, i., 272; Courtenay's Temple, i., 82; Col. Doc., iii., 120, 137; Col. Rec. Conn., ii., 514; Shea's note to Miller's N. Y., 113, 114.

CHAP. III. 1666. New York and Canada.

being treated as equals, would be claimed as English subjects, and used as barriers against the neighboring French in Canada. Between New France and New Netherland there had been little if any disagreement, while many acts of kindness shown by the Dutch were long remembered by the French authorities. But now, instead of placid Holland, aggressive England was sovereign of New York. Where there had been friendship was soon to be discord; and national antipathies, which could not be repressed in Europe, were destined to begin, in the country of the Iroquois, an eventful struggle for ultimate supremacy in North America.

French policy in Canada.

It had been the policy of France to obtain a spiritual as well as temporal dominion over the savages who encompassed her colonists in the New World. Wherever the lilies were planted, there was set up the cross. With heroic devotion the missionaries of Christianity pushed on their labors among the tribes south of the Saint Lawrence and "the beautiful lake" which the Iroquois called "Ontario."* Of all these confederated tribes the Onondagas were the most friendly to the French. This was chiefly owing to their greatest orator, Garakontié, "the sun that advances," who had nothing savage in him "except birth and education." A nephew of the "Atotarho," or great sachem of the Iroquois, but himself neither sachem nor chief, Garakontié had acquired immense power over his countrymen by his eloquence and his political wisdom. He had protected the Jesuit father Simon le Moyne at Onondaga, and had induced the remote Cayugas and Senecas to join his own nation in releasing their French prisoners, with whom the missionary returned to Canada in the summer of 1662.†

But the nearer Oneidas and Mohawks cherished enmity, and even threatened Montreal. This aroused the Canadian government. The Baron Pierre du Bois d'Avaugour, who had succeeded D'Argenson in 1661, was a soldier, who

* "Ontario" signifies in Indian "the beautiful lake:" Col. Doc., ix., 16; Hennepin's Louisiana, 5. The note in Col. Doc., ix., 76, which renders Ontario "the Great Lake," is contradictory, and seems to be erroneous.

† Col. Doc., ix., 13, 16, 76; Relation (ed. Quebec, 1858), 1661, 32–38; 1662, 10–12; Hennepin, Desc. de la Louisiane, 5; Charlevoix (ed. 12mo), ii., 88, 108–119, 144; Shea's Catholic Missions, 242, 248; Ferland, Histoire du Canada, i., 470–477; Faillon, Hist. de la Col. Française en Canada, ii., 450; iii., 2, 92; Sparks's Life of La Salle, 71; Bancroft, iii., 120–162; *ante*, vol. i., 84, 704. Le Moyne died at the Cap de la Madeleine, 24 November, 1665: Col. Doc., iii., 123; ix., 38; Shea's Missions, 248.

thought it his chief duty "to plant effectually the *fleur de lys*" in New France. He recommended to Louis a scheme of fortifications by which Quebec would be made impregnable, and the king "master of America, where all the heretics would remain only so long as might please him." The Iroquois he considered a rabble to be destroyed. To this end forts should be built on the Richelieu River, and at the upper part of the Hudson, near Fort Orange. Three thousand men should be sent to Canada to rout the Iroquois, hinder the progress of the heretics, and open a direct communication with the sea through the more genial region of New Netherland. Should his bold plan be vigorously prosecuted, D'Avaugour prophesied that his ambitious sovereign would be "master of the finest and greatest empire in the world."

1663. 4 August. D'Avaugour advises the destruction of the Iroquois.

On the other hand, the Jesuit missionaries insisted that their greatest obstacle was the drunkenness of the Indians, who were supplied with liquors by the Europeans, and especially by the Dutch at Fort Orange. The French colonists had been forbidden by severe edicts from engaging in this traffic. But D'Avaugour would not enforce the prohibition; and a quarrel broke out between him and the ecclesiastics, headed by Laval de Montmorency, the titular Bishop of Pétrée, *in partibus infidelium*, who had come out to Quebec in 1659 as Vicar Apostolic of New France. Laval complained to the king, who, at his suggestion, appointed the Chevalier Augustin de Mezy, an apostate Calvinist, to succeed D'Avaugour as Governor of Canada. De Mezy arrived at Quebec in the summer of 1663, accompanied by the Royal Commissary Du Pont Gaudais, who organized the colonial government which Louis had established after the surrender to him of all their rights by the old Canada Company.*

The Jesuits oppose the liquor trade.

1 May. De Mezy Governor of Canada.

The administration of De Mezy was short and troubled. Its most important event was an embassy sent by the Iroquois to Montreal, in the summer of 1664, to treat for peace. The Mohawks had been weakened and their pride humbled by their war with the Mahicans, or "Loups."†

1664. Iroquois embassy to Montreal.

* Col. Doc., ix., 7–17, 25, 59, 783, 784; Relation, 1661, 10; Quebec MSS., ii. (ii.) 170; Garneau, Hist. du Canada, i., 140–146, 155; Ferland, i., 447, 448, 476–483, 494–500; Faillon, ii., 322; iii., 30–69; Charlevoix, ii., 88, 105, 120–123, 135, 137, 140, 145; *ante*, vol. i., 705.

† The Mahicans or Mohegans were originally settled on the Hudson River, and were

CHAP. III. 1664. The far-off Senecas were in arms against their fierce neighbors, the Andastes, or Conestogues, or Susquehannas, who inhabited the region west of the Swedes on the Delaware, near what is now Lancaster in Pennsylvania, and were thought "the most capable of all others to exterminate the Iroquois."* The confederate nations therefore desired that the French should live among them and supply them

18 Septem. with European weapons. De Mezy was assured by the upper tribes that all except the Oneidas desired peace; and the friendly disposition of the Mohawks was vouched for by a letter from "one of the notables of New Netherland." But the governor let the Iroquois see that the French were resolved to rid themselves of such treacherous enemies.†

De Mezy, however, quarreled with the Jesuits, as his predecessor had, and was recalled by Colbert. The Chev-

1665. alier Daniel de Remy de Courcelles, a brave officer of

23 March. Courcelles governor of Canada, and Talon intendant. merit and experience, was commissioned to succeed him as governor of Canada. The Sieur Jean Talon, formerly of Hainault, a man of large views and enterprising mind, was also appointed intendant of justice, police, and finance. D'Avaugour's plans of fortification, which he had explained more fully on his return to France, and the advice of D'Estrades to destroy the Iroquois in a year, were now favorably considered. The king's instructions to Ta-

27 March. lon declared the five nations to be "perpetual and irreconcilable enemies of the colony," and ordered that war should be carried "even to their firesides, in order totally to exterminate them." A thousand veterans of the Carignan regiment, which had just distinguished itself against the Turks in Hungary, were detached, under the command of

therefore often called the "River Indians." Their Indian name "Mahigan" was the Algonquin word for "wolf," which the French translated into "Loup:" Relation, 1660, 31; 1661, 39; 1664, 33; Charlevoix, v., 178; Col. Doc., ix., 38, 66; *ante*, vol. i., 72, 183, 232, 733.

* Relation, 1660, 6; 1661, 31; 1663, 10; 1664, 33; Charlevoix, i., 134; Col. Doc., iii., 74, 125, 417, 797; v., 486; ix., 45, 66, 84, 227, 665; Doc. Hist., i., 259; Shea, 24, 249, 291. Mr. Gallatin erroneously places the Andastes on the Alleghany and Ohio Rivers, and calls them Guyandots. The Mengwe, Minquas, or Mingoes were the Andastes, or Gandastogues, or Conestogas, who lived on the Conestoga Creek, which empties into the Susquehanna. Upon their reduction by the Five Iroquois Nations in 1675, the Andastes were to a great extent mingled with their conquerors; and a party removing to the Ohio, commonly called Mingoes, was thus made up of Iroquois and Mingoes. The celebrated Logan was a real Andaste: Colden, i.; Shea's note on Washington's Ohio Diary, p. 224; Historical Magazine, ii., 294–297.

† Relation, 1663, 11; 1664, 26, 32–36; Charlevoix, ii., 134, 141, 142; Garneau, i., 156; Shea, 250, 251; Faillon, iii., 83–100; *ante*, vol. i., 733.

the Sieur de Salières, and Courcelles set sail with his ex- CHAP. III.
pedition for Canada.*

In the mean time, Louis had commissioned Alexander 1663. 19 Novem.
de Prouville, Marquis de Tracy, to be his lieutenant gen- Tracy viceroy of New
eral in America, in the absence of the Count D'Estrades, France.
whom he had appointed viceroy, but who was now his ambassador in Holland. Tracy embarked with four companies of infantry, and, after visiting the West Indies, sailed for the Saint Lawrence. Among other things, the act- 1664.
ing viceroy was instructed to avoid quarreling with the 15 Novem.
Jesuits, but not let them encroach too much. Their inter-
diction of the liquor trade had injured Canada, because the
savages carried all their peltries to the Dutch, who supplied them with brandy in exchange. Another consequence followed: the Iroquois allowed themselves "to be
catechized by the Dutch ministers, who instruct them in
heresy." In the opinion of Lyonne, the Jesuits should
have "closed the eye to one evil to avoid a greater." 1665.

Soon after Tracy reached Quebec, he was joined by 30 June.
Courcelles and Talon. The squadron in which they came
brought over, besides the Carignan regiment, a number of 14 Septem.
mechanics and cattle, and the first horses that had been
seen in Canada; "in a word, a more considerable colony
than that which it came to re-inforce." No time was lost
in executing the vigorous policy which Louis had adopted.
The viceroy, with all his soldiers, went up to the mouth of 23 July.
the Richelieu, when the fort which Montmagny had estab- Forts built on the
lished in 1642 was at once rebuilt by the able engineer Richelieu, or Sorel
Saurel, or Sorel, whose name is commemorated in that River.
which the river now bears. A second fort was erected by
Chambly at the foot of the rapids, about half way to Lake
Champlain, which at first was called Saint Louis, but was
soon known as Fort Chambly. Three leagues farther south
a third fort was built, called Sainte Therèse, because it was
finished on the fifteenth day of October. Here Salières
took his post as colonel; and the way to Lake Champlain 15 October.
was now commanded by the French.†

* Col. Doc., ix., 20–29, 785; Faillon, iii., 100–116; Charlevoix, ii., 145–147, 150; D'Estrades, ii., 576, 577; Garneau, i., 188, 189; *ante*, p. 78. De Mezy died at Quebec on the 5th of May, 1665, a short time before Courcelles arrived there.

† Col. Doc., ix., 18, 19, 22; Relation, 1665, 3, 4, 7, 10–13, 25; La Potherie, i., 319; ii., 82, 83; Charlevoix, i., 357; ii., 151, 152; v., 221; Doc. Hist., i., 43–45; Warburton, i., 373; Garneau, i., 190; Ferland, i., 320; Faillon, iii., 117–126; Shea, 251. On the map in the

CHAP. III.

1665. December. The Western Iroquois visit "Onnontio."

These vigorous measures impressed the savages. Deputies from the Onondagas, who also represented the Cayugas and Senecas, hastened to Tracy at Quebec, led by Garakontié, "the father of the Frenchmen." An Oneida chief joined the Western ambassadors, and spoke for his nation. Presents were interchanged between the Iroquois plenipotentiaries and "Onnontio,"* by which name they distinguished the governor of Canada. A treaty was made, by which Louis was declared the protector and sovereign of the four Iroquois nations, and they his vassals and allies. French families and missionaries were to be settled among the savages, and farms near Montreal, Three Rivers, and Quebec assigned to emigrants from the four Iroquois nations. Thus these nations would "hold the French, not merely by the hem and fringe of the garment, but clasp them cordially around the waist." The Mohawks were not included in the treaty. The representatives of the other confederates promised to return to Quebec "within four moons," and ratify this acknowledgment of their vassalage to France.†

3/13 Decem. Treaty made.

The Mohawks not included.

Canada ignorant of the English conquest of New Netherland.

Up to this time the French in Canada were ignorant of the political changes in New York. They supposed that it was still a Dutch province. The boundaries between New France and the neighboring English colonies were indefinite; but while the Oneidas, Onondagas, Cayugas, and Senecas had just given to Louis a nominal sovereignty over much of the territory south of Lake Ontario, the Mohawks had never acknowledged their subjection to any European master. Tracy therefore resolved to treat them as enemies.

1666.

An expedition into the Mohawk country was organized, and Courcelles was directed to take the command. In the depth of winter he began his march with three hundred regular soldiers and two hundred Canadians. The Father

9 January.

Relation of 1665, the name of Sorel is spelled "Saurel," which seems to be the true orthography according to Col. Doc., ix., 52, 53, 139.

* This word, derived from "Onnonta," a mountain, signifies, in the Iroquois tongue, "Great mountain." It was a literal translation of the name of Montmagny, who was governor of Canada from 1636 to 1648; and the savages, having become familiar with the word, applied it to his successors in office. By the same rule they called the King of France "Grand Onnontio." The English, who did not understand its etymology, wrote the word "Yonnondio:" Relation, 1641, 22; 1658, 8; Doc. Hist., i., 32, 33, 35; Col. Doc., iii., 489, 733, 735; iv., 893; ix., 37; La Potherie, i., 303, 348; Charlevoix, i., 350; Colden, i., 29, 62, 70; *ante*, vol. i., 591, *note*.

† Col. Doc., iii., 121–125; ix., 37, 38; Relation, 1661, 38; 1664, 32; 1665, 5; Charlevoix, ii., 154, 155; Doc. Hist., i., 46; Garneau, i., 193; Shea, 251; Faillon, iii., 127, 128.

CHAP. III.

1666.

Courcelles's expedition against the Mohawks.

Pierre Raffeix went along as chaplain. Snow four feet deep covered the ground, so that no horses could be used. Light sledges, drawn by mastiffs, were the only mode of conveying provisions. Each officer and soldier was also obliged to carry a weight of thirty pounds, and to walk on large Canadian snow-shoes, to the use of which the heroes from Hungary were not accustomed. It required "a French courage" to sustain their long and difficult march through American forests, over deep snow, and across frozen lakes and rivers, and to sleep in the woods, where the cold was more severe than the rudest winters in Europe. From Fort Sainte Therèse they passed southward, 30 Jan'y. over Lake Champlain, toward the Mohawk villages. But, in the absence of their expected Algonquin guides, they missed their way, and wandered in the wilderness until, without knowing where they were, they encamped about $\frac{9}{19}$ Febr'y. The French at Schenectady. two miles from Schenectady, or Corlaer.* A party of Mohawks appearing, a detachment of fusileers was sent against them, which, falling into an ambuscade, lost several killed and wounded. The Mohawks reported their victory at Schenectady, and exhibited the heads of four Frenchmen as trophies. The news was dispatched to Albany, and the next day three of the "principal inhabitants" came to in- $\frac{10}{20}$ Febr'y. quire why the French commander had brought "such a body of armed men into the dominions of his majesty of Great Britain without acquainting the governor of these parts with his designs?" Courcelles replied that he had come to attack and destroy his enemies, the Mohawks, but not to molest the English; and that he "had not heard of the reducing those parts to his majesty's obedience." Seeing that the English, instead of the Dutch, were masters, he was "disturbed in mind," and prophetically remarked "that the King of England did grasp at all America." As it was reported that France and Holland had united against England, Courcelles inquired particularly about the force at Albany, thinking that he might take the place by a rapid movement. But, learning that the fort was garrisoned by sixty English soldiers with nine cannon, and that Baker

* The French called this place "Corlaer," after Arendt Van Curler, who had begun a settlement there in 1661: see *ante*, vol. i., 345, 659, 691, 732; Colden, i., 31; Charlevoix, ii., 156; Col. Doc., ix., 467.

CHAP. III. had sent down to Brodhead at Esopus for a re-enforcement, he abandoned the project. At his request, seven of

1666.

The French kindly treated.

his wounded were taken to Albany for medical aid. Wine and provisions were cheerfully supplied, through the influence of Van Curler; but Courcelles declined the offers of accommodation for his troops in Schenectady, lest his half-starved followers, who had camped under the cold blue heavens for six weeks, might desert if brought "within the smell of a chimney-corner." Learning that most of the Mohawks and Oneidas had gone to attack the "wampum makers," while the rest had retired to their castles, and fearing that a sudden thaw might break up the ice, Courcelles "found it reasonable to return home, nothing effected."

The French retreat.

He began his retreat with a show of marching toward the Mohawk villages, but soon faced northward, and pushed rapidly for Canada. The savages pursued their enemies to Lake Champlain, and made some prisoners. The French supposed that they had terrified the Mohawks, who only took fresh courage because their vainglorious adversaries had "vanished like false fire."*

When the news of Courcelles's expedition reached Nicolls, he was "surprised" at such an invasion of "these His Majesty's dominions" in time of peace, which was "not conformable to the practice in Europe." Yet he commended the friendly conduct of the Albany officers, whose

Action of Nicolls.

predecessors had "in all former times been very affectionate with Christian charity to ransom or by any other means to convey divers French prisoners out of the hands of their barbarous enemies." The wounded Frenchmen who had been left there were carefully attended by Surgeon D'Hinse, who spoke their own tongue. With Nicolls's approbation, the officers at Albany exerted themselves so that the Mohawks "were at last wrought upon to treat of peace" with the French; and a letter from Baker and his colleagues,

26 March.

announcing the event to Tracy, was handed to the Oneidas to carry to Quebec. In consequence of the supplies which had been furnished to Courcelles, and of an anticipated

24 March.

short crop, the governor was obliged to prohibit the ex-

* Relation, 1666, 6, 7; Col. Doc., 118, 119, 126, 127, 133, 152, 395; Doc. Hist., i., 46, 47, 50, 51, 55, 100; Charlevoix, ii., 144, 156, 157; Colden, i., 31, 32; Mass. H. S. Coll., i., 161; Faillon, iii., 129–134.

CHAP. III.

1666.

portation of wheat from New York, except by special license.*

By this time apprehension of an attack by De Ruyter had ceased; but the want of trade, caused by the war and the English navigation laws, was grievous to New York. In letters to the Duke of York, and Clarendon and Coventry, Nicolls described the sad condition of the province. To Arlington he wrote, "In regard the inhabitants (at least three parts of four) being Dutch, though now His Majesty's subjects as native English, have been seated here divers years as a factory, and their estates as well as relations interwoven with their correspondents and friends in Holland, unless His Majesty pleaseth to grant them some extraordinary enfranchisement, the sudden interruption of their factory with Holland will absolutely destroy all the present inhabitants; who, setting aside the innate love to their country in this time of war after so sudden a change, will prove better subjects than we have found in some of the other colonies; and, with a moderate permission, both for time and trade, will support this government better than can be reasonably expected from new comers of our own nation, who at first, as we find by experience, are blown up with large designs, but not knowing the knack of trading here to differ from most other places, they meet with discouragements, and stay not to become wiser." After alluding to the action of the royal commissioners, and the "sophistry" and "pride" of Massachusetts, Nicolls remarked that New York "will withdraw, in short time, most of their trade hither, where I have begun to set up a school of better religion and obedience to God and the king." Again he urged that "a speedy consideration be taken of the necessities both of the soldiers and country. For myself," he added, "I am utterly ruined in my small estate and credit; and, which is worse, without very great supplies I shall not be able to secure or make an honest defence of his majesty's interest should we be attacked by a foreign force." The English soldiers, upon whom alone he could rely, were now dispersed into four garrisons, at New York, Esopus, Al-

9 April. Sad letters of Nicolls home.

* Col. Doc., iii., 126–134; Ord., Warr., Lett., ii., 30, 78, 157. Nicolls appears to have thought of sending Van Curler to Canada, but the latter did not go until the next year: Col. Doc., iii., 128, 156; *post*, 121.

CHAP. III. 1666. bany, and the Delaware. "My ignorance," he modestly suggested, "made me bold to undertake so great a charge, which will become a much wiser man and of a more plentiful fortune."*

The Delaware territory. The Delaware territory had meanwhile been governed by Nicolls on his own responsibility, without any directions 20 March. from England. To encourage its trade, he directed that no duties should be levied on any merchandise carried between it and New York. By Ensign Arthur Stock, who had acted 9 April. as commissary there, Nicolls wrote to Arlington, exposing the fallacy of Lord Baltimore's pretensions to the Delaware country, and urging that it might be granted to Berkeley and Carteret in place of New Jersey. "If some course be not taken to rectify these great mistakes," he added, "New York, Delaware, and the Lord Berkeley's interest will destroy each other." Sir Robert Carr, who was now at New 9 April. York, also renewed his suggestion that Delaware should be united with some of the Eastern colonies, and himself made the governor, which he thought would be "both useful and beneficial." Nevertheless Delaware long remained an inconvenient appendage to New York.†

In spite of the admonitions of Nicolls, few patents for lands were yet issued. An important one, however, was 18 May. Haerlem patent. granted to the inhabitants of Haerlem, or "Lancaster," which confirmed their former privileges, but in subordination to the city of New York, "as being within the liberties thereof."‡

Following the example of Gardiner, the owners of Shelter Island patent. Shelter Island obtained a confirmation of their title. This beautiful spot, formerly known as "Farret's Island," had come into the possession of Thomas Middleton, and Constant and Nathaniel Sylvester, of Barbadoes. The latter, who professed to be a Quaker, settled himself at Shelter Island. In consideration of one hundred and fifty pounds, paid "one half in beef and the other half in pork," toward 25 May. the support of the New York government, Nicolls released

* Col. Doc., iii., 114, 115. This letter, being addressed to Lord Arlington as Secretary of State, is preserved in the British State Paper Office. Those of the same date, which Nicolls wrote to the Duke of York, Lord Clarendon, and Secretary Coventry, were not deposited there: see N. Y. H. S. Coll. (1869), 113–120.

† Ord., Warr., Lett., ii., 43; S. Hazard, 369, 370; Col. Doc., iii., 105, 109, 113–115; R. I. Col. Rec., ii., 137, 138; Chalmers, i., 634.

‡ Patents, i., 57–60; Hoffman, i., 131; *ante*, p. 76; vol. i., 674, 675.

CHAP. III.

1666.

the island forever from all taxes and all military duty. A patent was also issued confirming it to the Sylvesters as an "entire enfranchised township, manor, and place of itself," with equal privileges with any other town in the province.*

31 May.

Visiting Hempstead again at the time of the annual races, Nicolls made a treaty with Tackapausha, the chief sachem of the Marsapeagues, and other Long Island tribes, by which they covenanted to be at peace with the English and submit to their government.†

11 June.

Discontent on Long Island.

In the mean time there was great discontent on Long Island, especially in its eastern towns, which were vexed at being no longer under the government of Connecticut. Southampton, Southold, and Easthampton refused to choose the local officers required by the duke's laws, and would not pay their rates. Nicolls therefore warned them against sedition, and that the duke's authority would be enforced. The oath required from the overseers seemed to be the chief stumbling-block, and this the governor prudently waived. The authors of the trouble were Howell, of Southampton, and Younge, of Southold, whose rival and colleague at the Hempstead meeting, William Wells, had been made high-sheriff of Yorkshire. In the judgment of Nicolls, Younge was "a bad instrument," but had no brains "to carry on such a business." Underhill, the high-constable of the North Riding, whose "reall hart" inclined to Connecticut, likewise wrote from Oyster Bay representing "the distempers of the people against the present form of government, by which they are inslaved under an arbitrary power," and intimated that there were some who would "hazard both life and estate in a mutiny and rebellion rather than bear the burden of the public charge." Nicolls peremptorily denounced the complainants as calumniators or traitors, and made known his purpose to act vigorously, but justly, in every case.‡

19 April.

21 April.

3 May.

7 May.

29 April.

Nicolls warns the seditious.

7 May.

Cause of the discontent.

Much of this ill feeling arose from the discontent of the eastern Long Island towns with the result of the Hempstead meeting. They disliked various provisions in Nicolls's

* New Haven Col. Rec., ii., 51, 89, 92, 122, 190–194, 364, 380, 412; Col. Rec. Conn., i., 386, 390, 400, 427; Oldmixon, ii., 28; Fox's Journal (Philad. ed.), 438, 442, 453; Patents, i., 65, 133; Thompson, i., 364–367, 392; Wood, 6, 9; *ante*, p. 90; vol. i., 292, 300, 301.

† Wood, 79; Thompson, i., 94; ii., 8.

‡ Ord., Warr., Lett., ii., 46, 47, 50, 54, 55, 58, 59, 60, 61; Mass. H. S. Coll., xxxvii., 192.

CHAP. III. 1666. code, and pined for a legislative assembly after the manner of New England. Above all, they were mortified by what they thought was servile language in the address of their delegates to the Duke of York. This feeling grew when it was seen that several of those delegates had been appointed to office by the governor. Censures were so freely uttered by the disaffected, that the delegates, to justify themselves, drew up a "Narrative and Remonstrance," in which they detailed what had occurred at Hempstead, and declared that their address to the duke could not "bear any other natural sense and construction than our obedience and submission to His Majesty's letters patent, according to our duty and allegiance." This narrative they published and recorded in each town, "that future ages may not be seasoned with the sour malice of such unreasonable and groundless aspersions."*

21 June. "Narrative" of the Hempstead delegates.

Yet this did not satisfy the people. Disaffection became so general that the governor was obliged to interfere. At the autumn session of the Court of Assizes, it was accordingly decreed "that whosoever shall reproach or defame any person or persons who have or shall act in any public employment, either in court or otherwise, or shall vilify their proceedings who serve the public in this Government by authority under His Royal Highness the Duke of York, or whoever hereafter shall any ways detract or speak against any of the deputies signing the Address to His Royal Highness at the General Meeting at Hempstead, they shall be presented at the next Court of Sessions, and if the Justices shall see cause, they shall from thence be bound over to the Assizes, there to answer for the slander upon plaint or information." Sedition was most violent at Setalcott, or Brookhaven. Arthur Smith, of that place, was convicted at the Assizes of saying that "the King was none of his King, and the Governor none of his Governor," and sentenced to be put in the stocks. Richard Woodhull was also fined five pounds, and required to make a public acknowledgment. The same punishment was awarded to William Lawrence, of Flushing.†

September. Action of the Court of Assizes against sedition.

29 Septem.

1 October.

* Deeds, ii., 43–48; Wood, 87, 173, 175; Thompson, i., 137; ii., 323–326.

† Court of Assizes, ii., 82, 83, 84, 94; Col. MSS., xxii., 107; N. Y. H. S. Coll., i., 417; Thompson, i., 137, 409, 410; ii., 364, 398.

1666. 27 Septem. to 2 October.

Several amendments of the code were made at this session of the Assizes. Public rates were required to be paid every year in wheat and other produce, at certain fixed prices, "and no other payment shall be allowed of." As the law against selling liquor to the savages was disregarded, owing to the difficulty of proof, it was ordered "that although the testimony of heathens against Christians may not altogether be allowed, yet, when it meets with other apparent circumstances, such as may be sufficient to convince a jury, in such cases the Indian testimonies shall be admitted as good proofs against the persons accused." Perhaps the most important decree related to land patents. "The Court having taken notice of the defects and failings of both towns and persons in particular of not bringing in their grants or patents to receive a confirmation of them, or not coming to take out new grants where they are defective, or where there are none at all, according to former directions in the Law, As also taking it into their serious considerations that several towns and persons within this Government, as well English as Dutch, do hold their lands and houses upon the conditions of being subjects to the States of the United Belgic Provinces, which is contrary to the allegiance due to his Majesty, They do therefore Order that all grants or patents whatsoever formerly made, shall be brought in, to be confirmed or renewed by authority of his Royal Highness the Duke of York, and all such as have not patents shall likewise be supplied therewith by the first day of April next after the date hereof; after which time neither town nor private person, whether English or Dutch, shall have liberty to plead any such old grants, patents, or deeds of purchase in law, but they shall be looked upon as invalid to all intents and purposes."*

Amendments to the code.

Land patents to be renewed.

This stringent ordinance made great commotion. It was vigorously enforced, because the quit-rents and fees on renewals were necessary for the support of the government. In the course of the next few months, Neperhaem, Pelham, Westchester, Eastchester, Huntington, Flushing, Brookhaven, Easthampton, New Utrecht, Gravesend, Jamaica, Hempstead, Newtown, Flatlands, Bushwick, Flat-

New patents granted.

* Court of Assizes, ii., 80; Col. MSS., xxii., 107; N. Y. Hist. Soc. Coll., i., 414–419; Hoffman's Treatise, i., 97.

CHAP. III. 1666. bush, and Brooklyn, paid new fees and obtained new charters which generally confirmed to each of them their old boundaries, and "all the rights and privileges belonging to a town within this government." But Southold and Southampton refused to comply with this law; and it was not until several years afterward that they were finally obliged to yield.*

Nicolls, however, made allowances in special cases. In the city of New York, where all land titles were derived from the Dutch West India Company, the payments for new patents were greatly eased. The magistrates of Albany were granted a month's delay, "in regard 'tis uncertain whether the river will be open before the time prefixed by the Court of Assizes for bringing in your groundbriefs under a penalty." They were also desired to keep a strict hand upon the authors or reporters of strange news, "that amongst yourselves no quarrels or disputes may arise, and to the end that English and Dutch may live as brothers." At the same time Nicolls advised Jeremias van Rensselaer, who claimed Albany as a part of Rensselaerwyck, "not to grasp at too much authority," as the question was to be settled by the Duke of York, to whom it had been referred. "If you imagine," he added, "there is pleasure in titles of Government, I wish that I could serve your appetite, for I have found only trouble."†

New York City and Albany patents. $\frac{6}{16}$ Novem.

The roguery of some of the soldiers gave Nicolls much annoyance. Thomas Weall and two others of the garrison at New York were convicted of having stolen some goods "out of Captain Carteret's cellar," and it was determined that one of them should die. The fatal lot fell to Weall. But on the Sunday evening before he was to be executed, "a company of the chief women of the city, both English and Dutch," earnestly besought the governor to spare his life. The next morning they again interceded, accompanied by "many others of the better sort, and a greater

9 Novem. Thievish soldiers.

11 Novem.

* Col. Doc., ii., 473; viii., 441; Patents, i., 88, 91, 99, 102, 105, 108, 111; iv., 50, 51, 53, 54, 56, 58; Bolton's Westchester, i., 125, 375, 517; ii., 171, 412; Riker's Newtown, 74, 75; Thompson's L. I., i., 311, 312, 334, 335, 384, 385, 411, 467; ii., 81, 159, 171, 177, 183, 201, 220; Stiles's Brooklyn, i., 154–156; *ante*, vol. i., 762.

† Court of Assizes, ii., 443, 444; Col. Doc., iii., 143, 144. Jeremias van Rensselaer seemed to claim a right to succeed his brother John Baptist as proprietor, but Nicolls advised him to apply the line of Ovid—*Filius ante diem patrios inquirit in annos*—and not to inquire prematurely, like a grasping son, how long his father was to live. See Barnard's Sketch of Rensselaerwyck, 131–133.

number of the ordinary Dutch women." All the privates in the garrison, headed by Sergeant Thomas Exton, joined in a petition for their comrade's release. Yielding to these influences, Nicolls drew up the soldiers on parade, and pardoned the prisoners.* CHAP. III. 1666. 12 Novem.

The governor's prudence was generally appreciated, and his influence grew stronger every day. "Many old matters are ripped up and misinterpreted," wrote Van Ruyven to Stuyvesant in Holland, "but they are wisely disregarded by Governor Nicolls, so that a man remarked to me that it was the Governor's policy to follow the same course you had observed in the case of Governor Kieft."† 7/17 Aug't. Prudence of Nicolls.

On reaching London after his captivity, Cartwright had explained the condition of affairs in New York, and the duke had licensed two ships to sail thither with necessary supplies; but Nicolls could not yet be spared from his government. In very friendly terms Clarendon intimated to him that he might before long expect to return to England, "and then I hope some others will receive encouragement by your example to look a little abroad, and imploy themselves in doing good for their country." Secretary Morrice also wrote him a flattering letter on behalf of the king, and enclosed a present of two hundred pounds, which Nicolls gratefully received as given "at a time when money can be least spared."‡ 13 April. Nicolls commended in England. 12 April.

Finding that it was useless to continue them in New England, the king, in gracious words, recalled his commissioners with "considerable gratuities." Letters expressing the royal approbation were likewise addressed to the submissive colonies of Connecticut, Rhode Island, and Plymouth; but Massachusetts was ordered to send over Bellingham, Hathorne, and others, to answer for her to the king. Maverick and Carr, one, or both, were also directed to return as witnesses. These letters were sent under cover to the commissioners at Boston, where they were received by Maverick early in August. By order of Secretary Morrice, a duplicate of the one to Massachusetts, "signed and sealed," 10 April. Royal commissioners recalled. 6 August.

* N. Y. Surrogate's Rec. Wills, i., 13-18; Val. Man., 1847, 354, 355, 356.

† Col. Doc., ii., 473. Stuyvesant's policy had been to sustain the acts of his predecessor Kieft: see *ante*, vol. i., 468, 469, 472.

‡ Col. Doc., iii., 116, 136; Chalmers, i., 578; Ord., Warr., Lett., ii., 87; Mass. H. S. Coll., xxxvii., 312.

CHAP. III.

1666.

6 Septem. Dissimulation of Massachusetts.

was delivered the next month by Maverick to Governor Bellingham. But the General Court, "with an uncommon strain of dissimulation," affected to doubt its genuineness, notwithstanding a copy had been "surreptitiously conveyed over to them by some unknown hand before the

11 Septem.

original came to Boston." An answer was addressed to Secretary Morrice, "in all humility" refusing to obey the royal directions; but, to avert the king's displeasure, a present of "two very large masts" for his navy was prepared at great expense, and sent to England, which it was hoped would prove "as a cloud of latter rain." The dis-

3 Novem.

obedience of the Puritan colony was rebuked by Nicolls, Carr, and Maverick, but without effect.*

24 October. Suggestions of Nicolls to the English government.

In writing to Secretary Morrice, Nicolls sharply reviewed the "false sophistry" of Massachusetts, and suggested that the king might "easily chastise their undutifulness, not by force, which might frighten the innocent as well as nocent, but by a temporary embargo upon their trade, 'till such and such persons are delivered into the hands of justice. The numerous well-affected people in that and other colonies would soon give up the ringleaders at His Majesty's disposal. Neither would His Majesty lose any of his customs by that embargo; for if strict care were taken to send a convenient number of ships with goods suitable to this port, all the trade of Boston would be brought hither, and from thence carried into England; in which case, a frigate of countenance for convoy or any emergent occasion would be necessary, if possibly to be supplied out of His Majesty's more immediate service. Indeed, in the posture we are, every small picaroon of the enemy's is master of all our harbors and rivers, from the Capes of Virginia to Piscataway."†

6 Novem. Nicolls's report on New York.

At the same time, Nicolls sent to the British government an interesting autograph report of the condition of New York, in the form of "Answers to the several queries relating to the planters in the Territories of His Royal Highness the Duke of York in America." Among other things,

* Col. Doc., iii., 116, 136, 140, 141, 142, 160, 173; Mass. H. S. Coll., xxxvii., 312–314; Chalmers, i., 149, 277, 390; Hutch., i., 253, 257, 546–543; Coll., 408–410; Mass. Rec., iv. (ii.), 314–318, 327; Col. Rec. Conn., ii., 514; R. I. Rec., ii., 149; Pepys, iii., 24; Bancroft, ii, 87–89; Barry, i., 400–403; Palfrey, ii., 606, 624–630.

† Col. Doc., ii., 473; iii., 136, 137; Ord., Warr., Lett., ii., 85; Chalmers, i., 578, 590; N. Y. H. S. Coll. (1869), 125–131, 157–159.

1666.

he explained that the governor and council, with the high-sheriff and justices in the Court of Assizes, "have the supreme power of making, altering, and abolishing any laws in this Government;" that "the tenure of lands is derived from His Royal Highness," who would grant them at rents of one penny an acre, when purchased by himself from the Indians, and of two shillings and sixpence for a hundred acres when so bought by the planters; that "liberty of conscience is granted and assured," provided the peace of the government be not disturbed; that the rate for public charges had been agreed to "in a General Assembly, and is now managed by the Governor, his Council, and the Justices in the Court of Assizes;" and that "the obtaining all these privileges is long since recommended to His Royal Highness as the most necessary encouragement to these his territories, whereof a good answer is expected."*

In the mean time, the war in Europe between England and Holland and France seriously affected the American colonies. Suspicious of the Canadians, Nicolls engaged Winthrop and the Connecticut magistrates to mediate with the Mahicans for a peace between them and the Mohawks. The king's letters of the 22d of February, directing hostilities against Canada, being now received, measures were taken to stir up the Mohawks to war with the French. Information soon afterward reached Nicolls that a large force was marching from Canada "towards Albany." The garrison at Esopus was at once ordered to strengthen that place. The governor also urged the authorities of Connecticut and Massachusetts to raise a cavalry expedition, which could "cut off the whole strength of Canada at once." Connecticut pleaded that all her hands were occupied in the harvest; and suggested that as she wished to promote peace between the Mohawks and the Mahicans, it would be well "to let the French and Mohawks try it out a while," by

June.

5 July.

6 July. Proposed attack of Canada.

11 July. Connecticut refuses.

* Col. Doc., iii., 188; Chalmers, i., 596, 597; Whitehead's Index N. J. Col. Doc., 4. Chalmers says that Nicolls transmitted these answers in July, 1665. They are not dated, but they appear to have been sent by him in November, 1666, as they are placed in the volume in the State Paper Office next to his letter to the commissioners at Albany of 6 November, 1666: Col. Doc., iii., 136, 143, 188; New York Papers, i., 28, 30, 31. It was first intended that Sir Robert Carr should convey these papers to England, and then that Maverick should, as one or both had been ordered home. But both were "taken sick," and neither could go. Carr, however, sailed from Boston on 20 March, 1667, for Bristol, where he arrived on the first of June following, and died the next day: Col. Doc., iii., 160, 161; Hutch. Mass., i., 250; Morton's Mem., 315, *note;* Smith, i., 33; Mass. H. S. Coll., xxxvii., 312, 313.

CHAP. III. 1666. 26 July.

which both would be weakened. Winthrop, however, learning from Baker at Albany that the French were endeavoring to gain the Mahicans, interfered so seasonably as to prevent the going over of "many hundred" expected auxiliaries. Horsemen were likewise sent out from Hartford and Springfield, who penetrated with great difficulty one hundred and twenty miles through the wilderness as far as Lake Champlain, "to discover the way toward Canada," and procure intelligence. Winthrop also went to Boston to consult with the Massachusetts authorities and Sir Thomas Temple, the Governor of Nova Scotia. It was there unanimously agreed "that at present there could be nothing done by these colonies in reducing those places at or about Canada." The General Court of Massachusetts notified Lord Arlington that the reduction of Canada was "not at present feazable, as well in respect of the difficulty, if not impossibility, of a land march over the rocky mountains and howling desarts about four hundred miles, as the strength of the French there, according to reports." Winthrop also wrote to the same effect. Privateers, however, were commissioned at Boston, which made prize of several French fishing vessels.*

September.

24 October. Massachusetts refuses.

25 October. Privateers commissioned.

On their side the French had not been idle. As soon as the Saint Lawrence was clear of ice, ten Seneca sachems came down to Quebec to ratify the treaty which the Onondagas had made in their behalf with Tracy the previous December. They now promised to send some of their families to settle in Canada as hostages, and to acknowledge the King of France "henceforth as their sovereign." Tracy, on his part, agreed to send French colonists and Jesuit missionaries to the Senecas, who stipulated to build cabins for their shelter and forts to protect them from "the common enemy the Andastes and others."†

12/22 May. Submission of the Western Iroquois to the French

Thus the Upper Iroquois confirmed their vassalage to France. But no overtures came from the Mohawks. Tracy now resolved to extend his permanent military occupation further to the south, and directed Captain La Motte to build a new fort on an island in the upper part of Lake

* Col. Doc., iii., 117, 120, 121, 137, 138, 141; Col. Rec. Conn., ii., 40, 43, 45, 514; Mass. Rec., iv. (ii.), 316, 317, 328, 329; Mass. H. S. Coll., xviii., 101–109; xxx., 63; Hutch. Mass., i., 256, 257; Coll., 407; Bancroft, ii., 88; Palfrey, ii., 630; iii., 114–116; *ante*, p. 97.

† Col. Doc., iii., 125; ix., 44, 45; Doc. Hist., i., 47; Faillon, iii., 134; *ante*, p. 100, *note*.

Champlain. This post, which was the first one possessed by the French within the ancient limits of New York, was named Fort Sainte Anne, but was afterward better known as Fort La Motte. Intended to command the Mohawk country, it soon caused uneasiness to the neighboring English colonies.*

CHAP. III. 1666. Fort Sainte Anne, or La Motte.

Soon afterward Oneida envoys came to Quebec, tardily bringing the letter of the Albany officers assuring Tracy that the Mohawks wished peace with the French. Two detachments of two hundred men each had meanwhile been ordered to march, under Courcelles and Sorel, from the forts on the Richelieu, against that nation. Understanding the Albany letter as a guarantee for the good faith of the Mohawks, Tracy countermanded the expeditions, and signed a treaty covenanting peace between the French and the Oneidas and Mohawks. Prisoners were to be mutually restored, and trade with Canada by way of Lake Saint Sacrement was to be open to the Oneidas, who now ratified the treaty made two months before by the Western Iroquois, and, like them, acknowledged the King of France "from this time as their sovereign." It was also agreed that Jesuit missionaries should be sent "to make known to them the God of the French, whom they promise to love and adore." Hostages were left with Tracy for the faithful performance of these conditions. At the request of the Oneidas, the Father Thierry Bechefer, with Hertel and two other Frenchmen, were sent, under their escort, to visit the soldiers whom Courcelles had left at Albany, and treat with the Mohawks there, or assure them that they might safely come to Quebec at any time within forty days. The letter of the Albany authorities was also published at the several French garrisons; and all felt confident that peace between Canada and the Iroquois was secured.†

27 June / 7 July.

2/12 July. The Oneidas and Mohawks agree to submit to the French.

14 July.

But scarcely had Bechefer and his companions gone three days' journey from Quebec, when news came that several French officers, who had gone out a hunting from

* Relation, 1665, 10; 1666, 7, 8; Doc. Hist., i., 43, 48; ii., 162; Col. Doc., iii., 141, 145, 146, 155, 803; iv., 195, 404; ix., 601, 1050; Faillon, iii., 126, 135. Fort Sainte Anne, or La Motte, appears to have been built on Isle La Motte, which, being east of the present boundary-line between New York and Vermont, belongs to the latter state: N. Y. Revised Statutes, i., 64.

† Col. Doc., iii., 126-132, 153; ix., 45, 46, 52, 169, 786; Doc. Hist., i., 47, 51, 52; Relation, 1661, 34; 1666, 7; 1670, 45; Charlevoix, ii., 110, 111, 155; Shea, 252, 500; *ante*, p. 104.

CHAP. III. 1666. French officers killed. the new Fort Sainte Anne, had been waylaid and murdered by the Mohawks, and some others taken prisoners. One of the chief victims was a nephew of the viceroy, the Sieur de Chazy, whose name is yet commemorated in that of one of the towns in the county of Clinton. Bechefer and the other Frenchmen on their way to Albany were at once recalled, and the Oneidas who escorted them were imprisoned. Sorel quickly collected three hundred men, with whom he pushed on toward the Mohawk country, intending to lay "a heavy hand every where." But when he had come within twenty leagues of their villages he met a party of Mohawks, who declared that they were on their way to Quebec to restore the Frenchmen captured near Fort Sainte Anne, and offer satisfaction for those who had been slain, as well as new guarantees for peace. The party was led by a half-breed known among the Indians as "Smits Jan," and among the French as "the Dutch Bastard."* Believing their statement, Sorel turned about, and conducted Smits Jan and his followers to the viceroy, by whom they were well received. A few days afterward, Agariata, a Mohawk chief, came to Quebec and announced himself as also a delegate from his nation. Negotiations for peace went on prosperously, until one day, Tracy having invited the two pretended ambassadors to his table, the talk fell upon the death of De Chazy. The Mohawk chief, lifting up his arm, exclaimed, "It was this which broke the head of that young officer!" All present were filled with indignation. "You shall kill no more," said the viceroy to Agariata, who was at once hung in the sight of his comrades, and Smits Jan was committed to prison. (Tracy's vengeance.)

22 July. Tracy now sent William Couture, who had been a prisoner with Jogues among the Mohawks, with a letter to the Albany officers, complaining that they had deceived him as to the peaceful disposition of that nation. Learning that a courier had come from Quebec, Nicolls voyaged up the river, which was "pleasant enough at that season of the year," to meet him. But before the governor reached Albany, Couture had returned to Canada. Nicolls, however, (Nicolls at Albany.)

* This "Smits Jan" was the son of a Hollander and a Mohawk squaw, and had been brought up among the savages. He was one of the witnesses to Cartwright's treaty at Albany in September, 1664, and was in the English interest: Col. Doc., iii., 68, 146, 148, 151, 435; Charlevoix, ii., 54, 69, 155, 161; Relation, 1654, 10, 11.

CHAP. III.

1666.

wrote courteously to Tracy, expressing his surprise at Courcelles's inroad into New York the last winter, but declaring his purpose to promote "the European interest amidst the heathen in America, as becomes a good Christian, provided that the bounds and limits of these His Majesty's of England's dominions be not invaded, or the peace and safety of his subjects interrupted." Baker and the Albany magistrates also wrote to the viceroy, justifying their conduct respecting the Mohawks, and stating that they would not intermeddle with French affairs in future.*

$\frac{20}{30}$ August. Answers to Tracy.

Ambassadors from all the nations but the Mohawks having met Tracy and Courcelles in the Park of the Jesuits at Quebec, the Cayugas renewed their request for missionaries, and the Fathers Jacques Frémin and Pierre Raffeix were chosen to go to them. Seeing no reason to hope for peace with the Mohawks, the viceroy determined to chastise them effectually. Colbert had insisted upon a prudent administration "in the present conjuncture, when His Majesty is obliged to maintain a heavy war against the English, whom none of his predecessors had ever before attacked on the sea." Talon accordingly submitted to Tracy and Courcelles various considerations for war and for peace. It was argued, among other things, that a successful attack on the Mohawks would open the door for the seizure of Albany, where the Dutch might be found inclined to aid the French against the English, upon whom they wished "to avenge the usurpation unjustly committed upon them," and of whose "insupportable dominion" they were weary. An expedition against the Mohawks was ordered, and six hundred soldiers of the Carignan regiment, with an equal number of militia, and one hundred Hurons and Algonquins, were soon collected. Notwithstanding he was more than seventy years old, Tracy set out from Quebec to lead his forces in person. The Jesuit Fathers Charles Albanel and Pierre Raffeix, and two secular priests, Du

$\frac{21}{31}$ August. Jesuit missionaries. 5 April. 1 Septem. French expedition against the Mohawks. 14 Septem.

* Col. Doc., iii., 68, 131–134, 146, 151, 153, 157; ix., 52; Doc. Hist., i., 47, 48, 56; Relation, 1645, 23; 1647, 19, 24; 1648, 11; 1666, 7, 8; La Potherie, ii., 85; Charlevoix, i., 409; ii., 54, 69, 155, 156; Colden, i., 33, 34; Garneau, i., 193; Ferland, i., 317; Faillon, iii., 135–137; *ante*, vol. i., 346, 347, 373. The Albany letters of 20 August, 1666, did not reach Tracy until April, 1667: Col. Doc., iii., 146, 147, 148, 151, 152.

CHAP. III. Bois D'Esgriselles, and Dollier de Casson, accompanied the expedition.

1666.

The general rendezvous was Fort Sainte Anne, on Lake

3 October. Champlain. It was October before the main body of troops was ready to advance; but Courcelles, with characteristic impatience, pushed forward with four hundred men.

Tracy's advance. The rear-guard followed four days after the main column, under Tracy. Three hundred light bateaux and bark canoes were prepared, each of which could convey five or six persons; and two pieces of artillery were carried along with great labor. The viceroy endeavored to advance cautiously, so as to surprise the Mohawk castles; but the watchful Iroquois scouts on the mountain tops saw the French flotilla afar off, as it swept southward over Lake Champlain, and the alarm was quickly spread. As the troops debarked the savages whooped on the hill-sides, and fired random shots at the invaders. Expecting to find abundance of corn in the Mohawk villages, the French carried only small supplies of provisions. These were soon exhausted, and the army was on the point of disbanding to seek food, when it fortunately entered a forest of chestnut-trees, the just ripening fruit of which relieved the famishing troops.

After marching thirty or forty leagues from the lake, the French reached the first Mohawk village, which they found abandoned. Entering it in order of battle, with flags flying and drums beating, the hungry army discovered abundance of corn buried in the earth. A second and a third village farther west were found deserted like the first. At length, guided by an Algonquin, who had long been a prisoner in the canton, the French reached the fourth Mohawk village. Here the savages were observed in great

Mohawk villages destroyed. force, and, by their heavy fire, appeared disposed to defend their fortress with desperation. The invaders prepared to attack it in regular form; but, as their van came on to attack, the Mohawks fled in terror into the forest, whither the French could not pursue them. An old man and two old women, too infirm to escape, and the half-roasted remains of two or three prisoners, were found in the deserted stronghold. It was surrounded by a triple palisade twenty feet high, flanked by four bastions, and abundantly supplied with water in bark tanks to extinguish fire. Prodigious quantities of provisions had been stored. Some of the cabins, which were one hundred and twenty feet long, and proportionably wide, and were planked on the inside, moved the admiration of the Frenchmen. CHAP. III 1666.

The cross was planted, mass said, a Te Deum sung, and formal possession was taken for the King of France of "The Fort of Andaraque," as well as all the other conquered Iroquois strong-holds, "and of all the lands in the neighborhood as far and in as great a quantity as they may extend." A post, with the king's arms affixed, was erected, amid the shouts of "*Vive le Roi!*" The palisades and cabins, with vast stores of corn, beans, and other provisions, were then burned. On its return, the expedition completed the devastation of the other villages; and grain "enough to sustain the whole colony for two years" was destroyed. 17 October. French possession of the country taken.

Supposing that famine and the terror of the French arms would overawe the Mohawks and keep them peaceful, Tracy judged it unnecessary to establish a fort in their country. Those on the Richelieu River were thought sufficient to maintain the sovereignty of France. Colbert's policy was against extending the Canadian settlements too far from each other. For the present, the Jesuit missionaries were to form the advanced guard of the French among the Mohawks. The viceroy would nevertheless have pushed on westward, and humbled the Oneidas also, if the approach of November had not warned him to return. The paths were now much more difficult to travel, and the swollen rivers hindered the march of the troops. On Lake Champlain two canoes and several soldiers were lost in a storm. Throughout the whole march of three hundred leagues, and during fifty-three days, Tracy, who was a very large man, shared all the fatigues of his army, submitting to be borne in a litter for two days only, when crippled by the gout. Courcelles, attacked by a nervous disease, had to be carried in the same manner. On reaching Quebec, the viceroy hung two or three of his prisoners by way of example, and sent the rest back to their cantons, with Smits Jan, the Dutch bastard, after having shown them many kindnesses. The returning Iroquois carried the terms of peace which Tracy offered to the Mohawks, Tracy returns to Canada. November

CHAP. III. and which they were expected to accept before the end of the next June.*

1666. After their severe humiliation by the French, the Mohawks came to confer with the Albany officers. It was now supposed that Tracy, wearied with his "two fruitless

1667. voyages," would hardly attempt another expedition. Yet no precaution was neglected. Nicolls had visited the garrisons on the North River the previous autumn, and had given the Albany magistrates full directions in case the French should attempt to do them harm. Captain Brodhead was now ordered to be "ready, upon an hour's warning," with all his soldiers at Esopus, and as many of the burghers as possible, to assist Albany in case of need, because it was "impossible" to send any from New York during the winter. Van Curler was also desired to prepare a map of Lake Champlain, with the French forts, showing "how it borders upon the Maquas's River."†

Precautions of Nicolls.

7 January.

When Nicolls received the news from Canada brought by Smits Jan, he directed that the Mohawks should be counseled to insist that the French must demolish all their new advanced forts on Lake Champlain. Baker was specially instructed to advise the Mohawks to "make a good peace, or none, with the French, such as may bring in beaver to Albany, and leave them without fear or jealousy of the French;" and also that they "should declare to the French that the King of England is the great king of all their country and parts adjacent, and unto him they are subordinate, living in peace and trading with all his subjects; and now they are willing to make peace with the French, and will resolve to keep it, if the French will demolish their forts, and bring no more troops of soldiers into the King of England's country or their Plantation."‡

11 Jan.

Nicolls's instructions respecting the Mohawks.

On receiving the letters of Nicolls and the Albany officers written the previous August, Tracy explained the inroad of Courcelles into the Mohawk country, and declared

* Relation, 1666, 8, 9; Charlevoix, ii., 157–161; La Potherie, ii., 123; iii., 55; Col. Doc., iii., 135, 146, 151; iv., 352; ix., 41, 52–57, 786; Doc. Hist., i., 48, 49, 53, 54; Colden, i., 33; Shea, 252; Faillon, iii., 138–155. The map of Tracy's route is in the Library of Parliament at Quebec: see Catalogue (1858), p. 1614.

† Col. Doc., iii., 143, 144, 145; Col. MSS., xxii., 22. The letters of Nicolls to Van Curler and the Albany magistrates were translated into Dutch, at the governor's request, by Counselor Van Ruyven.

‡ Col. Doc, iii., 146–148. Colden says nothing of this.

1667.

that until then he did not know that New Netherland was not under the dominion of the United Provinces. "The French nation," he added, "is too much inclined to acknowledge courtesies not to confess that the Dutch have had very much charity for the French who have been prisoners with the Mohawks, and that they have redeemed divers, who had been burned without their succour. They ought also to be assured of our gratitude towards them, and to any others who shall exercise such Christian deeds as they have done." The viceroy also absolved the Albany officers from blame in regard to the murder of his officers by the Mohawks near Fort Sainte Anne, and invited Van Curler to visit him the next summer at Quebec.*

30 April. Tracy writes to Nicolls.

Van Curler, accompanied by La Fontaine, a young Frenchman whom he had rescued from the savages, now went to Canada, with passports from Nicolls, who wrote a kind letter to Tracy. Embarking in a canoe on Lake Champlain, he had a prosperous voyage as far as "a great bay" on its western side, opposite the "Isles des quatres vents." While crossing this bay the canoe was upset by a tempest, and Van Curler was drowned. The memory of this estimable Hollander was long preserved by the Iroquois, who insisted upon calling the successive governors of New York "Corlaer." For years Lake Champlain was known among the English as "Corlaer's Lake." The bay in which he was drowned—long called by the French "Baye Corlar"—is now known as "Peru Bay," in Essex county, New York.†

28 May. Van Curler goes toward Canada.

Drowned in Lake Champlain.

"Corlaer."

Soon after Nicolls left Esopus, in the previous autumn, the ill feeling which had been growing between its inhabitants and the garrison broke out into open hostility. The soldiers, who, as well as their officers, were all Englishmen, did nothing to conciliate and much to offend the Dutch burghers. Disturbances occurred both at the village of Wildwyck and at the redoubt on the creek. When, in obedience to Nicolls's orders, Captain Brodhead was "gathering some of the young burghers together" to go to Albany, Antonio d'Elba, a French refugee, openly said, "Shall we go and fight our friends, and leave our enemies at home?"

Disturbances at Esopus.

* Col. Doc., iii., 133, 134, 150–154; Doc. Hist., i., 55; *ante*, vol. i., 402.

† Map in Charlevoix, i., 226; Rel., 1668, 5; Ord., Warr., etc., ii., 159, 160; Col. Doc., iii., 128, 156, 157, 322, 395, 558, 559, 815, 817; Colden, i., 32; O'Call., i., 323; Smith, i., 65.

CHAP. III. 1667. Brodhead's overbearing conduct. 14/4 Feb.

Much of the ill feeling was due to the overbearing conduct of Brodhead, who did not hesitate to commit to the guard any who offended him. He imprisoned a burgher who would keep Christmas according to the Dutch and not the English style. He quarreled with and arrested Cornelis Barentsen Slegt, the village brewer, and a sergeant of its militia. Slegt's wife and children thereupon ran crying through Wildwyck. The excited villagers rushed to arms. Finding some sixty of them drawn up before their lieutenant's door, Captain Brodhead marched thither with a few of his soldiers, and ordered them to disperse. The local magistrates asked Brodhead to release his prisoner and have him tried before them, which he refused, and threatened to resist any attempt at a rescue. The people would not disperse until late at night, and then only with the understanding that the whole matter should be laid before the governor. What added to the bitterness was that Hendrick Cornelissen, the village ropemaker, was killed by William Fisher, one of Brodhead's soldiers.*

16 April. Special commission sent to Esopus.

Reports were sent down to Nicolls, who issued a special commission empowering Counselors Needham and Delavall and Justice Van Ruyven to go to Esopus, and "hear, receive, and determine such and so many complaints as they shall judge necessary or of moment, and to pass sentence of imprisonment, fine, correction, or suspension of office against such who shall be found guilty." At the same time the governor guided the action of his commissioners by private instructions. They were to be attended by a file of soldiers, and were to admit but "very few" into the room in which they might sit. The case of Fisher was "to be the first tried, because a man is killed." But he could only be convicted of manslaughter; and it might turn out that he had acted in self-defense. In regard to the "first occasion" of the mutiny, as Slegt, the brewer, had first assaulted Captain Brodhead, they were "to declare that the king's officer is not of so mean a quality as to be struck by a burgher," and were to enlarge their discourse on this point as they should "find fit." But as the captain had broken his instructions several times, they were to suspend him

Nicolls's private instructions.

* Col. MSS., xxii., 14, 21–32; Alb. Rec., xviii., 327–330, 470; Esopus Records; Col. Doc., iii., 144, 149.

from his command for "that only fault" of keeping the brewer in prison after the schout and commissaries had asked for his release. A few of the "most notorious" insurgents were to be found guilty of "a treasonable and malicious Riot," and were to be brought to New York for "final sentence of punishment" by the governor. "Discourage not the soldiers too much in public," added Nicolls, "lest the boors insult over them; appear favorable to the most of the boors, but severe against the principal incendiaries; and, in general, you may tell them freely that I will proceed against every man that shall lift arms against His Majestie's garrison, as rebellious subjects and common enemies."*

CHAP. III. — 1667.

The commissioners sat three days at Esopus. Captain Brodhead frankly admitted the charges against him, and was suspended from his command, which was intrusted to Sergeant Beresford. The burghers excused their being in arms because the soldiers had threatened to burn the town, and because Brodhead had imprisoned their sergeant. Four of the movers of the insurrection, Antonio d'Elba, Albert Heymans, Arent Albertsen, his son, and Cornelius Barentsen, were found guilty of a "rebellious and mutinous Riot," and were carried down to New York for sentence by the governor. Nicolls was of opinion that they deserved death. But, on the petition of the inhabitants and by the advice of his council, he sentenced Heymans to be banished for life out of the government, and the others, for shorter terms, out of Esopus, Albany, and New York. These sentences were afterward modified; and Heymans, the chief offender, became a prominent officer at Esopus.†

25 April. 26 April. 27 April. Brodhead suspended.

3 May. Chief rioters sentenced.

The soldiers at Albany also gave the governor much trouble. Several of them were convicted of stealing wampum from the inhabitants, and, upon Captain Baker's report, Nicolls, with the advice of his council, decreed prompt satisfaction.‡

Soldiers at Albany.

* Patents, i., 145; Col. Doc., iii., 149, 150.

† Col. MSS., xxii., 24, 28, 31, 32, 99; N. Y. Surr. Rec. Wills, i., 22–25; Val. Man., 1847, 357, 358; Col. Doc., ii., 627; iii., 150; Ulster Hist. Coll., i., 50, 51; Esopus Records. Fisher, the soldier who killed Cornelissen, appears to have been acquitted, and afterward obtained a lot of land at Marbletown: Val. Man., 1847, 361; Patents, iii., 43. Captain Brodhead died at Esopus on the 14th of July, 1667, about two months after his suspension from command, leaving his widow, Ann, and three sons, Daniel, Charles, and Richard.

‡ The details of these cases are given in N. Y. Surrogate's Records, Wills, i., 19, 20, 21, 32; Val. Man., 1847, 356, 357, 361.

CHAP. III.

1667. 3 July. Long Island.

Discontent was still manifested in Long Island. While the governor was attending "a public meeting" at Flushing, he offered to furnish the people with powder for their own use, and receive pay for it in firewood. This friendly proposition was covertly represented by William Bishop as "another cunning trick." It was accordingly ordered in Council at New York, that for his "seditious words" Bishop should "be made fast to the whipping-post, there to stand, with rods fastened to his back during the sitting of the Court of Mayor and Aldermen, and from thence to be removed into the common Gaol, till further orders." This sentence seems to have effectually quelled sedition during the rest of Nicolls's administration.*

9 July. William Bishop punished for sedition.

Meanwhile England had been at open war with Holland and France. But before France engaged in hostilities she made another attempt to pacify England and Holland. A conference was held at Paris between Lord Hollis, De Lionne, and Van Beuningen, in which the latter offered, on the part of the States General, "either to restore all things to the same state they were in before the war, or to take them as they now stand, and every one keep what he hath." But neither of these alternatives suited Charles, who directed his ambassador to leave Paris.†

1666. 6/16 April. Dutch offers to England.

1/11 June. Battle between the Dutch and English.

Another naval engagement followed off the mouth of the Thames, between the English fleet under Prince Rupert and the Duke of Albemarle, in place of the Duke of York, who refused to command, and the Dutch under De Ruyter, Evertsen, and Tromp. The contest lasted four days, and the English Vice-Admiral Sir John Berkeley and other officers were killed. Both sides fought with proverbial courage; but the chain-shot which De Witt is said to have invented, and now introduced, cut to pieces the rigging of the English, and the Dutch remained conquerors. They had never gained such a triumph since the foundation of the republic. In London, "orders were given for

Chain-shot.

The Dutch victorious.

* N. Y. Surr. Rec. Wills, i., 28, 29; Val. Man., 1847, 359, 360. On the third of July, 1667, the mayor and aldermen of the city of New York, with the approbation of Nicolls, sold to Johannes Verveshe, of Harlaem, for five years, the ferry thence to Bronck side, provided he maintained proper ferry houses, and carried over free "all men going or coming with a packett from our Governor of New Yorke, or coming from the Governor of Connecticott:" Val. Man., 1849, 362; N. Y. City Rec.

† D'Estrades, iv., 167, 253, 257, 263, 276, 524; Lister's Clarendon, iii., 431–434; De Witt, ii., 253, 255.

CHAP. III. 1666.

bonfires and bells." But even Charles became "melancholy," wrote Pepys in his cipher diary, "under the thoughts of this last overthrow, for so it is, instead of a victory." A month afterward the fleets engaged again. On this occasion the English were victorious. Evertsen and other Dutch admirals were killed, and De Ruyter and Tromp became bitter enemies. The next week Sir Robert Holmes made a piratical descent on the island of Schelling, on the coast of Friesland, which was chiefly inhabited by unwarlike Mennonists, and, after burning several Dutch merchantmen, destroyed nearly a thousand houses in the unfortified town of Brandaris. The Tower guns at London were fired for this "late good success." But the English government could send no supplies to the American Plantations, and especially to the Carribee Islands, which were exposed to great danger from the French. Arlington therefore urged the New England colonies to fit out, if possible, an expedition for the relief of those threatened places, which would be considered by the king as a marked expression of their "good affection and loyalty."

25 July. / 4 August. Another battle. The English victorious. Holmes at Schelling. 28 August.

In Holland, the conduct of Holmes at Schelling embittered the national resentment against England. De Witt, who felt the unpopularity which threatened to overthrow his administration, vowed that he would never sheathe the sword until he had obtained revenge. But before his vow was fulfilled, London was visited by a calamity scarcely less appalling than the pestilence by which she had been desolated the year before. A great fire, which lasted for three days, consumed every house, church, and hall in ninety parishes, between the Tower and Temple Bar. This "marvellous year" was commemorated by Dryden in magnificent verses, full of bitterness against the Dutch, which before long won for him the laurel crown.*

September. Fire of London. Dryden's "Annus mirabilis."

1667. January.

When the news tardily reached the North American colonies by way of Barbadoes, Massachusetts set the example in contributing for the relief of the sufferers. Not

* Aitzema, v., 697–731; Basnage, i., 772–784; Kennett, iii., 259–262; Clarke's James II., i., 423, 424; Burnet, i., 228–232; Rapin, ii., 642, 643; Pepys, ii., 391, 431, 435, 439–448; Evelyn, ii., 6, 11–17; D'Estrades, iv., 322, 402, 432; Davies, iii., 45–54; Martin, i., 273, 274; Dryden's Annus mirabilis; Lister, ii., 360–365; Knight, iv., 279–290; Col. Doc., ii., 661; iii., 147, 154; Mass. H. S. Coll., xxx., 66; Col. Rec. Conn., ii., 515, 516. Dryden's patent as Poet Laureate was dated 18 August, 1670, but his salary began immediately after the death of Sir William Davenant, his predecessor, in 1668.

CHAP. III. 1667. March. Colonial apprehensions.

long afterward, upon the receipt of Arlington's letters, Winthrop went from Connecticut, and Maverick from New York, to consult with the authorities at Boston in regard to sending aid to the Carribee Islands. But there was too much danger to be apprehended near home, both from Canada, and from the Dutch and French ships at sea, to justify an expedition for the relief of the "dear countrymen" in the West Indies. This was communicated by 7 May. Winthrop to Arlington in a very loyal letter excusing the apparent indifference of the New England colonies. Maverick June. also informed the secretary that such were the straits to which Nicolls had been reduced for want of supplies in New York, that he had been obliged to pledge his personal credit for more than a thousand pounds, to carry on his government.*

The apprehensions of the English that the Dutch and French might attack their West India colonies were well founded. Commander Abraham Krynssen, sailing from 6 March. Krynssen takes Surinam. Flushing with three ships, surprised the English colony of Surinam, in Guiana, and left a military force to secure it, under the command of Maurice de Rame, and Ensign Colve. Not long afterward, a frigate belonging to the Duke of York, coming from Guinea with a cargo of ivory and negroes, was captured by the Dutch at Surinam. Krynssen had meanwhile joined the French squadron commanded by Lefebvre de la Barre, and assisted in defeating the English off the island of Nevis. Thence the June. Krynssen in Virginia. Dutch commander sailed to Virginia, where he captured, in the James River, twenty-six English vessels, one of which was a man-of-war. After scuttling most of them, Krynssen returned to Flushing, bringing along with him eleven prizes laden with tobacco.†

This daring exploit so near home alarmed and mortified Nicolls, who attributed it to the "negligence and ill conduct" of the officers in Virginia. Every precaution was therefore taken for the defense of New York. The magistrates of Southampton, Easthampton, and the other towns

* Col. Doc., iii., 154–156, 161; Hutch. Mass., i., 250, 257; Coll., 411, 412; Mass. Rec., iv. (ii.), 310, 311, 335, 345, 347; 547; Palfrey, ii., 631.

† Wagenaar, xiii., 406–408; Richesse de la Hollande, i., 213; Basnage, i., 809; D'Estrades, v., 83, 250, 261, 262; De Witt, iv., 642, 677; Aitzema, vi., 123, 426–428, 438, 440; Burk, ii., 149; Campbell, 267; Pinkerton, xii., 292; Col. Doc., ii., 518–522; iii., 155, 161, 167; ix., 167; N. Y. Senate Doc., 1844, No. 42, p. 5.

at the east end of Long Island were ordered to turn one third of their militia into cavalry, and to be ready at an hour's notice; while the other two thirds were to remain at their homes for the security of their estates. Connecticut, fearing a French incursion from Canada, did the like. But "the grandees of Boston were too proud to be dealt with," alleging that the king was well satisfied of their loyalty, and had recalled and disgraced his commissioners. Nicolls, however, anxious to harass the enemy, commissioned Sergeant Thomas Exton, of the garrison at Fort James, to be captain of the privateer Cedar, of New York, and sent her under his command to act against the French and Dutch. Exton soon captured and burnt two French forts, Saint Mary and Du Coudray, in Acadia, and came to Boston with "as many guns and other plunder" as his ship could carry. On reaching New York, Exton reported his proceedings, and the spoil he had taken was condemned as good prize.*

CHAP. III. 1667. 19 July. Precautions of Nicolls. 30 July. New York privateer in Acadia. 14 October. 4 Novem.

In their war against the Mahicans during the summer, the Mohawks had committed some depredations at Hadley and Northampton, in Massachusetts, and had murdered a young savage, whose scalp they exhibited at Albany. The victim "was servant to an Englishman at Northampton." On learning this outrage, Nicolls went to Albany to interpose his authority with the native belligerents. The General Court of Massachusetts, however, conceiving that they could treat independently with the New York Iroquois, wrote to "the chief sachem of the Mohawks" that such doings were contrary to their promise not to molest any Indians "that woare English cloakes, or that had their haire cutt short;" and hoping for satisfaction and better behavior in future.†

30 August. 10 October. Nicolls at Albany.

The war in Europe had meanwhile obliged Louis to recall Tracy to France, with several companies of the Carignan regiment. These orders surprised the viceroy, who was expecting Van Curler to visit him at Quebec, and was obliged to embark just as his coming guest was meeting his death on Lake Champlain. Courcelles was now left in command as governor general of Canada. The

Tracy leaves Canada. May. Courcelles governor.

* Col. Doc., iii., 157, 158, 161, 162, 167; Col. Rec. Conn., ii., 69, 81; Val. Man., 1847, 355, 362; N. Y. Surr. Rec. Wills, i., 16, 35; Patents, i., 171, 172; Court of Assizes, ii., 154, 155. I do not find any reference in the French authorities to Exton's exploits in Acadia.

† Col. Doc., iii., 162; Relations, 1667, 28; 1668, 4; Mass. Rec., iv. (ii.), 359-361.

CHAP. III. 1667. king had approved the treaties made with the Western Iroquois the year before, because he expected thereby "to acquire a possession adverse to the actual or future pretensions of the European nations." But, as the Mohawks had shown no disposition to submit to the French, Colbert directed Courcelles to undertake a new expedition against that nation during the next summer, "for the purpose of utterly destroying them if possible, or at least of increasing the terror they entertain of His Majesty's forces, and placing them in a position not to trouble the country." (6 April.)

Courcelles had "a sufficiently strong inclination to return to the charge." But, a few days after the viceroy's departure, Mohawk and Oneida deputies came to Quebec to declare their submission to the French, and solicit that missionaries might be sent to their cantons. The Canadian expeditions the year before had so awed these proud nations that, in spite of the efforts of Nicolls and his officers at Albany, they showed their sincerity by bringing several of their families to Canada as hostages. Talon, suspecting that the Mohawks had "yielded considerably to existing circumstances, and to the war with the Mahicans, from which they were suffering," thought that they had not brought hostages enough. But, as Colbert desired to "Frenchify" the savages, a treaty was concluded to the apparent satisfaction of both parties. Jesuit missionaries were at once selected to go among the several Iroquois nations. The Father Jacques Frémin, who had been with Dablon at Onondaga in 1656, and the Father Jean Pierron, who had just arrived from France, were assigned to the Mohawks. Father Jacques Bruyas, who had been about a year in Canada, and had already given proof of that talent which was to make him so distinguished as an Indian philologist, was appointed to go to the Oneidas. Three other Jesuit fathers held themselves ready to work among the Onondagas, Cayugas, and Senecas.*

June. Mohawks and Oneidas at Quebec.

Missionaries assigned to the Iroquois.

The next month the Mohawk and Oneida envoys set out with Frémin, Pierron, and Bruyas for their mission grounds. On reaching Fort Sainte Anne, at the foot of Lake Cham-

14 July. Frémin, Pierron, and Bruyas.

* Relation, 1657, 9; 1667, 2, 28; 1668, 3; Charlevoix, ii., 161, 163, 164, 176, 178; Col. Doc., iii., 151, 152; ix., 58, 59, 60, 130, 720, 787; Doc. Hist., iv., 190; Shea, 254, 274, 294, 500; Garneau, i., 195; Faillon, iii., 156–158; *ante*, vol. i., 644.

plain, they were delayed a month by apprehension of a Mahican ambuscade. At length, on the eve of Saint Bartholomew's day, finding that the Mahicans had retreated, the party embarked, and followed the north coast of the lake. From morning to night, the fathers, unused to the toil, rowed "like poor galley-slaves," for every hand in the light birch-bark canoes was obliged to work. In this manner they "traversed gaily the whole of this great lake, already too renowned by the shipwreck of several of our Frenchmen, and quite recently by that of the Sieur Corlaer." On reaching the outlet of Saint Sacrement* they crossed the portage, and at the head of the lake met fourteen Mohawk warriors, who were stationed there as sentinels to watch for a new army of Frenchmen. But, on learning the peaceful errand of the missionaries, they "made themselves their valets," and joyfully carried their luggage. A few days of pleasant journeying brought the party near the first palisaded village of the Tortoise tribe of the Mohawks, on the north bank of the river, "called Gandaouague,† which is that which the late Father Jogues moistened with his blood, and where he was so badly treated during eighteen months of captivity." The missionaries were received with all honor by the savages, who were delighted to see among them peaceful Frenchmen in place of those who so recently appeared "as furies, setting every thing on fire." Two leagues further to the west they came to the village called "Gandagaro," or "Kanagaro," belonging to the Bear tribe.‡ Thence they proceeded four leagues more, passing beyond Canajoharie, to the village of the Wolf tribe, and the capital of all the Mohawk country, called "Tionnontoguen,"§ which that nation "had rebuilt at a

1667. 23 August.

Gandaouague, or Caghnawaga.

Tionnontoguen.

* This was called by the Indians "Tionderoga," meaning in their language "the place where two rivers meet." The French called it "Carillon," on account of the noise of the waterfall in the outlet: see Benson's Mem., 96. The English called it "Ticonderoga:" see Col. Doc., vii., 399, 795, 984; x., 721; *ante*, vol. i., p. 18, *note*.

† Relation, 1668, 6; 1670, 23. This village, called "*Oneugiouré*" by Jogues, and "*Kaghnewagé*" by the Dutch, was the site of the modern village of "Caghnawaga," in the county of Montgomery: Relation, 1646, 15; Col. Doc., ii., 712. Want of taste has recently belittled this sonorous, significant, and historical name into "*Fonda*:" see Hist. Mag., ix., 371, 372; x., 20, 115, 321, 322. The word "Caghnawaga" (which was afterward transferred to the Catholic "Reduction" on the Saint Lawrence, near Montreal) means, in the Mohawk language, "the Rapids," or "a carrying place:" Col. Doc., ii., 712; iii., 250, *note;* Index, 282; Doc. Hist., iii., 674; N. Y. H. S. Coll., iii. (ii.), 159, 171; Shea's Catholic Missions, 256, 304; *ante*, vol. i., 423, 659.

‡ Col. Doc., ii., 712; iii., 250.

§ This village seems to have been not far from Fort Plain, or Palatine. It was removed, in 1689, "an English mile higher up," and was again burned by the French in 1693: Doc.

CHAP. III. 1667. quarter of a league from that which the French had burned the year before." It was situated on a hill, about a bowshot from the north bank of the Mohawk River. Like Caghnawaga, the capital was "double-stockaded round;" and it contained about thirty cabins. Here the missionaries were received with a grand fusillade, "each one firing from his cabin, and two swivels going off at the extremities of the village."

14 Septem. On the day of the exaltation of the Holy Cross, the six Mohawk villages assembled at Tionnontoguen, and were harangued by Frémin, after the *Veni Creator* had been chanted. Having reproached them for their cruelties to the French, the father declared that their Great Onnontio would receive them as his subjects. To enforce his speech, Frémin planted a tall pole, at the top of which was a wampum belt, and explained that the first Iroquois who should kill a Frenchman would be thus hung. The awed savages offered a place for a chapel; mass was soon celebrated in the rude building, at which all had worked with zeal; and the Mission of Saint Mary of the Mohawks was established.*

Mission of Saint Mary of the Mohawks.

Leaving Frémin and Pierron among the Mohawks, Bruyas now went thirty leagues farther west to found a new mission among the Oneidas, who were esteemed "of all the Iroquois the least numerous in fact, but the most proud and insolent." A small chapel, quickly built by the savages, was consecrated on the feast of Saint Michael the Archangel. Here Bruyas labored diligently; but the Mission of Saint Francis Xavier of the Oneidas never answered French hopes.†

Bruyas at Saint Francis Xavier of the Oneidas.

29 Septem.

The Jesuits soon found that the strong liquors which were sold to the savages by their European neighbors greatly hindered conversions. Pierron therefore asked an interview with the English authorities. Nicolls, who was

13 Septem.

Hist., ii., 50, 88; Col. Doc., iv., 16, 82. A note in Col. Doc., ix., 762, erroneously states that Tionnontoguen (which was on the *north* side of the Mohawk, and several leagues *west* of Caghnawaga) was the site of Fort Hunter, which was built in 1712, on the *south* side of the river, *east* of Caghnawaga, at the mouth of the Scoharie Creek. The note appears to confound "Tionnontoguen" with "Tiononderoge," the castle of the "Praying Maquas," which was built in 1690, and was the site of Fort Hunter: compare Col. Doc., iii., 163, 250, 483, 559, 565, 771, 772; iv., 16, 64, 81, 82, 391; v., 279, 280, 349, 372, 960; vi., 15, 16; vii., 577; ix., 550, 558; x., 677; Doc. Hist., i., 340; ii., 50, 88; iii., 543, 631; Munsell's Annals, ii., 67, 93, 99, 108; *post*, 583.

* Relation, 1667, 28; 1668, 4–13; 1670, 23; N. Y. H. S. Coll., iii. (ii.), 159; Col. Doc., ii., 712; iii., 163, 250; Shea, 254–258.

† Relation, 1668, 13–16; Shea, 259, 275.

then at Albany, invited the father to meet him at Schenectady, and a pleasant conference followed. The French missionary did not fail to acknowledge that the kindness he had received among the Dutch at Schenectady had kindled a friendship which "diversity of religion should not quench." Leaving Frémin alone at Tionnontoguen, Pierron then returned to Quebec, which he did not reach until early the next year.*

CHAP. III. — 1667. — $\frac{10}{20}$ Octob'r. — Pierron meets Nicolls at Schenectady. — 6 Novem.

Meanwhile there had been little direct intercourse between England and her North American colonies. The only vessel that had reached New York for many months (7 May.) was Sir William Davison's ship, the "Orange Tree," which came from Hamburg under the king's special license. Necessaries of all kinds grew very scarce; and, although rumors came by way of Bilboa and Fayal that peace had been concluded between England and France, it was feared that "some extraordinary disaster" had befallen the king. In writing to Lord Arlington, Nicolls reported the military precautions he had taken during the summer, and with just pride in New York, observed that "when His Majesty is truly informed how advantageously we are posted by situation to bridle his enemies and secure all his good subjects, I humbly presume to think that His Majesty would afford much of countenance and regard unto us, notwithstanding that His Majesty hath granted the whole tract to His Royal Highness."†

Want of supplies in New York. — 12 Novem. — Nicolls's report to Arlington.

There was, indeed, reason to apprehend that some great disaster had happened to the King of England. He had expressed his desire to make peace with the Dutch, and the States General had renewed their offers of reciprocal restitution or retention of all that either had taken before or during the war. At the suggestion of Charles, plenipotentiaries were appointed on each side to negotiate at Breda.‡

1666. — $\frac{6}{16}$ Septem. — 1667. — $\frac{18}{28}$ March. — Plenipotentiaries at Breda.

In the mean time Stuyvesant had reached the Hague, and presented to the States General his report of the surrender of New Netherland. This having been referred to

1665. — 19 October.

* Relation, 1668, 12, 13, 62; Col. Doc., iii., 162, 163; Renss. MSS. in O'Call., i., 337, 338; Shea, 258, 259.

† Col. Doc., iii., 162, 167; Ord., Warr., Lett., ii., 165, 166.

‡ Aitzema, v., 724, 732, 750–766; vi., 4, 9, 12, 236–239; D'Estrades, iv., 391, 469, 515, 609; v., 8, 26, 63, 109; Basnage, i., 790, 801; Lister's Clarendon, ii., 368–374; iii., 443, 453; Rapin, ii., 644; Courtenay's Temple, i., 99, 112; Martin, i., 276; Pepys, iii., 66, 67, 72, 82, 94; *ante*, 78, 93, 96, 124.

CHAP. III. the West India Company, they insisted that their late director had not done his duty, and prayed the States to disapprove of "the scandalous surrender of the aforesaid country, and consider such example detrimental to the state." Stuyvesant urged that his case should be promptly decided, so that he might return to New Netherland, and bring back to Holland "his sorrowful wife and family, with his property." The States General, however, required him to answer the objections of the West India Company. After six months' delay, in order to procure additional testimony from New York, Stuyvesant submitted an able vindication of his conduct, supported by proofs. Among others was a letter from his former subordinate, Van Ruyven, "still the Company's resident and agent" in New York, and, at the same time, high in the confidence of Nicolls. "I can not myself imagine," wrote the late secretary of New Netherland to his old chief, "on what pretext the loss of the country can be laid to your charge. Was not every possible effort used for its preservation? And was not its dangerous and ruinous condition notified, and assistance for redress solicited? and was it not protested that otherwise every thing would be lost? Certainly yes; not once, nor one year, but for several years, and by almost every ship. What more can be demanded from a Governor?"*

1666. 11 Jan'y. Stuyvesant and the W. I. Co. 2 April. 17 April. 29 October. Stuyvesant's reply. 17 August.

1667. 12 March. The W. I. Company's rejoinder.

In a long and petulant rejoinder, the West India Company labored to shift the responsibility for the loss of New Netherland from themselves to Stuyvesant. But it was now useless to prolong discussion. The States General had offered to Charles the alternative of reciprocal restitution or retention of conquests as the basis of a treaty. They had triumphantly established the Dutch title to New Netherland against the asserted claims of England, but they could not make its restitution the only condition of peace.

25 March. The importance of New Netherland.

Finding how the case stood, the West India Directors represented to their High Mightinesses that they had reared New Netherland "like a foster child," at an "excessive expense," for forty-six years, and urged that its restitution by England should be insisted upon. To this was appended a memorial from many prominent merchants of Holland, setting forth the importance of regaining New Neth-

* Col. Doc., ii., 361-379, 419-425, 427-488; *ante*, p. 60, *note*.

erland, possessed by the Dutch for nearly half a century "by a just and indisputable title," and "inhabited by more than eight thousand souls, consisting of about fifteen hundred families, all natives and subjects of this state, who went thither formerly to gain a livelihood and to settle, on a promise of being sustained and protected." Its restoration by treaty was urged, "the rather that in case the aforesaid country be left to and remain in the power and hands of the English nation, it could gain and obtain therefrom, in time of war, considerable advantages over this state and its inhabitants, as well because it will be able to draw and receive thence, and therefore from its own lands and colonies, almost all the wares which, being necessary for its equipments, it has hitherto been obliged to obtain from the Baltic, as that, whenever it shall possess and be master of nearly the entire northern part of America (for the French will be illy able to hold Canada against that nation), it can, without people here in Europe having the least knowledge of the circumstance, fit out a considerable fleet of large and small ships there, * * * whereby said English nation then would found, and extend considerably, its pretended dominion over the sea."*

But these statesmanlike arguments were now too late. Charles accepted the alternative which he pretended the States General had proposed, "namely, that each party should remain in the possession of all things which had been acquired on one side or the other during this war." On the other hand, the States instructed their ambassadors at Breda to adhere to their offer actually made on the sixteenth of the previous September, namely, "that it be left to His Majesty's choice to make peace by a reciprocal restitution, on both sides, of what is seized by force of arms or detained from the other, either before or after the commencement of the war; or else that the one party retain what it hath taken by force of arms, or otherwise seized from the other, as well before as after the commencement of the war." The plenipotentiaries were also directed to procure, if possible, from the King of France, the cession to the republic of some of the colonies which he had taken from the English, as some equivalent for the relinquish-

12/22 April.

5 May. Negotiations at Breda.

* Col. Doc., ii., 491-515; Res. Holl., 1667, 120, 133.

CHAP. III. ment of New Netherland by the Dutch, which sacrifice
Louis had first suggested.*

1667. By this time the real importance of New York had become better appreciated by the European powers which
1666. were chiefly interested in its fate. From Quebec, Talon
13 Novem. had suggested to Colbert that Louis should, after an ar-
Talon wishes France to gain New Netherland. rangement with the Dutch government, procure the cession
from England of New Netherland to himself, by which
means he "would have two entrances into Canada, and
would thereby give the French all the peltries of the North
—of which the English have now partly the advantage, by
means of the communication with the Iroquois which they
possess by Manatte and Orange—and would place those
barbarous tribes at His Majesty's discretion; who could,
moreover, approach New Sweden when he pleased, and
1667. hold New England confined within its limits." This idea
27 October. Talon reiterated the next year; but Colbert was obliged to
6 April. content himself with directing the subjugation of the Iroquois by the French. Louis, now engaged in active hostilities in the Spanish Netherlands, could do nothing to obtain the cession of New York either from Holland or England, and limited his efforts to regaining Acadia, which Cromwell had wrested from France.†

20 May. A difficult point soon occurred at Breda. The Dutch offer was craftily misstated by Charles, and the negotiations were delayed. Observing this, De Witt, who could not forget his vow to avenge the outrage which the English had perpetrated the year before at Schelling, thought that the time had come for a memorable retaliation. The large sums voted by Parliament for the fleet had been squandered by the king on his unworthy favorites, and most of the English ships were laid up in ordinary. The Grand Pen-
The Dutch in the Thames. sionary accordingly dispatched De Ruyter and Cornelis de
Witt to the Thames. Sheerness and the dock-yard at Chatham were surprised; several of the finest vessels in the En-
12/22 June. glish navy were burned; and the "Royal Charles," which
had brought back the restored king in triumph from Scheveningen, was carried off as the chief prize of the Dutch

* D'Estrades, v., 175, 201; Aitzema, vi., 27–31; Sec. Res. Holl., ii., 528–552; Col. Doc., ii., 516, 517; Rapin, ii., 645; Martin, i., 275; Courtenay's Temple, i., 100; *ante*, p. 131.

† Col. Doc., ix., 56, 57, 58, 60; D'Estrades, v., 181, 208, 250, 333, 344.

1667.

avengers.* London was deprived of its supplies, and threatened for several weeks by the blockading Hollanders, who, had they been better informed of the condition of the capital, and acted with prompt vigor, might from the White Tower have dictated their own terms of peace to the fugitive sovereign at Windsor. While his ships were burning at Chatham, Charles was gayly supping with his parasites at Whitehall, and all were "mad in hunting of a poor moth." But the nation felt, with Evelyn, that Englishmen had suffered "a dishonor never to be wiped off." Well might Nicolls, at New York, after waiting the whole summer for a ship from England, apprehend that "some extraordinary disaster" had befallen his majesty.†

Fright in London.

12 Novem.

De Witt's galling success in the Thames had a marvelous effect at Breda. The English ambassadors agreed to the principle that each party should retain the places it had occupied, and Charles was obliged to recede from his position and accept the terms insisted upon by the Dutch. A treaty between England and Holland was soon concluded. By the third article it was stipulated that "each of the said parties shall hold and possess in future, in perfect right of sovereignty, propriety, and possession, all such countries, islands, towns, forts, places, and colonies, and so many as each, whether during this war or before, in whatever time it may have been, shall have taken and retained from the other, by force and by arms, or in whatever manner it may have been, and that in the same manner as they shall have occupied and possessed them on the $\frac{10}{20}$th of May last, none of the said places excepted." The same day another treaty was signed between France and England, by which Acadia was restored to Louis, in exchange for Antigua, Montserrat, and a part of Saint Christopher's.‡

Effect at Breda. 30 June.

$\frac{21}{31}$ July. Treaty made.

Acadia restored to France.

By the treaty of Breda the Dutch West India Company lost New Netherland, while the East India Company gained

New Netherland given up by the treaty of Breda.

* A part of the stern of the Royal Charles is still preserved as a trophy in the dock-yard at Rotterdam.

† Aitzema, vi., 35–46, 109–120; D'Estrades, v., 246–361, 382, 390; Kennett, iii., 265; Lister's Clarendon, ii., 376–381; iii., 454–463; Basnage, i., 803, 804; Evelyn, ii., 27, 28; iii., 214; Pepys, iii., 142–155, 164; Rapin, ii., 645; Burnet, i., 250; Clarke's James II., i., 425, 426; Martin, i., 286; Col. Doc., iii., 167; *ante*, p. 125, 131.

‡ Dumont, vii., 45; Aitzema, vi., 55; D'Estrades, v., 333, 384, 385, 462, 464, 476; Basnage, i., 806, 807; Temple, i., 481; Courtenay's Temple, i., 112; Lister's Clarendon, ii., 381; De Witt, ii., 537; Charlevoix, ii., 204; Hume, vi., 400-402; Lingard, xii., 211–215; Hazard's Reg. Penn., iv., 120; Rapin, ii., 645, 646; Anderson, ii., 4[illegible]2, 493; Martin, i., 287.

CHAP. III. 1667. Poleron. Surinam, having been conquered before the 10th of May, was also confirmed to the United Provinces. Its acquisition somewhat reconciled the Dutch people to the loss of New Netherland; and all, except the West India shareholders and the regents of the city of Amsterdam, 24 August. seemed to be content when the peace was proclaimed at the Hague.

Feeling in London. But in London the feeling was very different. The church-bells rang out merry peals. Yet no bonfires showed the national joy—"partly," wrote Pepys, "from the dearness of firing, but principally from the little content most people have in the peace." They lamented "the giving away Poleron and Surinam, and Nova Scotia, which hath a river 300 miles up the country, with copper-mines, more than Swedeland, and Newcastle coals, the only place in America that hath coals that we know of; and that Cromwell did value those places, and would forever have made much of them." In this feeling Massachusetts shared when it became known that England had parted with "a place so profitable to them, from whence they drew great quantities of beaver and other peltry, besides the fishing for cod." Public sentiment, both in and out of Parliament, strongly condemned the king. A scape-goat Fall of Clarendon. became necessary at Whitehall; and Clarendon, who had served his sovereign with austere fidelity, was meanly de- 30 August. prived of the great seal, which, at the very moment it was demanded from him, he was affixing to the proclamation of the Peace of Breda. This was followed by a quarrel between the Duke of York and his secretary, Sir William 2 Septem. M. Wren the duke's secretary. Coventry, who gave up his place, and was succeeded in it by Matthew Wren, a son of the Bishop of Ely, and secretary to the fallen chancellor, upon whose recommendation James made him his own most confidential officer.*

The Peace of Breda finished the controversy between the West India Company and Stuyvesant. As the fatherland had relinquished its ancient province to England, the veteran felt no scruple about ending his days under a govern-

* Lambrechtsen, 80; Aitzema, vi., 54; Basnage, i., 809, 810; Lingard, xii., 215–226; Hume, vi., 402–406; Lister, ii., 383–414; Chalmers, Ann., i., 393, 578; Rev. Col., i., 118; Pepys, ii., 361; iii., 227, 233–236, 240, 242, 244, 247; Evelyn, i., 335, 409; Campbell's Chancellors, iii., 232; Clarke's James II., i., 426–433; Col. Doc., iii., 241; Hutch. Coll., 489; Life of Clarendon, Cont. (Oxf.), iii., 292, 293, 294.

CHAP. III. 1667.

ment to which he had already sworn a temporary allegiance. But, before returning to America, he tried to obtain a relaxation of the English navigation laws in favor of New York by allowing it a direct commerce with Holland; urging to the Duke of York that the capitulation should be ratified, and that its sixth article especially—which allowed a free trade with the Netherlands in Dutch vessels—should be "observed, or in some measure indulged." This was very necessary, because the Indians, in trading their beavers, especially prized Holland duffels and Utrecht ironware, and, for want of them, would traffic with the French of Canada, "who are now incroached to be too neare neighbours unto us;" and because, as no ships were to go to New York from England this season, there would be destitution unless it should be relieved from Holland. Stuyvesant therefore asked permission to dispatch two Dutch vessels from Holland to New York, that so "the inhabitants, being plentifully supplied, may cheerfully follow their vocations, and bless God for the opportunity of enjoyment of all peace and plenty under the auspicious wings of your Royal Highness's paternal care and protection."*

Stuyvesant asks for free trade.

As the Duke of York could not grant such a request, Stuyvesant petitioned the king in council. On the report of a special committee, without reference to the Council of Trade, Charles ordered that "a temporary permission for seven years, with three ships only," be granted to the Dutch "freely to trade" with New York; and the duke was authorized to grant his license to Stuyvesant pursuant to Nicolls's passport. The capitulation of New Netherland was not formally ratified, but it was recognized as obligatory. Having gained for his countrymen this concession in their favor, Stuyvesant returned to spend the remnant of his days calmly in New York.†

17 Oct.

23 Oct. Permission given.

Stuyvesant's return to New York.

The Peace of Breda brought welcome relief to Nicolls. The duke yielded to his many requests to be recalled from an administration which he had conducted so well. It was difficult to find a proper successor in a court thronged with needy place-hunters, few of whom were qualified to govern an American province. James selected Colonel Francis

Nicolls relieved.

* Col. Doc., ii., 251; iii., 163, 164; *ante*, vol. i., p. 762.

† Col. Doc., iii., 164–167, 175–179, 237; v., 496; vii., 586; Val. Man., 1847, 370.

CHAP. III.

1667. Lovelace.

Lovelace, a brother of John, Lord Lovelace of Hurley, and a favorite of the king, of whose "honorable privy chamber" he was one of the gentlemen. It seems to have been Lovelace's chief "affliction" that at his departure from England he was unable to see Secretary Arlington.*

1668. 1 January. Peace proclaimed in New York.

At length official intelligence of the Peace of Breda reached Nicolls, whose pleasant duty it was, at the opening of the new year, to announce the good news in his government. This was done by warrants addressed to each justice, requiring a general publication of the proclamations announcing the auspicious event.†

Commercial enterprise.

A new order of things at once opened. The success of Stuyvesant at London aroused the repressed commercial enterprise of the Dutch merchants; of whom Van Cortlandt, Cousseau, Ebbing, and others set sail for Holland during the summer, to settle old accounts and prepare for increasing trade.‡

Grants of land. 3 Febr'y.

The peace also enabled Nicolls to reward some of his English subordinates. Among the effects of Dutch subjects which had been confiscated by the decree of 10th of October, 1665, were Hog Island, and the two "Barent's" Islands in the East River. Hog Island was now granted to Captain John Manning, whom the governor had just before appointed sheriff of New York. The Barent's Islands were at the same time patented to Collector Thomas Delavall.§

Martha's Vineyard and Nantucket.

A question respecting the jurisdiction of New York was now settled by Nicolls. The islands of Martha's Vineyard and Nantucket, although contiguous to the coast of New Plymouth, were included by name in the Duke of York's patent. In 1641 they had been conveyed by Stirling and Gorges to Thomas Mayhew and his son, who, after 1654, finding that they were out of the jurisdiction of Massa-

* Chalmers, i., 578, follows the error of Smith, i., 42, in stating that Lovelace assumed the administration of New York in May, 1667. He appears to have arrived at New York in the spring of 1668, and did not relieve Nicolls until August of that year. See N. Y. Surrogate's Records, Wills, i., 35; Val. Man., 1847, 362; Col. Doc., ii., 580; iii., 174.

† Ord., Warr., etc., ii., 193; Col. Doc., ii., 522.

‡ Col. Doc., iii., 178.

§ Patents, i., 129, 131; Ord., Warr., Lett., ii., 177; Col. Doc., ii., 654; Val. Man., 1847, 351; 1853, 380; 1855, 493-497; Smith, i., 299; Hoffman's Treatise, i., 147, 148; Benson's Mem., 96; C. Wolley, 90; *ante*, p. 91. Hog Island was known as Manning's Island, and afterward as Blackwell's Island. The "Barent's Islands" became Englished into Great and Little "Barn" Islands, one of which is now known as Ward's Island, and the other as Randall's Island. All the three now belong to the city of New York. See the "Nicolls Map," Val. Man., 1863.

chusetts and New Plymouth, exercised a kind of independent government in their remote habitations. An English vessel having been driven ashore on one of the neighboring Elizabeth Islands, and seized by the Indians, the matter was reported to Nicolls, who sent a special commission to Mayhew, and instructed him to summon the offending sachems before him at "Martin's Vineyard," and also to request Governor Prince, of New Plymouth, to reprove the disorderly savages within his jurisdiction. "I have not been forward," he added, "in trivial cases, to contest for my master's bounds; knowing, however, that all the islands, except Block Island, from Cape Cod to Cape May, are included in my master's patent. The first scruples will be soon removed; however, in cases of this consequence, I must declare myself both in point of power and readiness to protect and defend my master's honor and interest.* (3 January.)

Another case of "scruple" was decided without difficulty. A few miles from Stonington, in Connecticut, is an island, about nine miles long and one broad, which the Dutch discovered in 1614, and named the "Visscher's" or Fisher's Island. As it was near the mouth of the Mystic, John Winthrop obtained a grant of it in 1640 from Massachusetts, and in the following year the assent of the Hartford Court; and in 1644 he bought it from the savages. But, as it was included in the Duke of York's patent, Winthrop procured from Nicolls a confirmation to himself of Fisher's Island "as an entire enfranchised township, manor, and place of itself; and to have, hold, and enjoy equal privileges and immunities with any other town, enfranchised place, or manor, within the government of New York; and to be in nowise subordinate or belonging unto, or dependent upon any riding, township, place, or jurisdiction whatsoever." In vain Connecticut afterward attempted to assert her authority over Fisher's Island. It still forms part of Suffolk County, in the State of New York, and was, until recently, owned by Winthrop's descendants.† (Fisher's Island granted to Winthrop. 28 March.)

For some time after his arrival at New York, Lovelace

* Col. Doc., iii., 168–170; Hough's "Nantucket Papers," x.–xv., 1–22, 70; Mass. Rec., iv. (i), 199; Palfrey, ii., 196, 330; Hutch. Mass., i., 161; Mather's Mag., ii., 424, 427.

† Patents, iii., 5; Col. Rec. Conn., i, 64, 65; iii., 64, 283; Mass. Rec., i., 304; Mass. H. S. Coll., xxx., 54, 78; xxxvi., 368; xxxvii., 83; Palfrey, ii., 234, 624; Thompson, i., 388–390, N. Y. Rev. Stat., iii., 2; *ante*, vol. i., 57.

CHAP. III. 1668. 13 April. Admiralty Court in New York.

occupied himself in becoming familiar with the government he was soon to administer. One of his duties was to preside in the Admiralty Court; and a case having been removed from the Mayor's Court to that tribunal, Lovelace took his seat with Nicolls on the bench. A controversy had arisen between the owner of the ship Cedar and the privateers who went in her to Acadia the year before, and who had taken a Spanish prize which they brought into New York. After several hearings the court pronounced a sentence, a remarkable feature of which was, that an Indian man, who had been taken "as part of their prize," should be sold, to defray the charges on both sides.*

18 April.

Delaware affairs.

Affairs on the Delaware had meanwhile gone smoothly along. A new church had been built by the Swedes in 1667 at Crane Hook, near Fort Christina or Altona, now known as Wilmington, in which Lokenius, the Lutheran clergyman, who appears to have led rather a godless life, continued to minister. By an order of Nicolls, the local government of the Delaware territory was now regulated more clearly. Captain John Carr was to remain as commander-in-chief at Newcastle, assisted by Alricks and others as counselors, and the Duke's laws were to be published and observed. In all cases of difficulty the directions of the governor and council at New York were to be sought and followed. Not long afterward, the Mantes, or Red Hook Indians, having committed several murders, Nicolls and Lovelace, in a joint letter, directed Carr and his counselors to make all necessary rules for the government of both Christians and Indians, and report them to New York for confirmation.†

21 April.

8 June.

Military arrangements in the province.

The military establishment of the whole province was now settled. The garrison at Newcastle was to have a lieutenant, a corporal, and eighteen men; that at Esopus, a sergeant and twenty-one men; and that at Albany, a lieutenant, a sergeant, a gunner, a drummer, and twenty men. At Fort James, in New York, there were to be a lieutenant,

* N. Y. Surr. Rec. Wills, i., 35–51; Val. Man., 1847, 362–369; Col. MSS., xxii., 46–49; Ord., Warr., Lett., ii., 191; *ante*, p. 127. Captain Richard Morris, formerly of Barbadoes, first appears as a New Yorker in connection with this matter of the ship Cedar: compare Dunlap, i., 272; Bolton's Westchester, ii., 284, 286; Col. Doc., ii., 595, 619.

† Ord., Warr., Lett., ii., 207, 208; S. Smith, 51, 52; S. Hazard, Ann. Penn., 140, 332, 348, 371, 372; Reg. Penn., i., 37, 38; iv., 74; Proud, i., 124; Upland Records, 24, 25; *ante*, vol. i., 225, 248, 511, 616, 631, 734.

an ensign, a gunner, a marshal, a surgeon, four sergeants, four corporals, and eighty men. As a special encouragement to the settlement of the newly-purchased country back of Esopus, Nicolls granted thirty lots of thirty acres each to the soldiers in the garrison there.* 6 April.

After the recall of the royal commissioners, Massachusetts extended her authority over Maine, which drew from Nicolls a strong remonstrance. But this was unheeded. In a farewell letter the Governor of New York sharply admonished the Boston Court, avowing himself "concerned during life in the affairs of New England;" adding, "You know that my station hath been a frontier place towards the Indians, who had too much influence upon the spirits of the Dutch in former times, but are now in a competent measure reduced to a better compliance in their behaviours towards us, and have given me some testimonies of their desires to live in peace with our nation; for they have made me a present of two youths which have been their prisoners a few years: they were taken in Maryland. Also they have promised to bring me another young man remaining with them. So that though they have a warr with the English in Maryland, because the English there do take part with their Indians, yett you may guesse these heathens are yet desirous of peace with the English, of which I have long since advertised the Governour of Maryland."† 12 June. 30 July. Nicolls's letter to Massachusetts.

In company with his successor, Nicolls made a last visit to Albany, against the monopoly of the Indian trade at which place the magistrates of New York had protested. While there, the two governors jointly issued new instructions to Captain Baker for the regulation of the garrison and in regard to transactions with the Indians, and other matters growing out of the treaty of Breda. There was now to be a general amnesty and oblivion of all "seeds of distrust and jealousy;" and, in future, no complaints were to be brought before the governor at New York "but such as are of high nature, and the proofs grounded upon sufficient testimonies."‡ 7 July. August. Albany affairs.

* Col. MSS., xxii., 50; Ord., Warr., etc., ii., 206; Coll. Ulster H. Soc., i., 50, 72; *ante*, 89.

† Col. Doc., iii., 170–173; Hutch., i., 260–267; Coll., 427, 428; Mass. Rec., iv. (ii.), 370–373, 400, 404; Chalmers, i., 484; Palfrey, ii., 632–634; Williamson, i., 431–438.

‡ Ord., Warr., etc., ii., 229–233; Col. MSS., xxii., 10; Munsell, vii., 100, 101; New York City Rec., vi., 387; *ante*, p. 88.

CHAP. III.

1668.

8 August.

On his return to New York, Nicolls prepared to take leave of his government. His predecessor Stuyvesant, having irregularly sealed some patents after the surrender of New Netherland, received a formal pardon for himself and his secretary Van Ruyven. A new patent was also given to De Sille, Cortelyou, and others, confirming the town privileges of New Utrecht. At the same time, Samuel Edsall received a patent for Bronck's land, opposite Haerlem. As a crowning act of grace and justice, Nicolls released Ralph Hall and his wife from the recognizances which they had been required to give when charged with witchcraft in 1665, "there having been no direct proofs nor further prosecution of them, or either of them, since."*

15 August.

21 August. Case of Hall.

17 August. Nicolls leaves New York.

The authorities of the city of New York now signed a loyal address, which they asked Nicolls to deliver to the duke, near whose person he was to resume his service. All the freemen of the metropolis were divided into two companies, and ordered to appear in arms at the governor's departure. A few days afterward, Nicolls, having transferred his functions to Lovelace, embarked for England, with every demonstration of respect and regret from those who, receiving him as a conqueror, bade him farewell as a friend. Invested with extraordinary powers, he had used them with the moderation and integrity of a true gentleman; and the people, whose prejudices he had avoided wounding, "loved the man whose orders they disliked." His former colleague, Maverick, thus wrote to Lord Arlington: "After his abode here four years (where he hath lived with great reputation and honour), he is now returning home. I must needs accompany him with this character—that he hath done His Majesty and His Royal Highness very considerable service in these parts, having, by his prudent management of affairs, kept persons of different judgments and of diverse nations in peace and quietness, during a time when a great part of the world was in warrs. And as to the several nations of the Indians, they were never brought into such a peaceable posture and faire correspondence as by his means they now are."†

28 August.

25 August. Maverick's letter about Nicolls.

* Ord., Warr., etc., ii., 216, 217, 220; Patents, iv., 54; Thompson, ii., 191; Bolton, ii., 283, 284; Doc. Hist., iv., 86; *ante*, p. 91; vol. i., p. 268.

† N. Y. City Rec., vi., 397, 489; Col. Doc., iii., 174, 175; Chalmers, i., 578; Smith, i., 42; Hutch. Coll., 428.

CHAPTER IV.

1668–1673.

CHAP. IV.

1668.

ABOUT thirty miles west of London, on the Berkshire side of the Thames, in the parish of Hurley, there stood, until a few years ago, a large country house, built in the Elizabethan style, and called "Lady Place." Covering the site of an ancient Benedictine monastery, from which it was named, it had been erected by Sir Richard Lovelace, a lucky comrade of Drake. With the rich Spanish spoil he had won, the retired adventurer had laid out terraced gardens around his Tudor mansion, the wide hall of which opened on the placid river, and had adorned its stately gallery with beautiful Italian landscapes. The heir of the old knight greatly improved this place, and was created, by Charles the First, Baron Lovelace, of Hurley. His sons, John, the second Lord Lovelace, and Francis, a colonel in the army, adhered to the royal cause. Francis Lovelace appears to have visited "Long Island" in 1650, under a pass from Cromwell's Council of State, and to have gone thence to Virginia. At its surrender to the Commonwealth forces in 1652, he was chosen by Sir William Berkeley to convey the tidings "to the late King of Scots." The zeal of Lovelace in the interest of Charles the Second led to his being committed a prisoner to the Tower by Richard Cromwell, on a charge of high treason. This only increased his favor with the king at the Restoration. He was enrolled as one of the knights of the "Royal Oak," an order which Charles proposed to institute as a reward to his faithful followers in adversity, but was more substantially recompensed by being made "one of the gentlemen of His Majesty's Honorable Privy Chamber." In due time, the king's favor induced his appointment by the Duke of York as the successor of Nicolls in his government.*

Lady Place at Hurley.

Colonel Francis Lovelace.

Appointed governor of New York.

* Lyson's Magna Brit., i., 299; Burke's Dormant Peerage, iii., 498, 499; Sainsbury's Cal-

CHAP. IV. — 1668. Character of Lovelace.

Lovelace was in many respects unlike his predecessor. He was phlegmatic rather than enterprising, and lacked the energy and decision so necessary in a provincial governor far removed from the observation of his superiors. Yet he was of "a generous mind, and noble;" upright and good-natured, and by the very moderation of his character unwilling to disturb the policy by which Nicolls had administered the government of New York with such success. For several months he had enjoyed the opportunity of studying his predecessor's conduct. With a commission similar to that of Nicolls, Lovelace also brought with him to New York a formal confirmation by the duke of the code of laws established at Hempstead. Lovelace's instructions, among other things, required him "to make no alterations in the Laws of the government settled before his arrival."*

28 August. Lovelace installed.

Having received from Nicolls the cipher in which he was to correspond with the secretary of state in case of necessity, Lovelace announced to Lord Arlington his installation in the government of New York, "being the middle position of the two distinct factions, the Papist and Puritan," and asked "some instructions" how he might steer his course, so as most to advance the interest of the king and the duke.†

2 Septem. Lovelace's council.

Lovelace's council, at various periods, consisted of Cornelis Steenwyck, the mayor of New York; Thomas Willett and Thomas Delavall, former mayors; Ralph Whitfield, Isaac Bedlow, Francis Boone, and Cornelis van Ruyven, aldermen; Captain John Manning, the sheriff of the city; Dudley and Thomas Lovelace, the governor's brothers; and Matthias Nicolls, the provincial secretary. Van Ruyven

24 Novem.

was also appointed to succeed Delavall, who went on a

endar, i., 339, 361, 376, 379; Chalmers, i., 124; Beverly (ed. 1855), 50, 51; Burk, ii., 81–91; Thurloe, vi., 151; vii., 558, 598, 622; Col. Doc., ii., 580; Macaulay, ii., 494; Knight's England, iv., 430; Lond. Quart. Rev., July, 1859. The nephew of Governor Francis Lovelace was John, the third lord, who was prominent in the Revolution of 1688. Upon his death without issue, the barony descended to his second cousin, John, the grandson of Francis, who became the fourth Lord Lovelace, and was appointed by Queen Anne governor of New York, where he died in May, 1709.

* Court of Assizes, ii., 231; MSS., Secretary's Office, Albany; Journals Leg. Council, i., Int., v., vii.; Col. Doc., iii., 104, 218, 226, 260; Mass. H. S. Coll., xxx., 78; Smith, i., 42, 46; S. Smith, 73; N. Y. H. S. Coll. (1869), 32; *ante*, 18, 73.

† Col. Doc., iii., 174, 175. The erroneous statements of Smith, i., 42, and Chalmers, i., 578, which have been so generally copied, that Lovelace began his administration in 1667, have been already noticed, *ante*, p. 138, *note*.

visit to England, as collector of the duke's revenue at New York; and Bedlow was made comptroller or naval officer, and Nicholas Bayard surveyor. The customs' rates were regulated by a new order from the governor.* CHAP. IV. 1668. 18 Novem.

Affairs at Esopus required Lovelace's earliest attention. Conflicting claims were made for the lands in the "New Dorp;" and the governor, finding it necessary to go thither in person, left Captain Manning in charge of Fort James, with full instructions. At Esopus, Sergeant Beresford was directed to disband the garrison, and cause their duty to be performed by the burghers; but, to induce the soldiers to remain, liberal grants of land were assured to them, and arrangements made to found two new villages farther inland along the fertile borders of the Esopus Creek. Soon afterward, Henry Pawling was appointed to lay out lots at the new "furthest dorp."† 5 Septem. Esopus affairs. 10 Septem. 25 Septem. 9 Novem.

A severe epidemic—fever and ague, and fluxes—visited New York this autumn, which caused the governor to proclaim a day of humiliation and prayer. In his proclamation, Lovelace reproved the swearing, intemperance, and impiety which he observed to prevail throughout the province.‡ 21 Novem. Epidemic in New York.

The want of a printing-press in New York was now much felt, and, as the only one in the English colonies was at Cambridge, Lovelace sent to obtain a printer from there. But he did not succeed; and it was a quarter of a century before the "master art" began to be practiced in New York. This was not, however, owing to the duke, who never instructed any of his governors to restrain printing. The immediate cause of Lovelace's enlightened effort was his desire to have published a catechism which the Reverend Thomas James, the first minister at Easthampton, encouraged by the friendship of Nicolls, had prepared for the use of the Indians, and translated into their tongue, with some chapters of the Bible. For this and other labors James was warmly thanked by the governor.§ A printing-press wanted. 19 Novem.

* Council Min., iii., 1; Court of Assizes, ii., 200, 293, 619, 635; Ord., Warr., etc., ii., 297, 298, 322; Col. MSS., xxii., 51–53, 108, 109; Val. Man., 1853, 328, 379–383; Munsell, iv., 22.

† Ord., Warr., etc., ii., 206, 241–258, 279; Esopus Records; Ulster H. S. Coll., i., 50, 72.

‡ Ord., Warr., etc., ii., 294, 295; Col. Doc., iii., 185; Val. Man., 1856, 514.

§ Ord., Warr., etc., ii., 290–293; Mass. H. S. Coll., xxxvii., 485; Wood, 41; Thompson, i., 317; Dunlap, i., 126; Thomas's Hist. Print., i., 275; ii., 90, 286. The Duke of York has been unjustly charged with discouraging printing in his province. The fact is, that neither

CHAP. IV.

1668.

Jesuit mission among the Mohawks.

7 October.

The Jesuit "Mission of the Martyrs," now named Saint Mary of the Mohawks, had meanwhile prospered greatly. After visiting Quebec, Frémin's colleague, Pierron, returned to Tionnontoguen, and resumed the care of the mission. He soon acquired the Mohawk language well enough to be understood, and, by means of little pictures which he painted himself, explained more readily the Christian doctrines. Every week he visited seven Mohawk villages, which extended over a distance of seven leagues and a half. But the war now raging between the Iroquois and "the nine nations of Mahicans who were scattered between Manhattan and the environs of Quebec," hindered the progress of religion. Hostilities were carried to the neighborhood of Albany, and prisoners taken on either side were burned or eaten. Being more numerous, the Mahicans had the advantage. One of Pierron's chief encouragements was that the savages themselves observed that they had among them a "foreign Demon" who was more to be feared than those which they adored in their dreams. This demon was intoxicating drink, which came to them from Albany,* hindered religion, and ruined their youth. At Pierron's suggestion, several sachems came to New York with a petition to the governor, accompanied by a letter from the father, asking him to arrest the evil. Lovelace at once directed

12 Novem. the officers at Albany to execute the laws against selling

18 Novem. liquors to the Indians. He also wrote to Pierron: "I have taken all the care possible, and will continue it under the most severe penalties, to restrain and hinder the furnishing of any excess to the Indians. And I am very glad to learn that such virtuous thoughts proceed from infidels, to the shame of many Christians. But this must be attributed to your pious instructions; you who, being well versed in a strict discipline, have shown them the way of mortification, as well by your precepts as your practice."†

Andros nor Dongan, the successors of Lovelace, were at all restricted on this subject: see Col. Doc., iii., 216–219, 331–334. It was not until 1686 that James the Second restrained the liberty of printing in New York; and the instruction then given to Dongan followed the precedents of the Plantation Committee respecting other royal governors: Col. Doc., iii., 375. The restrictive policy of Massachusetts has been adverted to, *ante*, p. 89, *note*.

* The French furnished the Indians with brandy distilled at Rochelle; the English and Dutch with rum imported into New York from the West Indies, which the savages preferred, as "more wholesome:" Col. Doc., iii., 463, 797; ix., 36, 979, 1073; Doc. Hist., i., 140.

† Ord., Warr., Lett., ii., 281; Col. Doc., ix., 883; Relation, 1669, 1–6; Charlevoix, ii., 183; Shea, 263, 264.

CHAP. IV.

1668.

At Saint Francis Xavier, among the Oneidas, Bruyas suffered many discouragements. He was obliged to live upon dried frogs and herbs, while few baptisms rewarded his zeal. Of all the Iroquois, the Oneidas were the most intractable. The hostile Mahicans, and the Andastes or Conestogues, however, filled the canton with continual alarms.*

Bruyas at the Oneidas.

June.

Early in the summer, Bruyas was joined by the youthful father Julian Garnier, the first Jesuit ordained at Quebec. After remaining a short time at Oneida, Garnier set out for Onondaga, a day's journey farther to the west, to the old mission of Saint Mary of Gennentaha, from which the French had been expelled ten years before. Received with every mark of good will, Garnier was constrained by "a gentle violence" to remain among the Onondagas. At his request, Garakontié caused a chapel to be built, and with four others then visited Quebec. His request for another "black robe" to be sent as a companion to Garnier was granted by Courcelles, who did not fail to impress upon the savages the power and glory of the "Great Onnontio Louis." Loaded with presents, Garakontié and his colleagues returned to Onondaga, escorting the Fathers Etienne de Carheil and Pierre Millet, and the Mission of Saint John the Baptist was happily established.†

Garnier and Millet at Onondaga.

20 August.

27 August.

October.

Carheil, however, did not remain long at Onondaga with Garnier and Millet. During the first mission of the French there, the Father René Ménard had founded a church at Cayuga, about thirty leagues farther west, and delegates now came from there to ask a renewal of missionary service. Conducted by Garnier, Carheil accordingly visited Cayuga. A chapel was soon completed and dedicated to Saint Joseph. Besides the village of Guyoguen, or Cayuga, which was the seat of the mission, there were two others a few leagues apart, Kiohero or Tiohero, and Onnontaré. These villages were near the Lake Tiohero—now known as Cayuga Lake—upon the banks of which David le Moyne had died in 1657. In this most beautiful region of Western New York Carheil began a laborious service among

6 Novem.

9 Novem.

Carheil at Cayuga.

* Relation, 1669, 7, 8; Charlevoix, ii., 185; Shea, 275.

† Relation, 1658, 3, 4; 1662, 8–13; 1668, 6–19; 1669, 10; Charlevoix, ii., 176, 177; Col. Doc., ix., 227, 665; Shea, 259, 260, 277, 287, 289, 294; *ante*, vol. i., 643, 646, 704.

Chap. IV. 1668. the docile but superstitious Cayugas, and Garnier returned to assist Millet at Onondaga.*

Twelve years before, Chaumonot had proclaimed the faith to the Senecas at their principal village of Gandagaré. The most numerous of all the confederates, the Senecas, whom the French called "the Upper Iroquois," were the most gentle and tractable. They were rather laborers and traders than warriors, and many Christian Hurons had been adopted by them after 1649. Frémin, who was now the superior of all the Iroquois missions, thought that the time had come to "begin a new church" among the Senecas. 10 October. Leaving Pierron in charge of the Mohawks at Tionnontoguen, the superior accordingly passed westward, visiting the other missionary stations. After twenty days' travel 1 Novem. Frémin among the Senecas. he reached the Senecas, who received him with the honors which the savages show to ambassadors. The chiefs quickly built him a chapel, and many converts, especially among the domiciled Hurons, rewarded his labors. The mission was named in honor of Saint Michael. Thus in 1668 the Jesuits had established five stations among the Iroquois. Frémin, the superior, however, found his labors among the Senecas hindered by a projected war against the Ottawas. But this he was able to prevent, aided by the opportune arrival, the next spring, of the Father Allouez from Canada, with some restored prisoners; and it was hoped that the Iroquois, who had now both "the Mahicans and the Andastes on their hands, would fear more than ever the arms of France."†

Iroquois colony at Quinté Bay. A colony of the Cayugas, which had been formed on the northern shore of Lake Ontario, at Kenté or Quinté Bay, was placed in 1666, for a short time, under the care of Frémin and some other fathers of his order; but, on the conclusion of the peace with the Iroquois the next year, the Jesuits, who were to occupy the more important field south of the lake, resigned the Quinté mission to the Sulpitians of Montreal. Two young "Levites" of that order, Francis Salignac de Fénelon and Claude Trouvé, had recently ar- 11 June. rived in Canada, the latter of whom was ordained a priest

* Relation, 1657, 19, 43; 1668, 20; 1669, 12–16; 1670, 63, 69; 1672, 22; Map in Rel., 1665; Col. Doc., iii., 251; Charlevoix, ii., 80, 81, 185; Shea, 232–234, 261, 287, 356; *ante*, vol. i., 644.

† Relation, 1649, 3–33; 1657, 43, 45; 1668, 32; 1669, 17; 1670, 69, 77; Charlevoix, ii., 8, 183; Shea, 191, 192, 198, 226, 232, 234, 263, 290; *ante*, vol. i., 644.

1668. 28 October.

by Bishop Laval; and in the autumn of this year they went to Quinté, where they began their missionary labors. In this station they were succeeded by Francis Lascaris D'Urfe, De Cice, and others; who for several years struggled with many difficulties, until the Sulpitians at length resigned their enterprise to the Recollets.*

New Jersey affairs.

New Jersey, under the government of Philip Carteret, had now for three years been quietly growing. But it was a constant eyesore to the authorities of New York; and, although Nicolls had ceased to allude to its dismemberment, Maverick could not refrain from writing by him to Lord Arlington that the duke's grant to Berkeley and Carteret had "proved very prejudicial to this place and government. Their bounds reach from the east side of Delaware River to the west side of Hudson's River, including a vast tract of the most improveablest land within his Royal Highness his patent. It hath taken away some Dutch villages formerly belonging to this place, and not above three or four miles from it. The Duke hath left of his patent nothing to the west of New York, and to the east upon the main about sixteen miles only from Hudson's River, whereon is but one poor village. Long Island is very poore and inconsiderable; and beside the city there are but two Dutch towns more, Sopus and Albany, which lie up north on Hudson's River. I suppose when the Lord Berkeley had that grant, it was not thought he should come so neare this place, nor were the inconveniences of it known or considered."†

25 August.

This letter of Maverick, in connection with Nicolls's personal representations on reaching London, caused the duke to try to regain New Jersey. One point was promptly settled. As Nicolls had confiscated to his royal highness, in 1665, the estate of the West India Company in Staten Island, and as one of the outlets of the Hudson River ran around the island, it was "adjudged to belong to New York." Philip Carteret, the Governor of New Jersey, had probably

Staten Island adjudged to New York.

* Relation, 1668, 4, 20, 31; Col. Doc., ix., 91, 97, 101, 102, 112, 132; Faillon, iii., 171–173, 189–198; La Potherie, iii., 216; Doc. Hist., i., 283; Charlevoix, ii., 177, 256; Shea, 254, 283, 309; N. Y. H. S. Proc., 1848, 199–209; 1849, 12; Sparks's Life of La Salle, 16, 17; Shea's note in N. E. Hist. and Gen. Reg., xvii., 246, 247. Fénelon, of Quinté, has been confounded by Hennepin and other later writers with his younger half-brother, the famous author of Telemachus, the Archbishop of Cambray. Another blunder places the scene of the Quinté Fénélon's labors among the parent tribe of the Cayugas, instead of among their colonists on the northern shore of Lake Ontario.

† Col. Doc., iii., 174; *ante*, p. 85.

CHAP. IV. — 1668.

anticipated this decision when he took title from Nicolls, in 1667, for land on that island. Lord Berkeley, one of the commissioners of the Duke of York's estate, having been detected in "the basest" corruption, was now "under a cloud, and out of all his offices." Berkeley therefore offered to surrender to James his patent for New Jersey. Carteret, lately made Treasurer of Ireland, agreed to do the like; and it was arranged that the two proprietors should, in exchange for New Jersey, "returned to his Royal Highness," receive the territory on the Delaware which Nicolls had so shrewdly and earnestly recommended. This determination was promptly notified by Carteret to his cousin at Elizabethtown. Had it been carried out it would have relieved the duke of much future anxiety.*

Berkeley and Carteret agree to return New Jersey to the Duke of York.

But, owing probably to Lord Baltimore's claim to the west side of the Delaware, the proposed arrangement fell through, and New York was not "inlarged" by the restoration of her old territory. In the spring of this year Carteret called an assembly, in which each town in New Jersey was represented, while Staten Island, being conceded to New York, was not. But in the next autumn dissensions grew so strong that the governor was obliged to adjourn the Assembly without day.†

The proposed restoration fails. May. November.

The order of the king in council, which allowed three Dutch ships "freely to trade" with New York for seven years, had meanwhile caused jealous complaints; and the Council for Trade reported that English merchants were "altogether discouraged and withdrawing their respective estates" from New York, and that the sixth and seventh articles of the capitulation bound the king to grant freedom of trade no longer than for "the first six months after the rendition of the place." They therefore advised that, as there had been "a mistake in the drawing" of the order, it should be revoked, and that all persons trading to New

November.

* Mass. H. S. Coll., xxxvii., 315, 319; N. J. H. S. Proc., i. (ii.), 32–36; Pepys, iii., 167, 172, 331; iv., 28; Col. Doc., iii., 105, 114; Yonkers Gazette, No. 686, for 8 July, 1865; Newark Town Records, 21, 22; *ante*, p. 59, 71, 85.

† Col. Doc., iii., 113, 186, 340; Penn. Archives, i., 70; Leaming and Spicer, 77–92; Gordon, 28; Whitehead, 42–48, 51–53, 188–190; Newark Town Rec., 21; Chalmers, i., 526, 528, 634; Yonkers Gazette, 8 July, 1865. Lord Berkeley was made Lieutenant of Ireland in 1670, when, on the death of the Duke of Albemarle, he also became Palatine of Carolina; and doubtless he and Carteret thought that their interests would be better served by retaining New Jersey than by taking the Delaware territory, and with it a controversy with so important an Irish peer as Lord Baltimore, who could be easier dealt with by the king's brother.

York contrary to the navigation acts should be prosecuted. This was the more necessary because the trade of England was "now in great measure upheld" by the American plantations. The king in council therefore ordered that all passes granted under the order of 23d October, 1667, be recalled and annulled; yet, out of regard to those who had relied on it, the Duke of York might license one of the ships now preparing in Holland to make one voyage to New York.

CHAP. IV. 1668. 18 Novem. The English refuse free trade to New York.

Sir William Temple was directed to notify this decision to the interested parties in Holland. Relying on the previous order, Van Cortlandt, Cousseau, and several other "loyal subjects now residing in New York," had dispatched one ship from Amsterdam, with the duke's pass, and were preparing another, which was nearly ready to sail. Upon their representing this to the king, backed by the personal efforts of Nicolls, an order in council was obtained, "with much difficulty," allowing the second "permissionated ship" "to make one voyage and no more;" and the Duke of York was at the same time directed not to grant "any other Passe or Passes to any Dutch shipp or shipps whatsoever to trade to New Yorke." Lovelace proclaimed the royal pleasure on the arrival of what was understood to be the last Dutch ship that would "ever come on that account" to Manhattan.*

24 October. 11 Decem. A Dutch ship specially permitted. 1669. 24 Feb.

This ending of the old commercial intercourse between New York and Holland followed one of the best acts of Charles the Second. Soon after the peace of Breda, the ablest English statesmen saw that the only way to curb the arrogance of France was to form an alliance between Great Britain and the Dutch Republic. Sir William Temple—in many respects the opposite of Downing—was accordingly sent with special powers to the Hague. He had already won the confidence of De Witt, and in a few days a treaty was made which bound Great Britain and the United Provinces to act, if necessary, in concert against France. The accession of Sweden shortly afterward gave to this famous coalition the name of the "Triple Alliance."

1668. $\frac{13}{23}$ Jan'y. The "Triple Alliance."

* Col. Doc., iii., 175–179; Chalmers's Rev. Col., i., 117; Mass. H. S. Coll., xxx., 77, 78; xxxvii., 315; Hist. Mag., viii., 230; *ante*, 137. Lovelace, at the same time, "granted free trade to the merchants at New York, and took off the wonted recognition."

CHAP. IV.

1668.

Foiled and mortified, Louis was obliged to suspend his conquests and make peace with Spain. In England, the Triple Alliance became very popular. The two great Protestant states of the world were now close friends, and outspoken members of Parliament declared that the king had done his only good act. "It was certainly," says Burnet, "the master-piece of King Charles's life; and if he had stuck to it, it would have been both the strength and the glory of his reign. This disposed his people to forgive all that was passed, and to renew their confidence in him, which was much shaken by the whole conduct of the Dutch war." The real merit of Temple's diplomacy was the ratification of the commercial stipulations in the treaty of Breda, by which England recognized the great principle so earnestly contended for by the Dutch, that "free ships make free goods."*

Principle of the Triple Alliance.

17 Febr'y.

1669. March.

Fishing-bank discovered off Sandy Hook.

New York was now prosperous, and Lovelace was sincerely anxious to aid its progress. Under his encouragement, a fishing-bank—now the favorite sporting-ground of the metropolis—was discovered, about two or three leagues from Sandy Hook, on which, in a few hours, some twelve hundred "excellent good cod" were taken. At the east end of Long Island the whale fisheries promised great results, and even in the harbor of New York several whales were struck. More than twenty of them were taken during the spring. In partnership with some others, Lovelace built a ship, "by Thomas Hall's house,"† on the East River, and a smaller one was launched at Gravesend. The governor's was "a very stronge and handsome vessell, but costly," named "the Good Fame, of New York," and was sent to Virginia, and afterward to Europe. It was noticed that there were at one time nine vessels in port which brought tobacco from Virginia, and others were employed in carrying more than ten thousand schepels of New York wheat to Boston. Several people in and about Boston

Ship-building in New York.

* Aitzema, vi., 383–398; Sylvius, i., 2–6; De Witt's Letters, iv., 609–651; Basnage, ii., 8-13; D'Estrades, vi., 222, 229, 233, 248–253, 267, 286, 291; Rapin, ii., 650, 651; Kennett, iii., 270; Anderson, ii., 495-497; Dalrymple, i., 37; Burnet, i., 254; Temple, i., 312–384; Courtenay's Temple, i., 117–201, 433; ii., 440, 452; Davies, iii., 67–71; Hume, vi., 411–413; Lingard, xii., 228–232; Macaulay, i., 202, 203; Campbell's Chancellors, iii., 304; Bancroft, ii., 325.

† Hall's house was near the present Beekman Street, so named after William Beekman, of Esopus, who purchased Hall's property in 1670: see Valentine's New York, 72, 133; Val. Man., 1860, 539, 540; Benson's Memoir, 129; *ante*, vol. i., 517.

showed inclination to come and live in New York, one of them having bought five houses. Many others, attracted by the reports of Sylvester and Morris, and the earnest recommendations of Maverick, prepared to remove from Bermuda and Barbadoes, and bought houses and plantations. The genial hospitality which had hitherto distinguished New York seems to have been encouraged by Lovelace. "There is good correspondence," wrote Maverick to Nicolls, "kept between the English and Dutch; and to keep it the closer, sixteen (ten Dutch and six English) have had a constant meeting at each other's houses in turns, twice every week in winter, and now in summer once. They meet at six at night, and part about eight or nine." Generous Madeira wine, and rum and brandy punch, "not compounded and adulterated as in England," were the usual beverages of the colonial metropolis.*

CHAP. IV.

1669.

April.

Hospitality in the metropolis.

Aspect of the city of New York.

The city itself was described by Daniel Denton, of Jamaica, in the earliest separate account of New York ever published, as "built most of brick and stone, and covered with red and black tile; and the land being high, it gives at a distance a pleasing aspect to the spectators." The king's cosmographer, John Ogilby, more elaborately pictured it as "placed upon the neck of the Island Manhatans, looking towards the sea, encompassed with Hudson's River, which is six miles broad: the Town is compact and oval, with very fair streets and several good houses; the rest are built much after the manner of Holland, to the number of about four hundred houses, which in those parts are held considerable: Upon one side of the town is James'-Fort, capable to lodge three hundred souldiers and Officers: It hath four bastions, forty pieces of cannon mounted; the walls of stone, lined with a thick rampart of Earth; well accommodated with a spring of fresh water, always furnished with arms and ammunition against accidents: Distant from the sea seven leagues, it affords a safe entrance, even to unskilful pilots: Under the town side, ships of any burthen may ride secure against any storms, the current of the River being broken by the inter-

* Col. Doc., iii., 182–185; Gen. Ent., iv., 149; Court of Assizes, ii., 455, 561; Mass. H. S. Coll., xxx., 80; xxxvii., 316–319; Wolley's New York, 35, 55.

CHAP. IV. position of a small Island, which lies a mile distant from the Town."*

1669. April. Nutten, or Governor's Island. The "small island," just below the city, known as Nutten, or the Governor's Island, "by the making of a garden, and planting of several walks of fruit-trees on it," wrote Maverick to Nicolls, "is made a very pleasant place." The metropolis was admirably protected by nature. About ten miles to the northeast was "a place called Hell Gate, which being a narrow passage, there runneth a violent stream, both upon flood and ebb, and in the middle lieth some Islands of rocks, which the current sets so violently upon that it threatens present shipwreck; and upon the flood is a large Whirlpool, which continually sends forth a hideous roaring, enough to affright any stranger from passing any further, and to wait for some Charon to conduct him through; yet to those that are well acquainted, little or no danger; yet a place of great defence against any enemy coming in that way, which a small fortification would absolutely prevent, and necessitate them to come in at the west end of Long Island, by Sandy Hook, where Nutten Island doth force them within command of the Fort at New York, which is one of the best pieces of defence in the North parts of America."†

Hell Gate.

Long Island. Long Island, although thought by Maverick to be "very poore and inconsiderable," was described by Denton, of Jamaica, as almost a paradise. Crops of all kinds came up

* Daniel Denton's "Brief Description of New York," London, 1670 (republished by W. Gowans, New York, 1845), p. 2; Ogilby's America, 1671, 169, 170. Ogilby's account is compiled chiefly from Denton and from Montanus, who seems to have described the Dutch engraving of New Amsterdam, rather than the reality of New York, as follows: "On the Manhattan's Island stands New Amsterdam, five [Dutch] miles from the ocean. Ships run up to the harbour there in one tide from the ocean. The city has an earthen fort. Within the fort, upon the outermost bastion towards the river, stand a wind-mill and a very high staff, on which a flag is hoisted whenever any vessel is seen in Godyn's [the lower] Bay. The church rises with a lofty doubled roof, between which a square tower looms up. On the one side is the prison, and on the other side of the church is the Governor's house. Outside of the walls are the houses, mostly built by Amsterdammers. At the waterside stand the gallows and the whip. A handsome city tavern adorns the furthest point. Between the fort and this tavern is a row of proper dwelling-houses, among which are conspicuous the warehouses of the West India Company." Montanus, 123; N. Y. Doc. Hist., iv., 75. I do not quote the description of Edward Melton, Amsterdam, 1681, who was in New York from 2 July, 1668, to 6 July, 1669—(and, being an Oxford scholar, ought to have written an original account)—because he merely copies Montanus. John Josselyn, *Gent.*, who published his two voyages to New England in 1674, describes New York as "built with Dutch brick, *alla-moderna*, the meanest house therein being valued at one hundred pounds. To the landward it is compassed with a wall of good thickness. At the entrance of the River is an island well fortified, and hath command of any ship that shall attempt to pass without leave:" see extract in N. Y. H. S. Coll. (ii.), i., 384; also Oldmixon, i., 239, 271.

† Col. Doc., iii., 183; Denton, 2; Benson's Mem., 94, 97; *ante*, vol. i., 56, 267.

in plenty. Many fruits grew spontaneously, especially strawberries; of which there was "such abundance in June, that the fields and woods are died red: Which the country-people perceiving, instantly arm themselves with bottles of wine, cream, and sugar, and, instead of a coat of Male, every one takes a Female upon his horse behind him, and so rushing violently into the fields, never leave 'till they have disrob'd them of their red colours, and turned them into the old habit." Trout and other delicious fish abounded in the crystal streams which "keep their course throughout the year;" and multitudes of seals, producing "an excellent oyle," sported on the beaches. The vast smooth plains on the island encouraged the breeding of swift horses; and upon that at Hempstead, Nicolls had already established a race-course, and directed that a yearly plate should be run for. Lovelace now ordered that trials of speed should take place every May; and the justices of Hempstead were directed to receive subscriptions from all disposed to run "for a crown of silver, or the value thereof in good wheat." The swiftest horse was to be rewarded by a silver cup. The general training being ordered for the same time, the governor attended it himself.*

CHAP. IV. 1669. Strawberries and trout. 1 April. Races. 18 May.

An extraordinary panic now occurred at the eastern end of Long Island. The Indians of "Meontawket" or Montauk, who were tributary to Ninigret, the Narragansett sachem, being in arrear, collected a quantity of wampum, which, with an old gun-barrel, they sent over to the chief, who received the messengers graciously, and pardoned the defaulters. This at once excited suspicions of a great Indian plot. The constable of Easthampton required the Montauks to give up their arms, which they reluctantly did. The clergyman James, with several of the inhabitants of Southold, wrote to Major John Mason, of Connecticut, one of the Pequod war heroes, and to Lovelace, charging Ninigret with organizing an extensive conspiracy to cut off all the English. The governor at once communicated with the Rhode Island authorities, who directed that Ninigret should be brought before them at Newport. But

Panic on Long Island. 29 June. 5 July.

* Col. Doc., iii., 174; Denton's N. Y., 2–6; Thompson, i., 271, 272; ii., 63; Dunlap, i., 119; Ord., Warr., etc., ii., 416; Farmer and Moore's Coll., iii., 189; Oldmixon, i., 275; *ante*, p. 74.

CHAP. IV. 1669. 28 July. 24 August. 8 Novem.

the sachem explained every thing so satisfactorily that the court "saw no just grounds of jealousy as to his intentions." The whole story was evidently a "panic fear of some over-credulous persons." In order, however, to prevent future jealousy, the Montauk chiefs soon afterward acknowledged the governor of New York as "their chiefest sachem."*

Scotch ships. 5 April. 23 April.

As the Navigation Laws prevented direct trade between Holland and New York, the Duke of York asked of his brother that "such of His Majesty's subjects in Scotland as shall be induced to take conditions as planters at New York" might be allowed to go there and trade in Scotch vessels to the West Indies and other plantations. The king accordingly authorized two Scotch ships to trade between Scotland and New York. The farmers of the customs objected that this would be a breach of the Navigation Laws. It was replied that the duke's design was for the general good of the king's "late acquired dominions," and that natural-born British subjects should be encouraged to emigrate to New York and its dependencies, so as to counterbalance its "forraigne" population, which consisted of Dutch, Swedes, and Finns. The objections of the farmers of the English revenue seem to have defeated the enterprise. In expectation of their arrival, Lovelace made arrangements to settle two hundred Scotch families at Esopus; but no ship came from Scotland this year.†

Not allowed to come to New York. 25 July.

9 Septem. Esopus affairs. 11 Septem.

Lovelace now ordered that "the garrison at the Esopus shall be henceforth disbanded and dismissed of their military employment, they being a needless charge to the Duke." A commission and instructions were likewise issued to Counselor Ralph Whitfield, Captain John Manning, Captain Thomas Chambers, William Beekman, Christopher Beresford, and Henry Pawling, to regulate affairs at Esopus and the new villages adjoining. The commissioners accordingly went to Esopus and organized two new villages, the farthest of which they named "Marbletown," from the blue limestone which abounds there; the nearer one they called "Hurley," after Lovelace's ancestral home on the

17 Septem. Marbletown. Hurley.

* Ord., Warr., Lett., ii., 461, 519; Court of Assizes, ii., 431; R. I. Rec., ii., 263-268; Col. Rec. Conn., ii., 548-551; Thompson, i., 92, 298-306; Wood, 65, 66, 79; Hough's Philip's War, 33-37; Arnold's R. I., i., 338, 339; *ante*, vol. i., 271, 550-554.

† Col. Doc., iii., 180, 181, 182, 186; Ord., Warr., etc., ii., 482-484.

CHAP. IV.

1669.

25 Septem. Kingston.

Thames. A few days afterward, "the town formerly called Sopes was named Kingston" by the commissioners, in farther compliment to the governor, whose mother's family had a seat at Kingston, l'Isle, near Wantage, in Berkshire. Beresford was appointed chief magistrate of Hurley and Marbletown, and Pawling officer over the Indians. Lewis du Bois and Albert Heymans, who was now restored to favor, were made overseers for Hurley; John Biggs and Frederick Hussey for Marbletown; and Thomas Chambers and William Beekman for Kingston. The "Duke's Laws" were directed to be enforced, and instructions were given to the new officers respecting their conduct toward the Indians. Separate lots in the two new villages were parcelled out to the disbanded soldiers. The governor having specially directed that "a very good provision at the furthest dorp" be made for Mrs. Ann Brodhead, "in regard of her great charge, and of her being a commissioned officer's widow," a tract at Marbletown was allotted to her.*

New officers.

Lands granted at Esopus.

In the mean time, Lovelace, sorely troubled that no instructions had come to him from England, in the absence of which he conceived "the whole frame of government at this time standing still," prorogued the Assizes from October to November. His reasons were that "new Instructions and directions from His Royal Highness" were daily expected from England, "and the Generall Court of Assizes being thought the most proper place for the publishing of business of such publique concern."†

23 Septem. Assizes prorogued.

Not long afterward Delavall returned from England, bringing the expected dispatches. Nicolls having explained the condition of New York, the duke caused a seal to be engraved for the province, and another for the city, which he directed should be used for all public purposes. James also presented to the city authorities a silver mace, and

4 July. Provincial and city seals.

* Council Min., iii., 11; Ord., Warr., etc., ii., 530–536; Col. MSS., xxii., 99, 1–27; Ulster H. S. Coll., i., 50, 51; *ante*, p. 123, *note*. Descendants of Captain Brodhead have continued to reside at Marbletown, where, in 1776, his great-grandson, Captain Charles W. Brodhead, raised a company of grenadiers, in command of which he was present at the surrender of General Burgoyne at Saratoga, in October, 1777: American Archives, v., 1382; Journals of N. Y. Prov. Congress, i., 295, 374; ii., 130, 150; *ante*, 89; N. Y. H. S. Coll. (1868), 185.

† Ord., Warr., etc., ii., 504; Court of Assizes, ii., 414, 415; S. Hazard's Ann. Penn., 376; Council Journals, i., Int., vi. It seems that Alderman John Lawrence, while in London in the spring of 1669, had been asked by Nicolls to take letters from him to New York; but on his calling for them, "Coll. Nicolls being not out of bed, and his man unwilling to awake him, he came away without them." So New York, through a valet's scruples, had no letters by Lawrence: Col. Doc., iii., 183; Mass. H. S. Coll., xxxvii., 319.

CHAP. IV. 1669. 10 July. 6 October.

seven gowns for the mayor, aldermen, and sheriff, and sent them a letter acknowledging the satisfaction which their loyal address had given him. Lovelace presented these to the corporation in behalf of the duke, who, "although he esteems some of these but as the gaiety and circumstantial part of Government, yet, you may be assured as to what is more essential and substantial, it shall receive all encouragement and hearty assistance from him."*

The city petitions for free trade.

Thus encouraged, the corporation petitioned the duke that—as the limited permission for Dutch ships to trade between Holland and New York had been withdrawn—a free commerce might be allowed to the province, according to the Navigation Acts, by vessels "touching in some port in England as they came from Holland, and paying His Majesty's customs there; as also touching in England as they go for Holland." This was indispensable if the Indian trade was to be retained, which required "Dutch duffels and blancoates," not made in England, and which, if prohibited, would be procured through Canada, to the injury of New York.†

Since the departure of Nicolls, Maverick had lived in
5 July. New York, whence he wrote that he had never received any thing "to the value of sixpence, one horse excepted, which Mr. Winthrop presented me with, among the rest. And what I had by His Majesty's order, I have spent as much since I came over, and four hundred pounds besides in England, in prosecution of this design." Nicolls now obtain-
12 July. ed for his former associate the gift, from the Duke of York, of a "house in the Broadway" of the city. In acknowl-
15 October. Maverick on New England. edging this favor, Maverick urged Nicolls and Cartwright to do all they could for the relief of their "poor friends in New England," whose spirits were drooping in the "bondage they live," and who were "now in a far worse condition" than that in which the royal commissioners had found them. The king, in truth, had, by this time, become "very intent about settlement of his collonies" in

* N. Y. City Rec., vi, 488–490; Mass. H. S. Coll., xxxvii., 316, 319; Val. Man., 1849, 343; 1850, 490; 1853, 380; Doc. Hist., iii., 241; iv., 1, *; *ante*, p. 142. The seal of the province of New York, thus authorized by the Duke of York's warrant of 4 July, 1669, to be used for all public instruments, was so used until replaced by the new seal which James the Second substituted for it on 14 August, 1687: Col. Doc., iii., 427.

† Col. Doc., iii., 187; Val. Man., 1850, 423.

America, and a select council was appointed to consider their affairs.* Chap. IV. 1669.

The Duke of York, by conviction a Roman Catholic, felt a sympathy with all who dissented from the Established Church of England. This feeling led him, in apparent contradiction to the arbitrary impulses of his nature, to become the friend of religious toleration. Soon after Nicolls came to New York, he allowed the Lutherans in the province to send to Germany for a minister. The Reverend
Jacobus Fabricius accordingly came over, and Lovelace 20 Febr'y.
gave him leave to exercise his office as long as he and his Fabricius Lutheran minister.
people should behave themselves orderly. At first Fabri-
cius labored at Albany; but his conduct was so offensive to 19 April.
the magistrates and the Dutch congregation that the governor was obliged to suspend him from his functions there, 28 May.
allowing him, nevertheless, to preach at New York. On
receiving his dispatches from England, Lovelace wrote to 13 October.
the Albany magistrates "that His Royal Highness doth
approve of the toleration given to the Lutheran Church Religious toleration.
in these parts. I do therefore expect that you will live friendly and peaceably with those of that profession, giving them no disturbance in the exercise of their religion; as they shall receive no countenance in, but, on the contrary, strictly answer any disturbance they shall presume to give unto any of you, in your divine worship."†

The provincial ministers of the Reformed Dutch Church Ministers of the Reformed Dutch Church.
at this time were the Domines Schaats at Albany, Polhemus at Flatbush and Brooklyn, and Megapolensis and Drisius, colleagues at New York. Blom's place at Esopus
remained vacant. Samuel Megapolensis had returned to 9 April.
Holland in the spring, under a pass from the governor.
The following winter, Domine Johannes Megapolensis was December.
"snatched away by death," after twenty-seven years' ministerial service in the province; and the metropolitan church was left in care of Drisius, whose declining health almost prevented his doing active duty. Privileged by the articles of capitulation, the Dutch churches in New York maintained their former discipline, and remained for a century in

* Col. Doc., iii., 184, 185; Mass. H. S. Coll., xxxvii., 311, 316; *ante*, p. 54.

† Gen. Ent., i., 71; Ord., Warr., etc., ii., 335, 394, 423; Court of Assizes, ii., 424; S. Hazard, 373; Dunlap, i., 120, 126, 484; Munsell, iv., 24; *ante*, vol. i., p. 634, 642, 656, 681.

CHAP. IV.

direct subordination to the mother Classis of Amsterdam, in Holland.*

1669.
4 Novem.
Meeting of the Assizes.

At the Court of Assizes it was ordered that uniformity of weights and measures should be enforced throughout the province. But as there were not enough English standard weights and measures in the country, the governor was

1670.
1 January.

obliged to suspend the execution of the law by his proclamation, "sealed with the seal of the colony."†

1669.
5 Novem.
Petitions from Long Island towns.

At the same Assizes petitions from East and West Chester, Hempstead, Oyster Bay, Flushing, Jamaica, Newtown, and Gravesend, against several grievances, were presented. These grievances were "that what was promised upon our submission by Governor Nicolls and the rest of His Majesty's Commissioners should be made good to us: —Namely, That we should be protected by His Majesty's lawes, and enjoy all such priviledges as other, His Majesty's subjects in America, do injoye;—which priviledges consist in advising about and approving of all such lawes with the Governor and his council as may be for the good and benefit of the common-wealth, not repugnant to the Lawes of England, by such deputies as shall be yearly chosen by the freeholders of every Towne or parish; and likewise to be informed what is required of us His Majesty's subjects by virtue of the Commission granted from His Royal Highness the Duke of York." Some of the smaller grievances complained of were remedied. But Lovelace had no power to grant the demand for an Assembly to make laws with the governor and council. Indeed, Nicolls had distinctly refused it at the Hempstead meeting in the spring of 1665. To the statement of the petitioners

Answer of the Court of Assizes.

the Court of Assizes replied: "It doth not appear that Colonel Nicolls made any such promise; and the Governor's Instructions directing him to make no alterations in the Lawes of the Government settled before his arrivall, they cannot expect his Honor can comply with them therein;—And for their desire to know what is required of them, there is nothing required of them but obedience and submission to the Lawes of the Government, as appears by His

* Ord., Warr., etc., ii., 381; Corr. Cl. Amst.; Col. Doc., ii., 251; iii., 189; vii., 586; N. Y. H. S. Coll., iii. (ii.), 144, 145; *ante*, vol. i., 614. 724, 762.

† Court of Assizes, ii., 226; Col. MSS., xxii., 88, 96, 98; Munsell, iv., 8, 9, 11; N. Y. H. S. Coll., i., 421.

Royal Highness's Commission, which hath often been read unto them."*

1669.

The Mohawk Mission.

In the spring of this year a Mohawk embassy asked Courcelles, at Quebec, that other missionaries might be sent to assist Pierron, and that their nation might be protected from the Mahicans by the King of France, to whom their country now belonged "by the force of arms." Father Francis Boniface was accordingly selected to help in the mission, the prosperity of which, piously attributed to the death of Jogues at Caghnawaga, seemed to verify the words of Tertullian, that "the blood of martyrs is the seed of Christians."†

18 August. Mahican war with the Mohawks.

But the Mohawk country was a battle-ground. At daybreak, toward the end of summer, three hundred Mahican warriors attacked the palisaded village of Caghnawaga, which the Mohawks bravely defended, while their squaws made balls for their firelocks. The news was quickly carried to Tionnontoguen, and at eight o'clock a large force, accompanied by Pierron, set out to relieve their beleaguered friends. The enemy had retired, however, after two hours' fighting; and the Mohawks, descending the river in canoes, hid themselves below the Mahicans in an ambuscade which commanded the road to Schenectady, at a place called "Kinaquariones." A conflict followed, in which the Mohawks put the Mahicans to flight. The Mohawks then induced the Oneidas, Onondagas, and Cayugas to make common cause; and four hundred confederate warriors went to surprise a Mahican fort "situated near Manhattan." But this enterprise failed, and the Iroquois came home with two wounded. They quickly appealed to Lovelace, who—anxious that they should hunt beaver rather than fight—endeavored, in concert with Winthrop, to make peace between them and the Mahicans.‡

19 August.

27 October. Lovelace and Winthrop try to make peace.

Frémin, the New York Jesuit superior, now summoned his missionary brethren to meet him at Onondaga. Pierron from the Mohawks, Bruyas from Oneida, Garnier and

* Court of Assizes, ii., 228–234; Journals Leg Council, i., Introd., vi., vii.; Wood, 91; Thompson, i., 145, 146; Dunlap, i., 120; *ante*, p. 33, 66, 69.

† Relation, 1669, 2–6; Shea, 264; *ante*, 129; i., 423.

‡ Relation, 1670, 23–27; 1671, 17; Col. MSS., xxii., 132; Court of Assizes, ii., 426; Ord., Warr., etc., ii., 485; Munsell, iv., 10, 26; Mass. H. S. Coll., i., 166, 167; xxx., 79; Holmes, i., 352; Col. Rec. Conn , ii., 549.

CHAP. IV.

1669.

29 August. Jesuit council at Onondaga. 6 Septem. 27 Septem. Garnier with Frémin among the Senecas.

Millet of Onondaga, and Carheil from Cayuga, accordingly met Frémin, from the Senecas, in council. After deliberating for a week, the superior detached Garnier to assist him among the distant Senecas, leaving Millet alone in charge of the Onondagas. On reaching their remote station, Frémin assigned Garnier to the village of Gandachiragou, himself remaining in charge of the mission of "Saint Michael," at Gandagarae. This village was composed of refugees from three different nations, the Neutres or Attiwandaronk, and the Hurons, which had been conquered by the Iroquois.*

15 May. Talon in France.

Talon now went for a short visit to France, where he induced Colbert to instruct Courcelles to visit the Iroquois country at least once in two years, with all his forces, so as to impress the savages with respect for the French. Six companies of the Carignan regiment, which had returned with Tracy, were also ordered back to Canada.†

Jesuit explorations in the West.

Meanwhile Talon's energy had aroused enterprise in Canada. The Jesuit Father Claude Allouez had, in 1665, visited Lakes Huron and Superior, or Tracy, by way of the Ottawa River, and had heard of "the great River called Messipi." In 1667 he was again on his way to the West with Father Louis Nicolas. The next year Nicolas returned; and Allouez, after a short visit to Quebec in 1669, went back to the Falls of Saint Mary, accompanied by Father Claude Dablon, where, with Father James Marquette, who had meanwhile arrived there from the Ottawas, they established a mission among the Chippewas.‡

Up to this time the disciples of Loyola had been the pioneers of western exploration in New France. Their honors were now to be shared by others. A young man of a good family at Rouen, Robert Cavelier de la Salle, after studying with the Jesuits, had emigrated to Canada in 1667, and had established himself on a fief granted to him,

* Relation, 1641, 72; 1651, 4; 1670, 26, 45, 46, 69, 72–77; Shea, 279, 290, 291. In Barber and Howe's N. Y. Hist. Coll., 393, and Clark's Onondaga, i., 194, is an extract from Governor Clinton's Memoir, giving an account of the massacre of a French and Spanish party at the Butternut Creek, near the present village of Jamesville, on the first of November, 1669. The story rests on the traditionary statements of some Onondaga sachems, and is not alluded to in the contemporary Relations of the Jesuits.

† Col. Doc., ix., 62, 86, 787; Charlevoix, ii., 166, 188, 189; Garneau, i., 198–201.

‡ Relation, 1667, 2–26; 1668, 21; 1669, 17–20; Charlevoix, ii., 167–176, 186, 187; La Potherie, ii., 124; Bancroft, iii., 149–152; Shea's Missions, 357–361; Discovery of the Miss., xxiv., xlvii., 67, 68, 69; Sparks's Life of La Salle, 2, 3.

which he named Saint Sulpice, at the head of the Rapids of Saint Louis, just above Montreal.* Enterprising, meditative, and abounding in courage and resources, La Salle thought that there must be a route to China and Japan through the Saint Lawrence and the unknown countries to the south and west of the great lakes. He talked so much about discovering it, that his home on the Saint Lawrence got the derisive name of "La Chine," which it bears to this day. Champlain had early heard of a great dividing cataract; and in 1641 the Jesuit missionaries had argued that if the French were once the masters of the shore of Lake Ontario nearest to the Iroquois, they could easily go up by the Saint Lawrence beyond "Onguiahra" to the farther savage tribes. The information which La Salle gained from "many savages of different nations" satisfied him that "by means of a great River, which the Iroquois call *Hohio*, emptying into the Meschasipi (which in the Illinois tongue signifies Great River), one could penetrate even to the sea." In the summer of 1669, La Salle, encouraged by Courcelles, joined the Sulpitian fathers François Dollier de Casson and René de Galinée, of Montreal—whose brethren had already established a mission at Quinté, on the northern shore of Lake Ontario—"in an expedition to explore a passage which they expected to discover, communicating with Japan and China." They proposed to visit "divers Indian nations situated along a great River, called by the Iroquois, Ohio, and by the Ottawas, Mississippi." Ascending the Saint Lawrence in canoes, they coasted along the southern shore of Lake Ontario, and visited the Seneca village just at the time Frémin was absent at Onondaga. After observing the Falls of Niagara, La Salle was seized with a violent fever, which obliged him to return to Montreal. Dollier and Galinée, however, continued their explorations, and visited the country between Lakes Ontario and Erie, of all of which they took possession in the name of the king. The royal arms were erected, and a map was prepared showing the new discoveries.

CHAP. IV.

1669.

La Salle at "La Chine."

The "Meschasipi," or Great River.

6 July. La Salle, Dollier, and Galinée explore Lakes Ontario and Erie.

August.

Septem.

Possession taken by the French.

* La Salle does not appear to have actually entered the Society of Jesus. Mr. Shea informs me that Father F. Martin, of Quebec, could not find La Salle's name in the Catalogues of the Order, all of which he examined. See also Shea's note to his "Early Voyages," etc.: Munsell, 1861. Faillon, iii., 228, says that La Salle was a "novice," by becoming which he lost his patrimony.

CHAP. IV. 1669. These events occurred while Talon was yet in France. But the act of possession, drawn up by the Montreal Sulpitians, was held to be good evidence of the French title to the countries around Lakes Ontario and Erie.*

Jegow's inn at Lazy Point, on the Delaware. Intercourse overland with the Delaware had become so constant, that a grant was obtained in 1668 from Governor Carteret by Peter Jegow, who had been a member of the New Jersey Assembly of that year, to take up the land at "Lazy Point," now known as Burlington, opposite Mattinecunk, or "Chygoes" Island, and keep a house there for the entertainment of travelers. 21 May. Lovelace now ordered that all the inhabitants on the Delaware should take out new patents from himself. William Tom, who had come over with Nicolls, and who had served as commissary there, 2 August. Delaware affairs. was appointed collector, and families from Maryland were encouraged to settle on the creek near Apoquinimy. This, however, excited the jealousy of the Maryland authorities, and White, their surveyor general, coming to Newcastle, Lord Baltimore's claim. laid claim "to all the west side of Delaware River, as belonging to the Lord Baltimore." Maryland also sent persons to exercise jurisdiction at the Hoarkill, but none of the inhabitants would submit to it until the matter should be decided in England. Nicolls had written that the question about the Delaware territory, which was to be transferred to Berkeley and Carteret in exchange for New Jersey, would be settled "in some short time;" and Lovelace 15 October. now dispatched to the duke "the original claim" made by White in behalf of Lord Baltimore by a ship "bound away for London."†

Disaffection had meanwhile appeared among the people on the Delaware. A Swede, whose real name was Marcus

* Faillon, iii., 151, 189, 228, 229, 284–307, 312–314; Col. Doc., ix., 66, 80, 81, 138, 305, 335, 382, 706, 787, 789; Champlain's Map, 1632; Relation, 1641, 71, 72; 1668, 4; Hennepin's Desc. de la Louisiane, 2, 3; Charlevoix, ii., 263, 264; Catalogue of Library of Parliament, Canada, p. 1615; Raynal, viii., 145; Kalm, in Pinkerton, xiii., 699; Bancroft, iii., 122, 129, 162; Sparks's Life of La Salle, 5–7; Shea's Desc. Miss., 83, 84, 100; note on Washington's Diary, 1753, 320; *ante*, p. 118; vol. i., p. 344. The statement in Col. Doc., ix., 335, and Doc. Hist., i., 150, that La Salle visited Niagara, and "established quarters and some settlers there," in 1668, seems to be a clerical error for 1678.

† Records of Upland Court, 140, 141; Elizabethtown Bill, 4; Ord., Warr., etc., ii., 234, 267, 268, 269; Col. Doc., iii., 185, 186; Col. MSS., xx., 2, 3; S. Hazard, 373, 374, 396, 402, 442, 466; Gordon, 22; Gazetteer, 112, 113; S. Smith, 69, 74, 93; *ante*, p. 150; vol. i., 183. It appears that New Jersey was understood to be restored to New York, from Newark Town Records, p. 21, that on 28th July, 1669, the town appointed Crane and Treat "to goe over to York, to advise with Col. Lovelace concerning our standing, whether we are designed to be part of the Duke's colony or not:" compare Mass. H. S. Coll., xxxvii., 319.

Jacobsen, but who pretended to be a son of the famous CHAP. IV.
Count Königsmark,* went about uttering seditious speeches, and with Henry Coleman, a Finn, endeavored to excite 1669.
an insurrection against the English authority. "They pre- Revolt of Königsmarke, or "the Long Swede."
tended an expectation of some Swedish ships to come and
reduce that place." The news reaching New York, Lovelace ordered the arrest of the ringleaders, and the confis- 2 August.
cation of Coleman's estate if he should abscond among the
Indians. Jacobsen, or "the long Swede," was soon taken, 15 Septem.
and kept in custody until he and his associates could be
tried by special commission from New York. "For the
rest of the poor, deluded sort," added the governor in his Lovelace's orders.
directions to Carr, "I think the advice of their own countrymen is not to be despised, who, knowing their temper,
could prescribe a method for keeping them in order, which
is severity, and laying such taxes on them as may not give
them liberty to entertain any other thoughts but how to
discharge them."† "I perceive the little *Domine*‡ hath
played the trumpeter to this disorder. I refer the quality
of his punishment to your discretion."

The council at New York ordered that although "the 18 October.
long Swede" deserved to die as a rebel, yet, as others were
involved with him, he should be whipped, branded, and
sold at Barbadoes. Secretary Nicolls and some others
were commissioned to go to the Delaware and try the 22 Novem.
insurgents. This they did, and brought back to New York 6 Decem.
Jacobsen, the ringleader, in irons, who was temporarily 20 Decem.
imprisoned in the City Hall. The next month "the long 1670.
Swede" was sent to Barbadoes and sold as a slave. Cole- 26 Jan'y. The insurgents sentenced.
man, his accessary, lived for several years among the In-
dians, and afterward became a landholder in Delaware.§

Another troublesome person, William Douglas, was sent William Douglas.

* Evelyn, ii., 168, 174; Reresby, 139–143; Kennett, iii., 402; Rapin, ii., 726; Hargrave's State Trials, iii., 466.

† It appears from this that the Swedes themselves advised severity and heavy taxes as a means of preserving order on the Delaware. Yet Wood (95), Thompson (i., 149), Dunlap (i., 121), and Bancroft (ii., 321) give Lovelace the credit of the idea, and seem to make the specific instructions which he gave to Carr at Newcastle his general principle of government in New York.

‡ "The little Domine" here referred to was Laurentius Carolus Lokenius, the Lutheran minister of the Swedish Church at Crane Hook, near Wilmington: *ante*, p. 140; vol. i., p. 577, 606, 616, 734.

§ Council Minutes, iii., 13–16; Ord., Warr., etc., ii., 500, 503–506; Court of Assizes, ii., 440, 460, 464; Col. MSS., xx., 4–8; xxviii., 163; Col. Doc., iii., 186, 343; S. Smith, 53, 54; S. Hazard, 375–379; Dunlap, ii., App. cxvii.; G. Smith's Del. Co., 93.

CHAP. IV. 1670. 26 Feb'y. 28 Febr'y. 15 March. Customs at the Delaware. 22 October. 16 Novem.

to New York, whence he was banished to New England, and warned not to come again within the duke's territories. A court was also established at the Hoarkill, and Martin Kregier appointed collector of the customs there, which were fixed at ten per cent. This duty, however, was soon abolished, upon condition that liquors were to be sold to the Indians very cautiously, and no prejudice be done to the trade at Newcastle, where Carr was directed to be vigilant, and send at once to New York for assistance in case of need.*

Lovelace now accomplished "the most memorable act" of his administration. After the return of Nicolls to London in the autumn of 1668, Staten Island having been "adjudged to belong to New York," Lovelace took measures for its settlement, as it was considered "the most commodiosest seate and richest land" in America. Its chief sachem, in the summer of 1669, had solemnly renewed the covenant between its aborigines and the English and the Iroquois.

7 April.

Several of its sachems, however, insisted that they were "the very true, lawful, and sole Indian owners" of the island, who were told that their predecessors had sold it to the Dutch.

Staten Island purchased from the Indians for the duke. 13 April.

To quiet their claims, satisfactory presents were promised; and they accordingly executed a deed by which, for a quantity of wampum, coats, kettles, guns, powder, lead, axes, hoes, and knives, they conveyed to Lovelace, in behalf of the Duke of York, "all that Island lying and being in the Hudson's River† — commonly called Staten Island, and by the Indians *Aquehonga Manacknong*—having on the south the Bay and Sandy Point, on the north the River and the City of New York on Manhattan's Island, on the east Long Island, and on the west the mainland of After Coll, or New Jersey." Possession was formally given "by turf and twigg;" and it was covenanted that on the first of May in each year the Indians should go to Fort James and acknowledge their sale; which was done.‡

* Council Minutes, iii., 17, 32; Court of Assizes, ii., 475, 611; S. Smith, 55, 56; Hazard's Reg. Penn., i., 76; Ann. Penn., 379, 380, 382; Proud, i., 130; Whitehead, 69, *note*. It seems that Douglas, not liking his banishment into New England, returned to Newcastle in 1672, whence he was sent to New York, and from there was shipped in February, 1673, to Barbadoes, to be sold: Gen. Ent., iv., 244; Council Minutes, iii., 131; S. Hazard, 403.

† By this it appears that the New York Hudson was then understood to encircle Staten Island: in other words, that "the Kills" north of that island were a part of the great Hudson River.

‡ Mass. H. S. Coll., xxxvii., 315, 317; Munsell, iv., 9; Chalmers's Ann., i., 599; Council

1670. 17 March. 30 March. Esopus affairs.

As soon as the river opened, Captain Dudley Lovelace, with Cortelyou, Beekman, Beresford, and Pawling, met at Kingston, under a commission of the governor, and granted lands at Hurley and Marbletown, chiefly to the discharged soldiers, who were required not to sell them for three years. Town boundaries were established, local regulations were made, and Beresford was sworn chief officer of Hurley and Marbletown. At the adjournment of the commission the laws were read, and an artillery salute was fired "when the president took horse to depart for New York."* (11 April.)

Commissioners sent to Albany. 11 April.

Captain Baker had meanwhile behaved so badly that he was bound over to answer at the Assizes; but the governor, finding it "not only difficult, but too tedious" to decide the case at New York, referred it to the Albany magistrates, with Delavall and Lovelace as commissioners. The latter were instructed, among other things, to make a peace between the Mohawks and Mahicans, arrange the garrison, the excise, and the Indian trade, and inform the magistrates that the governor looked upon the Dutch Church and ministry, which was "found established" by Nicolls and himself, as the parochial church of Albany, which was to be maintained at their discretion, by tax or otherwise, "and that no inhabitant, of what opinion soever, be exempt, but bear his proportion."

14 May.

The result of Baker's case was his dismissal from military employment "at Albany and elsewhere." As his place was one of the most important in the province, the governor promoted Ensign Sylvester Salisbury to fill the vacancy, with a commission as lieutenant of infantry; and Dudley Lovelace naturally succeeded to Salisbury's ensigncy on the duke's establishment.†

13 July. Baker succeeded by Salisbury.

Minutes, iii., 19–25; Court of Assizes, ii., 518; Land Papers, i., 34; Patents, iv., 62; Val. Man., 1857, 544–547; Hist. Mag., x., 375–377; Dunlap, ii., App. cxviii.; Whitehead, 17, 19, 216; N. Y. H. S. Coll., ii., 41; Col. Doc., ii., 706; iii., 304, 352, 354; *ante*, p. 149, 150; vol. i., 73, 202, 203, 525, 641, 642, 692. It does not seem that there could have been a better European title to Staten Island than that now held by the duke as proprietor of New York. Yet Carteret's heirs afterward suggested that it belonged to New Jersey.

* Court of Assizes, ii., 476, 481, 482, 581; Col. Mass., xxii., 99, 100; Patents, iii., 43; Ulster H. S. Coll., i., 51, 72; N. Y. H. S. Coll. (1868), 185.

† Ord., Warr., Lett., ii., 514–516; Court of Assizes, ii., 418, 489, 490, 500; Council Min., iii., 27; Col. MSS., xxii., 78–94, 104; S. Hazard, 373; Munsell, iv., 9, 12, 13, 14; vii., 101; Hist. Mag., iv., 50; i. (ii.), 323; Val. Man., 1847, 354, 361. After his disgrace Baker appears to have sought a refuge at Elizabethtown, New Jersey, in which he had a joint interest: Col. Doc., ii., 571; *ante*, p. 49.

CHAP. IV.

1670.

27 June. Trading vessels on the Hudson River.

The Corporation of New York, jealous of any infringement of the ancient "staple right" of Manhattan, now represented that many vessels not belonging to the province "do frequently go up Hudson's River to Esopus and Albany, there to trade and traffic, contrary to former constitutions and customs." Lovelace accordingly ordered "that no stranger or strange vessel shall be permitted, from and after the date hereof, to pass up the said River to either of the places aforesaid, there to trade or traffic, upon any pretence whatsoever. However, such vessels, unloading their goods in this city, and paying the duties required, the owners of such goods have liberty to transport them into these parts in any other vessels belonging to this port, and may go up themselves, with leave to negotiate there, having first obtained the privilege of being free Burghers of this city."*

24 March. New York Exchange.

There was, at this time, no exchange or place of meeting for the merchants of New York. Lovelace therefore directed that they should come together every Friday, between eleven and twelve of the clock, at the bridge which crossed the canal.† The governor also gave by patent, to

10 Feb. Bark mill.

Adriaen and Christofell van Laer, the exclusive privilege of maintaining a rasp mill to grind the bark used in tanning leather in the city.‡ Another order of Lovelace di-

19 August.

rected that "Love Island," in the bay, owned by Isaac Bedlow, alderman, counselor and comptroller of the revenue, should be a privileged place, where persons were free from warrants of arrest.§

Their war with the Mahicans prevented the Mohawks from reaping all the advantage expected from the presence of Pierron and Boniface. Yet many converts were

* Court of Assizes, ii., 559; Munsell, iv., 18, 19; *ante*, vol. i., 243, 628.

† Court of Assizes, ii., 478, 479; Dunlap, ii., App. cxvii.; Hist. Mag., x., 381. This place was at the corner of the present Bridge and Broad Streets: see Val. Man., 1862, 515, 555. The canal or creek at that time ran up from tide-water through Broad Street as far as "Verletten Berg," or "hindering hill," which the unknowing English, who caught the sound, but not the meaning, nonsensically called "Flattenbarrack Hill," and which is now known as "Exchange Place." It was a favorite sport of New York boys to "coast" on their sledges from Broadway down the steep descent of Verletten Berg.

‡ Court of Assizes, ii., 471–474; Val. Man., 1851, 401, 402.

§ Court of Assizes, ii., 576; Dunlap, ii., App. cxvii. Governor Nicolls granted this island to Captain Needham on the 23d of December, 1667, and he sold it to Bedlow, after whom it was named. Bedlow's widow sold it to James Carteret on 20 April, 1676. In 1800 the State ceded to the United States jurisdiction over it, and Ellis or Oyster, and Governor's Islands in the bay, provided that New York process, civil or criminal, should still continue to be executed on them: Benson's Mem., 121; 1 R. L., 1813, 189, 190; Col. MSS., xxv., 102.

made; and even the worship of Aireskoué, their great dæmon, was renounçed when Pierron threatened to leave them, after witnessing one of their solemn "feasts of the dead" at Caghnawaga. So zealous were some of the proselytes that they took pride in displaying their crucifixes at Albany, and in arguing with the "heretics." A converted squaw went into the church while Domine Schaats was preaching, and recited her chaplet during the whole of divine service. The Mohawk mission promised so well that the Fathers Bechefer and Nicolas were assigned to assist Pierron and Boniface.*

CHAP. IV.

1670.

Mohawk converts at Albany.

Bruyas had little success among the intractable Oneidas; but he edified himself by keeping Easter and Pentecost with Millet at Onondaga, where Carheil came from Cayuga to meet them. The little bell which, fourteen years before, had called the faithful to prayer, was begged back from the Onondagas and used again for Christianity. Many new converts were made, chiefly by the influence of Garakontié who had declared himself a Christian at a Mohawk council on his way back from Albany. About midsummer, an Iroquois embassy, headed by him, set out for Canada with a letter from Millet, in which Garakontié was described as an "incomparable man," who might justly be called "the protector of the French crown in this country." A council was held at Quebec with all the Iroquois except the Senecas, and Frémin was directed to leave his mission if the Senecas did not come and give satisfaction. At this visit Garakontié was baptized by Bishop Laval, and took the name of "Daniel," from Courcelles, who acted as his sponsor.†

Oneida and Onondaga missions.

25 March.

15 June.

July.

August.

Baptism of Garakontié.

Talon now returned from France, where he had informed Colbert that there was a copper mine‡ near Lake Huron, which, in connection with "the communication supposed to exist between Canada and the South Sea," it was desirable to explore. The Intendant was accompanied by several Recollet§ or Franciscan fathers, among whom was

* Relation, 1670, 27–45; Charlevoix, ii., 223–226; N. Y. H. S. Coll., iii. (ii.), 158; Shea, 265–268.

† Relation, 1670, 4–7, 43, 47–63; 1671, 3; 1673–9, 186; Charlevoix, ii., 220, 221, 227, 230; Faillon, iii., 227–230; Col. Doc., ix., 788, 789; Shea, 278, 280; *ante*, vol. i., 647.

‡ Col. Doc., ix., 63, 787. Allouez, in the Relation for 1667, p. 8, spoke of the masses of copper reported by the savages in Lake Superior.

§ The Recollets, or Gray Friars, were a branch of the Order of Saint Francis, and were so

CHAP. IV. 1670. French explorations. Gabriel de la Ribourde, and by some companies of the Carignan regiment. Delighted with the progress of Western discovery during his absence, Talon dispatched two "persons of resolution," La Salle, to explore farther in the southwest, and his own deputy, Saint Lusson, to the northwest. They were encouraged by the promise of the king to reward nobly him who should reach the Pacific. Saint 3 Septem. Copper mines on Lake Superior. Lusson was instructed to go to Lake Superior, and "make search and discovery there for all sorts of mines, particularly that of copper;"* take possession of all the countries through which he might pass, and plant the cross, with the escutcheon of France, in confirmation of the king's dominion. The Intendant's deputy was accompanied by the experienced interpreter Nicholas Perrot, who was directed to visit the Northern nations, and invite them to meet, the next spring, at the Falls of Saint Mary, the delegate of the 10 October. Great Onnontio. 10 Novem. French projects on Lakes Ontario and Erie. Talon also sent to Paris the maps and records made by Dollier and Galinée, as evidences of the French title to the regions round Lakes Ontario and Erie, and proposed that a galley should be maintained on Ontario to secure the fur trade, as the English at Boston, and the Dutch at New York, now drew to themselves more than twelve thousand livres of beaver "trapped by the Indians in the countries subject to the King."†

The movements of the French among the Iroquois were 3 October. Jealousy of Lovelace. reported to Lovelace, who wrote to Secretary Williamson that four Jesuits, with their servants, in all eleven, had "settled themselves on this side the Lake of Irecoies. They pretend it is no more but to advance the kingdom of Christ, when it is to be suspected it is rather the kingdom of his most Christian Majesty." The "legionary soldiers" whom Louis was sending over might be dangerous to the English Plantations, and should be looked after in Europe.

called because they were first instituted in solitary convents devoted to recollection: Col. Doc., ix., 88, *note; ante*, i., p. 67.

* In the Relation of 1670, 83–86, in a very interesting account of the copper mines on Lake Superior, particularly that at "Nantonnagan," or Ontonagon, sent by Dablon from the Falls of Saint Mary to Le Mercier at Quebec, and by him communicated to Talon before the dispatch of Saint Lusson.

† Col. Doc., ix., 63–67, 70, 76, 88, 97, 382, 626, 787, 789, 803, 804; Relation, 1670, 2; 1671, 26; Faillon, iii., 255, 256, 305–307; Colden, i., 35; Charlevoix, ii., 216, 217, 234, 237; Hennepin, New. Disc., 32; La Potherie, ii., 89; Hist. Mag., ix., 206; Shea's Cath. Miss., 412; Disc. Miss., 79, 80, 89, 159; Garneau, i., 204. The maps and description of Lake Ontario, prepared by Dollier and Galinée, are in the Parliament Library at Quebec: see Catalogue, p. 1615; also in Faillon, iii., 305.

CHAP. IV. 1670.

In consequence of a letter from Pierron, orders were sent to Salisbury, at Albany, to keep a vigilant watch over him, and report all his actions. 22 October.

Lovelace visits Connecticut.

Lovelace, at the same time, expecting leave to return home, went, with several of his council, as far as Milford to meet Winthrop, "and discourse all affairs that may tend to the mutual convenience of each other." Among these was the settlement of the boundary-line between New York and Connecticut, which the Hartford Court had proposed should be run by a joint committee from each government. 13 October. But Winthrop, intending to visit England, had vainly endeavored to resign his office of governor, and was unable to meet Lovelace, whose winter journey was thus 9 Decem. made fruitless.*

Katherine Harrison's witchcraft case.

At the Court of Assizes another case of reputed witchcraft was disposed of. Katherine Harrison, a widow, of Wethersfield, in Connecticut, having been convicted of witchcraft, was obliged to leave that town, and came to May. Westchester, the Puritan inhabitants of which complained 7 July. to Lovelace, who warned her to return to Connecticut. Upon her refusal she was cited before the governor, who referred her case to the Court of Assizes, upon her giving 25 August. security for good behavior. The court, finding nothing against her, directed her release, and gave her liberty to October. reside where she chose in the government. But the people of Westchester became so "uneasy" at her remaining amongst them, that Lovelace was obliged to order the poor widow to leave that infatuated town.†

Ordered to leave Westchester.

Contribution for palisades at Fort James ordered.

An interesting political event now occurred. The palisades around Fort James being decayed, the Court of Assizes ordered that a levy, or contribution for their repair, 8 October. should be made in the several towns of Long Island, and the justices in each riding were directed to find ways and means at the next courts of Sessions. But the rejection of the petitions which some of the Western towns had presented for redress the last autumn, left the people in no mood to comply with this extraordinary demand. They

* Col. Doc., iii., 190; Court of Assizes, ii., 445; Council Min., iii., 27, 32, 34; Col. Rec. Conn., ii., 145; Mass. H. S. Coll., xxx., 80–82.

† Council Min., iii., 28–31; Court of Assizes, ii., 255, 563, 577, 584, 585; Doc. Hist., iv., 87, 88; Col. Rec. Conn., ii., 118, 132; Dunlap, ii., App. cxviii.; Bolton, ii., 181, 182; *ante*, 91, 142.

CHAP. IV. 1670. were persuaded that the principle of "Taxation only by consent"—which Holland had maintained since 1477, and England had adopted in her Petition of Right in 1628—was their own birthright as British subjects. They had, for several years, paid a direct tax of a penny in the pound to defray their town charges. They had also submitted to the duke's customs' duties for the support of his government. But this last order of the Court of Assizes, where they were not represented, would, if yielded to, become a dangerous precedent: they might next be required to maintain the garrison, and they knew not what else. Southold, Southampton, and Easthampton, in a joint meeting of their delegates, agreed to contribute, provided that they might have the privileges which the king's other subjects in New England enjoyed. Huntington refused, because her people "were deprived of the liberties of Englishmen." Those of Jamaica declared that the order of the Assizes was inconsistent with the British Constitution; but if it was the king's absolute pleasure to "disprivilege" them, they would bear their burthens with patience until they could address him for relief. Flushing and Hempstead concurred with Jamaica; and the constables of the three towns laid their votes before the Court of Sessions of the North Riding, which was held at Jamaica; where, however, no action was taken. They were again presented the following week, at the Sessions of the West Riding, which met at Gravesend. At that court Secretary Nicolls presided, and Counselors Van Ruyven, Manning, and Thomas Lovelace were present as justices. It was there unanimously adjudged "that the said papers are in themselves false, scandalous, illegal, and seditious, tending only to disaffect all the peaceable and well-meaning subjects of His Majesty in these His Royal Highness's Territories and dominions;" and they were referred to the governor and his council for such action as should "best tend to the suppression of such mischief as may arise by the impression of false suggestions and jealousies." Upon this reference, Lovelace and his council ordered that these "scandalous, illegal, and seditious" papers should "be openly and publicly burned" before the Town Hall of the city of New York, at the next Mayor's Court, and that "the principal

Action of the Long Island towns.

16 Decem. Votes laid before the Sessions.

21 Decem.

Adjudged to be seditious.

29 Decem. Ordered to be burned in New York.

1670.

contriver thereof be inquired into, and proceeded against according to their demerits, and the laws of the land established."*

It was easier to burn "seditious" votes than to subdue opinion. Most of the Long Island towns had, as we have seen, taken out new patents, in conformity with the law of 1666. But Southampton and Southold refused to comply. The latter claimed that their title from the Indians and from New Haven was sufficient. Southampton relied upon theirs from Lord Stirling. The Court of Assizes therefore declared invalid the titles to lands in Southampton, unless a patent from the duke's government should be obtained for them within a certain time. This produced a spirited remonstrance from fifty of the inhabitants of that town, in which, among other things, they set forth that a new patent would be a grievance, and might make them and their posterity "groan like Israel in Egypt;" that they could not acknowledge the Duke of York to be the "sole Proprietor of the whole Island;" that, although Nicolls had promised them as great privileges as any colony in New England, they had no deputies at the courts, and were "forced to pay customs for goods imported, for which custom hath before been paid to His Majesty's use in England;" and that the royal commissioners, in August, 1664, had proclaimed that all should enjoy "whatsoever God's blessing and their own industry had furnished them withal." Lovelace, expecting leave to run over to England, replied that, to avoid "prolix debates," he would appoint commissioners to confer with them, and meanwhile recommended that they should observe the "golden rule of the Apostle, which is—be not high-minded, but fear." Counselors Delavall, Nicolls, and Bedlow were accordingly deputed to examine the cases of the recusant towns; but no other steps to enforce a compliance with the law were taken until several years afterward.†

8 October.

1671.

15 Febr'y. Southampton Remonstrance.

9 March. Referred to commissioners.

The isolated inhabitants of Martha's Vineyard and Nantucket, however, were more tractable. Nicolls had ap-

* Court of Assizes, ii., 650, 651, 652, 653; Col. Doc., iii., 303; Wood, 92–95, 151; Thompson, i., 146–149, 284; Dunlap, i., 121; ii., App. cxvii.; Bancroft, i., 321; Council Journals, i., Int., vii., viii.; *ante*, p. 160; vol. i., 437, 442.

† Court of Assizes, ii., 591, 661–664; Wood, 91, 92, 175–177; Thompson, i., 146, 334, 384; ii., 326–328; *ante*, 25, 110; vol. i, 300, 301.

CHAP. IV. 1671. June. pointed Thomas Mayhew to superintend affairs there; but as the relations between those islands and New York were vague, the governor notified their landholders to take out fresh patents. Mayhew accordingly came to New York in behalf of Martha's Vineyard, and Tristram Coffin, with 28 June. Nantucket and Martha's Vineyard incorporated. Thomas Macy, represented Nantucket. Lovelace readily made Nantucket a township, and commissioned Coffin its chief magistrate, in subordination to New York. A similar 8 July. patent was granted to Martha's Vineyard, of which the venerable Mayhew was appointed governor during his life. His grandson, Matthew Mayhew, was also commissioned as collector of the duke's customs for the several islands.*

Lovelace proved himself no bigot. John Booth, of Southold, whose children had been refused baptism by the Puritan minister, John Younge, declined to pay his tax for Younge's salary, and his cattle were distrained. Booth pe- 8 July. titioned the governor and council for relief. Lovelace 10 July. Lovelace rebukes Younge, of Southold, for intolerance. could not lawfully interfere; yet he wrote to Younge, reproving his want of Christian charity, reminding him that the indulgence granted by Nicolls and himself was not intended to justify such severity toward others "of a different persuasion;" and adding, "I desire you not to insist on such rigorous courses against those who desire to live under the known and established laws of His Majesty's dominions, lest I be forced to represent to His Royal Highness the great inconveniences that may arise by it, and you be interrupted in the exercise of that Christian function you now so peaceably enjoy."†

Lutherans. The Lutherans in the province gave Lovelace the greatest trouble. He had been obliged to suspend their minister, Fabricius, from preaching at Albany, but allowed him to exercise his function in New York. A quarrel broke out before long between Fabricius and his congregation, who 10 July. Fabricius and Arensius. were building a church "on ground without the gate," and Lovelace was obliged to interfere. Another Lutheran clergyman, Bernardus Arensius, "a gentle personage and of a very agreeable behaviour," fortunately arrived about

* Council Min., iii., 26, 67, 68; Court of Assizes, iii., 533, 538; Deeds, iii., 58–63, 70–75; Hough's Nantucket Papers, 20–41, 70, 71, 129–131; Mass. H. S. Coll., xiii., 85; xxxvii., 30; *ante*, p. 139.

† Court of Assizes, ii., 735–737; Doc. Hist., iii., 209; Thompson, i., 383, 395; Wood, 34; Farmer and Moore's Coll., iii., 189.

CHAP. IV. 1671. 11 August.

this time at New York. Fabricius, having already received the governor's passport to go to the Delaware, was allowed, as his last clerical act, "to give his congregation a valedictory sermon, and to install the new-come minister, according to the custom used by those of their religion."*

Reformed Dutch Church in New York.

The Reformed Dutch Church in the city had meanwhile wanted a colleague for Drisius, whose ill health prevented his doing much duty. Polhemus, of Flatbush, preached occasionally; and Ægidius Luyck, the former teacher of the grammar-school in New Amsterdam, who had returned from Holland, after studying divinity for a time, assisted by the foresinger Evert Pietersen, conducted divine service on Sundays. The Consistory, in January, 1670, had called Selyns, who formerly preached in Brooklyn, and was now settled at Wavereen, in Holland, to supply the place of Megapolensis, but he had declined their invitation. At the joint request of "the Elders and Deacons of the Church," and of the mayor and aldermen of the city, who desired that "some care may be taken for the supply of this place with an able and orthodox minister, of which they are at present wholly destitute," Lovelace, in June, 1670, declared, under his hand and the seal of the province, "that whensoever such a minister shall come over to this city, and undertake the charge aforementioned, I shall take care that there shall be duly and justly paid unto the said minister, or to his order, the value of One Thousand Guilders Holland's money, each year, and likewise that he shall have the accommodation of a convenient dwelling-house, rent free, together with his provision of firewood gratis." This being sent to Holland, Domine Wilhelmus van Nieuwenhuysen, an accomplished scholar and divine, was induced by his relative Selyns to accept the call, which was approved by the Classis of Amsterdam. On his arrival at New York he was installed as a colleague with Dris- 24 August.

Van Nieuwenhuysen called.

* Court of Assizes, ii., 500, 503, 702, 725; Gen. Ent., iv., 15-17, 19, 304; Doc. Hist., iii., 242, 245, 525; Col. Doc., iii., 415, *note;* Munsell, iv., 14, 22, 23; S. Hazard, 381, 385, 388; C. Wolley's Two Years in New York, 57; Dunlap, i., 127; *ante,* 150. On the 18th of October, 1672, Arensius had a pass from the governor to go to Albany for the winter. The "Aanspreker," or Sexton of the Dutch Church there, had claimed the right enjoyed by such officials in Holland to conduct the funerals of all decedents in his parish; but on the 10th of June, 1672, it was ordered in Council that, as the Lutherans have a toleration for their religion, they may bury their own dead; and Delavall, in the following November, declared in open court at Albany, "Let the dead bury their dead:" Gen. Ent., iv., 228; Council Min., iii., 103; Doc. Hist., iii., 525; Dunlap, ii., App. cxix.

CHAP. IV. ius, to the "highest acceptance" of the people. The Con-
1671. sistory of the Dutch Church were soon afterward author-
26 Septem. ized by an order in council to lay taxes on the congregation for the support of the ministers and of the poor. Dris-
5 Decem. ius was also allowed one hundred pounds out of the public
revenue for the partial services he had rendered during
the last two years. By these various measures the Reformed Dutch Church was virtually "established" in New
York by its English rulers.*

Although the Dutch inhabitants of New York had little
cause for complaint, the inducements offered by the proprietaries of Carolina, where Sir John Yeamans had just
arrived with slaves from Barbadoes, attracted some to em-
Port Royal, in Carolina. igrate thither. Two ships were accordingly sent by the
proprietaries to convey them to Port Royal. But Love-
lace, disliking the "fair and specious pretences" which
were robbing his own government of its population, order-
9 Novem. ed that all persons resident in New York for more than six
months should notify the secretary of their intended departure, and procure passports. Captains of vessels were
13 Novem. also directed not to receive passengers on board unless
duly authorized. Notwithstanding these restraints, nine-
20 Novem. Emigrants from New York to Carolina. teen heads of families obtained the necessary passports and
embarked for Carolina, where they settled themselves on
the Ashley River, and were afterward joined by others of
their countrymen from New York and Holland.†

New Jersey. In New Jersey, the proposed restoration of which to the
Duke of York had not been executed, Carteret's government went well, until the first payment of quit-rents to the
proprietors became due on "Lady-day," or the 25th of
March, 1670—the Old Style New-year's day. Open opposition was then shown, especially by those who held their
lands under patents from Nicolls, or direct purchases from
the savages. The governor could not prevail on them to

* Corr. Classis of Amst.; Records of Collegiate R. D. C., N. Y.; N. Y. City Rec., vi., 562, 563, 653, 665, 679–681, 750; Gen. Ent., iv., 47; Council Min., iii., 82; Col. Doc., ii., 470, 475; iii., 189; Hist. Mag., i. (ii.), 323, 324; Dunlap, i., 127; ii., App. cxix.; C. Wolley, 56, 93; Murphy's Anthology of N. N., 146, 178; *ante*, 159; vol. i., 633, 694, 734. The elders and deacons of the "Reformed Christian Church in New York," who wrote to the Classis of Amsterdam on 5 June, 1670, were Petrus Stuyvesant, Oloff Stevensen van Cortlandt, Paulus Leendertsen van de Grist, Boele Roelofsen, Jacob Teunissen Kay, and Jacob Leisler.

† Gen. Ent., iv., 62, 69, 72; Chalmers, i., 530, 531, 557; Oldmixon, i., 464; Hewat, i., 5[illegible], 73; Holmes, i., 357, 367; Grahame, i., 360, 361, 420, 422; Bancroft, ii., 170, 171; Smith, i., 47; Riker's Newtown, 100, 101; Gentleman's Magazine, 1740, p. 104.

recognize the rights of the proprietors, and anarchy began. Elizabethtown became the focus of disaffection, while Bergen and Woodbridge alone remained loyal.*

Captain James Carteret.

About this time a young man, destined to cause great trouble in the province—Captain James Carteret, the weak and dissolute second son of Sir George, and who, with John Locke, Sir John Yeamans, and others, had been created a landgrave of Carolina—stopped, on his way thither, at New Jersey. Some murders having been committed by the Indians on the Delaware, near Mattinicunk Island, Lovelace ordered Governor Carteret and his kinsman to advise with the council at New York. Carteret at once promised to call an extraordinary Assembly at Elizabethtown, and ascertain how far the people of New Jersey were willing to contribute for a general war with the savages. It was also agreed that a good correspondence should be kept up between the two governments, and nothing be done without a mutual understanding. At the appointed day Lovelace met Carteret at Elizabethtown; but the season being too far advanced for an effectual campaign, the officers on the Delaware were directed to enrol their militia, and engage the Susquehannas on their side. On this occasion Carteret was "ready with a handsome party to have stepped into the work;" and Lovelace was obliged to reprove his own subordinate, Carr, because "the backwardness of the inhabitants on the Delaware has put a stop to the forwardness of those in New Jersey."†

25 Septem.

Agreement between New York and New Jersey.

7 October.

9 Novem.

1 Septem. to 1 October.

Batts's Virginian discoveries.

This autumn, Thomas Batts, with several Englishmen and Indians, under a commission from the authorities of Virginia, made an interesting tour "behind the Apuleian Mountains." The party appear to have gone from the Appomattox to the head waters of the Great Kenhawa; and, as the first European explorers, they took possession of the whole country in the name of their king.‡

French movements.

The movements of the French now caused much excitement in New York. Courcelles's imperious message to the

* Eliz. Bill, 35; Chalmers, i., 616; Gordon, 29; Grahame, i., 466; Bancroft, ii., 319; Whitehead, 54, 55; Mass. H. S. Coll., xxxvii., 319; *ante*, 150, 164.

† Gen. Ent., iv., 35, 42, 45, 50, 67; Council Min., iii., 71–73, 77–81; S. Smith, 69, 70, 71; S. Hazard, 388–392; Col. MSS., xx., 24, 25; Whitehead, 55, 59; Oldmixon, i., 464; Eliz. Bill, 35; Douglas, ii., 272; Collins, iv., 213; Chalmers, i., 528, 530, 616; *ante*, 164.

‡ Beverly, 58, 60; Burk, ii., 149–151; and Campbell, 268, 269, refer briefly to this expedition. The original journal of Batts was first published in N. Y. Col. Doc., iii., 193–197.

CHAP. IV. 1671. Senecas determined them to restore some of their Algonquin prisoners, whom they intrusted to the great Cayuga chief, Saonchiogoüa, to convey to Canada. On reaching Quebec, the Cayuga mediator arranged every thing satisfactorily with Courcelles; and, having declared himself a Christian, was baptized by Bishop Laval, receiving from Talon, his sponsor, the name of "Louis."*

Prairie de la Madeleine.

In 1669 the Jesuits had founded a "residence" at their Prairie de la Madeleine, on the south bank of the Saint Lawrence, a little below the Rapids of Saint Louis, and nearly opposite Montreal. It was intended as a place of repose for their missionaries, and Father Pierre Raffeix was appointed its first superintendent. Converts from the Oneidas, Mohawks, Mahicans, and other nations, on their way to the Huron colony of Notre Dame de Lorette, near Quebec, soon began to stop at the nearer Prairie; and Courcelles, observing the political importance of the "Reduction," it was established as a mission, under the name of "Saint Francis Xavier, des Prés." In 1671 Raffeix was sent to Cayuga, and Frémin was recalled from the Senecas to take charge of the new mission, which soon became very important, both to the Jesuits and the civil authorities of Canada.†

Iroquois missions.

On the recall of Frémin, Bruyas became superior of the Iroquois missions, and, leaving Oneida, he went to the Mohawks to take the place of Pierron at Tionnontoguen, who now returned to Quebec. Millet, at Onondaga, encouraged by Garakontié, labored with such zeal that the savages, who always gave descriptive names, called him, as they had formerly called Le Mercier, *Teharonhiagannra*, or "the looker up to heaven." Bruyas, however, transferred him to his own former mission at Oneida; and John de Lamberville, who had come out to Canada in 1668, succeeded Millet at Onondaga. Carheil, forced by a nervous disease to leave Cayuga, was replaced by Raffeix, who came from the Prairie de la Madeleine. After the departure of Frémin from the Senecas, Garnier was left in sole charge of the three stations of Conception, or Totiakto, Saint

* Relation, 1671, 3, 4; Charlevoix, ii., 230, 231; Shea, 289; *ante*, 169.

† Relation, 1671, 12, 13, 15; 1672, 16, 18; Douniol's Mission du Canada (Paris, 1861), i., 179, 180; ii., 49; Charlevoix, ii., 233, 257; v., 261; Col. Doc., ix., 116, 130; Shea, 288, 296–298; Faillon, iii., 316, 317; Colden, i., 53, 54; Smith, i., 69; Garneau, i., 203.

Michael, or Gandagaraé, and Saint James, or Gannagaro. CHAP. IV.
In the spring of this year the village of Saint Michael, or Gandagaraé, was burned, and the chapel, with all Garnier's effects, were destroyed. But the greatest grief of the lonely missionary was the drunkenness "caused by the liquors which the savages brought from the Hollanders for more than eighty leagues over land."* 1671.

11 March. Colbert's orders to Talon.

In writing to Talon, Colbert recommended that a good correspondence should be kept up with the English, and a mutual trade established. The dispatch of La Salle to the South, and of Saint Lusson to the North, was approved; "but the principal thing to which you ought to apply yourself in discoveries of this nature, is to look for the copper mine. Were this mine once discovered, and its utility evident, it would be an assured means to attract several Frenchmen from Old to New France."†

Meanwhile Perrot, after visiting the copper mine in Lake Superior, had summoned the Western Indians to meet at the Falls of Saint Mary; and Saint Lusson, who had wintered on Lake Huron, went thither to join the Fathers Dablon, Druillettes, Allouez, and André. Soon fourteen different savage nations were represented in an assembly. The arms of France were placed on a cross on the top of a hill; the "Vexilla" and the "Exaudiat" were chanted, the "Te Deum" was sung, and possession was taken, in the name of the king, "with all the pomp and éclat the country could afford." Talon exultingly prophesied to Louis that this part of his monarchy would "become something grand." The foreign colonies, "so long settled on the sea-board, already tremble with affright in view of what His Majesty has accomplished here in the interior within seven years." * * * "They are already aware that the King's name is spread so far abroad among the savages throughout all those countries, that he alone is there regarded by them as the arbiter of Peace and War. All detach themselves insensibly from the other Europeans; and, with the exception of the Iroquois, of whom I am not yet assured, we may safely promise our-

May.

14 June.

2 Novem. The French in the Northwest.

* Relation, 1671, 14–24; 1672, 12, 21; Col. MSS., xxxv., 160; Col. Doc., iii., 251, 252; ix., 171, 366, 367, 665; Shea, 268, 276, 277, 281, 282, 288, 291; *ante*, 148, 162. Mr. Shea's note (56) to his edition of Colden, p. 135, is evidently erroneous.

† Col. Doc., ix., 63, 64, 70, 787, 789; *ante*, 170.

1671. 11 March. Colbert's orders to Courcelles.

selves to make the others take up arms whenever we please."*

When he wrote to Talon, Colbert also instructed Courcelles that he need not visit the Iroquois, and, as troops could not be sent from France, he and the Intendant might do as they thought best on Lake Ontario. This piqued the governor, whom Talon had represented as being sluggish. He therefore determined to make a showy voyage up the Saint Lawrence; to strike terror into the Senecas and other remote tribes; to establish a post which would prevent the Iroquois — who had exhausted the country south of Lake Ontario, and were now hunting elk and beaver among the Hurons and Ottawas—from taking their peltries to the Dutch and English; and to ascertain whether a colony near the foot of Lake Ontario would not aid future explorations of his countrymen toward the Mississippi. A large plank bateau was accordingly built at Montreal, in which Courcelles proposed to ascend the Rapids of the Saint Lawrence, to convince the savages—who thought that their own light bark canoes could alone perform the feat—"that the French could accomplish something they were incapable of." In spite of all sneers, a flat-boat of two or three tons burthen was loaded with provisions, and thirteen Indian canoes carried the rest of the expedition, which was fifty-six men in all. Courcelles embarked at La Chine, accompanied by Perrot, the governor of Montreal, and other French officers, and by the Sulpitian Father Dollier — who had already visited Ontario with La Salle—as chaplain. With great labor the heavy bateau was dragged up the several rapids as far as "Otondiata," now called Grenadier Island, a few leagues above Ogdensburg. There it was left under a guard, while Courcelles went in his bark canoe through "beautiful tranquil waters almost without a ripple," past the "Thousand Islands," to the mouth of Lake Ontario, which appeared "like an open sea without any bounds." Charles le Moyne, the inter-

3 June. Courcelles's voyage to Lake Ontario.

10 June.

11 June.

* Col. Doc., ix., 72, 73, 97, 304, 383, 626, 790, 803, 804; Relation, 1671, 26–28, 31, 35, 42, 43; La Potherie, ii., 124–130; Charlevoix, ii., 234–238; Hist. Mag., ix., 206; Bancroft, iii., 154, 155; Faillon, iii., 307, 308; Shea's Missions, 361–365; Disc. of Miss., 69. On this visit, Perrot appears to have discovered the long-talked of Ontonagon copper mines near Keewena Point, on Lake Superior, which Colbert and Talon were so anxious to find out, and which have since developed such wonderful riches: see Relation, 1667, 8; 1670, 83–86; 1671, 25; 1672, 2; *ante*, 170.

preter, soothed by judicious presents the jealousy of some Iroquois who were catching eels, which abounded there; and letters were sent by them to the missionaries, direct- 12 June.
ing that the reasons of Courcelles's voyage should be published in the several villages. After enjoying the astonishment of the savages at the sight of his heavy bateau tri- 13 June.
umphantly reposing at Otondiata, the governor safely descended the rapids; and in three days reached Montreal 17 June.
without the loss of a man. The flat-boat of Courcelles was the first European-built vessel which ever accomplished the adventure, now safely performed every summer's day in vast steamers, guided by the confidence of practiced skill. The effect of the expedition was at once apparent. Several of the missionaries, on their return from the Iroquois country, reported that it had alarmed the cantons so much that they recalled their warriors from an expedition against the Andastes, and resolved to send an embassy the next spring to learn from Onnontio the reasons of his voyage, and what they must now expect.*

Effect of Courcelles's expedition on the Iroquois.

The influence of Courcelles's expedition was not confined to the savages. Exaggerated accounts of it were sent to New York, where a panic broke out, and some prepared to move away before the French could reach them. Lovelace, returning in haste from Staten Island, where he was looking for a mill-seat on his farm, wrote to Delavall 6 July.
at Albany that, as there was peace in Europe, Courcelles would not dare to "commence a warr on his own head." A fortnight afterward, the governor, having appointed Steenwyck to act in his absence, left the fort in charge of 19 July.
Manning, and went up to Albany. Various arrangements were made for its better government. Deputies from the 2 August.
several Iroquois nations having arrived there, peace was made between them and the Mahicans; which, however, proved to be as annoying to the French as it was welcome to the English.†

Effect of Courcelles's expedition at New York.

Peace between the Iroquois and Mahicans.

* Col. Doc., ix., 70, 71, 75–85, 96; x., 349; Relation, 1671, 2; Charlevoix, ii., 188, 190, 191; v., 286; Gent. Mag., xxvii., 74; Sauthier's Map in Doc. Hist., i.; *ante*, 162. Charlevoix erroneously dates Courcelles's voyage in 1670 instead of 1671. It was my good fortune to discover, in the Royal Library at Paris, the original and very interesting account of this voyage, by Dollier, of which a translation is printed in N. Y. Col. Doc., ix., 75–85: see also Faillon, iii., 331–336.

† Court of Assizes, ii., 732; Gen. Ent., iv., 10, 282–284; Munsell, iv., 21, 24–26; Relation, 1671, 17; 1672, 21; Faillon, iii., 336; Douniol, i., 4, 5; Shea, 281; Mass. H. S. Coll., i., 169;

CHAP. IV. 1671.

9 March. North River vessels.

Notwithstanding the orders of the previous year, vessels not belonging to the city of New York continually went up the North River to trade at Esopus and Albany; and the governor, on the complaint of the metropolitan burghers, renewed the prohibition, with directions to the custom-house officers to take a strict account. As a special favor, Counselor Willett's sloop was declared a privileged vessel, although it had not been built in the province. Isaac Grevenraet, who had just been appointed to succeed Beekman, as sheriff of Esopus, was directed to keep an account of all vessels coming there.*

12 July.

According to the Duke's laws, the high-sheriff of Yorkshire was to be appointed every year from each of the ridings in turn. Warned by the recent exhibitions of the temper of the Long Island people, Lovelace thought that this office should now be held by one of his own immediate dependents. He accordingly commissioned Captain John Manning in place of Robert Coe. The captain, who had been sheriff of the metropolis since 1667, was succeeded in that office by Allard Anthony.†

7 Septem. Manning high-sheriff of Yorkshire.

John Archer, of Westchester, having purchased a part of the old estate of Van der Donck, built a new village "near unto the passage commonly called Spiting Devil;" the place being "the road for passengers to go to and fro from the main, as well as for mutual intercourse with the neighboring colony" of Connecticut. Lovelace therefore made Archer's property an enfranchised township, with the usual immunities, by the name of the Manor of Fordham, upon condition that its inhabitants should always send forward to the next town all public packets and letters coming to New York, or going thence to any of His Majestie's colonies.‡

13 Novem. Fordham patent in Westchester.

The Peace of Breda brought advantage to the banished New Netherland Counselor, John de Decker, whom the

Colden, i., 35; Col. Doc., ii., 580. It is a hardly excusable blunder in Dunlap, i., 125, 126, to make Lovelace go to Albany in 1671, to meet Kendall and Littleton, of Virginia, who did not visit that place until September, 1679: Colden, i., 42, 43.

* Court of Assizes, ii., 559, 657, 659, 660; Gen. Ent., iv., 3; Val. Man., 1860, 540; Val. N. Y., 72, 133; Munsell, iv., 18, 21, 22; *ante*, 168.

† Court of Assizes, ii., 554; Gen. Ent., iv., 26, 201; Council Min., iii., 148; C. Wolley, 89; Val. Man., 1853, 328, 329; N. Y. H. S. Coll., i., 385; Wood, 150; Thompson, i., 284; *ante*, 70, 138.

‡ Patents, iv., 79–82; Bolton, ii., 179, 320–322; Col. Doc., iii., 303; *ante*, vol. i., 421, 561; ii., 124, *note*.

Duke of York referred to Lovelace for the redress of any grievances he might have suffered. De Decker's case was accordingly considered by the governor, who gave him, as a peace-offering, a tract of land on Staten Island. The settlement of Deckertown, in Sussex County, New Jersey, perpetuates the name of Stuyvesant's honest, and perhaps too patriotic commissioner.*

CHAP. IV.

1671.
9 January.
De Decker's case.

Perhaps the most interesting domestic transaction of this year was the purchase by Lovelace of the greater part of "the Domine's Bouwery," or about sixty-two acres of land, between the present Warren and Christopher Streets, in the city of New York, which had formerly been in the possession of the Dutch Domine Everardus Bogardus and his widow. This property had been confirmed to their heirs, by Nicolls, in 1667. It adjoined the old West India Company's farm, which the duke now held by virtue of its confiscation by Nicolls. But in the spring of 1671 several of the heirs of Bogardus and his wife sold the old domine's estate to Lovelace, who appears to have held it for some time in his own right. It was afterward vested in the Duke of York, and then in the crown; and, by a curious train of events, the original Bouwery of the Dutch clergyman of Manhattan at length made part of the estate now enjoyed by the corporation of Trinity Church.†

9 March.
Purchase of the "Domine's Bouwery" by Lovelace.

1672.

The new year was marked by an impressive local event. Since his return from Holland, Stuyvesant had remained for four years quietly at his "Bouwery," taking no part in public affairs. Having made his will, the veteran calmly died at the age of eighty years, and was buried in a vault under the little chapel he had built near his country house. Crowded thoroughfares now surround the spot where his ashes rest; and a pear-tree from the fatherland, planted by his own hands, until recently put forth its annual foliage, amid the hum of busy multitudes.‡

February.
Death of Stuyvesant.

* Court of Assizes, ii., 635, 636; N. Y. Surr. Rec. Wills, i., 52, 53; Val. Man., 1847, 369, 370; O'Call., ii., 305; Gordon's Gaz. of N. J., 127; *ante*, 46.

† Rec. Clerk's Off., City and County of N. Y.; Val. Man., 1855, 531, 532; 1860, 548; Valentine's N. Y., 132; Sandford's Chancery Rep., iv., 633, 726; Paige, iv., 178; Hoffman's Treatise, i., 116, 117; ii., 180–189; Col. Doc., iii., 226; *ante*, vol. i., 266; ii., 80.

‡ N. Y. H. S. Coll. i. (ii.), 399, 400, 454; N. Y. Surr. Rec. Wills, i.; Smith, i., 33; Dunlap, i., 118; Thompson, i., 129, *note;* Val. Man., 1852, 413; 1861, 532; Barber and Howe's N. Y. Coll., 339. The pear-tree, surrounded by an iron railing, stood at the corner of Third Avenue and Thirteenth Street, until it was destroyed in February, 1867. The inscription on the tablet in the wall of Saint Mark's Church, over the vault in which Stuyvesant was

CHAP. IV.

1672.
8 March.
Lovelace visits the Delaware.
12 March.

Affairs on the Delaware requiring his personal attention, Lovelace set out overland, with an escort of horse, under the command of Captain Nicolls. Passing in great state from Neversink through New Jersey, he crossed the Delaware at Jegow's new house, near Mattinicunk Island, and reached Newcastle. On his return to New York, Newcastle was incorporated as a bailiwick; English laws were established on the Delaware; and the officers at the Hoarkill were directed to oppose all pretenses of the Maryland authorities, and obey only the orders of the Duke of York's governor, "until His Majesty's or His Royal Highness's pleasure be signified to the contrary."*

17 May.

26 Febr'y.
Military arrangements in New York.
24 April.

Rumors of a new war in Europe now made Lovelace take special care for the defense of New York. A third company of foot was organized in the city, which Martin Kregier was commissioned to command. A volunteer troop of horse was also raised, of which Cornelis Steenwyck was appointed captain, Dudley Lovelace lieutenant, and Gabriel Minvielle cornet; and the new forces were ordered to be ready for the next General Training in May.†

There was need of precaution. Charles the Second disliked the Triple Alliance; he hated the Dutch, who had burned his ships at Chatham; he wanted money for his pleasures, and was restive under the restraint of the House of Commons. The Duke of York, who had become a Roman Catholic, encouraged his brother to carry on a clandestine negotiation with Louis, and a secret treaty was signed between them in May, 1670, by which, among other things, the King of England agreed to profess the Roman faith, and join the King of France in making war against the Protestant Dutch Republic. In return for this, Charles was to receive enough money from Louis to make him independent of Parliament. Another treaty was openly negotiated in January, 1671, by which it was stipulated that England was to annex Zealand, and France all the other Dutch provinces except Holland, which was to be the

England and France unite against the Dutch.

buried, erroneously states that he died in "*August, A.D.* 1682," instead of February, 1672. An epitaph on Stuyvesant, written by Domine Selyns, is in Murphy's Anthology of New Netherland, 160.

* Council Min., iii., 92, 93, 94, 97; Gen. Ent., iv., 110–114, 184; Col. MSS., xx., 26–35; S. Hazard, 395–397, 400; Eliz. Bill, 4; Bancroft, ii., 319; *ante*, 164.

† Gen. Ent., iv., 105, 128; Mass. H. S. Coll., xxx., 80; *ante*, vol. i., 631, 665, 712, 724.

William, Prince of Orange.

share of the Prince of Orange if he would come into the arrangement. William—who had been declared entitled to precedence next after the Duke of York, "as nephew to His Majesty, and a grandchild of England"—was invited to London, where his birthday was celebrated with extraordinary pomp. A marriage between him and his beautiful cousin Mary was projected. But the Dutch prince was not to be bought. "The King of England," wrote Colbert de Croissi from London, to Louis, in December, 1670, "is much satisfied with the parts of the Prince of Orange. But he finds him so passionate a Dutchman and Protestant, that even although your Majesty had not disapproved of his trusting him with any part of the secret, those two reasons would have hindered him." Temple was now recalled from the Hague, and in July, 1671, was replaced by Downing, the mean-spirited enemy of Holland. It was agreed that the Dutch should mainly be fought by England at sea, and by France on land. To obtain money for equipping his fleet, Charles adopted the iniquitous expedient, foreseen by Ashley, suggested by Clifford, and recommended by the "Cabal," of closing the English Exchequer, and seizing the moneys loaned to the nation by its confiding creditors.*

2 Jan'y. English Exchequer closed.

With characteristic perfidy, the English captured the Dutch Smyrna fleet, which was coming home, unconscious of danger. "No clap of thunder on a fair day," wrote Temple, "could more astonish the world." But the captors received "little save blows, and a worthy reproach." A few days afterward Charles declared war against the Dutch; and Louis soon followed. The young Prince of Orange was made captain general of the Dutch army; but their navy was intrusted to the veteran skill of De Ruyter. James, Duke of York, and Lord High Admiral of England,

3 March.

17 March.

7 April. England and France declare war against Holland.

* Temple, i., 463; ii., 173, 178, 180, 181, 251; Reresby, 18; Dalrymple, i., 42–47, 96–129; Clarke's James II., i., 440–457; Courtenay's Temple, i., 271, 338–352, 415; ii., 481; Basnage, ii., 59, 60, 98–107, 110, 116–118, 133–141, 182–192; Kennett, iii., 279, 284; Burnet, i., 300–308; Rapin, ii., 655, 656, 660–662; Anderson, ii., 522; Evelyn, ii., 76; Davies, iii., 71–89; Lavallée, iii., 219, 220; Martin, i., 306–319; Lingard, xii., 239–273, 369–380; Hume, vi., 433–440, 445–448; Mackintosh, 314–319; Macaulay, i., 204–216; King's Life of Locke, 35, 36; Campbell's Chancellors, iii., 305. It has been commonly supposed that the word "Cabal" was derived from the initials of Clifford, Ashley, Buckingham, Arlington, and Lauderdale, who were the ministers of Charles the Second in 1672. But that term was used in England as early as 1665, to signify what is generally called "the Cabinet:" Pepys, ii., 312; iii., 328; *ante*, 5.

CHAP. IV. commanded its fleet, while the French ships were led by
D'Estreés. De Ruyter quickly attacked the combined En-
1672. 28 May. glish and French fleet lying in Southwold Bay, or Solebay,
7 June. on the coast of Suffolk. A bloody, but indecisive action
Battle of Solebay. followed. The Duke of York was attended on board his
flag-ship by Colonel Richard Nicolls, his late governor of
Death of New York, who was killed by an avenging Dutch cannon
Nicolls and Wren. ball. The duke's secretary, Matthew Wren, was mortally
wounded at his side. The Dutch had the advantage; and
the French prudently looked on while the naval rivals destroyed each other. Yet all this carnage was caused, said
the calm and candid English Evelyn, "for no provocation
but that the Hollanders exceeded us in industry, and in all
things but envy."*

In the mean time, Charles, "very intent" about the set-
1670. tlement of his American colonies, had appointed a new
30 July. Council for Foreign Plantations, and made the Duke of
1671. 4 April. York and others, of whom one was John Evelyn, addition-
26 May. al members. The first inquiry of the council was into the
New Plantation condition of the "peevish and touchy" colonies in New
Council in England. England. Colonel Cartwright, Nicolls's old colleague, gave
21 June. the council "a considerable relation of that country;" and
it was determined to send new commissioners, with secret
3 August. instructions, to ascertain whether those colonies were able
12 August. to resist the king and "declare for themselves as independent of the crown."

1672. The Dutch war, however, postponed action on this point;
although orders were sent to the plantations that none of
their ships should venture home without convoys; and it
12 Feb'y. was considered who would be fit commissioners to go to
New England. The affairs of New York were also noticed. Dissatisfied with Lovelace's government, Easthamp-
3 July. ton, Southampton, and Southold represented to the king
that they were more heavily taxed than his subjects in
New England, were not represented by "deputys in Court,"

* Basnage, ii., 192–209; Sylvius, i., 191–208, 243–249; Clarke's James II., i., 456–481; Evelyn, i., 335, 409; ii., 75, 76, 80, 82; Pepys, ii., 361; iv., 235; Kennett, iii., 285, 287, 288; Rapin, ii., 662–664; Lyson's Mag. Britt., i., 39; Davies, iii., 90–104; Lingard, xii., 265–283; Hume, vi., 449–456; Anderson, ii., 522; Martin, i., 327, 328. In the Ampthill Church, Bedfordshire, England, is a mural monument to Richard Nicolls, on which is represented a cannon ball, with the inscription "*Instrumentum mortis et immortalitatis.*" A copy of Nicolls's epitaph is in N. Y. Hist. Soc. Proc. for 1844, p. 117. It is a curious coincidence that the conqueror, Nicolls, should have followed Stuyvesant to the grave within a few months.

and were obliged to obey laws imposed by others, who insulted over them, and threatened to cut down their timber. As they had purchased their lands from Lord Stirling's deputy, and had formerly been under Connecticut, they prayed that they might "be continued under the Government and Patent of Mr. Winthrop, or else that they may be a free corporation as His Majesties subjects." The king referred the petition to the Plantation Council for a report, and directed that notice should be given to the Duke of York's commissioners that they might attend when it should be considered. The council accordingly read Lord Stirling's conveyances, on which the petitioners relied; but as the whole of Long Island was clearly within the Duke of York's patent, no farther action appears to have been taken.*

CHAP. IV. 1672. The Long Island representation disregarded in England. 19 July.

The next autumn the supervision of trade and commerce was added to the former functions of the Plantation Council. Of this new council the versatile Ashley, recently created Earl of Shaftesbury, was made president; and, through his influence, John Locke, "an excellent learned gentleman and student of Christ Church," at Oxford, was appointed its secretary, while John Evelyn continued to be a member. The first business of the council was to warn the governor of Jamaica of a design of the Dutch against that island.†

27 Septem. 24 October. Locke and Evelyn in the English Plantation Council.

Meanwhile the king had directed Lovelace to take care that all ships bound for Europe should sail in company, in March, June, and September, that an additional battery should be made at New York, and that the whole government should be put in a condition of defense. As soon as war was declared, the several colonies were warned against the private men-of-war which were being prepared in Holland and Zealand, and were directed to take effectual precautions for their own safety, as well as to seize all Dutch ships and property within their territories.‡

10 March. Precautions in the English American colonies ordered. 3 April.

When the king's letter reached Lovelace, prompt meas-

* Col. Doc., iii., 21, 22, 190–193, 197, 198; Sainsbury, i., 298; Evelyn, ii., 60, 62–66, 74; Palfrey, iii., 33, 273, 274; Mass. H. S. Coll., xxxii., 285; xxxvii., 316; *ante*, 158.

† Col. Doc., iii., 228; Evelyn, ii., 83, 85, 86; Anderson, ii., 522, 523; Palfrey, iii., 33. Locke gave up his secretaryship when his patron, Shaftesbury, quarreled with the court in November, 1673. King's Life of Locke (Bohn's ed.), 34; Evelyn, ii., 74, 94. 95; *post*, p. 249.

‡ Evelyn, ii., 74; Council Min., iii., 99, 100; Col. Rec. Conn., ii., 559, 560.

CHAP. IV. ures were taken for defense. Younge, at Southold, was warned to be on his guard. Instead of a compulsory tax,
1672. a contribution, or "benevolence" from each town, was
24 May. asked by the governor for the repair of Fort James.
30 May. Lovelace's action in New York. Thomas Lovelace, High-sheriff Manning, Allard Anthony,
24 June. 3 July. Captain Richard Morris,* Thomas Gibbs, and Francis
11 July. Rombouts were appointed commissioners to receive and expend the moneys collected. On the king's declaration
6 July. of war coming to hand, it was proclaimed at the Fort Gate and the City Hall, and the fortifications vigorously pushed forward. Counselors Delavall and Steenwyck were dis-
18 July. patched to put Albany in a state of defense. Already the commerce of New York suffered; and Lovelace's own ship, the "Good Fame," with three others belonging to the port, were seized in Holland.†

The restriction of the navigation of the Hudson to New York vessels brought up an interesting question. Massachusetts had insisted, in 1659, that her territory extended as far as the Hudson, and Stuyvesant had distinctly rejected her claim. But the Massachusetts governor now wrote
12 March. to Lovelace, desiring that her boundary might be settled,
Territorial question between New York and Massachusetts. and free passage up and down the Hudson be allowed to her people. This letter was brought to New York by John Paine, of Boston, who was interested in the Massachusetts
8 August. grant of 1659. Lovelace, however, declined to recognize any rights claimed by Massachusetts, which ought to have been settled by the royal commissioners; and he referred the whole subject to the Duke of York. On his re-
23 October. turn to Boston, Paine obtained the grant of a tract of land ten miles square, "at or near Hudson's River," and free trade with the Indians forever. But, as Massa-
1673. chusetts vessels could not navigate that river, and "be-
7 May. cause a hill of a vast extent impedes the passage to that

* Captain Richard Morris died soon after this, leaving an only son, Lewis; and administration of his estate was granted to Secretary Nicolls and others, by whom word was sent to Lewis Morris, of Barbadoes, an elder brother of the deceased: N. Y. Surr. Rec. Wills, i., 173; Bolton, ii., 287, 288; Col. Doc., ii., 595, 617; *ante*, 140, *note*.

† Council Min., iii., 99, 100, 108, 114, 115; Gen. Ent., iv., 57, 139, 148, 149, 156, 161, 165, 170; Col. MSS., xxii., 130, 134; Thompson, i., 150; Col. Doc., iii., 185; *ante*, 152. The declaration of war against the Dutch was proclaimed at Boston on the 28th of May, 1672, the first instance of such a measure; Connecticut called a special court for 26 June, and Rhode Island took similar precautions: Mass. Rec., iv. (ii.), 517; Hutch., i., 283, 284; Coll., 441; Palfrey, iii., 120; Col. Rec. Conn., ii., 180–183, 559–561; Mass. H. S. Coll., xxx., 82, 83; R. I. Rec., ii., 461–464.

CHAP. IV. 1672.

place," Paine was allowed to take up another tract, "into which passage may be found for transportation overland."*

Question about Prudence Island, in Rhode Island.

The visit of Paine to New York, however, gave rise to another claim of territory. He had bought Prudence Island, in Narragansett Bay, from the representatives of Williams and Winthrop, and was astonished to find that Lovelace claimed it as belonging to New York under the duke's patent. The pretension was as absurd as that of Massachusetts to any part of the Valley of the Hudson. Nevertheless, Paine thought it best to take a patent for his island from Lovelace, who readily gave it, in consideration of liberal contributions to the repair of Fort James. By
Lovelace's patent, Prudence Island was made a free town- 25 July.
ship, under the name of "Sophy Manor," of which Paine
was appointed governor for his life, subordinate to the 7 August.
jurisdiction of New York. But Rhode Island, very prop-
erly resenting Lovelace's usurpation, arrested the unfortu- 6 Septem. 9 Septem.
nate Paine; who, not long afterward, was convicted of at- 23 October. 29 October.
tempting to introduce a foreign jurisdiction.†

In New Jersey, disaffection had meanwhile grown so strong that those who desired to escape paying the proprietors' quit-rents sent deputies to an anarchical assembly
at Elizabethtown, which deposed Governor Philip Carte- 14 May.
ret, and appointed in his place his newly-arrived cousin,
Captain James Carteret, the "weak and dissolute," but legitimate younger son of Sir George. Lovelace and his
council did their best to reconcile the dispute; but the 11 June.
usurper rejected the friendly offices of New York, and
claimed that he was justified by the instructions of the 14 June.
proprietors of New Jersey. Philip Carteret therefore ap- 1 July.
pointed Captain John Berry to be his deputy, and sailed for 20 July.
Guernsey under a passport from Lovelace, accompanied by 18 Septem.
Secretary James Bollen, to state the case at London. After Philip Carteret's departure, James, who usurped his of- 12 October.
fice, corresponded with Lovelace; but without any result.‡ 13 October.

James Carteret assumes the government of New Jersey.

* *Ante*, 168, 182; vol. i., 655, 671, 672; Col. Doc., vi., 143, 159; vii., 224, 334, 563, 564, 596, 597; viii., 371, 439; Hutch., i., 159, 160; Gen. Ent., iv., 177, 178, 179; Col. MSS., xxii., 137, 149; Mass. Rec., iv. (i.), 395, 396 (ii.), 548, 558, 570; Mass. H. S. Coll., xxxvii., 512. The Western Railroad from Springfield to Albany now triumphantly surmounts this "hill of a vast extent."

† Patents, iv., 86-90; Col. MSS., xxii., 138, 139; R. I. Col. Rec., i., 45, 46; Arnold, i., 87, 105, 362, 363; Palfrey, iii., 109.

‡ Council Min., iii., 101; Gen. Ent., iv., 142-143, 171, 207, 208, 218; Eliz. Bill in Chan-

CHAP. IV.

1672.

Fresh troubles now occurred on the Delaware. A party of Marylanders came to the Hoarkill, and, assisted by Daniel Brown, a planter, assaulted the magistrates, and carried off all the plunder they could. Brown was afterward sent a prisoner to New York, where he was tried and convicted, but was released on promise of amendment.

1 July.

12 August.

Maryland truculence rebuked by New York.

Lovelace quickly rebuked Calvert for allowing his people to commit, for a second time, such outrages in the Duke of York's territories "in these portending troublous times, wherein all true-hearted Englishmen are buckling on their armour," and required him to punish the offenders. The New York governor's prompt intervention saved Delaware from "the imminent peril of being absorbed in Maryland." The Duke of York was soon advised of the truculence of Lord Baltimore's agents; and Carr was directed to guard against the Maryland people, who, following up "their former violent action" in 1669, had again invaded a dependency of New York, "after so long quiet possession of those parts by His Royal Highness's deputies under His Majesty's obedience, and by other nations before that, several years before the date of the Lord Baltimore's patent, whom they never disturbed by arms, and whose right is now devolved upon the Duke."*

7 October.

A memorable event of this year was the visit of the English Quaker, George Fox, to America. Sailing to Barbadoes, he spent several months there with Lewis Morris and other "Friends." Early in 1672 he went to Jamaica, and thence to Maryland. Passing through Newcastle, Fox traversed the wilderness of New Jersey to Middletown,

March.

April.

cery, 35; N. J. H. S. Proc., i. (ii.), 23, 30; Douglas, ii., 269, 271, 272; Chalmers, i., 616; S. Smith, 68; Gordon, 29; Bancroft, ii., 319; Whitehead, 55–57; Collins's Peerage, iv., 213; *ante*, 177. James Carteret seems to have enjoyed the genial society of New York during the winter, as he was married, by license from Lovelace, on 15 April, 1673, to Frances, daughter of Counselor Thomas Delavall: Gen. Ent., iv., 277; N. Y. Marriages (1860), 68, 105. He appears to have been a sad rake, and "a very profligate person," but of "a good understanding." He was afterward separated from his wife and allowed an annuity by his father, who would not "acknowledge him as his son, as before:" see Dankers's and Sluyter's Journal (1867), 137, 138. See also Hist. Mag., x., 157, for a notice of the descendants of James Carteret and Frances Delavall. There is no reason for the brand of *illegitimacy* which Whitehead, 55, and Mulford, 152, have endeavored to stamp on James Carteret: compare Eliz. Bill, 35; Collins's Peerage, iv., 213; Douglas, ii., 272; Chalmers, i., 616, 625. "Natural," as used by Chalmers, does not mean "illegitimate;" Hist. Mag., ii. (iii.), 110.

* Council Min., iii., 110; Gen. Ent., iv., 188, 189, 211–213; S. Smith, 72–76; Hazard's Ann. Penn., 397–402, 405; Bancroft, ii., 238, 319, 320; Proud, i., 131, 132; Col. MSS., xx., 37, 38; Col. Doc., iii., 186; *ante*, 164. Yet Chalmers, i., 361, 634, affirms that Calvert took possession of the country around Cape Henlopen, which the Dutch "had relinquished;" and Grahame repeats Chalmers's falsehood.

and went from there to Gravesend, on Long Island. At Oyster Bay he calmed the quarrels of the "Friends." At Rhode Island he met several Connecticut Quakers. From there he crossed over to Shelter Island, accompanied by several "Friends," one of whom was "John Jay, a planter in Barbadoes." He visited Oyster Bay, Flushing, and Jamaica again, and held several "precious meetings." On his return through New Jersey, Fox came near losing his companion, Jay, who was thrown from his horse, but was restored by the skill of the Quaker apostle. At Newcastle, Fox was lodged by Carr in his own house, where the first Quaker meeting in Delaware was held. After revisiting Maryland, Fox passed on to Virginia and North Carolina, and in the spring of the following year sailed from the Chesapeake for England.*

CHAP. IV. 1672. June. Visit of George Fox to America. August. Septem.

There were, at this time, seven Jesuit missionaries among the five Iroquois nations. Bruyas, the superior, remained with Boniface among the Mohawks, who still kept on their guard against their old enemies, the Mahicans. At Oneida, Millet found the savages as obdurate as the rock from which they derived their name. John de Lamberville, at Onondaga, aided by the active zeal of Garakontié, had better hopes.†

Jesuit missionaries among the Iroquois.

Carheil, now cured of his disease, returned to the Cayugas, and Raffeix was transferred to assist Garnier among the Senecas. In a letter to Dablon, Raffeix described Cayuga as "the most beautiful country I have seen in America. It is situated in latitude 42 degrees and a half, and the needle dips there scarcely more than ten degrees. It lies between two lakes, and is not more than four leagues wide, with almost continuous plains, while the woods which border them are very beautiful. Mohawk is a narrow valley, often very stony, and always covered with fogs. The mountains which enclose it seem to me to be of very poor soil. Oneida and Onondaga appear to be a very rugged country, and little adapted to hunting. The same is true of Seneca. Every year they kill more than a thousand

24 June. Raffeix's description of Cayuga.

* Fox's Journal (Phil. ed.), 435–464; Sewell, 509–512; Col. Doc., ii., 619; Arnold, i., 360, 361; Thompson, ii., 82, 83; Hazard's Reg. Penn., vi., 181; Palfrey, iii., 106–108; Mass. H. S. Coll., xxxvii., 288; *ante*, vol. i., 635. Fox returned to Bristol on the 28th of June, 1673.

† Relation, 1672, 18–22; 1672–3, 33–39; Douniol, i., 4–8; Charlevoix, ii., 222, 231, 232; Shea, 198, 268, 281–283; *ante*, 181.

CHAP. IV. 1672. deer in the neighborhood of Cayuga. Fishing is as abundant here as at Onondaga, as well for salmon as for eels and other fishes. Four leagues from here I saw, on the brink of a River, within quite a small space, eight or ten very fine salt springs. It is there that they spread numbers of nets to catch pigeons, of which they often take seven or eight hundred at one haul. The Lake of Tiohero [Cayuga], one of the two which border on our village, is fourteen leagues long, by one or two wide. Swans and bustards abound there all the winter; and, in the spring, one sees nothing but continual clouds of all sorts of game. The River of Ochouéguen [Oswego], which flows out of this Lake, divides itself at its beginning into several channels surrounded by prairies, with here and there very pleasant and pretty deep bays, where the wild fowl resort. I find the inhabitants of Çayuga more tractable and less fierce than the Onondagas and Oneidas; and, if God had humiliated them as much as the Mohawks, I believe that the faith would be established there more easily than in any one of the Iroquois nations. They reckon more than three hundred warriors among them, and a prodigious multitude of small children."*

20 July. Garnier's account of Seneca. From Seneca, Garnier sent his superior a discouraging account of the three missions of Conception, Saint Michael, and Saint James. The expedition of Courcelles to Lake Ontario, which at first had been thought to be an intended invasion, retarded conversions; and an ill feeling arose against the "black robes," who were charged with being sorcerers and spies to report every thing to Onnontio. 31 July. With great joy, Garnier welcomed Raffeix to assist him among the Senecas, who now numbered from twelve to thirteen thousand souls.†

The war against the Andastes was still carried on, chiefly by the Cayugas and the Senecas. During the summer,

* Relation, 1672, 22, 23; Col. Doc., iii., 251. The salt springs which Raffeix describes are those at Montezuma.

† Relation, 1672, 18, 24–26; 1672–3, 108; Col. Doc., ix., 97, *note;* Shea, 292; *ante*, 179. The Annual Relations of the Jesuits were not printed later than this year at Paris, owing to the request of Courcelles: Faillon, iii., 312. Dablon, however, who remained superior general, at Quebec, until 1693, compiled several others. Two of these, for 1672–1673, and 1673–1679, have been published from the originals at Quebec, by Mr. John G. Shea. Mr. James Lenox has likewise printed the Relation for 1676–1677. Charles Douniol, of Paris, also published two volumes in 1861, entitled "Mission du Canada," containing the Relations from 1672 to 1679, copied from the originals at Quebec and at Rome.

1672.

The war between the Iroquois and Andastes.

an Iroquois party descending the Susquehanna River were attacked and routed by sixty young Susquehannas. The sympathies of the French missionaries were with the latter. "God preserve the Andastes, who have only three hundred warriors, and bless their arms to humiliate the Iroquois and preserve to us peace and our missions," wrote Raffeix to Dablon, his superior general, at Quebec.*

6 April. Courcelles recalled, and Frontenac appointed governor of Canada. 7 April.

Courcelles's expedition the last year to Lake Ontario so affected his health that he asked to be relieved; and the king appointed in his place Louis de Buade, Count of Frontenac, a veteran lieutenant general in the French army. Frontenac was quick, firm, penetrating, domineering, and a scholar. He was instructed, among other things, to keep his government prepared to repel, and, if necessary, to attack the Iroquois; to favor "contiguous clearances" rather than scattered settlements; and to counterbalance the influence of the Jesuits by encouraging the Sulpitians and Recollets.†

July.

August.

Courcelles projects a fort at Cataracouy, or Kingston.

The summer before Frontenac reached Canada, a congress was held at Montreal, to which more than five hundred red men came in one hundred and fifty canoes. A new treaty of peace was confirmed in the presence of Courcelles. At the same time, the governor invited the principal Iroquois chiefs to meet him at Cataracouy, on the northern shore of Lake Ontario. Having assembled there, Courcelles flattered them by presents, and got their consent to build a fort at that place, where they might come to trade with the French. They did not perceive that the object of the Canadian governor was really "to hold them in check," after they should have ended their war with the Susquehannas, and provide an entrepôt for himself. The work was at once projected by Courcelles; but its completion was left to other hands.‡

Septem.

On his return to Quebec, Courcelles met Frontenac, who had just arrived, and easily convinced him of the importance of the enterprise he had begun on Lake Ontario.

* Relation, 1672, 20, 24. It has been supposed by Charlevoix, ii., 244, that the Susquehannas, or Andastes, were subjugated by the Iroquois in 1672. But this event does not seem to have happened until 1675: see Douniol, i., 267; ii., 44, 99; Hist. Mag., ii., 297; Col. Doc., ix., 110, 111, 227; *ante*, 100, *note*.

† Col. Doc., ix., 85–88, 791; Charlevoix, ii., 191, 247; Garneau, i., 201, 205, 207; Sparks's La Salle, 15, 16; Faillon, iii., 416–418; *ante*, 181.

‡ Relation, 1672, 21; Charlevoix, ii., 244, 245; Shea, 282; Garneau, i., 206.

CHAP. IV. 1672. 17 Septem. Frontenac governor of Canada. 2 Novem.

Frontenac's first act was to publish his king's declaration of war against the Dutch. In his dispatches to France, he approved of Courcelles's projected fort at Cataracouy "to prevent the Iroquois carrying to the Dutch the peltries, for which they go to the Ottawas;" and as it might strengthen the mission at Quinté Bay, he promised to go there himself the next spring.*

Courcelles soon afterward returned to France, accompanied by Talon, in a new ship of five hundred tons burthen, which had been built at Quebec. As the Mississippi was supposed to empty into the Gulf of California, Talon recommended to Frontenac that its exploration should be intrusted to Louis Jolliet, of Quebec, an "aspirant to the Ministry," who had accompanied Saint Lusson the year before to Lake Superior, and who had "already been almost at that great river, the mouth of which he promises to see." Jolliet was accordingly dispatched to Michilimackinac, with orders to Marquette to join the expedition. On the feast of the Immaculate Conception he reached the Jesuit missionary, who longed to visit the Mississippi; and the winter was spent in preparations for their journey.†

Jolliet sent to explore the Missis-sippi with Marquette.

8 Decem.

While Lovelace was at Albany the last year, he regulated the Indian trade at Schenectady as the frontier. The people of that town now bought from the Mohawks the land on both sides of the river, as far as "Kinaquariones," where the last battle was fought between the Mohawks and Mahicans in 1669. A separate court was soon afterward established at Schenectady.‡

13 July. Schenectady affairs.

6 Septem.

Under the new arrangements at Esopus, its three villages prospered abundantly, and twenty-five thousand "schepels" of corn were raised there this year. Not far from the village of Kingston, the land owned by Captain Chambers was erected into a manor, with the usual privileges, and

Prosperity of Esopus.

16 October. Fox Hall.

* Col. Doc., ix., 90–94, 791; Quebec MSS., ii. (ii.), 116; Charlevoix, ii., 245; Garneau, i., 207–210; Faillon, iii., 456, 457; *ante*, 148, 149.

† Relation, 1672, 1, 2, 36; 1672–3, 146; Col. Doc., ix., 89, 92, 121, 668, 793, 804; Charlevoix, ii., 245, 246, 248, 254, 255; Bancroft, iii., 153, 155, 156; Garneau, i., 205–207, 231, 232; La Potherie, ii., 130; Shea's Disc. Miss., xxvii., xxviii., lxv., lxxix., 4, 5, 6; Hist. Mag., v., 237; Douniol, i., 193, 194; Faillon, iii., 260, 312, 417–421; *ante*, 170, 179.

‡ Gen. Ent., iv., 90; Council Min., iii., 116; Col. MSS., xxii., 132; *ante*, 161. On the 27th of January, 1673, Anthonia van Curler, in consideration of her house and barns being destroyed, and of her husband, Arendt van Curler, being lost in the public service (*ante*, 121), was allowed to sell rum and lead, but not powder, to the Indians, for a year and two months: Council Min., iii., 120; Col. Doc., ii., 652.

named "Fox Hall." Soon afterward Counselor Delavall was authorized to build a store-house adjoining the redoubt at the Strand, near Kingston.* CHAP. III. 1672.

The provincial law, in cases of divorce, was now settled. Daniel Denton, of Jamaica, who had gone to London to publish his work on New York, found, on his return, that his wife, Abigail, had been unfaithful during his absence. He applied to the Court of Sessions for a divorce; but that tribunal having no jurisdiction, he laid his case before the governor and council. Lovelace, observing that it was "conformable to the Laws of this Government, as well as to the practice of the civil law, and the laws of our nation of England," granted Denton a divorce from his wife. But in this decision the governor seems to have followed the Dutch rather than the English law.† 19 March. The law of divorce in New York. 26 June.

At the autumn session of the Court of Assizes an interesting case was heard on appeal from the court on the Delaware. Amigart Pappegoya, the daughter of the former Swedish Governor Printz, brought an action in ejectment against Andrew Carr, to recover her patrimonial estate in the island of Tinicum. The plaintiff's attorney was John Sharpe, assisted by Samuel Edsall, and Jacob Milborne, who was specially admitted to plead. John Rider appeared for the defendant. The writings in German were translated for the court by the Lutheran "Domine" Arensius, and those in Low Dutch by Nicholas Bayard. After a full hearing the case went to the jury, who brought in a verdict for the plaintiff, and judgment was given in her favor.‡ 2 October. Interesting appeal in the Court of Assizes. 3 October. 4 October.

* Col. Doc., ii., 526; Lambrechtsen, 115; Gen. Ent., iv., 216, 273; O'Call., ii., 394, 395; Val. Man., 1853, 381.

† Gen. Ent., iv., 153; Dunlap, ii., App. cxviii.; Daly's Introd., 27. The Court of Assizes, however, in the following October, allowed the divorced Abigail Denton to marry again: Court of Assizes, ii., 317. In October, 1670, the Court of Assizes divorced Rebecca Leveridge from her husband, Eleazer, on account of his alleged impotence: Council Min., iii., 27; Court of Assizes, ii., 486, 519–522, 607, 608; Thompson, i., 256. The governor and council, in October, 1672, divorced Thomas Petitt, of Newtown, from his wife Sarah, because of her adultery; and Mary Cole from Daniel Sutton, because of his bigamy: Gen. Ent., iv., 213, 214, 215. The law, however, was afterward settled otherwise. Chancellor Kent observes that "for more than one hundred years preceding the Revolution, no divorce took place in the colony of New York;" and that there was no way of dissolving a marriage in the lifetime of the parties but by a special act of the Legislature. The Court of Chancery was not authorized to grant divorces *à vinculo* until 1787, and then only for adultery: Kent's Commentaries, ii., 97, 98.

‡ Court of Assizes, ii., 293–300; Gen. Ent., iv., 260–262; Col. MSS., xx., 26; S. Hazard's Ann. Penn., 400, 401, 404; *ante*, vol. i., 397, 557. Sharpe and Rider appear to have been regular practitioners: Col. Doc., ii., 617, 709, 718; iii., 202; Doc. Hist., iii., 58, 60; Mass.

CHAP. IV. 1672. 2 October to 7 October. New laws enacted at the Court of Assizes.

Several important public measures were adopted at the same session of the Court of Assizes. As servants frequently ran away from their masters into other governments, it was ordered that all strangers without passports should be liable to arrest. English weights and measures only were to be used throughout the province before the next Old Style New-year day, on the 25th of March. The laws as to parochial churches were to be duly observed, and "although divers persons may be of different judgments, yet all shall contribute to the minister established and allowed of, which is no way judged to be an infringement of the liberty of conscience to the which they may pretend." The contributions for the renovation of the fort were to be sent to New York, or to "the Ferry," before the next Christmas. It was also ordered that a Boston shilling should pass for one shilling, and a good Spanish piece of eight, whether of Mexico, Seville, or a pillar piece, should be valued at six shillings in all New York transactions.*

10 Decem. Monthly post to New England established by Lovelace.

Lovelace now issued a proclamation that, conformably to the king's commands to promote correspondence, and the advancement of commerce and general intelligence between his colonies, a monthly post should be established to go from New York to Boston; and that, accordingly, a sworn messenger would be dispatched on the first of the next January, to convey letters or small packets to Hartford, Boston, and other places on his way. All letters were to be deposited in the secretary's office, and the postage to be prepaid before the bag was closed. In a private letter which Lovelace intended to dispatch by his pioneer post, he wrote to Winthrop: "I here present you with two rarities, a pacquett of the latest intelligence I could meet withal, and a Post. By the first, you will see what has

27 Decem.

H. S. Coll., xxx., 108. Edsall afterward became quite prominent in colonial affairs: Col. Doc., ii., 576, 720; iii., 75, 589, 683, 789. Jacob Milborne, who became still more prominent, was a young Englishman, who had been convicted of clipping the king's coin, and sold as a servant in Barbadoes. He was afterward bought by a Hartford man; but because of his stubbornness and disobedience, was transferred several times from one master to another. Having finally got his liberty, he came to New York in 1668, being then twenty years old, and was employed by Counselor Thomas Delavall to keep his books and manage his affairs; in which service he remained until this year: Col. Doc., iii., 301, 621, 674, 727, 755, 789; Doc. Hist., ii., 28, 42; Col. MSS., xxvi., 139; Gen. Ent., xxxii., 19.

* Court of Assizes, ii., 323; Col. MSS., xxii., 9, 142; N. Y. H. S. Coll., i., 420–424; Thompson, i., 150. Frequent cases of the prohibition of the export of grain, either by order of the governor and council, or of the Court of Assizes, occurred from time to time in New York.

1672. Lovelace's postal regulations.

been acted on the stage of Europe; by the latter you will meet with a monthly fresh supply; so that if it receive but the same ardent inclinations from you as first it hath from myself, by our monthly advisoes all publique occurrences may be transmitted between us, together with severall other great conveniencys of publique importance, consonant to the commands laid upon us by His sacred Majestie, who strictly injoins all his American subjects to enter into a close correspondency with each other. This I look upon as the most compendious means to beget a mutual understanding; and that it may receive all the countenance from you for its future duration, I shall acquaint you with the modell I have proposed; and if you please but to make an addition to it, or substraction, or any other alteration, I shall be ready to comply with you. This person that has undertaken the imployment I conceaved most proper, being both active, stout, and indefatigable. He is sworne as to his fidelity. I have affixt an annuall sallery on him, which, together with the advantage of his letters and other small portable packes, may afford him a handsome livelyhood. Hartford is the first stage I have designed him to change his horse, where constantly I expect he should have a fresh one lye, *leger*. All the letters outward shall be delivered gratis, with a signification of *Post Payd* on the superscription; and reciprocally, we expect all to us free. Each first Monday of the month he sets out from New York, and is to return within the month from Boston to us againe. The maile has divers baggs, according to the townes the letters are designed to, which are all sealed up 'till their arrivement, with the seale of the Secretarie's Office, whose care it is on Saturday night to seale them up. Only by-letters are in an open bag, to dispense by the wayes. Thus you see the scheme I have drawne to promote a happy correspondence. I shall only beg of you your furtherance to so universall a good work; that is to afford him directions where, and to whom to make his application to upon his arrival at Boston; as likewise to afford him what letters you can to establish him in that imployment there. It would be much advantagious to our designe, if in the intervall you discoursed with some of the most able woodmen, to make out the best and most facile

CHAP. IV. 1672. way for a Post, which, in processe of tyme would be the King's best highway; as likewise passages and accommodation at Rivers, fords, or other necessary places."*

Lovelace is certainly entitled to the credit of having established the first post between New York and New England. But the pioneer whom he intended to dispatch on New-year's day was kept back until the Albany news reached the capital. He was then sworn, and instructed to behave civilly; to inquire of Winthrop "how to form the best post-road;" to mark trees "that shall direct passengers the best way;" and "to detect, and cause to be apprehended all fugitive soldiers and servants" who might run away from New York. By him the governor wrote again to Winthrop that the last ships from England to Maryland and Virginia brought "little tidings save the despair of a peace between the Protestant nations. Presses, both by sea and land, are very vigorously prosecuted. The Hollander has absolutely lost three of their Provinces. They have disposed of all their men-of-war, and given liberty to all that will venture on privateering; in so much that forty saile, well fitted, are dispatched towards the West Indies. If so, it will be high time for us to beginne to buckle on our armour, and to put ourselves into such a posture of defence as is most suitable to our severall conditions. However, it will be absolutely necessary that in the first place, a good understanding be made and preserved amongst us, conformable to His Majestie's gracious care and good pleasure; to which end I have erected a constant post, which shall monthly pass betwixt us, or oftener, if occasion requires. I desire of you to favour the undertaking by your best skill and countenance. I have writt to you my more particular desires in a former letter which this bearer brings likewise."†

1673. 22 Jan. First post messenger from New York.

22 Jan. Lovelace to Winthrop.

Murder case at Albany. 27 Jan.

The delayed messenger from Albany brought news of the murder of a soldier there by two "North Indians," who were promptly arrested by Pynchon, at Springfield. Lovelace at once commissioned Salisbury to try them at a spe-

* Gen. Ent., iv., 243, 244; Barber and Howe's N. Y. Coll., 290; Val. Man., 1857, 542; Bolton, i., 139; ii., 321, 322; Mass. H. S., Trumbull Papers, MSS. xx., 110; *ante*, 182.

† Gen. Ent., iv., 252, 253; Val. Man., 1857, 543, 544; Mass. H. S., Trumbull Papers, MSS. xx., 109; Hist. Mag., iv., 50. Massachusetts does not appear to have taken any steps respecting a post until 1677: see Mass. Rec., v., 147, 148; Palfrey, iii., 306, 548.

cial court at Albany. The murderers were convicted and executed; and the savages retained a lasting memory of the sure and swift justice of the English.* CHAP. IV. 1673.

Lovelace had given no attention to the duke's territory at Pemaquid. Massachusetts, however, had claimed jurisdiction over that region; and after the Peace of Breda, the French insisted that Acadia extended as far west as the Kennebec River. Saint Lusson had visited Pemaquid after his return from the West, and found the colonists there apparently glad to come under French authority. Lovelace therefore wrote to them to send to New York "a modell of such a government as shall be most conducing to the happiness of that colony, both to its safety, traffic, and increase of inhabitants; promising, upon the reception of that scheme, not only to invest you with ample power to exercise your authority both to ecclesiastick as civill affairs, but will be ready on all occasions to be assisting to you in the preservation of all your rights and interest against any sinister obstructions."† 16 Febr'y. Lovelace's orders about Pemaquid.

At Martha's Vineyard affairs went quietly on under the government of Mayhew, and a code of laws was passed at a General Court held at Edgartown. Nantucket, however, "would not proceed" in the same way; and Lovelace appointed Richard Gardner its chief magistrate, in place of Coffin, with instructions. One of these was that the island should thereafter be known as the town of Sherborne.‡ 15 April. Martha's Vineyard and Nantucket.

Meanwhile, Philip Carteret had succeeded in England. At the request of the proprietors of New Jersey, the Duke of York wrote to Lovelace that the grants of Nicolls to Baker and others being made after his own conveyance to 1672. 25 Novem. The duke's orders to Lovelace about New Jersey.

* Gen. Ent., iv., 248–251; Col. Doc., iv., 994; Hist. Mag., iv., 50, 51. On the 28th of January, 1673, "Jo. Clarke," who appears to have belonged to the garrison of Fort James, wrote by the same post to Salisbury, among other things, the following city news: "The other day we had like to have lost our hangman, Ben. Johnson; for he, being taken in divers thefts and robberies, convicted and found guilty, 'scaped his neck through want of another hangman to truss him up; so that all the punishment he receaved for his 3 yeares' roguery in thieving and stealing (which was never found out 'till now) was only thirty-nine stripes at the whipping-post, loss of an ear, and banishment. Capt. Manning had likewise two servants that he employed at his Island, taken with him in their villainy; but they being not found so guilty as he, came off with whipping and banishment. All this happened about a fortnight since, but 'tis two months since they were apprehended."

† Gen. Ent., iv., 258, 259; Maine H. S. Coll., i., 130, 131; v., 6–8, 247, 248; Col. Doc., ix., 74, 75, 119, 265, 379, 433; Mass. Rec., iv. (ii.), 519; Charlevoix, ii., 256; La Potherie, ii., 130; Williamson, i., 440–442; Hutch. Mass., i., 325; *ante*, 141, 179.

‡ Deeds, i., 78; iii., 57, 85–89; Col. MSS., xxiv., 92; Hough's Nantucket Papers, 42–59, 71; *ante*, 174.

CHAP. IV. 1672. Berkeley and Carteret, were void; and as the latter had promised to instruct their agents to assist the governor of New York, "I do desire you," he added, "and all others herein concerned, in like manner effectually to assist them in furthering the settlement and maintaining the quiet of these parts." (9 Decem.) The king also directed Berry, the acting governor, to notify all the inhabitants of New Jersey to yield obedience to the proprietors, who had "the sole power" under him.*

1673. 5 May. When these documents were published by Berry, the insurgents submitted. James Carteret retired with his young bride to New York, whence he soon afterward sailed for Virginia. (15 May. James Carteret retires from New Jersey.) Lovelace read in council the duke's orders about New Jersey, and supported the proprietors' authority there. (2 July.) Willis and Winthrop also wrote to Berry and Sir George Carteret in favor of emigrants from Connecticut to New Jersey, and recommended convenient townships as "best conducing to safety and the advancing of civil societies."† (29 July.)

March. Panic in New York about Dutch attack. While Lovelace was at Anne Hook's Neck, or Hutchinson's Bay, on postal business, news came to New York that a Dutch squadron was coming from the West Indies to Virginia, and thence northward; and the governor was summoned back to the capital by express from Manning. Seeing no enemy, Lovelace "slited" his subordinate's care, and said "this is one of Manning's 'larrums." He did not even prepare the fort to withstand an enemy, although he had received the contribution money. Soldiers were, however, summoned from Albany, Esopus, and Delaware, and (1 May.) nearly one hundred and thirty enlisted men were mustered. (29 May.) At the general training the volunteer and regular force amounted to three hundred and thirty. But soon afterward, Salisbury, with his men, were sent back to Albany, (July.) and the whole number left in garrison at Fort James did not exceed eighty.‡

24 June. Precautions and war orders. The exportation of wheat, however, was prohibited, owing to "these times of trouble." On account of the scarcity of wampum, it was directed that six white and three

* Col. MSS., xxii., 144; Eliz. Bill, 35, 36, 37; Leaming and Spicer, 31–41; Whitehead, 57, 58; Hatfield, 149–154; *ante*, 49, 84, 189.

† Coun. Min., i. (ii.), 147; Gen. Ent., iv., 277; Eliz. Bill, 37, App. 31; Whitehead, 58, 59; Col. Doc., iii., 200, 214; Mass. H. S. Coll., xxx., 84, 85; *ante*, 190, *note*.

‡ Doc. Hist., iii., 54, 57, 59; Bolton, i., 518; *ante*, vol. i., 334, 366, 595.

black beads should pass for a stuyver or penny, instead of eight white and four black, as formerly. The Duke's Laws were also ordered to be enforced in Esopus.* CHAP. IV. 1673. 12 June.

Lovelace for some time intended to visit Winthrop, who had recently lost his wife; and now, "having urgent occasions," he set out for Connecticut, leaving Manning, as usual, in charge of Fort James; but "without any order to repair the same for to make defence against an enemy." Before the governor saw that fortress again, events occurred which he does not appear to have apprehended.† 15 May. 20 July. Lovelace visits Winthrop in Connecticut.

The "Cabal" of Charles the Second had, meanwhile, been the only gainers by his war with the Dutch. Parliament was asked by the king for assistance. Shaftesbury, his chancellor, bitterly denounced the Dutch, whose commerce he described, in glowing rhetoric, as leading them to "an universal Empire, as great as Rome." Following the key-note which Dryden had sounded ten years before, he compared Holland to Carthage, which England, like Rome, must destroy — "*Delenda est Carthago.*" Both Charles and Shaftesbury spoke to little purpose. Parliament suspected the orthodoxy of the Duke of York, and disliked the king's meretricious alliance with Roman Catholic France no less than his unjustifiable war with Protestant Holland. A supply was voted, but it was coupled with a condition to which Charles was obliged to give his reluctant assent. This was the "Test Act," which continued to be an English law until the reign of George the Fourth. It required all persons holding any civil or military offices in England, Wales, Berwick, Jersey, or Guernsey, to take the oaths of allegiance and supremacy; publicly receive the sacrament of the Lord's Supper according to the usage of the Church of England; and subscribe a declaration against the Romish doctrine of Transubstantiation. In consequence of this law, the Duke of York, who for some time had secretly been a Roman Catholic, candidly declared his religious faith, and in a flood of tears resigned all the offices which he held under the crown, including that of lord high admiral of England. But as the Test 4 Febr'y. Charles and Shaftesbury on the Dutch. 29 March. The English "Test Act" passed. Effect of the Test Act on the Duke of York.

* Council Min., iii., 129, 145, 146, 153-157; S. Hazard, 405; Proud, i., 133, 134.

† Council Min., iii., 147; Trumbull Papers, xx., 104, 109; Mass. H. S. MSS.; Col. Doc., iii, 198; Doc. Hist., iii, 57, 59; Col. Rec. Conn., ii., 242; Eliz. Bill, 6.

CHAP. IV. 1673.

Act did not extend to Scotland and Ireland, nor to the British Plantations, the duke's admiralty jurisdiction over them remained unimpaired.*

Parliament again turned its attention to the American colonies. Their commerce had already been restrained by the Navigation Laws; but "the avarice of English shopkeepers" now required that commerce to be taxed. It was observed that the British Plantations enjoyed a profitable intercolonial traffic, and sold their commodities to foreign nations, "to the diminution of the customs and the navigation of the kingdom." Parliament therefore enacted that sugars, tobacco, ginger, and certain other productions, when exported from any English colony, should pay the same duties to the crown as if they were landed in England; and that these duties were to be collected at such places and by such officers as the commissioners of the customs in England should appoint. This selfish measure "formed the seed-plot on which was raised the subsequent system of colonial revenue."†

29 March. Colonial policy of the English Parliament.

During the first year of the war the United Provinces suffered terrible calamities. Although the Dutch had, a century before, proved themselves the first soldiers in the world, they had, through a long interval of peace and prosperity, become unused to military service on land. Their whole energies had been directed to commercial and naval enterprise. Holland seemed almost like a rich galleon, with De Ruyter for captain, and De Witt for pilot. One of the Pensionary's maxims had always been to foster the sea rather than the land forces of the republic. The young Prince of Orange, on the other hand, chafed at his thraldom, and longed to be at the head of armies. It is

1672. The Dutch Republic again at war.

De Witt, De Ruyter, and William of Orange.

* Statute 25 Ch. II., cap. ii.; Parl. Hist., iv., 495, 502–585; Kennett, iii., 289–294; Clarke's James II., i., 483; Burnet, i., 346–352; Rapin, ii., 665–671; Basnage, ii., 395–399; King's Locke, 34; Evelyn, ii., 88, 89; Anderson, ii., 527; Hume, vi., 468–472; Lingard, xii., 289–298, 303; Campbell's Chancellors, iii., 314-317; Col. Doc., iii., 239; Leaming and Spicer, 46; *ante*, 3. The Test Act did not extend to the English Plantations of its own force, because they were not particularly named, or intended to be embraced in the statute: Col. Doc., iii., 357; Chalmers's Ann., i., 240; Rev. Col., i., 173, 236; Blackstone, i., 108, 109; Jacob, iv., 401; v., 15, 160. It was first extended to the American Plantations by William III., in 1689, of his own will, by clauses in the Royal Commissions and Instructions to the several Governors: Col. Doc., iii., 623, 685; *post*, p. 264.

† 25 Charles II., cap. vii.; Anderson, ii., 521, 522; Chalmers's Ann., i., 317, 320; Rev. Col., i., 125, 126, 152, 172; Kennett, iii., 295; Holmes, i., 360; Bancroft, ii., 44; Grahame, i., 92; Palfrey, iii., 33, 34, 279. Chalmers, and those who follow him, using the Old Style, erroneously date this act in 1672. The 25th year of Charles the Second was from 30 January, 1673, to 29 January, 1674.

not surprising that while the Dutch fleets gloriously maintained the honor of their flag against England, their militia, officered by incapable favorites, recoiled before the disciplined veterans of France, led by Condé, and Luxembourg, and Turenne. Before Holland knew it, the Gallic Hannibal was at her gates. Louis established his court at Utrecht. Almost in despair, De Witt opened negotiations with France and England. But the humiliating terms they offered could not be accepted; and spasmodic popular indignation broke out against the Pensionary and his brother. *Oranje Boven, De Witten onder!* "Up with Orange—down with the De Witts"—was the cry.*

CHAP. IV. 1672.

July. Louis at Utrecht.

"Oranje Boven."

William Henry, Prince of Orange, was now in the twenty-second year of his age. "A young man without youth," he concealed under a cold exterior a dauntless soul. But he had been deprived of the stadtholderate enjoyed by his ancestors, and its duties were performed by the Grand Pensionary of Holland, John de Witt, who administered the government with great success until the war with France. The people then began to murmur that their soldiers did not fight well because they were badly officered, and demanded that the Prince of Orange should be made captain general. This was done; and, at the popular cry of "Oranje Boven," William was appointed stadtholder. An army to protect the hearth was now more important than a navy to keep open the port. John de Witt resigned his office of Pensionary, and his brother

William, Prince of Orange.

Made captain general and stadtholder.

* Sylvius, i., 346; Hollandtsche Mercurius, 1672, 89–91; Basnage, ii., 183, 196, 211–260, 283, 284; Le Clerc, iii., 290; Wagenaar, xiv., 26–165; Davies, iii., 91–108; Hume, vi., 454; Lavallée, iii., 220; Martin, i., 345–352; *ante*, p. 185. On the 29th of June, 1672, the partisans of the prince welcomed him at Dordrecht, in Holland, with the old national song, "Wilhelmus van Nassauwen" (*ante*, vol. i., p. 442), and by hoisting an Orange flag above a white flag, the upper one bearing the inscription in Dutch:

"*Oranje boven, de Witten onder;*
Die 't anders meend, die slaat den Donder."

Which may be rendered in English:

"Orange above, the Whites under;
Who thinks not so, be struck by thunder."

The Dutch word *Wit* signifies "White." *De Witten*, or the De Witts, therefore means "the Whites;" and thus the Dordrecht flags, with their inscription, formed a popular double pun. Although the words "*Oranje Boven*" were thus adopted as a popular cry by the partisans of William the Third in 1672, they were known and used long before by the Dutch people, who applied them to their national flag, of which the upper stripe was orange, the middle one white, and the lower one blue (*ante*, vol. i., 19, *note*). These words were also shouted on the 15th of January, 1651, when the young prince was baptized at the Great Church in the Hague: *ante*, p. 2; Aitzema, iii., 551, 552; Basnage, i., 181; Le Clerc, ii., 292; J. C. de Jonge, Oorsprong (1831), 52; Rey's Histoire du Drapeau (1837), ii., 518, 519; J. Ter Gouw, Oorsprong (1863), 44, 45; De Navorscher for 1854, iv., 62, 63; and for 1857, vii., 371.

CHAP. IV.

1672.

The De Witts murdered. 20 August.

Cornelis was imprisoned. The Orangeists attributed the disasters of their country to the party which had lately governed it; and a band of ruffians, bursting into the prison where John de Witt was visiting his brother, butchered them both on the "Plaats" before the Buitenhof at the Hague.*

William's magnanimity.

In almost uncontrolled authority, William now showed the grandeur of his soul. To the desponding States he spoke encouragement. To the proposals of Louis and Charles he answered that, "rather than sign the ruin of the Republic and receive the sovereignty from the hand of its enemies, he would embark with his friends for Batavia." To the suggestion that Holland was lost if he did not accept the terms of France and England, he replied, "There is a sure way never to see it lost, and that is, I will die in the last ditch!"†

The Dutch encouraged.

The spirit of William roused his drooping countrymen. The Dutch remembered what their ancestors had done a century before. The sluices were opened, and the low lands became a vast lake, studded with cities and villages, rising here and there above the waters which washed their ramparts. Again the invaders were forced to retreat, and Holland was saved.‡

1673.

28 May. Naval actions.

4 June.

The Dutch navy was now commanded by De Ruyter and Tromp, who had been reconciled by the Prince of Orange. Prince Rupert took the place of the Duke of York in command of the English fleet, which, being joined by the French, attacked the weaker Dutch off the coast of Zealand. Tromp's division was almost overpowered by the French, when De Ruyter, who was conquering the English, magnanimously checked his own career and hastened to rescue his former rival. The battle was indecisive. Another engagement followed the next week, and the English retreated to the Thames. Two months afterward, one hundred and fifty English and French ships were encountered by seventy-five Dutch off the Helder. A terrible

* Basnage, ii., 284-322; Temple, ii., 257, 258; Wagenaar, xiv., 166-193; Davies, iii., 43, 107-118; Martin, i., 352-357; Sylvius, i., 346-409; D'Estrades, iv., 223, 242; Macaulay, ii., 180; *ante*, 2.

† Burnet, i., 327, 331, 332; Kennett, iii., 292; Dalrymple, i., 53; Rapin, ii., 664; Basnage, ii., 256; Temple, ii., 259; Hume, vi., 465-467; Davies, iii., 121-123; Mackintosh, 320; Macaulay, i., 218, 219; ii., 182.

‡ Burnet, i., 335-337; Temple, ii., 260, 261; Davies, iii., 123; *ante*, vol. i., 442, 443.

conflict followed, in which, as a last exhibition of courage, CHAP. III.
Hollanders and Englishmen rivaled each other in stubborn
valor. From morning until night the churches were filled 1673. 11 August.
with praying Dutch Protestants, while the sound of rapid Last battle between
guns boomed over the low coast of Holland. At length the Dutch and En-
the English retreated, and De Ruyter and Tromp shared glish.
with William of Orange the gratitude of their rescued
fatherland.*

While the countrymen of Grotius were thus fighting for
their hearths, a former province of the Netherlands was unexpectedly annexed to the Dutch Republic. Cornelis Evertsen, a son of the famous admiral, had been sent out from 1672.
Zealand with fifteen ships to harass the enemy in the West 15 Decem. Expedition
Indies, which was effectually done. At Martinico he fell of Evert- sen and
in with four ships dispatched from Amsterdam, under the Binckes.
command of Jacob Binckes. Joining their forces, the two 1673.
commodores followed Krynssen's track to the Chesapeake,
where they took eight, and burned five Virginia tobacco 11/21 July.
ships, in spite of the gallantry of the frigates which were
to convoy them to England. As they were going out of
the James River, the Dutch commodores met a sloop from At Virgin-
New York, conveying Captain James Carteret, with his ia.
bride, and Samuel Hopkins, of Elizabethtown, to Virginia.
The master of the sloop, Samuel Davis, on being questioned, stoutly insisted that New York was in a good condition
of defense, with one hundred and fifty mounted guns, and
five thousand men ready to answer the call of Governor
Lovelace in three hours. But Hopkins bluntly told the
truth. Davis's story was "altogether false;" there were
only sixty or eighty men in the fort, and thirty to thirty-six
cannon on its walls; three or four hundred men might be
raised in three or four days, and Lovelace was absent on a
visit to Governor Winthrop in Connecticut. Upon Hopkins's information, "all the cry was for New York." Car- Resolve to
teret and his young wife were set ashore in Virginia; but sail for New York.
Hopkins, with Davis and his sloop, were detained. In a
few days the Dutch fleet, which, with three ships of war 28 July/7 August.
from Amsterdam, and four from Zealand, was now swelled The Dutch
by prizes to twenty-three vessels, carrying sixteen hundred at Staten Island.

* Basnage, ii., 410–422; Sylvius, viii., 607-612; ix., 647-649; Davies, iii., 127-132; Kennett, iii., 295, 296; Rapin, ii., 671; Hume, vi., 473–476; Bancroft, ii., 324; Martin, i., 375, 376.

 men, arrived off Sandy Hook. The next morning they anchored under Staten Island.*

28 July. / 7 August. Manning's action. The tidings of their approach were soon brought to Manning, at Fort James, who, finding that the wolf was this time really at the door, hurried off an express to meet Lovelace at New Haven. Volunteers were sought by beat of drum, provisions were seized, and the arms in the fort repaired. Orders were sent to the nearest Long Island towns to forward re-enforcements, but none came. The

The Dutch welcome their country-men. Dutch inhabitants, rejoicing at the approach of their countrymen, had already begun to make "threatening speeches." The fleet was soon crowded with sympathizing visitors from New Utrecht and Flatbush. Learning from them how weak Fort James really was, the Dutch commanders came

29 July. / 8 August. up the bay, and anchored above the Narrows, in sight of the city. Lovelace's sheep and cattle on Staten Island afforded them an acceptable "breakfast." Already New York was substantially restored to the Dutch. In vain did Manning continue beating the drums for volunteers. Few appeared, and those that did only spiked the guns at the City Hall.†

The situation of the capital now resembled that of New Amsterdam nine years before. All that Manning could think of was to procrastinate, in hope that the governor might return, or aid come from Long Island. Captain John Carr, of the Delaware, who was now in New York,

30 July. / 9 August. Answer of the Dutch commodores to Manning's demand. was accordingly dispatched, with Counselor Thomas Lovelace and Attorney John Sharpe, to demand why the fleet had come "in such a hostile manner to disturb His Majesty's subjects in this place?" The Dutch commodores replied that they had come to take the place, "which was their own, and their own they would have." Meanwhile Evertsen and Binckes had sent a trumpeter with their joint summons from the flag-ship "Swanenburgh," requiring the surrender of the fort. To this Manning promised a reply on the return of his own messengers. When they did re-

* Basnage, ii., 456, 781, 782, 832, 834; Sylvius, ix., 660, 665; x., 23; xiv., 355; xv., 38, 94; Kok, vi., 562; xiv., 564; Davies, iii., 50, 132; Col. Doc., ii., 518, 527, 572, 579; iii., 199, 200, 201, 204, 205, 213, 214; Hist. Mag., i. (ii.), 297, 298; Hutch. Mass., i., 284; Mass. H. S., Trumbull Papers, xx., 103; Lambrechtsen, 82; Grahame, i., 420; *ante*, 126, 200. There is a portrait of Evertsen in Wagenaar, xv., 394. See also N. Y. H. S. Coll. (1868), 184.

† Doc. Hist., iii., 57, 59, 60, 65; Col. Doc., iii., 198, 199; iv., 1151; Hist. Mag., i. (ii.), 298; *ante*, 200.

turn, Carr declared that the Dutch were too strong to be withstood, and that they would only allow half an hour's delay. The fleet had meanwhile quietly tided up and anchored within musket-shot of the fort, without a gun being fired. Sharpe was sent on board a second time, to ask a stay of hostilities until the next morning, so that Manning might obtain the advice of the mayor and aldermen. But the Dutch commander, Evertsen, had already written to the city authorities, "promising to all men their estates and liberties," and this had been communicated to the burghers at the City Hall. On Sharpe's return, he reported that the commodores would give only a half an hour more, "and accordingly they turned up the glass." At the end of that time the ships fired their broadsides at the fort, which killed and wounded some of its garrison; "whereupon the fort fired upon them again, and shot the General's ship through and through." Six hundred men were now landed above "the Governor's Orchard," at "the new burial-place" on the shore of the Hudson, just north of the fort, and back of the present Trinity Church. The Dutch burghers, all armed, and about four hundred strong, encouraged their countrymen to storm the fort, promising that not one of its garrison would "look over their works." At Carr's instigation, Manning ordered a parley to be beaten, and a flag of truce exhibited; but Carr, exceeding his orders, struck the king's flag at the same time. Carr, Lovelace, and Gibbs were now dispatched to "make the best conditions they could." They met the Dutch "forlorn" storming-party advancing. Carr was sent back to inform Manning that the garrison must surrender as prisoners of war, while Lovelace and Gibbs were kept in custody under the Dutch standard. But Carr, never coming near the fort, fled away from the city. Manning then dispatched Sharpe with articles for the Dutch to agree to, who met their column marching down Broadway toward the fort. It was now about seven o'clock in the evening. Captain Anthony Colve, who commanded the Dutch forces, readily accepted the proposed articles, which merely surrendered the fort and garrison with the honors of war. Manning himself had meanwhile caused the fort gates to be opened, and the Dutch marched in, while the garrison

The Dutch fire on Fort James, which returns a shot.

Fort James surrendered.

CHAP. IV. 1673. marched out with colors flying and drums beating, and grounded their arms. The English soldiers were now ordered back into the fort, and committed to prison in the church. Before the sun went down, at the end of that

30 July. / 9 August. New York conquered by the Dutch. eventful summer's day, the three-colored ensign of the Dutch Republic rose to its old place on the flag-staff of her ancient fort, and New York reposed again under the dominion of her former lords.* Stuyvesant was avenged. THE DUTCH HAD TAKEN NEW YORK.

* Col. Doc., ii., 597, 659; iii., 199–206, 234; iv., 1151; Doc. Hist., iii., 53–65; Council Min., iii. (ii.), 18; Col. MSS., xxiv., 36–53, 97; Hist. Mag., i. (ii.), 298; N. Y. City Rec.; Dunlap, i., 129. Smith, i., 43, carelessly asserts that Manning "treacherously made his peace with the enemy," and that the Dutch "landed their men and entered the garrison without giving or receiving a shot." Smith's statement has been credulously adopted. The weight of authority, which I have followed, seems to be that the fort did actually return the fire of the Dutch fleet: compare Col. Doc., iii., 199, 201, 206; iv., 1151; Hist. Mag., i. (ii.), 298; Doc. Hist., iii., 62. Manning's real fault was that he allowed the ships to anchor before the fort without firing on them: see Doc. Hist., iii., 55, 56, 58. But, after all, he was as badly off as Stuyvesant, nine years before: see *ante*, 34. Compare Cadwallader Colden, in the Collections of the New York Historical Society for the year 1868, p. 184.

CHAPTER V.

1673–1674.

CHAP. V.

1673.

THE recovery of New York by the Dutch was an absolute conquest by an open enemy in time of war. All its circumstances differed from those which had disgraced the capture of New Netherland by the English nine years before. Then, while the mother-countries were at peace, a treacherous expedition, deliberately prepared, had seized the territory of an unsuspecting ally: yet the British commander felt it necessary to grant the most liberal articles of capitulation. But now, after proclaimed hostilities, and distinct warnings for more than a year, the ships of the Batavian Republic came boldly to recover what had been robbed from an insulted fatherland; and the English ensign fell beneath the Dutch avengers, who, welcomed by their countrymen, marched triumphantly into the old fortress, which surrendered to their discretion.

Character of the Dutch reconquest of New York.

"Not the smallest" article of capitulation, except military honors to the garrison, was granted by the victors. They had unexpectedly captured a prize from the aggressive enemy of their nation. Their reconquest annihilated British sovereignty over ancient New Netherland, and extinguished the duke's proprietary government in New York, with that of his grantees in New Jersey. Evertsen and Binckes for the time represented the Dutch Republic, under the dominion of which its recovered American province instantly passed, by right of successful war. The effete West India Company was in no way connected with the transaction.*

British sovereignty extinguished.

Evertsen and Binckes.

Never had the Bay of New York held so majestic a fleet

* Col. Doc., ii., 536, 611; iii., 202; Doc. Hist., iii., 55, 56, 61, 62; Eliz. Bill, 6, 7, 37. The old West India Company went into liquidation soon after the conquest of New Netherland in 1664, and the new corporation took no interest in its recapture: Murphy's Steendam, 12, 13; Col. Doc., ii., 564, 565.

CHAP. V.

1673.

The Dutch fleet in New York.

as that now anchored in its beautiful waters. Two ships loading for England were added as prizes to the force of the conquerors. The condition of the province, thus marvelously restored to the republican Netherlands, was far different from what it was when the English appropriated it to themselves. New York, including New Jersey and Delaware, now contained three chief towns and thirty villages, and its Dutch population was estimated at between six and seven thousand. The event which brought its Batavian inhabitants once more under the authority of the States General and the Prince of Orange, "their lawful and native Sovereigns," was hailed by them with boundless joy. It more than atoned for the bitterness with which they had endured "the insolent injustice of England's original acquisition." Once more, "The Fatherland" became a household word. The cry of "Oranje Boven" was soon as familiar in Manhattan as in that fatherland.*

Condition of the province.

The province again named New Netherland.

The name of "New Netherland" was of course restored to the reconquered territory, which was held to embrace not only all that the Dutch possessed according to the Hartford agreement of 1650, but also the whole of Long Island east of Oyster Bay, which originally belonged to the province, and which the king had granted to the Duke of York. Fort James was named "Willem Hendrick," in honor of the Prince of Orange. It was, first of all, necessary to extemporize a provisional government. No orders had been given to Evertsen or Binckes about New Netherland. Its recovery was a lucky accident, wholly due to the enterprise of the two commodores; upon whom fell the responsibility of governing their conquest until directions should come from the Hague. As commanders of separate Dutch squadrons, Evertsen, of Zealand, and Binckes, of Holland, alternately wore the admiral's flag for a week. Associating with themselves Captains Anthony Colve, Nicolas Boes, and Abram Ferdinandus van Zyll, as an advisory Council of War, they held regular sessions, first at the City Hall, and afterward at the fort. Their most important duty was to appoint "a fit and able person as Governor General, to hold the supreme command over this con-

Fort James named Willem Hendrick.

Evertsen, and Binckes, and Council of War in power.

* Col. Doc., ii., 526, 598; iii., 200; Doc. Hist., i., 467; Lambrechtsen, 84-86; Grahame, i., 422; *ante*, 203.

quest of New Netherland." Anthony Colve, of Zealand, who appears to have served as an ensign at the capture of Surinam in 1667, and was now a captain in the Dutch infantry, was chosen for the office. To him Evertsen and Binckes gave a commission "to be Governor General of this Country and Forts thereunto belonging, with all the appendencies and dependencies thereof, to govern, rule, and protect them from all invasions of enemies, as he, to the best of his ability, shall judge most necessary." Colve's commission described his government as extending from fifteen miles south of Cape Henlopen to the east end of Long Island and Shelter Island, thence through the middle of the Sound to Greenwich, and so northerly, according to the boundary made in 1650, including Delaware Bay and all the intermediate territory, as possessed by the English under the Duke of York. But Pemaquid, Martha's Vineyard, and Nantucket, not having been under Stuyvesant's jurisdiction when New Netherland was taken from him, were not comprehended in the Dutch province now organized.*

CHAP. V. — 1673. $\frac{2}{12}$ August. Anthony Colve appointed governor of New Netherland.

Extent of Colve's government.

Colve was "a man of resolute spirit, and passionate," whose arbitrary nature had not been improved by military service. He did not, however, assume the administration at once; for the naval commanders prudently determined to keep their ships in harbor until the new government should be firmly established. In the mean time they retained supreme authority in their own hands, assisted by the three captains whom they had adjoined, as a "Council of War." Matthias Nicolls, ousted from his office of provincial secretary, was replaced by Nicholas Bayard, the experienced clerk of the city, whom the Dutch commodores appointed to act as their own secretary, and as secretary and register of New Netherland under Colve.†

Council of War retain temporary power.

$\frac{10}{20}$ August. Bayard secretary of New Netherland.

The name of the city of New York was, at the same time, changed to "New Orange," in compliment to the prince stadtholder, and its magistrates were released from their oaths to the late English government. At the request of the commanders, six burghers were appointed to

$\frac{2}{12}$ August. City of New York named New Orange.

$\frac{4}{14}$ August.

* Col. Doc., ii., 528, 529, 571, 609, 610; iii., 201; Smith, i., 44-46; Wagenaar, xiii., 407; De Witt's Letters, iv., 677; *ante*, 126; vol. i., 519, 520.

† Col. Rec. Conn., ii., 565; Col. Doc., ii., 571, 573, 578, 612; Mass. H. S. Coll., xxx., 99, 108. Among other changes, the Dutch introduced again into New Netherland the New Style, which had so long been used in Holland: see *ante*, vol. i., 443, *note*.

CHAP. V. — 1673. 5/15 August.

confer with them respecting the restoration of the old municipal government, who were directed to convoke the commonalty and nominate persons "from the wealthiest inhabitants, and those only who are of the Reformed Christian Religion," out of whom the Council might select the magistrates for the city. From the nominations thus made, Johannes van Brugh, Johannes de Peyster, and Ægidius Luyck were chosen as burgomasters, and William Beekman, Jeronimus Ebbing, Jacob Kip, Laurens van der Spiegel, and Gelyn ver Planck as schepens. In place of Allard Anthony, the late sheriff, Anthony de Milt was appointed schout. The new magistrates were sworn to administer "good law and justice;" promote the welfare of the city; maintain "the upright and true Christian Religion agreeably to the Word of God and the order of the Synod of Dordrecht;" uphold the supreme authority of the States General and the Prince of Orange; and were empowered to govern for one year, "both burghers and strangers, conformably to the laws and statutes of our Fatherland." The next day John Lawrence, the displaced mayor, surrendered the gowns, mace, and seal which the Duke of York had presented to the city; all of which were carefully deposited in Fort Willem Hendrick.*

7/17 August. Burgomasters, schepens, and schout.

8/18 August. English insignia surrendered.

8/18 August. English and French property seized.

Evertsen and Binckes now issued a proclamation seizing all property and debts belonging to the kings of France or England, or their subjects, and requiring every person to report such property to Secretary Bayard. Under this edict—which only retaliated that of Nicolls against the Dutch in 1665—the estates of Thomas Delavall, the duke's auditor, and of William Dervall, his son-in-law, were especially attached. The houses of Lovelace and Manning had already been plundered by the Dutch troops in the heat of conquest; but Manning himself had been courteously allowed to wear his sword. Mayor Lawrence's house had been spared, at the request of the Dutch burghers. Van Ruyven, the receiver of the Duke of York's revenues, although an old Dutchman, was, nevertheless, required to render a strict account.†

11/21 August.

* Col. Doc., ii., 571–575; Doc. Hist., i., 390, 391; New York City Rec., vii.; Val. Man., 1850, 487–490; Valentine's New York, 173, 174; Moulton's New Orange, 6, 7; *ante*, 158.

† Col. Doc., ii., 578, 580, 591, 603, 608, 643; iii., 200, 206; Hutch. Coll., 468; Court of Assizes, ii., 589; Val. Man., 1853, 381, 384; *ante*, 89, 80, 91.

CHAP. V. 1673.

The metropolis being secured, two hundred men were sent up the river, in several vessels, to reduce Esopus and Albany. No opposition was shown. Salisbury at once surrendered Fort Albany "upon the same terms with New York, namely, at mercy," and all the English soldiers were brought down to New York as prisoners of war. As the number of these prisoners was now embarrassing, they were embarked for Europe, with Manning, Salisbury, Dudley Lovelace, and other subordinate officers, in three ships from Binckes's squadron, and one of Evertsen's, under the command of Captains Boes and Van Zyll. A small prize, taken in the West Indies, was also placed in charge of Andries Michielsen, and dispatched to Amsterdam with letters from Binckes, detailing the capture of New York.*

5/15 August. Albany and Esopus reduced.

8/18 August. English prisoners sent to Europe.

9/19 August.

Meanwhile Lovelace, after enjoying Winthrop's hospitality at Hartford, and arranging his favorite post-office project, had met, on his return to New Haven, Manning's "unwelcome news" of the Dutch approach before New York. On reaching Mamaroneck, he learned that they had taken the fort. Hoping to retrieve the calamity, the governor hastened over to Long Island to raise its militia. At Justice Cornwell's, near Flushing, he met Secretary Matthias Nicolls, who agreed to go over to the fort on the next Saturday, while the governor was to keep himself "out of the enemy's hand," and raise the country to reduce the place again. But, being "collogued with" by one of the Dutch domines, Lovelace weakly consented to revisit his old quarters in the fort "for three days." On the afternoon of Saturday, the third day after the surrender, one of the Dutch commanders accordingly went in his barge, with Orange flag and trumpet, over to Long Island; and Lovelace and Nicolls returned with him to the fort. The English governor was "peaceably and respectfully" entertained by his conquerors. But, before the three days were out, Lovelace's creditors arrested him for debt. The proclamation of Evertsen and Binckes soon afterward stripped

31 July/10 August. Lovelace on Long Island.

1/11 August.

2/12 August. Enticed over to New York and arrested.

8/18 August.

* Col. Doc., ii., 527, 576; iii., 202, 203, 205, 206; Hist. Mag., iv., 50; i. (ii.), 298; Sylvius, ix., 665; x., 23; Doc. Hist., iii., 54, 59. Michielsen was captured in the Channel, off Beachy Head, and obliged to throw his dispatches overboard. He got to Amsterdam on 24 October, 1673; but the Admiralty there found him "a man of so little curiosity that he had no particulars to report" about the reconquest of New York: Col. Doc., ii., 527, 528, 529. The original dispatches of Nicolls, detailing his capture of New York in 1664, were also lost at sea: *ante*, 50, *note*.

Chap. V. 1673. 15/25 August. Lovelace's letter to Winthrop.

him of all his property; but the commanders told him that, on paying his debts, he might leave the country within six weeks. With touching simplicity the ruined Lovelace wrote to Winthrop: "I am now intending for England, with all the conveniency I may, unlesse prevented. Albany is surrendered on the same termes this did, which was too lean and poor for persons of Honour. However, they would willingly frame some excuses, and shoulder the blame and burthen from one to the other. Some shelter themselves under the shields of my absence, which, though (it is confes't) it proved unfortunate, yet the means that were afforded them to a handsomer resistance and prudent managery can plead no excuse. To be brief—it was *digitus Dei*, who exalts and depresses as he pleases, and to whom we must all submit. Would you be curious to know what my losses might amount to—I can in short resolve you. It was my all which ever I had been collecting; too greate to misse in this wildernesse."*

Long Island and Staten Island towns.

No sooner had the Dutch commanders established themselves in the metropolis than the nearest six Long Island towns—Midwout, Amersfoort, Brooklyn, New Utrecht, Bushwick, and Gravesend, together with Staten Island, submitted to their authority. These towns were chiefly settled by rejoicing Hollanders. Upon their nomination,
8/18 August. Jacob Strycker, of Brooklyn, was appointed schout, and Francis de Bruyn, of New Utrecht, secretary of the district; from each of the six towns, of which four persons
15/25 August. named by them were made schepens. Peter Biljou was appointed schout, and two others schepens of Staten Island.†

But the other towns of Long Island and Westchester showed no disposition to submit to the Dutch. They were
3/13 August. therefore summoned to send deputies to New Orange, with their constables' staves and English flags, in place of which they would be furnished with the prince's colors as soon as
4/14 August. Proclamation of Evertsen and Binckes.
possible. The commanders, in a proclamation, declared that although the fort and city on Manhattan Island had "surrendered themselves without any Capitulation or Articles," yet that no harm would be done to any of the in-

* Col. Doc., ii., 578, 583, 587, 603, 685; iii., 198, 200, 201, 202, 203, 205, 206; Mass. H. S. Coll., xxx., 86, 87; MSS. Trumbull Papers, xx., 104, 108; Hist. Mag., i. (ii.), 298; *ante*, 206.

† Col. Doc., ii., 573, 577, 580, 586, 643.

habitants of New Netherland who should submit to the Dutch government. Each town was required to send two delegates to the fort, authorized to take the oath of allegiance, and bring with them their English colors and constables' staves, "whereupon they shall be considered and governed, without respect of nations, as good and faithful subjects;" but, if they refused, they would be forcibly subdued.*

CHAP. V. 1673.

The fact that Lovelace was in the hands of the Dutch commanders added emphasis to their summons. Westchester, Eastchester, and Mamaroneck promptly sent delegates, and magistrates were selected from their nominations. The five Long Island towns—Flushing, Jamaica, Middelburg, Oyster Bay, and Hempstead—upon the petition of their delegates, were granted the usual privileges, but with a warning not to take up arms against the present Dutch government, as some of them had "formerly done, contrary to honor and oath," against that of Stuyvesant. From their nominations, William Lawrence, of Flushing, was chosen to be schout, and Carel van Brugge secretary of the district, and three schepens were selected for each of the five towns. At the same time Captain William Knyff and Lieutenant Jeronymus de Hubert were sent with Ephraim Hermann, a clerk in Secretary Bayard's office, to administer the oath of allegiance to the inhabitants of the neighboring towns, which was readily taken by all except the Quakers.†

20/30 August. Officers appointed on Long Island.

21/31 August.

19/29 August.

But the five towns in the East Riding were not disposed to submit to the Dutch commanders. On receiving their proclamation, Southampton, "struck with amazement," sent to Hartford "for their advice or help." Connecticut, however, would not encourage the "poore towne" to stand out alone. She was about to send messengers to New Orange on her own affairs, which had suddenly come to a critical point. John Selleck, of Stamford, going in a ketch to Long Island, was captured by a Dutch cruiser. Another sloop was taken, but, being neglected by her captors, was retaken on the "Sabbath day following." The

The Eastern towns on Long Island will not submit to the Dutch authority.

2/12 August.

* Col. Doc., ii., 572, 573; iii., 202; Mass. H. S. Coll., xxx., 87; Wood, 96.

† Col. Doc., ii., 580, 581, 582, 589, 591, 592, 596; Val. Man., 1850, 520, 521; *ante*, vol. i., 719, 723, 724, 726, 730, 733.

CHAP. V.

1673.

7/17 August. Connecticut letter to the Dutch commanders.

General Court met at Hartford; a military committee was organized; and troops were ordered to be ready. James Richards and William Rosewell were also sent with a letter to the Dutch commanders, which, with "amazing absurdity," lectured them for treating "His Majesty's subjects" in time of war, as Charles the Second had treated the colonists of Holland in time of peace, nine years before; inquired their "further intentions;" and declared that the United Colonies of New England would defend their sovereign's authority "in these parts." The Connecticut

14/24 August.

delegates delivered this letter to the Council of War at New Orange, and explained verbally that their colony would not molest the Dutch province if nothing hostile was done against her by New Netherland. They were courteously asked to put in writing what they had to say; but they declined to do this, because "such written negotiations might be turned to the worst use by any disaffected person of their colony." The Connecticut messengers

Answer of the Dutch commanders.

were then handed a reply, with which they returned to Hartford. In soldier-like style, the Dutch commanders answered that it was "very strange" that their enemies should object to the results of war; that the Republic of the Netherlands had commissioned them to do all manner of damage to its enemies, in consequence of which the neighborhood of the Hudson River had been reduced to obey Dutch authority; and they declared that, as the villages east of Oyster Bay "did belong to this Government," they would be likewise subjected, and prompt punishment would be visited on all "those that shall seek to maintain the said villages in their injustice."*

In the mean time, deputies from Southampton, Easthampton, Southold, Brookhaven, and Huntington had met

14/24 August.

at Jamaica, and drawn up a paper, in which, after stating that they had not heard from their governor, Lovelace, who was "peaceably and respectfully entertained" in the fort, they asked the Dutch commanders to allow them, upon their submission, to retain their ecclesiastical privileges, and enjoy several other particular liberties. On

* Mass. H. S. Coll., xxx., 87; xxxvii., 570, 571; Col. Rec. Conn., ii., 181–183, 204, 208, 561, 562; Plymouth Col. Rec., x., 387, 388; Col. Doc., ii., 584, 586, 602, 606; iii., 201, 203; Trumbull, i., 323, 324; Grahame, i., 421; Thompson, i., 153, 154; Palfrey, iii., 120; *ante*, 24, 25.

1673. Long Island delegates at New Orange.

reaching New Orange, the deputies met the Connecticut messengers, whom they found were "shy and cautious" about giving advice. But Captain Nathaniel Sylvester, of Shelter Island, who had come from Hartford with Richards and Rosewell, advised his Long Island neighbors "by all means" to submit to the Dutch government. The delegates accordingly "declared to submit themselves to the obedience of their High Mightinesses the Lords States General of the United Netherlands, and his Serene Highness the Prince of Orange." Upon this their petition was granted in all points, except that in regard to appointing officers and sending deputies they should have the same privileges enjoyed by the Dutch towns, and that their request to buy whaling tools in New England could not "in this conjuncture of time be allowed." The next day they ($\frac{15}{25}$ August.) were directed to nominate for approbation a schout and a secretary for the district, and four magistrates for each town, who should be "only such as are of the Reformed Christian Religion, or at least well affected to it."*

Nathaniel Sylvester now asked for a confirmation of the ($\frac{16}{26}$ August.) privileges which Nicolls had granted to Shelter Island in 1666. It was found, however, that the heirs of his deceased brother Constant, of Barbadoes, and Colonel Thomas Middleton, who lived in England, were part owners. Their share was accordingly confiscated, and Sylvester bought it ($\frac{18}{28}$ August. Shelter Island.) of the Dutch authorities for five hundred pounds "in this country's provisions." Upon his giving a bond for this payment, Shelter Island was duly conveyed to Sylvester, ($\frac{19}{29}$ August.) with all the usual privileges. David Gardiner, who had early offered his submission, was likewise, on his personal promise of obedience, confirmed in the possession of his ($\frac{20 \text{ Septem.}}{1 \text{ October.}}$ Gardiner's Island.) island, with "the same privileges and pre-eminences that may be granted to the other subjects of this Government."†

Upon the return of their deputies from New Orange, the five eastern towns of Long Island, having "duly weighed" their circumstances, and found that they must follow their "neighbour townes in submitting to the Dutch Government," ($\frac{28 \text{ August.}}{7 \text{ Septem.}}$ Submission of the Eastern towns.) nominated magistrates, and sent their discarded English flags and constables' staves to Fort Willem Hendrick.

* Col. Doc., ii., 583, 584, 586; Mass. H. S. Coll., xxx., 87.

† Col. Doc., ii., 587–590, 622; Thompson, i., 155, 367; Wood, 9; *ante*, 90, 107.

CHAP. V.

1673.

29 August.
8 Septem.
Officers appointed.

From these nominations the Council of War chose Isaac Arnold, of Southold, to be schout, and Henry Pierson, of Southampton, to be secretary of the five towns, and two from each town to be magistrates. A petition for a modification of the oath from some of the more scrupulous inhabitants was at the same time presented, which the council promptly granted, and instructed Schout Arnold to give notice that it would be administered by commissioners to be sent for that purpose. Nevertheless, the five towns were very reluctant to acknowledge the Dutch authority;

29 August.
8 Septem.
Southampton address.

and Southampton felt constrained to address a declaration to all his British majesty's subjects in Massachusetts, Connecticut, Plymouth, or elsewhere, "to take off an aspersion cast upon us, as though we should freely submit to this foreign government."*

22 August.
1 Septem.
Kingston named Swanenburg.

Albany named Willemstadt.

Delegates from Albany and Esopus had meanwhile appeared at the fort, and received prompt satisfaction. The name of Kingston was changed to "Swanenburg," after Evertsen's flag-ship; but the names of Hurley and Marbletown were not altered. Albany was ordered to be called "Willemstadt," and its fort was named "Nassau." A garrison was directed to be maintained, and presents made to the five Iroquois nations, "in order to prevent the designs and undertakings of our enemies the French." Schenectady was to observe the regulations established by Stuyvesant and Nicolls.

25 August.
4 Septem.
Rensselaerwyck.

Jeremias van Rensselaer was allowed to enjoy his previous privileges for a year, upon contributing three hundred schepels of wheat; but was required to obtain a new grant from the States General.†

New Jersey named "Achter Col."

2/12 August.

Dutch authority was quietly re-established over New Jersey, the name of which was changed to "Achter Col." The very day that Evertsen and Binckes began their sessions at Fort Willem Hendrick, delegates came to them from Elizabethtown, Newark, Woodbridge, and Piscataway, to treat for a surrender. They were partisans of James Carteret, and opponents of Berry, the acting gov-

* Col. Doc., ii., 601, 602; Mass. H. S. Coll., xxx., 86–88; Hist. Mag., i. (ii.), 298; Col. Rec. Conn., ii., 212, 563; Wood, 96.

† Col. Doc., ii., 559, 592–597; Doc. Hist., iii., 60; Val. Man., 1852, 431. Van Rensselaer was ordered to account to Joanna de Laet, wife of Schepen Jeronymus Ebbing, for the tenth part of the colony, which she had inherited from her father, John de Laet. The next year she sold her interest to Van Rensselaer: Col. Doc., i., 406, 407, 519, 534; ii., 549–561, 596, 597; Val. Man., 1855, 521; Barnard's Sketch, 109, 132; *ante*, vol. i., 204, 535.

ernor. A few days afterward delegates from these towns, CHAP. V.
and from Middletown and Shrewsbury, came to the fort,
and were granted the usual privileges. Berry and his 1673. $\frac{8}{18}$ August.
friends were treated with the same liberality. Bergen, of
which the population was chiefly Dutch, nominated offi- $\frac{11}{21}$ August.
cers, who were promptly confirmed; and every one of her
seventy-eight burghers who were present when the com-
manders visited the town the next Sunday, "after the ser- $\frac{17}{27}$ August.
mon," took the oath. John Ogden was appointed schout,
and Samuel Hopkins, whose timely information had $\frac{22 \text{ August.}}{1 \text{ Septem.}}$
brought the Dutch fleet from Virginia, was made secre- Officers appointed.
tary of the other six towns; from each of which three
magistrates were likewise chosen, among whom was Daniel
Denton, of Piscataway, the author of the recently published "Brief Description of New York." Bollen, the late
secretary of New Jersey, was directed to deliver his papers $\frac{28 \text{ August.}}{7 \text{ Septem.}}$
to Hopkins; but, as he was charged with "having made
away with some of them," the records were ordered to be $\frac{2}{12}$ Septem.
deposited with the provincial secretary Bayard, in Fort
Willem Hendrick.*

Deputies from the Delaware were promised freedom of $\frac{2}{12}$ Septem. Delaware affairs.
trade and commerce, and equal privileges to all the inhabitants who should take the oath of allegiance. Courts of justice were also established at New Amstel, Upland, and the Hoarkill; and the usual nominations of magistrates were ordered to be sent by the schout, Peter Alrichs, to New Orange, for approval.†

The affairs of the metropolis went on with great regularity. Measures were taken to improve the fortifications; and, as these were made chiefly of earth, owners of hogs $\frac{18}{28}$ August. New Orange regulations.
were directed to prevent them from roaming in the streets south of the "Fresh Water," or Kolck, lest they should damage the works. The Dutch Church having again become the establishment in New Netherland, its service The Dutch Church again established.
was conducted by Domine van Nieuwenhuysen, to the

* Col. Doc., ii., 571, 572, 576–580, 582, 587, 595, 598, 600, 602, 603, 606, 607; iii., 201, 203, 213, 214; Smith, i., 44; Whitehead, 60, 61, 62; *ante*, 154. The estate of Governor Philip Carteret was ordered to be inventoried; and Robert la Prairie, or Vanquellen, and Jonathan Singletary, who had tried to secrete some of it, were brought to the fort, where the latter was fined, and Vanquellen sentenced to banishment for publicly declaring "that the Duke of York had still an interest in Fort James, and that there would be another change within half a year."

† Col. Doc., ii., 604, 605; S. Hazard, 407, 408.

CHAP. V. great acceptance of Reformed Protestant Dutch people, in Kieft's old church in the fort.*

1673. 29 August. 8 Septem. Letter of the municipality of New Orange to the States General.

Van Ruyven now intending to return to Holland, the schout, burgomasters, and schepens of New Orange intrusted to him a letter to the States General, in which—after thanking them for reducing the inhabitants of New Netherland again under the obedience of "their lawful and native Sovereigns, from whose protection they were cut off, about nine years ago, in time of peace"—they represented how advantageous the province, which now consisted of three cities and thirty villages, might be made to the fatherland. Many private families there, ruined by the French invasion, could live easily in New Netherland, which, with a larger farming population, would soon become "a granary and magazine of many necessaries" which Holland ordinarily imported from the Baltic. Esopus alone, which the last year had produced twenty-five thousand schepels of grain, could supply the Dutch colonies of Curaçoa and Surinam. New Netherland could also, by its peltries, maintain the Dutch commerce with Muscovy; and the tobacco trade, besides many other interesting details, would be personally explained on his arrival by Van Ruyven, who had filled "divers respectable offices here." But, above all, the province would be especially important as a naval station, and as a watch-tower, from which a constant eye could be kept on the King of England, "who, in case he only came to be Lord and Master of this northern part of America, would be able to equip ships here, unknown to any Prince or Potentate in Europe, and thus, most unexpectedly, fall on our state or its allies." Yet, without speedy re-enforcements from the fatherland, its "good Dutch inhabitants," who were not more than six or seven thousand, and scattered over a vast country, could not resist "its numerous neighboring English and French enemies, by whom it is encompassed around on all sides." The States General were therefore urged to dispatch such aid as might, after the departure of the Dutch fleet, defend "this newly-recovered Province." This statesmanlike let-

Importance of New Netherland to Holland.

* New Orange Rec., vii., 16–20; Val. Man., 1850, 490–498; Corr. Classis of Amsterdam; Letter of Van Nieuwenhuysen, 26 July, 1674; Col. Doc., ii., 705, 730. The other Dutch clergymen in New Netherland were Polhemus on Long Island, and Schaats at Albany, or Willemstadt: Blom having left Esopus in 1667, and Drisius having died on 18 April, 1673.

ter could hardly have failed to produce a decisive effect in Holland. But a remarkable fatality prevented its delivery in time to advance "the Dutch interest."*

CHAP. V.

1673.

This appeal of the corporation of New Orange was quickened by the determination of Evertsen and Binckes to depart with all their ships of war, leaving New Netherland unprotected. Hearing of this, the city authorities represented the exposed condition of the country, surrounded by English and French colonies, and its scattered Dutch population of six thousand outnumbered, fifteen to one, by that of New England. These English and French subjects had now become enemies, and would endeavor to gain New Netherland as soon as it should be left to its own resources for defense. The Duke of York, and Berkeley, and Carteret were all alike interested in its recovery. "This, without doubt, renders some so bold as to say already that something else will be seen before Christmas, and that the King of England will never suffer the Dutch to remain and sit down here, in the centre of all his dominions, to his serious prejudice in many respects; so that we are inevitably to expect a visit from our malevolent neighbors of old, now our bitter enemies, unless they be prevented, under God, by your valiant prowess and accompanying force." Two ships of war, under the command of one of the superior officers, should therefore winter in the province, and not leave its inhabitants "a prey to be destroyed or to be sold as slaves to the English Plantations."†

27 August. / 6 Septem. The corporation of New Orange desires ships of war for its protection.

The commanders replied that the garrison in the fort could protect the place sufficiently against all enemies; but, as the petitioners were so urgent, the frigate *Surinam*, of forty guns, Captain Evert Evertsen, and the sloop or snow *Zeehond* (or *Seal*), Captain Cornelis Ewoutsen, would be left under the command of Governor Colve until the province should be "furnished with other help, either from Fatherland, or by the ships already sailed hence." As these vessels belonged to Evertsen's Zealand squadron, Binckes

27 August. / 6 Septem. Ships ordered to guard the metropolis.

* Col. Doc., ii., 526, 527, 532, 538; Lambrechtsen, 83-86; N. Y. H. S. Coll., i. (ii.), 115, 116. Van Ruyven embarked in the snow "Expectatie," Captain Martin Vonck, which, having lost her mast and sails in a storm, managed to get into Nantucket, whence Van Ruyven returned to New York in the following November: Col. Doc., ii., 532, 658, 662, 663; Col. Rec. Conn., ii., 565; Mass. Rec., iv. (ii.), 573, 574; Mass. H. S. Coll., xxx., 103. Vonck sailed again in the ketch "Hope" in January, 1674: Col. Doc., ii., 677; *post*, p. 258.

† Col. Doc., ii., 598-600; Doc. Hist., i., 467.

CHAP. V. 1673. 31 August. / 10 Septem. agreed that the Admiralty of Amsterdam should bear its just proportion of all expenses and damages which might happen to them during their special service in New Netherland.*

Some necessary police regulations were now adopted. 9 Septem. Police regulations. Resolved Waldron was directed "to forbid the ferry people at Haerlem and Spytenduyvel to put across any strangers from this Island, unless they first exhibit a pass to that effect." As many strangers were passing in and out of the 1/11 Septem. metropolis, it was ordered that all persons who had not taken the oath of allegiance should leave New Orange within twenty-four hours, and that none but Dutch subjects should visit it without license; and all the inhabitants were forbidden to harbor strangers without reporting them to the schout.†

13 Septem. Visit of Indian sachems to New Orange. Attracted by the fleet in the harbor, the Hackensack sachems came to the fort with several of their people, and declared their desire to live as before, in peace with the Dutch. The commanders made them presents, and promised that they should be considered "good friends" as heretofore. A few days afterward, the sachems of the 8/18 Septem. Mohawks, who had come "to see the naval force and make a report," were likewise dismissed with satisfactory presents. The people of Schenectady were also confirmed in the privileges formerly granted by Stuyvesant, and the local officers nominated by them were approved.‡

Colve's commission as governor general was now entered on the records of the province. The experienced Cor- 9/19 Septem. Colve's counselor and subordinate officers. nelis Steenwyck was appointed counselor of New Netherland, "to assist in the direction of all cases relative to justice and police, and further in all such military concerns both by water and by land, in which the Governor shall deem proper to ask his advice and assistance." Cornelis Ewoutsen, the commander of the snow Zeehond, was made superintendent of gunners and ammunition. Nicholas Bayard, who had been commissioned as secretary and reg- 10/20 Septem. ister of New Netherland, was also appointed receiver general of the provincial revenue. All these appointments

* Col. Doc., ii., 600, 611, 612, 649, 654, 658, 662, 664, 682, 702, 707, 715, 726; Val. Man., 1850, 522.

† Col. Doc., ii., 603, 604.

‡ Col. Doc., ii., 606, 608, 609.

were made subject to the approval of the "Lords Principals" in the fatherland.*

1673.

10/20 Septem.

Confiscation of English and French property.

The commanders now issued a proclamation, referring to their former one of the eighteenth of August, and declaring that, as "not the smallest capitulation" was entered into at the surrender of the fort and province to the States General and the Prince of Orange, all the property belonging to the kings of England and France, and their subjects, was liable to confiscation and forfeiture. They therefore confiscated all such property, especially that of the Duke of York, his governors, officers, and agents, to the benefit of the Dutch government. Nevertheless, they excepted the effects of "the actual inhabitants of the neighboring colonies of New England, Virginia, and Maryland," which, "for sufficient reasons," were for the present exempted from this confiscation.†

Exceptions made.

Lovelace's and others' property seized.

Under this act, the property of Lovelace, Delavall, Carteret, Manning, Willett, and others was placed in the hands of commissioners. Lovelace was also required forthwith to leave the province, and go either to New England or to Holland in one of the returning vessels. His request to go to Europe in Commander Binckes's ship was promptly granted. Delavall accompanied Lovelace. The Dutch commodores soon afterward sailed—Binckes directly to Holland; and Evertsen by way of the West Indies, Fayal, and Cadiz, to Zealand.‡

The Dutch commodores sail for Europe.

Colve assumes the government of New Netherland.

ANTHONY COLVE now assumed the government of New Netherland. To give greater state to his office, he set up a coach drawn by three horses. In all ordinary business he was assisted by Counselor Steenwyck and Secretary Bayard. On important occasions, the authorities of the

* Col. Doc., ii., 609–614; *ante*, p. 211.

† Col. Doc., ii., 578, 611, 612, 710; S. Hazard, 409; *ante*, p. 212. Palfrey, iii., 120, *note*, suggests that this forbearance on the part of the Dutch commanders may have arisen from the hope of the States General that New England would ally itself with them. But Virginian and Maryland property was at the same time exempted from forfeiture by the act of Evertsen and Binckes; and, moreover, the States General knew nothing about the matter.

‡ Col. Doc., ii., 580, 587, 591, 595, 597, 603, 608, 617, 638, 643, 644, 645, 647, 651, 667, 672, 687, 688, 720, 721; iii., 205, 206; Smith, i., 44. Binckes afterward commanded a squadron against the French in the West Indies, and was killed at Tobago in December, 1677. Evertsen rose to the rank of admiral, and, in November, 1688, commanded a division of the fleet which conveyed the Prince of Orange to England. He died in November, 1706, and was buried at Middelburgh, in Zealand: Sylvius, ix., 665; x., 23; Wagenaar, xiv., 376, 401, 443, 444; xv., 395; Lambrechtsen, 82, 86, 87, 88; Kok, vi., 562; xiv., 564; Col. Doc., ii., 572, 579; Col. MSS., xxv., 171; Doc. Hist., iii., 54, 59.

CHAP. V. 1673.

city of New Orange were consulted. When questions arose about the treatment of foreigners or their property, Captains William Knyff and Carel Epesteyn, of the Dutch infantry, were added as a Council of War.*

9/19 Septem. Alrichs commander on the South River.

Colve's first official act was to commission Peter Alrichs commander and schout "on the South River, in New Netherland, lately called Delaware," where he was to maintain the Established Dutch Church, keep his soldiers in discipline, the Indians in good temper, and obey all orders from New Orange. Walter Wharton was also commissioned (15/25 Septem.) to be surveyor of all the Dutch territory on the South River.†

16/26 Septem. Andries Draeyer commander at Willemstadt.

Lieutenant Andries Draeyer was appointed commander of Fort Nassau, and schout of the town of Willemstadt and the colonie of Rensselaerwyck. Draeyer was instructed, among other things, to maintain "the pure true Christian Religion agreeably to the Synod of Dort;" and, as much as he could, "keep the natives and Indians devoted to him, and, according to his ability, render the Dutch government agreeable to them, and obtain from them all the information he can respecting the trade and doings of the French, and present all correspondence they may carry on with the inhabitants of Willemstadt."‡

Lutherans at Willemstadt.

The Lutherans at Willemstadt, who had enjoyed much liberty under the Duke of York's government, petitioned Colve at the same time for the "free exercise of their religious worship, without let or hindrance, to the end that they may live in peace with their fellow burghers." Their request (16/26 Septem.) was granted, "on condition of comporting themselves peaceably and quietly, without giving any offence to the Congregation of the Reformed Religion, which is the State Church."§

* Col. Doc., ii., 630, 642, 644, 662, 664, 665, 710, 715; Doc. Hist., iii., 48.

† Col. Doc., ii., 614, 615, 618, 619; S. Hazard, 408, 409.

‡ Col. Doc., ii., 593, 596, 608, 618, 627, 659, 662, 676. On the 23d of January, 1674, Commander Draeyer was married in the Dutch Church to Gerritje, a daughter of Gosen Gerritsen van Schaick, and a sister of Levinus van Schaick: Holgate, 129, 144, 145, 146; Munsell's Collections, i., 361; MSS. of Matthew Clarkson, Esq., communicated to me. Draeyer afterward entered the Danish service, in which he became a rear-admiral; and in March, 1699, his widow, having returned to New York, was received, "with attestation from Copenhagen," into the membership of the Dutch Church. Her son, Captain Andries Draeyer, returned to Denmark in April, 1700: see Records of the Collegiate R. P. D. Church of New York, Liber A. The Widow Draeyer's daughter, Anna Dorothea, afterward married the Reverend Thomas Barclay, of Albany: Holgate, 129, 144.

§ Col. Doc., ii., 617; *ante*, 175. It appears, however, that the "Aanspreker," or sexton

To assure the safety of the metropolis, the magistrates at "the Nevesings," near Sandy Hook, were ordered to send the earliest information to the governor of the arrival of any ships from sea. Martial law was also necessary to check the unruly troops who had so recently spoiled the West Indies. Ensign Jan Sol, the major of the garrison in Fort Willem Hendrick, was accordingly directed to enforce it severely within the citadel; and the burghers were prohibited from selling liquors or giving credits to the soldiers.*

CHAP. V. 1673. 19/29 Septem. Military precautions. 21 Septem./1 October.

The fort itself was miserably insecure. Its condition, as described by Stuyvesant, had been very little strengthened by Nicolls and Lovelace, neither of whom seem to have apprehended its being again occupied by a foreign force, and certainly not by its old masters. Houses, gardens, and orchards were clustered thickly under its earthen walls. "The newly-begun fortification of New Orange" was in the same case. Obstructions were ordered to be demolished, and their owners summoned before the governor. At the same time, an extraordinary duty was laid to indemnify those whose property was to be taken. Several of the owners accordingly appeared; other lots were assigned to most of them; and all were promised satisfaction out of the new duties. Counselor Steenwyck, with Burgomasters Van Brugh, De Peyster, and Luyck, were directed to estimate the damages, and report to the governor. The demolition of the doomed houses was effected; and each owner was recompensed for the property which the public safety required should be taken. Among the buildings thus destroyed was the Lutheran Church, which had just been built "without the gate."†

Insecurity of Fort Willem Hendrick. 28 Septem./8 October. Incumbering houses demolished. 1/11 Oct. 6/16 Oct.

To establish a general system for the government of the towns in New Netherland, Colve drew up a "Provisional Instruction," some of the articles of which were annoying

21 Septem./1 October.

of the Dutch Church at Willemstadt required the Lutherans to pay fees to himself, as was the custom in Holland, notwithstanding they employed their own sexton; which produced a remonstrance to Colve from Arensius, their minister, and others: Doc. Hist., iii., 525; Col. MSS., xxiii., 296, 313, 408.

* Col. Doc., ii., 619, 622–625, 650.

† Col. Doc., ii., 440, 629–631, 633–637, 685, 688, 697, 699, 700, 710, 716; iii., 87; Val. Man., 1850, 511, 512, 521, 525, 530; 1851, 435, 447, 448; New Orange Rec., vii., 42; Moulton's New Orange, 11, 12; Valentine's New York, 175; *ante*, 26, 81. 200. The Lutherans were allowed another lot, "No. 5 in the Company's garden," within the gate, on which they built a new church. It was at the corner of Broadway and Rector Street, where Grace Church was afterward built: Col. Doc., ii., 636; Doc. Hist., iii., 245; *ante*, 174.

CHAP. V. 1673. Provisional articles for the government of towns.

to the English inhabitants. The local magistrates were, above all things, to "take care that the Reformed Christian Religion be maintained in conformity to the Synod of Dordrecht, without permitting any other sects attempting anything contrary thereto." Local ordinances must be conformable to the laws of Holland, and be approved by the governor. All officers must acknowledge the authority of the States General and the Prince of Orange, and "maintain their sovereign jurisdiction right and domain over this country." The magistrates were to nominate as their successors "a double number of the best qualified, the honestest, most intelligent and wealthiest inhabitants, exclusively of the Reformed Christian Religion, or at least well affected thereunto, to be presented to the Governor, who shall then make his election therefrom, with continuation of some of the old ones, in case his Honor may deem it necessary."*

Colve's municipal system was substantially a revival of that of Stuyvesant. The "Instruction" was ordered to be enforced in every town of the province except New Orange and Willemstadt, where some modifications were necessary. But the eastern towns of Long Island showed great disaffection, although their nominations of magistrates had been promptly confirmed. Colve therefore commissioned Captain William Knyff, Lieutenant Anthony Malypart, and the clerk, Abram Varlett, to visit all the towns east of Oyster Bay, and administer the oath to their inhabitants; and also directed their magistrates to publish his Instructions, with the proclamation for the seizure of the property of English and French subjects.†

24 Septem. / 4 October. Commissioners sent to Long Island towns.

9/19 Oct. Answers of the Long Island towns.

The commissioners reported that Oyster Bay had taken the oath, while Huntington desired to be excused, upon promising in writing to be faithful to the government of New Netherland. Setauket, or Brookhaven, apologized, and asked a suspension of censure, because her people wished to preserve their English allegiance, and yet to live in peace with the Dutch government. Easthampton acknowledged the "Christian and moderate" dealing of the

* Col. Doc., ii., 620–622, 653, 654, 678–680.

† Col. Doc., ii., 578, 586, 591, 601, 602, 616, 620, 622, 626, 628; Whitehead, 61; *ante*, 212; vol. i., 540, 548, 574, 613, 619, 640.

Dutch; but asked to be left as she was, as her letters had been opened and read at Southampton, where threats against her submission had been uttered by "several disaffected persons." Southold objected to several clauses in the "Instruction," but was "willing to submit" to the Dutch government, if the articles first promised should be performed, and the town be protected "from the invasion of those which daily threaten us." Knowing that Evertsen and Binckes had left New Netherland, Southampton declared that Colve's "Instructions" overthrew what had been previously agreed upon; that the town could not abjure its king, and swear allegiance to a foreign power; yet, that it would not disturb the Dutch, unless molested by them, or "called thereunto by His Majesty's power of England."*

On receiving this report, Colve called the burgomasters and schepens of New Orange to advise with the council, and was disposed to send the frigate Surinam, with a "considerable force," to the Eastern towns, and "punish them as rebels, in case they persist in refusing to swear obedience." The majority thought "that, in this conjuncture of war, it was not advisable to attack them by force of arms, as we should thereby be affording them, and the neighboring Colonies, occasion again to take up arms against us; but they judged it better to send a second delegation."†

10/20 Oct. Colve refrains from reducing the recusant towns.

It was gratifying, however, that Midwout, Bushwick, New Utrecht, Amersfoort, Brooklyn, and Gravesend, in Schout Jacob Strycker's district, declared that "the entire of the people" would observe their oaths, and, in case of attack, would assist New Orange in resisting the enemy. These loyal Dutch towns were accordingly allowed to select their own military officers.‡

10/20 Oct. The Dutch towns submissive.

15/25 Oct.

Lewis Morris,§ and Nathaniel Sylvester, with whom he

* Col. Doc., ii., 632, 638-642; Wood, 96.

† Col. Doc., ii., 642, 648.

‡ Col. Doc., ii., 577, 643, 645, 646; *ante*, 214.

§ Lewis Morris was a Welshman, a brother of Richard Morris, of Westchester, and a Cromwellian officer, who was sent to the West Indies, and settled himself at Barbadoes, where he became a Quaker, and entertained George Fox. After the death of his brother Richard in 1672, he was allowed by Colve to come to New Netherland, "on condition that he attempt nothing to its prejudice during his sojourn." Morris was accordingly granted the guardianship of his infant nephew, and custody of his brother Richard's effects, under the direction of the "Orphan Chamber" of New Orange, although his own estate was confiscated as belonging to a then Barbadian: Col. Doc., ii., 595, 617, 619, 631, 632, 645, 650, 664; Besse, ii., 288, 313, 314, 315; Fox's Journal, 442; Smith, i., 209; Bolton, ii., 280-300; Whitehead's Memoir of L. Morris, 1-5; *ante*, 140, 188, 190.

CHAP. V. 1673. was staying at Shelter Island, now asked the governor to send "a second embassy to the east end of Long Island, so that the innocent may not be punished with the guilty."

15/25 Oct. Oaths administered. Colve therefore dispatched Captain Knyff and Ensign Nicholas Vos to administer the oath to such as might "be free to take the same." Huntington and Setauket were accordingly visited; and their inhabitants and officers readily swore fidelity to the Dutch government.*

By advice of his council, which agreed with that of Morris and Sylvester, Governor Colve, instead of sending the

20/30 Oct. frigate Surinam, directed Counselor Steenwyck, with Captain Charles Epesteyn and Lieutenant Charles Quirynsen, to visit Easthampton, Southold, and Southampton, and "admonish the inhabitants of their duty and true submission, and also to establish the elected magistrates in their respective offices, and to administer the oath, as well unto them as the rest of the inhabitants there." If any New England vessels were met, they were not to be molested. If the people of the towns objected to swear, they were to be allowed to promise obedience; but their magistrates must take the oath, as the Schout Arnold had already done. Concessions were promised regarding trade with the New England colonies, the nomination of local officers, and whatever the people might "ask in fairness." But, if they should be obstinate, the chief mutineers were to be reported at New Orange. Steenwyck, with his colleagues, accordingly

21/31 Oct. embarked in the "Zeehond," under the command of Captain Cornelis Ewoutsen.†

The Eastern towns admonished.

In the mean time, Rhode Island, which did not belong

13/23 Aug. Rhode Island. to the New England confederation, had passed laws for the defense of the colony, in case it should be attacked by the Dutch. On receiving the answer of Evertsen and Binckes,

27 August./6 Septem. Connecticut. Connecticut summoned a meeting of the commissioners of the United Colonies at Hartford. A "remonstrance" was there adopted, recommending each confederate to take care for its own defense, and to aid any other which might be

15/25 Sept. Plymouth. first invaded. Plymouth did not see satisfactory grounds for a war upon the Dutch at New York "without express command" of the king, or the actual invasion of a New

* Col. Doc., ii., 645, 647; Wood, 96, 97; Thompson, i., 154, 155; *ante*, 217.

† Col. Doc., ii., 648, 649, 654; Wood, 97; *ante*, 218.

CHAP. V.

1673.

England colony. Massachusetts, characteristically selfish, notwithstanding the appeal of Southampton, "did not judge it expedient to engage" in the matter further than to provide for her own safety. This was owing, not to love of the Dutch, or hatred of the Duke of York, but to an ever-controlling thirst for individual aggrandizement. At this very time, Captain Cleyborne, of the English frigate Garland, being at Boston, offered to retake New York with his own ship, if Massachusetts would assist him with some sailors, soldiers, and provisions. But the General Court would do so only on condition that "the conquest might be added to Massachusetts; and if that were refused, it would rather that Manhattan remained in possession of the Dutch than that it should be put into the hands of Colonel Lovelace, the former governor." At the same time, upon the petition of John Payne, to whom a large tract had been granted, the Court ordered "the running of their southern line to Hudson's River." But this attitude of Massachusetts did her no good at Whitehall.*

19/29 Sept. Massachusetts.

17/27 Oct. Boundary to be run.

Connecticut, however, yearned after Long Island. Howell, Younge, and James, as representatives of the three eastern towns, petitioned for "protection and government" against the Dutch, and were received with great favor at Hartford. Letters were sent to Plymouth and Massachusetts, asking their concurrence; upon favorable answers to which, the governor and some other magistrates of Connecticut were authorized "to protect the people of the east end of Long Island, and to establish government amongst them." But the reply from Boston was unsatisfactory. In cloudy words it intimated that Massachusetts was "ignorant of the extent" of the Connecticut patent, yet admitted an obligation to aid the Long Island people, as Englishmen, against the Dutch, as a national enemy; while the Hartford "claim of jurisdiction over them" was testily rejected. Connecticut, nevertheless, commissioned Samuel Willys and Captain Fitz John Winthrop to go to Long Island with "necessary attendants;" treat with such Dutch forces as they might find there; and warn them that opposition

14/24 Oct.

17/27 Oct.

18/28 Oct.

24 October / 3 Novem. Massachusetts repels Connecticut.

22 October / 1 Novem. Connecticut sends commissioners to Long Island.

* Col. Rec. Conn., ii., 562, 563; iii., 486, 487; R. I. Rec., ii., 488–500; Plymouth Col. Rec., v., 134; x., 387; Mass. Rec., iv. (ii.), 548, 558, 561, 570; Arnold, i., 366, 367; Chalmers, i., 433, 434; Hutch. Coll., 443; Mass. H. S. Coll., xxx., 86–88, 96; Palfrey, iii., 121, 122, 304; *ante*, 188, 216.

CHAP. V. would provoke the Hartford authorities to consider what they were "nextly obliged to do."*

1673.

The Connecticut magistrates also lectured "the commander of the Dutch forces at New York" for urging his majesty's subjects on Long Island to swear allegiance against the King of England, and threatened that if he persisted, the New England colonies would attack him at "headquarters." These "animadversions" were sent to New Orange "by Mr. John Bankes," who was instructed to inform Colve how tender Connecticut was of the "effusion of Christian blood," yet how interested for her "dear neighbours, his Majestie's good subjects" on Long Island.

21/31 Oct. Connecticut lectures Colve.

Surprised at the insolent tone of this letter, Colve arrested its bearer, and replied to Winthrop that he could not believe such an "impertinent and absurd writing" came from him. Winthrop, in answer, complained of Bankes's detention at New Orange, and declared that the letter he bore contained "very pertinent and needful premonitions for the preventing a confluence of evill consequences."†

26 October. 5 Novem. Colve's answer.

Winthrop's reply.

Unappalled by this peculiar rhetoric, Colve denied the right of Connecticut to question his proceedings on Long Island, where the people would have peaceably taken the oaths to the Dutch "had not some evil-disposed persons gone from you and dissuaded them." He was in New Netherland, he added, "to maintain the right of their High Mightinesses and his Serene Highness the Prince of Orange;" and he would do it. The Dutch had always treated their enemies more humanely than the English, who had so barbarously used the "poor fishermen and farmers" on the island of Ter-Schelling. On his return to Hartford with this letter, Bankes reported that Colve was "a man of resolute spirit and passionate, that manageth the affaires now under his power so as is not satisfactory to the people nor soldiers; and that he is in expectation of strength from foreign parts, upon whose arrival he seems to be resolved to subdue under his obedience what he can, not only on the island, but he sayth he knowes not but he may have Hartford ere long."‡

8/18 Novem. Colve's pungent retort.

Report of Bankes about Colve and New Netherland.

* Col. Rec. Conn., ii., 212–216, 563, 564; Col. Doc., ii., 656; Col. MSS., xxiii., 281; Wood's Long Island, 96; Palfrey, iii., 121, 122.

† Col. Rec. Conn., ii., 216, 564, 565; Col. Doc., ii., 651, 652, 660.

‡ Col. Doc., ii., 660, 661; Col. Rec. Conn., ii., 565; *ante*, 125. On the 18th of May, 1675,

CHAP. V.

1673.

27 October / 6 Novem.

New Netherland commissioners at Southold.

After a boisterous voyage through the Sound, Colve's commissioners meanwhile met, near Plum Gut, the vessel conveying Willys and Winthrop to Long Island, which struck its colors to the Dutch. The Connecticut officers, on coming on board and producing their commissions, were courteously treated, and the Dutch, on their side, showed them their own papers. Both parties then landed on Long Island, Steenwyck and his colleagues spending the night with Sylvester. The next morning the commissioners on both sides rowed up to Southold. A large force was in arms. Steenwyck desired the inhabitants to be summoned; but the Connecticut officers urged the people to remain faithful to the King of England. Upon this, Moore, who had been named a magistrate of Southold, declined the Dutch appointment; and Arnold, although already sworn as schout, declared that he had resigned his office, because his neighbors threatened to plunder his house. Seeing that they could now do nothing at Southold, Colve's commissioners left the village, intending to go to Southampton. But, finding that they would "be unable to effect any thing, and rather do more harm than good," they came back to New Orange with an unsatisfactory report.*

28 October / 7 Novem.

Foiled by the Connecticut commissioners.

30 October / 9 Novem. Return to New Orange.

On the return of Willys and Winthrop, Connecticut, considering the condition of her "dear countrymen upon Long Island, their further motion for assistance, and the late attempts of their enemy the Dutch upon them," determined to send them help; and commissioned Captain Fitz John Winthrop "to be sergeant major over the military forces of his majesty's subjects on Long Island." Accordingly, adventurers were raised at Stonington and New London, and hurried across the Sound to Southold.†

13/23 Novem. Connecticut forces sent to Southold.

Meanwhile "the Dutch interest" in New Netherland was hoping that Van Ruyven would do much for them in the fatherland. But Van Ruyven returned unexpectedly to New Orange, reporting that the snow "Expectatie," in which he embarked, had been wrecked near Nantucket. Ewoutsen was dispatched thither with the Zeehond, to bring back the disabled vessel, but not to damage any New En-

Van Ruyven, shipwrecked, returns to New Orange.

6/16 Novem. Ewoutsen sent to Nantucket.

the Connecticut General Court granted Bankes "forty shillings towards his expences, when he was detained in Yorke, in the year seventy three:" Col. Rec. Conn., ii., 253.

* Col. Doc., ii., 654–658; Wood, 97; Thompson, i., 155; Palfrey, iii., 124; *ante*, 217, 218.

† Mass. H. S. Coll., xxx., 89, 91; Palfrey, iii., 125; Col. Rec. Conn., ii., 216.

CHAP. V. 1673.

gland craft, unless the Expectatie had been captured; in which case he was to take or destroy all English vessels, "whencesoever they may be." 15/25 Novem. New England vessels captured. Ewoutsen reported that the Expectatie had been taken by an English privateer, commanded by Joseph Dudson, and carried to Boston; and that, according to his orders, he had brought into New Orange four New England trading ketches. These vessels were detained "provisionally under arrest," and their masters 17/27 Novem. were sent to Rhode Island with a letter from Colve to Leverett, asking that the crew of the Expectatie might be allowed to return unmolested from Boston. Upon further Condemned. 20/30 Novem. consideration, the New England prizes were confiscated as belonging to "subjects of England actually in open war against our state."*

25 Novem./5 Decem. Threats of Massachusetts. These spirited Dutch reprisals waked up New England. Massachusetts demanded the release of its coasters, and threatened, otherwise, "a full reparation by force of arms." 3/13 Decem. Colve's reply. Colve replied that Massachusetts had seized a Dutch vessel and carried it to Boston, before any thing had been done by New Netherland to her prejudice; and that, in future, Massachusetts should employ as messengers "honorable people, and no spies."†

Connecticut now proposed to Massachusetts a "prevent- 21 Novem./1 Decem. ive expedition" against New Netherland, offering a "proportionable conjunction and compliance." Massachusetts 10/20 Decem. determined "that God doth call them to do something in a hostile way for their own defence," fitted out a ship and Action of Connecticut and Massachusetts. a ketch, and impressed soldiers. But, as Dudson had seized the Dutch vessel at Nantucket, which was "without the jurisdiction of this court," and had acted under a letter of marque from the king, and not from Massachusetts, it was thought "not convenient to proceed to a judication" of the 17/27 Decem. prize. Plymouth resolved that there was "just ground of a war," and that she should do her utmost against the Dutch in New Netherland. But Rhode Island, not belonging to the New England Confederation, took no action.‡

This state of war obliged Colve to adopt more severe measures toward strangers, especially English. Francis

* Col. Doc., ii., 526, 532, 658, 662, 663, 664; Col. Rec. Conn., ii., 565; Mass. Rec., iv. (ii.), 573, 574; Mass. H. S. Coll., xxx., 103; *ante*, 221. † Col. Doc., ii., 667, 668.

‡ Col. Rec. Conn., ii., 216–220, 555, 556; Mass. Rec., iv. (ii.), 572, 573, 574; Plymouth Rec., v., 135, 136; N. Y. Col. Doc., ii., 663; Palfrey, iii., 98, 122, 125; R. I. Rec., iii., 508–515.

Beado, an Englishman, had been convicted, on his own confession, of designing to burn the village of Fordham, and had been sentenced to be branded and banished from New Netherland for twenty-five years. In addition to the previous order of 11th September, a proclamation was now issued requiring all strangers who had not taken the oath of allegiance to leave the province at once, and forbidding all persons, not inhabitants and subjects, to come within the government without proper passports. The inhabitants were also forbidden to harbor such strangers, or hold any correspondence with the people of New England and all other actual enemies; and all letters to or from such persons were to be sent to the provincial secretary's office for examination.*

CHAP. V. 1673. 28 Novem. / 8 Decem. Colve's vigorous police measures. 2/12 Decem.

Colve also appointed Captain William Knyff, of the infantry in Fort Willem Hendrick, to be "Fiscal and Conservator of the Laws" in New Netherland. It was a revival of the office, held last by De Sille, under Stuyvesant; the duties of which were to promote the peace and prosperity of the province, maintain the jurisdiction of the home government, prosecute all offenders, and to take care "that good law and justice be administered, without respect of persons, in all courts of justice within this province, according to the laudable custom, laws, and ordinances of our Fatherland."†

5/15 Decem. Knyff fiscal of New Netherland.

Colve now visited Midwout, where he had invited the magistrates of the Dutch towns on Long Island to meet him. He informed them of the preparations making in New England, and recommended the towns to send grain to New Orange, repair thither whenever summoned, keep a good watch, and send horsemen occasionally to observe what was doing in the English towns. Steenwyck, Van Ruyven, and Van Brugh were directed to examine the houses in the city, and report what accommodation could be given to "outside people" seeking refuge from the enemy. The towns in Schout Lawrence's district, and Bergen, Haerlem, and Fordham, were also enjoined fidelity and vigilance.‡

9/19 Decem. Colve at Flatbush, or Midwout.

12/22 Decem.

* Col. Doc., ii., 665, 666; *ante*, 222.

† Col. Doc., ii., 668, 669; *ante*, vol. i., 164, 414, 532, 622.

‡ Col. Doc., ii., 669, 670, 672, 673. The burgomasters of the city, anxious for its safety, were alarmed that the frigate Surinam had left the harbor on the 2d of December, contrary to the promise of Evertsen and Binckes, *ante*, 221, and, on calling on Colve, were informed that he could not and would not explain his reasons, but that "with or without the ship

CHAP. V.

1673.

17/27 Decem. New Orange regulations.

The city fortifications being nearly completed, at "excessive expense, trouble, and labor of the burghery and inhabitants," regulations were made to secure the place. At sundown the gates were to be closed, and the burgher watch set; and no other person was to approach the batteries until sunrise. No one could enter or depart, except through the city gate, on pain of death. Jacobus van de Water was appointed town major of New Orange and auditor of its court-martial. The commissioned officers of the city militia were Captains Cornelis Steenwyck, Martin Kregier, Johannes van Brugh, and Ægidius Luyck, Lieutenants William Beekman, Jacob Kip, Christopher Hooghland, and Nicholas Bayard, and Ensigns Gabriel Minvielle, Stephanus van Cortlandt, and Gelyn Verplanck. They were thanked by the governor for the zeal they had shown in fortifying New Orange, and assured that the States General would not fail to "take the greatest interest in the preservation and prosperity of the city." But the event did not justify Colve's too ready words.*

Van de Water town major.

Militia officers.

Following the laudable practice of the fatherland, the governor issued a proclamation that, as the province was now blessed with "the free and pure worship of God," and other mercies, the first Wednesday in each month should be observed in New Netherland as "an universal day" of fasting, humiliation, and thanksgiving, on which all labor, gaming, or excess in drinking was strictly prohibited.†

5/15 Novem. Fasting and thanksgiving days ordered.

On the Delaware the Provincial Instruction was readily enforced by Schout Alrichs, and magistrates were established at the Hoarkill. Captain John Carr, who had gone to Maryland, was allowed to settle himself in New Netherland, if he took the oath of allegiance; but if he refused, his estate was to be seized. As several Marylanders had lately committed aggressions on the Delaware settlers, Colve invited the sufferers to New Orange, and directed all the inhabitants there to obey the orders of Alrichs.‡

6/16 Novem. Delaware affairs.

aforesaid, he should not undertake nor execute any thing except what his Honor should consider serviceable and expedient for the fort, the city, and the burghery :" New Orange Rec., vii., 72; Val. Man., 1850, 522. The Surinam was back again in harbor in January, 1674: Col. Doc., ii., 682.

* Col. Doc., ii., 670, 671, 674, 675, 677, 678; Val. Man., 1850, 523. Moulton, 7, 8, 11, 12, 21, mistakes the office of Van de Water for mayor, instead of major, of New Orange. The muster-roll of Captain Steenwyck's company, of which Bayard was lieutenant and Minvielle ensign, is in Val. Man., 1850, 424, 425.

† Col. Doc., ii., 658; Val. Man., 1850, 521.

‡ Col. Doc., ii., 597, 622, 632, 659, 663, 672, 673, 678; Col. MSS., xxiv., 97; S. Hazard, 409, 410.

In Achter Col, or New Jersey, Colve's instruction was cheerfully obeyed. Bergen enacted some local regulations. At an assembly called by Schout Ogden at Elizabethtown, several ordinances were adopted, much milder than the English laws. Before approving them, Colve had them translated into the Dutch language. Weary of their distractions under the government of Berkeley and Carteret, the people of New Jersey welcomed the regained authority of the Republican Netherlands.*

CHAP. V. 1673. 13/23 Oct. Achter Col, or New Jersey. 8/18 Novem.

The Esopus officers were confirmed by the governor; among whom were Cornelis Wynkoop, Roeloff Kierstede, Wessel Tenbroeck, and Jan Burhans, of Swanenburg, or Kingston; and Louis du Bois, Roeloff Hendricksen, Jan Joosten, and Jan Broersen, of Hurley and Marbletown; and Captain Albert Heymans, who had been prominent in the riot of 1667. William la Montagne was made secretary of the three towns, and Isaac Grevenraet their schout, in place of William Beekman, who had removed to New Orange. Two brass guns, useless at Swanenburg, were ordered to be sent down to the metropolis, "as the same are required here."†

6 October. Esopus affairs. 15/25 Oct.

Schenectady was made subordinate to Willemstadt; and Anthonia van Curler was allowed an extension of the privilege which had been granted by Lovelace. As New France was now hostile to New Netherland, Commander Draeyer was directed to "stop all correspondence with the Jesuit, and Frenchmen from Canada, whether runaways or others." He was again instructed to observe all military precautions at Fort Nassau; not to confide in any French from Canada; and "to break off all correspondence with the Jesuit, but to excuse himself in a courteous manner."‡

27 October / 8 Novem. Willemstadt and Schenectady. 6/16 Novem. 17/27 Novem. Draeyer's orders.

The Jesuit missionaries had meanwhile been active among the Iroquois. Bruyas, at Tionnontoguen, or Saint Mary's, and Boniface, at Caghnawaga, or Saint Peter's, labored among the Mohawks. Although the smallest of the Iroquois villages, Caghnawaga was esteemed by the Jesuits, like ancient Judah by the Israelites, as the greatest of all their stations. Prayer was offered there as constantly

Bruyas and Boniface among the Mohawks.

* Col. Doc., ii., 621, 633, 643, 658, 683, 706, 714, 726; Whitehead, 61, 62.

† Col. Doc., ii., 622, 626, 627, 629, 630, 644, 646, 649, 650; Esopus Records; Warr., Ord., Passes, iii., 147; *ante*, 123, 157, 218.

‡ Col. Doc., ii., 652, 653, 654, 659, 662, 675; Council Minutes, iii., 120; *ante*, 218, 224.

CHAP. V. 1673. "as in the best regulated families of France." Yet, while zealous Mohawk converts paraded their chaplets in the Dutch church at Albany, the Jesuit missionaries mistrusted their frequent visits to the "heretics," and lamented their "wretched peace" with the Mahicans, which, by making the paths safe, enabled the Iroquois to get brandy to their hearts' content. The most interesting incident was the departure of a number of Mohawks to the mission at the Prairie de la Madeleine, near Montreal. This settlement had received its first Iroquois accessions from Oneida, whose chief, Garonhiague, or "*La cendre chaude*," became a catechist. While on a visit there, Kryn, or "the Great Mohawk," had become converted by Frémin; and, on his return to Caghnawaga, so moved the village that forty Mohawks, with their squaws and children, went back with him to the Prairie. Their brethren at Tionnontoguen, "who were not yet disposed to embrace the faith," complained to Bruyas of the "black robes, who seemed to wish to make their country a desert and ruin their villages." The health of Boniface, however, soon failed; and he returned to Quebec to die—conducting "a great party" of converts, and leaving Bruyas alone, in charge of both the Mohawk stations. The intervals of missionary labor were employed by the Iroquois superior in preparing his immortal dictionary of the Indian tongue.*

Emigration to Canada from New York.

12 June.

Millet at Oneida.

Millet became so popular at Oneida that he persuaded many proselytes to renounce the invocation of Agreskoué. But he was much embarrassed by the efforts of the Hollanders against the Jesuits, "since they had retaken Manhattan and Orange, and driven out the English." In an interesting letter to Dablon, at Quebec, Millet described an eclipse of the moon on the 21st of January, 1674, which he had foretold, much to the amazement of the savages.†

Lamberville at Onondaga.

At Onondaga, John de Lamberville was cheered by some new converts. But his flock was diminished by several

* Relation, 1672–3, 33–55; 1673–9, 140, 142, 143–151, 175, 177; Douniol's Miss. Can., i., 4–21, 179–189, 235–239, 279–293, 345, 346; ii., 10; Shea, 269–272, 298, 299; Charlevoix, ii., 233, 257, 354, 357; Col. Doc., ix., 352, 474; *ante*, 190–192. I find no authority for the statement in the note in Col. Doc., ix., 720 (repeated in N. Y. Senate Doc., 115, April 16, 1863), that Bruyas was among the Senecas in 1673. He certainly wrote from Tionnontoguen, by Boniface, to Frontenac, on 12th June of that year: Col. Doc., ix., 792; Douniol, i., 345.

† Relation, 1672–3, 55–65; 1673–9, 140; Douniol, i., 22–30, 175–177, 239–256; Charlevoix, ii., 258; Shea, 276, 282; *ante*, 178, 181, 191.

proselytes from their native "Babylon," who went to live at the more attractive Prairie de la Madeleine. Carheil, at Cayuga, had little to break the monotony of his station except the baptism of three Andaste prisoners before they were burned by their Iroquois conquerors.*

Carheil at Cayuga.

Among the Senecas, Garnier had charge of Saint Michael and Saint James, while Raffeix labored at Conception. Wanting assistance, the lonely Jesuits applied to Dablon, and Pierron was sent to their aid, who took care of Saint James. After leaving the Mohawks in 1671, Pierron returned to Quebec, and from there went to Acadia, where he spent the winter of 1673. Thence he wandered over New England, Maryland, and Virginia, finding nothing "but desolation and abomination among those heretics." At Boston he was "much esteemed," although suspected of Jesuitism, because of "the uncommon knowledge which he exhibited." Pierron offered to establish a mission among the Maryland savages, "whose language he knew." But Dablon, scrupulous not to allow a Canadian missionary to interfere with the "English Fathers" in Maryland, ordered Pierron to assist Garnier and Raffeix among the Senecas.†

Garnier and Raffeix at the Senecas.

Pierron in Acadia, New England, and Maryland.

Among the Senecas.

During the winter the Jesuit missionaries had reported to Frontenac that the Iroquois were not well disposed toward the French. The new Onnontio therefore resolved to make a pompous visit to Lake Ontario, and impress the savages with the power of Canada. He built two bateaux similar to that of Courcelles, but of a peculiar model, each carrying sixteen men with their provisions, and each mounted with small cannon, and painted "in a fashion unlike any thing seen before in the whole country."‡

Frontenac's visit to Lake Ontario.

To disarm the suspicions of the Iroquois, Frontenac dispatched La Salle, who was well acquainted with them, and had just returned from the West, to invite the five nations to meet him at Quinté Bay toward the end of June. On his way from Quebec to Montreal, as he was passing the Cap de la Madeleine, the governor is stated to have met

24 May.
3 June.

* Relation, 1672–3, 65–108; 1673–9, 143–146, 152; Douniol, i., 30–62, 256–268, 347; ii., 11; Shea, 283, 289.

† Relation, 1672–3, 108–114; 1673–9, 140; Douniol, i., 63–68, 268–278; ii., 8, 9, 10, 11, 12, 44; Shea, 268, 292; *ante*, 178, 192.

‡ Col. Doc., ix., 91, 95, 96; Faillon, iii., 456–470; *ante*, 180, 193.

CHAP. V. 1673.

Dablon, the superior of the Jesuits, who informed him that he had learned from the Indians that some Dutch ships had captured Manhattan; and that it was to be feared that they might blockade the Saint Lawrence, or even attack Quebec. But Frontenac, "seeing no foundation for this intelligence," continued his route, requesting Dablon not to divulge the news; at the same time taking precautions for the safety of Quebec and Tadoussac.*

19/29 June.

Frontenac started from La Chine with one hundred and twenty canoes and four hundred men, and ascended the Saint Lawrence with "incredible labor," fifty men being required to drag each heavy bateau up the rapids. On his way he saw "the most delightful country in the world."

29 June. / 9 July. La Galette, or Prescott.

At length he arrived at "a point at the head of all the rapids," called "La Galette,"† which the Sieur la Valterie had previously chosen for a magazine of provisions. Here the governor received letters from La Salle, informing him that two hundred leading Iroquois had gone to meet him at Quinté. This obliged him to send the Sulpitian Abbés Fénelon and D'Urfé thither, to ask them to come twenty leagues nearer, at Cataracouy, which he judged to be the best place for the establishment which Courcelles had proposed. Passing Otondiata and the "vast group of Islands with which the river is studded," Frontenac reached the opening of Lake Ontario, and arranged his flotilla in order

2/12 July.

of battle. Here he met D'Urfé, who had overtaken the Iroquois on their way to Quinté, and caused them to turn back. The French flotilla followed them "to the mouth

Frontenac at Cataracouy.

of the River Cataracouy, into a bay about a cannon shot from the entrance, which forms one of the most beautiful and agreeable harbors in the world;" and Frontenac was

* Col. Doc., ix., 97, 98; *ante*, 179. This is a palpable anachronism. New York was recaptured by the Dutch on the 30th of July, or 9th of August, 1673 (*ante*, 208), which was eight or nine weeks after Dablon is said to have reported it to the governor at the Cap de la Madeleine! It seems that Frontenac got his first information in a letter from Lamberville, dated at Oswego, on the 30th of August, or 9th of September, 1673, and dispatched by La Salle, who, he states, was "in haste to depart, to carry the news of the reconquest of Manhattan and Orange by the Hollanders, and of the current rumour that they have twenty ships of war about to sail for Quebec:" Douniol, i., 347, 348; *post*, 239, 240.

† "La Galette" (the meaning of which French word is a flat cake, familiar to Parisians) seems to have been what is now called Wind-mill Point, a little below Prescott, in Canada West, the scene of one of the "patriot" movements in 1838: compare Col. Doc., ix., 77, 101, 114, 195, 241, 381; Charlevoix, v., 281–286, and Map; Gent. Mag., xxvii., 74, Map; Hough's Saint Lawrence, 41, 46; Barber and Howe's N. Y. Coll., 488. The name, however, was afterward transferred to Fort Présentation at Oswegatchie or Ogdensburg: see Smith, i., 69, *note;* Col. Doc., vii., 136, 573; x., 349; Doc. Hist., i., 281, and Sauthier's Map annexed.

"enraptured at finding a spot so well adapted for his design."* CHAP. V.

The next day Frontenac received the Iroquois with great pomp in front of his tent, called them his "children," and named a day for solemn conference. In the mean time the Sieur Rendin traced out a fort, and the troops worked at it with good will. At the appointed time Frontenac told the Five Nations that the Jesuits labored only to teach them, and should be respected; that Onnontio had proved his power by coming up all the rapids with bateaux carrying cannon; that he now ratified the treaties made by his predecessors; and he urged his "children" to let their youth learn the French tongue, promising to communicate with them either through the missionaries, or by some "person of character" like La Salle. The Iroquois "appeared highly gratified that Onnontio had, at the first and second audience, addressed them as Children, and thereby had bound himself to act towards them as a Father; the other Onnontios not having made use of that mark of authority, and they having never consented to be addressed otherwise than as Brothers." They expressed their joy at the establishment of a French fort at Cataracouy; yet they lamented the conquests of the French in Holland, and the ruin of the Dutch, who "had been friendly with them."† At the same time, they wished Frontenac to assist them against the Andastes, "the sole enemies remaining on their hands." This, however, the governor waived; and the Five Nations promised to consider his proposition in regard to their children learning French.

1673. 3/13 July. Fort traced out. 7/17 July. Conference with the Iroquois. The Iroquois called "children." 8/18 July Joy of the Iroquois.

The fort was soon completed; and, after settling its garrison, Frontenac returned to Montreal, delighted that he had accomplished his enterprise without any accident, and by the resources of Canada alone, without any aid from the court. Not long afterward La Salle came back from Oswego with a letter from Lamberville, reporting the re-

22 July/1 August. 30 August/9 Septem.

* Col. Doc., ix., 91, 98–103, 792; x., 349; Douniol, i., 172, 240, 250, 346; Charlevoix, ii., 245; *ante*, 180, 193. The admirable situation of Kingston, in Canada West, well deserves the praise bestowed by its founder, Frontenac. But in 1708, D'Aigremont reported to Pontchartrain that La Galette would be a much better place for the fort than Frontenac: Col. Doc., ix., 822; and Charlevoix adopted this opinion when he visited Cataracouy in 1721: Charlevoix, v., 281, 282.

† Col. Doc., ix., 110. It is clear from this that Frontenac could not yet have heard the news of the recapture of New York by the Dutch, referred to on the previous page.

CHAP. V. capture of New York by the Dutch, and their proposed attack of Quebec. La Salle was immediately appointed gov-
1673. La Salle governor of "Fort Frontenac." ernor of "Fort Frontenac," at Cataracouy, an interesting
detail of the establishment of which was sent to Colbert.*

In his letters home, Frontenac dwelt upon the inter-
$\frac{8}{18}$ Novem. meddling of the Jesuits with the Recollets. Colbert, in
reply, instructed him to form towns and villages in Cana-
1674. da, rather than prosecute distant discoveries, unless they
$\frac{7}{17}$ May. should open a nearer way to France than through the
Saint Lawrence. At the same time, he expressed surprise
Population of Canada. that the population of Canada was only six thousand seven
$\frac{4}{14}$ Novem. hundred souls.† Frontenac answered that his expedition
to Lake Ontario had made the Iroquois friendly, and in-
sured the safety of the Jesuit missionaries among them.
But the only way to build up Canada was to follow the
example of her neighbors at Manhattan and Orange. The
Jesuits only endeavored "to instruct the Indians, or rather
to get beavers, and not to be parish priests to the French."
But the Franciscans or Recollets, who, under the Father
The Recollets at Cataracouy. Gabriel de la Ribourde, were now transferred from
Quinté to Cataracouy, were laboring with great zeal, and,
if more numerous, "would assuredly do wonders in the
missions."‡

In the mean time the exploration of the Mississippi had
been partially accomplished. After spending the winter
at Mackinaw, Jolliet and Marquette left Green Bay in
1673. June, 1673, ascended the Fox River, crossed the portage
to the Wisconsin, down which they drifted in their birch
$\frac{7}{17}$ June. Jolliet and Marquette explore the Upper Mississippi. canoes until they reached the Great River, which the father called "the Conception," while his fellow-adventurer
wished to name it "the Colbert." Following its current,
they passed the mouth of the muddy "Pekitanoui," or
Missouri, and then that of the limpid "Ohio," which Bruyas—who literally translated its Mohawk name—called
"The Beautiful River." Having reached the mouth of

* Col. Doc., ix., 103–114, 122, 211, 792; Quebec MSS., ii. (ii.), 291; DounioI, i., 347, 348; Garneau, i., 112; Hennepin's Louisiana, 5, 6; Shea, 283; Discovery of the Mississippi, xxxiv.

† Col. Doc., ix., 88, 95, 115, 116, 792; Quebec MSS., ii. (ii.), 291; *ante*, vol. i., 67. The population of New Netherland at this time was estimated to be from six to seven thousand, and that of New England about one hundred and twenty thousand: Col. Doc., ii., 526, 598; Chalmers, i., 434.

‡ Col. Doc., ix., 95, 120, 121, 793; Quebec MSS., ii. (ii.), 57; Charlevoix, ii., 257; Sparks's La Salle, 16; Shea's Missions, 412; Discovery of the Mississippi, 85, 89, 159; *ante*, 149, 169, 170, 194.

the Arkansas, and satisfied themselves that the Mississippi CHAP. V.
emptied into the Gulf of Mexico, the explorers returned by 1673.
way of the Illinois River to Chicago, and thence to Green $\frac{7}{17}$ July.
Bay, having traveled nearly three thousand miles. Leav-
ing Marquette at Green Bay, Jolliet went homeward as far Septem.
as Mackinaw, accompanied by a young savage, who had
been given him by the chief of the Illinois, and spent the
winter there. Early the next spring he came down to Fort 1674.
Frontenac, where he communicated his discoveries to La
Salle, who was in command of the post. In descending
the Saint Lawrence, Jolliet safely passed all the rapids until he reached the Sault Saint Louis, just above Montreal,
where his canoe was overturned, all his papers lost, his July.
young Illinois companion drowned, and his own life barely
saved after a four hours' struggle with the waters.

Nevertheless, Jolliet was able to prepare from memory a Jolliet's map and
map and a narrative of his marvelous journey. From these narrative.
materials Dablon compiled a "Relation," which he dis- $\frac{22 \text{ July.}}{1 \text{ August.}}$
patched to the superior general of the Jesuits at Paris.
Not long afterward Jolliet was rewarded by a grant of the
island of Anticosti. By the Ottawa flotilla Dablon received copies of Marquette's journal and map, which he Mar-
forwarded to France. Frontenac also sent to Colbert the quette's journal
map and narrative of Jolliet, who had discovered an inland and map. $\frac{4}{14}$ Novem.
navigation from Lake Ontario to the Gulf of Mexico, with Frontenac recom-
only a short portage; and therefore he suggested that a mends a French
French settlement should be made at Niagara, and a bark post at Ni-
be built on Lake Erie. This idea was no doubt originated agara.
by La Salle, who had seen Jolliet at Cataracouy, fresh
from his Mississippi voyage, and who was now out of employment. La Salle therefore resolved to return to France La Salle re-
to plead his own cause with the king; and Frontenac cheer- turns to France.
fully recommended him as "the most capable for all the
enterprises of discovery."*

* Col. Doc., vi., 532, 545, 610; ix., 118, 119, 121, 122, 211, 216, 383, 668, 706, 787, 793, 886; Quebec MSS., ii. (ii.), 57; La Potherie, ii., 131; Douniol's Miss. Can., i., 193–204; ii., 5, 6, 241–330; Faillon, iii., 312–315, 472; Charlevoix, ii., 248–250; Hist. Mag., v., 237–239; Hennepin's Louisiana, 6, 13; New Discovery, 303–306; Sparks's La Salle, and Marquette; Bancroft, iii., 155-161; Garneau, i., 232–237; Shea's Disc. of the Mississippi, xxvii.–xxxiv., lxxv., lxxx., 4–52, 83, 84; and Catholic Missions, 405, 406, 435–437; *ante*, 163, 194. The copy of Marquette's Journal which Dablon sent to Paris was published by Thevénot, with curtailments, in 1681. An English translation was issued in 1698, annexed to Hennepin's "New Discovery," 306–349; and another in Dutch is contained in vol. xxviii. of Van der Aa's Collection of 1707. Another copy of Marquette's Journal was prepared for publication

CHAP. V.

1674.

While the dominion of France was thus indefinitely extended by her adventurous sons over the interior of North America, that of Holland over a modest space of its seaboard was firmly maintained by her patriotic children.

15 Jan. New Orange affairs.

The metropolis of New Netherland was brought more directly under the governor's authority by a "Provisional Instruction," which, among other things, authorized the Fiscal Knyff to preside over the court of Schout, Burgomasters, and Schepens. The city magistrates rebelled at
16 Jan. this; but, upon Colve's threat to dismiss them and convoke the burghers to nominate others, they yielded, under a protest.*

To provide for the "excessive expenses" of the city for-
1 Febr'y. tifications, Colve levied a tax on the estate of each citizen of New Orange worth over one thousand guilders. Com-
19 Febr'y. Tax for the city fortifications. missioners were accordingly appointed, and lists made out of the property of "the most affluent inhabitants;" which amounted to upwards of five hundred and twenty thousand guilders. But as it would take time to collect this tax,
17 March. each burgher assessed more than four thousand guilders was ordered to "advance, by way of loan," the hundredth penny of his capital, "for such is deemed to be necessary for the public good." Of this forced loan Major Jacobus
24 March. van de Water was appointed receiver.†

The city of New Orange being now "capable (under God) of resisting all attacks of any enemies," the "out
13 March. people" of the neighboring villages were directed to hasten there with proper arms on the first notice of the coming of any hostile ships. The citizens were also forbidden to
16 March. Military precautions. leave town without the consent of their magistrates. The sloops sailing up the North River to Esopus and Willemstadt, and to the Delaware, were required to go in rota-

by Dablon, which, however, was long buried, along with the original map, in the archives of the Jesuit College at Quebec. In 1844 they came into the hands of Father Felix Martin, by whom they were intrusted to Mr. John G. Shea, who published a fac-simile of the map and a translation of the Journal in 1853. The originals were privately printed, with great elegance, in 1855, by Mr. James Lenox. They were also reprinted at Paris in 1861, by Douniol, in his "Mission du Canada," ii., 241–331. Copies of Jolliet's map and letter to Frontenac, made from the originals at Paris, are in the Library of the Canadian Parliament at Quebec: see Catalogue (ed. 1858), p. 1615. Henri Martin, i., 491, insists that La Salle discovered the Mississippi before Jolliet and Marquette: compare Garneau, i., 236, *note;* and Douniol, ii., 375; Faillon, iii., 313.

* Col. Doc., ii., 678–681; Val. Man., 1850, 523–527; *ante*, 212, 226, 233.

† Col. Doc., ii., 685, 688, 697, 699, 700, 701; Val. Man., 1850, 525, 530; 1851, 435; Moulton, 14, 15, 16; Valentine's N. York, 319–330; *ante*, p. 234. The rate list is in Col. Doc., ii., 699, 700.

tion, so as not to weaken the capital. In case an enemy should arrive, all vessels were to haul behind the frigate Surinam, "near the circular battery."* CHAP. V. 1674. 27 March.

The towns on Long Island, with Bergen and Haerlem, were also directed to send each a militia officer and magistrate to a Convention in New Orange. Francis Bloodgood, one of the schepens of Flushing, was at the same time appointed "chief officer" of the Dutch people of Flushing, Heemstede, Jamaica, and Newtown, and charged with their military police. The Convention met accordingly, and every precaution was taken to provide sufficient defense for the capital in case it should be attacked.† 22 March. Convention at New Orange. 26 March.

The governor's attention had meanwhile been drawn to affairs at the eastern end of Long Island. Provisions being needed at the fort, Ewoutsen was ordered to receive them at Shelter Island from Sylvester, whose bond was now due. Some soldiers were sent along, in hope that the refractory towns might be reduced to subjection. Meanwhile Fitz John Winthrop had reached Southold with his Connecticut auxiliaries. On learning the approach of Colve's expedition, forces were hurried from Southampton and Easthampton; and it was determined not to hinder the Dutch from obtaining what they wanted at Shelter Island, but only to defend Southold. Sylvester promptly delivered his stipulated provisions to Ewoutsen. The next morning the Dutch flotilla ranged itself before Southold, and Sylvester was sent to demand the surrender of the English, who were promised the same privileges with other towns in New Netherland, but were threatened, in case of their refusal, "with fire and sword." He was answered that the Dutch commander would be received "as a person that disturbs His Majesty's subjects." Ewoutsen now ordered his boats to land, and a gun to be fired from his snow, the Zeehond, which did no harm. The fire was returned without effect. As the English were evidently too overpowering, it was thought absurd to attempt any thing farther; and the Dutch flotilla quietly returned to New Orange with the provisions for which it had come to Shelter Island safely on board.‡ Febr'y. Dutch expedition to Shelter Island. 23 Feb'y./5 March. 24 Febr'y./6 March. Attempt to land at Southold repulsed.

* Col. Doc., ii., 695, 696, 697, 702; Val. Man., 1850, 536, 537; 1851, 439, 440, 441; Moulton, 12; Wood, 97; Thompson, i., 156. † Col. Doc., ii., 103, 591, 701, 702; *ante*, 215.

‡ Col. Doc., ii., 588–590; Mass. H. S. Coll., xxx., 91–94; Col. Rec. Conn., ii., 566, 567; Wood,

CHAP. V. Winthrop's conduct at Southold was applauded by Connecticut, which directed him to continue "to assist and de-
1674. fend the people there 'till at least these present motions of
$\frac{2}{12}$ March. Connecticut. the Dutch be over." Application was also made to Massachusetts for a man-of-war "to cleare the coasts." But
$\frac{8}{18}$ March. Massachusetts. Governor Leverett replied that "the generall voague of the
averseness of the people to ingage in any acts of hostility
against the Dutch, occasions retardment of comeing to any
conclusion tending thereto." The General Court, however,
"after much and serious consideration of the condition of
$\frac{11}{21}$ March. these colonies," resolved to send out a vessel or two "to repress the insolence of the Dutch in the Sound, who are,
with an inconsiderable force there, triumphing to the
amazement and affrightment of our friends." Connecti-
$\frac{14}{24}$ March. cut was advised of this determination; but no cruisers appear to have been dispatched from Boston.*

$\frac{16}{21}$ March. It was now rumored that the King of England was
about to retake New Netherland. Some vessels having
$\frac{15}{25}$ April. arrived at Sandy Hook, Ewoutsen was dispatched to learn
what they were, but "not to imperil his snow." Soon aft-
erward it was reported that peace had been made between
Holland and England. Nevertheless, the property of in-
$\frac{2}{12}$ May. English colonial property confiscated. habitants of New England, Virginia, and Maryland found
within New Netherland, which had been excepted, was
now confiscated. The Zeehond was also ordered to cruise
in Long Island Sound, where Ewoutsen captured two Massachusetts craft, and in Narragansett Bay a Plymouth
$\frac{16}{26}$ May. sloop. The prizes were brought to New Orange and condemned. But this was the last act of hostility between
the Dutch and English colonies in North America.†

1673. The first intelligence of the reconquest of New York
$\frac{14}{24}$ Oct. came to Holland by way of England. Michielsen, who
had been sent home with dispatches from Binckes, was

9, 97; Thompson, i., 155, 367, 368; Trumbull, i., 324, 325; Palfrey, iii., 125, 126; *ante*, 217, 231. The Dutch Records (Col. Doc., ii., 688–707) do not mention this expedition, of which the reducing the towns at the east end of Long Island seems to have been "the chiefe part of their errand:" Mass. H. S. Coll., xxx., 99, 100.

* Mass. H. S. Coll., xxx., 95–98; Mass. Rec., iv. (ii.), 576, 577; Palfrey, iii., 122, 126; *ante*, 229, 232. The vessels ordered by Massachusetts for service in the Sound were the "Swallow," of 12 guns, Captain Richard Sprague, and the "Salisbury," of 8 guns, Captain Samuel Moseley: Mass. H. S. Coll., xxx., 100–102, 104.

† Col. Doc., ii., 611, 707, 710, 715, 716, 719, 725, 726, 727; iii., 208–212; Col. MSS., xxiii., 325; Mass. H. S. Coll., xxx., 99, 104, 107; Col. Rec. Conn., ii., 222; Moulton, 13; Palfrey, iii., 127; *ante*, 228.

1673.

15/25 Oct. News of the reconquest of New Netherland in Holland.

20/30 Oct. Action of the States General.

captured off Beachy Head, and threw them overboard to prevent their being read by the English. The States General deliberated "what further ought to be done for the protection and preservation of the Colony of New Netherland." Upon the petition of merchants interested in the colonial trade, the secret committee on foreign affairs was directed "to dispose of the matter as they shall think proper." Six weeks afterward, on the receipt of dispatches from Binckes, the States General resolved "that the superintendence of New Netherland, and whatsoever appertains thereto, shall be committed, as it is hereby committed, provisionally and until further order, to the Board of Admiralty at Amsterdam; Ordering and commanding the inhabitants of New Netherland aforesaid, and the military who shall be sent thither, absolutely, and without any reserve, to obey the orders which will be issued by or on behalf of the said Board, in their High Mightinesses' name: —That by Commission of their High Mightinesses, a proper person shall be sent thither, with the title of Governor or Commander, in order to clothe him with greater respect: —That the aforesaid Governor or Commander shall be chief and Supreme Ruler, both in civil and in military affairs; and that he shall by the aforesaid Commission, be instructed to obey the orders of said Board of Admiralty at Amsterdam:—That JORIS ANDRINGA, actually Secretary of the Provincial fleet, shall be appointed and commissioned to said government or command, and that the necessary commission shall be expedited to him:—That the Captain and officers of the Companies to be sent thither shall be given in charge, as they are hereby enjoined, precisely and punctually, to obey all orders that will be given them by said Board of Admiralty at Amsterdam."*

5/15 Decem.

Joris Andringa appointed governor of New Netherland.

By this action of the States General a regular government was established over New Netherland, and Joris Andringa took his place in her annals as the successor of Anthony Colve. The Amsterdam Board of Admiralty, after considering Binckes's dispatches, determined that, as the entire province had been surrendered at discretion, all the

1674.

19/29 Jan'y. Further action in Holland.

* Col. Doc., ii., 527–531; Sylvius, ix., 660, 665; Mass. H. S. Coll., xxx., 103; *ante*, 213. Joris is the Dutch for George. Andringa had formerly been secretary to De Ruyter, and had written interesting accounts of the battle of June, 1666, and of the Chatham expedition of June, 1667: Basnage, i., 781, 805; *ante*, 124, 134.

Chap. V.

1674.

property of the Duke of York, or his officers, was good prize, and should be applied to the benefit of the state; and that the governor of New Netherland should be authorized to "maintain some neutrality" with the English colonies north and south of him, and even to make a treaty of commerce with them. These points were approved by the Prince of Orange and the States General, and were ordered to be carried into effect by "Joris Andringa, Governor of New Netherland aforesaid."*

21/31 Jan'y.

Extraordinary vicissitudes in New York history.

Extraordinary vicissitudes have always marked the colonial life of New York. Another epoch appeared to be now opening in her history; and many in her Dutch fatherland looked forward to the establishment of their nation's power over the most important region in North America. That region, they knew, had formerly languished under the selfish rule of the West India Company. Now they hoped it would flourish as the rose under the more genial administration of the Dutch Republic itself. Midway between the Royalist and the Puritan colonies of England might grow up a valiant empire, to teach the world sublime lessons in civil liberty, religious freedom, and patriotic endurance. The descendants of the men who had first proclaimed the doctrine of "taxation only by consent;" who had banished the Inquisition, and established in its place liberty of conscience; and who were even now breasting the ruthless cohorts of France, could maintain and extend in the Columbian world the principles and the virtues which distinguished the grandest "United" nation in Christendom. Instead of emigrating to Batavia, the children of Holland might follow the sun toward the west, and on the great "River of the Mountains" which their fatherland had discovered, could build up "the Exchange of a wealthier Amsterdam, and the schools of a more learned Leyden."†

Holland hopes to retain New Netherland.

1673.

Providence decrees England to succeed Holland in America.

But these things were not to be. England must take the place of Holland in America. The Dutch Republic could not, single-handed, cope with France and Britain. Peace with the latter had become a necessity. William of Orange felt that, to secure the republic, Louis must be ef-

* Col. Doc., ii., 535–537; *ante*, 212, 223.

† *Ante*, vol. i., 224, 403, 436, 437, 441, 442, 443, 445, 746; ii., 204; Macaulay, i., 219.

CHAP. V.

1673.

fectually crippled. Alliances against France and England were accordingly made between the United Provinces on the one hand, and the Emperor of Germany and the King of Spain on the other. Europe wondered at the extraordinary spectacle of the Roman Catholic dynasty which had employed Alva to crush the young Protestant Dutch Republic, now hastening to support it against both the powers which had watched the cradle of its independence. Spain, however, made it a condition that the Netherlands should consent to a peace with England, upon the basis of a mutual restoration of conquests, the yielding to her of the honor of the flag, and the payment of an indemnity for the expenses of the war. Political necessity alone could bend the States General to these hard terms. They yielded:—just two months before they knew the reconquest of New Netherland, and just one month after that event happened. Had they known it they would hardly have given up their American acquisition. But when the news reached them they were too deeply committed to recede. The day it came to the Hague they sent a trumpeter to Charles the Second, with a firm but conciliatory letter, which offered him every reasonable satisfaction.*

Alliance between Holland, Germany, and Spain.

$\frac{20}{30}$ August. Conditions imposed by Spain.

Dutch necessity yields.

$\frac{15}{25}$ Oct.

This letter reached London just as the news came that the Dutch had reconquered New York. Memorials were quickly presented to the Plantation Council for the recovery of the province, where the Dutch, it was said, were about to send men-of-war and soldiers "to fortify themselves in those parts." William Dyer, of Rhode Island, urged that "New York, being the centre of His Majesty's western Dominions, and furnished with so excellent a harbour to secure shipping, also a pleasant town and beautiful country round about," should be retaken at once. For this purpose frigates and fire-ships should be sent to New England, where they could be manned; and a militia force from there could then besiege the town, while the vessels blockaded the harbor. Sir John Knight, of Bristol, which was at that time largely interested in colonial commerce, also explained to Lord Shaftesbury the defenseless condi-

News in London of the Dutch reconquest of New York.

22 October.

26 October.

Its recovery urged by Dyer and Knight.

20 October.

* Basnage, ii., 440, 441, 458–460; Sylvius, ix., 632, 633, 654–658, 665, 684, 685; Col. Doc., ii., 529; Dumont, vii., 240–243; Davies, iii., 133, 134; Lingard, xii., 306, 318; Macaulay, ii., 181–185; Temple, ii., 230, 246; Martin's Louis XIV., i., 377; *ante*, 245.

CHAP. V. 1673.

tion of Virginia, where the planters "doe generally desire a trade with the Dutch and all other nations," and counseled the recovery of New York as the best means of preserving "the rest of the plantations." The Council reported to the king that New York was "the only fortified harbor in all the Northern Plantations of America," which, if the Dutch were allowed to retain, would be ruinous to the English. Virginia and Maryland would suffer the most; but "the inhabitants of New England, being more intent upon the advancement of their own private trade than the publique interest of your Majesty's crowne and government, may, if the Dutch continue a quiet possession there, enter into commerce with them, whereby it is to be feared they will at present divert a great part of the trade of England into those countries, and lay a foundation for such an union hereafter, between them and Holland, as will be very prejudiciall to all your Majesty's Plantations, if not terrible to England itself." Its speedy reduction by an overwhelming combined force was therefore recommended, as well as the removal of its Dutch colonists "farther up into the country from the sea-side, at least as far as Albany; their inhabiting the town of New York being a great cause of the loss of both Town and castle now, and as long as they shall stay there, there will be the like danger upon any occasion for the future."*

15 Novem. Report of Plantation Council in favor of regaining New York.

But never was the British government less able to act with vigor. Charles was anxious to continue the war with the Dutch. On the other hand, he desired the friendship of Louis, their most determined foe. Through the influence of the French king, who gave the bride a splendid dowry, the Duke of York had just been married to the Roman Catholic Princess Mary of Modena, a niece of Mazarin. James, who had been deprived of his English offices only in the spring before, by the Test Act, was doubly mortified at the loss of his American province, the prompt regaining of which was even more important than wedding festivities at Whitehall.†

30 Septem. Second marriage of the Duke of York to Mary of Modena.

Charles's treasury, however, was exhausted. It was dif-

* Col. Doc., iii., 207–213; Hist. Mag., i. (ii.), 299, 300; Index N. J. Col. Doc., 5; Evelyn, ii., 95; Pepys, iii., 464; Macaulay, i., 335; iv., 486; Valentine's N. Y., 233, 234; R. I. Col. Rec., i., 266; ii., 108, 396; Palfrey, ii., 360, 558; iii., 34; *ante*, vol. i., 557.

† Clarke's James II., i., 484, 485, 486; Martin's Louis XIV., i., 380; *ante*, 201.

ficult for him to procure the ships and men necessary for an expedition against New Netherland. The war with the United Provinces had become very unpopular in England. Its real statesmen were disgusted with a strife in which the English and Dutch fleets had been made "gladiators for French spectators;" while its merchants were almost ruined by the privateers of Holland and Zealand, which had captured twenty-seven hundred British ships. Apprehending a change in the national religion, which the recent marriage of the presumptive heir to the crown rendered more probable than ever, Parliament saw with chagrin the league of Charles and Louis against the republic, which it regarded as the "Bulwark of the Reformation;" and it insisted that the king should break away from France, and make a separate treaty with the Netherlands.

20 October. Parliament opposed to war with the Dutch.

In vain did Charles and Shaftesbury demand a new subsidy. The House of Commons absolutely refused to grant any more supplies, "unless it shall appear that the obstinacy of the Dutch shall render it necessary; nor before this kingdom be effectually secured from the dangers of Popery and Popish Counsels and Counsellors, and the other present grievances be redressed."*

27 October.

31 October.

In great displeasure, the king prorogued his fractious Parliament, and dismissed his versatile chancellor, Shaftesbury, who, up to this time, had been the most rhetorical enemy of the "Carthage" of England. In reply to the Dutch overture, Charles captiously questioned its sincerity. The States General repelled this imputation, and distinctly offered to renew the treaty made at Breda in 1667; adding that, "in order to manifest to your Majesty the special esteem which we entertain for your friendship, we hereby also offer the restitution of New Netherland, and of all the other places and colonies which we have won by our arms during the present war; being fully persuaded that your Majesty will be unwilling to refuse a reciprocal engagement to restore to us such lands and forts as your subjects may have taken from us."†

4 Novem. Shaftesbury dismissed.

$\frac{7}{17}$ Novem.

$\frac{9}{19}$ Decem. Offer of the States General to restore New Netherland to England.

* Basnage, ii., 460, 461, 483; Sylvius, ix., 647, 687-689; Kennett, iii., 296; Burnet, i., 366; Rapin, ii., 672; Parl. Hist., iv., 585, 586, 593, 597, 602; Lingard, xii., 308; Davies, iii., 137; Clarke's James II., i., 485; Martin, i., 380, 383.

† Sylvius, ix., 690-692, 708, 709; Basnage, ii., 460, 463-467; Col. Doc., ii., 529, 531; Parl. Hist., iv., 610; Campbell's Chancellors, iii., 320. One of the consequences of Shaftesbury's dismissal was Locke's resignation of his place as Secretary of the Council for Plantations,

CHAP. V. 1673. This offer to restore New Netherland to England—made only four days after the States General had appointed Andringa governor of their reconquered province—was extorted from the necessities of the republic, and its engagement with Spain. With the consent of the States General, $\frac{10}{20}$ Decem. Spanish offers. the Spanish ambassador offered advantageous articles to the British government. Charles, finding that Louis refused him further supplies, and that he could not expect $\frac{16}{26}$ Decem. any from Parliament, replied that he was willing to accept reasonable conditions.*

1674. $\frac{7}{17}$ Jan'y. But when Parliament met, a few days afterward, the king again charged the Dutch with insincerity, and begged for means to continue his war. Finch, who had succeeded Shaftesbury, harangued for a supply, which might save England from being found, "like Archimedes, drawing lines in the dust while the enemy is entering into our ports." But Finch's pedantry had no effect. The House of Commons refuse supplies. The House of Commons would grant no money to Charles unless the Dutch should reject a peace."†

Negotiations, under the mediation of Sweden, had meanwhile been going on at Cologne. The Dutch plenipoten- $\frac{8}{18}$ Jan'y. tiaries there were instructed to explain the importance of New Netherland, which, "although it be their own domain," the States General were to relinquish to England. At this critical moment the king's speech to Parliament was received at the Hague. The States General refuted $\frac{14}{24}$ Jan'y. his charge of insincerity, and sent him the draft of a treaty which they were ready to sign. One of its articles, they explained, "demonstrates sufficiently to what a degree we wish to deserve your Majesty's affection; since we offer you the restitution of so considerable a conquest as New New Netherland to be restored to England. Netherland is, without the hope of receiving any thing in exchange for it." Nothing but the murder of John de Witt, and the paramount influence of William of Orange, could have brought the Dutch government to write this letter.‡

in which he was succeeded by Benjamin Worsley: King's Life of Locke, 34; Col. Doc., iii., 228; *ante*, 187, 201.

* Dalrymple, i., 137; Basnage, ii., 467, 468; Sylvius, ix., 709, 710; Col. Doc., ii., 531; *ante*, 245.

† Basnage, ii., 493–495; Sylvius, x., 4–12; Burnet, i., 365; Rapin, ii., 673, 674; Kennett, iii., 297; Parl. Hist., iv., 611–618.

‡ Sylvius, x., 12–14; Basnage, ii., 492; Col. Doc., ii., 533–535, 537, 538; Temple, ii., 246, 247; Clarke's James II., i., 489.

Chap. V. 1674. 24 Jan'y. / 3 Feb'y.

Charles instantly laid it before Parliament, and asked their "speedy advice." He was answered that he ought to make a treaty. Louis, apprehending the consequences of a separate peace between England and Holland, hastened to offer Charles five millions and a half of money and forty ships of war if he would break off his negotiations. The Duke of York strongly opposed a peace. But Charles could not now recede. Sir William Temple was summoned from his retirement, and instructed to confer (5/15 Feb'y.) with the Spanish ambassador at London, the Marquis del Fresno, to whom the States General had sent full powers. In three days all the points were arranged, and a treaty was signed at Westminster by Arlington and four other (9/19 Feb'y. Treaty signed at Westminster.) commissioners on the part of Great Britain, and by Fresno on the part of the United Netherlands. The honor of the flag, which had been refused by De Witt, was yielded to England; the Treaty of Breda was revived; the rights of neutrals guaranteed; and the commercial principles of the Triple Alliance renewed. By the sixth article it was covenanted that "all lands, islands, cities, havens, castles and fortresses, which have been or shall be taken by one party from the other, during the time of this last unhappy war, whether in Europe or elsewhere, and before the expiration of the times above limited for the duration of hostilities, shall be restored to the former Lord and Proprietor in the same condition they shall be in at the time that this peace shall be proclaimed." This article restored New Netherland to the King of Great Britain. (Restoration of New Netherland to England.) The Treaty of Breda had ceded it to him on the principle of "*uti possidetis*." The Treaty of Westminster gave it back to him on the principle of reciprocal restitution.*

Peace was soon proclaimed at London and at the Hague. (28 Feb'y. / 6 March. Peace proclaimed between England and Holland.) The Treaty of Westminster delivered the Dutch from fear of Charles, and cut off the right arm of Louis, their more dreaded foe. England, on her part, slipped out of a disastrous war. But Charles told Rouvigny, the ambassador of France, that in making peace with the Netherlands "he

* Sylvius, x., 14–19; Basnage, ii., 406, 408; Temple, ii., 247–250; iv., 10–20; Courtenay's Temple, i., 194, 419–421, 433; ii., 460, 461; Burnet, i., 366, 367; Parl. Hist., iv., 660, 665; Dalrymple, i., 137; Kennett, iii., 297; Rapin, ii., 674, 675; Anderson, ii., 529, 530; Wagenaar, xiv., 298–300; Lingard, xii., 318, 319; Martin, i., 383; Smith, i., 46; Mass. H. S. Coll., xxx., 104, 105; Bancroft, ii., 325; Col. Doc., vii., 586; Eliz. Bill, 7; *ante*, 135, 152.

CHAP. V. 1674.

had been doing a thing that went more against his heart than the losing of his right hand." The war had been begun by "the Cabal" of England, as Temple acknowledged, "with two unusual strains to the honour of the crown;" and, instead of making her king "great," had made "only four great subjects." During the course of it Holland had lost her ablest statesman, and in his place had raised to her highest post of authority the young representative of the Silent founder of the republic. She had recovered, and had resigned, her ancient trans-Atlantic province.

Holland, and American history.

For a season she retired from prominence in American history. But it was only to return, in the fullness of time, as the fatherland of a sovereign appointed by Providence to maintain civil and religious liberty on both shores of the Atlantic, and once more to govern the countrymen who never forgot their own Batavian prince.*

When rumors of these events reached New Orange, Colve was still strengthening it "against the coming of the New England army." This was done so thoroughly that one hundred and ninety guns, some of which came from Esopus, were mounted on Fort William Henry and about

2/12 June. New Orange affairs.

the town. The dilatory victims of the forced loan ordered in March were compelled to pay their assessments. This was the more hard, because the expense which had been devoted to the fortifications was now of no avail. John

28 April / 8 May.

Sharpe, having come from New England with Isaac Melyn, in violation of the edict of December, news of the peace and of the surrender of the province was soon noised through the city. Melyn taunted its Dutch burghers with having "slaved and wrought too hard and too long for the King of England." This threw them "into such a distracted rage and passion that they cried, 'We'll fire the town, pluck down the fortifications, and tear out the governors' throats' who had compelled them to slave so, contrary to their native privileges." Having no official information of what had happened in Europe, Colve determined to punish the "fomenters of mutiny and disturbance." Melyn

2/12 May. Cases of Melyn and Sharpe.

was accordingly sentenced to "come personally every day, when the burgher companies are employed at the city for-

* Rapin, ii., 675; Sylvius, x., 20, 21; Col. Doc., ii., 726; Basnage, ii., 499; Burnet, i., 367; Temple, ii., 251; Clarke's James II., i., 489; *post*, 536.

1674. $\frac{12}{22}$ May.

tifications, and work with them until said fortifications are completed." Sharpe was banished out of the province for ten years. On reaching Milford, he reported that the Dutch in New Netherland were so enraged that they declared they would not, "on demand and by authority of the States or Prince, surrender, but keep it by fighting, so long as they can stand with one leg and fight with one hand."*

Feeling of the Dutch in New Netherland.

$\frac{7}{17}$ June. $\frac{1}{11}$ July.

Authentic intelligence of peace was soon received from Massachusetts and Connecticut. A few days afterward the Treaty of Westminster was proclaimed at the City Hall of New Orange. Connecticut, however, after news of the restoration of New Netherland to the king had reached Hartford, resolved that, as Southampton, Easthampton, and Southold had asked it, they should continue under her government. John Howell, John Younge, and John Mulford were accordingly appointed commissioners for the three towns, and were "invested with magistraticall power" by the Hartford Court. Samuel Willys, John Talcott, and Secretary Allyn were also empowered to go to Long Island, "to order and settle the affairs of those people, and to establish such military officers amongst them as they shall see reason and judge necessary." Easthampton, on her part, appointed a committee, in conjunction with Southampton and Southold, to petition the king to allow them to continue under the jurisdiction of Connecticut. Thinking it was now a good opportunity to extend their bounds westward on the main land, the Hartford Court, at their autumn session, appointed commissioners "forthwith to run the line between this colony and the colony of New York from Momoronock River to Hudson's River." At the same time, it was well known that it had been settled in 1664 that the boundary should be "twenty miles every where from Hudson's River."†

$\frac{19}{29}$ May. Action of Connecticut about Long Island. $\frac{20}{30}$ May. $\frac{22 \text{ May}}{1 \text{ June}}$. $\frac{13}{23}$ June. $\frac{8}{18}$ Oct. Boundary with New York.

The Jesuit missionaries, Bruyas and Millet, were now apprehensive of being driven away by the savages, who declared themselves the friends of the Dutch. Several

* Col. Doc., ii., 617, 666, 697, 707–711, 719; Col. MSS., xxiii., 334, 338, 340, 397; Mass. H. S. Coll., xxx., 108–110; Moulton, 14; Palfrey, iii., 126, 127; *ante*, 206, 233.

† Col. Rec. Conn., ii., 222, 226, 229, 242; Mass. H. S. Coll., xxx., 104–106; Trumbull, i., 325; Wood, 98; Thompson, i., 156, 335, 367, 383; Col. MSS., xxiii., 376; Col. Doc., ii., 719, 723, 726; iii., 231, 235; New Orange Rec., vii., 201; *ante*, 56, 222.

CHAP. V. — 1674. — $\frac{15}{25}$ April.

emissaries were sent by Draeyer to engage the Iroquois against the French; and some Canadian prisoners were carried down to New Orange. Mohawk chiefs from Caghnawaga and Gandagaro, accompanied by Jan Jansen Bleecker and Henry Lansing as interpreters, also visited Colve. They had come, they said, "as to their brethren; for the Dutch, both at Nassau and here [New Orange], have been always one flesh with them." The new bond of peace, made at the "last harvest," was confirmed, and the chiefs declared that if the French should come to injure their brethren, then they would "side with the Dutch, and live and die with them." After visiting some of the neighboring tribes, the Mohawk sachems were conveyed back to Fort Nassau, loaded with presents, and assured that they would be shown all possible favor, "as brethren of the Dutch."*

($\frac{9}{19}$ May. Mohawk chiefs at New Orange. — $\frac{26 \text{ May}}{5 \text{ June}}$.)

The Treaty of Westminster, leaving the Dutch at war with the French, really made them more bitter enemies. Colve, of course, held all the subjects of Louis in America to be hostile to the government of his fatherland. Some Frenchmen at Hurley, having refused to swear allegiance, were ordered to be sent away unless they took the oath, and promised "to remain quiet in case of any attack by their nation."†

(5 June. French at Hurley.)

Not long afterward, a Dutch privateer, "The Flying Horse," Captain Juriaen Aernouts, commissioned by the Prince of Orange, came from Curaçoa and Saint Domingo to Boston, where she obtained a pilot, and then sailed to Acadia. There Aernouts attacked and captured the French forts of Penobscot, commanded by Chambly, and "Gemsec," on the Saint John's, commanded by Marson. Possession was taken, in the name of the Dutch government, of the coasts and country of Acadia, and the plunder was brought to Boston. Frontenac complained of this to Governor Leverett, but seems to have obtained no satisfaction; because Massachusetts coveted Maine, and wished the Dutch conquest of it to inure to her own benefit.‡

(10 August. Capture by the Dutch of French forts in Acadia. — Septem.)

* Col. Doc., ii., 594, 608, 618, 659, 662, 712, 713, 716, 717; iii., 250; ix., 97, 110, 117; Charlevoix, ii., 258, 259; Bancroft, ii., 322.

† Col. Doc., ii., 646, 676, 718; Esopus Records.

‡ Col. Doc., iv., 476; ix., 119, 120, 547, 793; Charlevoix, ii., 255, 256, 360; Quebec MSS., ii. (ii.), 57; Williamson, i., 580; Hutchinson, i., 311, *note*, Coll., 464; Mass. H. S. Coll., xxxii., 286; Mass. Rec., v., 116, 118; Depeyster's "Dutch in Maine," 45, 73–76; *post*, 296.

Colve and his council were meanwhile occupied in de- CHAP. V.
ciding important cases affecting lands in Achter Col, Long 1674.
Island, and elsewhere. Order and decorum were enforced
occasionally by severe penalties. Samuel Forman, of Oys- Case of Samuel Forman.
ter Bay, having made a great uproar in the streets of New
Orange, and even come into the Dutch Church during divine service on Sunday, "abusing with great levity the 19 April.
word of God, and blaspheming his holy name," was condemned to be whipped, and banished out of the province.
Daniel Lane, of Setalcot, or Brookhaven, charged with in- Case of Daniel Lane.
cest, having escaped from prison before trial, his estate was
seized, and half of it allowed to his wife, to whom a divorce was promised if the accused did not appear within 12 April.
six months and purge himself from the crime.*

The Lutheran Domine Fabricius, who had gone to the
Delaware territory, coming back to New Orange, irregu- 5 Feb'y.
larly and without authority married Ralph Doxy, of Newtown, on Long Island, to Mary Harris. The court, aware
of his "previous ill conduct," but unwilling, "out of respect for his old age and the office he last filled," to pro-
ceed rigorously, suspended Fabricius from the ministry for 1 March. Case of Fabricius.
one year. The marriage of Doxy was declared unlawful,
but the parties were allowed to marry again "according to
the laws of the Government." The domine petitioned that 18 April.
his sentence should be modified so far as to allow him "at
least to baptize;" but the court declined his request.†

The Dutch churches, fostered by Colve, foresaw that
they would not be so comfortable under the English, who
were soon to repossess the province. To guard themselves
as much as possible, the Consistory of New Orange asked 7 July. The Reformed Dutch Church.
that their old church in Fort William Henry, which, at the
surrender in 1664, had been stipulated should continue in
its then use, might be confirmed to them; and the govern-
or promptly ordered "a Deed in form" to be granted,
which was accordingly duly executed. As Van Ruyven 23 July.

* Col. MSS., xxii., 147; xxiii., 330, 331; Col. Doc., ii., 606, 661, 668, 694, 704-728; Whitehead, 61; Moulton, 13.

† Col. Doc., ii., 686, 689, 691, 692, 693, 706; S. Hazard's Ann. Penn., 410, 411, 412; Moulton, 8; *ante*, 175. Fabricius appears to have behaved very badly to his wife, and was fined by the Court of Burgomasters and Schepens of New Orange: see Col. MSS., xxiii., 311, 314, 315; N. O. City Rec., vii., 201, 202; Doc. Hist., iii., 242, 243; Val. Man., 1850, 528; 1851, 428, 431, 432, 435, 441-450; 1853, 497. He then went back to the Delaware, where he again got into trouble: S. Hazard, 419, 420.

CHAP. V. 1674. was about to return to Holland with his mother-in-law, the widow of Domine Megapolensis, the arrears of salary due to that clergyman were recommended to be paid to her.

26 July. Feeling of the Dutch about the restoration of New Netherland to England. In writing to the Classis of Amsterdam, Domine Van Nieuwenhuysen expressed the general feeling of the Dutch: "We are greatly pleased at the peace arranged between our country and the kingdom of England, but we should have been the more touched if we were not apprehensive that this country is included in the scope of the sixth article of the sealed Treaty, and must be restored back to that crown. It is not less agreeable to us to understand how God Almighty has been pleased to put a hook in the nose of the haughty French Sennecherib, and thus far to stay the wasting of his dearly-bought Church in our various cities particularly, and in our Fatherland generally."*

The city government had now been in office for nearly
11 August. a year, and it was necessary to make new appointments. From the nominations submitted, Van Brugh and Beek-
13 August. New city government of New Orange. man were accordingly selected as burgomasters, and Kip, Verplanck, Rombouts, Hoogland, and Stephanus van Cortlandt, as schepens of New Orange. Knyff was continued as schout-fiscal. Very little, however, was left the mu-
7 Septem. nicipal officers to do. They obtained an order from Colve for the produce of the scales and tapster's excises, to pay the city debt of upward of six thousand guilders for work done on the fortifications. New "church-wardens" were
3 October. nominated by the metropolitan authorities and confirmed by the governor.†

While the Treaty of Westminster was yet in suspense, Manning reached London in great distress from Fayal, where he and his soldiers had been landed, and was sum-
11 Jan'y. moned before the Duke of York, who, after hearing his story, at first censured him. At Lord Arlington's office he
13 Jan'y. Manning in London. was again closely examined by the king and the duke. "Brother," said Charles to James, "the ground could not

* Col. Doc., ii., 721, 722, 730; Col. MSS., xxiii., 269, 433–446; N. Y. H. S. Coll. (ii.), iii., 142; Corr. Cl. Amsterdam. Van Ruyven, who never returned to New York, was living at Amsterdam in 1698: Col. Doc., iv., 353.

† Col. MSS., xxiii., 371; New Orange City Rec., vii., 208, 211, 212, 218; Val. Man., 1850, 538; 1853, 472, 473, 476, 477, 487, 488, 492; Moulton, 14; *ante*, 212, 233, 242. Among the rules adopted by the burgomasters and schepens of New Orange was one that whoever should smoke tobacco in the court while it was engaged in business should forfeit two and a half guilders: Val. Man., 1853, 483.

be maintained by so few men;" and Manning was dismissed without reprimand. For more than two months he waited the pleasure of the duke, who at length paid his expenses from Fayal.*

Major Edmund Andros.

31 March. / 9 April. Commissioned to receive New Netherland.

But who should be sent to receive and govern New York? was the question. Lovelace was unfit; Nicolls was dead; a new man must be named. The person selected was Edmund Andros, a major in a dragoon regiment, disbanded after the Westminster Treaty. Charles accordingly commissioned Andros to receive New Netherland from the Dutch; and he asked the States General to direct their "Governor or Commandant of the place called New York, in the West Indies," to surrender it to Andros, whom he had appointed to go there and take possession in his name.†

$\frac{10}{20}$ April. Massachusetts and New York.

Thinking that the re-establishment of the duke's authority over his former province would be hurtful to Massachusetts, John Collins, its agent at London, wrote to Governor Leverett that "New York being restored by the peace, one Mr. Andrews is appointed governor, a man I know not; and some rumour is maliciously spread at court that you have made peace with the Dutch there, which is obviated by the readiness of some persons to show the falsehood of it. I hope nothing will for this year further disturb you; and if any thing do arise, it will be from New York and the Government there. I have therefore greatly encouraged some gentlemen, your friends, who would purchase it of His Royal Highness, as thinking it will be much for your peace, who are about it; but how it will issue, I know not." This project, however, if seriously entertained, came to naught. The king was now the only English proprietor of New York under the Treaty of Westminster; and while Charles was offended at the insubordination of his subjects in Massachusetts, he had "little time to mind such minute things" as theirs.‡

New York not to be bought.

5 March.

Meanwhile the delayed letter of the municipality of New Orange reached the States General only the day before the

* Col. MSS., xxiv., 36–51; Doc. Hist., iii., 53, 54, 59; Sylvius, x., 23; *ante*, 213. It is difficult to understand how Dunlap (i., 130) could venture the preposterous conjecture that "*the needy and profligate Charles was pacified by receiving part of the bribe Manning had taken from the Dutch*:" compare *ante*, 206–208.

† Col. Doc., ii., 544, 740, 741; ix., 403; Col. Rec. Conn., iii., 376; Temple, ii., 78.

‡ Hutchinson's Coll., 443, 444; Mass. H. S. Coll., xxx., 106; Palfrey, iii., 22, 312.

CHAP. V. Peace of Westminster was proclaimed—too late for any
effect. The several Boards of Admiralty had been asked
1674. to advise what should be done in favor of the relinquished
20 March. province. The Rotterdam Board thought that the King
of England should consider the Dutch in New Netherland
not as "a conquered people, but as men who have passed by
conveyance and convention under another sovereignty."
Advice of the Admiralty Boards about New Netherland. That at Amsterdam submitted a memorial from the merchants trading to New Netherland that the province should
be repurchased; but, if that could not be done, the King of
England should be required not to molest its inhabitants
for what they had done during the war; that their rights
should be respected, and a free trade be established; and
that the old articles of capitulation in 1664 should "remain valid and be faithfully executed." The Zealand
$\frac{18}{28}$ March. Board at Middleburg knew "no fitter means than to furnish said inhabitants with ships and craft for their conveyance, either to this country, or Surinam, or some other
colony dependent on the jurisdiction of this State."*

$\frac{6}{16}$ April. Request of the States General about New Netherland. The States General promptly complied with Charles's
request to order the surrender of New Netherland to Andros, but desired the king to leave the people of the province "in full and entire possession of the lands, property,
and rights they possess in those parts, in the same manner
$\frac{16}{26}$ April. Promise of Charles. they held them before the rupture." Charles assured their
high mightinesses "that all the inhabitants there should
enjoy all their rights and privileges, of which they were in
the enjoyment before the war." This declaration substantially gave new effect to the articles of capitulation in 1664.
$\frac{25 \text{ May.}}{4 \text{ June.}}$ Rensselaerwyck. The Dutch ambassadors at London were also instructed to
do all they could in aiding the proprietors of Rensselaerwyck to obtain from the king a confirmation of their ancient privileges.†

At the request of Secretary Coventry, the West India
$\frac{4}{14}$ June. Company also wrote to Colve to surrender New Netherland, although the matter was "wholly beyond their controul." The ship "Muyll Tromp" [Jews' Harp], Captain
Hendrick Toll, being now reported ready to take out orders for the evacuation, and bring home the Dutch soldiers

* Col. Doc., ii., 526, 532, 538–544, 658, 662, 664, 677; Col. Rec. Conn., ii., 565; Mass. H. S. Coll., xxx., 103; *ante*, 220, 221.

† Col. Doc., ii., 545–548, 549–561; *ante*, 218.

CHAP. V.

1674.

27 June. / 7 July. Orders of the States General to Colve about the surrender of New Netherland.

in the province, the States General directed Colve "to restore and surrender the aforesaid New Netherland to Edmund Andros, or such other person as the King of Great Britain shall have deputed for that purpose; that, in case the above-named Edmund Andros should not have as yet arrived yonder, and no one have order from the King of Great Britain to receive the aforesaid country, the above-named Governor Colve shall, pursuant to the last Treaty concluded with the said King in February last, and agreeably to their High Mightinesses' aforesaid Resolution of the Sixteenth of last April, vacate said New Netherland, and place it—having made an inventory and obtained a receipt—in the hands of the political Government there, to the end that thus possession may be taken for the behoof of the King of Great Britain." The Dutch ambassadors at London, having communciated these orders, were informed that Andros was authorized to receive New Netherland, and would proceed thither at once, with "a number of new colonists" from England.

7/17 July.

5/15 Oct. Colve's orders received.

In due time the Dutch frigate reached New Orange; and Colve announced his orders to the burgomasters and schepens, who voted him two hundred and fifty florins "for his last year's services." A few days afterward he requested the court to name ten persons, from whom he would select five, "who, after his departure, shall exercise and possess the executive authority until the arrival of the expected ships and the Governor of His Majesty of England, who shall be also authorized to surrender the country to whomsoever exhibits His Majesty's Commission." Steenwyck, Bayard, Van Brugh, Beekman, Luyck, Kregier, De Peyster, Van Cortlandt, Kip, and Rombouts were accordingly nominated. But the proposed provisional government was not organized. Before Colve was ready to embark the expected British frigates anchored at Staten Island; and Andros notified him that, pursuant to the late treaty of peace, he was ready to receive possession for the King of England of "the New Netherland and dependances, now under" the Dutch governor's command.*

15/25 Oct.

16/26 Oct. Proposed provisional government of New Netherland.

22 October. / 1 Novem. Arrival of Andros.

* Col. MSS., xxiii., 412, 413; Col. Doc., ii., 544, 564–568, 730–733; New Orange Rec., vii., 237, 244–247; Val. Man., 1853, 489, 493, 494; Doc. Hist., iii., 45; *ante*, 257.

CHAPTER VI.

1674–1678.

CHAP VI. 1674. Effect of the Treaty of Westminster.

By the Treaty of Westminster the United Provinces relinquished their conquest of New Netherland to the King of England. The sovereign Dutch States General had treated directly with Charles as sovereign. A question at once arose at Whitehall about the subordinate interest of the Duke of York. It was claimed by some that James's former American proprietorship was revived. Yet, while the Treaty of Westminster re-established the Articles of Capitulation agreed to by Nicolls and Stuyvesant, who represented their sovereigns in 1664, it did not cure the imperfections subject to which the duke had for nine years governed his American province. James's patent had been sealed while the Dutch were in quiet possession of New Netherland; and no new grant was made to him after the Treaty of Breda, which confirmed to the English king his conquest of the Dutch province. Eminent lawyers "very justly questioned" the duke's pretension to the territory which England had recently recovered; because its cession to her sovereign by the Dutch government "had given no strength to original defects." James was now obliged to give up the claim of English right which he and his brother had formerly maintained. Moreover, the duke wished to regain New Jersey, which he had so foolishly squandered on Berkeley and Carteret. Besides this, the boundary agreement with Connecticut, which had never been ratified by the crown or by himself, was a sore point. The opinion of counsel having been taken, they advised that the duke's proprietorship had been extinguished by the Dutch conquest, and that the king was now alone seized of New Netherland, by virtue of the Treaty of Westminster. The "*Jus Postliminii*" did not obtain in New York.*

Defects in James's title.

No *jus postliminii.*

* Col. Doc., ii., 739; iii., 166, 176, 235, 236, 237; v., 596; vii., 586, 596, 597; Eliz. Bill, 7,

A new patent to the Duke of York was therefore sealed. By it the king again conveyed to his brother the territories he had held before, and granted him anew the absolute powers of government he had formerly enjoyed over British subjects, with the like additional authority over "any other person or persons" inhabiting his province. Under the same description of boundaries, New Jersey, and all the territory west of the Connecticut River, together with Long Island and the adjacent islands, and the region of Pemaquid, were again included in the grant. The new patent did not, as has been commonly, but erroneously stated, "recite and confirm the former." It did not in any way allude to that instrument. It read as if no previous English patent had ever existed. It was a second grant; in almost the same terms with the first; and it conveyed to the duke, ostensibly for the first time, a territory which the Dutch government, after conquering and holding, had by treaty "restored to His Majesty."*

CHAP. VI. 1674. 29 June. New patent to the Duke of York.

Thus James again became the proprietor of a vast American province, over which he was to domineer, until his delegated authority from the king was merged in his inherited right as successor to the crown. His private revenue continued to be managed by a board of commissioners, of which his brother-in-law, Lawrence Hyde, was one; Sir Allen Apsley was his treasurer and receiver general, Sir Thomas Wynnington his attorney general, and Sir John Churchill his solicitor general. In place of Matthew Wren, who had been killed at his side in 1672, the duke's secretary was Sir John Werden; although James frequently wrote letters to his governors with his own hand.†

James's commissioners and officers.

Werden, the duke's secretary.

As his colonial lieutenant and deputy, the duke, almost

37; Leaming and Spicer, 50; Vattel, 212, 362; Kent, i., 108–111; Douglas, ii., 224, 268; Smith, i., 48; Chalmers's Ann., i., 579–581, 617; Rev. Col., i., 143; Proud, i., 282; Grahame, i., 422, 467; Spectator, No. xx.; *ante*, vol. i., 4, 141, 143, 144; ii., 36, 56, 135, 209, 251, 258.

* Col. MSS., xxiii., 362; Eliz. Bill, 7; Deeds, i., 1; Leaming and Spicer, 3–8, 41–45, 50; Col. Doc., ii., 295–298, 539; iii., 215, 234, 235; vii., 597; Chalmers's Ann., i., 579, 580; Whitehead's E. J., 63, 264; Yonkers Gaz., 4 Nov., 1865; Hist. Mag., i. (ii.), 89–91; *ante*, 16.

† Werden was a son of Colonel Robert Werden, of Chester, one of the duke's commissioners, and, before he became his secretary, had been *chargé d'affaires* at Madrid in 1667; special messenger to Temple at the Hague in 1669; at Stockholm in 1670; was made a baronet in 1672; and in 1673 was appointed a commissioner of the navy: Temple's Works, i., 487; ii., 195, 196; Courtenay's Temple, ii., 400; Pepys, iii., 167, 231, 235; iv., 25; Beatson, i., 208, 350; *ante*, 4, 136, 186. The first regular Entry Books relating to New York, in the State Paper Office at London, begin in 1674. None of the duke's letters before that date seem to be preserved there; and the few documents of an earlier period which I found are chiefly those sent by Nicolls and Lovelace to the English secretaries of state.

CHAP. VI. 1674. Major Edmund Andros.

necessarily, appointed Major Edmund Andros, whom the king had directed in the previous March to receive New Netherland from the Dutch. Born in London in 1637, Andros had been brought up in the royal household, of which his father was lieutenant of the ceremonies. During the exile of the court, Andros began his military life in Holland, under Prince Henry of Nassau. After the Restoration he was favored by Charles; distinguished himself in the first Dutch war; and in 1669 was commissioned major in Prince Rupert's regiment of dragoons. In 1672 Andros commanded the English forces in Barbadoes, where he got reputation for skill in American affairs. The proprietors of Carolina made him a landgrave, and granted him four baronies in their province. Andros was married, in 1671, to Mary, daughter of Sir Thomas Craven. On the death of his father in April, 1674, he succeeded to the office of bailiff of Guernsey, and became hereditary seigneur of the fief of Sausmarez. Like his predecessors, Nicolls and Lovelace, Andros was an English Episcopalian, but no bigot. Moreover, he was a good Dutch and French scholar. Of unblemished private character; with talents, energy, and zeal in his master's service, he was as fitting an instrument as the Duke of York could have chosen to confirm arbitrary government in his regained province. Andros was accordingly commissioned by James to be his "Lieutenant and Governor" within the territories covered by his patent; to hold office during his pleasure, and to obey all orders that he might give. Andros's commission was almost exactly similar to those of Nicolls and Lovelace.*

1 July. Andros commissioned governor of New York.

1 July. Andros's Instructions from the duke.

The duke's Instructions to Andros, minute and specific, formed the temporary political constitution of New York. The governor was to satisfy the inhabitants that his coming was "for their protection and benefit, for the encouragement of planters and plantations, and the improvement of trade and commerce, and for the preservation of religion, justice, and equity among them." Strict discipline was to be maintained among the soldiers, so as to avoid all

* Col. Doc., ii., 544, 740, 741; iii., 215, 224, 291, 308; ix., 403; Letter of Selyns to Cl. Amst., 10 Oct., 1688; Mem. of Penn. H. S., vii., 36, 37; Col. Rec. Conn., iii., 376; Temple, ii., 78; Pepys, i., 69; ii., 167, 231, 331; Chalmers's Ann., i., 580; *ante*, 18, 144; *post*, *note* B. A memoir of Andros, and an engraved portrait of him, from an original in England, has been published by the Prince Society at Boston, in Massachusetts.

causes of complaint. None of the inhabitants were to be molested for assisting Evertsen in taking the fort, except in the case of Englishmen, whose estates might be forfeited; but the Dutch who had been active were to be observed "more circumspectly" thereafter, and to be removed from places of strength. Special care was to be taken of the forts at New York and New Albany, "upon which, in a manner, wholly depend the safety and trade of the whole country." Planters of all nations, but especially Englishmen, were to be offered "all manner of encouragement" to settle in New York, by assigning them lands according to the rules observed "by those of New England and Maryland," so that the province should, in that respect, be at least equal to "any other neighboring colony." The quit-rent reserved to the duke was left to the discretion of the governor, who was directed "to settle a good correspondence with the neighboring English Plantations, as well those of New England as those of Maryland." As it was "necessary to make some abatement in the customs," James established a new "tariff," or declaration of the duties on imports. All goods brought into New York were to pay two per cent. if shipped from England or any English plantation, and ten per cent. if coming from a foreign country. All imports, except farmers' tools going up the Hudson River, were to be charged three per cent. in addition. Wines were to pay ten shillings a pipe, and brandy or other European spirits fifteen shillings a hogshead; while rum—which came from the West Indies—was favored by the lower rate of six shillings a hogshead. All liquors sent up the Hudson River were charged double these rates. Exported beavers were to pay fifteen pence on each skin, and other peltry in proportion; while New York tobacco was charged two shillings a hogshead if sent to England, and a penny a hundred weight if sent elsewhere. The same regulations were to apply "in Delaware River as in Hudson's River." These rates were "to hold good for three years, to commence from the arrival and publication of them at New York." Excise and other internal taxes, which had been imposed by Nicolls and Lovelace, were to be temporarily continued until farther orders from the duke. All these duties were calmly laid by

Planters to be encouraged.

Tariff of duties.

Rates to last for three years after publication.

CHAP. VI. 1674.

James, at Windsor Castle, on the people of New York. At the same time, he directed his provincial governor to lessen the charge of government there as much as possible, "that so, by degrees, I may reap from thence some advantages, in return for the great expence and trouble I have been at in protecting that colony." Justice was to be administered "with all possible equality, without regard to Dutch or English," so that all might see "their just rights preserved to them inviolably." The laws and orders established by Nicolls and Lovelace were not to be varied from "but upon emergent necessities," and with the advice of the council and the gravest and most experienced inhabitants; and no alteration was to be valid unless confirmed by the duke within a year. All writs were to run in the king's name. Magistrates were to be chosen "for their abilities and integrity," and no officers were to be appointed "for above one year, or otherwise than during pleasure." The governor was to choose a council, not exceeding ten, out of "the most prudent inhabitants," with whom he was to "consult upon all extraordinary occasions" relating to the public service. They were to hold their places during the duke's pleasure; and they, as well as all other officers, were to take oaths of allegiance to the king, and of fidelity to the proprietor, as also one peculiar to the office. Freedom of conscience was secured. "You shall," were James's orders to Andros, "permit all persons, of what Religion soever, quietly to inhabit within the precincts of your jurisdiction, without giving them any disturbance or disquiet whatsoever, for or by reason of their differing opinions in matter of Religion: Provided they give no disturbance to the public peace, nor do molest or disquiet others in the free exercise of their religion."

Equal administration of justice.

Magistrates and officers.

Counselors.

Freedom of religion in New York.

In case of the death of Andros, Lieutenant Anthony Brockholls was to succeed him in his government. Brockholls was of a Roman Catholic family in Lancashire, England, and was himself "a profest Papist." The "Test Act" of 29 March, 1673, would have excluded him from holding office in England. But, as that statute did not extend to the British American Plantations, the duke, himself a victim of Protestant intolerance, was able to illustrate his own idea of "Freedom to worship God," by ap-

Brockholls lieutenant under Andros.

pointing a member of the Church of Rome to be his second colonial officer in New York.*

CHAP. VI.

1674.

By the king's special permission, the Duke of York raised a company of infantry, consisting of one hundred men, besides officers, to serve in his province. Of this company he commissioned Andros to be captain, and Brockholls lieutenant. Christopher Billop, who had "served the king," and whose father was an importunate office-seeker, was appointed second lieutenant, and Cæsar Knapton ensign. A surgeon and a chaplain were likewise established for the forces in New York.†

1 July. 2 July. Regular military officers in New York.

James also chose William Dyer, or Dyre, formerly of Rhode Island, and who, the autumn before, had planned reconquest, to be the collector of his provincial customs. Dyer was instructed to receive all the customs' duties accruing to the duke within the territory granted to him by the king, and pay them over to Andros, whose farther directions he was to follow, and to whom he was to report from time to time. No trust was to be allowed to any one, and all duties were to be paid in money or goods. The collector was not to trade as a merchant; and all revenue differences with importers were to be determined by "the ordinary magistrates of the place, or otherwise, as hath been hitherto accustomed."‡

2 July. Dyer collector of New York.

One of the motives to the Duke of York's second patent was the peculiar condition of New Jersey. James considered that his former release of that region to Berkeley and Carteret was annulled by the Dutch conquest—just as his own grant from the king had been. But both his grantees were old courtiers, and more than his match, where their own interests were at stake. They played

New Jersey affairs.

* Col. Doc., iii., 216–219, 657, 674; iv., 166; Burke's Commoners, iv., 491; *ante*, 202. Brockholls, although a Roman Catholic, was married to Susanna Maria, daughter of Paulus Schrick, of New York, and a member of the Reformed Dutch Church, in which their children were all baptized. One of these children, Susanna Brockholls, married Philip French, Jun., and their daughter Susanna married William Livingston, governor of New Jersey, by whom she had Judge Henry Brockholst Livingston, and others: N. Y. H. S. Coll. (ii.), i., 395; Col. Doc., iv., 664; Val. Man., 1863, 748, 809; Sedgwick's Livingston, 59, 60, 236, 239. The usual English spelling of the name was "Brockholes;" but the major's autographs in the Secretary's Office at Albany are written "Brockholls." The Dutch Church Records make the name "Brockholst," and this appears to have been preferred by his descendants.

† Col. Doc., iii., 219–221, 230, 276, 284; Pepys, iv., 53. It is not known what chaplain accompanied Andros to New York in 1674: Hist. Mag., v., 153, 156, 189; Col. Doc., iii., 415, *note;* Gen. Ent., xxxii., 93; N. Y. H. S. Coll. (1869), 157: *ante*, 45, *note.*

‡ Chalmers, i., 580; Col. Doc., ii., 721; iii., 207, 221–223, 318; iv., 353; R. I. Col. Rec., i., 266; ii., 108, 396; Val. Man., 1853, 387; *ante*, 247, 263; vol. i., 557.

CHAP. VI. their own separate games with skill, and eventually they beat the duke.

1674.

After returning from his lieutenancy of Ireland, Berkeley was appointed ambassador in France. He had found that his American proprietorship verified the prediction of Nicolls, that its profit, if any, would only benefit his grandchildren. Berkeley, therefore, shortly after the Treaty of Westminster, in consideration of one thousand pounds, conveyed to John Fenwick, an old Cromwellian soldier, in trust for Edward Byllinge, a broken-down London brewer, his undivided half of New Jersey, together with such "franchises, liberties, governments, and powers" as had been granted to him by the Duke of York in 1664. Both of Berkeley's grantees were Quaker disciples of George Fox, who had just returned from America. They probably calculated that they had secured a bargain. Yet Berkeley's conveyance to Fenwick was a very doubtful parchment. If, by reason of the Dutch reconquest of New York and New Jersey, the Duke of York was obliged to procure a new patent from the king, it was much more necessary for Berkeley to obtain a new release from his own grantor. Nevertheless, the bargain stood as it was thus concluded, just three months before Charles made his second grant to his brother; and Berkeley rejoiced that he had touched his thousand pounds, and was rid of any concern in New Jersey.*

John Lord Berkeley.

18 March. Conveys his undivided half of New Jersey to Byllinge and Fenwick.

But Berkeley's old copartner, Sir George Carteret, was differently situated. He had no motive to part with his interest in New Jersey. He had come back from Dublin to resume his place near the person of his sovereign. It was not difficult for the domineering courtier to warp his easy king. Charles, accordingly—a fortnight before his own second patent to his brother for New York and New Jersey had passed the great seal—was prevailed upon to sign a letter declaring that Sir George was "seized of the Province of New Cæsarea or New Jersey, in America, and of the jurisdiction thereof," and commanding its inhabitants to obey his government, "who hath the sole power,

Sir George Carteret.

13 June. The king's letter in Carteret's favor.

* Leaming and Spicer, 64, 65, 413; Chalmers, i., 617; S. Smith, 79, 89, 567; Gordon, 34; Burnet, i., 267; Col. Doc., iii., 105; Fox's Journal, 465; Sewell, 512; Bancroft, ii., 365; Grahame, i., 467, 473, 474; Whitehead, 65, 67; Dixon's Life of Penn (ed. Philad., 1851), 136; Dankers's and Sluyter's Journal, 241-243; *ante*, 85, 150, 260, 261.

under us, to settle and dispose of the said country, upon such terms and conditions as he shall think fit."* CHAP. VI.

1674.

Fallacy of Charles's letter in favor of Carteret.

Yet, when this letter was written, the king knew that the only way in which Carteret could be "seized" of New Jersey was by the duke's release in 1664, which made him a joint owner with Berkeley, who had just sold his undivided interest to Fenwick. How, then, could Carteret have "the sole power" which Charles's letter attributed to him? Moreover, at that very time the king had ordered a new patent, which he afterward sealed, granting to his brother "full and absolute power and authority" over all the territory between the Connecticut and the Delaware which had been relinquished to him by the Dutch in the Treaty of Westminster. New Jersey was a part of that territory; and after James's patent was sealed, he stood, in place of the king, as its only proprietor. Carteret, therefore, had no "power" at all in New Jersey. Whatever equitable claims Berkeley and Carteret, or their assigns might have had to the personal favor of James, they had no legal rights whatever to New Jersey after its conquest by the Dutch, and its second grant by King Charles to the Duke of York.

What followed is less clear. All that we know is, that the Duke of York—three weeks after he had commissioned Andros to be governor of the whole of his American territory—was induced to direct his attorney general and his solicitor general to prepare a grant to Sir George Carteret, *in severalty*, of a part of the portion which, ten years before, he had conveyed to Berkeley and Carteret *jointly*. 23 July.

29 July. Grant by the Duke of York of New Jersey to Carteret in severalty.

Accordingly, James—referring to the king's second patent to him of 29 June, 1674—granted to Carteret and his heirs the tract of land "westward of Long Island and Manhattas Island, and bounded on the east, part by the main sea and part by Hudson's River, and extends southward as far as a certain creek called Barnegat, being about the middle between Sandy Point and Cape May; and bounded on the west in a strait line from the said creek called Barnegat to a certain creek in Delaware River next adjoining to and below a certain creek in Delaware River called Rankokus Kill; and from thence up the said Delaware River to the

* Col. MSS., xxii., 166; Eliz. Bill, 38; Leaming and Spicer, 49; Whitehead, 64.

CHAP. VI. 1674.

northermost branch thereof, which is in forty-one degrees and forty minutes of latitude; and on the north crosseth over thence in a strait line to Hudson's River in forty-one degrees of latitude: which said tract of land is hereafter to be called by the name or names of *New Cæsarea*, or *New Jersey*." But—as in the case of the duke's original release of 24 June, 1664—his second grant did not convey to Carteret any of the "full and absolute power and authority to govern," which the king had intrusted to his brother.*

No powers of government granted.

Whatever may have been the scope of this instrument, its history is remarkable. Before he granted it, James is said to have "hesitated long, and at length sacrificed his personal interest, as well as the prosperity of New York, to his fatal esteem for Carteret." The duke himself afterward declared that the grant was obtained from him "by surprise." The probability is that James found that he could not safely thwart his brother's imperious vice-chamberlain, for whom, besides, he cherished "much esteem and regard." So, to make things easy at Whitehall, he gave away to Carteret the largest half of New Jersey, which that experienced courtier flattered him he chose "because near unto his government of New York;" while it was really preferred "on the account of its being well settled with a sober and industrious people, which would invite others to come there, whereas the other was a desart." Yet James did not intend to "let go any part of his prerogative;" for he made no alteration in the commission he had given to Andros. Berkeley's conveyance of his undivided interest to Fenwick was disregarded; because, if the duke had been evicted by the Dutch conquest, much more so were his grantees in 1664. Carteret, however, took his new title, in severalty, knowing that in 1668 Staten Island had been "adjudged to belong to New York," and that it had been purchased for James in 1670.†

Effect of the duke's grant to Carteret.

31 July. Carteret's new concessions to New Jersey.

Esteeming himself, nevertheless, the sole proprietor of New Jersey, Carteret drew up some explanations of the former "concessions" of himself and Berkeley. In this instrument Sir George distinctly recognized the annihilation

* Col. Doc., iii., 223, 224; Eliz. Bill, 7; Leaming and Spicer, 42, 46, 47, 48; *ante*, 82, 83.

† Chalmers, i., 617; Col. Doc., iii., 229, 240; S. Smith, 548; Whitehead, 65, 67; Mass. H. S. Coll., xxxvii., 315; Yonkers Gazette of 8 July and 5 August, 1865; *ante*, 149, 150, 166.

CHAP. VI. 1674.

of his old rights by the Dutch conquest, and the recent fresh grant from the duke to himself. At the same time he commissioned his cousin Philip to be his provincial governor, and procured for him a passage in the frigate which was to convey Andros to New York.*

30 July. Lord Stirling's pension.

It was necessary for the duke to do another act before he could feel at ease about his title to Long Island and Pemaquid. The consideration which he had promised to Lord Stirling in 1664 had never been paid. To obtain a release from the earl of "all his pretence of right and title," James granted to him for life a pension of three hundred pounds a year, "out of the surplusage of the neat profits of the revenue arising out of the said colony, all manner of charges, be it civil or military, first deducted and allowed." At the same time, Lord Stirling agreed that, if the duke should procure for him "any employment or other satisfaction to the like value," he would release the grant of his annuity.†

6/16 Aug. Final instructions to Andros from the duke.

James now gave several final directions to Andros. As soon as he should arrive at New York, the governor was to seize the estate of Lovelace, who was charged with being about seven thousand pounds in debt to the proprietor. Andros was also furnished with a copy of the "Duke's Laws," as established in New York by Nicolls and Lovelace, which, it was thought upon consideration, might be amended "in some particular clauses thereof." His original instructions were therefore modified so as to require him "to put in execution the said laws, except such as shall have apparent inconveniences in them;" and, after his settlement in New York, he was, with the advice of his council, to make such amendments as might be found necessary "for the ease and benefit of the people," and the good of the proprietor's service. These alterations were to be at once reported to the duke for his authority to put them in execution. Shortly afterward James's new governor set sail, accompanied by his staff and military forces, and by "a number of new colonists." They were conveyed by

* Eliz. Bill, 7, 38–40; Leaming and Spicer, 50–60; Doc. Hist., iii., 45; Whitehead, 65, 66; *ante*, 83–86, 189, 199, 200. Carteret was a kinsman of Andros: Hatfield, 178.

† It seems that there never was any "surplusage of the neat profits" arising out of the revenue of New York, and that the duke neither got any office for Lord Stirling, nor paid him any part of his stipulated annuity: see Col. Doc., iii., 42, 225, 606, 607; v., 330, 331; vii., 430–432; Duer's Life of Stirling, 37–49; *ante*, 15, 16.

CHAP. VI. 1674. the frigates Diamond, Captain Richard Griffith, and Castle, Captain Cassibelan Burton. Besides Philip Carteret, the governor of New Jersey, Captain John Manning, who had been waiting for some months in England, returned to New York in the Diamond with Andros.*

22 October. 1 Novem. Andros notifies Colve to give possession of New Netherland. In due time the British frigates anchored at Staten Island; and Andros sent Governor Carteret with Ensign Knapton to notify Colve that he was ready to receive from him "The New Netherland and dependances," now under his command. The Dutch governor, however, declined yielding possession at once, and required eight days to complete the necessary preliminaries. These were not mere formalities. They touched what the Dutch considered their essential rights, chiefly affecting religion and property. The burgomasters and schepens of the metropolis appointed Steenwyck, Van Brugh, and Beekman to welcome the English governor on board the Diamond, and request from him some privileges "for the advantage of the commonalty." Andros desired them to "assure the inhabitants of the Dutch nation that they should participate in the same privileges as those of the English nation, and that his Honor would, as far as possible, promote their interests; referring himself further to the Instructions given him by His Royal Majesty and Highness the Duke of York." Wishing more certainty, Colve sent Steenwyck and Captain Eppsteyn to Andros with several articles, to which he desired answers for the satisfaction of the Dutch government, and for "the greater tranquillity of the good People of this Province." These articles related chiefly to the settlement of debts; the validity of judgments during the Dutch administration, and the maintenance of owners in the possession of property; "that the inhabitants of the Dutch nation may be allowed to retain their customary Church privileges in Divine service and Church discipline, besides their Fathers' laws and customs in the division of their inheritances;" that they might not be forced to serve "against their own nation;" that each congregation might support its own poor; besides several other particulars.

24 October. 3 Novem.

The city authorities request privileges for the Dutch.

27 October. 6 Novem. Colve's demands.

The Dutch Church in New York.

* Col. Doc., ii., 733; iii., 226, 227; Doc. Hist., iii., 45, 54; Council Min., iii. (ii.), 6; Warr., Ord., Pass., etc., iii., 51; *ante*, 256. There is a copy of "the Duke's laws" in the State Paper Office, London: Board of Trade, N. Y., No. 110, 15[illegible].

Andros replied the next day by a general assurance that he would give satisfactory answers to most of the points, being ordered to observe the articles of peace "in the best and most friendly manner" toward the Dutch inhabitants, and that he had directed Captain Matthias Nicolls personally to confer with Colve on the subject. At this conference Nicolls satisfied Colve that Andros would give the desired answers as soon as he had assumed the government. This assurance was honorably fulfilled.*

CHAP. VI. 1674. 28 October / 7 Novem. Andros's reply. 29 October / 8 Novem.

All preliminaries being now satisfactorily arranged, Colve assembled the burgomasters and schepens, with the burgher court-martial, at the City Hall, and announced that on the morrow he would surrender the fort and province to Andros on behalf of the King of Great Britain; and, after thanking them for their past services, absolved them from their oaths of allegiance to the States General and the Prince of Orange. The banners of the "Out people," and the cushions and table-cloth in the City Hall, were intrusted to Burgomaster Van Brugh until they should be claimed by "superior authority;" and Colve then took his "farewell of the Assembly." The next day, being Saturday, the tenth of November, according to the New Style, "The Province of New Netherland was surrendered by Governor Colve to Governor Major Edmund Andros on behalf of His Britannic Majesty."†

30 October / 9 Novem. Colve's farewell to New Netherland. 31 October / 10 Novem. New Netherland restored to England.

Thus England once more became predominant over North America. From Carolina to Acadia its Atlantic coast obeyed the servants of her king. On taking possession of his government, Andros's first official act was to swear in Captain Matthias Nicolls as one of his council, and appoint him to be again secretary of the province of "New York." The governor's other counselors, from time to time, were Brockholls, Dyer, Phillipse, and the several mayors of the metropolis, Lawrence, Dervall, De Meyer, Van Cortlandt, and others. A proclamation was immediately issued, charging all persons to be peaceable.‡

31 October / 10 Novem. Andros assumes the government of New York, and appoints officers.

* Col. MSS., xxiii., 412–420; New Orange Records, vii., 253; Doc. Hist., iii., 45–51; Val. Man., 1852, 415–421; 1853, 498; *ante*, 259. See Appendix, Note C, for the documents illustrating this negotiation between Colve and Andros.

† New Orange Rec., vii., 254, 255; Val. Man., 1852, 421, 422; 1853, 498, 499; Doc. Hist., iii., 51, 52; Col. MSS., xxiii., 423.

‡ Council Min., iii. (ii.), 1; Gen. Ent., iv., 295; Warr., Ord., Passes, iii., 1; S. Hazard's Ann. Penn., 413; Mass. H. S. Coll., xxx., 112; *ante*, 211.

CHAP. VI.

1674.

Domine Nicolaus van Rensselaer.

A quiet Sunday followed. Whoever was British chaplain at the fort, it especially interested Domine Van Nieuwenhuysen to learn that the Reverend Nicolaus van Rensselaer, a younger son of the first patroon of Rensselaerwyck, and an ordained clergyman in both the Dutch and the English churches, had come over with Andros, recommended by the Duke of York to be made "minister of one of the Dutch churches in New York or New Albany, when a vacancy shall happen."*

2/12 Novem. Letter of Andros to Colve.

Early on Monday morning Andros wrote a courteous letter to Colve, acknowledging his "generosity in all his proceedings" since the arrival of the English frigates; not the least touching mark of which seems to have been the gift by the Dutch governor to his successor of his coach and three horses. Andros likewise returned to Colve the articles proposed before the surrender; almost all of which were agreed to, and certified by Secretary Nicolls, "pursuant to the assurance given by those employed."†

Colve's coach and horses given to Andros.

2/12 Novem. Andros notifies the governors of the English colonies.

At the same time Andros notified the governors of the neighboring English colonies of his arrival, and of his assumption of the government of New York. Dyer was installed as collector, and the duke's customs' rates published. Various local officers were also appointed. But, as these could not all be selected at once, the governor, by proclamation, authorized the English magistrates who were in office in the several towns at the time of the Dutch conquest, to act for six months, as before.‡

4/14 Novem. Proclamation to continue English officers.

3 Novem.

The most important point to be regained was Albany. Ensign Cæsar Knapton was accordingly sent thither, with Sergeant Thomas Sharpe and eighteen men, to take com-

* Van Nieuwenhuysen's Letter to Cl. Amst., 30 May, 1676: Col. Doc., iii., 225; Doc. Hist., iii., 526; O'Call., i., 122, 212; ii., 552; Holgate, 42; Smith, i., 49, 388; N. Y. Christ. Int., 2 Nov., 1865; Hist. Mag., ix., 352. It appears that Van Rensselaer had luckily prophesied to Charles the Second, at Brussels, that he would be restored to his throne. When that event occurred the Domine accompanied the Dutch ambassador, Van Gogh, to London, as chaplain to the embassy; and the king, recollecting his prediction, gave Van Rensselaer a gold snuff-box, with his likeness in the lid, which is still preserved by the family at Albany. After Van Gogh left London because of the Dutch war in 1665, Domine Van Rensselaer received Charles's license to preach to the Dutch congregation at Westminster; was ordained a deacon in the English Church by the Bishop of Salisbury; and was appointed lecturer at Saint Margaret's Lothbury.

† Col. MSS., xxiii., 419, 420, 421; Doc. Hist., iii., 48, 49, 50; Val. Man., 1852, 418–421. Andros appears to have been the first English governor who used a coach and horses in New York, and they were a present from Colve: see Col. Doc., iv., 221, 275; *ante*, 223.

‡ Gen. Ent., iv., 296–299; Council Min., iii. (ii.), 2, 3; Warr., Ord., etc., iii., 2, 3; Riker's Newtown, 90; Col. Rec. Conn., ii., 569; Col. Doc., iii., 217, 246; *ante*, 263, 265.

CHAP. VI.

1674.

4 Novem. Albany officers.

6 Novem. Arensius.

19 Novem.

mand of the fort. Michael Siston was appointed schout, or sheriff, and Richard Pretty collector of the excise. George Hall was made schout of Esopus. Andros also wrote to the Dutch commissaries at both places, inclosing Colve's orders for their surrender. Domine Bernardus Arensius, the Lutheran minister, was at the same time licensed to go to Albany in the sloop which conveyed the new officers, and officiate there "as formerly under the English Government." The surrender was happily accomplished; and the reinstated Albany commissaries expressed their satisfaction at being settled again under the Duke of York's authority.*

9 Novem. Proclamation of Andros confirming all former grants.

16 Novem.

To quiet any controversy about the "*Jus Postliminii*," Andros now issued a proclamation that "all former grants, privileges, or concessions heretofore granted, and all estates legally possessed by any under His Royal Highness before the late Dutch Government, as also all legal judicial proceedings during that Government to my arrival in these parts, are hereby confirmed, and the possessors by virtue thereof to remain in quiet possession of their rights: It is hereby further declared that the known Book of Laws formerly established and in force under His Royal Highness's government, is now again confirmed by His Royal Highness, the which are to be observed and practiced, together with the manner and time of holding Courts therein mentioned, as heretofore." The next week, to settle some farther doubts, the governor declared that his proclamation of the ninth of November was "to be understood with due regard of the Articles of Peace in every particular."†

10 Novem. City officers of New York.

The city of New York being the metropolis, Andros, by a special commission, appointed Secretary Matthias Nicolls to be mayor, John Lawrence deputy mayor, and William Dervall, Frederick Phillipse, Gabriel Minvielle, and John Winder aldermen, who were to hold their offices until the

* Council Min., iii. (ii.), 2, 3; Gen. Ent., iv., 300–304; Warr., Ord., Passes, iii., 2–8, 38, 39; Doc. Hist., iii., 51, 525. It appears that Arensius afterward spent his summers in New York, and his winters at Albany, ministering alternately to the Lutherans in each place: Letter of Selyns to Cl. Amst., 26 October, 1682; Murphy's Anthology, 94; C. Wolley, 57. Captain Knyff, on his departure for Holland, made several donations to the Lutheran Church: Col. MSS., xxiii., 424.

† Warr., Ord., Pass., iii., 13, 19; Col. MSS., xxiv., 8; Col. Doc., iii., 227; Doc. Hist., iii., 52; Min. of N. Y. Com. Council, i., 12, 13; Val. Man., 1845, 1846, 330, 331; *ante*, 260.

CHAP. VI. 1674. next October. Thomas Gibbs, who had been one of Lovelace's counselors, was also commissioned as sheriff. Yet care was taken that the English element should prevail.*

13 Novem. Mayor's Court of New York. A few days afterward the "Mayor's Court" of the city of New York was convened. Its records were ordered to be thereafter kept in English, and every paper offered to the court to be in that tongue, except in the case of poor people who could not afford the cost of translation. This introduced more of the English form in legal proceedings. But it was several years before the system was settled.†

12 Novem. Lovelace's estate seized for the Duke of York. Pursuant to the duke's order, Andros seized the estate of Lovelace, and required all persons having any of it in their hands to render accounts. The governor thus obtained possession of the "Bouwery," which some of the heirs of Domine Bogardus and his widow conveyed to Lovelace in 1671. It formed a part of "the Duke's farm," then esteemed to be one of the least valuable perquisites of the actual governor; but which has since become the subject of much avaricious strife.‡

When the governor's proclamation of the fourth of November, reinstating the old officers under Lovelace, was received at Southampton, Easthampton, and Southold, these towns held meetings, and directed Mulford, Howell, and Younge, the magistrates appointed by Connecticut, to sign a memorial to Andros, stating that, by the aid of that colony, they had repelled the Dutch; that they were now under her government, and that they could not secede without her consent. It was at once ordered in council that the three towns should reinstate their former officers, according to the proclamation, "under the penalty of being declared rebels." Andros also wrote to Governor Winthrop, of Connecticut, counseling him to disabuse his would-be subordinates of their "notion" that they could exercise

(Margin notes: Eastern towns on Long Island. — 18 Novem. — 4 Decem. Action of Andros.)

* Council Min., iii. (ii.), 3; Warr., Ord., Pass., iii., 12. These particulars are not stated in Valentine's Manual. While the provincial seal was saved, the city's seal and mace had disappeared, and Andros "bespoke" new ones: Col. Doc., iii., 230; *ante*, 157, 158, 212.

† Records of the Mayor's Court, ii.; Daly's Int., 28, 29; Council Min., iii. (ii.), 148; C. Wolley, 57. In May, 1677, it was ordered that "pleading attornies" be no longer allowed to practice their profession in New York, "but for the depending causes."

‡ Col. Doc., iii., 226, 291; iv., 327, 393, 448; Warr., Ord., Passes, iii., 15, 16; Col. MSS., xx., 14, 15, 72; Hoffman's Treatise, ii., 182, 183; Val. Man., 1860, 548; *ante*, 183, 269. Trinity Church, in the city of New York, now enjoys the benefit of this action of Governor Andros in 1674. Lovelace died before 21 January, 1679, on which day the accounts of his estate were exhibited: Col. MSS., xxvi., 43; xxviii., 50.

1674.

power in any part of New York. Sylvester Salisbury, who had returned from England with the governor, was accordingly dispatched to execute the orders of the council. To give him more dignity, Salisbury was also commissioned to be high-sheriff of Long Island.*

5 Decem. Salisbury high-sheriff.

Andros himself appears to have visited the eastern towns of Long Island, which prudently avoided any farther opposition to his authority. They soon learned that Winthrop had sent his son, with Mr. Willys, to explain the proceedings of Connecticut at New York, where they arrived during the governor's absence. The recusant towns seem to have been soothed by Salisbury's declaration that he accepted their return to New York "from under the colony of Connecticut, by whose help and protection they have been secured from the Dutch invasion unto the obedience of His Royal Highness." On his return to the capital, Andros wrote to Winthrop that every thing was satisfactorily arranged at the eastern end of Long Island; and that Connecticut, by her interference against the Dutch in the previous February, had done well for the restoration of his master's royal authority.†

Connecticut messengers to Andros.

10 Decem. Submission of recusant towns.

28 Decem. Andros writes to Winthrop.

By direction of the people of Newtown, their clerk, John Burroughs, replied to the governor's proclamation, speaking very plainly of the grievances they had suffered under Lovelace, and reflecting on the authority of the Court of Assizes. Andros at once demanded whether Burroughs had expressed the voice of the town, and an unsatisfactory answer was returned. The offending clerk was brought before the council at New York, and sentenced to stand an hour on the whipping-post before the City Hall, with a paper on his breast, setting forth that he had signed seditious letters against the government; and Burroughs was farther declared incapable of holding any public trust in the province. This sentence was executed under the direction of Sheriff Gibbs, at the metropolis.‡

16 Novem. Letter of Newtown to Andros.

27 Novem.

5 Decem.

1675.

15 Jan'y. Its clerk, Burroughs, punished.

* Council Min., iii. (ii.), 6–9; Warr., Ord., Passes, etc., iii., 4, 28, 29, 30, 31, 41, 42, 53; Gen. Ent., iv., 299; Wood, 98, 99; Thompson, i., 158, 335, 383; *ante*, 253, 272.

† Mass. H. S. Coll., xxx., 113, 114, 117; Warr., Ord., Passes, iii., 48; Thompson, i., 383; Dunlap, ii., App. xxxviii.; *ante*, 243.

‡ Warr., Ord., Passes, iii., 25; Council Min., iii. (ii.), 14, 15; Riker's Newtown, 90–92. Several interesting details respecting Jamaica, Francis Bloodgood, of Flushing, and Thomas and Mary Case, Samuel Scudder, and Samuel Furman, or Forman, may be found in Col. MSS., xxiv., 25, 171; xxv., 2; Warr., Ord., Passes, iii., 52; Riker, 92–95; *ante*, 243, 255.

CHAP. VI. 1675. 8 Jan'y. Council meetings. Fishery established.

The council was now directed to meet for the transaction of business every Friday morning at nine o'clock. A charter was also passed, authorizing a joint-stock company "for settling a fishery in these parts" for cod. It is supposed that this was the first commercial corporation ever created within the province of New York.*

16 Jan'y. 2 Feb'y. Manning arraigned before a court-martial. 4 Feb'y. 5 Feb'y.

Among those who had lost heavily by the surrender to the Dutch was Alderman Dervall, who attributed it directly to the "treachery" of Manning. This charge against an Englishman made it necessary for the governor "to proceed against him," according to the duke's instruction. Manning was brought before a court-martial, composed of the Council, Captains Griffith, Burton, and Salisbury, and the mayor and aldermen of the city; and six charges were exhibited against him, involving neglect of duty, cowardice, and treachery. A number of witnesses testified strongly against the prisoner. Manning endeavored to explain his conduct; at the same time, acknowledging himself "blameworthy to all" the charges except those of treachery and cowardice; and, pleading that his errors had been occasioned by his "poor broken head and disquieted spirit," he threw himself on the mercy of the court. His judges acquitted him of treachery, but found him guilty of the other charges. It was agreed that he deserved death; but as he had been in England since the surrender, and had seen the king and the duke, he was allowed the benefit of the proverb, "*King's face brings grace.*" Manning was therefore sentenced "to be carried back to prison, and from thence brought out to the publick place before the City Hall, there to have his sword broken over his head, and from that time be rendered uncapable of wearing a sword or serving His Majesty in any publick employ or place of benefitt and trust within this Government."†

Sentence of Manning.

5 March. Vessels to enter at the New York Custom-house.

To secure the duke's customs' duties a proclamation was issued requiring all vessels trading within the government of the province to enter at the custom-house in New

* Col. MSS., xxiv., 67; Council Min., iii. (ii.), 10; Col. Doc., iii., 234, *note*.

† Col. Doc., ii., 638, 643; iii., 206, 216; Council Min., iii. (ii.), 15, 18, 20–24; Col. MSS., xxiv., 36–53, 97; Doc. Hist., iii., 53–65; Smith, i., 48, 49; Thompson, i., 159; Dunlap, i., 130; Val. Man., 1853, 384; C. Wolley, 47, 89, 90; *ante*, 208, 257, 263, 270. After this sentence Manning retired to his island in the East River, now known as Blackwell's Island (*ante*, 138), where he entertained his friends with bowls of excellent rum punch, according to the testimony of Chaplain Wolley, in 1679.

York. Dyer, the collector, accordingly executed his office so stringently as to give occasion, not long afterward, to serious complaints.*

13 March. Oaths of allegiance required.

Andros now issued a proclamation requiring "all such persons as doe intend to continue under His Majesty's obedience within His Royal Highness's government, that they appear at such times and places as the magistrates within the respective towns and places where they live shall appoint, to take the usual oaths of allegiance and fidelity." The mayor and aldermen of the city of New York accordingly appointed the next Monday for the purpose. Early on that morning many of the citizens appeared at the Mayor's Court, and were directed to take the same oath which Nicolls required from the Dutch residents in 1664. Several of the leading burghers† readily agreed to do this, provided Andros would confirm what his predecessor had declared, namely, that the capitulation of August, 1664, was "not in the least broken or intended to be broken by any words or expressions in the said oath." This capitulation they thought was confirmed by the sixth article of the Treaty of Westminster in 1674; and such was the opinion of the duke and his officers. Mayor Nicolls, however, was "ignorant of any such declaration," and was quite surprised when a copy of it was produced. The burghers insisted that they only wished Andros's confirmation of their "freedom of religion and from being pressed in time of war." But the governor refused to make any explanation, and required them to take the oath without qualification, charging the recusants with being mutinous. Accordingly, Steenwyck and his associates petitioned Andros either to be satisfied with the oath as accepted by Nicolls, or to allow them to dispose of their estates and remove elsewhere with their families. This petition was "not only ill received, but peremptorily rejected;" and its eight signers, Steenwyck, Van Brugh, De Peyster, Bayard, Luyck, Beekman, Kip, and De Milt, were imprisoned on a charge of disturbing the government and endeavoring a rebellion.

15 March.

Objections of some of the Dutch.

16 March. Petition to Andros.

18 March.

* Warr., Ord., Passes, iii., 63; Col. Doc., iii., 229, 233, 239, 240, 316; Col. MSS., xxiv., 132; *ante*, 263, 272.

† These were, Cornelis Steenwyck, Johannes van Brugh, Johannes de Peyster, and Jacob Kip, who had objected in 1664, and Nicholas Bayard, Ægidius Luyck, William Beekman, and Anthony de Milt, who had not: *ante*, 47, 48.

CHAP. VI.

1765. 18 March. 19 March. The petitioners ordered to be tried. 20 March.

The governor at the same time issued a proclamation warning all against like practices. The prisoners having been examined before the council, where Governor Carteret, of New Jersey, and Captains Griffith and Burton, of the English frigates, were present, were ordered to be tried at the next Court of Assizes; and were released from close confinement only upon giving heavy bonds.*

Martha's Vineyard and Nantucket.

Although Pemaquid, Martha's Vineyard, and Nantucket had been included in the Duke of York's patent, and had been governed by Nicolls and Lovelace, they were not comprehended in Colve's commission. This produced a sort of interregnum in those secluded regions, and many disorders occurred. Some of the "opposition" inhabitants of Martha's Vineyard and Nantucket riotously endeavored to "transfer" them under the government of Massachusetts; but, through the firmness of the venerable Thomas Mayhew, they were held for the duke—the arrival of whose new governor was patiently waited for, "as in time of great

1674. 7 Novem.

drouth, for the latter raine." Mayhew was accordingly reinstated in his "first right;" and the ringleaders in the late disorders were directed to be punished. Nantucket

1675. 12 April.

soon afterward declared that the coming of the duke's governor was to them "as the rising sun after a dark and stormy night." It was therefore ordered that the two isl-

29 April.

ands should continue to enjoy their former privileges in subordination to the government of New York, and that the old magistrates should remain in their places.†

Delaware affairs.

On the Delaware, Captain Edmund Cantwell, the sheriff, and all the other magistrates in office at the time of the Dutch conquest, were reinstated, except Alrichs, who had offered them his friendship on their first coming, and had acted violently as their chief officer. Captain Carr, the former English commander, had now gone to Maryland,

3 Novem.

and his estate was seized. Andros also informed Governor Calvert that he had directed his officers on the Delaware to prevent any injuries to the neighboring colonies, and did "not doubt the like on the Governor of Maryland's part."

* Warr., Ord., Passes, iii., 65, 66, 67, 74, 75; Council Min., iii. (ii.), 27–31; Col. MSS., xxiv., 73, 76, 77–84; Col. Doc., ii., 738–744; iii., 237; v., 496; vii., 586; Val. Man., 1845, 331, 332; 1861, 605–607; Minutes of C. C., vol. i., 9–11; *ante*, 46, 47, 260.

† Warr., Ord., Passes, iii., 19, 21, 77, 84; Council Min., iii. (ii.), 36–38; Col. MSS., xxiv., 6, 16–18, 92, 93, 100–102; Hough's Nantucket Papers, 60–88; *ante*, 1[illegible]9, 211.

The murder of Doctor Roades by the Indians, and other important matters, requiring his own presence on the Delaware, the governor went thither, through New Jersey; thirty horses being furnished for his journey by Governor Carteret. After settling matters there, and writing to Lord Baltimore, Andros returned to New York, where Brockholls had acted for him during his absence.*

CHAP. VI. 1675. 3 May. 15 May.

The Diamond and the Castle frigates were sent back to England, the latter with a load of timber for the king's dock-yard. Its value was allowed to the duke; who nevertheless found himself more than two thousand pounds out of pocket on account of the expedition "for the repossessing New York." Andros soon afterward received James's autograph reply to his letters of the previous November and December. His conduct was approved, especially in reducing to obedience the three "factious towns at the east end of Long Island," which he was to treat so that their people should "be without apprehensions of any injustice towards them." In regard to "General Assemblies, which the people there seeme desirous of, in imitation of their neighbour Colonies, I thinke," wrote the duke, "you have done well to discourage any motion of that kind; both as being not at all comprehended in your Instructions, nor indeed consistent with the forme of government already established, nor necessary for the ease or redresse of any grievance that may happen; since that may be as easily obtained by any petition or other addresse to you, at their Generall Assizes, (which is once a yeare,) where the same persons (as Justices) are usually present, who in all probability would be their representatives if another constitution were allowed." The question of an Assembly had been raised under Nicolls and Lovelace:—but James now clearly announced his disapprobation.†

1 April. 20 April. Timber sent to England.

6 April. The duke's letter to Andros.

A popular Assembly disapproved by James.

Respecting the boundary arrangement with Connecticut in 1664, the duke thought it best "only to make accommodations of this kind temporary, if possible, to preserve the utmost limitts for me that my Patent gives me a title to."

6 April. The Duke of York disallows the Connecticut boundary.

* Council Min., iii. (ii.), i., 35; Gen. Ent., iv., 305, 306; Warr., Ord., Passes, iii., 34, 69, 80, 81, 89–92; Col. MSS., xx., 50–65; xxiv., 97, 105; xxv., 54; Col. Doc., ii., 597, 659; iii., 203, 233, 254; Hazard's Reg. Penn., i., 93; iv., 56; Ann. Penn., 398, 413–418; *ante*, 190, 224, 234.

† Warr., Ord., Passes, iii., 51, 60, 70, 72; Col. Doc., iii., 230, 231, 232, 237; Chalmers's Annals, i., 581; Mass. H. S. Coll., xxx., 115; *ante*, 64, 68, 69, 160.

CHAP. VI. 1675. But Andros had already acted on that subject. Connecticut had recently appointed commissioners "to runn the lyne between this Colony and the Colony of New York, from Momoronock River to Hudson's River;"—which she had done in violation of the clear understanding that she was not to approach that river nearer than twenty miles. Seeing that the king, in 1674, had again granted to the Duke of York the territory as far east as the Connecticut River, 1 May. Andros sent to the General Court at Hartford copies of the duke's patent and of his own commission, and requested them to give orders for his receiving that part of his royal highness's territories as yet under their jurisdiction.*

17 May. The Connecticut Court, in answer, set up their charter from the king, and the boundary arrangement of 1664. 25 May. Andros maintains the rights of New York. Andros replied that the award by the royal commissioners "was an evident surprise," and "never confirmed;" and that whatever pretenses Connecticut had made before 1674 were "sufficiently cleared by His Majesty's reiterated Letters Patents." He therefore again demanded possession, and protested against all who might thus disobey their 16 June. king's commands. Connecticut rejoined, denying any "undue surprise" in the boundary determination, and insisting on her own charter. The New York Council thereupon re- 28 June. solved that such disobedience to the king's pleasure as expressed in his patent to the duke was "rebellion."†

30 June. 2 July. Salisbury dispatched to England. Andros now sent Captain Salisbury with dispatches to the duke and Sir John Werden, and directed him to inform them fully of every thing relating to New York; especially about its people, their trade, the French in Canada; the "Bostoners' trading-house at Springfield," and their claiming "to Albany itself;" and of the recent contempt of the duke's authority in "that part of His Royal Highnesses' territories as yet under Connecticut, their many harbors, and plenty of corn and provisions." By the same vessel, Steenwyck and his associates, who had been bound over for trial, sent a memorial to the Dutch States General, setting forth their own hard case.‡

* Warr., Ord., Passes, iii., 2, 3, 112–114; Col. Doc., iii., 215, 231, 235; vii., 597; Col. Rec. Conn., ii., 242, 569; Mass. H. S. Coll., xxx., 116; *ante*, 55, 56, 253.

† Council Min., iii. (ii.), 39, 41, 42; Warr., Ord., Passes, iii., 104, 115, 116; Col. Rec. Conn., ii., 252, 570–574, 581; Col. Doc., iii., 235, 236, 238; Col. MSS., xxiv., 121.

‡ Warr., Ord., Passes, iii., 106, 116; Col. Doc., ii., 739, 744; iii., 234, 235, 236, 237, 415.

CHAP. VI. 1675.

In this posture of affairs, intelligence reached New York that the Wampanoags and Narragansetts, who owned most of the territory of Rhode Island, had revolted against the Europeans. The Narragansett sachem, Ninigret, had been suspected, in 1669, of plotting against the English colonists. Two years afterward, Metacomet, or Philip, the sachem of the Wampanoags, who inhabited the region of Pokanoket, around the eastern and northern shores of Narragansett Bay, was obliged to give up most of his guns and acknowledge his subjection to the Plymouth government. This galled the soul of the American chief. He was the youngest son of Massasoit, who had made the first treaty with the English "Pilgrims." Massasoit's eldest son, Wamsutta, or Alexander, succeeded to the sachemship; but he soon followed his father to the grave, broken-hearted, at being dragged a prisoner to answer before the European new-comers at Plymouth. Philip was a youth when he became sachem in place of Wamsutta. Yet he had heard of the prompt kindness of his father, Massasoit, to the forlorn English Pilgrims, and naturally contrasted it with the characteristic arrogance which repaid savage hospitality with British truculence. He saw that the Europeans had crowded his people into narrow necks of land, where they were jealously watched. In vain had Eliot and Mayhew solicited the Wampanoags to become Christians. The well-remembered injunctions of Massasoit kept the tribe firm in heathenism. A few savages were nevertheless converted. Among these was John Sausaman, who, after being partially educated at Cambridge, relapsed from Christianity, and was employed by Philip as his secretary. The Puritan colonists had generally disregarded the feelings of the Americans. Instead of adopting the conciliatory policy of New Netherland and New York toward the natives, they followed—without any warrant from the God of Israel—the aggressive method of that peculiar host which went out of Egypt to possess the promised land. As Puritanism had already exterminated or sold the Pequods, so it now doomed the other native owners of New England to destruction or bondage. The pride of the aborigines was wounded without remorse; for the white English Pharisee, holding the imported black African in slavery, would not

Philip of Pokanoket.

New England policy.

CHAP. VI. 1675.

brook the equality of the noble red American, whose lands he covetously appropriated. While at Albany the autochthones of America were addressed as "Brothers," every where in New England, except in Rhode Island, they were offensively reminded of their inferiority. These memories stirred the mind of Philip. Cautiously visiting the neighboring tribes, he urged them to drive out the destroyers of their race. The Narragansetts were won by his eloquence; and secret preparations were made for a rising of the native Americans against their British foes in the spring of 1676.*

Philip prepares for war.

An unexpected event precipitated the crisis. Sausaman, reclaimed from his apostasy by Eliot, revealed Philip's plot to the Plymouth governor. Not long afterward the informer's body was found under the ice in Assawomsett Pond, midway between Plymouth and Rhode Island. It was suspected by the English that the savages had punished, after their own laws, a renegade and a traitor. Three of Philip's subjects were accordingly tried at Plymouth; convicted of the murder of Sausaman; and executed. The Wampanoag chief now remained on guard within his strong-hold at Mount Hope, near Bristol, in Rhode Island. There he soon gathered seven hundred warriors, the younger of whom were eager to avenge the death of their three countrymen by the forms of Puritan law, which they did not recognize. They were restrained from attacking by a belief that the side which shed the first blood in the strife would be conquered.† Hoping to prevent hostilities, John Easton, "Deputy Governor," and several magistrates of Rhode Island—which colony had always been friendly with the Indians—visited Philip at the Ferry. "We sat," wrote the honest Quaker, "very friendly together. We told him our business was to endeavour that they might not receive or do wrong. They said that was well: they

29 Jan'y. John Sausaman murdered.

8 June. Indians tried and executed at Plymouth.

Rhode Island magistrates visit Philip.

* Bradford's Plymouth, 94-97; Hutch. Mass., i., 275-285; Colden, i., 40; Mather's Magnalia (ed. 1853), ii., 429, 430, 434, 558, 559; Mather's History of New England (ed. 1864), 226-234; Easton's Narrative of Philip's Indian War (ed. 1858), viii.-xii., 3, 6, 12-14, 33-39; Court of Assizes, ii., 678; Holmes, i., 325, 369, 383; Belknap, i., 102-107; Bancroft, ii., 92-100; Palfrey, iii., 141-151, 218, 221, 298; Arnold's Rhode Island, i., 23, 87, 212, 339, 387-395; Plymouth Col. Rec., v., 76-80; Hazard, ii., 531-534; Moore's Notes on Slavery in Mass., *passim*; *ante*, i., 171; ii., 155, 156, 254.

† Hutchinson, i., 286, *note*, calls this "a whimsical opinion." It certainly was the converse of the augury prevailing in the Highlands of Scotland:

"Which spills the foremost foeman's life,
That party conquers in the strife."—*Lady of the Lake*, Canto iv., vi.

had done no wrong; the English wronged them. We said, we knew the English said the Indians wronged them and the Indians said the English wronged them; but our desire was the quarrel might rightly be decided in the best way, and not as dogs decided their quarrels." The Indians then asked "how right might take place?" The Rhode Islanders proposed arbitration. The Americans replied that all the English were "agreed against them," and would insist upon English arbitrators, by whom they already had much wrong. The Rhode Island men suggested that they might choose an Indian king, and the English the governor of New York, both of whom would be indifferent. This pleased the savages; and "if that way had been tendered, they would have accepted." Philip then told the grievances of his people. When the first colonists came, his father, Massasoit, "was as a great man, and the English as a little child," to whom he freely did good; but now the Americans were insulted and cheated in bargains, until "they had no hopes left to keep any land." Again the Rhode Island men urged the Indians to accept the arbitration of Andros and a native king; to which they did not object. Easton and his friends then endeavored to persuade them "to lay down the war; for the English were too strong for them." With logic as keen as it was just, Philip replied, "then the English should do to them as they did when they were too strong for the English." So ended this memorable interview. It was a virtual protest, by Rhode Island and Philip, against the doctrine of the Puritan colonists of New England, that they were the sole judges between themselves and Americans. If those colonies had accepted the arbitration of Andros and a native chief, justice might have been done, and war avoided.*

Arbitration proposed.

Philip's reply.

Philip's young men could not be restrained. Some of them plundered a house at Swansey, within the Plymouth government, and one of the marauders was killed by an

20 June. Hostilities begin.

* Plymouth Col. Rec., v., 167–174; Mather's Early History, 235–237; Mather's War, 48–53; Magnalia, ii., 559, 560; Hutch., i., 284–286; Bayley's Plymouth, ii., 27; Easton's Narrative, by Hough, 1–15; "A true Relation," etc., in N. Y. Col. MSS., xxv., 29. This Rhode Island negotiation with Philip is not noticed by most New England writers. Mr. Palfrey, iii., 180, *note*, pronounces that Easton's Narrative adds "nothing of importance" to our historical knowledge; and in a note to page 227, he says of the speech of Philip to John Borden, given in Arnold, i., 394, 395, "I have made no account of it. It is no material for history." Perhaps a New Yorker may venture to dissent from this Massachusetts judgment.

Englishman. This made the savages hope that they would triumph in the end, because the English had shed the first blood. 24 June. Swansey was attacked, and several of its inhabitants killed. Massachusetts and Plymouth called out large forces. 29 June. An express was sent to Hartford for aid, and 1 July. Winthrop dispatched the news to Andros at New York.*

4 July. Action of New York.

The Metropolitan Council thought "that Connecticut doth not expect nor desire assistance from us in relation to the Indian disturbances at this time." But it was "Resolved that the Governor do proceed on his intended voyage to Connecticut forthwith, and do take a force with him to be in a capacity to protect that part of His Royal Highness's Government, as there may be occasions." So, Andros wrote to Winthrop:—"I am very much troubled at the Christians' misfortunes and hard disasters in those parts, being so overpowered by such heathen. Hereupon, I have hastened my coming to your parts, and added a force to be ready to take such resolutions as may be fit for me upon this extraordinary occasion, with which I intend, God willing, to set out this evening, and to make the best of my way to Connecticut River, His Royall Highnesses bounds there."†

4 July. Andros's letter to Winthrop.

7 July. Action of Connecticut.

Andros's letter made great trouble at Hartford. The Council of War hastened Captain Thomas Bull to Saybrook, and recalled the forces sent forward to fight against Philip. Bull's instructions were cunningly drawn. He was to keep Saybrook and its neighborhood from any enemy, "by force of arms," if necessary; and while his orders appeared to require him to repel the savages only, they really meant that the officers of the Duke of York were to be treated as the special foes of Connecticut.‡

8 July. Andros at Saybrook.

The next morning, Andros, with three sloops, appeared off Saybrook, and desired a "direct and effectual answer" to his former letters. Meanwhile the Hartford authorities had ordered their subordinates at Saybrook to "carry it warily and prudently" with Andros, forbid his landing, and advise him to send his forces eastward and assist the

* Mather's History, 53–58; Magnalia, ii., 561; Hutch., i., 286, 287; Hough's Easton, 16–21, 40–43; Barry, i., 410, 411; Mass. H. S. Coll., xxx., 117, 118; R. I. H. S. Coll., iv., 127; Col. MSS., xxiv., 119, 121; Col. Rec. Conn., ii., 332, 579; Palfrey, iii., 129, 155.

† Council Min., iii. (ii.), 44; Warr., Ord., Passes, iii., 117; Col. MSS., xxiv., 121; Hough's Easton, 44–48; Col. Rec. Conn., ii., 579; Col. Doc., iii., 254, 264; Palfrey, iii., 129.

‡ Col. Rec. Conn., ii., 333, 579.

"good people" at Seaconk or Swansey. The next day they wrote to Andros himself, resenting his "hypotheticall expressions and injurious imputations," and desiring him not to "molest" the king's good subjects in Connecticut, or put them "into a discomposure, at such a time as this." They also drew up "a Protest," denouncing the governor of New York as a disturber of the king's peace, and appealing to the Connecticut charter as their warrant for refusing obedience to the duke's representative.*

CHAP. VI. 1675. 9 July. Connecticut protests against discomposure by Andros.

Andros had meanwhile remained quietly at Saybrook, anxious about his suffering countrymen at the East, to whom he sent forward a sloop with supplies; and wondering that the Connecticut forces did not move to their relief. When the dispatches from Hartford were communicated to him, the governor landed, with his attendants, and was received by the Connecticut officials, who desired "to tender him a treaty." This Andros declined; but he ordered the Duke of York's patent and his own commission to be read; which was accomplished, while the Connecticut officials "withdrew a little," declaring that they "had nothing to doe to attend it." Andros then told them that he had now done, and would sail immediately unless they desired him to stay. The Connecticut officers answered that they were not ordered to ask him to remain; and they then read the protest of the Hartford authorities. This Andros at once denounced as "a slander, and so an ill requital for his kindness;" and being refused a copy of it, he went on board his sloop again, and sailed to Long Island, whence he intended to send a force to Martin's Vineyard, and then to return to New York. As he passed below the fort, salutes were fired on both sides.†

13 July. Andros lands at Saybrook.

His commission read.

The Hartford protest "a slander."

The Hartford authorities regretted that their subordinates at Saybrook had not interrupted Andros "in commanding there so usurpingly;" which "might have been done by shouts, or sound of drum, etc., without vio-

14 July. Action of Connecticut.

* Col. MSS., xxiv., 121; Warr., Ord., Passes, iii., 118, 119; Hough's Easton, 49–56; Col. Rec. Conn., ii., 260–263, 334, 335, 579, 580, 581; Trumbull, i., 329, 330; Palfrey, iii., 129, 130; *ante*, 280.

† Col. Rec. Conn., ii., 582, 583, 584; Col. Doc., iii., 254, 264, 415; Warr., Ord., Passes, iii., 119, 120; Hough's Easton, 56–60; Mass. H. S. Coll., xxxvii., 137; Palfrey, iii., 130, 131. The romantic account of this transaction, which the Reverend Doctor Trumbull has dressed up in his History of Connecticut, i., 328–330, is so erroneous that Mr. Palfrey is "obliged to omit some striking circumstances in the sketch by that usually cautious historian:" Hist. N. E., iii., 131, *note*.

CHAP. VI. 1675. 24 July.

lence."* An elaborate "narrative" of the Connecticut version was sent to Major Robert Thompson, of Newington Green, near London, with a request for his help against Andros, who, it was thought, "must be necessitated to misrepresent" the colony.†

14 July. New York soldiers sent to Martha's Vineyard and Nantucket.

Andros, meanwhile, went over to Southold, whence he dispatched a sloop, with some soldiers and ammunition, to Martha's Vineyard and Nantucket. "To satisfy the great jealousy" of his neighbors, the governor came through Long Island to New York, disarming the Indians every where, and reviewing all the militia. On his reporting "the several passages of his voyage," the council resolved that the several towns on Long Island should maintain a good watch, and take care that the disarmed Indians "be not any wise injured, but assisted, upon any occasion requiring it."‡

24 July. Long Island Indians.

23 July. New Jersey Indians.

The governor also sent for all the Indian sachems of New Jersey and other parts, most of whom had been with him before, and they all "again renewed their submissions and engagements."§

At the same time, Andros did not neglect the immediate interests of the province. Accordingly, the council, "upon a proposal to give public notice what encouragement will be given to persons that shall come out of Europe hither, to inhabite and plant in this His Royal Highness's Province, Resolved that every freeman shall have for himself the proportion of sixty acres of land of inheritance, and for his wife and every child fifty acres per head; and every working servant that shall be brought over shall have each of them fifty acres after the expiration of their service, according to the custom of the country." A copy of this order was sent to England by the ship Good Hope,

5 August. New York lands offered to emigrants from Europe.

* Col. Rec. Conn., ii., 335, 584. It would seem that this hint was remembered in 1693, when Fletcher, one of the successors of Andros, visited Hartford; although the "tradition" related by Doctor Trumbull, i., 393, does not agree with the official account in Col. Doc., iv., 69–71.

† Col. Rec. Conn., ii., 96, 103, 263, 264, 338–344; iii., 261; Trumbull, i., 331; Mass. Rec., v., 408, 409, 426, 467; Hutch. Coll., 449, 463, 469, 473; Col. Doc., iii., 355. Winthrop, who intended to take the Connecticut "Narrative" to England, died at Boston on the 5th of April, 1676: Col. Rec. Conn., ii., 273; Palfrey, iii., 233–238.

‡ Warr., Ord., Passes, iii., 119, 120, 121; Council Min., iii. (ii.), 44; Hough's Easton, 54–64; Col. Doc., iii., 254, 264. On the 21st of July, Governor Coddington, of Rhode Island, complained to Andros of the invasion of its territory by Massachusetts and Connecticut: Col. MSS., xxiv., 128.

§ Col. MSS., xxiv., 117, 130; Council Min., iii. (ii.), 44; Dunlap, ii., App., cxxii.; Col. Doc., iii., 254; Hough's Easton, 76.

1675.

Captain George Heathcote, a Quaker, who had been imprisoned at Boston by Governor Bellingham "for delivering him a letter, and not putting off his hat."*

16 April.

The intrigues of the French missionaries, Bruyas and Lamberville, among the Iroquois, having caused complaints, the council resolved that the Mohawks should be encouraged to friendship, and the Jesuits be sent for, to explain themselves at Albany. Leaving Brockholls in charge at New York, Andros now went up the river. After regulating affairs at Schenectady, he visited the "most warlike Indians near one hundred miles beyond;" and at Tionnontoguen, the third castle of the Mohawks, he accepted the name of "Corlaer," who, they told him, was "a man that was of good dispositions and esteemed deare amongst us."† On his return to Albany, the Five Iroquois nations applied to Andros "declaring their former alliance, and now submitted in an extraordinary manner, with reiterated promises." Perhaps the governor's most important measure at this time was to organize a local board of commissioners for Indian affairs, composed of some of the Albany officers.‡ Of this board he appointed as secretary the town clerk of Albany, Robert Livingston, a shrewd young Scotchman, who had come over from Rotterdam the year before, and who was destined to become prominent in colonial affairs.§

30 August. Andros visits the Mohawks, and receives the name of "Corlaer."

Indian commissioners at Albany. R. Livingston, secretary.

10 Septem. Indian orders.

The Council now "Resolved that we ought not to break with our Indians upon account of the war between our neighbors and their Indians." The selling of powder to

* Council Min., iii. (ii.), 45, 46; Col. MSS., xxiv., 127; xxv., 25–42, 221, 235–241; Farmer and Moore's Coll., iii., 190; Besse, ii., 259; C. Wolley, 12, 97; Holmes, i., 377.

† This name "Corlaer" was given by the Iroquois to the governors of New York, until, in 1693, they made a special one for Fletcher: compare Col. Doc., iii., 254, 322, 327, 395, 559; iv., 22, 85; Colden, i., 32, 41; *ante*, 121.

‡ Warr., Ord., Passes, iii., 77, 122, 125, 126, 129, 224, 225; Council Min., iii. (ii.), 34; Col. Doc., iii., 254, 323, 559; Hist. Mag., ii. (i.), 301. Regular minutes were kept of the transactions of the Albany commissioners, beginning with 1675, which in 1751 were bound up in four large folio volumes. But they have disappeared from our State Archives: see Colden, i., Preface, ix., 94; Smith, i., 251, *note;* Col. Doc., i., Gen. Introd., viii., xxxi.; v., 983, *note;* vi., 439, 731, 739.

§ Col. MSS., xxiv., 140. Robert Livingston was born on 13 December, 1654, at Ancram, in Roxburghshire, Scotland, where his father, the Rev. John Livingston, was the Presbyterian minister. After the Restoration the father went to Rotterdam, where he died on 9th of August, 1672. After his father's death, Robert, who had learned the Dutch language, came to Albany, probably accompanying Domine Van Rensselaer thither in the autumn of 1674: *ante*, 272. There is a biographical sketch of him in Doc. Hist., iii., 434: see also Col. Doc., iii., 315, 401, 699; iv., 203, 251, 253, 720; v., 196; Smith, i., 142, *note;* Sedgwick's Life of W. Livingston; Hunt's Life of E. Livingston.

CHAP. VI. 1675. 16 Septem.

the savages was "regulated as formerly;" each town was to provide a block-house as a refuge for women and children; and all New York Indians were to be "friendly treated, and have equall justice according to law." A sloop was also ordered to cruise in the Sound; and, as the natives were very strong near Martha's Vineyard and Nantucket, great guns were sent to each of those islands. These measures, however, made Connecticut fear that Andros would again threaten Saybrook.*

New York sloop in the Sound. 28 Septem. Guns sent to Martha's Vineyard and Nantucket.

Domine Nicolaus van Rensselaer, who had come from London under the special patronage of the Duke of York, was soon afterward inducted by Andros to minister in the Reformed Dutch Church at Albany, as a colleague of Domine Schaats. This was done without regard to the Classis of Amsterdam, which governed the Reformed Dutch churches in New York, under the eighth article of the capitulation of 1664, confirmed by Andros's stipulation with Colve. It occasioned much ill feeling, and Van Rensselaer was forbidden to baptize children in the metropolitan Reformed Dutch Church by Domine Van Nieuwenhuysen, who denied the lawfulness of his induction at Albany. Instead of showing that he had been ordained as a minister in Holland, Van Rensselaer complained to Andros that the Church of England and the Duke of York's recommendation had been contemned. Van Nieuwenhuysen was summoned to explain himself before the Council. He admitted the validity of English Episcopal ordination, but insisted that every minister serving any Reformed Dutch congregation in the king's dominions must promise conformity to the Holland Church. This explanation was accepted; and Van Rensselaer, having solemnly promised to conduct his ministry "conformably to the public Church service and discipline of the Reformed Church of Holland," the question was satisfactorily adjusted.†

Case of Domine Nicolaus van Rensselaer.

25 Septem. 30 Septem. 1 October. 2 October.

* Council Min., iii. (ii.), 50, 51, 52, 57; Warr., Ord., Passes, iii., 132, 133, 134; Col. MSS., xxiv., 138, 139, 141; Hough's Philip's War, 71-82; Nantucket Papers, 88, 89; Rec. Conn., ii., 369-371; C. Wolley, 95; *ante*, 278.

† Corr. Cl. Amst., Letter of Van Nieuwenhuysen of 30 May, 1676, and Inclosures; Council Min., iii. (ii.), 54-59; Doc. Hist., iii., 526, 527; Col. Doc., iii., 225; Col. MSS., xxiv., 158; Yonkers Gazette, 21 October, 1865; Hist. Mag., ix., 352, 353; N. Y. Christ. Int., 2 November, 1865; *ante*, 270, 272. The account of this matter in Smith, i., 49, 50, is very erroneous. Domine Van Rensselaer improved his visit to New York by procuring Andros to appoint him director of Rensselaerwyck in place of his deceased brother, Jeremias: Col. MSS., xxiv., 158; xxv., 145. The domine married Alida, daughter of Philip Pietersen Schuyler, of Albany, and died there in November, 1678: O'Call., i., 212; ii., 552; Holgate, 40, 42, 163; *ante*, i., 533.

CHAP. VI.

1675.

At the first regular session of the Court of Assizes under Andros, the case of Steenwyck and his Dutch associates, who had been bound over for "sedition," was taken up, and De Peyster was acquitted on his taking the oath. The other seven were convicted of "not being obedient to His Majesty's laws," in having traded without taking the oath, in violation of the act of Parliament. Their goods were accordingly forfeited; but eventually all penalties were remitted upon the prisoners taking the required oaths. Thus ended the question; and on the proclamation of the new mayor, William Dervall, the inhabitants of the metropolis who had hitherto refused, came forward and swore allegiance to English authority.*

6 October to 13 Oct. 12 October. Case of Steenwyck and his associates. 3 Novem. 30 October.

Among other things, the Court of Assizes—upon the petition of the coopers of South and East Hampton, on Long Island, that, owing to their "great deceipt," stranger coopers should not come from Boston and work there in the winter—Ordered "that noe cooper shall be admitted to make casks without the consent of the magistrates" of the respective towns. A yearly fair for grain, cattle, or other produce, was established "at Breucklyn, neare the ferry." By reason of its separation by water, it was ordered that "Staten Island shall have a jurisdiction of itself, and to have noe farther dependence on the courts of Long Island;" and John Palmer was appointed its "Ranger." Palmer was an English lawyer, who had recently come to New York from Barbadoes. A double rate was also levied "upon all those townes that have not already a sufficient maintenance for a minister."†

13 October. Massachusetts coopers not liked on Long Island. Fair at Brooklyn. Staten Island. John Palmer ranger. Church rates.

The New York Court ordered all canoes east of Hell Gate to be laid up, because the savages were said to be plotting to attack the English as far west as Greenwich. Brockholls was also sent to Albany with "reiterated orders" for the advantage of Connecticut. The burning of Hadley, Deerfield, Northfield, and Springfield induced An-

6–11 Oct. Canoes on the Sound to be laid up. 10 October. Brockholls sent to Albany. 19 October.

* Col. MSS., xxiv., 172–178, 186, 196; xxv., 1, 2, 5–14; Warr., Ord., Passes, iii., 142, 157; Min. of Common Council, i., 9–11; Col. Doc., iii., 233, 237, 239; *ante*, 277, 278. Dervall now succeeded Nicolls as mayor of New York, and John Sharpe was made sheriff; Samuel Leete was appointed clerk of the city and of the Court of Assizes: Min. of C. C., i., 1, 2, 9; Val. Man., 1845, 309, 331, 332; *ante*, 252, 253.

† Col. MSS., xxiv., 164, 185; xxv., 70; xxvi., 155; xxvii., 35, 36, 57, 59; Warr., Ord., Passes, iii., 196; N. Y. H. S. Coll., i., 425–428; Val. Man., 1844–5, 310, 311; Yonkers Gazette, 25 Nov., 1865; Stiles's Brooklyn, i., 198. Palmer afterward rose to distinction in New York and New England, in both of which he was made a judge.

1675.

dros to think of encouraging the Iroquois to attack the Eastern savages. But, as the Mohawks had renewed their former peace with the Mahicans "without leave," it was

24 October. Orders about powder.

ordered to be kept. It was farther directed "that there be at this juncture a prohibition of selling powder and lead to any Indians whatsoever at Albany, unless it be to the Maquas and Senecas." The commander there might, however, allow a small quantity to be sold to any well known Mahican beaver-hunter. As the magistrates at Esopus had shown great apprehension of the Indians, they were reproved "for their needlesse feares." But they

Esopus affairs.

were required to explain what was meant by the savages offering to deliver up the articles made between Nicolls and them in 1665, and which had "been renewed with those Indians this very spring."*

2 Novem. New York sends supplies to Rhode Island.

The confederated colonies having declared war against the Narragansetts, Andros spontaneously sent six barrels of powder and other ammunition to Rhode Island, "which they thankfully accepted, and afterwards lent part of it to New England forces in want, at their fight in Narragansett

19 Decem. Narragansett fight.

country." In this engagement nearly a thousand savages and two hundred English colonists were killed and wounded. The Rhode Island Quakers still desired the arbitration of the governor of New York; thinking that Puritanic New England ministers had urged on hostilities, "and

1676.

9 Jan'y. Rhode Island rebukes Massachusetts.

that the war had not been, if there had not been a hireling, that, for his money, giving, what he calleth the Gospel, by violence." Governor Coddington, of Rhode Island, accordingly rebuked Massachusetts for having "departed from the Lord."†

1675.

8 Novem. Pierce and Pennyman.

Nehemiah Pierce and James Pennyman, charged with "writing false storeys to Boston," were sent down from Albany to New York, and bound over. Massachusetts, on

7 Decem.

similar information, published a declaration that Philip had been "supplied with ammunition from Albany, whereby

* Warr., Ord., Passes, iii., 139, 141, 142, 143, 145, 146, 147, 148, 151, 155, 156; Council Min., iii. (ii.), 65, 66; Col. MSS., xxiv., 157, 172; N. Y. H. S. Coll., i., 425-428; Col. Rec. Conn., ii., 372-378; Col. Doc., iii., 254, 264; Wood's L. I., 80; Hough's Philip, 83-119; Hutch. Mass., i., 294, 295; Trumbull, i., 333-335; Holland's Western Mass., i., 95, 105; *ante*, 89, 181, 192.

† Col. Doc., iii., 254, 265; Col. Rec. Conn., ii., 383-391; Council Min., iii. (ii.), 74; Warr., Ord., Passes, iii., 169; Hough's Philip's War, 26-31, 125, 129-135; Hutch. Mass., i., 297-301; Trumbull, i., 337-342; Arnold, i., 401-406; Col. MSS., xxv., 67.

he was enabled to prosecute his bloody design against the CHAP. VI.
English." This was such an "aspersion" that Andros sent 1676.
an express to Boston to vindicate the duke's government. 17 Jan'y.
The Puritan Bostonians cleared the magistrates of New 24 Jan'y. Massachu-
York, yet continued to asperse her people "without any setts continues to
known cause, complaint, or notice." The metropolitan "asperse" New York.
council thereupon resolved "That for the present no further 24 Febr'y.
application be made to the Government of Boston." Andros's action was "very well looked on" in London.*

Philip being now reported within forty or fifty miles of
Albany, Andros sent fresh orders to Brockholls, and again 6 Jan'y.
notified the Hartford authorities. They prudently suggested that the Mohawks should be employed to "utterly 13 Jan'y. Connecti-
extirpate" the natives in New England, and hinted that cut and
Albany had supplied the "common enemy" with arms or
ammunition. Andros satirically repelled this "great re- 20 Jan'y.
flection on the Dutch," and demanded explanations. The
Connecticut Council could only give rumors. The governor then demanded whether Connecticut would allow 4 Febr'y. New York
the New York Iroquois to pursue their enemies in her ter- about Philip.
ritory? This she declined, but suggested that the Mo- 10 Feb'y.
hawks had better attack Philip "near Albany."†

Good correspondence, however, was maintained between New York and Rhode Island, the people of which were informed "that any in their parts driven by the Indians from 17 Jan'y. Friendship
their habitations or plantations shall be welcome here, and between New York
have land assigned them upon this, Long Island, or Staten and Rhode Island.
Island." But Massachusetts, Connecticut, and Plymouth,
having shown no desire for the friendship of New York,
the council resolved "to continue our endeavors as Chris- 26 Feb'y. New York
tians and the King's subjects, for the good of this Govern- "Christians" re-
ment, without further application to the said Coloneys." prove New England
The governor was also advised to "go forthwith to Al- Puritans.
bany, to settle matters there, it being of very great import;" as news had just come of the Mohawks "being moved in a warlike manner against the North Indians."‡

The Hudson having opened unexpectedly soon, Andros

* Council Min., iii. (ii.), 68, 69, 70, 81, 85; Col. Doc., iii., 238, 242, 254, 258, 266, 267; Hough's Philip's War, 120–142; Hutch. Coll., 476–490; Mather's War, 117, 129, 254.

† Col. Doc., iii., 255, 265; Col. Rec. Conn., ii., 397, 398, 404, 406, 407; Hutch. Mass., i., 305; Palfrey, iii., 229.

‡ Council Min., iii. (ii.), 81, 85, 86, 97; Col. MSS., xxv., 81; Hough's Philip's War, 136, 137, 143–147, 160, 164.

CHAP. VI. went up to Albany with six sloops and additional men.
He found that some three hundred Mohawks had just re-
1676. Andros again at Albany. turned from the pursuit of Philip, and had brought back
several scalps. They had been supplied with arms and
ammunition by Brockholls, who had also received their old
sachems, squaws, and children within Albany. Lieutenant
4 March. Teunise was at once dispatched "to the farthest part of
the Government, or as far as Connecticut River," to demand from Philip any Christian prisoners. The governor
11 March. also directed William Loveridge to be arrested for having
Loveridge arrested for slander. slanderously affirmed that the Dutch inhabitants of Albany had supplied the North Indians with arms and am-
27 March. munition. Sergeant Sharpe was left in command of the
3 April. garrison, as Brockholls was needed at New York.*

7 March. Connecticut had meanwhile asked to be allowed to talk
19 March. with the Iroquois at Albany, and threatened that, if her
Connecticut agents at New York. "historians" should report to England, the conduct of Andros "would look dark, and be displeasing both to His
Majesty and all true Englishmen; yea, His Highness would
take no pleasure in the consequences of such services by
his ministers." Samuel Willys and William Pitkin came
1 April. on her behalf to ask the desired permission. After full
explanations before the council, the Connecticut agents
10 April. were told that New York had already "taken fitting or-
Answer of New York. ders" with regard to its own Indians, and that it was
"strange" that their colony, which had been so jealous
about all their own concerns, should "ask to treat with any
branch of this Government apart." Andros also wrote
10 April. that he was ready to do all he could to procure a peace between the Connecticut authorities and their savage enemies, "and wholly to remove all manner of jealousys, shall
suspend all further demands of that part of your colony
claimed by His Royal Highness, (to remain as it is,) 'till a
determination from England."†

5 May. To carry out his humane intentions toward Rhode Isl-
and, the governor sent his sloop there to bring back as

* Col. Doc., iii., 255, 265, 708; Council Min., iii. (ii.), 87, 101; Warr., Ord., Passes, iii., 146, 223; Col. MSS., xxv., 88, 90, 184; Hough's Philip's War, 103, 148–153, 167.

† Council Min., iii. (ii.), 90–93; Col. Rec. Conn., ii., 414, 419, 420, 426, 435, 436, 437; Col. Doc., iii., 255, 265; Hough's Philip's War, 155–159. The Connecticut correspondence was now conducted by her new governor, William Leete, who succeeded the deceased Winthrop: Col. Rec. Conn., ii., 273; Trumbull, i., 345, 346; Palfrey, iii., 233–238; Arnold, i., 411, 412; N. Y. H. S. Coll. (1869), 374–376; *ante*, 286, *note*.

many of her people as wished to come to New York. At the same time, it was "Ordered that upon this extraordinary occasion of the warre, and other late intelligences, the severall townes upon Long Island be sent to, to represent the same unto the inhabitants, in order to a levy, and to know what they will give towards a supply." Collector Dyer was accordingly dispatched to urge each town to grant "such a suitable supply as may be proper." But this appeal was poorly answered. The contribution, like that proposed by Lovelace in 1672, was viewed as "a kind of benevolence—the badge of bad times."*

CHAP. VI. 1676. Friendly action of New York toward Rhode Island. 8 May. 13 May.

On Salisbury's return, Andros received fresh instructions from the Duke of York. Referring to his former directions of the 6th of April, 1675, concerning Assemblies, James added, "I have since observed what several of your latest letters hint about that matter. But unless you had offered what qualifications are usual and proper to such Assemblyes, I cannot but suspect they would be of dangerous consequence; nothing being more knowne than the aptness of such bodyes to assume to themselves many priviledges which prove destructive to, or very oft disturbe the peace of the government wherein they are allowed. Neither do I see any use of them, which is not as well provided for, whilst you and your council govern according to the laws established (thereby preserving every man's property inviolate), and whilst all things that need redresse may be sure of finding it, either at the Quarter Sessions or by other legall and ordinary wayes; or lastly by appeal to myselfe. But, howsoever, if you continue of the same opinion, I shall be ready to consider of any proposalls you shall send to that purpose."

28 Jan'y. The Duke of York again disapproves of Assemblies.

At the same time the duke approved of Andros's demand "of all the land on the west side of Connecticut River." "But," he added, "at the present, for other reasons, I am not willing you should proceed further, in regard I hope for hereafter more convenient means of adjusting the boundaries in those parts; and in the interim, though the agreement by the Commissioners in 1664 were never confirmed by me, I soe far approve of the prudence of Colonel

28 Jan'y. The duke sustains Andros's action about Connecticut.

* Council Min., iii. (ii.), 94, 95; Warr., Ord., Passes, iii., 193; Hough's Philip, 137, 160–163; Smith, i., 51; *ante*, 171, 188.

CHAP. VI. 1676. Nicolls, at that time, as to admitt by no means of any nearer access of those of Connecticut than to the mouth of Marinac (or Mamaronocke) River, and along the edge of it; provided they come to noe place within twenty miles distance of Hudsons' River. But this I hint to you only for the present, not intending thereby to conclude myself as to the right of the case." Secretary Werden wrote more fully that the duke was "willing things should rest as they are at present; but he is not sorry you have revived this claim, because possibly some good use may be hereafter made of it." Werden also called Andros to account for permitting "the Bostoners and other strangers to go up in their small vessells to Esopus and Albany and elsewhere, as freely as the very natural subjects of his Royal Highness's Colony," which was "a new thing," forbidden by Lovelace, and to the disadvantage of the metropolis.*

Secretary Werden's directions.

31 Jan'y. "Bostoners" on the North River.

News having come that Massachusetts was making a separate peace with the North Indians, the Council resolved that the Mohawks should be restrained from farther prosecuting them, and that arms be restored to the Long Island savages. As Connecticut was advising with Uncas about sending a present to the Mohawks, they were summoned to meet the governor at Albany. The Mahican and other eastward Indians were also invited to come in, and "live under the protection of the Government," as both Canada and Connecticut had solicited them.†

28 May.

30 May. The Iroquois summoned to meet Andros at Albany.

At Albany the governor built a new stockaded fort, with four bastions, and mounted twelve guns, so as to defend and command the whole town. Salisbury, who was a favorite of the duke, was now reinstated in his old place of commander, Sergeant Sharpe remaining under his orders. The local militia was put under Captain Goosen Gerritsen van Schaick, and Lieutenants Martin Gerritsen and Jan Jansen Bleecker.

June. Fort and officers at Albany.

On this occasion Andros went up to Schaghticook, a pleasant place, in the present county of Rensselaer, near the confluence of the Hoosic with the Hudson River, where

Andros at Schaghticook, or Scatacook.

* Col. Doc., iii., 230, 235–238, 241; Council Min., iii. (ii.), 99; Chalmers, i., 581, 600; Bancroft, ii., 406; *ante*, 55, 56, 168, 182, 188, 260, 279.

† Council Min., iii. (ii.), 99, 100, 101; Col. Rec. Conn., ii., 443; Col. MSS., xxv., 116, 121, 124; Hough's Philip's War, 164–168; Nantucket Papers, 89–103.

he "planted a tree of welfare," and invited all the Northern and River Indians to come and live.*

5 July. Connecticut and New York.

Having informed the Hartford authorities of the "very great execution" done by the Mohawks on their savage enemies, Andros desired to know whether the New York Indians would be admitted into their towns. This, however, was declined; while Connecticut sent word that some of Philip's warriors were about to cross the Hudson River near Esopus, "to seek for 'complices of their straine," and, if they should escape southward, "it may be a great occasion to animate the Virginia Indians." Convinced of "the improbability" of this suggestion, Andros replied that as Connecticut declined the assistance of the Mohawks, he dared not "presume further, than as formerly, by encouragements and gifts, to assure their constant fidelity."†

8 July. 20 July. 26 July.

Indians killed at Stockbridge.

Not long afterward a large party of savages were surprised at Stockbridge, on the Housatonic, and the survivors were reported to be attempting their escape "over Hudson's River to a place called Paquiage." The Connecticut Council asked Andros either to grant "liberty to pass up your river, with some vessels from hence and the Bay, with men and provision, to pursue and destroy those of the enemies that are in those parts, or doe something effectual yourself for the utter suppression of the enemy in those parts." The governor replied that he would dispatch proper orders to Albany, but he would not allow Connecticut to send forces up the Hudson, or her agents to treat with the Mohawks, "as it would breed distraction."‡

19 August. 25 August. 11 October. Connecticut not to talk with the Iroquois.

12 August. Philip slain near Mount Hope.

In the mean time, Philip was slain in a swamp near Mount Hope, whither he retreated after having defended "what he imagined to be his own, and the just rights of his countrymen, to the last extremity." War was now ended. "A handsome penny" was turned by exhibiting the man-

* Council Min., iii. (ii.), 140; Warr., Ord., Passes, iii, 175, 223; Col. Doc., iii., 235, 255, 260, 565, 713; iv., 248, 576, 744, 902, 991; v., 388; Hutch. Mass., i., 348; Colden, i., 101; Hist. Mag., iv., 50. Plans of Albany at this time, and of its fort, which stood near the present St. Peter's Church in State Street, are given in Miller's N. Y., and in Munsell's Ann. Alb., iii., 39; iv., 200.

† Col. Rec. Conn., ii., 461, 462, 466, 467; Council Min., iii. (ii.), 104, 105; Hough's Philip's War, 171.

‡ Trumbull, i., 348, 349, 350; Col. Rec. Conn., ii., 469, 471, 472, 477, 478, 480; Council Min., iii. (ii.), 128, 129. About two hundred of the fugitives from Stockbridge fled to the Mahicans on the Hudson River, and became incorporated with them: Col. Doc., iv., 744, 902, 991; Trumbull, i., 350. Hutch. Mass., i., 348, calls them "Scatacook Indians."

CHAP. VI. 1676. Fate of the captured Americans.

gled right hand of the son of Massasoit to New English "curiosity;" and the able-bodied native American captives who escaped the tender mercies of "the women at Marblehead," or the gibbets of Plymouth and Massachusetts, were exported to the West Indies and sold into slavery. Even the heir of the King of Pokanoket, and the grandson of the early friend of the shivering "Pilgrims" from Holland, was made a victim of Puritan avarice; and the latest historian of New England pronounces that there was no "peculiar aggravation in the circumstance that one of the sufferers was Philip's son."*

August. Pemaquid burned.

The Duke of York's eastern territory did not escape the consequences of Philip's war. Pemaquid was burned by the savages, who drove many of its colonists westward to Massachusetts. Hearing of this, the New York government voted land to the sufferers, and Andros dispatched

8 Septem. Andros's humanity.

his sloop to Boston, "offering free passage and relief to any driven from His Royal Highness's territories about

12 October. Opposed by Massachusetts.

Pemaquid." But Massachusetts, not relishing the humanity of New York, thought it better that all his Majesty's subjects should join in hunting the aborigines out of Maine, and that every effort should be made "to engage the Mohawks or other Indians, friends of the English, for their help and assistance therein."†

Massachusetts, indeed, always coveted Maine. After the Dutch had conquered from the French the region east of the Penobscot, they were driven off by Boston vessels, the crews of which, nevertheless, "kept no possession." The States' ambassador at London, however, complained of this aggression, and charged that the Bostoners "would not suffer any Hollanders there." Charles accordingly or-

11 Feb'y.

dered the Massachusetts magistrates "to return their answer to the said complaint, that so his Majesty, understanding the nature of the fact, may give such order as is agreeable to justice therein."‡

* Hutch. Mass., i., 306, 307; Trumbull's Conn., i., 348, 349; Mather, 188, 194, 195; Davis's Morton, 453–455; Everett's Bloody Brook Address, 1835; Arnold's R. I., i., 416, 417, 418; Plymouth Col. Rec., v., 174, 210; Hough's Philip's War, 21, 25, 188; Col. Rec. Conn., ii., 471; Palfrey, iii, 205, 206, 216–221; Moore's Notes on Slavery in Massachusetts, 35–48.

† Council Min., iii. (ii.), 117; Col. Doc., iii., 241, 255, 265; Mass. Rec., v., 123; Williamson's Maine, i., 515–537; Maine H. S. Coll., v., 8, 9, 255, 256; Palfrey, iii., 208–211.

‡ Williamson's Maine, i., 580; Hutch. Mass., i., 311; Coll., 464, 489; Mass. H. S. Coll., xxxii., 286, 287; Mass. Rec., v., 114, 116, 118; Palfrey, iii., 295; *ante*, 254. On the 27th of October, 1676, the Dutch West India Company commissioned CORNELIS STEENWYCK, of New

CHAP. VI.

1674. 21 Decem. 1675. 12 March. New committee for trade and plantations. 11 August.

After the Peace of Westminster, the British king gave more thought to his American colonies. His former Council of Trade and Plantations was dissolved, and its records were transferred to the Privy Council, a committee of which Charles directed to oversee "matters relating to trade and his foreign plantations." Thus American affairs were restored to the immediate control of the crown. The strict enforcement in her colonies of the Navigation and the Customs' laws of England was the motive. So the Plantation Committee addressed a circular letter to the several North American colonies requiring answers to various questions. A royal proclamation followed, which prohibited the importation into the plantations "of any merchandize but what should be laden in England, and for putting other branches of those acts into strict execution relating to America." This appears to have been drawn by Attorney General Sir William Jones, and was communicated to the colonial governors. At the same time it was determined "that no Mediterranean passes should be granted to New England, to protect its vessels against the Turks, until it is seen what dependence it will acknowledge on his Majesty, or whether his custom-house officers are received as in other colonies."*

24 Novem. Proclamation to enforce the Navigation Laws.

1676. 20 March. No Mediterranean passes for New England.

30 March. Edward Randolph sent to Massachusetts.

10 June. Randolph insulted at Boston.

Edward Randolph—a kinsman of Robert Mason, one of the claimants of Maine, a servant of the Duke of York, shrewd, active, and intensely devoted to his king—was sent with these dispatches to Massachusetts, which was thought to be the most "prejudicial plantation." On reaching Boston, Randolph was treated with coarse incivility by Leverett, its governor, who seems to have supposed that good breeding was inconsistent with Puritanism. Relying on its royal charter, the Corporation of Massachusetts — a creature of Charles the First—assumed that it could settle "all matters in difference" with Charles the Second by its

York, to take possession, in its behalf, of the conquered territory east of the Penobscot, and govern it as captain. This project, however, was never executed: see J. W. de Peyster's pamphlet, "The Dutch in Maine," 45, 73–77; Append., 7, 8, 9, 10, 11; Valentine's Manual, 1853, 352; 1864, 661; Col. MSS., xxvii., 125; Pemaquid Papers, 29, 30.

* Col. Doc., iii., 228, 229, 230, 231, 232; Evelyn, ii., 86, 95; Anderson on Commerce, ii., 531; Mass. H. S. Coll., xxvii., 136, 137; Chalmers's Ann., i., 319, 323, 324, 400, 402; Rev. Col., i., 128, 129; Hutchinson's Coll., 444, 463, 503; Barry, i., 453; Palfrey, iii., 33, 275, 279–283. Chalmers, in the Preface to his Annals, erroneously states that Locke was Secretary of the Committee for Trade of March, 1675. Sir Robert Southwell, the Clerk of the Privy Council, was secretary of that committee. and afterward William Blathwayt: Col. Doc., iii., 228, 230, 271; Evelyn, ii., 104, 279; King's Locke, 34; *ante*, 187, 249.

1676. July. Opinion of Winslow, of Plymouth. 30 July. Randolph's report on his return to England.

own "final determination." Governor Winslow, of Plymouth, reproved the absurdity of his neighboring fellow-subjects, and told Randolph that New England would never flourish until its several colonies were reduced under his majesty's "immediate government." Randolph returned to London, satisfied that most of the inhabitants of Massachusetts abhorred the "arbitrary government and oppression of their magistrates," and hoped that the king would free them "from this bondage" by establishing his direct authority among them. The Navigation Laws, however, were so faithfully executed by Andros and Dyer as to cause a stoppage of trade between New York and Massachusetts. No European goods were allowed to be imported from Boston into New York unless they had paid customs in England, and this caused a "misunderstanding" between those colonies. Plymouth and Connecticut "duly observed" the laws.*

12 Oct. Randolph sustains Andros.

Concerning the Indian war, Randolph testified that the Massachusetts complaints that Philip and his countrymen had been encouraged and supplied by the people of Albany were "without any just cause or ground, but rather a report raised out of malice and envy." Governor Andros had proved himself "very friendly and serviceable" to Massachusetts. Had his advice been taken, the war would have been less destructive, for he would have overpowered Philip by the New York Indians; "but his friendship, advice, and offers were slighted."†

9 August. Massachusetts sends Stoughton and Bulkley to England. 16 Septem.

Having consulted her "reverend elders," Massachusetts sent William Stoughton and Peter Bulkley after Randolph to England. They were instructed to evade all "clamors and accusations," and to promise "a full answer" to the complaint of the Dutch government that the Hollanders had been driven out of Maine. This "answer," however, does not appear to have been given.‡

1675. 13 May.

Meanwhile La Salle had obtained from Louis a grant of Fort Frontenac and its neighborhood, with the monopoly of hunting and fishing on Lake Ontario, on condition that

* Chalmers, i., 403; Hutch. Mass., i., 311, 319; Coll., 477–513, 534, 564; Col. Doc., iii., 239–244; Bancroft, ii., 111; Barry, i., 454–458; Palfrey, iii., 284–289; Col. Rec. Conn., ii., 484; Hist. Mag., ii. (iii.), 70, 71; *ante*, 294.

† Randolph's "Narrative" of 12 October, 1676, in Hutch. Coll., 490; Col. Doc., iii., 242.

‡ Mass. Rec., v., 99–116; Hutchinson, i., 311, 312; Palfrey, iii., 291–295.

CHAP. VI.

1675.

La Salle ennobled by Louis. 13 May. 30 May. Franciscan missionaries.

1676. New fort at Cataracouy.

he should pay its cost, maintain a garrison, build a church, and support Franciscan missionaries. The king also made him a French nobleman. La Salle hastened back to Canada in company with Laval de Montmorency, who had been created Bishop of Quebec, and Jacques Duchesnau, who succeeded Talon as intendant, as well as with the Franciscan fathers Louis Hennepin, Christian Le Clercq, and Zenobius Membré. A new stone fort, with four bastions, was quickly built by La Salle around the old palisades at Cataracouy; a chapel was prepared; and the fathers Hennepin and Luke Buisset were installed as assistants of Ribourde in the mission.*

Jesuit missionaries among the Iroquois.

After establishing the Franciscans at Cataracouy, Frontenac took little interest in the French missions south of Lake Ontario. Bruyas remained at Tionnontoguen, and James de Lamberville, who had just come over from Paris, replaced Boniface at Caghnawaga. The large secession to the Prairie de la Madeleine nevertheless troubled the Mohawk missionaries. Millet labored among the Oneidas with tolerable success. At Onondaga, John de Lamberville was comforted by the steadfast faith of Garakontié until the death of that eminent proselyte early in 1676. Carheil's chapel at Cayuga was burned by drunken savages. Among the Senecas, Pierron, Raffeix, and Garnier labored diligently. But that distant tribe, having subdued the Andastes, now talked only of war, "even against the French, and to begin by the destruction of the fort of Cataracouy."†

The Andastes conquered.

Prairie de la Madeleine.

The "Residence" of the Prairie de la Madeleine had prospered, and Bishop Laval visited it in great state. But, as the land was not fertile, the mission was, in 1676, removed farther up the St. Lawrence, near to the rapids of St. Louis. There a new village was founded, which the French named "St. Francis Xavier du Sault;" while the Iroquois proselytes, remembering their old home on the Mohawk, called it "Caghnawaga," which in their language means "the rapids," or "a carrying-place." A stone church

Caghnawaga, on the St. Lawrence.

* Col. Doc., ix., 118, 119, 120, 122–125, 126, 213, 216, 794; Charlevoix, ii., 256, 265; Faillon, iii., 472, 473, 474, 537; Hennepin's Louisiana, 2, 3, 7–14; New Discovery, 7–16; Hist. Coll. Louisiana, i., 195, 196; Sparks's La Salle, 8–17, 181; Shea's Disc. Miss., 78, 84, 85, 89, 103, 147, 159, 265, 266; Missions, 309, 412; Bancroft, iii., 162; Garneau, i., 237; *ante*, 99, 241.

† Relation, 1673–9, 140, 194, 195, 204; Douniol, ii., 10, 35–45, 99, 106–114, 197; Shea, 272, 274, 277, 285, 289, 292, 293; Hist. Mag., ii., 297; Col. Doc., ix., 227, *note; ante*, 100, 193, 238–240.

CHAP. VI.

was soon built at this Residence, which was put in charge of the fathers Frémin and Cholenec.*

1676.

13 August. Domine Nicolaus van Rensselaer's case.

This year marked the domestic annals of New York. Domine Nicolaus van Rensselaer, whom Andros had installed as colleague of Schaats in the Reformed Dutch Church at Albany, was accused of "false preaching" by Jacob Leisler, one of the deacons in the Dutch Church in New York, and Jacob Milborne, a young Englishman, who had formerly been the book-keeper of Thomas Delavall. On their complaint the Albany magistrates imprisoned Van Rensselaer for having uttered "some dubious words." An appeal was taken to New York, where the case was heard

23 Septem.

before the governor and council, the mayor and aldermen, and the "ministers of the city," and sent back for the authorities at Albany to determine. Domine Schaats accordingly proved his colleague's heterodoxy. Yet the Al-

28 Septem.

bany court thought it best that all differences "should be consumed in the fire of love," and enjoined perpetual forbearance on both sides, "for edification to the Reformed

23 October. Leisler and Milborne.

Religion." Their action was confirmed by the governor, council, aldermen, and "ministers of New York," who ordered Leisler and Milborne to pay all costs, "as giving the first occasion of the difference."†

10 Novem. New dock in New York.

The increasing commerce of the metropolis requiring larger accommodation, a mole or dock was built under the encouragement of Andros. Its expense was paid by a city tax levied on the residents, and timber was furnished by the North and West Ridings of Long Island. The "Heere Gracht," or canal in Broad Street, was also filled up and leveled, and a market-house was established at the "plaine afore the fort."‡

* Relation, 1673-9, 231-240; 1676-7, 122-145; Douniol, ii., 49-70, 167-179, 217-227; Shea, 298-304, 307, 308; Col. Doc., iii., 251; ix., 95, 116, 130; Index, 282; Colden, i., 54; Smith, i., 69; Charlevoix, i., 352; ii., 258; v., 261; Hist. Mag., x., 322, 323; *ante*, vol. i., 423, 659; ii., 129, 178.

† Council Min., iii. (ii.), 118-125, 131, 132; Doc. Hist., ii., 42; iii., 527-530; Smith, i., 50; Col. MSS., xxv., 166; xxvi., 139; Col. Doc., iii., 301, 680, 727, 755; N. Y. Christ. Int., 2 Nov., 1865; *ante*, 196, *note*, 272. Domine Van Rensselaer acted as one of the managers of Rensselaerwyck after the death of his brother Jeremias in 1674. In 1677 Andros deposed him from his ministry "on account of his bad and scandalous life." The domine died the next year; and his widow, Alida Schuyler, married, in 1683, Robert Livingston, the astute young Scotch town clerk of Albany: Cor. Cl. Amst., Letter of Domine Van Zuuren, 30 Sept., 1677; Holgate, 42, 163; O'Call., i., 122, 212; ii., 177, 552; Col. MSS., xxiv., 158; xxv., 145; xxxi., 90; xxxii., 175; *ante*, 287, 288.

‡ Col. MSS., xxv., 98, 155; Col. Doc., iii., 303, 309, 313, 314, 412; Min. of N. Y. C. C., i., 61; Val. N. Y., 181; Dunlap, ii., App. cxxv.-cxxvii.; Hoffman's Treatise, ii., 5.

CHAP. VI.

1676.

At the Court of Assizes, William Loveridge, who had been arrested for slandering the Dutch at Albany, was fined twenty beavers, and allowed six months to make good his charge against Arnout Cornelissen Viele, the interpreter. Several of the inhabitants of Hempstead, having entered into an unlawful combination, were tried, convicted of riot, and variously sentenced. George Heathcote, the Quaker ship-captain, being charged with talking seditiously, was also heavily fined.*

7 October. Loveridge. 25 October. Hempstead. Heathcote.

Southampton and Southold, which for ten years had refused to take out new patents according to the Duke's Laws, were now obliged to submit. They sent up various reasons for their contumacy, which Andros treated more cavalierly than Lovelace. The Court of Assizes gave judgment that Southampton and Southold "for their disobedience have forfeited all their titles, rights and privileges to the lands in said township;" but a fortnight was allowed them to acknowledge their faults and obey. This was decisive, and the towns prudently obtained new patents.†

28 Septem. 7 October. Southampton and Southold. 31 October. 1 Novem.

The Delaware territory, after the governor's visit in the spring of 1675, had been disturbed by Ogle and the Lutheran minister Fabricius. They were cited to appear before Andros at New York, and it was ordered that Fabricius, "in respect of his being guilty, and his former irregular life, be suspended from exercising his functions as a minister, or preaching any more within this government, either in public or private." This sentence appears to have been modified, and the Lutheran clergyman preached for several years in the church which Andros directed to be built at "Wickegkoo."‡

Delaware affairs. 15 Septem. Fabricius.

1675.

In the mean time, Fenwick, to whom Lord Berkeley conveyed his undivided interest in New Jersey, had quarreled with Byllinge, for whom he was trustee, and this Quaker dispute had been arranged by William Penn. Berkeley's grantees assigned their estate in North America

New Jersey. 10 Feb'y William Penn.

* Col. MSS., xxv., 90, 184, 185, 211, 220, 226–241; *ante*, 287, 292. On the 25th of Sept., 1676, Andros wrote (in French) to Commander Binckes that he had supplied one of his ships with provisions, and thanked him for having reported favorably of him to the Prince of Orange: Col. MSS., xxv., 171; *ante*, 223, *note*.

† Col. MSS., xxv., 173–176, 222; Patents, iv., 103, 105; Thompson, i., 146, 334, 335, 384, 385; Dunlap, ii., App. xxxviii.; *ante*, 110, 173, 275.

‡ Council Min. (iii.), ii., 53; S. Hazard, 417, 419, 420, 438; G. Smith's Delaware County, 102, 115, 124; *ante*, 255, 279.

1675. 25 June. Fenwick sails to the Delaware. 5 Decem. 10 Decem.

to William Penn, Gawen Laurie, and Nicholas Lucas, all of whom were Quakers. Under their auspices Fenwick sailed for the Delaware with his family and some colonists, and landed at the old "Varcken's Kill" of the Dutch and "Elsingburg" of the Swedes, which he named "Salem." Cantwell, the New York sheriff at Newcastle, reported this intrusion to Andros, who directed that as Fenwick had not produced any authority, he "was not to be received as owner or proprietor of any land whatever in Delaware, but to be used civilly, paying all duties as others His Majesty's subjects;" and that, "as to any privilege or freedom of Customs, or trading on the Eastern Shore, none to be allowed in any case to the smallest vessel, boat, or person." The same duties levied at New York were to be exacted on the Delaware.*

1676. 23 Septem. Collier commander in Delaware. 25 Sept.

Captain John Collier was not long afterward commissioned as the New York commander and sub-collector on Delaware Bay, and carefully instructed as to his duties. Three subordinate local courts were also established at Newcastle, at Upland, and at Hoarkill. The Duke's Laws, with certain exceptions, were directed to be enforced, and Cantwell was made high sheriff.†

25 Sept. Fenwick contumacious. 3 Decem. 7 Decem. 8 Decem. 1677. 12 Jan'y. Fenwick imprisoned in New York.

In spite of Andros's warning, Fenwick, "a litigious and troublesome person," continued to act as proprietor at Salem, and was summoned to answer at New York, but he refused to obey. Collier was then directed to send him to Fort James; and he accordingly visited Fenwick, who denied that the governor of New York had any thing to do with him. The recusant was brought to Newcastle, whence he was conveyed a prisoner to New York. At a special Court of Assizes Fenwick was fined, and ordered to give security for his good behavior. Refusing to do this, he was kept in custody.‡

* Council Min., iii. (ii.), 71, 72; Warr., Ord., Passes, iii., 163; Dankers and Sluyter, 242, 243; Leaming and Spicer, 65; S. Smith, 79, 89; Hazard's Rec. Penn., vi., 182; Proud, i., 136, 137; Dixon, 137; S. Hazard, 410, 419, 421, 422; N. J. H. S. Proc., ii., 8, 9; *ante*, vol. i., 322, 338, 380; ii., 266, 278.

† Warr., Ord., Passes, iii., 115, 116, 211–213; Col. MSS., xx., 84–98; Hazard's Reg. Penn., iv., 57; Ann. Penn., 425–429; G. Smith's Del. Co., 105–107; Upland Records, 35–43. This last book was published by the Pennsylvania Historical Society. Scholars must regret that its editor, Mr. Edward Armstrong, has so carelessly repeated the stale errors that De Vries visited the Delaware in 1630, whereas it was Heyes; and that Lovelace succeeded Nicolls in May, 1667, whereas it was in August, 1668.

‡ Ord., Warr., Passes, iii., 231; Col. MSS., xx., 102, 103; xxv., 242; xxvi., 11, 12, 14; S. Smith, 94; Haz. Ann., 429–434, 453; N. J. Proc., ii., 9–11, 17; Dixon, 136; Eliz. Bill, 8.

CHAP. VI.

1676.

Carteret's government in New Jersey.

Meanwhile Philip Carteret had quietly governed that part of New Jersey north of Barnegat and the Renkokus Creek, which the Duke of York had conveyed, *in severalty*, to Sir George Carteret. James, however, did not suppose that his new deed of lands transferred to his grantee the "full and absolute power and authority" which the king had vested in him personally. The most important sovereign prerogative which Charles had delegated to his brother was that of taxing the inhabitants of a British-American province for the support of its government. To this end the duke's governor had ordered that all vessels trading within his original territory should enter at the New York Custom-house. After Andros reached New York, James's secretary wrote him that nothing had been done in England toward "adjusting Sir George Carteret's pretensions in New Jersey, where, I presume, you will take care to keep all things in the same posture (as to the Duke's prerogatives and profits) as they were in your predecessors' time, until you shall hear of some alterations agreed to here." This led to a "bickering" between Collector Dyer and Governor Carteret, who was made to pay duties to the duke on "a present" sent to New Jersey, and was "obstructed" by Andros from clearing a sloop from Elizabethtown to Carolina.*

1675.

13 Feb'y.

Customs' duties levied by New York on New Jersey importations.

The subordinate title to New Jersey, however, had now become so doubtful that its various claimants found it necessary to make a compromise. This was accomplished "after no little labour, trouble, and cost;" and, as is said, through the interposition of the Duke of York, who induced Sir George Carteret to relinquish his separate ownership. A "Quintipartite" deed, in partition, was accordingly made between Carteret, and Penn, Laurie, Lucas, and Byllinge, by which it was agreed that their division line should run from Little Egg Harbor to the northernmost branch of the Delaware River, in forty-one degrees and forty minutes of latitude. All the territory north and east of this line, called "East New Jersey," was vested in Carteret. All the remainder, to the south and west of it, named "West New Jersey," was conveyed to Penn and his associ-

1676.

1 July.

Quintipartite deed for East and West New Jersey.

* Leaming and Spicer, 91–111; Eliz. Bill, 8; Col. Doc., iii., 229, 240, 316; iv., 382; Chalmers's Annals, i., 617, 618; Grahame, i., 468; S. Smith, 68; Whitehead's East Jersey, 66, 69, 70, 190, 191; *ante*, 267, 268, 277.

CHAP. VI. 1676. ates. Yet this famous instrument was based wholly on the king's effete patent to the Duke of York in March, 1664. It did not allude to the Dutch reconquest in 1673; nor to the Dutch reconveyance of New Netherland to Charles the Second, by the Treaty of Westminster, in February, 1674; nor to Charles's second patent to his brother in the next June; nor to the Duke of York's release of a part of New Jersey to Sir George Carteret, individually, in the following July. In these respects the "Quintipartite" New Jersey deed of 1676 is perhaps the most faulty English secondary parchment in American annals.*

31 August. The Duke of York maintains his prerogative.

Two months afterward Secretary Werden wrote to Andros that the duke was not "at all inclined to let go any part of his prerogative, which you and your predecessors have all along constantly asserted in his behalf; and so, though at present, in respect to Sir George, we soften things all we may, not to disturb his choler (for in truth the passion of his inferior officers so far infects him as puts him on demands which he hath no colour of right to), I verily believe, should his foot chance to slip, those who succeed him must be content with less civility than we show him in this point; since then we should exercise that just authority His Royal Highness hath without such reserves as, though intended but as favours now, may, if confirmed, redound too much to the prejudice of your Colony."

Indeed, James now contemplated obtaining a new patent, "either for the better ascertaining the boundaries, or for any other cause," which should confirm to him Delaware, as well as the region eastward as far as the Connecticut. But the duke's political situation in England did not permit him to move in the matter at this time; although

1677. 7 May. James contemplates a new patent.

his secretary informed Andros that "a time may come, either upon a regulation of matters in New England, when His Majesty shall please to take that into his consideration, or some other way, when His Royal Highness may without scruple thinke it convenient to insist on all those rights that were intended him by his Patent from the Crowne."†

The Quintipartite deed, however, induced Governor Carteret to claim a distinct port and custom-house in New

* Leaming and Spicer, 61–72; Eliz. Bill, p. 8; Answer to Bill, p. 18; S. Smith, 80, 89, 546, 548; Gordon, 38; Proud, i., 142; Dixon's Penn., 138; Whitehead, 67, 68; *ante*, 260, 261, 265–268.

† Col. Doc., iii., 237, 239, 240, 247; Chalmers, i., 618.

Jersey. The New York authorities resolved "That they find no port or harbour granted to Sir George Carteret (distinct or independent from this); but all ships or vessels, as hitherto, to enter and clear at the Custom-house here, or subordinate officers thereof, with due regard to Governor Carteret's or others' authority, for the duties on tobacco and other produce of America, according to acts of Parliament and orders thereupon."*

CHAP. VI.
1677.
11 July.
New York refuses New Jersey a separate port.

Penn and his co-proprietors of West Jersey, having prepared some "Concessions and Agreements," dispatched commissioners to organize its government and arrange matters with Fenwick. As the ship Kent, in which they were embarked, was lying in the Thames, King Charles came alongside in his pleasure barge, and seeing a great many passengers, and learning where they were bound, "asked if they were all Quakers, and gave them his blessing." After a tedious voyage the Kent anchored at Sandy Hook, and the commissioners went up to New York to wait on Andros. "He treated them civilly, but asked them if they had any thing from the Duke, his Master? They replied, Nothing particularly; but that he had conveyed that part of his country to Lord Berkeley, and he to Byllinge, etc., in which the Government was as much conveyed as the soil. The Governor replied: *All that will not clear me; if I should surrender without the Duke's order, it is as much as my head is worth; but if you had but a line or two from the Duke, I should be as ready to surrender it to you, as you would be to ask it.* Upon which, the commissioners, instead of excusing their imprudence in not bringing such an order, began to insist upon their right, and strenuously to assert their independency. But Andros, clapping his hand on his sword, told them, that should defend the government from them, till he received orders from the duke, his master, to surrender it. He, however, softened, and told them he would do what was in his power to make them easy till they could send home to get redress; and in order thereto, would commissionate the same persons mentioned in the commission they produced. This they accepted, and undertook to act as magistrates under him, till further orders came from England, and pro-

3 March.
Quaker emigrants to West New Jersey.

August.
Their treatment by Andros.

7 August.

* Warrants, Ord., Passes, iii., 63, 103, 254; *ante*, 276, 277.

CHAP. VI.

1677.

16 August. 14 Novem.

ceed in relation to their land affairs according to the methods prescribed by the proprietors." The Kent then went on to Newcastle. A site for a new town was chosen near "Jegow's Island," or Mattiniconk, which was leased to Robert Stacey, and a village soon arose, at first called

Burlington founded.

"New Beverley," and then "Bridlington," or "Burlington," after the town in Yorkshire from which some of the emigrants came. Fenwick was at the same time released from his imprisonment and allowed to return to Salem upon promising to appear again at New York in the following October. This he honestly did, and Andros then

14 August. Billop commander on the Delaware.

set him free. The governor also appointed one of his lieutenants, Christopher Billop, now of Staten Island, to succeed Collier as commander and sub-collector for New York, on Delaware Bay and River.*

Among other reasons for a new patent, the Duke of York desired more definite limits for his province, which he considered as having always been bounded northward by Canada, "the Dutch having ever claimed and never lost the possession of the same." "As for the northern

7 May. Boundary between New York and Canada.

bounds," wrote Werden to Andros, more explicitly, "there is no question but they have always been esteemed to extend as far as the Lake (or River of Canada), and the French have no colour to pretend right of conquest from any of their invasions there, unless they had such possession before the Dutch were settled in Albany, which I believe is nothing soe."†

Knowing the duke's views as to territory, Andros was sorely annoyed at the presence of the Jesuit missionaries among the Iroquois, of whom John de Lamberville at Onondaga had now become superior, in place of Bruyas at Tionnontoguen. Indeed, the French fathers were all jealously watched as intruders within the province of New

12 March. Andros asserts English sovereignty over the Iroquois.

York. Salisbury, the commander at Albany, was instructed "that the Maquas Indians and associates on this side the Lake (having been always under a part of this government) have nothing to do with the French, only as

* Warrants, Ord., Passes, iii., 259, 263; Council Min., iii. (ii.), 166–168; Col. MSS., xx., 136, 140; xxi., 35, 112; xxvii., 6; Col. Doc., iii., 221, 239, 240, 276; Dankers and Sluyter, 174, 235; Leaming and Spicer, 382–409; S. Smith, 69, 80–94, 99, 521–538; Proud, i., 144; Gordon, 22, 38, 39; Gaz., 112, 113; Hazard's Reg. Penn., iv., 57, 73; Ann. Penn., 373, 374, 396, 443, 444, 453, 466; Thomas's West Jersey, 14, 15; N. J. H. S. Coll., ii., 17; Upland Rec., 140, 141; *ante*, 164, 184, 265, vol. i., 183. † Col. Doc., iii., 233, 237, 247; v., 531; ix., 305.

they are friends, but in no case are to be commanded by them. And that the Commissaries do send for the Maquas Sachems and Father Bruyas, and signify this to the said Sachems before him, and to the said Father that the Governor desires, and does not doubt, his comport accordingly, for the quiet of these parts, pursuant to the friendship of our Kings at home."*

April. Hennepin among the Mohawks.

Andros's messengers found Bruyas entertaining as his guest the Franciscan Father Hennepin, who had walked over the snow from Fort Frontenac, and tarried to copy "a little Iroquois Dictionary" which the Jesuit had compiled. When the Dutch envoys heard Hennepin, who was a native of Hainault, speak Flemish, they showed him much friendship, and invited him to return with them to Albany, where they wished him to settle, "for the spiritual consolation of several Catholics" from the Netherlands who lived there. They even alighted from their horses to induce the father and his companions to mount in their places and go back with them. Hennepin would willingly have yielded to their urgency had he not feared giving umbrage to the Jesuits and injuring the Canadian fur trade. He therefore "thanked these estimable Hollanders," and, bidding farewell to Bruyas, returned to Cataracouy.†

18/28 April. France denies English sovereignty over the Iroquois.

The territorial pretensions of New York were not, however, recognized by Louis, who insisted that the expeditions of Champlain, Courcelles, and Tracy, followed by the submission of the savages and the settlement of Jesuit missionaries among them, had given him the sovereignty over the Iroquois. But it was not the time to bring this question to an issue. Louis, still at war with the Dutch, and anxious for the friendship of Charles, directed Frontenac "to cultivate a good understanding with the English,

* Council Min., iii. (ii.), 135; Col. Doc., ix., 171, 720; Douniol, ii., 195–205; Shea, 274, 286; *ante*, 294. Mr. Shea, in a note to the reprint of the first edition of Colden's Five Nations, 139, erroneously attributes to Dongan the assumption of English sovereignty over the Iroquois which was due to Andros: compare Hist. Mag., x., 268, *note.*

† Hennepin's Nouvelle Découverte, 10, 25–30; New Discovery, 16–20; Col. Doc., iv., 689; ix., 720; Shea's Discovery, 104; Catholic Missions, 274; Sparks's La Salle, 17; *ante*, 299. Bruyas's Dictionary, or "*Racines Agnieres*," was published in the Appendix to the Report of the Regents of the University of New York of 15 April, 1863: Senate Document, 1863, No. 115. The general opinion, derived from the English translation (1698) of the "Nouvelle Découverte," is that Hennepin visited Albany: Sparks's La Salle, 17; Shea's Discovery, 104. A careful examination of the French original, however, convinces me that Hennepin did not go to Albany, but returned from Bruyas's cabin at Tionnontoguen directly to Fort Frontenac: see Hist. Mag., x., 268.

CHAP. VI. 1677. and to be careful not to give them any cause of complaint; without, however, permitting any thing contrary to the treaties I have concluded with the king their master."*

La Salle builds barks on Lake Ontario. La Salle had meanwhile built at Cataracouy three barks with decks, the first ever seen above the rapids of the Saint Lawrence, intending to use them for trading on Lake Ontario. But Jolliet's accounts of the vast buffalo countries in the West convinced him that a more lucrative and direct traffic with France than that through Canada could be opened by way of the Gulf of Mexico, into which it was supposed the Mississippi emptied. La Salle had already attempted to reach that river by way of the Ohio in 1669, and he now burned to demonstrate the truth of De Soto's early discovery, and extend actual French exploration from the mouth of the Arkansas down to the open sea. But
1676. Louis having declared himself against "new discoveries,"
$\frac{5}{15}$ April. and instructed Frontenac not to countenance them "without urgent necessity and very great advantage," La Salle determined to revisit France and impress his own views on
1677. the court. The jealous policy of Andros in prohibiting
16 May. French traffic with the Iroquois south of Lake Ontario was
November. another reason. As soon as his fort at Cataracouy was
La Salle returns to France. walled up, La Salle returned to France, carrying the warmest letters from Frontenac.†

In the mean time, Massachusetts and Connecticut had engaged some Mohawk warriors to help them fight the Eastern Indians, who were ravaging Maine. The Con-
19 March. necticut Council renewed their request for leave to treat directly with the Iroquois at Albany. Andros at once di-
28 March. rected the Mohawks to recall their parties from the East, and notify his officers if any Christians or Indians should
3 April. tamper with them. He also informed Governor Leete that he was going to Albany, where, "if you please to depute and send a fitt person, he may be present and say any thing [that] may be proper from yourselfe or colony to our Indyans, Maquas, etc." Pynchon and Richards were
10 April. accordingly appointed to make a treaty with the Mohawks

* Col. Doc., ix., 126, 267, 304, 305, 380–382, 702, 703, 783–803.

† Hennepin's Louisiana, 2, 3, 8–15; New Discovery, 15–25, 40, 41, 44; Faillon, iii., 473, 474; La Potherie, ii., 135; Col. Doc., ix., 126, 213, 216; Council Min., iii. (ii.), 148; Charlevoix, ii., 264. 265; Sparks's La Salle, 10, 11; Shea's Discovery, 84, 85, 88; Bancroft, iii., 163; *ante*, 163, 241, 299.

on the part of Massachusetts and Connecticut, under the advice of the governor of New York, or, if he should "obstruct," to take "what opportunity" they could to gain their end. Andros received the New England agents kindly at Albany; allowed them all freedom to speak "to what Indians they pleased;" and informed Leete that they had been "denied nothing here to their content." A handsome present was made by Pynchon, on behalf of Massachusetts, to the Mohawks, who covenanted peace with her friendly Indians. For the first time, New York permitted her Iroquois to treat with a New England colony. The League was sealed with the characteristic gift of "a fish painted on paper" to the savages, who, according to their custom, distinguished their new Eastern friends, whom Pynchon represented, by the descriptive name of "Kinshon."*

CHAP. VI. 1677. 25 April. Massachusetts and Connecticut agents at Albany.

Conference with the Iroquois.

The subjugation of the Andastes or Susquehannas by the Senecas led to a correspondence between Andros and Governor Calvert of Maryland, in which the friendship of New York toward her sister English colonies at the South was fully manifested; although Virginian historians have somewhat blamed her for the "rebellion" which broke out in the Old Dominion under the lead of Nathaniel Bacon. In their warfare the Iroquois did not always discriminate between their savage enemies and the English colonists around the Chesapeake, among whom they dwelt; and both Virginia and Maryland felt the necessity of a peace with the Five Nations of New York.†

New York and Maryland.

Charles Calvert, now Lord Baltimore, having returned to England, Notley, his lieutenant governor of Maryland, accordingly commissioned one of her council, Colonel Henry Coursey—who, in 1659, had hospitably treated the envoys of New Netherland—to go to Albany and "make a league

30 April.

* Council Min., iii. (ii.), 140, 141, 144, 145; Col. MSS., xxvi., 46, 52; Col. Doc., iii., 328; Col. Rec. Conn., ii., 483, 488, 489, 491-496, 507; Mass. Rec., v., 165, 167; Hutch. Mass., i., 348; Williamson's Maine, i., 548; Colden, i., 116, 180; *ante*, 296, 298. As the Iroquois had no labials in their language, they were obliged to say "Quider" instead of "Peter:" Hennepin's New Discovery, 24; Colden, i., 16, 116. For this reason, I think it probable that "Kinshon" was the nearest they could come to "Pynchon." Being great generalizers of names, they used that of "Pynchon" to denote New England, just as they substituted "Onnontio" for Canada, and "Corlaer" for New York; *ante*, 102, 287. Father Millet, in his letter of 6 July, 1691, p. 48, wrongly applies the name "*Le Poisson*," or "*Kinshon*," to New York instead of New England.

† Warr., Ord., Passes, iii., 152, 163, 164, 214; Col. MSS., xxv., 124; Col. Doc., iii., 245; Hough's Philip's War, 124, 125; S. Hazard, 421-426; Beverley, 62, 63; Burk, ii., 156, 157; Force's Tracts, i., viii., ix.; Douniol, ii., 44, 45, 99, 197; Hist. Mag., i., 65-73; ii., 297; Campbell's Virginia, 284-323; *ante*, 100, 193, 299.

CHAP. VI. of friendship" with the New York Iroquois. After entertainment at Newcastle, Coursey was cordially received at Fort James. In anticipation of his coming, Andros dispatched "two Christians," one of whom was Wentworth Greenhalgh, to summon the Senecas and their confederates to meet Coursey at Albany, and announce the governor's intention to be there in August. When Coursey reached New York, another message was sent to hasten the interview. This was accordingly held, and the agent of Maryland and Virginia, in several conferences with the Iroquois sachems, "had answers to his satisfaction."*

1677. 23 May. Coursey sent to New York. 16 May. Greenhalgh's tour in Western New York. 6 June. 21 July. Coursey at Albany.

The savages in Maine were meanwhile doing great mischief. Andros therefore resolved "to take possession, and assert the Duke's interest at Pemaquid, and parts adjacent Eastward;" and that if New York should make peace with the Indians there, "the Massachusetts to be comprized, if they please." Brockholls, Knapton, and Secretary Nicolls were accordingly commissioned to go to Pemaquid with four sloops, one hundred men, and a framed redoubt, to be set up in the most convenient place. They were directed to make peace with such Indians as delivered up their prisoners, and to include the New England colonies if they so desired. Any Mohawks who might come to them were to be received and used kindly, "as at Albany." The redoubt, which was named "Fort Charles," was quickly built at Pemaquid, mounted with seven guns, and placed under the command of Knapton, the brother-in-law of Andros, with a garrison of fifty men. Peace was arranged with the Indians, and several Christian captives rescued. Stringent orders were adopted in New York for the government of Pemaquid. None could treat with its aborigines except through the governor at the metropolis. The trading-place was to be at Fort Charles, where alone Christians were allowed to inhabit; and all entries were to be made in the New York Custom-

9 June. 16 June. Andros takes possession of Pemaquid. July. Fort Charles established. 2 August. 22 Septem. Regulations for Pemaquid.

* Council Min., iii. (ii.), 142, 147, 148, 151, 152, 160, 161, 164; Deeds, vi., 28; Col. MSS., xxvi., 66, 69; Col. Doc., ii., 94; iii., 250–252, 256, 321; ix., 227; Colden, i., 38; first ed., p. 31, 46; Chalmers, i., 364, 365, 366, 606–609; S. Hazard, 437, 438; Upland Rec., 49; Clinton, in N. Y. H. S. Coll., ii., 80; Davis's Day Star, 113; *ante*, i., 666. I am indebted to Mr. Brantz Mayer, of Baltimore, for the communication of interesting memoranda from the State Paper Office relating to Coursey's mission. Greenhalgh's Journal of his visit to the Five Nations, from 28 May to 14 July, 1677 (in Col. Doc., iii., 250–252, and Chalmers, i., 606–609), is the earliest English account we have of the strength and condition of the Iroquois.

house. Fish might be cured upon the islands, "but not upon the Maine, except at Pemaquid, near the fort." This regulation mortified Massachusetts, which claimed that its people should be allowed their ancient privilege "to improve themselves and estates in the honest and industrious labour of fishing."*

CHAP. VI. 1677. 17 October. Massachusetts offended.

Andros now went up to Albany and held another conference with the Iroquois. The Oneidas had been "diverted from the southward;" but they and the Mohawks still suspected the Mahicans. On his return to the metropolis Andros indignantly rebuked Connecticut for "falsely and unchristianly" censuring his Indian policy. Not long afterward Massachusetts undertook to reprove the New York savages for breaking the treaty which Pynchon had made with them in April, and suggested that they would do "an acceptable service" if they should destroy "a parsell of Indians who came lately from Canada," and attacked Hatfield on the Connecticut. A similar lecture was addressed to the New York commander at Albany. Andros accordingly instructed Salisbury to send any interfering strangers who might come there, down to New York for examination.†

28 August. Andros at Albany. 24 Septem. 12 October. Precautions against the New Englanders. 30 October.

This year witnessed fresh discoveries in the interior of New York. While Greenhalgh was exploring the West, nearer regions were not neglected. The search led by Louis du Bois after the prisoners captured at Wyldwyck in 1663 had revealed the beauty of the rich valley of the Wallkill, and a second exploration was made through the more rugged neighborhood of the river. A large tract of land was purchased from the Indians by Dubois, Hasbrouck, and other French and German Protestants, to whom the governor gave a patent. The grant extended along the Shawangunk Mountains from "Mohunk" to "Tower-a-tauch," and along the Hudson River from "Rapoos" down to "Jeffrouw's Hook." Several of the grantees settled themselves at once on the tract, which was

29 Septem. Patent for New Paltz.

* Col. Doc., iii., 248, 249, 256, 265; Council Min., iii. (ii.), 153, 163, 169; Warrants, Ord., Passes, iii., 251; Col. MSS., xxvii., 130; Maine H. S. Coll., v., 14–23, 30, 259; Mass. Rec., v., 162, 164, 168, 169; Hutch. Mass., i., 325, 347; Williamson's Maine, i., 552; Belknap, i., 129; Palfrey, iii., 213; *ante*, p. 308.

† Col. Doc., iii., 256; Col. MSS., xxvi., 135, 136, 141; Col. Rec. Conn., ii., 502, 503, 506, 507, 508; Council Min., iii. (ii.), 170; Mass. Rec., v., 165–168; Hutch., i., 348; Trumbull, i., 354.

CHAP. VI.

1677.

named the "New Paltz," in memory of their former home in the Palatinate, which had just been so awfully ravaged by Turenne. The first settlement was made near an ancient Indian mound on the Wallkill, where Dubois and his associates were required to build a redoubt "for a place of retreat and safeguard."*

2 Novem.

The provincial customs' rates, which had been established in November, 1674, were now renewed for three years, by a proclamation from the governor, under the duke's special instructions to "continue the same rates and other duties for three years longer, to commence from the end of these now running."†

November. Customs' rates renewed.

Meanwhile Andros had received permission to spend the winter in England, "to look after his own concerns," provided he took care to settle every thing during his absence "in the best and safest manner." After advising with his council, the governor commissioned Brockholls to be commander-in-chief, and Secretary Nicolls next in authority, with instructions to consult the council and the metropolitan mayor, Stephanus van Cortlandt, on extraordinary occasions. He also gave his wife a power of attorney to manage his private affairs during his absence. Having visited Carteret at Elizabethtown, Andros embarked from Staten Island for England, accompanied by William Nicolls, son of the provincial secretary.‡

7 May. Andros allowed to return to England.

7 Novem. Brockholls commander-in-chief.

16 Novem.

17 Novem. Andros sails for England.

After the governor's departure the affairs of New York were quietly administered by Brockholls, who was chiefly engaged in strengthening Fort James and remounting its guns. Correspondence with Frontenac in Canada, Leverett in Massachusetts, Knapton at Pemaquid, Bruyas in the Mohawk country, and Salisbury at Albany, also taxed the attention of the Duke of York's temporary commander-in-chief during the next winter and spring.§

Brockholls's temporary administration of New York affairs.

* Patents, iv., 234; Warr., Ord., Passes, iii., 286; N. Y. H. S. Proceedings for 1848, 81; Ulster H. S. Coll., i., 34, 35, 41–48, 80, 187–191; Martin's Louis XIV., i., 394; *ante*, vol. i., 712, 713. The New Paltz Academy, in Ulster County, now stands on the site of this old Indian mound.

† Col. Doc., iii., 217, 246, 289, 292; Col. MSS., xxiv., 1; xxvi., 5; Ord., Warr., etc.; xxxii½, 43, 44, 45; Council Journals, i., Introd., viii.; *ante*, 263.

‡ Col. Doc., iii., 246, 256, 257, 709; Council Min., iii. (ii.), 175, 176; Warr., Ord., Passes, iii., 286, 287; Col. MSS., xxvi., 151; Col. Rec. Conn., ii., 508; Hazard's Reg. Penn., iv., 73, 74; Thompson, ii., 391; Whitmore's Memoir of Andros, xix.

§ Col. Doc., iii., 307, 311; Col. MSS., xxvi., 149, 150, 152, 161, 162; xxvii., 1–178; Council Min., iii. (ii.), 176, 177; Maine H. S. Coll., v., 9–18, 23–32; Col. Rec. Conn., iii., 258; Mass. Rec., v., 300.

1678. April. New York as described by Andros.

New York, as described by Andros in London the next April, contained twenty-four towns, villages, or parishes, in six precincts, or Courts of Sessions. Its population had increased of late, consisting of old inhabitants, chiefly Dutch, with colonists from England, and "some few of all nations." Servants were much wanted, there being "but very few slaves," most of whom were brought from Barbadoes, and were worth from thirty to thirty-five pounds each. A merchant having five hundred or a thousand pounds was thought substantial, and a planter worth half that "in moveables" was accounted rich. The value of all the estates in the province was about 150,000 pounds. From ten to fifteen vessels, of one hundred tons each, traded to the province each year from Old and New England. Five small ships and a ketch belonged to New York, of which four were built there. The exports were chiefly provisions, furs, tar, and lumber; and the imports of English manufactures amounted to 50,000 pounds yearly. The customs, excises, and quit-rents were all applied to the public charges; but they did not suffice "by a greate deale." The chief trading-places were New York and Southampton for foreign commerce, and Albany for the Indian traffic. There were about two thousand males able to bear arms, of whom one hundred and forty were horsemen, in three troops. Fort James was a square of stone, with four bastions, and mounting forty-six guns. Fort Albany was a small stockade, with four bastions and twelve guns, "sufficient against Indians." Fort Charles, at Pemaquid, was a "wooden redoubt," with seven guns. These forts were garrisoned by regular English soldiers. Ministers "were scarce, and religions many," so that there were no records of marriages or births in New York. The duke maintained an Episcopalian chaplain, which was "all the certain allowance or Church of England." There were about twenty churches in the province, most of which were Presbyterians and Independents, with Quakers, Anabaptists, and Jews; and all were supported by "free gifts to the ministry." In New York there were "noe beggars, but all poore cared for."*

Value of estates.

Ships and commerce.

Militia.

Forts James, Albany, and Charles.

Religions various, and "noe beggars."

* Col. Doc., iii., 245, 246, 260–262; Doc. Hist., i., 60–62; Chalmers's Pol. Ann., i., 600–604.

CHAPTER VII.

1678–1683.

CHAP. VII.

1678.

England gains by the Treaty of Westminster.

DURING the four years which followed the Treaty of Westminster, England reaped the fruits of her peace with the Dutch Republic in the growth of her own trade, and in a higher consideration by other nations. As a neutral between France and the United Netherland States, she engrossed nearly all the commerce of the world. Yet French cruisers would capture English trading ships, and Charles was forced to ask Parliament for supplies to repair his neglected navy. But English commoners were too jealous of the influence of Louis over Charles to intrust their sovereign with a power which he might prostitute for the benefit of France. The British House of Commons represented then—as it generally represents—the temporary sentiment of insular England. On the broader continent, the Dutch, seeing their commerce languish while that of England flourished, were naturally anxious for a peace with France. So negotiations were opened at Nimeguen, on the Rhine; and the Prince of Orange, determined to engage his uncle as a mediator or an ally, revisited England. A marriage between William and his cousin Mary, the eldest daughter of his uncle James, of York, had long been contemplated. Before the Dutch war of 1672, when the princess was only twelve years old, Charles suggested the match to his brother, who bitterly opposed such a heretical alliance. After the Peace of Westminster the king again spoke to the duke in favor of the project, which was approved by his own ministers. At their first audience Charles told the ambassadors of the Republic that he loved his Dutch nephew "like a son." But the Duke of York was ambitious to give his daughter to the Dauphin of France, while Louis wished her to accept his inferior sub-

William of Orange revisits England.

ject, the Prince of Conty. Rouvigny, the French ambassador at London, warned James to dread the proposed marriage "as death;" to regard the Prince of Orange as "the idol of England;" and he predicted to the duke that "such a son-in-law would inevitably be his ruin." William at first rejected his uncle Charles's overture. Political and personal interests now combined to make him anxious for the splendid alliance. The Stuart cousins understood each other at once; Charles's command compelled James's reluctant consent; and the Reformed Protestant Dutch champion espoused the future heiress of the British crown. Little did Charles or James foresee the momentous consequences of these Dutch and British nuptials. Louis observed the advancement of his greatest enemy with prophetic vexation. But England rejoiced in growing sympathy with Holland; and Parliament, while voting liberal supplies for an expected war with France, resolved that all English soldiers and sailors should be recalled from duty under Louis. A struggle was at hand between the Protestant convictions of England and the Popish inclinations of its anointed sovereign.*

CHAP. VII.
1678.

1677.
4/14 Novem.
William of Orange married to Mary of England.

1678.
5/15 Feb'y.
Effect of William's marriage.

After the marriage of William and Mary, the limping conferences at Nimeguen sprung briskly. The English auxiliaries of Louis were mustered out of his service; but his parsimonious treatment of them caused just complaints, and disgusted the king and the Duke of York. At length peace was covenanted between France and the Protestant Dutch Republic, which, at the end of the long struggle, found herself far better off than she was when her Popish adversary began his ruthless attack.†

1/11 August.
Peace of Nimeguen between the Dutch and French.

Andros had meanwhile landed in Ireland, whence he hastened over to London. On reaching court he was knighted by the king, and allowed a short holiday to look after his private affairs at Guernsey; where, however, he

5 Jan'y.
Andros in London, and knighted.

* Col. Doc., ii., 563; Rouvigny to Louis XIV., 23 April, 1674, in Mignet's Negotiations, iv., 232; Martin's Louis XIV., i., 409, 410, 456, 457; Temple, ii., 252–430; Dalrymple, i., 148, 155–164; Clarke's James II., i, 500–502, 508, 510; Burnet, i., 367–412; Kennett, iii., 297–362; Macpherson, i., 202, 211, 224–231; Courtenay's Temple, i., 424–510; Rapin, ii., 675–685; Parl. Hist., iv., 907, 925; Basnage, ii., 499–870, 902–907; Sylvius, x.–xvi.; Davies, iii., 138–168; Hume, vii., 1–34; Lingard, xiii., 1–43; Macaulay, i., 224–229; *ante*, 185.

† Parl. Hist., iv., 943, 952, 964, 983, 1005; Martin's Louis XIV., i., 462–468; Dumont, vii., 350; Temple, ii., 430–455; Courtenay's Temple, ii., 13; Dalrymple, i., 164–169; Macpherson, i., 233–235, 244; Clarke's James II., i., 511, 512; Kennett, iii., 363; Burnet, i., 422, 423; Basnage, ii., 907–937; Anderson, ii., 537, 548, 549; Col. Doc., iii., 423, 456, 460, 462, 463.

CHAP. VII.

did not tarry long, because the duke required him to return quickly to his government.*

1678.

Massachusetts agents in trouble.

The new-made knight found the Massachusetts agents, Stoughton and Bulkley, in tribulation because of the ill favor of their colony at Whitehall. They could not answer the telling testimony of Randolph, which, in the opinion of Jones and Winnington, the king's attorney and solicitor general, contained "sufficient matter to avoid the patent" of Massachusetts by a writ of "*Quo Warranto.*"

8 April. Andros's account of his government.

By the Duke of York's order, Andros attended the Plantation Committee, where he gave an account of his government, and exposed the behavior of the Eastern Puritan colonies toward New York about the Indian War. In answer to particular inquiries, he suggested that the various sub-governments in New England should be made "as one people and country" by the king's "asserting and regulating" their militia forces, otherwise "every colony may be a prey to an invader." From his information, Andros thought that "the generality of the magistrates and people are well affected to the king and kingdom; but most, knowing noe other government than their owne, think it best, and are wedded to, and opiniate for it. And the magistrates and others in place, chosen by the people, think that they are obliged to assert and maintaine said government all they can, and are church members, and like so to be; chosen, and to continue without any considerable alteration and change there, and depend upon the people to justifie them in their actings."†

9 April. Andros suggests a consolidation of the New England colonies under the king.

16 April. Andros's report about New York.

Andros also submitted to the committee full replies about New York, to the specific inquiries which each royal governor in the Plantations was required to answer. For the first time since Nicolls's report in 1666, the internal administration of the duke's province came directly under the observation of the king's Privy Council.‡

There was an unsettled account between New York and

* Col. MSS., xxvii., 124; Maine H. S. Coll., v., 26; Whitmore's Andros, xix.

† Col. Doc., iii., 254–258, 262–264, 578; Mass. H. S. Coll., xxxii., 287; Hutch. Mass., i., 312–322; Chalmers, i., 403, 404, 405, 436–447; Palfrey, iii., 303–317; Hist. Mag., ii. (iii.), 70, 71; *ante*, 298.

‡ Col. Doc., iii., 188, 260–262; Chalmers, i., 600–604; Doc. Hist., i., 60–62; *ante*, 113, 298. The twenty-seven official "Heads of Inquiry," which were sent to the several colonial governors, are in Col. Rec. Conn., iii., 292–294; see also Arnold's Rhode Island, i., 460, 488–491. The substance of Andros's answers has already been given; *ante*, 313.

Massachusetts which Andros did not fail to adjust. In America, the "aspersions" of Boston could not be corrected, because the Puritan press, which uttered the falsehood, had not the manliness to publish the truth. But now both colonies stood face to face before a supreme tribunal. Andros accordingly petitioned for an inquiry into the truth of the charges of Massachusetts while her agents were yet in London to answer. This was granted at once. Stoughton and Bulkley, after meditation, evasively replied that they had no proofs to offer, and hoped that New York had not been "prejudiced" by the libel against those who were "never discovered" to "your Majesty's Government of the Massachusetts." This acknowledgment was fatal to the would-be independence of the royal corporators in Boston. The king declared that he found "no cause to believe that any of his subjects from the parts of Albany did supply any powder or other materials for war to Philip or other Indian enemies in those parts, neither could he perceive any cause or ground for the imputation laid upon his said subjects of Albany by the Massachusetts;" and he therefore ordered that no Albanian should be liable to such "imputation," unless the authorities in Massachusetts should prosecute him within a year. It does not appear that any prosecution was instituted, nor any apology or retraction offered by the Boston court, whose printers were now more rigorously fettered by colonial censors than any of the craft were restrained in Old England by Sir Roger L'Estrange.*

9 April. Andros desires the charges of Massachusetts to be proved.

24 April.

24 April. The king absolves New York from the "imputation" of Massachusetts.

Having been absent from his government as long as the duke thought prudent, Andros prepared to return. Hitherto he had exercised Admiralty powers in New York only under his "general commission." The Duke of York, who was yet Lord High Admiral of England in its Plantations, now gave Andros a special commission as Vice-Admiral throughout his colonial government, and authorized him to appoint a Judge, Register, and Marshal in Admiralty, to hold their offices during his pleasure.†

20 May. Andros's Commission in Admiralty.

The next week Andros sailed for Sandy Hook, accom-

27 May.

* Col. Doc., iii., 258, 259, 266, 267; Mass. H. S. Coll., xxxii., 287, 288; Whitmore's Andros, 18, 20; Macaulay, i., 248, 390, 580; iv., 349; *ante*, 89, 290–292.

† Col. Doc., iii., 215, 239, 260, 268; *ante*, 87, 202. The first part of the Duke of York's Admiralty Commission to Andros (in Latin) is recorded in N. Y. Patents, iv., 146–153. The record is not complete, nor does the date appear; but it is entered next after a local patent, dated 20th October, 1678.

Andros returns to New York.

panied by several residents of New York, among whom were William Pinhorne, James Graham, and John West, all of whom became prominent in the affairs of the province. The Reverend Charles Wolley, a recent graduate of Cambridge University, whom the duke had appointed chaplain to the forces in New York, also came out with the governor. 7 August. After a nine weeks' voyage Andros reached port, 8 August. and the next day landed in the metropolis.*

8 August. Albany trade.

The first business of Andros, on resuming his government, was to order that none but New Yorkers should trade at Albany. The commissioners for Indian affairs there, having complained of the French intrigues among 22 August. the Mohawks, were also directed to do every thing to encourage the New York savages.†

Bolting of flour.

Another measure, necessary to help the provincial trade, was met by remonstrances from Albany, Esopus, and other inland towns. The previous direction that all flour exported from the city of New York should be bolted fine, and the barrels branded, appears to have been evaded, and the reputation of its great staple was jeoparded in foreign 24 August. ports. The Council therefore ordered that no inland towns should "trade over sea," and that no flour should be inspected within the province except in the metropolis. Honest manufacture was thus secured; and, for some years, "no bad commodity was suffered to go out."

Condition of the metropolis.

At this time the city contained three hundred and forty-three houses, each of which, on the average, had ten inhabitants, making its whole population three thousand four hundred and thirty.

Population and shipping.

There belonged to the metropolis three ships, seven boats, and eight sloops. Four hundred beeves were killed for its yearly supply. The whole revenue of the province was about two thousand pounds. But, from the time of the metropolitan flour-law, the revenue of the city, as well as that of the proprietor, began to improve.‡

An interesting incident now occurred. After his theological defeat in 1676, Leisler went to trade in Dela-

* C. Wolley's Journal (Gowans's ed., 1860), 10, 21, 65, 68, 69, 70; Dankers and Sluyter, 148; Col. Doc., iii., 271, 303, 657, 716; iv., 847; General Entries, xxxii., 1; *ante*, 45, *note*.

† Col. MSS., xxvii., 175, 187; Council Min., iii. (ii.), 179, 180; Col. Doc., iii., 315.

‡ Warrants, Ord., Passes, iii., 40, 287; Col. MSS., xxvi., 147; xxviii., 3, 78, 83, 95, 99; xxix., 29, 32; Col. Doc., iii., 315, 338, 797; iv., 333, 375, 461, 1133; v., 57; Minutes of Common Council, i., 143; ii.; Dunlap, ii., App., cxlvii.; Chalmers's Ann., i., 597, 598; Valentine's New York, 180: compare Andros, in Col. Doc., iii., 260–262, and *ante*, 313.

ware, Maryland, and Virginia, and afterward sailed in his "Pincke" for Europe, with several other New Yorkers. On their way they were taken by the Turks, whose corsairs commanded the ocean, and Andros at once ordered "that a brief be granted for the Church officers (and recommended by the ministers) to collect the benevolence of well-disposed persons in this Government toward the redemption of these captives." This was an imitation of the familiar practice in England, where such letters are usually issued by the sovereign. The appeal was effectual, and the captives were soon redeemed; Leisler paying two thousand pieces of eight (or Spanish dollars) for his own ransom.*

CHAP. VII.

1678.

17 August. Letter in favor of captives by the Turks.

Pursuant to his new commission and the duke's special warrant, Andros now appointed the mayor, Stephanus van Cortlandt, to be judge, and the aldermen of the city of New York to be assistants of the Provincial Court of Admiralty. Samuel Leete, the city clerk, was likewise appointed register, and Sheriff Thomas Ashton the marshal of the court. This organization substantially existed for several years, the mayor of the city, for the time being, always receiving a commission as judge in Admiralty.†

5 October. Admiralty Court in New York.

Affairs in Pemaquid seemed now to require the governor's presence; but, by the advice of his Council, Andros deferred going thither until the spring. Knapton, his commandant at Fort Charles, had diligently executed his instructions, to the discontent of Massachusetts; a vessel belonging to which had been seized for illegally trading within the duke's territories. It was accordingly ordered in Council that the former regulations should continue in force, and that "no Indian trade be admitted at Pemaquid but from and to this place, to prevent inconvenience."‡

Pemaquid affairs.

23 August.

On the Delaware, Billop, the commandant, had misconducted himself, so that Andros was obliged to order him

3 Septem.

* Ord., Warr., Passes, iii., 210; Council Min., iii. (ii.), 178; Gen. Ent., xxxii., 65; Col. MSS., xxvii., 179, 188; xxviii., 26, 27, 30; xlix., 138; Mass. Rec., v., 289; Col. Doc., iii., 717; Doc. Hist., ii., 2; iii., 253; Laws of Maryland, 1681. A surplus of this collection remained after the captives were redeemed, and this Andros directed to be applied toward the building of a new Dutch Church in New York: Col. Doc., iii., 717.

† Minutes of Common Council, i., 122, 124; Gen. Ent., xxxii., 4; Col. Doc., iii., 268; Dunlap, ii., App., cxxviii.; Daly's Sketch, 30, 51. Delavall having succeeded Van Cortlandt as mayor on 14 October, 1678, was commissioned judge in Admiralty in his place.

‡ Col. Doc., iii., 272; Council Min., iii (ii.), 180, 181; Col. MSS., xxvii., 2, 5, 63, 64, 125, 126, 143; Mass. H. S. Coll., xxviii., 338; Pemaquid Papers, 9-14, 15, 16, 23-33; *ante*, 310.

CHAP. VII. back to New York, leaving Alricks in charge. On his return to the capital, Billop was dismissed his military em-
1678. Delaware affairs. ployment, for "extravagant speeches in public," at the Cus-
24 Septem. tom-house. This action of Andros was approved by the
1679. duke, who ordered the vacant commission of lieutenant in
10 March. the regular service to be given to Salisbury; and Billop retired to his plantation on Staten Island to nurse his anger
against the governor.*

1678. Notwithstanding his experience at New York, Fenwick,
on his return to Salem, persisted in acting as an independent proprietor. He was complained of to the Council, who
29 May. Fenwick's case. directed "that, according to his parole, he forbear the assuming any power of government to himself on the east
side of Delaware River, or any where else in those parts."
3 June. This he refused to do, alleging that he was answerable
24 July. only to the king, and was again arrested and sent to New
York. His case was considered by the Council, which de-
22 August. nied his appeal to the king, but referred him to the judgment of the Court of Assizes. This being adverse, the
October. governor appointed six commissioners to act at Elsingburg,
or Salem, in subordination to the court at Newcastle. The
28 October. Newcastle court was also instructed to take care that the
inhabitants of the east side of Delaware River "be not disturbed in their possession upon any pretence whatsoever by
the said Major Fenwick, or others."†

The governor's attention was quickly called to the relations between New York and New England. The commissioners of the three Eastern United Colonies, meeting at
5 Sept. Hartford, complained to him of the "frivolous answers"
which their agents, Ely and Wayte, had received from the
Mohawks at their recent visit to Albany. Andros re-
25 Sept. New York and New England colonies. proved them for treating surreptitiously with the New
York Indians, but offered to give full liberty to talk with
the savages "through the government," and proposed a
meeting at New Haven "to advise on the matter," if it be
"necessary for the public good of these colonies." Leete
9 October. and Allyn, on behalf of Connecticut, thought the proposed

* Col. Doc., iii., 276, 284, 350, 356; Col. MSS., xxvii., 9, 11; xxviii., 13; Council Min., iii. (ii.), 185; S. Hazard, 448–458; Newcastle Rec.; Upland Rec.; Chalmers, i., 363, 375; Anderson's Col. Ch., ii., 395; *ante*, 306.

† Council Min., iii. (ii.), 180; S. Hazard, 452–459; N. J. Hist. Soc. Proc., ii., 12–21; Col. MSS., xx., 145, 146, 147, 148, 149, 150, 155, 156; xxvii., 106; xxviii., 1; *ante*, 302, 306.

meeting "will little avail," and that the conferences at Albany, if not known to Andros, had been with the "privity and allowance" of Salisbury, his subordinate there.* CHAP. VII. 1678.

In his letters to Secretary Blathwayt, Andros dwelt on the relations between the duke's province and its eastern neighbors, and insisted that troubles with the savages must be expected "so long as each petty colony hath, or assumes, absolute power of peace and warr, which cannot be managed by such popular governments; as was evident by the late Indian wars in New England." He charged the Puritan colonies with making the New York Indians "lie, if not insolent, which they never were afore; nor did I ever make treaty with, but dealt with them as being under, or part of the Government." All his hope now was, "regulations and orders from the king, as the only means to keep us well in peace, and preserve or defend us of wars." These opinions had much effect in England, where measures for the reform of the Massachusetts corporation were at this moment under consideration.† 16 Sept. 12 October. Complaints of Andros to England.

Jacob Milborne, who, after his theological trouble in 1676, had left the province in November, 1677, now returned, on his way to Boston, where his brother William was an Anabaptist preacher. Behaving himself "scandalously and reproachfully in relation to the Government," he was desired to attend the governor, "to give an account of his coming," as was the usual custom. But Milborne refused, saying that "he had nothing to do with the Governor or Government." Mayor Delavall accordingly brought him before the Council, who, finding him to be "a troublesome and mutinous person," committed him to the sheriff. The next day Milborne was set at liberty, and soon afterward returned to London, where he annoyed Andros.‡ 26 Decem. Case of Jacob Milborne. 27 Decem.

* Gen. Ent., xxxii., 1; Col. Doc., iii., 273-276; Col. MSS., xxvii., 154, 155, 160, 167, 168; Col. Rec. Conn., iii., 258, 259, 490, 491, 494, 495, 503; Mass. Rec., v., 209, 300; *ante*, 312.

† Col. Doc., iii., 272, 276. Blathwayt, who had been secretary to Sir William Temple in Holland, raised himself from humble circumstances, and was "a very proper, handsome person, very dexterous in business:" Temple, ii., 140, 176, 201; Evelyn, ii., 279.

‡ Col. Doc., iii., 277, 300, 301, 582, 621, 680; Doc. Hist., ii., 42; Col. MSS., xxvi., 139; Gen. Ent., xxxii., 19; *ante*, 196, *note*, 300. Andros's warrant of 27 December, 1678, directed Sheriff Ashton to take into his custody Jacob Milborne, "for clamoring and writing scurrilously against the magistracy and government of this place, particularly at his going off in November, 1677, and afore and since, without any complaint or known cause given, and now being arrived in the Beaver as a passenger to Boston, and upon examination by and before the Governor concerning the above, showing no cause or reason for his so doing, but giving further occasion by his comport."

CHAP. VII.

1678.

The English claim of sovereignty over the Iroquois, which Andros had asserted in the spring of 1677, roused Louis. In the unsettled condition of European politics, the French king could not take a decided stand about his interests in America. Nevertheless, he wrote to Frontenac, "I am well pleased to learn that you have always maintained my authority in the different treaties you have made with the Iroquois and other Indian tribes;—and in regard to the pretension of the English Major General [Andros], my intention is that you always contribute whatever lies in your power to maintain peace between the two nations, without, however, allowing any thing to be undertaken against the countries under my dominion." In the same spirit, Colbert instructed Duchesnau that French explorations toward Hudson's Bay were advantageous for the king's service, "in order to be able to contest the title thereto of the English, who pretend to take possession of it, although it lies within the limits of the countries appertaining to the Crown."*

12 May. Canadian affairs.

15 May. Hudson's Bay.

La Salle had meanwhile satisfied Colbert that a great trade might be established for the benefit of France in buffalo skins—called by the Spaniards "Cibola," after the town of that name on the Gila—one of which he brought to Paris as a sample, and from which hats were soon made "as beautiful as those from beaver." The only difficulty was that of transportation, for these skins were too bulky to be profitably carried in canoes through the Ottawa and the Saint Lawrence to Quebec. They must be shipped to Rochelle by a more direct route. La Salle therefore petitioned the king to let him "go and discover the mouth of the great River Meschasipi, on which vessels might be built to come to France." As he had been at great expense in maintaining Fort Frontenac, he also asked the exclusive privilege of trading in buffalo skins. Colbert gladly countersigned the decree of Louis, which authorized La Salle "to labour in the discovery of the western part of New France," and build necessary forts; and likewise granted him the monopoly of the buffalo fur trade.†

La Salle again in Paris.

12 May. La Salle authorized to explore the Mississippi.

* Col. Doc., ix., 128, 268, 794; La Potherie, i., 140, 143; Charlevoix, ii., 290–298; Oldmixon, i., 544, 545; *ante*, 307.

† Col. Doc., ix., 127, 795; Hennepin's Louisiana, 14, 15; Sparks's La Salle, 12, 13, 181–

CHAP. VII.

1678.

4/14 July. La Salle embarks with Tonty and La Motte. 8 August.

At the request of the Prince of Conty, who had befriended him at court, La Salle took into his enterprise Henry de Tonty, a son of the famous Italian author of the system called "Tontine," and who had served in the French army until its reduction at the Peace of Nimeguen. Embarking at Rochelle with Tonty, and La Motte as his lieutenant, and with abundant means of equipping vessels on the lakes, La Salle safely reached Quebec. His arrival startled the New York authorities, who heard that he had brought over five ships and two thousand men. Materials and artisans were quickly sent up to Fort Frontenac, where the Franciscans Hennepin, Membré, and Watteau now joined Ribourde and Buisset. An advanced party was dispatched to Michilimackinac, and one of La Salle's barks was sent with Tonty, La Motte, and Hennepin to Niagara. Sailing along the north shore of Lake Ontario — which the Iroquois called "*Skannadario*" — they entered the Niagara River on Saint Nicholas's Day, when a *Te Deum* was sung, and thanks were offered to God. The Senecas, who inhabited a little village on the shore of the green, deep river below the cataract, wondered at the "great wooden canoe" in which the strangers had come, and gave them three hundred delicious whitefish just taken from the lake. La Salle's vessel was secured from the floating ice; the first mass was said by Hennepin; and a bark cabin was built near the present village of Lewiston, under the awful roar of the falls.*

8/18 Nov.

6 Decem. The French at Niagara.

11 Decem.

19 Decem.

La Salle's mistake in his route.

In executing his combined scheme of discovery and trade, La Salle now made the decisive mistake which produced most of the troubles he afterward suffered, and influenced, perhaps unhappily, the colonization of Western New France. A fort or magazine at Niagara was, of course, necessary. But the exploration of the Mississippi down to its mouth would have been most readily effected by descending the Alleghany from its near head-waters, and then the Ohio, which it was long ago known emptied

183; Louisiana Hist. Coll., i., 35, 36; Shea's Discovery, 18, 88; *ante*, 308. The account in Charlevoix, ii., 265, is full of errors.

* Hennepin's Louisiana, 15–30; Nouvelle Découverte, 62–77; New Discovery, 40–51, 63; Col. MSS., xxvii., 177, 178; Shea's Discovery, 89, 90; N. Y. H. S. Coll., ii., 219–230; Louisiana Hist. Coll., i., 52, 53, 79, 196; Charlevoix, iii., 381, 385; Sparks's La Salle, 13–19, 203, 204; *ante*, i., 612; ii., 299.

CHAP. VII. 1678. into the Great River. Instead of this, La Salle adopted Jolliet's roundabout plan, and resolved to build a vessel above Niagara, to traverse the upper lakes, and bring back thither cargoes of furs from the neighborhood of Chicago.*

27 Dec. La Motte and Hennepin among the Senecas. To quiet the jealousy of the savages, La Motte and Hennepin, with seven men, visited the Senecas. After five days' march over the snow and through forests, they reached the great village of "Totiakto," or "Tegarondies."†

1679. 1 Jan'y. Conference with the Senecas. On New-year's day Hennepin preached in the bark chapel of the Jesuits in presence of the fathers Garnier and Raffeix. A conference was then held with the great Seneca Council, which, in its gravity, resembled the Venetian Senate. Before any thing was said, La Motte declared that he would enter into no particulars in presence of Garnier, "whom he suspected." The Jesuit was ordered to withdraw, and Hennepin went out at the same time, "to bear part of the affront put upon him." After handsome presents, the Senecas were told that the French intended to build "a great wooden canoe" above the falls, by means of which they could be supplied with European commodities cheaper than by Boston and New York. A blacksmith and a gunsmith would also be settled at the mouth of the 2 Jan'y. Niagara River. The Senecas replied, apparently approving the French proposals. But they really had a greater inclination for the Dutch and English, who afforded them European goods at cheaper rates. After witnessing the torture of a prisoner, whom one of the Seneca war-parties had taken "towards Virginia," La Motte and Hennepin re- 14 Jan'y. traced their way through the woods to the Niagara River.‡

20 Jan'y. La Salle at Niagara. La Motte now returned to Canada, and soon afterward La Salle's cheerful voice was heard again at Niagara. He

* Hennepin's Louisiana, 2; Nouvelle Découverte, 25; Col. Doc., ix., 66, 80, 81, 789; Shea's Discovery, xxxv., xxxvi.; *ante*, 163, 241.

† Nouvelle Découverte, 81; New Discovery, 53, and Map; Pownall's Map of 1776. La Hontan, i., 101, calls the village "Thegaronhies." I think it must be another name for the chief Seneca village of Todehaeckto or Totiakto, or Conception, near Mendon, in Monroe County; although Mr. Marshall refers it to Gannagaro, or Saint James, near Victor, in Ontario County: see N. Y. H. S. Coll., ii. (ii.), 160, 162, 180, 191; Marshall's "Niagara Frontier," 14; Col. Doc., ix., 334, 364–367; Col. MSS., xxxv., 160; *ante*, 179.

‡ Hennepin's Louisiana, 31–40; Nouvelle Découverte, 78–92; New Discovery, 29–61; Lou. Hist. Coll., i., 197–199. With his constitutional tendency to falsehood, Hennepin represents the Falls of Niagara to be "more than five hundred feet," and "above six hundred foot high." The exaggeration is copied in the spurious work attributed to Tonty, in N. Y. H. S. Coll., ii., 228. The Jesuit Relation of 1648, p. 46, described it, thirty years before, as "*une cheute d'eaux d'une effroyable hauteur*." The actual average height of the cataract is one hundred and sixty feet.

1679.

Fort Conty. 22 Jan'y. 26 Jan'y. Keel of a vessel laid above Niagara. Chapel.

had come from Fort Frontenac in one of his barks with supplies for his projected vessel on Lake Erie, but he had been wrecked by his pilots within two leagues of the mouth of the river, at a place which his sailors named the "Mad Cape." On his way La Salle revisited the Senecas, and gained them so that they consented to his designs. Yet "certain persons" made it their business to thwart him, and filled the savages with such jealousy of a fort, that La Salle was obliged to content himself with "a habitation encompassed with palisades." With a fine harbor and excellent fishing, it commanded the New York side of the Niagara River mouth, and was named Fort Conty. La Salle then went two leagues above the cataract, and laid out a dock in which to build his vessel, upon a stream flowing into the river on its west side, now known as Cayuga Creek. The keel was quickly laid by La Salle, who, leaving Tonty in command, hurried back over the snow to Fort Frontenac. During the rest of the winter, which was not half as severe as that in Canada, bark cabins were built by Mahican savages who had accompanied Hennepin. One of these was used as a chapel, in which, for the first time on the western border of New York, Gregorian music was given by practiced European tenors, with the tremendous bass of Niagara.*

Enmity of the Senecas. May. Launch of the Griffin.

The Senecas, who had faithfully reported La Salle's movements to Andros, now refused to sell corn to the French, and threatened to burn their little ship in her dock. This quickened Canadian work; and, under Hennepin's blessing, the singing of "*Te Deum Laudamus*," and the firing of guns, the first European vessel built in Western New York was launched on the upper Niagara. It could carry sixty tons, and it was named the "Griffin," to compliment Frontenac, whose armorial supporters were two griffins. Amazed to see this brigantine afloat, the savages pronounced its French builders "Otkon," which meant, in their tongue, *most penetrating wits*. Pictorially they described the vessel as "a moving fort."

* Hennepin's Louisiana, 25, 31, 32, 41, 42; Nouvelle Découverte, 93–96; New Discovery, 50, 61–63; Lou. Hist. Coll., i., 198; N. Y. H. S. Coll., ii., 230; Col. Doc., iii., 510; v., 633; ix., 335, 381, 382; Doc. Hist., iii., 726; Marshall's Niagara Frontier, 28, 29; Bancroft, iii., 163; Sparks's La Salle, 20, 21, 22; *ante*, 163, 164. The name of La Salle is commemorated in that of the village at the mouth of the Cayuga Creek, in the County of Niagara; and the dock which he built there is still known as "the old ship-yard."

CHAP. VII. 1679. 27 May. La Salle among the Senecas.

Hennepin now hastened to Cataracouy to bring some of his Franciscan brethren; and Ribourde, Membré, and Watteau accompanied him to Niagara. La Salle followed them in a canoe along the southern shore of Ontario. On his way he visited the Seneca villages again, where he met Garnier and Raffeix, and learned that the Miamis and Father Allouez were endeavoring to rouse the Iroquois to war with the Illinois. This purpose was checked by the timely presents of La Salle. On reaching the Niagara River, he stationed the Father Melithon Watteau at the magazine there. Meanwhile the Griffin—completely equipped, and armed with five small guns—had been towed up to the outlet of "the beautiful Lake Erie," where the savages "cried several times *Gannoron*, to signify their admiration." News of the event was quickly sent by them to Andros at New York. At length, all things being ready, La Salle went on board with Hennepin, Ribourde, and Membré, and thirty others; and the Griffin set sail with a favorable wind up Lake Erie, which was now named "Conty," in honor of the great French subject who had befriended the enterprise at Paris.*

3 July.

7 August. La Salle embarks on Lake Erie, or Conty.

25 April.

Louis now directed Frontenac again to "constantly maintain peace, friendship, and good correspondence with the English and Dutch, without, however, foregoing any of the rights and advantages appertaining either to my crown or my subjects in that country." In his reply, the governor complained of the intrigues of Andros among the Iroquois to make them "break" with the French, and of his efforts to thwart La Salle. At the same time, he urged that a French garrison should be maintained at Chambly, through which almost all the communication was carried on between Canada and the English colonies. As there were now rumors of fresh hostilities in Europe, Duchesnau, the intendant, sent an interesting dispatch to Seignelay, who had succeeded Colbert, his father, in the ministry of the colonies, showing that a war with New York and New England would be to the advantage of Canada.†

6 Novem. Frontenac complains of Andros.

14 Nov.

* Hennepin's Louisiana, 43–50; Nouvelle Découverte, 97–121; New Discovery, 63–78, 314; Lou. Hist. Coll., i., 199, 200; La Potherie, ii., 136; Col. Doc., iii., 278; ix., 118, 167, 204, 214, 216, 382; Shea's Discovery, 69, 90, 91, 154; Missions, 411, 412; N. Y. H. S. Coll., ii., 228–231; Sparks's La Salle, 22–26; Bancroft, iii., 164; Hist. Mag., v., 198.

† Col. Doc., ix., 128–139, 140, 411, 795; Martin's Louis XIV., i., 121, 496; ii., 1.

1679.

Jesuits among the Iroquois.

The Jesuit missionaries among the Iroquois were now somewhat changed. Bruyas, to whom Andros had always been civil, left Tionnontoguen, where he was replaced by the Father Vaillant de Gueslis, and took charge of the Residence at the Sault Saint Louis, in place of Frémin, who returned to France. James de Lamberville remained at Caghnawaga. Millet continued in charge of the Oneida mission. John de Lamberville, the superior of the Iroquois missions, labored at Onondaga. Carheil ministered quietly to the Cayugas. Pierron having left the Senecas, Garnier and Raffeix remained in charge of all the villages of that nation. At this period the "Relations" close, and we miss hereafter their interesting details.*

1678.

23 August. Correspondence with Maryland and Virginia.

The Governor of Maryland had meanwhile written to New York that "strange Indians" had again done mischief along the Susquehanna; and Sir Edmund had assured him that the Senecas and Mohawks, "having been always very good and faithfull to this Government," could not have been the offenders. Colonel Herbert Jeffreys, the acting governor of Virginia, also complained of the mischiefs done to that colony and Maryland by "unknown Indians," in breach of Coursey's treaty; and Andros sent the two Indian interpreters, Arnout and Daniel, in the depth of winter, to invite the Iroquois to Albany. Swerise, one of the sachems of the Oneidas, accordingly came there, and excused his nation by laying the blame on the people of Schenectady, who, they said, had misrepresented the designs of the English. Some captives were restored, and Andros received the thanks of Virginia and Maryland. A few months afterward the Oneidas again visited Albany, and Swerise, as their spokesman, declared to Sir Edmund's commissioners, "Corlaer governs the whole land from New York to Albany, and from thence to the Seneca's land; we, who are his subjects, shall faithfully keep the covenant chain." * * * * "Corlaer's limits, as we have said, stretch so far even to *Jacob* my Friend, or Jacob Young." But, as the Onondagas and Cayugas claimed the land lying on the Susquehanna River by right of conquest

1679. 15 Feb'y. Iroquois at Albany.

24 May.

"Corlaer governs the whole land."

* Col. Doc., iv., 607; ix., 129, 130, 171, 194, 239, 720, 762, 838; Rel., 1673–9, 140, 204, 283; Douniol's Missions, ii., 196, 197, 359; Shea's Missions, 274, 277, 286, 289, 293, 294; *ante*, 299, 307. Colden, i., 44, errs in stating that in 1679 there were French priests among the Oneidas, Onondagas, and Cayugas only, and none among the Mohawks and Senecas.

CHAP. VII. 1679.

from the Andastes or Conestogas, they now transferred it to the government of New York "to rule over it," so that it could not be sold "without Corlaer's order."*

Virginia, being still troubled, sent Colonels William Kendall and Southley Littleton to confer with the New York Indians. They were courteously received by Andros and his Council, and then went up to Albany, where Salisbury was instructed to aid them all he could. The Iroquois were accordingly summoned to a conference; but they were delayed by the small-pox, which desolated their villages, and Littleton died at Albany before the savages arrived. Kendall, however, renewed a peace with the Oneidas, Mohawks, and Senecas. The Onondagas came later, and Kendall addressed them as he had done their brethren. Yet, in spite of all promises, the young Iroquois braves could not be restrained from new incursions toward the South.†

31 July. 8 August. Virginian agents in New York and Albany. 5 Novem.

By advice of his Council, Andros meanwhile visited Pemaquid to "take order about the settlement of planters or inhabitants, trade, and all other matters." On his return to the metropolis, after attending to local affairs, and the autumn session of the Court of Assizes, the governor went up to Albany, where Iroquois complications and the regulation of the frontier towns of the province demanded his personal presence.‡

August. Andros at Pemaquid. October. At Albany.

In the autumn of this year two Dutch "Labadists," Jasper Dankers and Peter Sluyter, came from Wiewerd, in Friesland, to view the New World, and select a place to establish a colony of their religious community. These Labadists were disciples of Jean de Labadie, a French enthusiast, holding the doctrines of the Reformed Dutch Church, but adopting other opinions and practices not recognized by that Church. The travelers were shrewd and observing men, and the narrative of their journey is an interest-

13 Septem. Dankers and Sluyter in New York. Labadists.

* Col. Doc., iii., 271, 277, 278, 322, 417; Council Min., iii. (ii.), 182; Col. MSS., xxviii., 2; Colden, i., 38–42, 55; first edit., 32–42, 64; Doc. Hist., i., 261; Hennepin, Nouv. Déc., 90; Chalmers, i., 339, 351; *ante*, 102, 287, 309. Jacob Young was an Indian interpreter who lived at the head of the Chesapeake Bay, back of Newcastle: Col. Doc., iii., 322, 328, 344; S. Hazard, Ann., 473.

† Col. Doc., ix., 120, 131; Col. MSS., xxviii., 120–122, 125, 131; Colden, i., 42, 43, 44; first ed., 42–48. Neither Beverley nor Burk notice this mission from Virginia.

‡ Council Min., iii. (ii.), 180; Pemaquid Papers, 32, 33; Col. Doc., iii., 272; Col. MSS., xxviii., 2, 123, 131–134; R. I. Rec., iii., 54; Arnold, i., 455; Dankers and Sluyter's Journ., 111, 167, 258; *ante*, 319.

ing contemporaneous account of the condition of New York and its neighborhood.* CHAP. VII. 1679.

The four Dutch ministers in the province were now called on to perform a very important office. Before the arrival of Van Gaasbeeck, the church at Kingston had been supplied by Petrus Tesschenmaeker, a young "Proponent," or licensed Bachelor in Divinity, who had recently been graduated from the University of Utrecht, and had come from Guiana to New York in the spring of 1678. The following autumn Tesschenmaeker went to Newcastle, where the congregation called him to be their minister, although he had never been ordained. To remedy this, the delegates from that church asked the provincial Dutch clergymen to form themselves into a "Classis" and ordain the candidate, without obliging him to go to Holland for holy orders. This was a novel question. Up to this time the Classis of Amsterdam alone had sent over Dutch ministers to New York, and those now settled there did not assume the power of ordaining others. Andros, who was anxious to have a Dutch clergyman settled on the Delaware, relieved the New York domines from responsibility by an official direction to Van Nieuwenhuysen, and "any three or more of the Ministers or Pastors within this Government," to examine Tesschenmaeker, and, if they should find him qualified, to ordain him "into the ministry of the Protestant Reformed Church." Accordingly, the Dutch clergymen, Schaats of Albany, Van Nieuwenhuysen of New York, Van Zuuren of Long Island, and Van Gaasbeeck of Esopus, met at New York, with their elders; formed themselves into a Classis; and, after examining Tesschenmaeker, ordained him as a minister of the Gospel, according to the ritual of the Reformed Dutch Church. None of the other provincial clergymen assisted; neither the English chaplain Wolley, nor the Lutherans Arensius and Lokenius, nor the Presbyterians on Long Island. It was wholly a Classis of the Reformed Church of Holland—the first ever held in America—and its proceedings, which had been originated by the Episcopalian governor of New York, were approved

Petrus Tesschenmaeker.

30 Septem. Andros directs the examination of Tesschenmaeker.

9 October. The Dutch ministers ordain Tesschenmaeker.

* The Journal of Dankers and Sluyter, in 1679 and 1680, was published in 1867 by the Long Island Historical Society, under the supervision of Mr. Henry C. Murphy, who procured the original manuscript in Holland, and translated and annotated this precious memorial with excellent scholarship.

CHAP. VII. by the supreme ecclesiastical judicature at Amsterdam charged with the affairs of colonial Dutch churches.*

1679.

The law of New York was now settled on an important

17 Decem. point. Twenty-one metropolitan coopers signed an agreement to charge certain prices for their labor; and that, if any of them should sell his work under their own arbitrary prices, he should be fined fifty shillings "for the use of the

1680. poor." For this agreement the conspiring laborers were

8 Jan'y. Coopers fined for unlawful combination. summoned before the governor and council, and Mayor Rombouts, who adjudged them guilty of an unlawful combination, and sentenced each signer to pay a fine of fifty shillings "to the church, or pious uses." This decision was founded on the laws of England, which declared such confederating modern "strikers" to be "infamous," and punished them by fine and imprisonment.†

The previous legislation in regard to the bolting and inspection of flour having been ineffectual, and complaints

17 Jan'y. 20 Jan'y. New regulations about bolting and exporting flour. being made of the loss which trade suffered, it was ordered in council that for the future no mills be allowed to bolt, nor flour to be packed for exportation, but at the city of New York; and that all bolting or exporting that commodity must be freemen or burghers. This new regulation was strictly enforced. For fourteen years the metropolis enjoyed a monopoly which helped her inevitable growth, and especially advantaged her coopers, who had just been punished for "striking." But her shoemakers were

24 Jan'y. Shoemakers not to tan hides. forbidden to tan hides; and it was proposed to require all leather to be imported. Happily, this restriction—intended to benefit the merchant at the expense of the producer—was not carried into effect.‡

An important measure in regard to Indian slaves was now adopted. It had been the practice to discriminate be-

* Corr. Class. Amst., Letters of 25 October, 1679, 2 April, 1680; Dankers and Sluyter's Jour., 111, 222; Col. MSS., xxviii., 132; Gen. Ent., xxxii., 61; Doc. Hist., iii., 583, *note;* Murphy's Selyns, 82, 101; Demarest's Hist. Ref. D. C., 183, 184; N. Y. Christ. Int., 19 Oct., 1865; Hist. Mag., Nov., 1865. Laurentius van Gaasbeeck came to Kingston as the successor of Blom in September, 1678, at the request of the elders and deacons of the Dutch Church there, with the approbation of Andros, and under the authority of the Classis of Amsterdam: Cor. Cl. Amst., MSS.; O'Call., ii., 432. Van Gaasbeeck died in February, 1680, and was succeeded by Johannes Weecksteen, from Harlaem, in 1681: Col. MS., xxix., 205; Doc. Hist., iii., 583; Cor. Cl. Amst.; Dankers and Sluyter's Journal, 276; Hist. Mag. (ii.), i., 333.

† Col. MSS., xxix., 2, 3, 19; Val. Man., 1850, 425, 426; Statutes 2 and 3 Edw. VI., cap. 15, 22 and 23 Charles II., cap. 19; Saint Paul's Epistle to Timothy 1, iii., 3, and to Titus, i., 7.

‡ Col. MSS., xxix., 2, 19, 29, 32, 39, 84, 187; Minutes of Com. Council, i., 143; Col. Doc., iii., 315, 338, 351, 797; v., 57, 58; Dankers and Sluyter's Jour., 354–357; Dunlap, ii., App., cxxvi.; *ante*, 318.

tween the free natives of New York and others, especially those of the Spanish West Indies, many of whom were held in bondage. It was now resolved in council that all Indians are free and not slaves, and can not be forced to be servants, unless those formerly brought from the Bay of Campeachy or other foreign parts. This was followed by a formal order "That all Indians here have always been and are free, and not slaves, except such as have been formerly brought from the bay or other foreign parts. But if any shall be brought hereafter into the government, within the space of six months, they are to be disposed of, as soon as may be, out of the government. But after the expiration of the said six months, all that shall be brought here from those parts and landed, to be as other free Indians."*

CHAP. VII. 1679. 5 Decem.

1680. 20 April. Imported Indian slaves declared free.

The Dutch Church in the fort had now become too small to accommodate its congregation, and its present condition was not convenient either for the people or for the government. At the suggestion of Andros, a meeting was held to consider the best means to build a new one, which was attended by several members of the council and other leading citizens, besides Domine van Nieuwenhuysen and the Episcopalian chaplain Wolley. It was determined, by a vote of ten to three, to raise money by "free will or gift," and not by a public tax; but, if that should fail, to appeal to the governor. It was agreed that the new church should be a quarter larger than that in the fort, which was fifty-four feet wide. Andros, warmly approving the project, directed that the surplus moneys raised under his letter of August, 1678, for the redemption of the captives in Turkey, should be applied toward the new church, and contributed fifty pounds himself. The mayor and aldermen also appropriated certain fines, and a plot of ground was selected on which to build the church as soon as possible.†

30 June. Arrangements for building a new Dutch church.

Wolley, the duke's Episcopalian chaplain, soon afterward went home to seek preferment in England, with a

* Col. MSS., xxviii., 161, 173; xxix., 86; Min. of N. Y. Com. Council, i., 142; Dunlap, ii., App., cxxix.; *ante*, 140. Notwithstanding this order, foreign Indians were for a long time held as slaves in New York, as they were in Massachusetts and other English dependencies.

† Doc. Hist., iii., 244, 265; Col. MSS., xxviii., 26, 27; xxix., 141; Gen. Ent., xxxii., 65; Col. Doc., iii., 315, 415, 717; Letter of Selyns to Classis, 28 October, 1682; *ante*, 319. Dr. De Witt, in his sermon (August, 1856, p. 26), erroneously places "the first steps" in 1687: see Records of the Collegiate Dutch Church, Liber A., p. 161, 169.

CHAP. VII. certificate from Andros that he had "comported himself unblameable in his life and conversation." After his return

1680. 15 July. Chaplain Wolley returns to England. Wolley prepared "A two years' Journal in New York," etc., which was published in London in 1701. Encumbered with pedantry, and fuller of detail about the native savages than the European colonists, Wolley's Journal, nevertheless, gives valuable information concerning the province in 1680. In respect to the metropolis, where he lived for two years, the lately returned chaplain declared New York to be "a place of as sweet and agreeable air as ever I breathed in, and the inhabitants, both English and Dutch, very civil and courteous, as I may speak by experience, amongst whom I have often wished myself and family, to whose tables I was frequently invited, and always concluded with a generous bottle of Madeira."*

1679. The Duke of York's customs' regulations had meanwhile proved so annoying to East Jersey, that its Assembly

3 April. Trouble between New York and New Jersey. passed an act to indemnify any vessel which, coming into that province by way of Sandy Hook, and entering and clearing at Elizabethtown, might be seized by the government of New York. Carteret accordingly proclaimed that all bottoms coming to East Jersey should be free. Upon this, one Mr. Hooper ordered a ketch from Barbadoes to go thither; but Andros made her enter and pay duties in New York before he would allow her to proceed to Jersey and land her cargo of rum. Sir Edmund also sent Collector Dyer to England to answer any complaints. The Duke of York being absent in Flanders, Secretary Werden appears to have given directions to Dyer, with which he returned to New York in the following December. Andros soon afterward went over to Staten Island, and invited Carteret to meet him there, "to negotiate in peace and friend-

1680. ship." The Jersey governor having declined this over-

8 March. Andros notifies Carteret. ture, Sir Edmund sent him copies of Charles's patent to James, and of the duke's commission to himself; and he directed Carteret to forbear exercising "any jurisdiction"

* Gen. Ent., xxxii., 93, 94; Hist. Mag., i., 371; *ante*, 318. A reprint of Wolley's Journal was published by W. Gowans (who misprints the name "Wooley") in 1860. It does not equal in interest the contemporaneous observations of Dankers and Sluyter; but, in connection with that book, and Secretary Nicolls's account in Scot's "Model" (128–144), it leaves little unknown about New York and New Jersey in 1680. I regret that the limits of this volume do not allow me to quote some interesting descriptions of the metropolis, and of Esopus, Albany, and Long Island, their people, magistrates, and others.

in any part of the territory thus granted by the king to the duke, without due authority recorded in New York. Moreover, Andros added, "it being necessary for the king's service, and welfare of his Majesty's subjects living or trading in these parts, that beacons for land or sea marks for shipping sailing in and out, and a fortification, be erected at Sandy Point, I have resolved it accordingly;—but, having due regard to all rights or proprieties of land or soil, shall be ready to pay or give just satisfaction."*

CHAP. VII. 1680. Andros proposes beacons and a fort at Sandy Hook.

This letter made a hubbub at Elizabethtown. After advising with his council, Carteret informed Andros that if he attempted to build a fort at Sandy Hook he would be resisted until the proprietor's pleasure be known, "he having reserved that for a fortification, when the king shall command it." In the mean time, Sir Edmund had sent Secretary Nicolls with a proclamation forbidding Carteret from exercising any jurisdiction within the duke's province, and commanding all persons to submit "to the king's lawful authority" as established in New York. On receiving this, Carteret protested, and appealed to the king, "who only can determine this matter."†

20 March. Carteret's reply to Andros.

13 March. Andros's proclamation.

29 March.

Andros soon went over to New Jersey. The rumor of his coming went before him, and Carteret gathered a large force to oppose the Governor of New York. But, as he came without soldiers, Andros was invited ashore with his attendants, and went up to Carteret's house. Patents and commissions were produced on each side, and long arguments followed, without result. After dinner, Carteret accompanied Sir Edmund Andros back to his sloop. Three weeks afterward, having tried various devices, Governor Andros ordered some soldiers to Elizabethtown, who broke open Carteret's house in the dead of night; "halled" him out of his bed; and brought him a naked prisoner to

7 April. Andros at Elizabethtown.

30 April.

* Leaming and Spicer, 112–137, 673; Col. MSS., xxix., 55; Col. Doc., iii., 268, 392; iv., 382; Warr., Ord., Passes, iii., 63, 254; Chalmers, Ann., i., 618; Index N. J. Col. Doc., 7; Whitehead's E. J., 70, 77–79, 82; Hatfield's Eliz., 189, 190; Evelyn, ii., 136; Dankers and Sluyter, 196, 255, 261, 347; *ante*, 261–270, 303, 305, 312. It is stated, in Collins's Peerage, iv., 212 (2d ed., 1741), that the king's vice-chamberlain, Sir George Carteret, died on the 13th of January, 1679, in the eightieth year of his age. There seem to be some writers who do not yet apprehend that the "*old style*" prevailed in England until 1753; so that the English year 1679 ended on 24 March, 1680, "*new style*," and that consequently Sir George Carteret died 13 January, 1680, according to our present reckoning.

† Gen. Ent., xxxii., 72, 73; Col. MSS., xxix., 61–64, 68, 69; Min. of N. Y. Common Council, i., 137, 138; Leaming and Spicer, 674–677; Whitehead, 71, 72; Newark Town Rec., 78; Dankers and Sluyter, 277, 347.

CHAP. VII. 1680. 1 May. Carteret a prisoner in New York. 27 May. 28 May.

New York. There, ill and forlorn, Carteret was committed to the custody of Sheriff Collyer, on a charge of unlawfully assuming jurisdiction over the king's subjects. A special Court of Assizes was ordered; before which Carteret was arraigned for trial, on an indictment for riotously presuming "to exercise jurisdiction and government over his Majesty's subjects within the bounds of his Majesty's letters Patents granted to His Royal Highness." Sir Edmund was conducted by trumpeters to the tribunal, over which he presided on a higher seat than usual. Carteret protested against the jurisdiction of the New York court. Being overruled, he averred his conduct as Governor of New Jersey "to be legal, and by virtue of power derived from the King." His commission and other documents were submitted to the jury, which brought in a verdict of "Not Guilty." This did not satisfy Andros, who sent the jurors out twice and thrice; each time with new charges.* At length a verdict of acquittal was recorded. Nevertheless, Carteret was obliged to give security that, if he went to New Jersey, he would not "assume any authority or jurisdiction there, civil or military."†

Carteret tried and acquitted.

2 June. Carteret again in New Jersey.

Sir Edmund, accompanied by Lady Andros, now escorted Carteret back to Elizabethtown with great pomp, and endeavored to induce the Assembly to confirm his proceedings, and adopt the Duke's Laws, in force in New York, with such amendments as might be desirable. The Jersey Assembly, however, adhered to their own laws, which they presented to Andros for his approval. Yet the authority of the Governor of New York was not disputed, and civil and military officers were commissioned by him to act in Newark, Elizabethtown, Woodbridge, Burlington, and elsewhere. An account of these transactions was sent by the deposed governor to Lady Carteret; and Bollen, who was now in London, was desired to move the Commissioners of Customs and others in favor of East Jersey, and watch Dyer, who was intending to return to England, "that he

11 June. Andros's government. 9 June. 25 July. 9 July.

* It was said that "one Jackson, a juryman, occasionally speaking to the Governor, said that he hoped they had the same privileges as the other Plantations. The Governor answered that their privileges hung on a slender thread, and that he was chidden for giving them such liberties." But Andros afterward denied that he "ever spoke any such words;" and Nicolls and Dyer, who were present in court all the time, heard nothing from the governor to any such purpose: Col. Doc., iii., 315.

† Leaming and Spicer, 678–684; Gen. Ent., xxxii., 77, 78; Col. MSS., xxix., 78, 93, 102–104; Whitehead, 73, 74; Dankers and Sluyter, 347–351.

doth not swear and romance against us, as he did the time CHAP. VII.
before."*

1680.

The spring of this year was marked by an attempt of
Connecticut to include Fisher's Island within her jurisdiction. Andros at once wrote to Leete that the island had 29 March.
been granted by Nicolls to the late Governor Winthrop, Fisher's Island.
and that any proceedings "intrenching" on the authority
of New York must be forborne, "to prevent greater inconveniences." The Connecticut court resolved that they 20 May.
would exercise government over the island, and prohibited
obedience to Sir Edmund. This bluster ended the matter.
The son of Winthrop was obliged to recognize the juris- 24 June.
diction of New York, under which the island has ever since
remained without question.†

The affairs of Pemaquid requiring attention, Knapton, 26 June.
the late commander, and John West, were commissioned as Knapton and West
special justices of the peace, and Henry Jocelyn and others at Pemaquid.
appointed a Court of Sessions. The commissioners were
also directed to visit Fisher's Island, Martha's Vineyard,
and Nantucket, and see that proper officers were established there. On their return, Knapton and West reported 14 Septem.
their proceedings; and Ensign Thomas Sharpe, the present commander at Pemaquid, and the justices there, were
ordered to inform the Eastern savages that the governor 15 Septem.
had forbidden the Mohawks to make incursions, and that
there must be no more "warring" between the Indians
subject to New York.‡

At the Court of Assizes this autumn, besides the usual 6 October.
members, justices attended from New Jersey, Nantucket, Court of Assizes.
and Pemaquid. There were thirty members present, including Sir Edmund Andros, "who was a good lawyer."
John West was now appointed clerk of the court, as well

* Leaming and Spicer, 680–685; Col. MSS., xxix., 98–101, 106–124, 127, 144, 153, 154, 169, 175, 179, 184, 194, 199; Gen. Ent., xxxii., 94, 95, 97; Whitehead, 74, 75; Newark Town Rec., 79; Dankers and Sluyter, 346, 351. It appears that when Carteret was seized at Elizabethtown, Bollen and Vauquellen secured his most important papers, and hastened to England, the former by way of Boston, and the latter by Maryland: Dankers and Sluyter, 349; Hatfield, 193.

† Gen. Ent., xxxii., 75, 90; Col. MSS., xxix., 136; Pemaquid Papers, 35; Col. Rec. Conn., iii., 64, 283; Dankers and Sluyter, 370; Trumbull, i., 375; Thompson, i., 389, 390; N. Y. Revised Statutes, iii., 2; *ante*, 139.

‡ Gen. Ent., xxxii., 92, 93; Col. MSS., xxix., 99, 136, 137, 213; Ord., Warr., etc., xxxii½, 1–4; Pemaquid Papers, 33–44; Nantucket Pap., 116–123. West had been a lawyer at New York, deputy clerk of the Mayor's Court, and clerk of Sessions on Long Island, and had returned from England with Andros in 1678: C. Wolley, 5, 70; *ante*, 319.

1680. 8 Novem.

as clerk of the council, and also provincial secretary in place of Nicolls, who was about going to England. At the request of the metropolitan mayor and aldermen, West was soon afterward appointed clerk of the City and County of New York.*

As soon as the Court of Assizes adjourned, Sir Edmund hastened to Boston, by invitation of Lord Culpepper, the Governor of Virginia, who was there on his way back to

13 October. Andros at Boston.

England. The General Court of Massachusetts was then in session; and Pynchon, who had written to Andros for leave to treat with the Mohawks at Albany, was directed to go thither, and, with the advice of the New York authorities there, procure a renewal of the covenant made in

9 Novem.

April, 1677. An interview was accordingly held, in the presence of Brockholls and the Albany officers, at which the Mohawks, whom Andros had forbidden to send parties

10 Novem.

eastward, agreed to lay down the axe, and be at peace with the New England Indians.†

After the return of Andros, Randolph remained in London more than a year, occupied by the affairs of Massachusetts. The intended alterations in the government of that colony were, however, avoided by the skill of her agents, Stoughton and Bulkley, in disposing of her bribes "to persons then in a great station at Court." Having been ap-

Randolph returns from England. 28 Jan'y.

pointed collector of the customs in New England, Randolph returned with Dyer to New York, whence he went to Boston. There he was so obstructed in executing his office, that he sent home bitter complaints. As the best

8 April.

remedy, Randolph recommended the abrogation of the

* Ord., Warr., etc., xxxii½, 6, 7; Col. MSS., xxix., 234; Col. Doc., iii., 303, 314, 315, 657; Wood, 149; Val. Man., 1853, 330, 331; Bancroft, ii., 428; C. Wolley, 70. Besides Governor Andros, the members of the Court of Assizes, in October, 1680, were Secretary Nicolls, Counsellors Dyer, Phillipse, Dervall, and Van Cortlandt, Mayor Rombout, and the metropolitan aldermen Beekman, Van Brugh, Lewis, Marius, Verplanck, and Wilson; Richard Betts, high-sheriff of Long Island, or Yorkshire; Justices Topping, Arnold, Woodhull, and Wood, of the East Riding, Willett, of the North Riding, and Hubbard, Elbertsen, and Palmer, of the West Riding of Long Island; Teller and Van Dyck, of Albany; Delavall, of Esopus; Spaswill, Browne, and Parker, of New Jersey; Gardiner, of Nantucket; and Knapton and West, of Pemaquid. Salisbury, the commandant at Albany, having died in the winter, was succeeded by Brockholls in the spring of 1680: Hist. Mag., iv., 50; *ante*, 312, 328.

† Col. Doc., iii., 244, 302, 308; ix., 140-145, 795, 796; Chalmers, i., 344, 438; Hutchinson, i., 332; Burk, ii., 226; Palfrey, iii., 343; Mass. H. S. Coll., xxxv., 52; Mass. Rec., v., 299, 300, 319, 320; Col. MSS., xxix., 196; *ante*, 309. Colden does not mention this conference. As Robert Livingston was then in New York, asking leave to buy lands on Roeloff Jansen's kill, his duties as secretary were performed by Richard Pretty: Ord., Warr., etc., xxxii½, 13, 14; Doc. Hist., iii., 367. An account of Culpepper's visit to Boston is in Campbell's Virginia, 312, 329, 330, 349-355: see also Mass. H. S. Coll., v., 124.

Massachusetts charter by a writ of *Quo Warranto*. That result, indeed, could scarcely have been averted, except by the submission of the recusant corporation. Yet it obstinately disobeyed the king's orders to send over new agents; and, while it could afford to buy territory in Maine, and bribe venal courtiers in London, pleaded poverty to excuse contumacy. This policy was neither manly nor wise. The local rulers of Massachusetts knew that they were the creatures of the King of England. Nevertheless, they affected a braggart independence of him. Neither ready nor willing to renounce subjection to England, the Puritan corporation clung to her royal charter as "the ark of her safety." If the inhabitants of Massachusetts had then been allowed to make a Constitution for themselves, they would hardly have intrusted to a sectarian oligarchy the power which had been abused by the grantees of "Charles the Martyr." Yet, as an English corporation, the ruling power in Massachusetts tried to maintain the inconsistent attitude of loyalty and rebellion; and, professing to be "humbly bold," demonstrated absurd weakness. Bradstreet, the governor of the corporation, however, sent a dutiful reply to the inquiries of the Plantation Committee at London. In this interesting paper he complained that Andros had laid heavy duties on the Pemaquid fishermen for the benefit of the Duke of York; and, at the same time, reported that a Boston vessel brought from Africa "betwixt forty and fifty negroes, most women and children, sold here for ten, fifteen, and twenty pounds apiece, which stood the merchants in near forty pounds apiece, one with another. Now and then, two or three negroes are brought hither from Barbadoes, and other of his Majesty's Plantations, and sold here for about twenty pounds apiece; so that there may be within our government about one hundred, or one hundred and twenty." At this time a good negro was worth about thirty-five pounds in New York; but, as the climate of Massachusetts was less genial to the African, he did not sell for quite so much there, when freshly imported into slavery.*

11 June.

Policy of Massachusetts.

18 May. Bradstreet's report.

Negro slaves in Massachusetts.

* Mass. H. S. Coll., xxviii., 330–340; xxx., 256; xxxii., 288–292; Mass. Rec., v., 270–289; Hutch. Mass., i., 324–332; Coll., 485, 495, 519–526; Chalmers, i., 405–410, 438–440, 509; Barry, i., 462–464; Palfrey, iii., 314–340, 367, 368; Col. Doc., iii., 261, 263; Story's Miscellanies, 66; Moore's Notes on Slavery in Mass., 49; *ante*, 313, 319.

CHAP. VII. 1680. 8 May. 30 June. 15 July. Reports of Rhode Island, Plymouth, and Connecticut.

Rhode Island reported to the Plantation Committee that there were "only a few blacks imported" into that colony. Plymouth represented that "slaves we have very few, except Indian women and boys taken in the late war." Connecticut answered that since Sir Edmund Andros came to New York, her correspondence with him was not "like what it was with his predecessors in that government;" that her chief trade was with Boston; that she had about thirty slaves; and that sometimes three or four blacks a year were imported from Barbadoes, who were usually sold at the rate of twenty-two pounds apiece.*

1679. 29 May. Habeas Corpus Act in England.

In the mean time, England had been convulsed by Titus Oates's story of a "Popish Plot," and its Protestantism was whipped into violent excess. In the height of this fanaticism the king prorogued Parliament, after assenting to what is familiarly known as the "Habeas Corpus" Act —chiefly due to Shaftesbury, and which may be considered to be, perhaps, the most meritorious work of his life. This statute, however, did not extend to the English Colonies or Plantations; just as the Test Act of 1673 did not affect them, as has been already explained. The same day the censorship of the English press expired with the law which authorized the abomination.†

Freedom of the press.

Tories and Whigs.

These events gave rise to two remarkable party appellatives, which have ever since been familiar in England. The friends of the king and his brother were nick-named "*Tories*," as were the Roman Catholic Irish Robbers, known as "Rapparees" and "White Boys;" while those who desired a Protestant English sovereign were designated "*Whigs*," as the persecuted Scotch Covenanters were then called. These political epithets—at first given in derision and accepted in bravado—have continued to distinguish the conservative and the progressive parties in English local strifes.

The Duke of York.

The Duke of York, threatened by the House of Commons with exclusion from the throne on account of his

* Chalmers's Ann., i., 282-284, 307-310; Arnold, i., 488-491; R. I. Rec., iii., 78, 86; Col. Rec. Conn., iii., 290-303; Mass. H. S. Coll., xxxv., 52; Palfrey, iii., 420-428; Moore's Notes on Slavery in Mass., 41; *ante*, 296.

† Statute 31 Charles II., cap. ii.; Parl. Hist., iv., 661, 1148; Kennett, iii., 377; Rapin, ii., 675, 707; Lingard, xiii., 133, 134, 165; Macaulay, i., 248; Burnet, i., 485; ii., 103; Jacob., iii., 227; Chalmers's Ann., i, 56, 74; ii., 72, 113; Rev. Col., i., 236, 308, 395, 412; N. Y. H. S. Coll., 1868, 72, 113; Coll. Doc., iii., 357; iv., 264; *ante*, 201, 202, *note*.

Roman faith, was obliged to withdraw from England; first to Brussels, and then to Scotland, where he remained until February, 1680, when he returned to London. During these exciting movements James had little time for the affairs of his American province. But he was now compelled to look anxiously into them.* CHAP. VII. 1680.

The complaints which the Quakers settled in West Jersey had sent home of their treatment by Andros were so strongly supported, that Sir John Werden inquired officially of the English Secretary of State whether they were empowered, as grantees of the duke, to set up a distinct government, and whether they were not still liable to the laws established in New York. The king's secretary, however, does not appear to have answered these legal questions. Wishing to know the right of the matter, the duke ordered his commissioners "to hear and make report to him concerning the customs demanded in New West Jersey in America, by his governor of New York." This was accordingly done. The Quakers' case was elaborately argued by Penn and others, who insisted that, in Berkeley's conveyance to them, "powers of government are expressly granted;" that the Duke of York had no authority to levy duties on the colonists in West Jersey, or exclude them of their "English right of common assent to taxes;" and then, adroitly alluding to "the Duke's circumstances and the people's jealousies," they submitted that as he had now the opportunity to free that country with his own hand, "so will Englishmen here know what to hope for, by the justice and kindness he shows to Englishmen there, and all men to see the just model of his government in New York to be the scheme and draft in little, of his administration in Old England at large, if the crown should ever devolve upon his head."† 1679. 19 Septem. New Jersey affairs. Penn's argument for the Quakers.

This bold and able, but very sophistical argument, which so skillfully touched the duke's present "circumstances," would have been unanswerable, if its material allegation had been true, that powers of government were "expressly granted" in Berkeley's conveyance to Fenwick. But the

* Clarke's James II., i., 512–588; Temple, ii., 426–479; Courtenay's Temple, ii., 13–82; Burnet, i., 422–469; Dalrymple, i., 168–177, 261–274, 292, 327, 332, 335; N. Luttrell, i., 10, 20–22; Macaulay, i., 229–257; Martin, i., 503–506.

† Index N. J. Col. Doc., 7; S. Smith, 117–124; Gordon, 40–42; *ante*, 266, 305, 320.

CHAP. VII. 1680. Fallacy of Penn's argument.

facts were not what Penn and his friends asserted. Berkeley could only convey what the duke had granted to him; and the duke had never granted to Berkeley express powers of government. Moreover, the Quaker argument disingenuously avoided any reference to the duke's second patent from the king in 1674, while it maintained that the Peace of Westminster had reinvested Berkeley with his annihilated rights. By that treaty, however, as has been seen, the Dutch conquerors relinquished New Netherland to the king; and Charles afterward granted the whole of it to his brother.*

Opportunity of the Duke of York.

If the Duke of York had now been free from political anxiety, he might have settled this New Jersey question on the grounds afterward taken by the ministers of William the Third, and declared that his secondary releases neither did nor could transfer rights of government to his grantees; because such sovereign authority, having been intrusted to him personally by the king, was "inalienable from the person to whom it is granted."†

But James had again to seek refuge in Scotland from the furious malice of his enemies. In this strait the duke resolved to refer "the whole matter" of his right to customs' duties from West Jersey to the decision of "the greatest lawyer of England," Sir William Jones, who had, just before, resigned his place as attorney general, and was now a vehement opponent of the king. When it had been proposed to govern Jamaica without any Assembly, Jones advised his sovereign "that he could no more grant a commission to levy money on his subjects there without their consent by an Assembly, than they could discharge themselves from their allegiance to the English Crown." Yet Jones held it to be incontrovertible "that the Parliament might rightfully impose taxes on every dominion of the Crown." This fallacy was the "universal opinion" of English jurists at that time. An English Parliament might tax an unrepresented colony of England when her sovereign might not. Jones had been retained by Stoughton and Bulkley, the agents of Massachusetts, as their counsel,

The Duke's resolution.

Sir William Jones.

* S. Smith, 117, 121; Leaming and Spicer, 10, 41-45, 64, 413; Gordon, 42; *ante*, 83, 260, 261, 267.

† Representation of the Lords of Trade, 21 October, 1701, in Leaming and Spicer, 607, 608, 613; S. Smith, 669, 670; Gordon, 23, 54; Bancroft, iii, 47.

1680.

28 July.

Jones's wary and timorous opinion.

and aided them in preventing the change which the king meant to make in its government. And now, this "wary" and "timorous" Parliamentarian advocate uttered a cautious opinion: "I am not satisfied (by any thing that I have yet heard) that the Duke can legally demand that or any other duty from the inhabitants of those lands. And that which makes the case the stronger against his Royal Highness is, that these inhabitants claim under a grant from his Royal Highness to the Lord Berkeley and Sir George Carteret, in which grant there is no reservation of any profit, or so much as of jurisdiction."*

Jones's opinion fallacious.

This was a model report for a referee wishing to evade a decision or becloud the truth. Avoiding several material facts in the case, Jones cited only the duke's first grant to Berkeley and Carteret in 1664, and ignored both the Dutch conquest of 1673 (which annihilated that grant), and the king's second patent to his brother in 1674. Sir William must have meant either that James never had any "jurisdiction" under his first patent from the king (which was not suggested), or else that the duke had released—because he had not reserved—that jurisdiction. Yet Jones was too good a lawyer to affirm that a mere release of a "tract of land" with its "appurtenances," in "as full and ample manner" as they had been originally granted, could convey powers of government from one English subject to another. This fallacy would have been too transparent.

6 August. The Duke of York's decision as to West Jersey.

The Duke of York, however, had neither time nor inclination to contest the matter. Easily as he might have confuted its fallacies, he determined to give liberal effect to the late attorney general's cloudy opinion. Without waiting for his own counsel—Churchill and Jeffreys—to approve it, James executed a deed tendered by Byllinge, "the more firmly to convey the said West New Jersey to him and the rest of the Proprietors, and plainly to extinguish the demand of any customs or other duties from them, save the rent as reserved at the first." By this instru-

* Clarke's James II., i., 588–600; Col. Doc., iii., 284, 285; Force's Tracts, iv., No. ix., 45, 46; Mather's Magnalia, i., 178; Chalmers's Ann., i., 240, 619, 626; Rev. Coll., i., 150, 173; *ante*, 316. Jones succeeded North as attorney general in 1674; resigned in October, 1679; and was succeeded first by Sir Cresswell Levins, and then by Sir Robert Sawyer: N. Luttrell, i., 24; Beatson, i., 416, 433; Kennett, iii., 300, 379, 391; Burnet, i., 396, 433, 455, 532; Temple, ii., 532; Evelyn, ii., 159; Parl. Hist., iv., 1208. As to Jones's private employment as counsel for the Massachusetts agents, see Palfrey, iii., 326, 367, 368; *ante*, 316, 336.

CHAP. VII. 1680. The duke releases West New Jersey. ment — which carefully recited the reconquest by the Dutch, and the several conveyances of the territory—the duke transferred to Byllinge, Penn, Laurie, and their associates, all the authority and power of government which in the king's two patents to him "were granted or intended to be granted to be exercised by his said Royal Highness, his heirs, assigns, deputies, officers, or agents in, upon, or in relation unto the said premises hereby confirmed."*

September. The accounts which Philip Carteret sent over of his treatment by Andros soon afterward reached London, and 10 Septem. Lady Carteret, Sir George's widow, complained to the duke, who at once said that "the Lord Proprietor should have all right done him in the enjoyment of the Province and the Government thereof; and that his Royal Highness would not in the least derogate from what he had granted to Sir George Carteret, and doth wholly disown and declare that Sir Edmund Andros had never any such order or authority from him for the doing thereof." As he had just released all claim over West Jersey to Byllinge and his friends, he determined to do the same to the claimants of 6 Septem. The duke's release of East Jersey. East Jersey. James therefore directed his counsel to prepare a deed confirming to Sir George Carteret, the grandson and heir of the original grantee, his moiety of New 16 October. Jersey. The next month, a few days before he returned to Edinburgh, the duke executed an instrument by which he relinquished all his claims to East Jersey. These meas- 6 Novem. ures were notified by Werden to Andros, to prevent any doubt of the validity of the deeds when they should be produced in New York.†

Complaints against Andros. The enemies of Sir Edmund had meanwhile not been idle. Complaints were made to the duke not only by the Quakers, but by Billop, and various other "private men;" and "suggestions" were insinuated that the governor

* Col. Doc., iii., 285; Leaming and Spicer, 412–419; Chalmers's Ann., i., 619, 626; Rev. Col., i., 150, 173; S. Smith, 125, 567; *ante*, 83, 260–268, 303–306.

† Leaming and Spicer, 685, 686; Col. Doc., iii., 285, 286; Chalmers's Ann., i., 619, 626, 627; Commissions, i., 19; Ord., Warr., etc., xxxii½, 41; Gordon, 42; Whitehead's E. J., 81, 82, 192; Index N. J. Col. Doc., 8; Eliz. Bill, 8; *ante*, 333, 334. The duke's release of 16 October, 1680, to the youthful Sir George Carteret, seems to have been made without knowing that the trustees under the will of the deceased baronet had, on the 6th of March, 1680, conveyed East Jersey to Thomas Cremer and Thomas Pocock: Eliz. Bill, 8; Leaming and Spicer, 73, 145. When that became known, the release was probably revoked, or, at all events, considered inoperative. It is not alluded to in the duke's subsequent grant of 14 March, 1683, to the twenty-four proprietors: Leaming and Spicer, 145, 604; Whitehead's East Jersey, 82, 83; Eastern Boundary of N. J., 49, 50; N. J. H. S. Proc., x., 134–139.

favored Dutchmen in trade, made laws hurtful to the English, detained ships unduly for private reasons, admitted Dutch vessels to a direct trade, or traded himself in the names of others. Moreover, James had received offers to farm his revenue in New York, which differed "so vastly" from the accounts rendered by his governor, that he resolved to send out an agent to make "a strict enquiry" on the spot. As the duke and his officers had "but loose and scattered notions" respecting the government of Andros, he was directed to return "by the first convenience" to England; "that I may have," wrote James, "the better opportunity to be informed in all those particulars from yourselfe, and that you may also have the satisfaction to obviate such matters as, if unanswered, might leave some blemish upon you, how little soever you may (in truth) have deserved any." Sir Edmund was farther directed to commit his government to Brockholls, and to give such instructions for the public safety as circumstances might require.*

CHAP. VII. 1680.

24 May. Andros recalled.

John Lewin, supposed to be "a person wholly unconcerned," was at the same time commissioned by the duke as his "Agent and servant" in New York, Albany, and his other territories in America, to inquire into all his revenue accounts, examine records, and ascertain whether trade had been obstructed, and if so, how it might be encouraged. Lewin was minutely instructed as to his duties, which were, to make such diligent inquiries as might inform the duke "of the true state and condition of all those places, in relation to the trade thereof, and of all the parts and branches of the Revenue and other profits, as well certain, as accidental or casual, which doe properly and justly belong unto me, as I am the Proprietor of the said places, or otherwise. And alsoe, that I may have a true, full, and just information and knowledge, of the reall, constant, and necessary charge and expense, which must be laid out and issued, for the maintenance and support of the government of those places." Andros was farther directed to enable Lewin to take such examinations as he might desire, under oath, within the government of New York.†

24 May. John Lewin commissioned as agent.

24 May. Lewin's Instructions.

1 July.

* Col. Doc., iii., 283, 284; Chalmers, i., 532; Dankers and Sluyter, 380.

† Col. Doc., iii., 279–284; S. Hazard, 470, 471, 472. Lewin appears to have been a Lon-

CHAP. VII. 1680. 16 October. 29 October. Andros obeys his recall.

The duke's agent reached New York while Sir Edmund was absent at Boston, whither he had gone to meet Lord Culpepper, the governor of Virginia, who was on his way to England. When Andros returned, Lewin exhibited his commission, but not his instructions from James. This sudden recall surprised the Governor of New York, who could not anticipate what had occurred about New Jersey after Lewin had left England. But Sir Edmund was too good a soldier not to know that his first duty was obedience. He therefore summoned his council to meet "the same morning;" ordered Lewin's commission to be recorded; and directed it to be communicated to the "other jurisdictions of the government," and published at New York "by ring of bell." Andros also proposed to "go home" at once. To this the council objected that much must be done before the government could be properly settled. The next day Brockholls was ordered down from Albany to take chief command of the province. All its justices were summoned to meet at the metropolitan hall. On the appointed day, the justices who could be had "in so short a time, and at that season of the year," were present. Each of them certified to the "good state" of their several precincts; and, with the advice of his council, which Lewin attended, Sir Edmund ordered "the continuing all as then settled."*

30 October. Brockholls appointed commander-in-chief.

17 Novem. Meeting of the provincial justices.

By some accident, an important enactment was neglected. The customs' rates, which, under James's instructions, had been renewed for three years by his governor in November, 1677, now ceased, by the expiration of their limited term. No order to continue them had been received from the duke; and, in the hurry of preparing to return to England, Sir Edmund either forgot the matter, or supposed it to be settled by his recent general order in council, that every thing was to remain "as then settled." Could Andros have foreseen the trouble which this technical or formal omission produced, he would hardly

The duke's customs' duties not formally renewed.

don attorney, and was at this very time appointed by the Narragansett proprietors to be one of their agents to represent them before the council: Arnold's Rhode Island, i., 463. He seems to have felt aggrieved by some legal proceedings in the Mayor's Court of New York, in a suit to which he was a party; Col. MSS., xxiii., 174; xxix., 2, 8, 18.

* Col. Doc., iii., 244, 292, 302, 308, 309, 313; Col. MSS., xxix., 258; Ord., Warrants, etc., xxxii½, 8, 9, 14; Hazard's Ann., 481; Reg. Penn., iii., 32, 33; iv., 81; *ante*, 336.

have neglected to renew the duke's customs' duties by a temporary order, which his governor was always empowered to make, "with the advice of the council."* Chap. VII. 1680.

The end of this year was marked by the appearance of a "blazing star" of extraordinary brilliancy. A few days after Brockholls left Albany, the commissaries there reported that "a dreadful comet" had appeared in the southwest, about two o'clock in the afternoon, and asked for a day of fasting and humiliation to avert the "dreadful punishments" supposed to be threatened. This pious request was granted. The comet was also observed in New Jersey, the New England colonies, and the metropolis. In Europe the brilliant apparition caused as much terror as in America; and Evelyn, in London, prayed God to "avert his judgments." But the grander Newton, by careful study, made the phenomenon a useful servant of astronomy, by demonstrating that comets revolve around the sun in parabolic orbits and in regular periods.† (9 Decem. The great comet of 1680 observed in America and Europe.)

With the new year Andros made his last arrangements for his return to England, supposing it would be short, in spite of Lewin's declarations to the contrary. Sir Edmund therefore left his wife in New York. By a special commission he appointed Brockholls to be "Commander-in-Chief of the Militia in this City, Government, and dependencies, during my absence, or 'till further orders; and in any civil matter requiring the same, with the Council to act for the continued welfare of His Majesty's subjects, as a Commander, or Chief Officer may, and ought to do, according to law and practice." The next day the governor left the metropolis, and soon afterward sailed from Sandy Hook.‡ (1681. 6 Jan'y. Andros leaves New York. 11 Jan'y.)

Not long after Andros was recalled from the government of the duke's province, he described it as follows: "At my first comeing to New Yorke, I found the place poore, unsettled, and without trade, except a few small coasters; (December. Andros's description of New York in 1681.)

* Col. Doc., iii., 217, 218, 246, 289, 292; Col. MSS., xxvi., 5; Ord., Warr., etc., xxxii½, 43, 44, 45; Council Journ., i., Introd., viii.; *ante*, 312.

† Ord., Warr., etc., xxxii½, 31; Doc. Hist., iii., 532; Hutch., i., 348; Holmes, i., 399; S. Smith's New Jersey, 136, *note;* Evelyn, ii., 163; Grahame, i., 249. See also Sir J. W. F. Herschel's masterly account of this "magnificent" comet in his "Familiar Lectures" (London, 1866), 108–111.

‡ Col. Doc., iii., 286, 309; Ord., Warr., etc., xxxii½, 27, 31, 55, 74; Hazard's Reg. Penn., iv., 82; Annals, 485; Doc. Hist., iii., 532. Secretary Nicolls appears to have accompanied or soon followed Andros to England: Col. Doc., 314, 315; Wood, 150; Col. MSS., xxx., 14.

CHAP. VII. 1681. hardly any went or came from beyond seas; and severall parts of the government never before well subjected under his Royall Highness; since which, by his Royall H.'s favour, greatly increased in people, trade, buildings, and other improvements; new townes and settlements lately built, and the Colony improved in all other advantages beyond any of our neighbours. A mold or harbour made to the city, of generall advantage as aforesaid. A market house (the only one in all those parts), and now constantly well supplied; and the navigation increased at least ten times to what it was, and plenty of money (hardly seen there before) and of all sorts of goods at reasonable rates for our owne and neighbours supplies; and noe disaster happened in any part of the government during my command there, though constantly serviceable to our English neighbours both east and west, who suffered much by the Indian war; in the composing whereof, I was a principal instrument; and also freed neare one hundred of their captives, &c. I doe not know that any have been discouraged from going to trade or settle at New Yorke; but many hundreds (I may say thousands) have actually come traded and settled; and very few (if any) have quitted the place during my being there."*

4 March. Foundation of Pennsylvania. While Andros was on his way back to England, a British royal parchment founded a new American state. As one of the owners of West Jersey, William Penn had looked closely into the condition of its neighborhood. He saw that there was a vast forest, west of the Delaware River, unoccupied by Europeans, and which, although it had been a part of the ancient Dutch "New Netherland," had not been included within the patent of Charles the Second to the Duke of York. To enterprising British subjects this region was yet a *vacant domicile*. Nevertheless, the savage owners of the Susquehanna country had recently, as has been stated, transferred it to the government of New York. Moreover, James claimed the Delaware territory adjoining Maryland as an appendage to his own province. William Penn. But William Penn was one of the most adroit Englishmen of his time. Next to George Fox, he had become the ablest minister of Quakerism. Next to Robert Barclay, Penn was

* New York Colonial Documents, iii., 313; compare *ante*, 313.

1681.

its most learned and ingenious champion. His principles of passive obedience commended him not less to the graceful and perfidious Charles than to the more arbitrary yet honest James. Besides this, Penn had a special clutch on both. His father, Sir William Penn, "the greatest hypocrite in the world," had been an admiral of England, first under its Protector, and then under its King; and he had been wise enough to secure for himself and his son the friendship of the ever-constant Duke of York. At the admiral's death, the king owed his estate some sixteen thousand pounds. Of both these circumstances Sir William Penn's cunning heir took advantage. Charles had no money; but he claimed much wild land in North America, which he could give away to a favorite, or assign in discharge of a debt. So, while the younger Penn was arguing his case as a proprietor of West Jersey before the duke's commissioners, he petitioned the king to pay off his dead admiral by granting to that admiral's son the vast region "lying north of Maryland; on the east, bounded with Delaware River; on the west, limited as Maryland; and northward, to extend as far as plantable."*

May. Penn asks for much American ground.

These were vague and startling boundaries for a royal grant in North America. By the king's order, Lord Sunderland referred this petition to the Plantation Committee, who summoned Penn before them, and asked "what extent of land he will be contented with northerly?" Penn declared himself "satisfied with three degrees to the northward; and that he is willing, in lieu of such a grant, to remit his debt due to him from his Majesty, or some part of it." This was ordered to be communicated to the agents of the Duke of York and of Lord Baltimore, both of whom were concerned. On the part of James, Sir John Werden objected to any interference with the Delaware territory, which was "an appendix" to New York; and Lord Baltimore's agents prayed that there should be no encroachment on Maryland. Penn, however, represented "his case and circumstances" so skillfully that the duke, who had just resigned all claim over New Jersey, recommended the king to grant him the land north of Newcastle, on the west side

1 June.

14 June. Penn asked what will content him.

23 June.

Maryland and New York concerned.

16 October.

* Pepys, ii., 60; Hazard's Reg. Penn., i., 269, 341–343; Annals, 474; Proud, i., 167–170; Chalmers, i., 635; Dixon, 173, 174; Grahame, i., 492–499; Bancroft, ii., 330–362; Macaulay, i., 502; *ante*, 4, 328, 339.

CHAP. VII. 1680. of the Delaware, "beginning about the latitude of forty degrees, and extending northwards and westwards as far as his Majesty pleaseth."*

11 Novem. The draft of a patent, which Penn had himself modeled after Lord Baltimore's Maryland charter, was revised by Sir Robert Sawyer, the new attorney general, and its boundaries were adjusted. 1681. January. Chief Justice North added clauses to secure the king's sovereignty and the power of Parliament; and at the request of Bishop Compton, of London, the interests of the Church of England were specially guarded. 24 Febr'y. Penn's charter for his province. At length the charter was submitted to the king, that he might name his fresh American province. Penn suggested "New Wales." This was objected to by the Welsh secretary, Blathwayt. Penn then proposed "Sylvania," because of the magnificent forests of the region. But Charles, out of respect to his deceased admiral, "would give it" his name; and the new province was accordingly called "Pennsylvania."†

4 March. The English charter for Pennsylvania. The charter of Pennsylvania, as it passed the English great seal, granted to William Penn, and his heirs and assigns, "all that tract or part of land in America, with all the islands therein contained, as the same is bounded on the east by Delaware River, from twelve miles distance northward of Newcastle Town unto the three and fortieth degree of northern latitude, if the said river doth extend so far northwards; but if the said river shall not extend so far northward, then, by the said river so far as it doth extend, and from the head of the said river the eastern bounds are to be determined by a meridian line to be drawn from the head of the said river unto the said three and fortieth degree; The said lands to extend westwards five degrees in longitude, to be computed from the said eastern bounds; and the said lands to be bounded on the north by the beginning of the three and fortieth degree of northern latitude, and on the south by a circle drawn at twelve miles distance from Newcastle, northwards and westwards unto the beginning of the fortieth degree of northern latitude; and then by a straight line westwards

* Hazard's Reg. Penn., i., 269, 270; Annals, 475–480; Chalmers, i., 635, 636, 655–657; Proud, i., 170, 269.

† Hazard's Reg., i., 269, 270, 273, 274, 297; Annals, 480–500; Chalmers, i., 636, 657, 659; Dixon, 182; Sewel, 576; Hist. Mag., viii., 180, 181; Penn. Arch., i., 141.

to the limit of longitude above mentioned." Of this territory Penn was made the absolute proprietor, with power to ordain laws, appoint officers, and enjoy the general authority of a feudal chief. But all laws were to be assented to by the freemen of his province, and to be subject to the king's approval; and no taxes were to be laid nor revenue raised unless by a Provincial Assembly; reserving, always, the supreme power of the Parliament of England to regulate commercial duties. Episcopalian clergymen, approved by the Bishop of London, were also to "reside within the said Province, without any denial or molestation whatsoever."*

CHAP. VII. 1681. Episcopacy provided for in Pennsylvania.

After procuring a letter from the king declaring his patent, Penn appointed his kinsman, William Markham, to be his deputy governor, and dispatched him to take possession of his province. Andros, who was now in London, was also directed by Werden to notify his subordinates in New York of the Pennsylvania charter. Markham sailed at once to Boston, and, on reaching New York, received from Brockholls instructions to the duke's officers within the limits of Pennsylvania to obey the government of its actual owner. The surrender was accordingly completed; preliminary covenants were made with the savages; and Markham, in an interview with Lord Baltimore, found that a vexatious question of boundaries was to be settled between the proprietors of Maryland and Pennsylvania.†

2 April. 10 April. Markham comes to America. 12 May. 21 June. Brockholls relinquishes Pennsylvania to Markham. September.

Meanwhile, Philip Carteret, informed of the Duke of York's action in regard to East Jersey, had issued a proclamation disowning the authority of the Governor of New York. A few weeks afterward Brockholls sent to Carteret a copy of Warden's notification, and promised that when the duke's deeds were produced he would respect them. Until then he required Carteret to desist from meddling with the government.‡

2 March. 14 April. Carteret and East Jersey. 18 April.

* The Charter of Pennsylvania is printed at length in Colden, ii., 164–182; Proud, i., 171–187; Hazard's Register, i., 293–297; Annals, 488–499; Colonial Rec. Penn., i., 17–26; Chalmers, i., 636–639.

† Hazard's Register, i., 305; iii., 33; Annals, 501–516, 524, 538; Upland Records, 195, 196; Chalmers, i., 640, 641; Proud, i., 189–196; Dixon, 191; Colonial Doc., iii., 286, 290; Col. MSS., xxi., 143, 144; Ord., Warr., etc., xxxii½, 49, 50. Andros reached Portsmouth from New York on 1 March, 1681: Ord., Warr., etc., xxxii½, 46.

‡ Leaming and Spicer, 685, 686; Ord., Warr., etc., xxxii½, 41, 42, 43; Whitehead's East Jersey, 75, 76; *ante*, 342. Philip Carteret now followed the example of his kinsman, James, in 1673 (*ante*, 190, *note*), by wedding a New York wife. On the 26th of March, 1681, he obtained a license from Brockholls to marry Mary Elizabeth Smith, widow of William Law-

CHAP. VII. About the middle of July Secretary Bollen returned from London with the desired papers, and with orders

1681. Carteret claims Staten Island. from Lady Carteret "to lay claim to Staten Island, as belonging to us, according to His Royal Highness's grant." This was an ill-founded pretense. As early as 1669 Staten Island had been "adjudged to belong to New York." This judgment had been respected by all parties; and in 1670 Lovelace had bought the island for the Duke of York from its savage claimants. With a knowledge of these facts, Sir George had obtained from the duke, in 1674, a new grant of New Jersey to himself, in severalty. Yet now his widow, seeing that James was exiled in Scotland, thought that she might win Staten Island if she made a bold push. Accord-
21 July. ingly, Bollen, in behalf of the dowager, submitted various papers to Brockholls; claimed Staten Island for her as a part of East Jersey, and demanded its surrender. No notice being taken of this demand, Bollen was sent again to Fort James with more documents. These, being examined
26 July. in the New York Council, were found insufficient to enable Carteret "to act in or assume the government of New Jersey," and Brockholls required him to desist until he should, agreeably to his parole, "produce and show a sufficient authority." No allusion was made to the claim of Staten Island on the part of its deceased proprietor's dowager;
21 July. but in writing to Andros and to Werden, Brockholls de-
30 July. clared that he would not part with that island unless by special orders from the duke.*

28 July. Carteret naturally complained of Brockholls's "uncivil answer," and acquainted the grasping widow that the New York authorities would not surrender to her Staten Island, which, he pronounced, "is as much your Honor's due as
30 July. any other part of this Province." Brockholls, however, while denying Carteret's authority, did not disturb his local
23 July. government. An East Jersey Assembly was quietly held at Elizabethtown, which voted the proceedings of Andros
19 October to 2 Novem. illegal. Nevertheless, the old spirit of discord broke out again. In the autumn, the Assembly quarreled with Car-

rence, of Flushing, on Long Island, and the wedding took place the next month: Ord., Warr., etc., xxxii½, 39; Thompson's Long Island, ii., 364, 365; Whitehead, 85; Hatfield, 195; Col. Doc., ii., 607, *note*.

* Ord., Warr., etc., xxxii½, 53, 54, 55, 57; Col. Doc., iii., 286; Leaming and Spicer, 686; Whitehead, 77, 216; Mass. H. S. Coll., xxxvii., 315; *ante*, 149, 166, 268, 334.

teret and his council, respecting the right of the proprietors to alter their "concessions," and the governor dissolved his refractory Legislature. This was Philip Carteret's last important public act. East New Jersey soon passed into other hands, and its first governor gave up the authority he had so long exercised.*

The recall of Andros, the presence of Lewin, and the incapacity of Brockholls, meanwhile produced insubordination throughout New York, which was weakly attempted to be checked. At length, provincial trouble culminated in the metropolis. In the hurry of his departure, Sir Edmund, as has been told, neglected to renew, by a special order, the Duke of York's customs' duties, which had expired, by their three years' limitation, in November, 1680. This oversight being "publicly known to the merchants," they refused to pay any duties to the duke on what they imported into his province. It does not appear that the recusants abated a farthing from the prices of the goods they sold to consumers; but they nevertheless seem to have thought—as, perhaps, modern smugglers and cheats often think—that any compensatory evasion of the revenue laws of a country is a proper, if not a patriotic felony. This seems to have been the moral philosophy of the "merchants" of New York in the spring of 1681. While Brockholls was at Albany, looking after Indian affairs, and Collector Dyer lay "ill of a fever" in the metropolis, a pink from London came into port, and her cargo was taken to the warehouses of her consignees, who "absolutely" refused to pay any customs' duties to the duke's provincial officers. In this quandary, Brockholls, when he got back to town, summoned his council. Wanting the guidance of the experienced Secretary Nicolls, that body decided that there was "no power or authority" to continue expired taxes "without orders from His Royal Highness." This may have been convenient shirking, but it was not even provincial statesmanship. James himself thought so when this

Insubordination in New York.

The merchants refuse to pay duties.

9 May.

14 May. Decision of Brockholls's Council.

* Ord., Warr., etc., xxxii½, 57; Leaming and Spicer, 137, 138, 687; Col. Doc., iii., 293–300; Chalmers, i., 620; Gordon, 48; Whitehead, 80, 192–195; Hatfield, 195, 210, 211, 212. It would seem that Lady Carteret did not know or recognize the conveyance to Cremer and Pocock of 6 March, 1680 (*ante*, 342, *note*); and Philip Carteret (who knew all the facts about Staten Island belonging to New York) may have been sarcastic when he told her ladyship that it was as much her "due" as any part of New Jersey: compare *ante*, 149, 150, 166, 268; Hist. Mag., x., 297–299; N. J. H. S. Proc., x., 88–158; i. (ii.), 31–36.

CHAP. VII. 1681.

"scruple" was reported to him. Yet the pusillanimity of Brockholls and his council made a colonial revolution. Their inaction may have been caused by the recent opinion of Sir William Jones, and the consequent freedom of trade which was already prospering New Jersey at the expense of New York.*

Dyer, who, besides being collector, was a counselor and the mayor of the city, was immediately sued in the ordinary courts, where he was "cast," for detaining goods for customs, and forced to deliver them without payment. This was decisive. An accusation of high treason was quickly brought in the mayor's court by Samuel Winder, of Staten Island, against Dyer, for having levied the duties he had recently taken. Thereupon the aldermen and court "intimated" the case to the commander and his council, who committed Dyer for trial at the next general assizes. But, upon his request, a special court was summoned. It met accordingly; a grand jury was sworn; witnesses were examined; and an indictment for traitorously exercising "regal power and authority over the King's subjects," contrary to Magna Charta, the Petition of Right, and the Statutes of England, was found against the duke's collector. He was taken into custody at once by High Sheriff Younge, and Brockholls demanded from him the seal of the city and his commission as mayor. These Dyer refused to surrender, because he had received them from their common superior, Andros.

31 May. Dyer sued, and charged with high treason.

29 June.

30 June.

The next day Dyer was arraigned. Instead of demurring, he pleaded "*not guilty*" to his indictment. A jury was sworn, and twenty witnesses were examined for the prosecution. The defendant then required to know "the authority and commission by which the court sat; saying if they proceeded by His Majesty's Letters Patents to His Royal Highness, he had the same authority;—and one part could not try the other." After consultation, the unlearned court decided that, as Dyer had questioned their authority, he should be sent to England, "to be proceeded against as his Majesty and Council shall direct." Samuel Winder, his accuser, was also required to give five thousand pounds'

1 July. Dyer tried, and his case referred to the king.

* Col. MSS., xxx., 26, 27; Ord,Warr., etc., xxxii½, 31, 43-46, 53; Col. Doc., iii., 246, 289, 292, 318; Doc. Hist., iii., 533, 534; Chalmers, i., 582; Wood's L. I., 99; Council Journals, i., Introd., viii.; *ante*, 341, 344.

security to prosecute Dyer in England. West, the clerk of the court, excused its irregular action because of the novelty of the charge of high treason, "and the present confusion and discord in the government here." Yet these proceedings against the duke's collector "had the greatest effect in laying in ruins that system of despotism which had so long afflicted the people." Trade was now substantially free; and the absence of both the governor and the secretary of the province gave an opportunity to utter freely the voice of the people of New York.*

CHAP. VII.

1681.

21 June. The Pennsylvania charter helps the movement in New York.

This opportunity was helped by the recent visit of Penn's deputy, Markham, to the metropolis. It was soon noised that in the last English-American province established by its sovereign, no laws could be passed, nor revenue levied, without the assent of a majority of colonial freemen represented in a local assembly. The popular sentiment of New York, which, from the days of Kieft and Stuyvesant, had maintained the Dutch principle of "taxation only by consent," was emboldened. The metropolitan jury which indicted Dyer accordingly presented to the Court of Assizes the want of a Provincial Assembly as a "grievance." Upon this, John Younge, the High Sheriff of Long Island, was appointed to draft a petition to the Duke of York, and his work was adopted by the court. It represented that the inhabitants of New York had for many years "groaned under inexpressible burdens, by having an arbitrary and absolute power used and exercised" over them; whereby a revenue had been exacted against their wills, their trade burdened, and their liberty enthralled, contrary to the privileges of a royal subject; so that they had become "a reproach" to their neighbors in the king's other colonies, "who flourish under the fruition and protection of His Majesty's unparallelled form and method of government in his realm of England." The duke was therefore besought that his province might, for the future, be ruled by a Governor, Council, and Assembly—"which Assembly to be duly elected and chosen by the freeholders of this, Your Royal Highnesses' Colony; as is usual and practicable within the realm of England, and other of his Majesty's planta-

29 June. Presentment of the grand jury.

Petition of the Court of Assizes to the duke.

* Colonial Doc., iii., 287, 288, 289, 291, 318, 320, 354; Ord., Warr., etc., xxxii½, 48, 53, 54; Chalmers, Ann., i., 582, 583, 619, 627; Rev. Col., i., 144; Wood's L. I., 150; Whitehead's East Jersey, 124; Contributions, etc., 81.

tions." This allusion to the king's "plantations," outside of his insular sovereignty, could hardly have meant his corporation of Massachusetts, where it was notorious that not "freeholders," but only puritanical church members (with rare exceptions) could vote for local magistrates. The examples of Pennsylvania, New Jersey, Maryland, and Virginia, in which no such sectarian exclusiveness existed, were probably in the minds of these early New York Democrats. The old Dutch province having never been governed by a royal English corporation, her people could not believe that a colonial minority should rule the roost.*

The New York idea of colonial government.

The same ship which took Dyer to England conveyed this action of the New York Court of Assizes. In writing to Werden, Brockholls attributed to want of orders from the duke the disorder of his province. "Authority and magistracy is grown so low that it can scarce maintain the public peace and quiet of the government; scurrilous persons daily laying charges of Treasôn against the magistrates, thereby to destroy authority, and bring all into confusion." * * * "I shall never make a perfect good settlement, 'till orders from His Royal Highness for the more strengthening and continuance or alteration of the Government as established, which is much disliked by the People, who generally cry out for an Assembly, and to that end a Petition was ordered to be drawn up and sent to His Royal Highness, from and in the name of the Court of Assizes."

21 July. Brockholls's complaints to England.

21 July. In his letter to Andros, Brockholls reported that the customs were "wholly destroyed." No revenue was left but the rates on Long Island, which the people might not pay; and the insolence of those who accused the magistrates of violating the English Magna Charta caused disorders in New York.†

2 May. Order from Andros.

Meanwhile, Andros, on reaching London, had authorized Brockholls to act as receiver general of all the duke's provincial revenues. Brockholls, hoping to give effect to this direction, sent orders to Delavall at Esopus, and Livingston at Albany. But Sir Edmund's after-thought was too late.

10 August. 17 August. 3 Septem.

* Ord., Warr., etc., xxxii½, 49, 50, 54; S. Hazard's Ann. Penn., 490, 495, 504, 515; Wood's L. I., 35, 99, 100, 150, 178, 179; Thompson's L. I., i., 160; Smith's N. Y., i., 67; Chalmers's Ann., i., 583; Rev. Col., i., 145; *ante*, i., 437, 442, 473, 572; ii., 349. The Petition of the New York Court of Assizes, of June, 1681, is in Appendix, Note D., p. 658.

† Ord., Warr., etc., xxxii½, 53, 54, 55; Council Journals, i., Introd., ix.

CHAP. VII.

1681.

17 Septem. Brockholls to Andros.

The whining commander-in-chief reported to Andros: "Nothing is paid in by any; and though since, I have done what was possible to get the excise kept up, my endeavors therein have proved ineffectual—the merchants taking advantage of Courts, who, being scared, refuse to justify and maintain my orders. * * * Here it was never worse. A Government wholly overthrown, and in the greatest confusion and disorder possible. Orders from the Duke for general material things, in your absence, are extremely wanting; nothing continuing as they were, nor can be again settled without it, which I hope shall not be long." To add to his other difficulties, Brockholls had been obliged to suspend Dervall from the council for misbehavior; and, in the absence of Nicolls and Dyer, his only advisers were the "small number" of Phillipse and Van Cortlandt.*

27 Sept. Long Island disaffected.

Long Island appeared to be the chief scene of disaffection. Persons had already been arrested at Huntington and elsewhere. It was accordingly ordered in council that the magistrates on Long Island should prevent any disorderly meetings, arrest such as might attend them, and keep the peace and quiet of the government as now established from any innovation or disturbance.†

6 October. The Court of Assizes rebukes disaffection.

At the regular session of the Court of Assizes, an order was made "against persons exhibiting and preferring divers causeless and vexatious accusations and indictments into the Courts within this Government, against magistrates and others concerned in the public affairs of the Government, thereby causing great trouble and disturbance." At the same court it was directed that "rude and unlawful sports, to the dishonor of God, and profanation of his holy day," which had become common among the negro and Indian slaves at their meetings on Sundays, should be prevented.‡

1 Novem. Sedition in New York. 30 Decem.

In spite of the Court of Assizes, the eastern towns of Long Island would be, what Brockholls thought, "seditious." Josiah Hobart, of Easthampton, who was accused of stirring up the people of Southold to oppose his administration, was ar-

* Ord., Warr., etc., xxxii½, 59, 60, 62, 63, 69, 70, 73, 74; Col. Doc., iii., 289, *note*. Andros seems to have determined not to return to New York, for his wife now sailed in the ship Beaver to join him in England: Ord., Warr., etc., xxxii½, 74, 93; Hough's Pemaquid Papers, 48; Whitmore's Andros, 21, 22.

† Ord., Warr., etc., xxxii½, 74, 75; Wood, 99; *ante*, 351.

‡ Colonial MSS., xxx., 36; Minutes of Common Council, i., 162–164; Dunlap, ii.; App., cxxix.; S. Hazard, 531; Newcastle Records.

CHAP. VII. 1681. rested and bound over to be tried at the next assizes. The feeling of discontent spread to Esopus, where Delavall was 10 Novem. directed to prevent "all undue and unlawful meetings of the people without authority." Much of this sentiment of insubordination arose out of the duke's own action in recalling Andros, and in sending over Lewin as his agent. Lewin showed himself unequal to his duty, and by his stupidity 15 Septem. must have disappointed his patron. The city authorities The metropolis rebukes Lewin. of New York took occasion, in his own presence, to protest against Lewin's unlawful proceedings, in taking private oaths and complaints, to the "scandal, blemish, and disparagement of several of his Majesty's servants." Well might 14 Decem. Brockholls end his correspondence for the year with Andros at London by a devout prayer for "speedy orders and directions for better settlement."*

Meanwhile Andros remained in London, without seeing the Duke of York, who was still in Scotland. Sir Edmund Andros annoyed in London. was annoyed by complaints of some he had offended in New York; and a verdict of forty-five pounds was recovered against him by Milborne, whom he had imprisoned in December, 1678.†

From Edinburgh, James, in answer to Brockholls's re- 8 August. The Duke of York's orders to Brockholls. port of affairs in New York, reproved him for not renewing the customs' rates, which, with the advice of the council, he had the power to do, adding, "I wonder you should thus long have left so material a point undetermined; and I expect you should settle and continue by some temporary order, the same payments of customs and other public duties, as have been lately established and collected, until further orders from me, who at the present have several things in my thoughts which I hope may conduce much to the good and satisfaction of all the inhabitants and traders within 27 August. that government." Brockholls was also authorized by the duke to continue all subordinate officers in their places.‡

Not long afterward, Dyer reached England, a prisoner, 14 Septem. Dyer set free. and, while the duke was absent in Scotland, his case was heard before the king in Privy Council. It was ordered

* Col. MSS., xxx., 47, 48, 49, 50; Ord., Warr., etc., xxxii½, 85, 86, 87, 88, 89, 93, 94, 95; Minutes of N. Y. Common Council, i., 155–158; S. Hazard's Ann. Penn., 481, 503, 531; Col. Doc., iii., 302–316.

† Col. Doc., iii., 286, 291, 300, 301, 621, 680, 727; K. B. Rep.; *ante*, 321, 342.

‡ Col. Doc., iii., 291, 292; Commissions, i., 27; Ord., Warr., xxxii½, iii.

that the defendant should go free upon his giving security to appear when summoned to answer the charge for which he had been prosecuted by Winder.*

CHAP. VII.

1681. December.

Lewin's report. 24 Decem.

At length Lewin returned to London, and submitted an unskillful report to the duke's commissioners. A copy of it was given to Andros, who answered its charges. Both parties were then heard by Churchill and Jeffreys, the duke's attorney and solicitor general. After examining Dyer, Nicolls, and others, they reported that Andros had not "misbehaved himself, or broken the trust reposed in him by his Royal Highness, in the administration of his Government, nor doth it appear that he hath any way defrauded or mismanaged his revenue." Dyer, they thought, "has done nothing amiss." Both he and the governor appeared to "have behaved themselves very well in their several stations."†

1682. January.

Report of the duke's commissioners.

Andros being thus cleared of blame, and complimented on his administration, was made a gentleman of the king's Privy Chamber, which post, of course, required him to live in or near London.‡ Werden accordingly instructed Brockholls "to keep all things within that government of New York and its dependencies in quiet and good order," and hinted that the duke would "condescend to the desires of that colony in granting them equal privileges in choosing an Assembly et cet, as the other English Plantations in America have. But if this be, it will be upon a supposition that the inhabitants will agree to raise money to discharge the public debts, and to settle such a fund for the future as may be sufficient for the maintenance of the garrison and government there." On this "great point" Brockholls was farther instructed "privately to sound the inclinations of the principal inhabitants there."§

11 Feb'y. Farther orders to Brockholls.

After much hesitation, the king had meanwhile resolved to stand up boldly against those of his subjects who plotted to exclude the Duke of York from the throne. Charles therefore dissolved the Parliament which he had summoned at Oxford, and determined to govern without any.

* Col. Doc., iii., 318, 320; *ante*, 352.

† Col. Doc., iii., 302–316; Chalmers's Ann., i., 582; *ante*, 300.

‡ Col. Doc., ii., 741. In 1683 the island of Alderney was granted, on a long lease, to Andros and his wife, and he spent much time there and in Guernsey, of which he was bailiff: Hutch. Coll., 542; Whitmore's Andros, 22; *ante*, 262.

§ Col. Doc., iii., 317; Chalmers's Ann., i., 583, 604.

CHAP. VII. 1682. 11 March. James in England again.

James now returned from Scotland, and the royal brothers met at Newmarket. While there, the duke considered the affairs of New York. He saw that no revenue could be collected in his province at present, unless he yielded to the wishes of its people for an Assembly; and James did not like popular gatherings. He had expressed his distrust of them to his provincial governor. But it was now a mere question of finance whether New York should be a drain on his purse, as it was, or whether he should sell it. Penn's closet-advice seems to have determined James to keep his province and give it some franchises.*

28 March. The duke's orders to Brockholls about New York.

So the duke, at Newmarket, instructed Brockholls, his representative in New York, "In confirmation of what my Secretary lately wrote to you, I send this to tell you that I intend to establish such a form of Government at New York as shall have all the advantages and privileges to the inhabitants and traders there which His Majesty's other Plantations in America do enjoy; particularly in the choosing of an Assembly and in all other things, as near as may be agreeable to the laws of England. But I shall expect that the country of New York and its dependencies shall provide some certain funds for the necessary support of the government and garrison, and for discharging the arrears which are or shall be incurred, since the obstructions that have lately been to the collection of the public revenue there. Wherefore you are to use all diligence to induce the people there of best note and estate to dispose themselves and their friends to a cheerful compliance in this point; and you may assure them that whatsoever shall be thus raised shall be applied to those public uses. For I seek the common good and protection of that country, and the increase of their trade, before any advantages to myself in this matter."†

But it was several months before James could execute

* Clarke's James II., i., 673–730; Dalrymple, i., 17, 106; Col. Doc., iii., 230, 235, 286, 355; ix., 165; Chalmers's Ann., i., 581, 583, 600; Rev. Col., i., 145, 152, 173; Mem. H. S. Penn., i., 444; Bancroft, ii., 413, 414; *ante*, 272. I can not see the propriety of the reference, in Introd. to Leg. Journals of Council of N.Y., xvi., to Pepys's Diary of January, 1668, as a reason for the Duke of York's action in 1682. If Anne Hyde, the first Duchess of York, saved £5000 a year, and laid it out in jewels, in 1668, it does not appear that the second duchess, Mary of Modena (*ante*, 248), did so in 1682, when the duke resolved to give an Assembly to New York. It is more likely that the Duchess of Portsmouth's importunity to Charles had something to do with the matter. The revenue of New York was £2000 in 1682, and did not reach £5000 a year until 1687: Dunlap, ii., App., cxlvii.

† Col. Doc., iii., 317, 318; Chalmers's Ann., i., 605.

the purpose he so clearly announced. He went back to CHAP. VII.
Scotland, and then returned to London. In that interval,
William Penn, under the pressure of "friends," and with 1682. 25 April.
the aid of Algernon Sidney, drew up and published a frame 5 May. Penn's
of government and laws for Pennsylvania, the large benev- frame of govern-
olence of which—surpassing the liberality of Maryland— ment.
furnished a model worthy to be carefully studied by the
proprietor of New York.*

After waiting in vain several months for his prosecutor
to appear, Dyer petitioned the king to be acquitted and al- 29 June.
lowed to proceed against Winder. It was accordingly ordered in council that he be discharged from his bond, which 30 Septem.
was delivered to him, so that he might take his remedy at Dyer discharged.
law. In recompense for his losses, Dyer was soon after- 1683.
ward appointed surveyor general of his majesty's customs 4 January.
in the American Plantations.†

In the mean time, Randolph, returning in disgust from 16 April.
his second visit to Boston, had urged legal proceedings to Randolph and Cul-
vacate the charter of Massachusetts. Lord Culpepper, of pepper against
Virginia, also advised that the king should send a governor Massachu- setts.
general to New England, without which his colonies "could
not be brought to a perfect settlement." Charles, now almost absolute, determined to act with effect against his father's corporation of Massachusetts Bay. He had already 1680.
granted a patent to Secretary Blathwayt to be surveyor and 19 May.
auditor general of all his revenues in America, with power
to appoint such inferior officers as the lords of the treasury
should direct. Blathwayt accordingly appointed Randolph 1681.
to be his deputy in all the New England colonies except 15 October. Randolph
New Hampshire. With this power Randolph went back deputy to Blathwayt.
to Boston, bearing a letter from the king requiring his cor- 21 October. The king's
poration of Massachusetts forthwith to send over agents to letter to Massachu-
excuse its irregularities, in default of which a writ of *quo* setts.
warranto would be prosecuted, and the charter granted by
his father be "legally evicted and made void." To this

* Colonial Rec. Penn., i., 29–42; Colden, ii., 182–206; Proud, i., 196–200; ii., App., 5–20; Chalmers, i., 642, 660; Dixon, 184–186; Grahame, i., 314, 506–509; Bancroft, ii., 366, 367; Kent's Commentaries, ii., 35, 36.

† Col. Doc., iii., 318–321; Chalmers, i., 583; Mass. Rec., v., 460, 530. After a cool reception in Massachusetts, in October, 1684, Dyer went to Pennsylvania, and thence to Jamaica: Penn. Coll. Rec., i., 148, 197, 198, 209–211; Val. Man., 1853, 388; 1864, 580. In June, 1683, Brockholls ordered the justices at Gravesend not to let Winder plead before them, because of his malicious behavior to Dyer: Entries, xxxiii., 65, 66; *ante*, 352, 353.

CHAP. VII. peremptory command the Puritan colony was obliged to
succumb. She could no longer pretend to be independent,
1681. while she set up her royal patent. Her only alternative
was open, manly rebellion. But this would have been by
1682. no means profitable; and so, with a very bad grace, her
23 March. corporate authorities deputed Joseph Dudley and John
Dudley and Richards agents. Richards to represent them in England. "Necessity, and
not duty," obliged this action. And now Massachusetts
adopted the maxim attributed to the Jesuits, "the end jus-
31 May. tifies the means." She accordingly provided her agents
with a "credit for large sums of money to purchase, if they
can, what their promises cannot obtain." This "singular
Bribery by Massachusetts. method" of Puritanism, in offering a bribe for the king's
"private service," was approved, if not advised, by Edward
Cranfield, the royal governor of New Hampshire, who had
just come from England.*

The domestic affairs of New York continued to be disturbed, in spite of Brockholls's efforts, and his announcement of the duke's orders to continue all magistrates in
9 March. Troubles in New York. their places until farther directions. Esopus and Albany
were troublesome, but Long Island was the chief scene of
17 Febr'y. 22 Feb'y. opposition; and Richard Cromwell and Thomas Hicks, two
of the justices of the North Riding, were ordered to be arrested for disaffection to the government. William Nicolls
2 October. and John Tudor were afterward directed to appear at the
next Court of Assizes, and prosecute for the king all indictments found.†

11 May. Connecticut now took the opportunity to revive her
boundary question. Counselor Frederick Phillipse, having bought of the Indians a tract of land on the Pocantico Creek, or Mill River, just above the present village of Tarrytown, "whereon to set a mill," had obtained a patent for
it from Andros; and began to improve his property. Hear-
Connecticut boundary. ing of this, the Connecticut authorities wrote to Brockholls,
claiming that, according to the boundary agreement of 1664,

* Chalmers's Annals, i., 410–413, 443–459; Hutch. Mass., i., 330–337; Coll., 526–540; Mass. Rec., v., 333, 334, 346–349, 521–529; Mass. H. S. Coll., xxxv., 52, 56; Col. Rec. Conn., iii., 303, 307; N.Y. Col. MSS., xxix., 97; Bancroft, ii., 123; Barry, i., 465–474; Palfrey, iii., 288, 342–369, 407, 410, 411, 424; *ante*, 336, 337.

† Ord., Warr., etc., xxxii½, 100, 108, 109, 111; Entries, xxxiii., 10, 11, 17; Col. MSS., xxx., 64, 65. Mr. H. P. Hedges, in his anniversary oration at Easthampton in 1850, says that an address to Brockholls was adopted in June, 1682, at the general training of the militia. But I think this address must have been drawn up in 1683, and was intended for Dongan, as it is word for word the same as that of 10 September, 1683, in Thomp. L. I., i., 315; ii., 228.

that colony, and not New York, owned the territory from Mamaroneck north-northwestward, touching the Hudson River southward of Phillipse's mills, and extending northward to the Massachusetts line; and they had the audacity to desire, in very careful words, that the duke's officers would countenance their attempted swindle. Brockholls knew that Connecticut was never to approach within twenty miles of the Hudson River. He therefore reproved her for so knavishly returning the "kind treatment" she had received from New York, and referred the question to the Duke of York, who soon caused it to be fairly settled.*

29 May.

Referred to the duke.

Another intercolonial incident happened this summer. John Williams, having captured a ketch from the Spaniards at Cuba, named her the "Ruth," turned pirate, robbed at Accomac in Virginia, and attempted to seize Lord Baltimore in Maryland, to get from him a large ransom. With another sloop, Williams then went to the east of Long Island, and captured several vessels, one of which belonged to Justice Arnold, of Southold. Brockholls at once directed all pirates to be brought to New York. The sloop Planter's Adventure, Captain Tristram Stevens, was also sent to cruise against the pirates. Several were secured by the authorities of Rhode Island and Connecticut; and Brockholls, having arrested two, dispatched them to Sir Henry Chicheley, the deputy governor of Virginia, to be dealt with there according to law.†

June.

New York and Maryland.

28 July.

7 August.

14 August.

Pirates sent back. 1, 8, 28, and 30 Septem.

The ecclesiastical affairs of New York also required attention. Eliphalet Jones, the minister at Huntington, on Long Island, was dealt with for denying baptism to the children of those whom he charged with "loose lives." At Staten Island and Albany there was trouble about their clergymen. In the metropolis, Domine Van Nieuwenhuysen, the patriarch, went to his rest; and the Consistory of the Dutch Church called, as his successor, Domine Henricus Selyns, who, having refused their invitation in 1670, now returned to America, and began a new and laborious service.‡

Church affairs in New York.

* Ord., Warr., etc., xxxii½, 121, 122, 123, 124; Colonial MSS., xxx., 87; lxix., 7; Col. Rec. Conn., iii., 100, 313, 314; Report of Boundary Commissioners, 1857, 42, 43, 105, 106; Bolton's Westchester, i., 175, 176, 316–319; Col. Doc., iii., 333; *ante*, 53–56.

† Ord., Warr., etc., xxxii½, 138–147, 156, 157; Entries, xxxiii., 2, 3, 8, 9; Col. MSS., xxx., 111, 117, 118, 119; Col. Rec. Conn., iii., 314–320; R. I. Rec., iii., 119, 120; Arnold, i., 469.

‡ Col. Doc., iii., 646; Doc. Hist., ii., 247; iii., 210, 244, 533–535; Thompson, i., 481; Col. MSS., xxx., 97; Murph. Anthol.; Dank. and Sluyt. Jour.; Corr. Cl. Amst.; *ante*, 175, 331.

CHAP. VII.

1682. The Jesuits among the Iroquois.

Meanwhile the Jesuit missions among the Iroquois had been declining. In 1680 James de Lamberville left Caghnawaga, and joined his brother John, the superior, at Onondaga; while Vaillant remained a year longer alone at Tionnontoguen, and then gave up the Mohawk mission. Millet staid among the Oneidas, and Carheil among the Cayugas. Raffeix having left the Senecas, Garnier remained alone among them, but with less influence—probably caused by the visit of La Salle, and, perhaps, by the presence of Father Melithon Watteau in Fort Conty, at Niagara.*

1679. 7 August. La Salle in the West.

After leaving the Upper Niagara, La Salle had sailed in the Griffin through Lake Erie, traversed the other lakes beyond, and anchored safely in Green Bay. The bark was

18 Septem.

quickly freighted with furs, and sent back to Niagara, with orders to return to the head of Lake Michigan; and La Salle, with his exploring party, coasted southward in canoes. But the Griffin was never heard of again, and the first decked vessel built in Western New York is supposed to

1680. January.

have foundered between Green Bay and Mackinac. Disheartened by his reverses, La Salle built a fort on the Illinois River, below Lake Peoria, which he appropriately

29 Feb'y. Hennepin's rascality.

named "Crèvecœur." Hennepin was now dispatched, with two Frenchmen, in a canoe, down the Illinois, to explore the Upper Mississippi. The father accordingly visited the great falls of the latter river, which he named after his patron, Saint Anthony of Padua. Afterward he met some Canadian fur-traders, under Daniel du Luth, with whom he

1681. 6 April.

came back to Michilimackinack. After remaining there until Easter, he returned to Niagara, whence he revisited the great Seneca village of Todehacto, or Conception,

26 May.

where, on Whitsunday, he conferred with Tegancourt, the chief of the tribe. At Montreal Hennepin was cordially received by Frontenac, to whom he gave "an exact ac-

November.

count" of his adventures; and he soon afterward sailed from Quebec to France, without having met La Salle since their parting at Fort Crèvecœur, in February, 1680.†

* Col. Doc., iii., 518; ix., 171, 190, 193, 762, 838; Shea's Missions, 274, 286, 289, 293, 294, 313, 374, 410; Disc. Miss., 91; Sparks's La Salle, 26; *ante*, 326, 327.

† Hennepin's Louisiana, 50–187, 188–312; New Discovery, 77–144, 145–299; La Potherie, ii., 137–140; Hist. Col. Lou., i., 54, 56, 200–214; N. Y. H. S. Coll., ii., 245, 246; Col. Doc., iii., 254; ix., 131, 132, 135, 141, 158, 334, 795; Col. MSS., xxxv., 160; Shea's Discovery, 91–147, 161; Sparks's La Salle, 26–59, 78–93; Charlevoix, ii., 267, 271; Garneau, i., 239–241; *ante*, 321, 324. It need hardly be repeated to scholars that Hennepin's afterthought, in his "New

After dispatching Hennepin up the Mississippi, La Salle CHAP. VII.
left Tonty in command of Crèvecœur, and returned on foot 1680.
to Fort Frontenac, after directing a new fort, which he 2 March.
named "Saint Louis," to be built near the present town of La Salle's adventures.
Peoria, in Illinois. Before this fort was completed, six hundred Iroquois and Miamis, commanded by the Seneca chief Tegancourt, attacked the weaker prairie warriors of 10 Septem.
the Illinois, of whom twelve hundred were slain or taken captive. La Salle, on reaching Cataracouy, had meanwhile found himself overwhelmed with misfortunes—"in a word, that except the Count de Frontenac, all Canada seemed in league against his undertaking." Duchesnau, the intendant, wrote to Paris that, under pretext of discoveries, the 13 Novem.
intrepid explorer of France in the New World was trading with the Ottawas, in violation of his patent from the king. After sending to Frontenac a memoir of his doings, in which he recommended the Ohio as a "shorter and better" 9 Novem.
route to the great West, La Salle went back to the Illinois December.
country, where he found his fort, Saint Louis, deserted. 1681.
Thence he returned to Michilimackinack, where he met his June.
lieutenant, Tonty, and then went down to Montreal to recruit his own forces. Embarking at the head of the Niagara, the undismayed adventurer returned to the Miami. 28 August.
Duchesnau, the intendant of Canada, had always been La Salle's backbiter. This was the inevitable antagonism of genius and inferiority. But the noble-minded Frontenac prophesied to his king that, despite of the obstacles and 2 Novem.
misfortunes he had encountered, La Salle would still "accomplish his discovery; and that, if he were a living man, Frontenac and Duchesnau differ.
he would proceed, next spring, to the South Sea."*

Frontenac's prediction that La Salle would succeed was fulfilled. Early the next year the follower of Jolliet and 1682.
Marquette floated down the Illinois River, and traced the 6 Feb'y. 7 April.
stream of the Mississippi until at last its yellow waters became salt, and the sea was discovered in the Gulf of Mexico. La Salle explores the Mississippi.
The American problem of the century was solved. Frenchmen had reached the outlet which Spaniards had

Discovery," of his having descended the Mississippi to the Gulf, is an audacious falsehood: see Bancroft, iii., 167, 202; Sparks's La Salle, 82–91, 186–193; Shea's Discovery, 103–106.

* Colonial Doc., ix., 147, 148, 158, 163, 164; Quebec MSS. (ii.), iv., 9, 51, 72; Charlevoix, ii., 272, 273, 275, 276; N. Y. H. S. Coll., ii., 246–263; Hist. Coll. Lou., i., 55–59; Hennepin's Discovery, 307–317; Sparks's La Salle, 59–78, 93, 94; Shea's Discovery, 147–165; Jesuit Missions, 411, 412; Garneau, i., 242, 243; Hist. Mag., v., 196–199.

CHAP. VII. 1682. explored one hundred and thirty-nine years before. With grateful hearts La Salle and his comrades chanted the sublime hymns, "*Vexilla regis prodeunt*," and "*Te Deum Laudamus*." A cross, bearing the arms of France, was set up on the "delta" of the Mississippi; and La Salle took formal possession of all the vast region he had been the first European wholly to traverse, which, in honor of his sovereign, he named "Louisiana." On his return to Illinois, he sent to France the details of his triumphant discovery.*

9 April.

"Louisiana" named by La Salle.

8 October.

In the mean time, the administration of Canada had been changed. The governor and the intendant had quarreled. Duchesnau recommended the purchase of New York, whereby the French would obtain "the most fertile and the finest country in North America." Frontenac asked for more soldiers, to occupy forts on Lakes Ontario and Erie, and prevent the savages from carrying their beaver to New York. To cut the knot, Louis recalled both Duchesnau and Frontenac, notwithstanding the latter was supported by the influence of his relative, Madame de Maintenon. War with the Iroquois appeared to be at hand. Irritated because La Salle and his men were cultivating friendship with the Illinois, who were their enemies, the Senecas and Onondagas robbed the French trading bark at Niagara, and cut her cable. This was done because Andros had ordered "not to suffer any French to trade there." The Iroquois were accordingly invited to send deputies to Montreal the next summer. But they insisted that Frontenac should visit them at Oswego, or at "La Famine," or the Salmon River, neither of which places suited the Onnontio of Canada. The next autumn, Teganissoren, or Dekanesora, an eloquent Onondaga chief, visited Frontenac, at the suggestion of Lamberville, and told him that the English had sent agents on horseback to invite the Iroquois to come to Albany, but that they had declined to go, and now asked Onnontio to visit them at Oswego. The speech was interpreted by the experienced Charles le Moyne, whom the Iroquois had named "Acossen," or "Oquesse," meaning, in English, "the partridge." Frontenac explained to Dekanesora why he could not go to Oswego, and promised to meet

13 Novem.

2 Novem.

Frontenac and Duchesnau recalled from Canada.

23 March.

11 Septem.

Teganissoren, or Dekanesora.

12 Septem.

Le Moyne, or "Oquesse."

* Col. Doc., ix., 198, 213, 214; Shea's Discovery, xii.-xv., 148, 165-184; N.Y. H. S. Coll., ii, 263-285; Hist. Coll. Lou., i., 45-50, 59-65; Sparks's La Salle, 95-108, 194-202; La Potherie, ii., 143-148; Charlevoix, ii., 276, 277, 285; Garneau, i., 243, 244; Bancroft, i., 51-59; iii., 168.

the Iroquois at Cataracouy the next spring, "at the first flowing of the sap."* CHAP. VII.

1682.

This was not so to be. Louis had already commissioned Le Febvre de la Barre to be his governor, and the Sieur de Meulles his intendant of Canada. The former had distinguished himself, in 1667, by his naval exploits against the English in the West Indies. Yet he had neither Frontenac's skill to elude obstacles, nor his ability to overcome them. De la Barre was authorized to attack the Senecas and Onondagas if he felt sure to succeed. But Louis directed his Canadian governor to "merely permit Sieur de la Salle to complete the discovery he has commenced, as far as the mouth of the said Mississippi River, in case he consider, after having examined it with the Intendant, that such discovery can be of any utility."† 10 May. Le Febvre de la Barre, Governor of Canada.

On reaching Quebec, De la Barre summoned an assembly of the chief officers of Canada, the Jesuit missionaries, and others, at which it was agreed that, to check English and maintain French influence among the Western savages, the Iroquois should be attacked by the Canadians; but regular French soldiers must be sent over to garrison Forts Frontenac and La Galette. In his reports to France, De la Barre pressed for supplies, and declared that La Salle's imprudence had provoked the hostility of the New York Indians, and that his discoveries in the West should not be considered "as very important."‡ 10 October. Assembly at Quebec. 12 Novem.

Meanwhile the Iroquois had troubled the Southern English colonies. The Senecas remained faithful to their treaty of 1677; but the other confederates let their young men make incursions into the Piscataway country, at the head of the Chesapeake, where they robbed and killed some English subjects. Lord Baltimore accordingly sent Colonels Henry Coursey and Philemon Lloyd to confer with the New York savages. Brockholls directed the officers at Albany to aid the Maryland agents, but to allow no talk with the Iroquois, unless in their presence. Inter- 15 May. Maryland and New York.

* Colonial Doc., iii., 442; iv., 122; ix., 139–166, 168–193, 796, 798; Quebec MSS. (ii.), iv., 51–136; La Hontan, i., 46; Colden, i., 65; Hennepin's New Discovery, 27, 28; Douniol, ii., 352–363; Charlev., ii., 278–285; Garneau, i., 214–221; Shea's Disc. Miss., 79, 80; *ante*, 325.

† Col. Doc., ix., 167, 168, 797; Doc. Hist., i., 65; Charlevoix, ii., 278; Garneau, i., 247, 248; Entick's British Marine, 489; *ante*, 126.

‡ Col. Doc., ix., 194–196, 798; Doc. Hist., i., 65–67; Quebec MSS. (ii.), iv., 137, 140; Charlevoix, ii., 285–289; Shea's Disc., 148; Garneau, i., 248, 249; Sparks's La Salle, 108.

CHAP. VII. 1682.

views were accordingly held, and Brockholls congratulated Lord Baltimore at the happy result of the negotiation. Not
3 August. long afterward the commander visited Albany, where an-
14 August. other Roman Catholic, Lieutenant Jervis Baxter, had been
19 August. commissioned by the Duke of York to do duty in place of Salisbury, "for his eminent services." Fourteen captives
17 Novem. taken by the Iroquois were released and quickly sent home to Maryland, with a friendly letter from Brockholls to Baltimore.*

New York and the Delaware territory.

The relation between New York and her territory on the Delaware meanwhile ended; and another North American state was founded in England. During the negotiations between New Netherland and Maryland in 1659, the Dutch insisted that, as Lord Baltimore's patent covered only savage or uninhabited territory, it could not affect their own possession of the Delaware region. Accordingly, they held it against Maryland until it was taken from them by the Duke of York in 1664. But James's title by conquest had never been confirmed to him by a grant from the king; and Cecilius Calvert, the second Lord Baltimore, insisted that Delaware belonged to Maryland. To quiet controversy, the duke had offered to buy off Baltimore's claim, to which he would not agree. Penn afterward refused a large offer by Fenwick "to get of the duke his interest in Newcastle and those parts" for West Jersey.†

Thus stood the matter when the Pennsylvania charter was sealed. Its proprietor soon found that his province, wholly inland, wanted a front on the sea. As Delaware was "necessary" to Pennsylvania, Penn "endeavored to get it" from the duke, by maintaining that Baltimore's pretension "was against law, civil and common." Charles Calvert, the third Lord Baltimore, was "very free" in talking against the Duke of York's rights; but he could not circumvent Penn. The astute Quaker readily got from James a
21 August. quit-claim of all his interest in the territory included within the proper bounds of Pennsylvania. After a struggle,
24 August. Penn also gained the more important conveyances to him-

* Ord., Warr., etc., xxxii½, 99, 113–115, 127–137, 150, 151; Entries, xxxiii., 5, 15, 18, 19, 47; Colonial MSS., xxx., 72, 101, 102; Col. Doc., iii., 323–328, 351, 423, 455, 593, 640, 1184; Doc. Hist., iii., 368; *ante*, 310, 327. Colden does not mention this embassy from Maryland.

† Col. Doc., ii., 74, 80–87; iii., 186; Mass. H. S. Coll., xxxvii., 319; Penn. Archives, i., 70; *ante*, i., 666–669; ii., 51, 85, 150.

1682.

self of the duke's interest in all the region within a circle of twelve miles diameter around Newcastle, and extending southward as far as Cape Henlopen.* 24 August.

Penn gains the Delaware territory.

The triumphant Penn set sail the next week. At Newcastle he received from James's agents formal possession of the surrounding territory, and of the region farther south. 1 Septem. 28 October. In honor of the duke, Penn directed Cape Henlopen to be 7 Novem. called Cape "James;" but posterity refused to confirm the courtly Quaker's decree, and HENLOPEN and MAY still retain the names which their Dutch discoverers first gave to the Capes of the Delaware.†

Cape May and Cape Henlopen.

Penn now hastened to "pay his duty" to the duke at the seat of his provincial government. At New York he was hospitably received by Brockholls, who, after inspecting his deeds from James, required the officers on the Delaware to 21 Novem. submit to their new Quaker chief. But in his report to 18 Decem. Werden, the duke's representative feared that what was left of his province would not defray the charge of its government.‡

Penn in New York.

After visiting his friends on Long Island, Penn came back to Upland, or Chester, where he held his first Assem- 7 Decem. bly, and organized his provincial government. He then visited Lord Baltimore, to confer about their respective 11 Decem. boundaries. On his return from Maryland, Penn went to Coaquannock, near Weccacoe, a neck of land where the Schuylkill flows into the Delaware, which had been occupied by the Dutch in 1646. It was now possessed by Swedes, who had built a church. From them Penn acquired the ground, and then planned a city, which he named "Philadelphia." This was just fifty-six years after Minuit had bought for the Dutch the island of Manhattan from its aboriginal owners.§

Philadelphia founded.

* Hazard's Reg. Penn., i., 375, 376, 429, 430; ii., 202; Annals, 586-593; Entries, xxxiii., 33; Col. Doc., iii., 290; Penn. Arch., i., 52, 53, 70; Mem. Penn. H. S., i., 444; Chalmers, i., 643; Proud, i., 200-203; *ante*, 348, 358. On the 22d of March, 1683, the duke obtained from the king a patent in fee for the Delaware territory, which he delivered to Penn in pursuance of his conveyance of the 24th August, 1682: Hazard's Reg. Penn., ii., 202; Ann. Penn., 588; Proud, i., 282.

† Proud, i., 204-209; Chalmers, i., 662; Dixon, 195-203; S. Hazard, Ann. Penn., 5, 593, 596, 597, 602, 603, 605, 612; Reg. Penn., i., 430; *ante*, vol. i., 79, 97.

‡ Proud, i., 208, 209, 268; Chalmers, i., 662; Hazard's Annals, 605, 606, 607, 635, 636; Reg. Penn., iii., 34; Entries, xxxiii., 20, 21, 33.

§ Proud, i., 206-209, 211, 233, 234, 268, 289; Hazard's Annals, 89, 417, 438, 447, 463, 467, 594, 607-634; Reg. Penn., i., 430, 436; Watson's Annals, 121, 133; Dixon, 204, 205; Upland Records, 67, 134, 153; G. Smith's Delaware County, 102, 115, 139-142; *ante*, vol. i., 164, 426, 427; ii., 301, 349.

CHAP. VII. 1683. Penn's treaty at Shackamaxon.

An event now took place of which no original record appears to have been preserved. Under a spreading elm-tree on the bank of the Delaware, at Shackamaxon, now known as Kensington, just north of the city of Philadelphia, William Penn made his first personal covenant with the native owners of his province. Declining to call the red men his "children," as did Onnontio of Canada, or "brethren," as did Corlaer of New York—even rejecting their own metaphor of a chain, which he suggested might rust—the adroit Quaker announced that Christians and Indians in his province "should be as one people." The sentiment touched the children of the forests, who vowed that they would live in friendship with "Onas"—which in their language signified "*a pen*"—as long as "the sun, moon, and stars endure."*

2 Feb'y. East Jersey affairs.

In the mean time the grantees under the will of Sir George Carteret had conveyed East Jersey to William Penn, Thomas Rudyard, and ten other Quakers. These twelve proprietors each sold half of his interest to a new associate, among whom were James Drummond, earl of Perth, the lord justice general of Scotland, John Drummond, his brother, afterward Earl of Melford, and Robert Barclay, of Ury, the famous author of the "Apology." Sir George Mackenzie, afterward Viscount Tarbet, the witty register and advocate of Scotland, was soon added as an associate.† The twenty-four proprietors made Barclay the governor of their province, with leave to execute his office

16 Septem. by deputy. Barclay therefore appointed Rudyard, who had been Penn's counsel in 1670, his representative; and Sam-

13 Novem. Rudyard succeeds Carteret.

uel Groom, another of the twelve first grantees, was made receiver and surveyor of East Jersey. The new officials hastened to Elizabethtown, where Philip Carteret at once resigned his authority to Rudyard.‡ Among the counsel-

* Hazard's Annals, 634, 635; Proud, i., 212–215; Watson, 125–131; Dixon, 210–216; Col. Rec. Penn., iii., 310–312; Bancroft, ii., 381–383; Chalmers, i., 644; *ante*, 282. I have a box made out of a piece of Penn's "treaty-tree," which was blown down on the 3d of March, 1810. There is a fine engraving of this elm in the frontispiece to Pinkerton's Voyages, vol. xii.

† Leaming and Spicer, 73, 145, 146; Col. Doc., iii., 329; Gordon, 50; Beatson, ii., 72, 87; Hatfield, 210, 211; *ante*, 342.

‡ Philip Carteret, who had married Elizabeth Lawrence, of New York (*ante*, 349, 351), died not long afterward, having made his will on 10th December, 1682, in which he directed his body to be buried in the city of New York: Whitehead's East Jersey, 85; Hatfield, 212, 213. 8 August, 1682, Carteret petitioned Brockholls for an order to enjoy the meadow-land on Staten Island which had been allowed to him by Nicolls in 1667 (*ante*, 150), and his request was granted: Col. MSS., xxx., 112; xxxi., 164; Hist. Mag., x., 297–299; N. J. H. S. Proc., i. (ii.), 31–36.

ors appointed by Rudyard were Lewis Morris, John Berry, and John Palmer. An Assembly was summoned to meet at Elizabethtown, at which East Jersey was divided into four counties. One of them, Bergen County, was carefully described as containing "all the settlements between Hudson's River and Hackinsack River, *beginning at Constable's Hook*, and so to extend to the uppermost bound of the Province Northward, between the said Rivers." By this act the East Jersey Legislature honestly admitted that Staten Island belonged, as it really did, to New York.* Rudyard was soon afterward visited by William Penn, who admired the land around Elizabethtown, "and said he had never seen such before in his life." But Amboy, at the mouth of the Raritan River, was meant to be the future great city of East Jersey. Delicious oysters abounded there, although clams were then esteemed "much better." Amboy was described as "extraordinary well situate for a great town." The oysters of the "Chingerora" Creek were, and are, supremely good, and the channel was "broad and bold" from Sandy Hook to Amboy Point, where three houses had already been set up. But workmen were scarce; and Groom prophetically remarked that, "if no help comes, it will be long ere Amboy be built as London is."†

CHAP. VII. 1682. 13 Decem. 1683. 1 March to 28 March. April. 30 May.

In spite of the efforts of Canada, the fur trade was attracted from Montreal to Albany. De la Barre attempted harsh measures, but only drove away his own colonists, of whom more than sixty went to live in New York. He therefore sent the Sieur de Salvaye to the governor of New York, asking him to prevent such desertions. In reply, Brockholls assured De la Barre that Andros had already done all he could to check runaways without passports to or from Canada; and that other measures must be left to his successor, Dongan, whose arrival was daily expected.‡

Canada and New York. 1 April. 15 April. 31 May.

* Leaming and Spicer, 229; Whitehead's E. J., 95, 97, 98; Yonkers Gazette of 25 November, 1865, and 20 January, 1866; *ante*, 149.

† Leaming and Spicer, 73, 141, 227-252; Entries, xxxiii., 48; S. Smith, 156, 166, 167-175, 539-546; Whitehead's East Jersey, 80, 83, 85, 89, 91, 95-98, 196-203, 211, 278-283; Contributions, 2-6; Sewell, 504; Scott's Model; Dankers and Sluyter.

‡ Charlevoix, ii., 305; Entries, xxxiii., 59, 60, 68; Col. Doc., iii., 455, 471; ix., 199, 200, 203, 205, 212, 215, 221, 326.

CHAPTER VIII.

1683–1685.

CH. VIII. — 1682.

DETERMINED to give his American province the franchises its people desired, the Duke of York sought an able colonial governor to take the place of Andros, who was now basking in London and in the Channel Islands. The man chosen by James was Colonel Thomas Dongan, born in 1634, a younger son of an Irish baronet, Sir John Dongan, and a nephew of Richard Talbot, afterward created Earl and Duke of Tyrconnel, in Ireland. William, the oldest son of Sir John, had been made, by Charles, Baron Dongan and Viscount Claine, in the Irish peerage. Thomas Dongan of course gained advancement by his brother's and his uncle's influence at the English court. Dongan was quickly promoted to be a colonel in the royal army, and, having been assigned to serve with his Irish regiment under Louis, was stationed for some time at Nancy. In 1678 he was ordered home from France, to his pecuniary loss; but was rewarded by Charles with a pension and the appointment of lieutenent governor of Tangier, in Africa, under Lord Inchiquin, whence he was recalled in 1680. Dongan was a Roman Catholic; enterprising and active; coveting money, yet "a man of integrity, moderation, and genteel manners." His experience in France was an important recommendation, because of the delicate relations between New York and Canada, and the necessity of managing them skillfully on the English side.*

Colonel Thomas Dongan, governor of New York.

* Col. Doc., ii., 741; iii., 423, 460, 462, 463; ix., 200, 298, 323; Hutch. Coll., 542; Smith, i., 66; Narcissus Luttrell, i., 36, 52; ii., 108; iv., 465, 625; Evelyn, ii., 151; Beatson, ii., 110, 112, 188; Macaulay, ii., 48–50; Kennett, iii., 387, 391; Liber Hiberniæ, i., 10, 25; Lodge, ii., 46; v., 42, 52; Memoirs of Lady Fanshawe, 177, 178, 182; N. Y. Coun. Jour., i., Introd., xxxiii.; *ante*, 357. In December, 1685, Lord Dongan was made Earl of Limerick; and in 1690 he commanded a regiment of dragoons under James at the battle of the Boyne, for which he was outlawed by the government of William and Mary. Lord Limerick died at Saint Germains in 1698, and was succeeded in his titles by his brother Thomas: Commons' Journal, xii., 278.

CH. VIII.

1682. 30 Septem. Dongan's commission.

Dongan was accordingly appointed governor of New York. With one exception, his commission was like that which James gave to Andros in 1674. The only difference was that East and West New Jersey, just released to others, were excepted from Dongan's jurisdiction. But the west side of the Connecticut River was still declared to be the eastern boundary of New York, and Pemaquid, Martha's Vineyard, and Nantucket were retained as its dependencies. The Delaware territory had been relinquished to William Penn. A separate commission as vice admiral, like that to Andros, was also given to Dongan by the Duke of York as lord high admiral. After some delay, Brockholls was notified that the new governor would soon be at his post, and, in the mean time, he would signify the duke's pleasure, in pursuance of his instructions.*

30 October. 1683. 4 Jan'y.

1682. 21 Decem. Dongan's instructions delayed.

The preparation of Dongan's instructions was retarded by the proprietors of East Jersey, on whose behalf Sir George Mackenzie, the lord register of Scotland, desired to have their government "rather holden by charter from His Royal Highness, than, as it is at present, by transmission from our authors, without any augmentation of our privileges, but, only to be under the Duke's immediate protection." This request was so vague that Werden had to inquire whether the proprietors of New Jersey desired "to join it to New York, as heretofore," and share in its advantages, or whether, in asking the duke's "protection," they wanted only a direct grant to them from himself. The latter being avowed as their real object, James readily executed an instrument by which, disregarding his release of October, 1680, to the young Sir George Carteret, he confirmed East New Jersey to the Earl of Perth and his associates, together with all the powers granted in the royal patents to himself. The king also commanded all persons "concerned in the said Province of East New Jersey" to yield obedience to its proprietors.†

1683. 4 Jan'y. 14 March. 23 Novem.

This Jersey episode having been arranged, Dongan's instructions were completed. They were carefully framed, apparently by James himself, as a full answer to the peti-

* Col. Doc., iii., 215, 328, 329, 330; Commissions, etc., i., 59, 61; *ante*, 262, 367.

† Col. Doc., iii., 329, 330; Leaming and Spicer, 141–152, 604; Beatson, ii., 72; Clarke's James II., i., 731; Grahame, i., 481; Gordon, 50, 51; Whitehead, 88, 195, 196; Eastern Boundary, 31, 49; Yonkers Gazette, 6 January, 1866; *ante*, 342.

CH. VIII. 1683. tion of June, 1681, and after Andros, Nicolls, Dyer, and Lewin had explained to his commissioners the real condition of New York. Perhaps the frame of government which Penn had published in the previous spring may have, in some degree, influenced the duke.* At all events, James instructed Dongan on his arrival at New York to call together Frederick Phillipse and Stephen van Cortlandt, its only actual counselors, and other "most eminent inhabitants," not exceeding ten in all, and swear them to allegiance to the king, fealty to the duke as "lord and proprietor," and official faithfulness as members of his council.† These counselors were to "enjoy freedom of debates and vote in all affairs of public concern;" but they might be suspended by the governor until the duke's pleasure should be signified. With the advice of his council, Dongan was, immediately after his arrival, to issue writs to the proper officers in every part of his government for the election of "a General Assembly of all the Freeholders by the persons who they shall choose to represent them," in order to consult with the governor and council "what laws are fit and necessary to be made and established for the good weal and government of the said Colony and its dependencies and of all the inhabitants thereof." This Assembly, which was not to exceed eighteen, was to meet in the city of New York. "And when," added the duke to Dongan, "the said Assembly so elected shall be met at the time and place directed, you shall let them know that for the future it is my resolution that the said General Assembly shall have free liberty to consult and debate among themselves all matters as shall be apprehended proper to be established for laws for the good government of the said Colony of New York and its dependencies, and that if such laws shall be propounded as shall appear to me to be for the manifest good of the country in general, and not prejudicial to me, I will assent unto and confirm them." All laws agreed to by the Assembly were to be submitted to the governor,

27 Jan'y. Dongan's instructions from James.

Counselors.

General Assembly.

Powers of the Assembly.

* *Ante*, 353, 354, 359. Several writers say that the Duke of York's instructions to Dongan were based upon the advice of Penn, after his visit to New York in November, 1682: *ante*, 367. I have seen no evidence to support this statement; and, from a comparison of dates and other circumstances, do not think it probable.

† The oath required by the "Test Act" of 1673 was not imposed on officers in the British colonies until after the accession of William the Third, in 1689: compare Col. Doc., iii., 331, 369, 543, 623, 685; *ante*, 202, 264; *post*, 628.

who could approve or deny them, according to his judgment. Such laws were to be confirmed or rejected by the duke; yet they were to be "good and binding" until he should signify his disapproval—then they should "cease, and be null and void." No man's life or property within the government of New York was to be taken away or harmed "but by established and known laws, not repugnant to, but as nigh as may be agreeable to the laws of the kingdom of England." None were to be admitted to public trusts "whose ill fame and conversation may bring scandal thereupon." With the advice of his council, the governor might establish courts similar to those in England, grant lands, set up custom-houses, regulate the militia, and build fortifications; but no war could be made without the duke's command, nor any duties levied until enacted by a colonial Assembly. Peculiar "immunities and privileges," proposed to be given to the metropolis, were to be reported. Pemaquid was to be regulated so as to secure "the best advantage" to New York. As soon as he could, Dongan must settle the boundaries of the "territories towards Connecticut." But no reference was made to religion, as in James's instructions to Andros.*

Effect of laws.

Dongan's powers.

New York city.

Pemaquid.

Thus the inhabitants of New York were enabled by James to share colonial authority. This event occurred at a remarkable period. The political corporations, which so largely influenced English politics, were being remodeled. Charles's "vigorous counsels and resolute methods" were chiefly owing to the advice of the Duke of York; and the abrogation of the New England charters, which contrasted unfavorably with that of Pennsylvania, was contemplated. These charters were prized by their grantees, not because they secured civil and religious liberty to all the inhabitants, but because they restricted colonial authority to the members of the corporations. The chartered oligarchies in New England had been watched with interest by the duke, who perceived that they were administered for the chosen few, and not for the unprivileged many. James was bigoted and imperious, but just. Excluded from holding office within England by its "Test Act," he naturally abhorred all laws which made distinctions in religion. In

Political considerations which moved James.

* Colonial Documents, iii., 218, 331–334; Council Journals, i., Introd., ix., x.; *ante*, 264.

CH. VIII.

1683.

his judgment, all British subjects in America were entitled to be governed impartially. His chief dislike of an Assembly in New York was because it might be an "imitation" of some of those in New England. He did not object to one like that which the king had recently granted to Pennsylvania, nor to those enjoyed by Virginia and New Hampshire. In the form of government which the proprietor now established in New York, he aimed to secure its dependence on the British crown, and the participation of all its freeholders in its local legislation. By retaining in his own hands the power to appoint its governor and counselors, James maintained the colonial subordination of New York. What its people desired was to levy their own taxes and make their own laws, by an Assembly elected by themselves, as in Virginia, New Hampshire, and Pennsylvania. In this respect their wishes were fully met by the duke, who established in his province a more democratic government than any of the chartered colonies in New England enjoyed. Freer than their fellow-subjects in these oligarchies, the freeholders of New York now gained the right to elect their own representatives in an Assembly.*

Freedoms in New York.

2 March. James's letter to New York.

In a letter to "The General Assembly of New York," James said that he had directed Dongan to call them together to "consult and propose all such matters as shall be for the public good." Instead of John West, who held Nicolls's old office, he also made John Spragg secretary of his province. As Dyer had been appointed surveyor general of the king's customs in America, Lucas Santen was made the duke's collector and receiver in New York and its dependencies, with instructions like those of his predecessor. The Reverend Doctor John Gordon was also commissioned to be chaplain of the soldiers in New York. An English Jesuit priest, Thomas Harvey, of London, likewise accompanied Dongan, who embarked for America in the old Parliamentarian frigate "Constant Warwick."†

27 Jan'y. John Spragg secretary.
4 Jan'y.
17 Feb'y.
28 April.
Lucas Santen collector.

* Col. Doc., iii., 230, 235, 317, 331, 677; Smith, i., 66; Chalmers's Ann., i., 274–277, 284, 605; Rev. Col., i., 109; Hutch. Coll., 328, 484, 534–538; Rapin, ii., 725, 726; Burnet, i., 523, 527, 528; Clarke's James II., i., 733–738; Dalrymple, i., 21–23; Story's Misc., 66; *ante*, i., 208, 331; ii., 202, 358.

† Col. MSS., xxxi., 13; Council Journals, i., Introd., x., xi.; Council Min., v., 242; Commissions, i., 71, 72; Minutes N. Y. Com. Coun., i., 171; Col. Doc., iii., 222, 335, 336, 415; Doc. Hist., iii., 73; Adlard's Sutton Dudley's, 75; Oldmixon, ii., 36; Pepys, i., 74; Letter of Selyns, 21 October, 1683; *ante*, 359. Chaplain Gordon appears to have been the successor

"With a considerable retinue," Dongan arrived at Nantasket, and set out for New York overland, accompanied some ten miles, to Dedham, by a troop of Boston militia, "besides severall other gents of the town." Crossing the Sound to Long Island, Dongan's attention was aroused by the disaffection of the people; and, "to extinguish the fire of discontent," he assured them that "no laws or rates for the future should be imposed but by a General Assembly."*

CH. VIII. 1683. 10 August. 15 August. Arrival of Dongan in Massachusetts.

The governor reached New York on Saturday, the twenty-fifth of August. The next Monday morning he met the magistrates at the City Hall, where he published his commission and exhibited his instruction respecting special privileges to the metropolis. The following day he dined with the city authorities, and, according to their record, "his honor received a large and plentiful entertainment, and they had great satisfaction in his honor's company."†

27 August. 28 August. Dongan in New York.

John Spragg was at once installed as secretary of the province, and Brockholls, with the former secretary, Matthias Nicolls, who had returned from England, and others, were directed to catalogue the records surrendered by West. Mayor Beekman, with Van Cortlandt, Santen the collector, Captain Mark Talbot, and Gabriel Minvielle, were appointed to survey Fort James, and Captain Thomas Young to be pilot of the port of New York.‡

29 August. Fort James. 31 August. Port pilot.

After a hurried visit to Albany, the governor summoned the freeholders of New York, Long Island, Esopus, Albany, Pemaquid, and Martha's Vineyard, to choose representatives to appear for them at a General Assembly to be held at the metropolis on the seventeenth day of October. John West, the clerk of the Court of Assizes, was also directed to deliver all its records to Secretary Spragg.§

13 Septem. A General Assembly summoned. 15 Septem.

The cause of Dongan's rapid visit to Albany was Penn's attempt to secure the upper Susquehanna valley to himself. Finding that some of the Iroquois nations claimed that region by right of conquest, Penn commissioned one of his

Penn and the Susquehanna.

of Wolley, who returned to England in 1680 (*ante*, 332), and was paid salary from 26 November, 1682, to 6 October, 1683: Camden Soc., Secret Services Charles II. and James II., 128.

* Adlard's Sutton Dudley's, 75, 76; Smith's New York, i., 67.

† Minutes of C. C., i., 171; Dunlap, i., 133; Smith, i., 66; Col. Doc., iii., 334; *ante*, 373.

‡ Entries, xxxiii., 79–81; Minutes of C. C., i., 171; Col. Doc., iii., 314, 315, 339; Colonial MSS., xxxiv., 1, 2.

§ Doc. Hist., i., 259, 260; Col. Doc., iii., 331; Council Minutes, v., 1, 2, 3; Journals of Legislative Council, i., Introd., xi.

CH. VIII. 1683. councilors, William Haige, with Alderman James Graham, of New York, to buy it for him from the savages. The Pennsylvania agents were at Albany on this business when Dongan reached New York. As soon as he could, the governor went up himself, and directed the Albany commissaries to examine the matter. They reported that a settlement on the Susquehanna would be "much nearer to the Indians" than Albany, and that Penn's purchase there would "be prejudicial to his Royal Highness's Government." Dongan accordingly ordered them "to put a stop to all proceedings in Mr. Penn's affairs with the Indians until his bounds and limits be adjusted." The Albany magistrates wrote, the next week, that "there hath not any thing ever been moved or agitated, from the first settling of these parts more prejudicial to his Royal Highnesses interest and the inhabitants of this Government, than this business of the Susquehanna River. The French, it is true, have endeavored to take away our trade by piece meals; but this will cut it all off at once." So, when Penn's agent solicited the Cayugas and Onondagas to sell their Susquehanna land to him, they refused, and told the Albany commissaries that the Senecas, Oneidas, and Mohawks had nothing to do with it; that the land "cannot be sold without Corlaer's order, for we transferred it to this Government four years ago;" that they "now convey and transport it again, and give it to the Governor General, or those who now represent him." Oreouaté, or Tawerahet, and two other Cayuga sachems, accordingly executed a formal "conveyance of the Susquehanna River, with the land situate thereupon," which the Albany commissaries accepted, "for Corlaer," and gave the savages a handsome present, "in full satisfaction."*

(Margin notes: 6 Septem. — 8 Septem. — 18 Septem. — 24 Septem. — 25 Septem. — 26 Septem. — Susquehanna lands.)

Penn had meanwhile come to New York, at Dongan's invitation, but remained only a short time, because of his boundary dispute with Lord Baltimore. Not long afterward the Mohawks visited Fort James, and agreed to give the Susquehanna River to New York. In announcing this to Penn, the governor said, "about which, you and I shall not fall out; I desire we may joine heartily together to

(Margin notes: 24 Septem. Penn in New York. — 3 October. — 22 October.)

* Doc. Hist., i., 259–261, 263; Col. Doc., iii., 393, 406, 523, 560; ix., 227, 360; Pennsylvania Archives, i., 62–75, 80; Proud, i., 235, 262; Whitehead's E. J. Contributions, 14; Colden, i., 55, 56, 103; ii., 64; *ante*, 328.

advance the interest of my master and your good friend." Dongan's action about the Susquehanna lands was approved by James, but it provoked the enmity of Penn.*

3 October. Dongan's orders to the Mohawks.

In his interview with the Mohawks, Dongan told them to deal no more with the French without his leave, allow no Frenchmen except the Jesuits to live among them, bring back as many of their friends as they could from Canada, make peace with those they were now at war with, and always to tell the governor of New York what the French said to them, adding that he would always look upon them as his "children." The Mohawks declared that they would "put themselves under his Honor's protection," and would "never suffer any straggling Frenchmen amongst them, but those Jesuits, who are very good men, and very quiet; and yet, if his Honor shall please, they will send them away also; and that none hath any land from them, and that they are resolved never to sell or give them any, or any others except the people of this Government." Dongan, renewing the claim which Andros had asserted in 1677, declared "that all on this side of the Lake of Canada belongs to the Government of New York, and that the Governor desires they may be all acquainted with it, and expects their submission;" gave the Mohawks "a ragged ship's flag," bearing the English arms, to be hoisted in their country, and soon afterward, by proclamation, forbade all persons to trade with the Indians without the governor's license.†

Dongan renews the claim of Andros.

26 Novem.

Jesuit missionaries among the Iroquois.

At the time of Dongan's arrival in New York, the Jesuit Father Vaillant was the only missionary among the Mohawks; but when the sachems returned with the English flag which Dongan had given them, and which they deposited in their "public chest," Vaillant abandoned his mission and went back to Canada. Millet remained at Oneida until the next July. The two Lambervilles also continued undisturbed at Onondaga. But on the return from Albany of the Cayuga chief Oreouaté, he drove the Father Carheil

* Proud, i., 276; Penn. Arch., i., 76, 77, 79, 81, 84; Council Min., v., 10, 11; Doc. Hist., i., 262, 263; Col. Doc., iii., 341, 350, 394, 397, 406, 418, 422. It was not until 1697 that Penn obtained a conveyance from Dongan of his Susquehanna lands: Pennsylvania Archives, i., 121-123; Col. Rec, iii., 101; Colden, ii., 64; N. Y. H. S. Coll. (1869), 378-383.

† Council Min., v., 7-12; Doc. Hist., i., 67, 262, 263; Col. MSS., xxxi., 94; Col. Doc., iii., 247; v., 731; ix., 208, 228, 800; Shea's Missions, 312, 313; Charlevoix, ii., 315; Colden, i., 44, 53, 54, 249, 250; *ante*, 307.

CH. VIII. 1683. out of that canton. Garnier, who for three years had been left alone among the Senecas, now felt no longer safe, and escaped from Niagara to Fort Frontenac.*

30 May. De la Barre's policy. De la Barre had meanwhile written to France that he must attack the Senecas; that over sixty "deserters" from Canada were now harbored by the English at Albany and New York; and that the Duke of York should be asked to prevent his subjects from "further aiding and stimulating the Iroquois against the French." 4 Novem. In the autumn he charged that the English had gained such an influence over the Iroquois that they now called Albany their "sixth cabin." They had even seduced "the captain" of the Prairie de la Madeleine, where there were now "two hundred good Iroquois soldiers," to return with his family to New York. Every effort had been made to secure friendship with the Senecas, who, hoping to gain by the war they were about to make in Virginia, demanded that La Salle should be withdrawn from Illinois, and refused to trade with the French at Niagara, or at Fort Frontenac.†

Jealous of La Salle, of whose "false discovery" of the Mississippi De la Barre "did not think much," he charged the great adventurer with trying to draw away French colonists from Quebec into the depths of the forest, "to build up an imaginary kingdom for himself." The truth was, De la Barre jealous of La Salle, that the sailor governor of Canada was narrow-minded and covetous of the gains which might be made by the fur traders. Accordingly, he sent the Chevalier de Baugy to supersede Tonty at Fort Saint Louis, and deprived La Salle himself of Fort Frontenac. This obliged that 9 Novem. who returns to France. grand discoverer to return to Quebec, whence he embarked for France to lay his case before the king. But Louis, trusting to De la Barre's representations, had, in the mean 5 August. Louis thinks La Salle's discovery "useless." time, pronounced that La Salle's exploration of the Mississippi was "very useless, and such enterprizes must be prevented hereafter;" and that, in consequence of his ambassador, Barillon's, complaints to Charles, Dongan had received "precise orders on the part of the said King to

* Col. Doc., iii., 518; ix., 171, 227, 228, 229, 360, 762, 800; Shea's Missions, 274, 289, 294, 313, 375; *ante*, 362.

† Col. Doc., iii., 451; ix., 197, 198, 202-210; Quebec MSS., iv. (ii.), 172, 174; Charlevoix, ii., 305-307; Shea's Missions, 313; *ante*, 369.

Ch. VIII.

1683.

maintain good correspondence with us, and carefully to avoid whatever may interrupt it."*

Pemaquid affairs.

The French had meanwhile encroached on the Duke of York's territory of Pemaquid, west of the Saint Croix; and Grand Fontaine, the governor of Acadia, had authorized the Baron Vincent de Saint Castin to be his lieutenant at Pentagouet, or Penobscot, which the Dutch had reduced in 1674. Castin had come to Canada as an officer in the old Carignan Regiment, with Courcelles, but, preferring a roving life among the Abenaqui savages, had so conformed himself to their ways as to be made their great chief. Gradually he saved a large fortune. His encroachments on the duke's territory had already startled Brockholls. A few days after he reached New York, Dongan accordingly wrote to "the French who live among the Indians at Pemaquid," desiring them to come under the duke's authority, or else quit his territory between the Kennebec and the Saint Croix before the next May; and offering them lands and kind treatment as Englishmen if they would come under his government.† As soon as he returned from Albany, Dongan appointed John Allen sheriff of Pemaquid; and Ensign Thomas Sharpe was afterward made commander. New trading regulations were also established; one of which was, that no license from Sir Thomas Temple's nephew, John Nelson, of Boston, or any one else not authorized by the Governor of New York, was to be good. At Dongan's suggestion, the merchants of the metropolis subscribed two thousand guineas in a stock company to manage the fisheries and Indian trade at Pemaquid, and the duke himself was asked to take a share in the adventure. These proceedings naturally stirred up jealousy in Boston.‡

Castin.

3 Sept. Dongan's warning.

13 Sept.

10 Novem.

22 Novem.

21/31 Oct. Selyns's letter to Holland.

In writing to the Classis of Amsterdam, Domine Selyns gave an interesting account of provincial Church affairs at

* Col. Doc., iii., 447, 451; ix., 198, 200, 203, 204, 214, 215, 216, 798, 799; La Hontan, i., 7, 8; Charlevoix, ii., 285, 286, 290, 307; Shea's Discovery, 185; Sparks's La Salle, 108, 109, 204; N. Y. H. S. Coll., ii., 285–287; Lou. H. S. Coll., i., 66; Garneau, i., 245.

† Col. Doc., iii., 450; ix., 263. By a very common error, this letter was dated in August instead of September. Dongan did not reach Nantasket until the 10th, nor New York until the 25th of August, 1683; *ante*, 375.

‡ Col. Doc., iii., 334, 349; iv., 207, 211; ix., 75, 918, 919; Charlevoix, ii., 274, 360; La Hontan, i., 223; Hutch. Coll., 562; Williamson, i., 429, 471, 472, 580, 581; Penn. Arch., i., 80; Council Min., v., 23–27; Col. MSS., xxxiv., 8, 10; Pemaquid Papers, Maine H. S. Coll., v., 59, 60, 69, 73–81, 89–91; *ante*, 254, 296.

CH. VIII. 1683. Tesschenmaeker. Dellius.

this time. At Schenectady, Domine Tesschenmaeker, who, after leaving Newcastle, had been preaching at Staten Island, was called. Domine Godfridus Dellius, a young clergyman who had just come out from Holland, was settled as colleague of Schaats at Albany. Weeksteen at Esopus, and Van Zuuren on Long Island, labored acceptably. At New York Selyns was much pleased: "My congregation," he wrote, "is engaged in building me a large house, wholly of stone, three stories high, and raised on the foundation of unmerited love. The surrounding villages—although too much for one person—I have not left neglected; preaching there on Mondays and Thursdays, administering the Communion, and attending the thanks-

Daillé.

preaching and Church ordinances. Domine Petrus Daillé, late professor at Salmurs, has become my colleague, and attends to the service in the French worship. He is full of fire, godliness, and learning. Banished on account of his religion, he maintains the cause of Jesus Christ with

Gordon.

untiring zeal. Domine John Gordon has come over to take charge of the English Church service. After my forenoon, and before my afternoon service, there is preaching in the English and French tongues. The Heer Dongan, our new governor, has at last arrived, and has told me and my consistory that his order from the Duke was to allow

Dongan.

freedom of conscience. His Excellency is a person of knowledge, politeness, and friendliness. I have had the pleasure of a visit from him, and can call on him when I choose. What is to be done for the good of our country and Church will be made manifest in the approaching Assembly, which is summoned to devise reasonable laws for us and our posterity."*

3 October. Court of Assizes.

At its usual day, the Court of Assizes met at New York, and Dongan, of course, presided. Although he may have appeared "rather as Mars than as Mercury, yet his behaviour was with discretion, patience, and moderation, showing in him that principle of honour not wilfully to injure any, and had a regard to equity in all his judgments."

9 October. Address to the Duke.

After the court adjourned, the sheriffs drew up an address to the Duke of York, in which they thanked him for sending over Dongan as governor of the province, "of whose

* Corr. Cl. Amst. MSS.; Murphy's Anth., 104, 105; Doc. Hist., iii., 265, 535, 536; *ante*, 329.

CH. VIII. 1683.

integrity, justice, equity and prudence, we have already had a very sufficient experience at our last General Court of Assizes. And that your Royal Highness might accumulate your gracious favours, and oblige, not only us, but succeeding generations, it has pleased your Royal Highness to grant us a General Assembly, to be held, the Seventeenth of this instant October, in your City of New York; a benevolence of which we have a larger and more grateful sense than can be expressed in this paper. And that it may appear that loyalty has spread as far into these parts of America, we will be always ready to offer up, with our hearty prayers, both our lives and fortunes for the defence of our most gracious Sovereign the King's Most Sacred Majesty, and your Royal Highness, against all enemies whatsoever."*

It is probable that John Younge, the high-sheriff of Long Island, drafted this address. At all events, its tone fairly set forth the general sentiment of the people of New York. Nevertheless, there was some show of dislike to a Roman Catholic governor among the remote Puritan towns of Long Island. Easthampton adopted an address to Dongan, apparently written by its minister, Thomas James, which, among other things, promised that if the governor was an "instrument under God" to relieve them, he would "firmly engage and oblige" them and their posterity to hold him in honorable remembrance, as the first restorer of their "freedom and privileges;" but if not, that they would appeal to their "most gracious Sovereign," and prostrate themselves "before the throne of his unmatchable justice and clemency, where we doubt not to find reliefe and restauration." What relief Easthampton could expect from the "unmatchable justice" of the Duchess of Portsmouth's paramour is not clear. However, the town directed their clergyman, James, to accompany and advise with their representatives at New York, "who are to stand up in the Assembly, for maintaining our privileges and English liberties, and especially against any writ going in the duke's name, but only in his Majesty's, whom only we own as our Sovereign. Also, in the town's name, to certi-

10 Sept. Easthampton's address to Dongan.

24 Sept.

* West to Penn, in Penn. Arch., i., 80; Smith's New York, i., 67, 68; Col. MSS., xxxi., 74, 78; xxxiv., 4.

CH. VIII. 1683. fy Captain Younge, the High-Sheriff, that they do not send these men in obedience to his warrant, but because they would not neglect any opportunity to assert their own liberties." It does not appear that the other Puritan towns on Long Island imitated Easthampton. The elections went quietly on, according to the mode ordered by Dongan and his council; and a majority of the Assemblymen chosen were "of the Dutch nation." Each of the three Ridings of Long Island returned two representatives; Staten Island, one; Esopus, two; Albany and Rensselaerswyck, two; Schenectady, one; Pemaquid, one; Martha's Vineyard and Nantucket, one; and New York, with Haerlem, four, making in all eighteen.*

A majority of the Assembly Dutchmen.

17 October. Meeting of the Assembly.

The seventeenth of October, sixteen hundred and eighty-three, is a memorable day in the history of New York. On that autumn morning the representatives of its freeholders first met together under British rule, and seventeen delegates to its General Assembly took their seats in Fort James. It was just seventy-four years after Hudson had explored the "Great River of the Mountains," and about thirty years after Stuyvesant's "Landtdag," or Convention, in 1653, had demanded laws for New Netherland, "resembling, as near as possible, those of the Netherlands." As the Journals of Dongan's first Assembly have not been found, the names of all its members are unknown. The experienced Matthias Nicolls, one of the representatives from the city of New York, was chosen speaker, and John Spragg, who was both a counselor and the secretary of the province, was made clerk. The Duke of York's letter of the second of March to the Assembly was read, and his resolution made known that it should have free liberty to propound laws for the government, and that if such laws should be for the good of the country, and not prejudicial to the proprietor, he would confirm them. The Assembly sat for three weeks, and passed fourteen several acts. Each of these acts, after three readings, was assented to by the governor and his council.†

Nicolls speaker, and Spragg clerk.

Laws passed.

* Thompson's Long Island, i., 314, 315; ii., 328–330; H. P. Hedges's Address, 1850, 19, 75–77; Penn. Arch., i., 80; Journals of Leg. Council of N. Y., i., Int., xi.; *ante*, 145, 360.

† Col. Doc., iii., 331, 332, 354, 355; Col. MSS., xxxi., 13; Council Journ., i., Int., x., xi., xii.; Wood's Long Island, 100, 164–167; Thompson, i., 161; Riker's Newtown, 104; Bancroft, ii., 306, 414; N. Y. H. S. Coll., ii. (ii.), 35; Manuscript Book, in Secretary's Office, Albany, "1683–1684;" *ante*, vol. i., 34, 570–575; ii., 374. Smith, i., 66, 111, 112, states that the

The first and most important of these laws was "The Charter of Liberties and Priviledges, granted by his Royal Highnesse to the Inhabitants of New Yorke and its dependencies." This venerable statute was simply, and clearly, and therefore ably worded, in good Saxon English. "For the better establishing the government of this Province of New Yorke, and that Justice and Right may bee equally done to all persons within the same," the charter enacted, "by the Governour, Councell, and Representatives, now in Generall Assembly met,"—among other things—"That the Supreme Legislative authority, under his Majesty and Royal Highness James, Duke of Yorke, Albany, etc., Lord Proprietor of the said Province, shall forever bee and reside in a Governour, Councell, and The People, mett in a Generall Assembly." It then ordained "That, according to the usage, custome, and practice of the Realm of England, a sessions of a Generall Assembly be held in this Province, once in three yeares at least." It likewise declared that "every freeholder within this Province, and freeman in any Corporation, shall have his free choice and vote in the electing of the Representatives, without any manner of constraint or imposition, and that in all elections, the majority of voices shall carry it." By other sections representatives were apportioned among the several counties, the usual privileges of Parliament were conferred on the members of Assembly, and the most liberal provisions of English law were declared to extend to the inhabitants of New York. Entire freedom of conscience and religion was guaranteed to all peaceable persons "which profess faith in God by Jesus Christ." The existing "Christian Churches" in the province were forever to be "held and reputed as priviledged churches, and enjoy all their former freedoms of their religion in divine worship and Church discipline." Following the words of the Petition of Right in 1628, the charter also ordained "that no aid, tax, tallage, assessment, custom, loan, benevolence, or imposition whatsoever, shall be laid, assessed, imposed or levied on any of his Majesty's subjects within this Prov-

CH. VIII.

1683.

30 October.

Charter of Liberties adopted.

Assembly.

Freedom of religion.

Taxes only by consent.

acts of the old New York Assembly "are for the most part rotten, defaced, or lost. Few minutes relating to them remain on the Council Books, and none in the Journals of the House." It is to be hoped that Mr. George H. Moore's long-promised work (*ante*, 73, *note*) will modify Smith's remark.

CH. VIII. 1683. ince or their estates, upon any manner of colour or pretence, but by the act and consent of the Governor, Council, and representatives of the People, in General Assembly met and assembled."*

30 October. A revenue granted to the duke. In conformity with this section, "a continued Bill" was appended to the New York Charter, by which—"for and in consideration of the many gracious and Royall favours expressed and extended unto the inhabitants of this his Province, and also for the bountifull confirming and restoring to them and their posterity, the rights, priviledges, liberties and immunities before recited and expressed, and also for the better defraying the necessary charge and expence of this Province, which cannot otherwise be effected without great charge unto his Royal Highness"—the Assembly granted to the duke and his heirs certain specified duties on importations. The act was declared to be in force "immediately after publication thereof."†

No time was lost in proclaiming this great event. Early
31 October. The charter proclaimed. on the following morning, "The Charter of Liberties and Privileges granted by his Royal Highness to the Inhabitants of New York and its dependencies, confirmed by Act of Assembly, with a continued act for defraying the requisite charges of the Government, were this day published at the City Hall, in the presence of his Honor the Governor, the Council and Representatives, and Deputy Mayor and Aldermen of this City, the inhabitants having notice by sound of trumpet, to hear the same." The appended rev-
1 Novem. enue act was put in force by a proclamation from Dongan, requiring all persons concerned to report to Santen, the duke's collector, "at the Custom House, near the Bridge."‡

Thus the representatives of New York asserted the great principle of "Taxation only by consent," which Holland had maintained since 1477, and appropriated the liberties allowed by English law to subjects within the realm of England. True ideas of popular government were now

* See Charter at length in Appendix, Note E.; N. Y. Revised Laws, 1813, ii., Appendix, iii., vi.; Munsell's Annals, iv., 32–39; Chalmers, i., 584; Dunlap, ii., App., xlii., xliii.; Bancroft, ii., 414; N. Y. H. S. Coll., ii. (ii.), 35, 41; Col. Doc., iii., 341, 357–359; Smith, i., 115; *ante*, 72, 84, 264, 373.

† MSS. Secretary's Office, Albany, Dongan's Laws, 1683, 1684, 7–12; Col. Doc., iii., 341, 357, 370, 400, 677, 678; Smith, i., 115; Journals of Leg. Council, i., 45, 46.

‡ Minutes of N. Y. Common Council, i., 175, 176; Col. MSS., xxxiv., 5.

1683. Democratic idea in New York.

more distinctly announced in the ancient Dutch province by its own freely-chosen Assembly—of which a majority were "of the Dutch nation"—than in any Northern colony of British America. In none of the charter governments of New England were "the people" recognized as having legislative authority. The first law made by the representatives of Dutch-English New York ordained that "The People met in a Generall Assembly" were to share in its colonial legislation. These memorable words, "The People," were so democratic, that the English king, at Whitehall, soon afterward objected to them, as being "not used in any other constitution in America."*

1685. 3 March. The king objects to "the People."

1683. 1 Novem. New York divided into counties.

The next law passed by the New York Assembly was "to divide this Province and dependencies into shires and counties." Twelve counties were established, the names of some of which appear to have been suggested by Dongan. The City and County of New York included Manhattan, Manning's, and the Barn Islands. Westchester contained all the land eastward of Manhattan, "as far as the Government extends," and northward, along the Hudson, to the Highlands. Ulster, which was named after the duke's Irish earldom, embraced all the towns on the west side of the Hudson, from the Murderer's Creek, near the Highlands, to the Sawyer's Creek, now called Saugerties. Albany included all the territory on the east side of the Hudson, from Roelof Jansen's Creek, and, on the west side, from Sawyer's Creek to "the Saraaghtoga." Dutchess extended from Westchester northward to Albany, and "eastward into the woods twenty miles." Orange, which was so called in compliment to the Dutch son-in-law of James, included the region on the west side of the Hudson, from the New Jersey boundary northward to Ulster, at the Murderer's Creek, and "westward into the woods as far as Delaware River." Richmond, apparently named in honor of the king's illegitimate son by the Duchess of Portsmouth,

* Col. Doc., iii., 357, 358; Rapin, ii., 270–277, 707; Penn. Arch., i., 80; Bancroft, i., 255, 256; ii., 304, 389, 414; Chalmers, i., 584, 649; Mather's Magnalia, i., 200; *ante*, i., 437, 573; ii., 374. "The People" always have been loved words in New York. Her first State Constitution of 1777 declared that the style of all her laws should be—"*Be it enacted by the People of the State of New York, represented in Senate and Assembly.*" Under her second Constitution of 1821 she adopted the more direct formula, "*The People of the State of New York, represented in Senate and Assembly, do enact,*" etc. The present Constitution of 1846 ordains that this form shall be observed in the enacting clause of all bills.

CH. VIII. 1683. contained "all Staten Island," with Shooter's Island, and the islands of Meadow on the west side. King's County, on Long Island, included Bushwick, Bedford, Brooklyn, Flatbush, Flatlands, New Utrecht, and Gravesend. Queen's contained Newtown, Jamaica, Flushing, Hempstead, and Oyster Bay. Suffolk, which commemorated the eastermost county of England, embraced Huntington, Smithfield, Brookhaven, Southampton, Southold, Easthampton to Montauk Point, Shelter Island, the Isle of Wight, Fisher's Island, and Plumb Island. Duke's County contained the islands of Nantucket, Martha's Vineyard, Elizabeth Island, and No Man's Land. Cornwall, named after the southwestern county of England, included "Pemaquid, and all his Royal Highnesses territories in those parts, with the islands adjacent." It was also enacted that every year a high-sheriff should be commissioned for each county.* (Sheriffs.)

(1 Novem. Courts of justice.) A third important act was "to settle Courts of Justice." This law established four distinct tribunals in New York: Town Courts, for the trial of small causes, to be held each month; County Courts, or Courts of Sessions, to be held at certain times, quarterly, or half yearly; a General Court of Oyer and Terminer, with original and appellate jurisdiction, to sit twice every year in each county; and a Court of Chancery, to be "the Supreme Court of this Province," composed of the governor and council, with power in the governor to depute a chancellor in his stead, and appoint clerks and other officers. But any inhabitant of the province might appeal to the king from any judgment, according to a clause in the Patent to the Duke of York. Dongan accordingly appointed the former provincial secretary, (29 Decem. 1684. 7 Febr'y.) Matthias Nicolls, and Captain John Palmer, of Staten Island—both of whom had been bred lawyers—to be the first judges of the New York Court of Oyer and Terminer.†

Another law was ordained at the same time "for naturalizing all those of foreign nations at present inhabiting

* MSS. Laws, Secretary's Office; Revised Laws, 1813, ii., App., vi., vii.; Thompson, ii., 319, 320; Dunlap, ii., App., xliii., xliv. The note at the foot of page iii., in Appendix to ii., Rev. Laws, 1813, is erroneous. Giles Goddard represented Cornwall County in the Assembly of New York for one session certainly: Maine H. S. Coll., v., 4, 94, 98, 263, 264; Williamson, i., 582.

† MSS. Laws, Secretary's Office; Rev. Laws, 1813, ii., App. viii.-x.; Col. MSS., xxxiv., 14; Council Min., v., 47, 48, 49; Col. Doc., ii., 296; iii., 389, 390, 412, 414, 417; N. Y. H. S. Coll., ii. (ii.), 35, 36; Daly's Sketch, 30, 31; Wood's Long Island, 100, 101, 144, 150; Thompson, i., 161, 162; ii., 390; *ante*, 289.

within this Province, and professing Christianity, and for encouragement of others to come and settle within the same." This statute was demanded by the general sentiment of "the people" of the most polygenous of all the British dependencies in North America. The Dutch inhabitants of New York rejoiced in knowing that the Stadtholder of their fatherland was the husband of the presumptive heiress of the British crown, and that he might, perhaps, become their own proper king. They saw that Louis was beginning to drive out of France every one of his subjects who did not profess that the Pope of Rome was the only vicar of Christ. Therefore the Assembly of New York ordained that all the actual inhabitants of the province, except bondmen, of what foreign nation soever, who professed Christianity, and who had taken, or should take the oath of allegiance, were naturalized; and that all Christian foreigners who should afterward come and settle themselves in the province might be naturalized upon their swearing allegiance to the king, and fidelity to the proprietor.*

Ch. VIII. 1683. 1 Novem. Naturalization law. 1 Novem.

After passing several other less important acts the Assembly adjourned; and the laws it had enacted were formally published in front of the City Hall. Not long afterward, Captain Mark Talbot was sent by Dongan to carry them to England for the duke's approval and confirmation.†

7 Novem. Laws published 4 Decem. and sent to the duke.

In the mean time, Connecticut, renewing the claim to a part of New York, which she had asserted to Brockholls the year before, complained to Dongan that Rye, Greenwich, and Stamford had been summoned to "make presentment" at the New York Assizes, and that as those towns "indubitably" belonged to Connecticut, they should not be "molested by any such injunctions." Dongan, who had been specially instructed to settle the duke's boundary toward the east, answered at once that the agreement was that Connecticut should not come within twenty miles of the Hudson River, and that she had "abused the former

5 October. Connecticut boundary. 9 October.

* MSS. Laws, Secretary's Office; Livingston and Smith's Laws, 113; Van Schaack, 97, 98; Col. Doc., iii., 114, 355, 370, 399, 478; v., 496; Council Journ., i., Int., xii., 387, 390; Assembly Journ., i., 95, 149, 151, 373, 377; Chalmers's Ann., i., 584; Rev. Col., i., 145.

† Minutes of N. Y. Common Council, i., 178, 179; Col. Doc., iii., 340, 349; Entries, xxxiii., 79; Council Journ., i., Int., xii.; Historical Magazine, vi., 233.

CH. VIII. 1683. 16 October 5 Novem. Dongan's letter.

contract." Attempting finesse, Connecticut replied that she had not violated that agreement. But Dongan wrote back very plainly—"The King's Commissioners, being strangers, and relying upon your people, were assured by them that the river Mamaroneck was twenty miles, every where, from Hudson's River, as we have very creditable witnesses can testify, and that it was Colonel Nicolls his intentions. Notwithstanding all that, you pretend to within sixteen or seventeen miles of this town, and, for ought we know, to Esopus and Albany also; which is argument sufficient it was none of Colonel Nicolls his intention. If you do not submit to let us have all the land within twenty miles of Hudson's River, I must claim as far as the Duke's Patent goes, which is to the River Connecticut. * * * Since you are pleased to promise to do me the honor to see me, pray come with full power to treat with me; and I do assure you, whatsoever is concluded betwixt us shall be confirmed by the King and his Royal Highness, which the other agreements, I hear, are not. If you like not of it, pray take it not ill that I proceed in a way that will bring all your patent in question."*

14 Novem. Connecticut's action.

But Connecticut had no notion to have her patent brought "in question" by the Duke of York, in such perilous times for charters in England. In great tribulation, Governor Treat summoned a special court at Hartford, and characteristic action was taken. Treat, with Gold, Allyn, and Pitkin, were commissioned to go to New York, and agree for a final settlement of the boundary, according to their "best judgment;" but with the proviso—which abandoned Connecticut pretenses—"that his Majestie and Royall Highness approve of and confirm the same." The agents were privately instructed not to yield to the Governor of New York more than twenty miles eastward from the Hudson River, "but get him to take up with as little as may be." These instructions were so framed as to allow Connecticut to gain every thing she could, and to take up with almost any thing—provided "His Majestie and the Duke's Highness shall please to ratify it."†

* Col. Rec. Conn., iii., 100, 131, 313, 314, 326–330; Col. Doc., iii., 106, 230, 231, 235, 236, 247, 333; vii., 597; *ante*, 360, 361, 373.

† Col. Rec. Conn., ii., 342, 514, 515; iii., 133–136, 328, 330; Trumbull, i., 364, 365; Col.

1683. 25 Novem. Connecticut agents in New York.

When the Hartford Commissioners reached New York, they found that Dongan was fortified with the testimony of Lawrence, Younge, and Nicolls, who personally knew that in 1664 it had been clearly understood that Connecticut was never to approach the Hudson River nearer than twenty miles. This truth, indeed, was too certain to be gainsaid. The pretenses of Connecticut to any territory on that river were proved to be "fraudulent or erroneous." And now the Connecticut agents appealed to Dongan's magnanimity, as their predecessors had to that of Nicolls, to be allowed to retain some of their settlements on the Sound, and to give in exchange for them an "equivalent tract" inland. It was accordingly agreed between Dongan, with his counselors Brockholls, Phillipse, Van Cortlandt, and Younge on the part of New York, and Treat, Gold, Allyn, and Pitkin on the part of Connecticut, that the boundary point between the two provinces should be removed several miles east from Mamaroneck to Byram River, between Rye and Greenwich, and the line run thence as it now remains; and that this new line should be properly surveyed the next October. On their return to Connecticut, her commissioners notified the Rye magistrates that they "could not help" giving up that town, but that Dongan was "a noble gentleman," and would do for their welfare whatever they should "desire in a regular manner."*

28 Novem. Agreement about the boundary.

3 Decem.

One of the duke's special instructions to his lieutenant governor, as has been seen, was to consider and report the advantage of granting to the city of New York "immunities and privileges beyond what other parts of my territories doe enjoy." Immediately after the adjournment of the Provincial Assembly, the mayor and aldermen of the metropolis accordingly petitioned Dongan that the "ancient customs, privileges, and immunities" which had been granted to them by Nicolls in 1665, should be confirmed by a charter from the Duke of York, with certain additions, including the division of the corporation into six wards;

9 Novem. New York City.

MSS., xxxi., 92; lxix., 8; N. Y. Senate Doc., 1857, No. 165, p. 43, 44, 107–109; Col. Doc., iii., 235, 362, 363; vii., 334, 563, 596, 597.

* Council Min., v., 27, 28, 29, 30, 31; Col. MSS., lxix., 9, 10, 11; Col. Rec. Conn., iii., 330–333; Bolton's Westchester, ii., 26, 27; Trumbull, i., 365, 366; Senate Doc., 1857, No. 165, 44, 45, 110–112; Smith, i., 285, 286, 287; Dunlap, ii., App. xliv.; Col. Doc., iii., 106; iv., 629; v., 950; vii., 564; viii., 442; *ante*, 55, 56.

CH. VIII. 1683. the annual election of aldermen and other officers by the freemen in each ward; the local government of the city to be intrusted to them, and to a mayor and recorder, to be annually appointed by the governor and council; that a sheriff, coroner, and town-clerk be appointed in the same way; that the corporation appoint their own treasurer; and, finally, that whatever else was necessary for its welfare should be confirmed to the old Dutch city as fully "as his Majesty hath been graciously pleased to grant to other corporations within his realm of England."*

10 Novem. Objections were made by the governor and his council to some of these proposed additional articles. But, after 19 Novem. full explanations, they were agreed to in "almost every particular." The existing metropolitan officers were ac- 24 Novem. Metropolitan officers. cordingly reappointed by the governor; who also commissioned John West, its actual clerk, to be "clerk of the city of New York," and John Tudor, one of the lawyers whom Brockholls had assigned to prosecute for the duke's government, to be its sheriff, in place of Collyer. The corpora- 27 Novem. tion soon afterward asked that it might choose its own 6 Decem. clerk, and have other privileges. Dongan answered that the clerk's nomination must be referred to the duke. But he allowed the corporation its ferry, dock, and market, and promised it a grant of lands on Manhattan Island.

8 Decem. The city of New York divided into wards. The mayor and aldermen accordingly divided the city into six wards, and assigned Nicholas Bayard to be alderman for the South Ward, John Inians for the Dock Ward, William Pinhorne for the East Ward, Gulian Verplanck for the North Ward, John Robinson for the West Ward, and 10 Decem. William Cox for the Out Ward. Dongan now ordered that the substance of the corporation's petition of the ninth of November be put in practice, "until such time as his Royal Highnesses pleasure shall be further known therein."

* Col. Doc., 334, 337–339; Val. Man., 1844–5, 312, 313; 1851, 397–399; Minutes of N. Y. Common Council, i., 179–182; Council Min., v., 16–19; *ante*, 76, 77, 373. This petition was signed by William Beekman, the mayor, and Johannes van Brugh, John Lawrence, Peter J. Morris, James Graham, Cornelis Steenwyck, and Nicholas Bayard, the aldermen of the city of New York: Ent., xxxiii., 79; Col. Doc., iii., 339. These names do not appear in Valentine's Manual. Between the 9th and the 24th of November, 1683, Dongan seems to have appointed Steenwyck mayor in place of Beekman, and Nicholas Bayard, John Inians, William Pinhorne, Gulian Verplanck, John Robinson, and William Cox to be aldermen: Min. of N. Y. Com. Council, i., 184, 185; Dunlap, ii., App. cxxxi. Mr. Murray Hoffman's "Treatise," vol. ii., 7–10, makes the petitions of the New York Common Council of 9 and 27 Nov., 1683, to Dongan, as governor for the Duke of York, appear as if they were addressed to him as governor under James the Second, in 1686.

He accordingly commissioned James Graham, one of its Ch. VIII.
late aldermen, to be the first recorder of the city of New
York. All its other officers were sworn to fidelity by the 1683. 4 Decem.
governor in Fort James; and Recorder Graham, coming 1684.
thence to the City Hall, "took his place on the bench on 16 Jan'y. Recorder
the right hand of the mayor."* Graham.

Dongan also allowed the metropolis to hold a Court of 1 Febr'y.
Sessions until the duke's pleasure should be known, and 31 March. Court of
commissioned its mayor and aldermen to be justices of the Sessions.
peace. As soon as it was organized, the common council 15 March.
adopted various by-laws for the government of the city.
It also asked Dongan to confirm the former orders of An- 17 March.
dros, especially that of the 20th January, 1680, prohibiting
the bolting of flour at any other place in the province than
the city. The governor required "reasons at large" for 18 March.
this request; and the corporation submitted that, as the 9 April.
manufacture of flour was the chief support of the trade of
the metropolis, the high reputation of its breadstuffs should
not be taken away, as it would be if bolting were allowed
elsewhere, and that Long Island enjoyed a peculiar advantage in its whaling, while the rest of the province was ag-
ricultural. Albany, however, objected to such a monopoly 16 April.
being allowed to the metropolis. But as Deputy Governor
Walrond, of Barbadoes, complained that some bad meal
had already been sent there from New York, Dongan is- 22 May.
sued a proclamation prohibiting the packing or bolting of Bolting of flour.
flour, or the making of bread for exportation, in any place
within the government, except the city of New York. This
action was approved by the duke's commissioners, who in- 1 Novem.
structed the governor "by all meanes chiefly to incourage
the City of New Yorke, according to the practice of your
predecessors, and particularly to observe how it was in Sir
Edmond Andros, his time."†

The shipping of the port of New York now consisted of 1 March.
three barks, three brigantines, twenty-seven sloops, and New York shipping.
forty-six open boats. But the trade of the city had lan-

* Council Min., v., 19, 20, 27, 31-35, 82; Col. MSS., xxxi., 95; xxxiv., 9, 10, 12; Min. of C. Council, i., 182-202, 207, 208, 253; Val. Man., 1844-5, 314-317; 1851, 399-401; 1854, 438, 440; Entries, xxxiii., 10; Dunlap, ii., App. cxxxi., cxxxii.; Daly's Sketch, 31; *ante*, 360.

† Min. of Com. Council, i., 143, 169, 210, 211, 230-245, 253, 255-257, 260, 261; Val. Man., 1851, 401; Council Min., v., 59, 62, 65, 71, 72, 83-85; Col. MSS., xxxi., 125, 126, 134, 144; xxxiv., 20; Col. Doc., iii., 315, 338, 351, 797; Dunlap, ii., App. cxxxii.-cxxxiv.; Hoffman's Treatise, ii., 6; Oldmixon, ii., 38; *ante*, 330.

CH. VIII. guished of late, owing to peculiar causes, one of which was the duke's alienation of East Jersey. At Dongan's

1684. 16 Feb'y. 7 March. New York City's address to the duke.

suggestion, under an opinion of Recorder Graham, the council and the city authorities drew up an address to the duke, in which was shown the convenient natural situation of Manhattan for commerce, and the hurtfulness of the "unhappy separation" of New Jersey from the ancient territory of New York, by reason of which its trade was diverted, to the injury of the proprietor's revenue. They therefore prayed that his royal highness would reannex East Jersey to his province "by purchase or other ways," and thus prevent the flourishing of the adjacent country by the ruin of New York. This address, the joint work of the New York Council—of which the elder Lewis Morris, of Westchester, and also of New Jersey, had just been sworn a member—was sent by Dongan to the duke and his commissioners, with a representation urging "the great inconveniences of having two distinct Governments upon one River," and "how convenient it would be to regain East Jersey."*

New York, indeed, had reason for annoyance. The proprietors of East Jersey removed Rudyard, and appointed Gawen Lawrie to be their governor, who, after visiting

23 Febr'y. Dongan, assumed his official duties at Elizabethtown.

2 March. New York and New Jersey.

Lawrie soon wrote home that the Governor of New York desired the boundary-line between the two provinces to be run, because several plantations were settled on the Hudson, and it was not known to which side they would fall. Amboy was now named "Perth," in honor of the earl, and a ferry was established there between Pennsylvania and

26 March. New York. A few weeks afterward, Lawrie reported that

29 March. several merchants of New York were leaving their plantations there and coming to East Jersey, because its land was

Penn and Dongan.

more productive. Even Penn and Dongan seem to have become rivals for the purchase of Baker's interest in Elizabethtown.†

* Council Min., v., 48; Min. of N. Y. Com. Council, i., 209, 222, 223, 225–227; Val. Man., 1860, 575; Col. Doc., ii., 619; iii., 341, 348, 354; Chalmers's Ann., i., 619, 621, 627, 628; Dunlap, ii., App. cxxxii.; Assembly Journals, ii., 527, *note;* Whitehead's East Jersey, 107, 215, 216; Eastern Boundary, 30. Lewis Morris was admitted into the New York Council on 17 January, 1684: Council Min., v., 43; Bolton's Westchester, ii., 290; Whitehead's Mem. of L. Morris, 3; *ante*, 188.

† Chalmers, i., 619–621; Leaming and Spicer, 168–185; Col. Doc., iii., 392; S. Smith, 170,

1684.

Penn had now become so involved in his controversy with Lord Baltimore that he sent two of his counselors, Lloyd and Welsh, to ask Dongan's friendly intervention. The governor promptly wrote to Maryland, as desired. 23 April. But when the Pennsylvania agents asked to be allowed to treat with the New York savages for their Susquehanna lands, Dongan told them "that they of Albany have sus- 24 April. Dongan opposes Penn's pretensions. picion it is only to get away their trade, and that Mr. Penn hath land already more than he can people these many years; that the Indians have long since given over their lands to this government; and advised them to write over to the duke about it." The agents then asked the governor to write to the Indians; but this was refused. Dongan's firm opposition to Penn's "coveting his neighbor's lands," made the latter his bitter enemy in England, whither he soon afterward returned "to improve his inter- 12 August. est" with the court. The duke's secretary, however, instructed Dongan "that no lands beyond the bounds of 10 March. James's orders to Dongan. East and West Jersey (betwixt the rivers) ought to be separated from your government upon any terms, and that you should use great care to hinder Mr. Pen and the inhabitants of both Jerseys from obstructing the peltry trade of New York; and that in order to this, you should prevent, all you can, the uniting of any part of either Jersey with Mr. Pen, who (as you observe) is very intent on his owne interest in those parts." Again Werden wrote, 27 August. The Susquehanna lands. "Touching Susquehanna River, or lands about it or trade in it, which the Indians convey to you or invite you to, we think you will doe well to preserve your interest there as much as possible, that soe nothing more may goe away to Mr. Penn or either New Jerseys. For it is apparent they are apt enough to stretch their priviledges, as well as the people of New England have been, who now probably will be reduced to reason by prosecution of the Quo Warranto which is brought against them."*

During the winter the savages in Maine were suspected 21 March. Pemaquid. of plotting against the English, and the New Hampshire

172, 175–180; Hatfield, 218–230; Whitehead's E. J., 38, 99, 100, 107, 161, 284–293; N. J. H. S. Proc., viii., 162; Council Min., v., 65; Penn. Arch., i., 80; *ante*, 49, 167, 368.

* Col. Doc., iii., 340, 341, 350, 422; Doc. Hist., i., 263, 265; Council Min., v., 73–79; Penn. Arch., i., 84–87; Col. Rec., i., 103, 104, 105, 109, 114, 117, 118; Proud, i., 265–287, 341; Mem. Penn. H. S., i., 442–449; Chalmers's Ann., i, 644, 650, 660–666; Dixon, 219, 220; *ante*, 377.

1684. Council asked Dongan to aid them with Mohawk warriors. To further this request, Governor Cranfield, with Dudley and Shrimpton, of Massachusetts, visited New York.

11 April. Dongan, however, would not irritate the Iroquois, especially as the Kennebec savages were "stout fellows, and feared not the Mohawks;" although he promised assistance if the Eastern Indians began hostilities. As Saint Castin was supposed to have instigated them, the governor again

May. Dongan again warns Castin. warned him and the French under his authority either to quit Pemaquid, or else swear allegiance to the King of England; promising not to interfere with their religion. Dongan's offer was considered by the French to be "the more dangerous," because of his "being a Catholic, and having a Jesuit and Priests along with him." Intending to visit Pemaquid, Dongan left its local government for the pres-

21 April. ent in the hands of Captain Nicholas Manning, Sheriff John

28 April. Allen, and Giles Goddard, its representative in the New

9 July. Orders for Pemaquid. York Assembly. Some of its inhabitants complained that the regulations of the previous November were "altogether arbitrary," and asked that the laws and tribunals of New York, although "over great distant," should be extended to them; but as the governor was now occupied with the Iroquois at Albany, the affairs of Pemaquid were postponed until he could himself go thither, "and in the mean time, the former orders to be observed."*

New York and Canada. Up to this time the relations between New York and Canada had been, upon the whole, friendly. The sympathy between Charles the Second and Louis the Fourteenth was not to be disturbed by any questions about their colonies in North America. But the Duke of York was anxious to gain all the territory he could; and his deputy, Andros, had claimed, in 1677, that New York included all the country south of the Saint Lawrence and Lake Ontario. This bold claim could not, however, be admitted by Canada. French missionaries had planted Christianity in that region long before any other Europeans had seen it; and the governors of New France had maintained the sovereignty of their king by warlike expeditions, and by treaties with the

* Council Min., v., 66–69, 72, 91; Col. MSS., xxxi., 166, 181; xxxii., 11, 37; xxxiv., 17, 18 (ii.), 2; Maine Hist. Soc. Coll., v., 70–72, 81–104, 263, 264; Mass. H. S. Coll., xxxv., 121, 122; Mass. Rec., v., 490; Col. Doc., iii., 364, 365, 406, 450; ix., 263, 265, 266, 800, 918; Belknap, i., 171, 172, 322; Williamson, i., 581; *ante*, 379.

savages, whom they overawed. But the appointments of De la Barre and of Dongan, to govern Canada and New York, brought to a crisis the question between those colonies, which could no longer be left undecided.

Dongan's Indian policy was simply to execute and extend that of his predecessor, Andros. In his earliest letters the duke's governor told De la Barre that "nobody hath a greater desire to have a strict union with you, and good correspondence, than myself, who served long time in France, and was much obliged by the king and gentry of that country." At the same time, Dongan claimed that all the territory "south and southwest of the Lake of Canada," belonged to the King of England. De la Barre, however, would not recognize the Iroquois as British subjects. Some Senecas and Cayugas having plundered French canoes on their way to the Sioux, assaulted Fort Saint Louis, but were repulsed by De Baugy, the successor of Tonty. De la Barre therefore resolved to attack the Senecas. He detained their ambassador, Tegancourt, who came to Quebec to ratify the agreement made the autumn before; and directed the Jesuit missionaries, Millet at Oneida, and the two Lambervilles at Onondaga, to intrigue so as to divide the Iroquois confederates. The savage allies of the French in the West were also ordered to be brought down, and Fort Frontenac was re-enforced. Some Caghnawaga converts were sent with friendly messages to the Mohawks, Oneidas, and Onondagas. The King of France was solicited to obtain an order from the King of England, prohibiting Dongan from assisting the Iroquois. De la Barre also sent the Sieur Bourdon to New York with a letter, advising Dongan of his intention to attack the Senecas and Cayugas, but not the Mohawks and Oneidas, "neighbors of Albany;" the people of which, he asked, might be forbidden to sell arms and ammunition to the Iroquois, which proceeding "can alone intimidate them, and when they see the Christians united on this subject, they will show them more respect than they have done hitherto."

February. Dongan's Indian policy.

28 March. De la Barre's conduct.

10 June.

5 June.

15 June.

But Dongan answered that all the Iroquois nations were under the government of New York, as appeared by its records; that the duke's territories reached "as far as the River of Canada; and that if the French did not come

CH. VIII. 1684. 24 June. 4 July. Dongan firm for New York.

south of the Saint Lawrence and Lake Ontario, "the people" of New York would not go north of them. "I am so heartily bent," he added, "to promote the quiet and tranquillity of this country and yours, that I intend forthwith to go myself to Albany, on purpose, and there send for the Indians, and require of them to do what is just, in order to a satisfaction to your pretences; if they will not, I shall not unjustly protect them."*

Dongan's promised visit to Albany had become more important, because some Iroquois war parties, said to have been instigated by the French missionaries, had gone down the Susquehanna, and committed outrages on the northern settlements of Maryland and Virginia. These hostilities violated the compact made at Albany in August, 1682.

28 Feb'y.

So Francis, Lord Howard of Effingham, who had succeeded Lord Culpepper as governor of Virginia, thought it necessary to instigate Dongan to join him in a war against the Five Nations. Accompanied by two members of his council,

29 June. Lord Howard of Effingham visits New York, and is made a freeman.

Effingham accordingly came to New York, where he was entertained, and was admitted by the city corporation to be a freeman of the metropolis. Lord Effingham appears to have been the first British peer upon whom this distinction was conferred. At Dongan's invitation he sailed with him in midsummer up the glorious Hudson to Albany, where the five Iroquois cantons of New York had been summoned to meet their "Corlaer."†

Deputies from the Mohawks, Oneidas, Onondagas, and Cayugas soon assembled there. Those from the far-off

30 July. Dongan and Effingham at Albany.

Senecas had not yet come. Lord Effingham opened the conference in presence of Dongan and two of his counselors, and the magistrates of Albany, by recapitulating the broken promises and recent outrages of the Iroquois, and proposed to make "a new chain" between them and Virginia and Maryland, "to endure even to the world's end."‡

* Col. Doc., iii., 233, 237, 247, 393, 394, 395, 447, 448, 449, 451, 467; v., 531, 731; ix., 200, 207, 226–228, 239, 240, 246, 247, 305; Doc. Hist., i., 67, 68, 73, 74, 262; Quebec MSS., iv. (ii.), 246, 248, 251; Council Min., iii. (ii.), 135; v., 40, 89, 90; Colden, i., 44, 53, 60, 61, 62, 249, 250; Charlevoix, ii., 290, 307–313; La Hontan's Voyages, i., 2–28; Pinkerton, xiii., 254–270; N. Y. H. S. Coll., ii., 286, 287; Shea's Missions, 312, 313; *ante*, 306, 307, 377.

† Council Min., v., 40, 93; Col. MSS., xxxi., 157, 174; Col. Doc., iii., 394, 406, 449; ix., 208, 228, 253; Colden, i., 44; ii., 80; Smith, i., 69; Chalmers, i., 346, 587; Burk, ii., 277, 281, 282; Beverley, 77; Oldmixon, i., 393; Campbell, 338; Collins's Peerage, v., 25; *ante*, 366, 377.

‡ In the *first* edition of Colden, p. 49, the date of this meeting is correctly given as "the

Dongan now accomplished an important purpose. Taking advantage of the presence of his brother governor from Virginia, he obtained from the Iroquois their written submission to "the Great Sachem Charles, that lives on the other side of the great lake." This was recorded upon "two white dressed deer-skins," which were "to be sent to the great Sachem in England, that he may write on them, and put a great red seal to them." All the Susquehanna River above the "Washuta," or Wyalusing Falls, and all the rest of the land of the Iroquois, was thus confirmed to the Duke of York, and "fastened" to his government.*

1684.

30 July. The Iroquois formally submit to the King of England.

Susquehanna lands.

At the same time, Counselor Van Cortlandt, whom the Massachusetts government appointed to be its agent, had an interview with the Mohawk sachems, and ratified "their former and happy friendship" by some small presents.†

30 July. Massachusetts and the Iroquois.

The next day the Mohawk sachem Odianne, who spoke for the four nations then represented, answered Lord Effingham that the Mohawks were free from blame, but that the Oneidas, Onondagas, and Cayugas had been "stupid, brutish, and void of understanding." In their name, however, he promised "*Assarigoa*," or "the big knife,"‡ that the covenant chain should thenceforth be kept "bright as silver" between Virginia and Maryland, and the Five Nations of New York, whose covenant house at Albany "must be kept clean." And then he offered to plant a tree of peace, "whose tops will reach the sun and its branches spread far abroad," so as to cover not only Virginia and Maryland, but Massachusetts, which Van Cortlandt represented. The Oneidas then gave beaver-skins to satisfy what they had promised Lord Baltimore two years before. An Onondaga followed for his own nation:—the Oneidas and Cayugas, asking to "lay hold of the chain," and that

31 July.

Lord Effingham named "Assarigoa" by the Iroquois.

thirtieth of July;" but the London editions of 1747, p. 47, and 1755, i., p. 45, erroneously print *thirteenth*. This error is followed by Burk, ii., 282; Bancroft, ii., 419; Dunlap, i., 136; and others.

* Col. Doc., iii., 347, 363, 394, 406, 417, 418, 508, 509, 515, 516; Colden (first ed.), 64, 65; ed. 1755, i., 55, 56; Doc. Hist., i., 261, 264, 266; Penn. Arch., i., 121–123; *ante*, 376.

† Mass. Rec., v., 461, 462; Colden (first ed.), 62; ed. 1755, i., 54; Col. Doc., iii., 394; *ante*, 309.

‡ The Mohawks, and Odianne their orator — misled, perhaps, by Arnout Cornelissen Viele, the Dutch interpreter—mistook Lord Howard's name for "Houwer," a Dutch word, which in English means a *hanger* or *cutlass*. This phonetic error made them call the Virginian governor "*Assarigoa*," which, in the Iroquois tongue, signifies "big knife." This term, "Assarigoa" (like that of "Corlaer" in New York), was long used by the New York savages to designate the governors of Virginia: Col. Doc., iii., 454; v., 670; viii., 119; ix., 706; Mass. Rec., v., 461; Colden, i., 50; ii., 48; Shea's ed., 57, 133.

CH. VIII. 1684.

an axe might be buried for each of them. But the Mohawks said that no axe need be buried for them, because they had never broken the first chain. Then the five axes —two for Maryland and Virginia, and three for the Oneidas, Onondagas, and Cayugas—"were buried in the south-east end of the court-yard, and the Indians threw the earth upon them. After which my Lord told them them that since now a firm peace was concluded, we shall hereafter remain firm friends, and Virginia and Maryland will send once in two or three years to renew it, and some of our Indian Sachems shall come according to your desire to confirm it." After this the Oneidas, Onondagas, and Cayugas "jointly sang the Peace Song, with demonstrations of much joy, and thanked the Governor of New York for his effectual mediation with the Governor of Virginia in their favour."*

Axes buried at Albany.

The four nations then asked to have "the Duke of York's arms put upon their castles," which they supposed "would save them from the French." So Dongan ordered Viele, the interpreter, to place them on "each castle, as far as Oneigra," which was accordingly done. Viele was instructed to forbid the Five Nations, "as subjects of the Duke of York," from holding any conference with the French without the governor's permission; and the Senecas were offered four hundred cavalry and as many infantry if they should be attacked by the French. Dongan likewise asked the savages to call home those of their nations who had settled at Caghnawaga, near Montreal. The sachems adroitly replied, "Corlaer keeps a correspondence with Canada, and therefore he can prevail more than we can. Let Corlaer use his endeavours to draw our Indians home to their own country."†

August. The Duke of York's arms put on the Iroquois castles.

The Onondagas and Cayugas now made "a remarkable speech" to the two English governors, whom they addressed as "Brethren," at the Town Hall of Albany—"Your Sachem," they said, "is a great Sachem, and we are but a small people. But when the English first came to Manhattan, Vir-

2 August. Speech of the Onondagas and Cayugas to Dongan and Effingham.

* Colden (first ed.), 55–61; ed. 1755, i., 49–53; ii., 80; Burk, i., 284–287; *ante*, 365, 366.

† Colden (first ed.), 61, 62, 63, 78 (ed. 1755), i., 53, 54, 65; Col. Doc., iii., 363, 396, 449, 473; v., 75, 76; ix., 242, 247, 251, 253, 257, 259, 261; Doc. Hist., i., 69, 76, 81, 87; Charlevoix, iii., 315. Viele's Journal of his expedition is in Col. MSS., xxxi., 159, and Albany Records, xviii., 461–464.

ginia, and Maryland, they were but a small people, and we a great people. And finding they were good people, we gave them land, and treated them civilly. And now, since you are a great people and we but a small, you will protect us from the French; which, if you do not, we shall lose all our hunting and beavers. The French will have all the Beavers, and are angry with us for bringing any to you."

1684. Speech of the Onondagas and Cayugas.

"We have put all our land and our selfs under the protection of the great Duke of York, the brother of your great Sachem;—We have given the Susquehanne River, which we won with the sword, to this Government, and desire that it may be a branch of that great tree that grows here, whose top reaches to the sun, under whose branches we shall shelter ourselves from the French, or any other people; And our fire burns in your houses, and your fire burns with us; And we desire that it always may be so, and will not that any of your Penn's people shall settle upon the Susquehanne River; for our young folks or soldiers are like wolfs in the woods, as you Sachem of Virginia know, we having no other land to leave to our wives and children."

"We have put ourselves under the Great Sachem Charles that lives over the Great Lake, and we do give you two white dres't deer-skins, to be sent to the Great Sachem Charles, that he may write upon them, and put a great red seale to them, that we do put the Susquehanne River, above the Washinta, or Falls, and all the rest of our land, under the great Duke of York, and to nobody else. Our Brethren, his servants, were as fathers to our wives and children, and did give us bread when we were in need of it; and we will neither join ourselves nor our land to any other government than this: And this Proposition we desire that Corlaer, the Governor, may send over to your Great Sachem Charles that dwells over the Great Lake, with this belt of Wampum-peeg, and another smaller belt for the Duke of York his brother; and we give a Beaver to the Corlaer to send over this Proposition."

"And you, Great Man of Virginia, We let you know that Great Penn did speak to us here in Corlaer's house, by his Agents, and desired to buy the Susquehanne River. But we would not hearken to him, nor come under his

CH. VIII. 1684.

government; and therefore desire you to be witness of what we now do, and that we have already done. And let your friend that lives over the Great Lake know that we are a free people, uniting ourselves to what Sachem we please; and do give you one beaver skin."*

5 August. Speech of the Senecas to Dongan and Effingham.

Three days after this speech the Seneca delegates reached Albany, and had an interview with the Governors of New York and Virginia. They asked Lord Effingham to include them in the "new chain" he had made with the other four nations, who, "from the Mohawks' country to the Cayugas, have delivered up the Susquehanna River and all that country to Corlaer's government. We confirm what they have done by giving this belt." And then, referring to their relations with Canada, they said that its governor was to blame; he furnished arms to their enemies, and enticed them to bring beavers to Montreal, which otherwise the Senecas would have brought to their own "brethren" at Albany. Onnontio called them his "children," and talked of protecting them; but at the same time he "knocked them on the head," by aiding their enemies. "Corlaer," they added, "hear what we say. We thank you for the Duke's Arms, which you have given us to be put on our castles, as a defence to them. You command them. Have we wandered out of the way, as the Governor of Canada says? We do not threaten him with war, as he threatens us. What shall we do? Shall we run away, or shall we sit still in our houses?"†

5 July. Dongan's notice to De la Barre.

Dongan had, meanwhile, notified De la Barre that the Senecas were under the government of New York; that "the Duke's territories" must not be invaded; and that the differences between the French in Canada and the New York Iroquois ought to be settled by the "masters in Europe, to whom we should properly refer." And he added, "I have ordered the coats of arms of his Royal Highness the Duke of York, to be put up in the Indian castles, which may dissuade you from acting any thing that may create a misunderstanding between us." De la Barre at

* See copy translated and revised by Secretary Robert Livingston, of this "Proposition," or "Oration," in Col. Doc., iii., 347, 417, 418, 508, 509; Doc. Hist., i., 263, 264, 265. Colden, in his first edition, 63–66, and in the ed. of 1755, i., 54–56, varies the wording.

† Colden (first ed.), 66–68, 74–77 (ed. 1755), i., 53–58, 62–64; Col. Doc., iii., 508, 509; ix., 297, 802.

once dispatched the Sieur de Salvaye to Albany with an answer to Dongan, that not the governors of New York and Canada, but only the kings of England and France, could decide "about pretensions to the possession of lands." Yet, although the Cayugas and Senecas had claimed the Governor of New York as their "intercessor," those "robbers, assassins, and traitors" would be attacked by the French toward the end of August. De la Barre's messenger came to Albany just as the Seneca delegates reached there, and was present at the conference with the two English governors. Dongan quickly sent him back to Canada with a letter to De la Barre, that the French claim to the Iroquois country by twenty-five years' possession, and sending Jesuit missionaries, was "very slender;" that he wished a "good correspondence;" but that as to all territorial claims, he had referred them, "with an entire submission, unto England."*

Ch. VIII. — 1684. — 15/25 July. De la Barre's answer. — 5 August. — August. Dongan's reply.

Accordingly, on returning to the metropolis, Dongan sent Baxter, the commandant at Albany, to London, with full accounts of what had just been done. Among other events which happened during the governor's absence, the Minisink sachems had appeared before the council, and declared themselves under the government of New York. The duke's commissioners approved of Dongan's doings with the Indians, "because they tend to the continuing that good correspondence which hath hitherto been held with them, and which is so necessary for the preservation of your peltry trade." But they cautioned him "to act so prudently" toward his European neighbors as to give them "no just cause of complaint."†

27 August. Dispatches to London. — 28 July. — 1 Novem. The duke's orders.

In spite of Dongan, De la Barre persisted to attack the Senecas, and went to Fort Frontenac with all the force of Canada, consisting of some twelve hundred men, who were pompously reviewed. On his way up the Saint Lawrence, the governor was joined by James Lamberville, who brought discouraging letters from his brother at Onondaga, and by Millet, who now abandoned his mission at Oneida. Lamberville was sent back with friendly messages to the Onondagas, and was followed by Charles le

14 August. De la Barre's expedition against the Iroquois. — 10–18 July. — 10 August. — 6/16 Aug.

* Col. Doc., iii., 449–452, 473; ix., 242; Doc. Hist., i., 69–72; Col. MSS., xxxi., 157; Colden, 74; i., 62; Smith, i., 70.

† Council Min., v., 93, 94; Col. Doc., iii., 351, 352.

CH. VIII. 1684.

Moyne, who invited the Iroquois to meet Onnontio at "La Famine," or the Salmon River, and took back Tegancourt, the Seneca ambassador, whom De la Barre had arrested at Quebec. A detachment was also sent forward from Fort Frontenac, to encamp at La Famine, so as to be "nearer the enemy," and be able, by hunting and fishing, to refresh the rest of the army.*

At Onondaga Le Moyne met Viele, whom Dongan had sent on horseback from Albany to warn the Five Nations not to speak to the Canadians without his permission. 7/17 Aug. Dongan's messenger succeeded very well with the Mohawks at Tionnontoguen, and with the Oneidas, "who promised that they would not go near the French Governor." 18/28 Aug. But, when Viele came to Onondaga, he was confronted, in a council of that nation and the Oneidas and Cayugas, by three French agents, much more able than himself. These were, De la Barre's messenger, Charles le Moyne, or *Acossen*, "the Partridge," with the Jesuit Father John de Lamberville—whom the Iroquois had named *Teiorensere*, which in their picturesque language meant "the dawning of the day"—and his younger brother James, whom they called *Onnissantie*. But Dongan's Dutch-English emissary did his work badly. In the Iroquois council, Viele, whom they called "Arie," spoke "like a master" to the American owners of New York, and told them that they belonged to the King of England and the Duke of York; that their council-fires were lighted at Albany; and that they must not talk with the Governor of Canada. This discourse offended the Onondagas, who replied that they would go and meet Onnontio. "You say we are subjects of the King of England and the Duke of York, but we say we are Brethren. We must take care of Ourselves. Those arms fixed upon the post without the gate cannot defend us against the arms of La Barre." Flattery and presents from Canada had meanwhile gained over one of the Onondaga chiefs named Outreouati, or Hoteouati, or

Viele, or "Arie," at the Onondaga council.

* Col. Doc., iii., 431, 445, 467, 473; ix., 172, 174, 234–236, 241, 242, 252–256; Doc. Hist., i., 74, 75, 83–86; Charlevoix, ii., 313, 314, 315; Shea's Charlevoix, iii., 248–251; Colden, i., 64, 181; La Hontan, i., 39–43; Shea's Missions, 277, 313; *ante*, 395. The Indian name of *La Famine*, now known as Salmon River, in Oswego County, was "Gainhouagué," or "Kaihohage," where Frontenac had been invited to meet the Iroquois in 1682: Col. Doc., iii., 431, 445; ix., 172, 174, 259; Colden, i., 64, 65, 181; *ante*, 364. In Doc. Hist., i., 63, it is incorrectly called Hungry Bay, in Jefferson County.

Grande Gueule opposes Corlaer.

Haaskouaun, whom the French called "*La Grande Gueule,*" because he had "the strongest head and loudest voice among the Iroquois." A few words "whispered in his ears" by the French agents made the Indian orator use "high words" against Dongan's messenger. "Learn," said he, "that the Onondaga places himself between Onnontio his father, and the Seneca his brother, to hinder them from fighting. I should have thought that Corlaer would have placed himself behind me, and cried 'Courage, Onondaga, do not let the father and the son kill each other.' I am very much surprised that his envoy talks to me quite otherwise. * * * I have two arms, one of which I extend to Montreal, to support there the tree of peace; the other is on the head of Corlaer, who for a long time has been my brother. Onnontio has been for ten years my father, and Corlaer for a long time my brother; and this, because I have willed it so. Neither the one nor the other is my master. He who made the world has given me the land which I occupy. I am free. I have respect for both. But nobody has the right to command me; and nobody should take it ill that I use every means to prevent the land from being troubled. I cannot any longer put off going to my father, since he has taken the trouble to come to my gate, and has only reasonable propositions to make to me." But, with "Iroquois cunning," the Onondagas asked Le Moyne to have their conference with De la Barre postponed until they could obtain Dongan's permission. This, however, was declined, and arrangements were quickly made for an embassy to meet Onnontio at La Famine.*

The Iroquois free.

De la Barre at Fort Frontenac,

The news was soon carried to De la Barre, at Fort Frontenac, where affairs were now bad enough. Fever had so reduced himself and his forces, both there and at La Famine, that it was out of the question to attack the Senecas. The Western auxiliaries assembled at Niagara were ordered to return home, and De la Barre hastened across the lake to Salmon River. Some of the sick were sent back to

* Col. Doc., iv., 122; ix., 185, 242, 243, 251, 257, 258, 386; Col. MSS., xxxi., 159; Albany Rec., xviii., 461; Doc. Hist., i., 76, 87, 88; Charlevoix, ii., 315–317, 370, 371; Shea's Charlevoix, iii., 351–353; Colden, 78–81; i., 65–67; La Hontan, i., 46, 125; Bancroft, ii., 421; *ante*, 364, 396, 398. As to the meaning of the Indian names of Lamberville and Millet, compare Shea's Colden, 79, 80, 135, and Catholic Missions, 277; Colden (ed. 1755), i., 66, 114; Col. Doc., iii., 453; ix., 665; Rel. 1672, 12, 21; *ante*, 178.

CH. VIII. 1684. Montreal, and messengers were dispatched to hurry forward the Indian delegation from Onondaga. Le Moyne, with nine Onondagas, three Oneidas, and two Cayugas, headed by Grande Gueule, and the younger Garacontie, soon came to La Famine. The French regaled them with abundant lake trout; and a conference was appointed for the next day. De la Barre was then sitting in an armchair, with his interpreters and officers on each side, while the Iroquois sat on the ground, "in the Oriental fashion," facing the French. Bruyas spoke for De la Barre; Outreouati, or Grande Gueule, and Garacontie for the Iroquois; and the Seneca Tegancourt was also present. In a bold harangue, Bruyas, on the part of Onnontio, charged the New York Iroquois with robbing and abusing the French traders among the Illinois and Miamis, and with introducing the English into the lakes belonging to the King of France; and threatened to destroy the villages of the Five Nations if they did not give satisfaction to the French. Amazed that the "soft words" of Lamberville and Le Moyne at Onondaga were turned into such threats at Salmon River, Grande Gueule, who had all the while kept his eye fixed on his calumet, or pipe of peace, arose, and, after five or six turns around the French and Indian circle, replied with telling sarcasm: "Onnontio, I honor you; but the Five Nations have not yet perished. I congratulate you that you have buried the murderous axe which has been so often red with French blood. I see you dreaming in a camp of sick men, whom the Great Spirit has allowed to live. We have introduced the English into our Lakes to trade with the Ottawas and Hurons, just as the Algonquins conducted the French to our Five Villages to carry on a commerce which the English say belongs to them. But we are born free. We no more depend on Onnontio than on Corlaer. We can go where we will, to take there what we think proper, and buy and sell as we please. We have attacked the Illinois and Miamis, because they cut down the trees of Peace on our frontiers. When we buried the axe in the middle of the Fort at Cataracouy, in the presence of your predecessor, we thought that the post would be a trading place, and not a garrison. Take care that the tree of peace planted there be not

3 Septem. and at La Famine.

4 Septem. Conference at La Famine.

Bruyas's speech for De la Barre.

Grande Gueule's reply to De la Barre.

choked by a crowd of your soldiers. Our warriors will not dig up the hatchet until their Brothers, Onnontio or Corlaer, shall undertake to attack the countries which the Great Spirit has allotted to our ancestors." On hearing this speech, De la Barre retired to his tent, and began to bluster. But in the afternoon he talked again for three hours with the savages, and then agreed to a peace, of which the main points were that his troops were to return at once to Quebec, and that, in fighting the Illinois, the Iroquois were not to hurt the French. On this basis a formal treaty was made. De la Barre hastened back to Canada, whence the best report that he could send to France was, that his campaign had "not been bloody." Yet, with characteristic folly, he declared that affairs in Europe alone prevented him from marching against Dongan, "who fain would assume to be sovereign Lord of the whole of North America, south of the River Saint Lawrence."*

5 Septem. De la Barre's treaty at La Famine.
7 October.

In later dispatches De la Barre laid the blame of his failure upon Dongan, who was "filled with chimerical pretensions," which ought to be stopped by orders from the King of England, or by force in America. But De Meulles, the intendant, declared that the governor had been fooled in the "most shameful manner" by a sycophantic buffoon. The Chevalier Hector de Callières, the newly-arrived governor of Montreal, also wrote that "the most intelligent in these parts believe this peace between us and the Iroquois uncertain, until they be obliged to leave the Illinois undisturbed."†

13 Novem.
14 Novem. Dongan's "pretensions."
10 Oct.
9 Novem. Hector de Callières's opinion.

La Salle had meanwhile laid his case before the king, and, supported by Frontenac and Zenobe, had convinced Louis that the discovery of the Valley of the Mississippi was not "very useless." So orders were sent to put La Salle again in possession of Fort Frontenac; and he was charged

10 April.

* Col. Doc., iii., 473; ix., 229–232, 236–239, 242–248, 259; Doc. Hist., i., 76–82, 89; La Hontan (ed. 1703), i., 43–57; Pinkerton, xiii., 273–278; La Potherie, ii., 157–165; iii., 57; Charlevoix, ii., 317–319; Colden, 81–90; i., 67–73; Smith, i., 71–77; *ante*, 299. La Hontan Latinized "Grande Gueule" into *Grangula;* and Colden, in 1727, or his printer Bradford, transformed La Hontan's "Grangula" into *Garangula.* Colden also took the liberty of altering the well-known *Onnontio* to "Yonnondio." Charlevoix, who charges La Hontan with irreligion, spite, and invention, also errs in saying that Haaskouaun, or "Grande Gueule," was a Seneca, when he was an Onondaga; and that "La Famine" got its name from the distress of De la Barre's troops in 1684, when it was so known in 1682: compare Charlevoix, ii., 319, 371; iii., 172; vi., 408, 409; Col. Doc., ix., 172, 174; *ante*, 364.

† Col. Doc., ix., 222, 244–264; Doc. Hist., i., 79–91; Charlevoix, ii., 318, 321; La Hontan, i., 57.

CH. VIII. 1684. Louisiana. 14 April.

to begin the colonization of "*Louisiana*" under the French government. La Salle's commission from Louis made him commander "from Fort Saint Louis on the River of the Illinois, unto New Biscay."*

10 April. "Loafing" Frenchmen in New York.

De la Barre was also instructed to enforce the ordinances, to punish all "vagabond and loafing Frenchmen" who should, without permission, emigrate from Canada "to Orange, Manatte, and other places belonging to the English and Dutch." But he might attack the Iroquois, and Louis gave him this extraordinary order: "To diminish as much as possible the number of the Iroquois, and moreover as these savages, who are very strong and robust, will serve usefully in my galleys, I will that you do every thing in your power to make a great number of them prisoners of war, and have them embarked by every opportunity that shall offer in order that they be conveyed to France." These instructions were a week in De la Barre's hands, when, at Salmon River, instead of making Iroquois prisoners, he was glad to escape from the sarcastic eloquence of Grande Gueule. But they led his successor into one of the worst errors ever committed by a Canadian governor. The king also directed Barillon, his ambassador at London, to ask the Duke of York to prohibit Dongan from aiding the Iroquois, and order him to act in concert with De la Barre, "to the common advantage of both nations." No such orders, however, were, or could be given at Whitehall, where Dongan's policy was cautiously but fully sustained.†

31 July. Louis orders robust Iroquois to be sent to his galleys. 31 July. 1 Novem. 4 Decem.

On his return from Salmon River, Garakontié hastened to Albany with news of De la Barre's wonderful treaty with the Five Nations. Dongan had gone down to New York; but the commissioners at Albany rebuked the savages for visiting Onnontio without the leave of Corlaer. "We are sorry and ashamed," answered the Onondagas, "for now we understand that the Governor of Canada is not so great a man as the English King that lives on the other side of the great water; and we are vexed for hav-

September. The Iroquois not to talk with Onnontio but by leave of Corlaer.

* Col. Doc., ix., 201, 213-223, 225, 233, 411; La Hontan, i., 7, 8; Charlevoix, ii., 287, 324, 436; iii., 2; Shea's Discovery, 185-188, 267; Sparks's La Salle, 109-113; Hist. Coll. Lou., i., 25-34, 37-44; Garneau, i., 245, 246; *ante*, 378.

† Col. Doc., iii., 351, 352, 353; v., 731; ix., 200, 203, 222-225, 232-234, 248, 250; Doc. Hist., i., 72, 73; Charlevoix, ii., 320, 321; La Hontan, i., 57, 62, 68; Colden, i., 249, 250; *ante*, 369.

ing given the Governor of Canada so many fine wampum belts."* CH. VIII.

1684.

The postponed affairs of Pemaquid were now resumed. The block-house at Merrymeeting was ordered to be immediately raised and garrisoned, and the duke's quit-rents "in the County of Cornwall" to be collected. Giles Goddard, the representative of the county in the New York Assembly, was also made a captain of its militia, and commissioned to be its surveyor of land.† Pemaquid. 8 Septem. 12 Septem. 22 October.

Some of the inhabitants of Esopus, in the new "County of Ulster," having petitioned the governor for the right to choose their own town officers, were bound over to keep the peace, because they were held to have committed "a riot," according to English law. Bail was given, and the petitioners were fined. But upon acknowledging that they had been "ill advised," they were relieved.‡ 18 Febr'y. Esopus rioters. 6 June. 6 Septem.

The magistrates at Southold, having fined Nathaniel Baker, of Easthampton, "only for bringing home an ox of his, on the Sunday," were ordered to show cause before the governor, and, on doing so, were "referred to law." The house of the Lutheran minister Arensius having been assessed by the Corporation of New York as that of "a private person," the governor and council declared their opinion that it should be as free and exempted from taxes as those of the Dutch and French ministers."§ Easthampton magistrates. 5 May. Arensius. 6 Septem.

The Reverend Josias Clarke, who had been commissioned by the duke to succeed Gordon as chaplain to the garrison, was engaged in a humane and interesting act soon after he reached his post. Among the passengers who had come over in the ship Seaflower, from Scotland, was David Jamison, who had been liberally educated, but held opinions which led him to join a company of enthusiasts called "Sweet Singers," who denounced the creeds of Christians, and the Protestant version of the Bible. Having been examined before the Duke of York, at Edinburgh, Jamison was ordered to be sent to America; and Doctor George Lockhart, one of the owners of the Seaflower, in which he came, was authorized to sell him, as a "Redemptioner," to 16 June. Josias Clarke chaplain. Sweet Singers. 17 May. David Jamison.

* Col. Doc., ix., 259, 261; Doc. Hist., i., 89, 91; Colden (first ed.), 90.

† Col. MSS., xxxiii., 40, 48, 61; xxxiv., 17, 18, 32 (ii.), 2; Maine H. S. Coll., v., 104–107; *ante*, 394.

‡ Council Min., v., 48, 49; Col. MSS., xxxi., 115, 149, 180.

§ Doc. Hist., iii., 213, 246; Council Min., v., 81; Col. MSS., xxxi., 98, 173; *ante*, 273.

CH. VIII. 1684. August.

any one who would pay the cost of his passage. With the impulses of a scholar, Clarke at once paid the demand, which the "chief men of the place" quickly reimbursed to the duke's liberal Episcopal chaplain; and the exiled Scotch "Sweet Singer" was set to teach a Latin school in New York, "which he attended some time, with great industry and success."*

Jamison teaches a Latin school in New York.

13 October. Common Council of New York.

At the usual time, new aldermen and common councilmen were chosen for the six wards of the metropolis, according to the "form and method" agreed to by Dongan the autumn before. The governor, in whose hands the appointment of mayor rested, made a grateful concession to the old Dutch feeling by allowing seven persons to be named to him, from which he chose Gabriel Minvielle to be the new mayor.†

14 October.

21 October to 29 October. Second Assembly of the province.

The second meeting of the New York Assembly was held, according to adjournment, and Matthias Nicolls continued to be its speaker. But, in place of Secretary Spragg, Robert Hammond was appointed clerk. Thirty-one laws were passed by the Assembly and assented to by the governor. Among them was an act to confirm previous judgments, and to abolish the General Court of Assizes. The Revenue Bill was also amended, in conformity to the "hint" of the duke's commissioners. An act was also passed "for the encouragement of Trade and Navigation within this Province," which laid a duty of ten per cent. upon all goods imported into New York from any other colony where such goods were not produced. The object of this law was to prevent the "refractory" people of Southold and other towns at the east of Long Island, who were "very loath to have any commerce" with the metropolis, from "carrying their oil to Boston, and bringing goods from thence into this Government."‡

Provincial Navigation Law.

* Col. Doc., iii., 352, 415; iv., 400, 429, 442, 823; v., 478; Doc. Hist., ii., 14; iii., 73, 245; Deeds, viii., 31; Col. MSS., xxxi., 147; xxxii., 29, 42; xxxiii., 75, 90, 304; xxxiv. (ii.), 23–33; Burnet, i., 526; Wodrow, iii., 348–355; iv., 85; Crookshank, ii., 135, 272; Whitehead's E. J. Contributions, 38–40, 367; Secret Services, Ch. II. and Jac. II., 88; *ante*, 374.

† Col. MSS., xxxiii., 57, 65; Min. of Com. Council, i., 267, 270; Val. Man., 1853, 331, 388; *ante*, 390. There is much curious and valuable information, which I have not the space to reproduce, in the N. Y. Common Council and Surrogate's Records; among other things, a report about Fort James: compare Val. Man., 1855, 551–553; 1864, 636, 637; Wills, iv., 1–15; Col. Doc., 390, 391; Col. MSS., xxxiii., 15; xxxiv., i., 23, 24.

‡ Council Journ., i., Int. xii., xiii.; Wood, 90, 101; Thompson, i., 162; Daly's Sketch, 31; Col. Doc., iii., 341, 349, 355, 383, 391, 399, 402, 797; v., 58; Coun. Min., v., 51, 52, 103, 108; *ante*, 384.

The Court of Assizes having "ceased and determined," Ch. VIII.
was replaced by the Court of Oyer and Terminer, of which
Nicolls and Palmer had been appointed judges. After his 1684. Court of
dismissal from the government of New Jersey, Rudyard Oyer and Terminer.
came to New York, and, having been a London lawyer, August. Rudyard.
was commissioned by Dongan "to act on all occasions" as
the duke's attorney general. It was also ordered that a 16 Febr'y.
Court of Chancery, to consist of the governor and his coun- Court of Chancery.
cil, should be held on the first Thursday of every second
month in the year, and Dongan appointed John Spragg to 29 Decem.
be master of the rolls, and John Knight and Recorder
James Graham to be its clerks. Under his Vice-Admiral-
ty Commission from the Lord High Admiral in English
Plantations, the governor appointed Justice Palmer, of the 30 May.
Oyer and Terminer, to be judge, in place of Collector Admiralty.
Santen, Secretary Spragg, register, and John Cavalier,
marshal. Dongan, however, following the practice of his
predecessors, acted as surrogate, before whom wills made in Surrogate.
the province were proved.*

Judge Palmer was soon afterward sworn a counselor. 1 Decem.
Jan Jansen Bleecker, and Johannes Wendell, who had long
been magistrates, were also appointed captains of infantry 15 Decem.
at Albany, and Peter Schuyler lieutenant of horse. The
people at the east of Long Island continued to give the
governor much trouble; and he was obliged to tell them 24 Decem.
that they would "neither be easy themselves, nor suffer Long Island troublesome.
others to be so." In spite of the Navigation Law of their
own province, they would smuggle and carry on illicit
trade with Boston. Dongan and his council were there- 1685.
fore forced to determine that "the inhabitants of East- 3 April.
hampton having refused to sell their oil and commodities,
unless Boston money was given for it, or pieces of eight
equivalent to them, and several abuses committed to the
prejudice of His Majesty's Customs' revenue being informed of, Ordered that a Proclamation be sent, prohibiting all

* Col. Doc., iii., 351, 352, 389, 412, 414; iv., 847; Council Min., v., 47, 48, 49, 86, 142; Col. MSS., xxxii., 32; xxxiii., 77, 79, 216; xxxiv., 3, 12, 13, 14, 21; Commissions, i., 61; N. Y. Surrogate's Office, Wills, i., ii.; Wood's Long Island, 90, 101, 102; Whitehead's E. Jersey, 99, 124, 125; Leaming and Spicer, 197; Daly's Sketch, 31, 32, 51, 52; Revised Laws, 1813, ii., App. ix.; *ante*, 386, 392. Judge Daly, in his Sketch, p. 30, 51, does not appear to have known that the New York Courts of Admiralty were appointed by the several governors, under their separate commissions from the Duke of York as Lord High Admiral of the English Plantations: *ante*, 319. When James became king, he gave his governor a larger commission: Col. Doc., iii., 380, 540; *post*, 452.

CH. VIII. vessels to come and trade at any port but the City of New York."*

1685. 2 Febr'y. The Corporation of the City of New York now voted that their governor should be "treated with," to confirm to it all the vacant land in and about the metropolis, as far as low-water-mark, and all the other franchises which it claimed. 23 March. Corporation of New York City. Dongan and his council soon afterward charged the Mayor of New York "not to give freedom to any but such as are qualified by Act of Assembly, and will give security to give 'scott and lott' for three years." This was in conformity with the ancient Dutch practice, which maintained that all traders must keep "fire and light" at home, and made the "hearth-stone" the only test of a multifarious citizenship.†

The proprietors of East Jersey, relying on the Duke of York's release to them of the 14th of March, 1683, had meanwhile revived the claim to Staten Island, which Lady Carteret had made in 1681. Their agents "dispersed printed papers" to the disturbance of the inhabitants and landowners there, so that even Judge Palmer thought it prudent to secure his own title by obtaining additional patents from the Jersey proprietors. Staten Island. Dongan is said to have done the same. Yet it was notorious that, after that island had been "adjudged to belong to New York" in 1668, it had been bought for the duke by Lovelace in April, 1670; and that in March, 1683, the East Jersey Assembly had conceded it to New York, by not including the island in either of the four counties then established. With full knowledge of the duke's release, Dongan had approved the law of November, 1683, which declared the New York County of Richmond to contain "all Staten Island" and the adjoining islands.

1684. 9 Febr'y. Samuel Winder, the former prosecutor of Collector Dyer, was accordingly commissioned to be clerk and register of that county, and directed to collect the quit-rents due within it; 23 Febr'y. Officers' duties. and Philip Wells, the surveyor general of the province, was ordered to lay out all the lands on Staten Island, according to each owner's patent. Thomas Love-

* Council Min., v., 100, 103, 108; Col. MSS., xxxiii., 81, 97, 103.

† Min. of Com. Coun., i., 272; Council Min., v., 107; Col. MSS., xxxiii., 104; *ante*, vol. i., 628, 694, 749; ii., 391. Hoffman does not notice, in his Treatise, this application of the Common Council of the city.

1684. 1 Decem. — 26 August. No "innovation" on the Hudson River to be suffered. — 27 August. — 1 Novem. Staten Island "without doubt" belongs to New York.

lace, the sheriff of Staten Island, was afterward directed to summon all persons not having land titles before the governor and council.* The metropolitan memorial in March, 1684, praying the duke to reannex East Jersey, appears to have brought the question to a crisis. "Because of some rumors I have met with," replied James to Dongan, "as if some of your neighbors, under colour of grants from myself, or upon some other groundless pretences, endeavour all they can to obstruct the trade of New York and Albany, I think it fit hereby to recommend that to you in an especial manner, that you may not suffer any innovation within that river." The next day, Werden added, with reference to a proposed sale of Billop's plantation on Staten Island, opposite Amboy, that Dongan should "endeavor to procure some inhabitant of New York rather to buy it, than suffer any of those of New Jersey to doe it; but whosoever buys land in that Island, it being under your government, he must be liable, as well as others, to the laws thereof." Not long afterward, when the claim of the East Jersey proprietors had been reported, Werden wrote more distinctly, "Staten Island, without doubt, belongs to the Duke; for if Sir George Carteret had had right to it, that would have been long since determined, and those who broach such fancies as may disturb the quiet of possessions in that Island are certainly very injurious to the Duke, and we think have no colour for such pretences." This was written by the duke's secretary, who witnessed his release to the proprietors of East New Jersey, and knew its true intent.†

But when Perth, and Mackenzie, and Drummond—the Scotch proprietors of East Jersey, and the personal friends of the duke—heard that Dongan had proposed that their colony should be brought again under the government of New York, they spoke to James, whom they found to be "verie just, and to abhorr the thoughts of allowing

* Col. MSS., xxxiii., 69; xxxiv., 11. On 27 August, 1684, Elizabeth, widow of the late Governor Philip Carteret, petitioned Dongan for some meadow-land on the island, formerly granted to her husband by the New York governors: Col. MSS., xxxi., 164; Hist. Mag., x., 297–299; *ante*, 150, 166, 350, 359, 369, 371, 386.

† Col. Doc., iii., 348, 349, 350, 352, 354; Col. MSS., xxxiii, 69; xxxiv., 14; Council Min., v., 102; Chalmers's Ann., i., 621, 628; Leaming and Spicer, 141–150, 229, 687; Whitehead's East Jersey, 124, 216, 217; Contributions, 94; Eastern Boundary, 30, 43, 44, 49, 50; Index N. J. Col. Doc., 1[illegible]5; *ante*, 3[illegible]2.

CH. VIII. 1684. any thing to be done contrary to what he hath past under his hand and seall." They also discoursed with his commissioners at London, whom they supposed they had convinced "of the reasons which induce us not to yield to such 22 August. Perth's letter to Dongan. a proposall." Accordingly, they wrote from Edinburgh "a very angry letter" to Dongan, in which they desired him to "lay aside all thoughts of attempting what may reflect upon the justice or honour of your master, or may give us 1685. 13 Feb'y. Dongan's reply. just reason to complain." Dongan, "mightily surprized" at this letter, replied that he had only done his duty in representing to the duke "the great inconveniencies of having two distinct governments upon one River, yours having the advantage of being some leagues nearer the sea than we are. Your agents have dispersed printed papers, to the disturbance of the inhabitants of Staten Island. It hath been in the possession of his Royal Highness above twenty years (except the little time the Dutch had it), purchased by Governor Lovelace from the Indians in the time of Sir George Carteret, without any pretences, 'till your agents 18 Feb'y. Dongan complains of New Jersey. made claime to it." At the same time, Dongan wrote to Werden, that if vessels were allowed to come to Amboy without entering at New York, it would be impossible to prevent smuggling into Staten Island. "The Quakers making continual pretences to Staten Island disturbs the people. More than two hundred families are settled on it. And in case his Royal Highness cannot retrieve East Jersey, it will doe well to secure Hudson's River, and take away all claim to Staten Island."*

1684. If New York was troubled about New Jersey, she was quieted about Connecticut. Under the agreement of No- 8 May. 26 Septem. vember, 1683, Dongan appointed commissioners to meet those of Connecticut, to lay out a boundary-line between 10 October. Connecticut boundary arranged. the two colonies. The joint commissioners accordingly met at Stamford, and went to the Byram River. From there they surveyed the proper courses, of which they made a map and report. These having been approved by the 1685. 23 Feb'y. council of New York, Dongan met Treat at Milford. The two governors there signed a ratification, which was order-

* Col. Doc., iii., 348, 353, 354, 356; Chalmers's Ann., i., 627, 628, 629; Whitehead's E. J., 214–217; Clarke's James II., i., 731. Chalmers conjectures that Dongan's "spirited answer" to Lord Perth "probably contributed to procure his recall" in 1688. This may be so; but the real reasons will be afterward explained; *post*, 501.

ed to be recorded in both colonies, and which was confirmed in England fifteen years afterward.*

1685. Postal affairs.

While at Milford, Dongan had conferred with Treat about establishing a regular post between New York and the neighboring British colonies as far eastward as Boston. The project had been started by Lovelace in 1673, but, owing to the Dutch war and other causes, it fell through, although Massachusetts afterward appointed a local postmaster at Boston. Dongan had proposed to set up post-houses along the coast from Carolina to Nova Scotia; and Werden instructed him to offer the privilege for a term of years to any one who would farm it from the duke, whose title to the profits of the English post-office was held to include all the British plantations. The governor, on his return from Connecticut, accordingly ordained in the New York Council, "that for the better correspondence between the colonies of America, a post-office be established; and that the rates for riding post be per mile three pence; for every single letter, not above one hundred miles, three pence; if more, proportionably."†

1684. 27 August.

1685. 2 March. Colonial Post-office established by New York.

Although the eastern boundary of New York was now arranged with Connecticut, her frontier toward Massachusetts remained unsettled. That colony had insisted that her territory extended westward beyond the Hudson River. The second grant of the king to the Duke of York in 1674, by which he again gave him all the lands between the Hudson and the Connecticut Rivers, was disregarded by Massachusetts; and Dongan notified Werden that he expected a dispute with that colony about them, it "pretending all along to the south sea, as Connecticut did." The governor accordingly commissioned Clerk West to claim, on behalf of the duke, Westfield, Northampton, Deerfield, and other towns, which Massachusetts had organized within his territory of New York, on the west side of the Connecticut River. But proceedings under this commission were made unnecessary by what had just been done in England.‡

Massachusetts boundary.

18 Feb'y.

Claims of New York on the Connecticut River.

* Council Min., v., 243, 244; Col. Doc., iii., 353; iv., 628–630; Col. Rec. Conn., iii., 142, 176, 337–339; Trumbull, i., 365, 366, 401; New York Boundary Report, Sen. Doc., 1857, No. 165, 7, 9, 45, 113, 114; Smith, i., 287; *ante*, 389.

† Col. Doc., iii., 349, 350, 355, 356; Council Min., v., 106; Val. Man., 1857, 542, 543; Mass. Rec., v., 147, 148, 273; Palfrey, iii., 306; Rapin, ii., 635; Anderson, ii., 475; *ante*, 4, 196–198.

‡ Col. Doc., iii., 112, 240, 356; vi., 508; vii., 564, 598; viii., 440; Mass. Rec., iv. (i.), 395, 396; (ii.), 548, 558, 570; C. Wolley, 70, *note*; *ante*, 188.

CH. VIII. 1683. In the mean time, political convulsions, which quickly affected the British colonies in America, had disturbed their motherland. A conspiracy against the lives of her sovereign and his heir was detected; which, because it had been hatched at a small farm near London, of that name, was commonly called *The Rye-House Plot.* Several Whigs—some of high social rank—were implicated, condemned, and executed. Among these victims were the patrician Lord William Russell, and the nobler Algernon Sidney. To exhibit its subserviency, the University of Oxford decreed that "the badge and character" of the Episcopal Church of England was absolute "submission and obedience" to her voluptuous king. Sir George Jeffreys, a brutal, impudent lawyer, who had been the Duke of York's solicitor general, was paid for his devotion to his patron by being made lord chief justice of the "Defender of the faith" of Protestant Englishmen. The "Franchise" of the City of London was adjudged to be "seized into the King's hands." Almost every corporation within his realm was deprived of its charter. The despotic power which Charles the Second now grasped in England was clearly demonstrated.

The Rye-House Plot.

21 July.

28 Septem. Jeffreys chief justice of England.

Yet the head of the Episcopalian English Church saw that he must give some pledge to his subjects for the security of their Protestantism. Charles therefore insisted that his brother's only remaining legitimate child, the Princess Anne—who, like her elder sister Mary, had been nurtured a Protestant—should be married, like her, to a Protestant husband. As the Prince of Orange was a Calvinist, it was thought desirable that the next son-in-law should be a Lutheran. The Crown Prince of Hanover—who afterward became King George the First of England—was discussed as a fitting match. But, on farther consideration, Prince George of Denmark—whose recommendations were his dullness and his Lutheranism—was preferred. The Duke of York—not yet despairing of a Roman Catholic male heir—ungraciously agreed to his daughter's marriage; which was solemnized to the satisfaction of most British subjects.

The Princess Anne married to Prince George of Denmark.

28 July.

1684. The king rewarded his brother's submission by dispensing with the "Test Act" in his favor, and by restoring to him his old office of Lord High Admiral of England, which that law had forced him to resign in 1673. Soon afterward, Charles called the duke back again to his Privy Council. These bold steps awoke jealousy; and even startled Tories balked at Oxford as they questioned the right of their anointed sovereign to violate a statute of the realm. But the season for Revolution had not come. God's field was not yet harrowed enough. In the fallow meantime, the sycophants of absolutism rejoiced. "And now," wrote James, in his own private memoirs, "the King had brought his affairs to a more happy situation than ever they had been since the Restoration:—He saw his enemies at his feet, and the Duke, his brother, at his side, whose indefatigableness in business took a great share of that burthen off his shoulders, which his indolent temper made uneasy to him."*

1684. 2 May. 28 May. The Test Act dispensed with, and James restored to his offices.

While these events shook England, the proceedings of the first Assembly in New York were brought over by Talbot to Werden. The duke's commissioners proposed several amendments to the revenue part of the charter; and Werden suggested to Dongan that they had better be passed at the next meeting of the Assembly. This, as has been seen, was done.†

New York laws. 10 March.

Several months afterward, James wrote to Dongan, "My commissioners are making what dispatch they can with those Bills that you have sent hither, and particularly with that which contains the Franchises and Priviledges to the Colony of New Yorke, wherein if any alterations are made (either in the forme or matter of it) they will be such as shall be equally or more advantageous to the people there, and better adjusted to the laws of England." At length, all the amendments thought necessary were completed, and the duke "signed and sealed the Charter of Franchises and Priviledges to New Yorke in America." The instrument

26 August. James's letter to Dongan.

4 October. James signs the New York Charter.

* Clarke's James II., i., 738–746; ii., 81; Dalrymple, i., 23–62; Burnet, i., 537–583; Reresby, 163–183; Rapin, ii., 725–734; Tindal, iv., 534; Kennett, iii., 408–423; Evelyn, ii., 186–206; Narcissus Luttrell, i., 272, 307; Hume, vii., 153–172; Lingard, xiii., 275–311; xiv., 89; Macaulay, i., 268–271; Knight, iv., 367–376; Campbell's Chancellors, iii., 509, 527; Martin's Louis XIV., ii., 27; Hargraves's State Trials, iii., 545–630, 706–824; *ante*, 201, 341, 373.

† Col. Doc., iii., 340, 341, 355; Chalmers, i., 585; Council Journ., i., Int., xiii.; *ante*, 387, 408. It was rumored, about this time, at Boston and Philadelphia, that the duke had sold New York to "one Colonel Thompson," probably Major Robert Thompson, of London, the friend of Massachusetts and Connecticut: see Col. Doc., iii., 355; Mass. Rec., v., 408, 409, 426, 467; Col. Rec. Conn., ii., 344, 528; Hutch. Coll., 473; *ante*, 257, 286.

CH. VIII. 1684. 1 Novem.

was ordered to be registered and taken to New York. In the mean time, "His Royal Highnesses' Charter" was considered to be in full operation. Indeed, under Dongan's instructions, every colonial law assented to by him, as this had been, was "good and binding" until the duke's negative should be signified. But before the amended charter was made "complete and irrevocable" by being sent to New York, great changes happened.*

The Massachusetts agents foiled in London.

Dudley and Richards, the agents sent by Massachusetts to England, had meanwhile found that their colony must either submit to her king, or be deprived of his father's royal charter, as the City of London had been of hers. In vain did they try to obtain a pardon for "all passed offences" from their licentious sovereign by a bribe of two thousand guineas, which the authorities at Boston had frugally authorized them to contribute "for his Majesty's private service." But the Boston agents found that they had not guineas enough to satisfy the Duchess of Portsmouth; and the "delicate transaction" was managed so awkwardly, by offering a Massachusetts price to "the wrong person," that the Puritanical tempters were laughed out of Whitehall. It did not please the Almighty "that devotional prayers, associated with such unholy exertions, should prevail."†

Charles determines to quell Massachusetts.

The king now determined to make void his father's patent to the Corporation of Massachusetts Bay by a writ of *Quo Warranto*, as advised by Jones and Winnington, his attorney and solicitor, in 1678. That colony was in a dilemma. She was either an independent sovereignty, or else the creature of her king. Yet, while Massachusetts affected independence, she insisted that, as an English corporation, she had properly used the delegated authority of her sovereign. On the other hand, Charles thought that those subjects who controlled his colony had abused their corpo-

* Col. Doc., iii., 332, 348, 351; Chalmers's Ann., i., 588; S. P. O., Board of Trade, N. Y. Entries, No. 49, p. 50; *ante*, 383. The official record is as follows: "*MD: That this day the 4th October 1684 His Royal Highness signed and sealed the Charter of Franchises and Priviledges to New Yorke in America; which was countersigned by Sir John Werden in the usuall forme, and sent the same evening to the Auditor (Mr. Aldworth) to be Registred by him, and then to be delivered to Capt. Talbott to carry to New Yorke.*" This interesting document was published for the first time in the Historical Magazine for August, 1862, vol. vi., page 233.

† Hutch. Mass., i., 337; Chalmers's Ann., i., 413, 450–462; Clarke's James II., i., 736–738; Kennett, iii., 405, 408; Macaulay, i., 264, 269; Bancroft, ii., 123; Barry, i., 474; Grahame, i., 337; Palfrey, iii., 356, 368–370, 410, 411; *ante*, 360.

1683.

rate privileges. If they had done so by excluding from the freedom of their corporation those who did not "agree in the Congregational way," or by other methods, it was his duty to resume the authority of the crown. The king's idea of a proper charter for an English colony in America may be inferred from the patent which he had just before granted to William Penn. The time had come when the government of Massachusetts should be made at least as liberal as that of Pennsylvania. Randolph, who had been ordered home from Boston, accordingly charged the Cor- 13 June.
poration of Massachusetts with assuming unwarranted powers; evading the Navigation Laws; opposing the Episcopal Church of England; and with various other offenses against British sovereignty. Sir Robert Sawyer, the attorney general, thereupon prosecuted a writ of "*Quo War-* 27 June.
ranto" in the King's Bench, to inquire into the alleged abuses. A Quo Warranto ordered.
After various delays the proceedings in the Common-law court were dropped, and a more searching writ 1684.
of "*Scire Facias*" in Chancery was issued. This was fol- 16 April.
lowed by a second, or "*alias*" writ; upon the return of 12 May.
which, the defendant not appearing, Lord Keeper Guilford, after hearing counsel, decreed, "*nisi*," in Trinity Term, that 21 June.
the Massachusetts patent "be vacated, cancelled and annihilated, and into the said court restored, there to be cancelled." The Massachusetts patent canceled.
In the following Michaelmas Term final judgment was entered in Chancery, and the Corporation of 23 October.
Massachusetts was dead.*

Thus, by the decree of the Keeper of the English Great Seal, a corporation, to which his official predecessor had given technical life, was annihilated. The separate name of Massachusetts no longer existed legally; and that part of New England which had been governed under the patent of Charles the First was left to the discretion of Charles the Second. The only English power that could review the judgment in Chancery was the House of Lords; and that house was not likely to reverse the decree. It now

* Mass. H. S. Coll., xxi., 96; xxxii., 246–278, 293, 294, 295; Mass. Rec., v., 382–468; Hutch. Mass., i., 337–340; Chalmers's Ann., i., 405, 414, 415, 440, 462; Rev. Col., i., 133, 134, 173; Palmer's Impartial Account, 10–12; Force's Tracts, iv., No. 9, p. 4, No. 71, p. 5, 6; N. Luttrell, i., 274; Barry, i., 474–478; Bancroft, ii., 124–127; Palfrey, iii., 371–394; Col. Doc., iii., 350, 578, 579; *ante*, 316, 337, 349. In the same Trinity Term, 1684, judgment was given against the Bermuda's corporation, chiefly because the inhabitants of those islands were opposed to the Church of England: Hutch. Mass., i., 336; Anderson's Col. Ch., ii., 87, 334, 335.

CH. VIII. 1684. Novem. Debate in the Privy Council.

became necessary for the king to determine how his subjects in Massachusetts should be ruled. The point, which was "carefully investigated" by his Privy Council, was, whether the English system of representation in Parliament should prevail in America, or whether the colonists should be governed directly by the Crown. Sir William Jones, the deceased attorney general, had maintained that Charles could no more levy taxes on his colonial subjects "without their consent by an Assembly, than they could discharge themselves from their allegiance to the English crown." At the same time, Jones maintained that the British Parliament "might rightfully impose taxes on every dominion of the crown."

These principles had been adopted by the king in his recent charter to Pennsylvania in 1681. Under the Royal Instructions to Cranfield in 1682, New Hampshire enjoyed a popular Assembly. In August, 1683, Charles had recognized such an Assembly in Virginia, by his Instructions to Lord Howard of Effingham. And now, in council at Whitehall, the Marquis of Halifax argued that the laws of England ought to prevail in "a country composed of Englishmen." He urged that an absolute government was neither as happy nor as stable as one in which the authority of the prince was limited; and he plainly declared that he could not live under a king who had the power to take at pleasure the money he might have in his pocket. But the Lord Privy Seal stood alone. James and all the other counselors "strongly withstood" Halifax's arguments, and maintained that the king should govern such distant countries "in the way which might appear to him the most convenient to maintain the mother country in the state in which she is, and to augment still more her power and wealth." So it was determined that the governor and council in New England "should not be obliged to call Assemblies of the whole country to lay taxes, and regulate other important matters, but that they should do what they might judge proper, without rendering an account of it, except to the king."*

Argument of Halifax.

Decision about New England.

* Barillon's dispatch to Louis XIV., 7 Dec., 1684, in Fox's James II.. 59, 60, App. vii., viii.; Chalmers's Ann., i., 345, 346, 416, 464, 465, 493, 497, 686, 690; Rev. Col., i., 173, 174, 309; Force's Tracts, iv., No. 9, p. 45, 46; Mather's Magnalia, i., 178; Grahame, i., 255; Burnet, i., 396, 532; Lingard, xiii., 316; Macaulay, i., 272; Palfrey, iii., 395, 514; *ante*, 340, 349.

This decision of the English Council was momentous. The period of royal American corporations had passed away. It was now settled that, in all colonies where it was convenient, the king's sovereignty was to be resumed, and his direct government established. As no Parliament had met in England for three years, its power to interfere with English Plantations was disregarded. To carry out Charles's arbitrary but simple policy, it was necessary for him carefully to choose his colonial officers. Andros was thought of as the first royal governor of Massachusetts. But, as Sir Edmund was occupied with his private affairs in the Channel Islands, Colonel Piercy Kirke was chosen. Kirke had just returned from the government of Tangier, where he had proved himself to be a licentious despot. But, being "a gentleman of very good resolution," it was considered that he would not fail "in any part of his duty to his Majesty." A commission and Instructions were accordingly ordered for Kirke, as "his Majesty's Lieutenant and Governor General" of "New England," including Massachusetts, New Hampshire, Maine, and New Plymouth; while for the present Rhode Island and Connecticut were excepted from his authority. It was, however, intended to form a royal government over all the New England colonies, of which the king appointed Randolph to be his secretary and register. Charles himself directed that in Kirke's Commission and Instructions "no mention be made of an Assembly, but that the Governor and Council have power to make laws and to perform all other acts of Government, 'till his Majesty's pleasure be further known."*

CH. VIII. 1684.

8 Novem. Kirke chosen to be governor of New England.

17 Novem.

22 Novem. No Assembly in New England.

The annihilation of the Massachusetts charter relieved New York from her anticipated boundary dispute with that colony, and confirmed to the Duke of York all the territorial rights, west of the Connecticut River, which he claimed under his patent.†

Boundary between New York and Massachusetts settled.

But how could James now complete the Instrument he had executed a few weeks before; which, nevertheless, had

* Chalmers's Ann., i., 416; Hutch. Mass., i., 341, 343, 344; Coll., 542, 543; Narcissus Luttrell, i., 52, 160; Anderson's Col. Church, ii., 282; Douglas, i., 413; Whitmore's Andros, 22; Rapin, ii., 732, 733; Kennett, iii., 423; Macaulay, i., 627, 628; Palfrey, iii., 394, 395, 396, 482, 483, 513; *ante*, 357.

† Col. Doc., iii., 350; vi., 508; vii., 564, 598; viii., 440; Smith, i., 297; *ante*, 413.

CH. VIII.

1684.

not been perfected by delivery? True, the Assembly of New York had voted a Revenue Bill, in consideration of his anticipated "bountiful confirming" of their charter. Yet James hesitated. He had thought of obtaining a grant of Rhode Island and Connecticut. The transmission of his sealed charter was therefore suspended. In writing to Dongan, Werden enjoined prudence in dealing with the Indians in New York and Pemaquid; "always avoiding, as much as possible, any proceedings on our part that may run us into disputes with the French, who, in our present circumstances, are not to be made enemies."*

James suspends the New York charter.

4 Decem.

Yet Halifax remained in Charles's council despite James's entreaties for his dismissal. Louis wrote to Barillon, at London, that "the reasonings of Lord Halifax on the manner of governing New England. little deserve the confidence which the King of England has in him; and I am not surprised to learn that the Duke of York has called the attention of the King, his brother, to their consequences." Halifax, on the other hand, urged the king to call a Parliament, and to dismiss James from his councils. It was thought by many that the royal brothers would soon be estranged. The Princess of Orange would probably be announced as the heiress presumptive of the crown. The illegitimate Duke of Monmouth might even be declared Prince of Wales. All forfeited charters would be restored. But Charles was weary of his brother's excessive zeal: perhaps he foresaw the result of his violent designs. Just after the dissolution of his last Parliament at Oxford, the king told the Prince of Orange that, should James come to the crown, he "could not hold it four years to an end." To the duke himself he said, "Brother, I am resolved never to go on my travels again:—you may, if you will."† The words of Charles were prophetic.

$\frac{3}{13}$ Decem.

Halifax, Louis, Charles, and James.

The king and the duke.

* Col. Doc., iii., 341, 348, 351, 353, 677, 678; Hutch. Coll., 543; Chalmers, i., 278, 416, 588; R. I. Rec., iii., 147; *ante*, 384, 401, 405, 408.

† Fox's James II., App. viii., ix.; Dalrymple, i., 63, 64; Macpherson, i., 419; Secret Hist. of Whitehall, Lett. lxxii.; Burnet, i., 575, 604, 605; Echard, 53; Rapin, ii., 725, 734; Kennett, iii., 423; Hume, vii., 175; Lingard, xiii., 316; Macaulay, i., 277, 278; Martin, ii., 27.

CHAPTER IX.

1685–1688.

CHAP. IX.

1685.

CHARLES the Second had now reigned for nearly a quarter of a century since his restoration. He was about fifty-five years old; and his strong constitution, helped by bodily exercise in the open air, promised him a length of days. But, early in the February of 1685, Charles was stricken by a disease which baffled the skill of his physicians. After suffering a short and sharp illness, the head of English Episcopalianism mumbled his reconciliation with the Church of Rome; wished the Duke of York a long and prosperous reign; and, after spending the life of an Epicurean Protestant, went to his judgment a pusillanimous, eleventh-hour Roman Catholic.

Decease of Charles the Second.

6 Febr'y.

The successor of Charles was a very different man: colder, more honest, more decided—a bigot in place of a shuffler. A quarter of an hour after the decease of his brother, James the Second of England and the Seventh of Scotland, came out of the closet whither he had retired to give "full scope to his tears." The Privy Counselors of the late king were already assembled, and their new master hastily told them that, although he had "been reported to be a man for arbitrary power," he would endeavor "to preserve the government, both in Church and State, as it is now by law established." Immediately afterward James was proclaimed king in the usual form. No opposition was made to the accession of a sovereign whom the Commons of England had so often attempted to exclude from its throne. The new ministry was arranged. Sunderland and Middleton were retained as secretaries of state. Rochester, the brother-in-law and old commissioner of James, was made the head of his treasury; Clarendon, also his brother-in-law, privy seal; and Halifax, although disliked, became lord president of his council. The king, who loved busi-

6 Febr'y. Accession of James the Second.

Ministers of James.

ness, took again the Admiralty into his own hands, and was assisted by the long experience of Samuel Pepys.*

Since the year 1675, Charles the Second had intrusted all matters relating to the Trade and Plantations of England to a committee of his Privy Council. Approving of this policy, James appointed a similar committee, which included the great officers of state. As the Duke of York had now become king, his rights as a subject proprietor were merged in his sovereignty; and New York, with her dependencies, having devolved to the crown of England, became a royal government, under the supervision of the Plantation Committee. A few days after the accession of James, the records belonging to the province were ordered to be sent to the Plantation Office; and Sir John Werden delivered all that were thought "material" to Secretary Blathwayt. Among these were thirteen of the acts passed at the first session of the New York Assembly, which had been transmitted for confirmation, and were readily approved. Another, and the most important, was "The Charter of Franchises and Privileges to New York," which, although it had been signed and sealed by the duke, and ordered to be delivered, had been kept back, and was "not yet perfected."†

17 Feb'y. New York Records sent to the Plantation Office.

The New York charter kept back.

Thus the political condition of New York was again changed. For twenty years—with a short interruption—the province had been the conquered dukedom of a royal English subject. At length her subordinate proprietor had become king; and New York — following his for-

* Clarke's James II., i., 746–750; ii., 1–8; Burnet, i., 606–621; Kennett, iii., 423–428; Rapin, ii., 734–742; Parl. Hist., iv., 1342; Lingard, xiii., 317–321; xiv., 1–8; Macaulay, i., 426–437, 440–446; Proud, i., 290, 291; Martin, ii., 28; Fox's James II., 73–81, App. xi.–xvi.; Dalrymple, i., 152–166; ii., 1–11; *ante*, 201.

† Col. Doc., iii., 229, 230, 354, 355, 357, 359, 363, 370; viii., 443; Chalmers's Ann., i., 584, 585; *ante*, 297, 416, 420. It is to be regretted that Werden, the Duke of York's secretary, did not transfer *all the papers relating to New York during its proprietary period*, whether thought "material" or not, to the Plantation Committee; in the archives of which they would have been carefully preserved. To this omission we probably owe much of the darkness which still obscures that period. Many of the documents relating to the governments of Nicolls, Lovelace, Andros, and Dongan—from 1664 to 1685—are now missing from the Records in the State Paper Office in London. The Duke of York, after he became James the Second, appears to have kept as souvenirs, in his own possession, much of the correspondence which his deputies had addressed to him as Proprietor; and it may be that these letters shared the fate of his other private papers, which were sent to Paris in 1688, and were afterward destroyed in the French Revolution: Fox's James II., Introd., xvi.–xix.; Clarke's James II., Preface, xiv.–xviii. In 1670 and 1671, Evelyn appears to have been furnished with some now well-known official documents, which he gave back to the Lord Treasurer Clifford, who took them with him to Devonshire: Evelyn, ii., 51, 55, 56, 59; iii., 221–223, 229–231, 238–242, 260–263; Pepys, iv., 221, 222; *ante*, 18, 187.

tunes — became an American province of the English crown. Out of a proprietorship came forth a royal government. Her "Charter of Privileges," which her late proprietor had sealed, required to be confirmed by her present king before that instrument could be "complete and irrevocable." But James, King of England, was a very different person from James, Duke of York. He presided in person at a meeting of his Plantation Committee, when the New York charter was considered. A series of "observations" upon several of its clauses was read, to which it was objected that they gave more privileges than had been "granted to *any of his Majesty's Plantations*, where the Act of Habeas Corpus, and all such other Bills do not take place;" that the words, "*The People, met in a General Assembly*," were "*not used in any other Constitution in America*;" in short: that some of its enactments were inconvenient, and tended too much to restrain the governor and "abridge the King's power." Moreover, the New York charter expressly recognized a "Lord Proprietor," who had now become sovereign. This was a fatal objection to that Instrument, as it had been sealed. The king therefore declared that he did "not think fit to confirm" the charter. "And, as to the Government of New York, his Majesty is pleased to direct that it be assimilated to the Constitution that shall be agreed on for New England, to which it is adjoining: And, in the mean time, his Majesty orders a letter to be prepared for his Royal signature, directing Colonel Dongan, Governor of New York, to pursue such powers and instructions as he shall receive under his Majesty's signet and sign manual, or by order in Council, until further order."*

CHAP. IX. — 1685. — New York a royal English province. — 3 March. — 3 March. — The New York charter not confirmed by James the Second. — 3 March.

By this action James the Second did not repeal the charter of New York. He merely declined to confirm it, and thus left it in force until his disapproval should be notified to Dongan. As the "Constitution" for New England had not yet been settled, the government of New York, under its late proprietor's Instructions, was not disturbed. So James wrote to Dongan: "Whereas, by the decease of the late King, our most dearly beloved brother, and our acces-

5 March. James the Second's orders to Dongan.

* Col. Doc., iii., 357–359; iv., 264; viii., 443; Chalmers's Ann., i., 56, 74, 588; ii., 72, 113; Rev. Col., i., 181; N. Y. Council Journ., i., 45; *ante*, 338, 416.

CHAP. IX. 1685. sion to the Imperial Crown of this Realm, our Province of New York—the Propriety whereof was by the letters Patents of his said Majesty vested in us—is now wholly devolved upon our royal person, and annexed to our other dominions, We do hereby signify our will and pleasure that you publish and make known the same to all our loving subjects within our Province. And as we have been pleased by our Royal Proclamation to direct that all men being in office of government shall so continue therein until further order, so we do hereby charge and require you to pursue such powers and instructions as we have formerly given you, and such further powers authority and instructions as you shall at any time hereafter receive under our royal signet and sign manual, or by our order in our Privy Council. And that you likewise give our said loving subjects to understand, that, having committed to our said Privy Council the care of our said Province, with the consideration of the several Bills and Addresses lately presented unto us from our Assembly there, they may shortly expect such a gracious and suitable return, by the settlement of fitting privileges and confirmation of their rights, as shall be found most expedient for our service and the welfare of our said Province."*

This letter of the king was equivalent to a new royal commission to Dongan. It recognized the existing Assembly of New York, while it foreshadowed such changes in the provincial government as might be "found most expedient." The Privy Council at the same time instructed Dongan to proclaim the new king "with the solemnities and ceremonies requisite on the like occasion," and inclosed the royal proclamation for continuing all persons in office in the same form as they had already notified the other American colonies. Dongan was also directed by Blathwayt, the secretary of the Plantation Committee, to correspond hereafter with him instead of Werden.†

5 March. Orders of the Privy Council.

6 March.

Although James the Second thus recognized a royal As-

* Col. Doc., iii., 332, 360, 361. The effect of this letter seems to have been misapprehended in 1689: Col. Doc., iii., 677, 678. Hoffman, in his recent "Treatise," i., 21, 22, appears to have overlooked it altogether.

† Col. Doc., iii., 357, 359, 360, 363; Council Min., v., 109; Col. Rec. Conn., iii., 339, 340; Mass. Rec., v., 473, 474; Chalmers's Ann., i., 346, 370, 417; *ante*, 416. Sir John Werden's occupation, as secretary of the Duke of York, being now gone, he was recompensed by being appointed a commissioner of customs: Beatson, i., 449–451; Col. Doc., v., 41.

sembly in New York, he did not mean it to last; for he had directed the "Constitution" of the province to be assimilated to that of New England, where there were to be no Assemblies. Home affairs, which crowded the beginning of his reign, prevented prompt action on colonial business; and the government of Massachusetts was meanwhile left in the hands of its late magistrates. Colonel Kirke, whom Charles had appointed to be governor of New England, was confirmed by James; and, after some delay, orders were given to complete his Instructions, and send him to America, with two frigates to maintain his authority. But the insurrections in Scotland, under Argyll, and in the west of England, under Monmouth, caused Kirke to be retained at home; and, while his throne was thus actually threatened, the king could bestow little thought on his distant American dominions.*

CHAP. IX. — 1685. No colonial Assemblies under James. 13 May. May. June. July.

The first dispatches from James the Second were brought to America by Captain Baxter, whom Dongan had sent to England in the previous August. The acting authorities of the late Corporation of Massachusetts hastened to proclaim their new sovereign "with all due solemnity." Connecticut did the same, "with great solemnity and affection." On receiving his letters, Dongan—now the royal governor of New York—ordered a parade of the metropolitan militia; and, two days afterward, James the Second was joyfully proclaimed sovereign of the province he had ruled so long as proprietor. It was natural that "the People" of New York should rejoice that their duke had become their king; for they hoped that the interest which James had shown in the prosperity of the province when it was his own property, would continue to be manifested after it devolved, as a colonial appendage of England, to her imperial crown.†

20 April. 22 April. 21 April. 23 April. James proclaimed in New York.

Quickly after his proclamation, the Corporation of the metropolis drew up an address to James, congratulating him on his accession, and wishing him "a long, peaceable,

May.

* Burnet, i., 623-646; Kennett, iii., 431-438; Rapin, ii., 743-749; Lingard, xiv., 33-65; Macaulay, i., 546-632; Clarke, ii., 14-47; Fox, 125-277; Mackintosh, 13-36; Hutch. Mass., i., 341, 342; Coll., 542; Chalmers, i., 416; Mass. H. S. Coll., xxxv., 142; Palfrey, iii., 480-482; *ante*, 419.

† Col. Doc., iii., 351, 357, 360; v., 651; viii., 443; Col. MSS., xxxiii., 113-117; Council Min., v., 109, 110; Mass. Rec., v., 473, 474; Col. Rec. Conn., iii., 340; Hutch. Mass., i., 340; Chalmers, i., 417; Penn. Col. Rec., i., 132, 133; Palfrey, iii., 481; *ante*, 401.

CHAP. IX. 1685. 13 May. The Corporation of New York's address to the king.

and prosperous reign," which, at Dongan's suggestion, they sent to his late Secretary Werden, for presentation. They also asked Werden to acquaint the king that since he had "been pleased to separate Delaware and the two Jersies from this, his Government of New York, this City hath apparently and extremely suffered in the diminution and loss of its trade, being thereby deprived of at least one third part thereof; and hath ever since much lessened and decayed, both in number of inhabitants, rents, and buildings; and his Majesty in his revenue likewise suffers thereby. And the remaining part of this Province, when less able the more burthened, which with great willingness and submission they bear; But now hope that this appearing to His Majesty, he will find it consistent with the ease and safety of his subjects, and his Majesty's interest and service, to reunite those parts and enlarge this government Eastward, and confirm and grant to this his City such privileges and immunities as may again make it flourish, and increase his Majesty's revenue." This letter Werden handed to the Plantation Committee, where it soon produced a decided effect.*

July.

An interesting point now came up to be settled. Saul Browne, a Jew, formerly of Rhode Island, complained that he had been hindered in his trade—apparently under the "scott and lott" regulation of the previous March—and Dongan having referred Browne's petition to the metropolitan authorities, they answered that "no Jew ought to sell by retail within the city, but may by wholesale, if the Governor think fit to permit the same." A question having also arisen, under the Charter of Liberties of 1683, whether others than those "which profess faith in God by Jesus Christ" were guaranteed freedom of conscience, the Jews petitioned the governor "for liberty to exercise their religion." This was referred to the mayor and aldermen, who returned their opinion "that no public worship is tolerated, by act of Assembly, but to those that profess faith in Christ; and therefore the Jews' worship not to be allowed." This severe construction, however, was contrary to the duke's policy in regard to New York, after he became a Roman

12 Septem. Jews in New York. 14 Septem.

* Col. Doc., iii., 361, 362; Index to N. J. Col. Doc., 11. The Corporation of the City of New York always exercised great influence in provincial affairs.

Catholic; and it does not appear to have been adopted by its provincial government.* CHAP. IX. 1685.

The events which had occurred in Scotland and England just after the accession of James were communicated to the several American governors in a circular letter from Secretary Sunderland. Dongan replied that "the people of this place express themselves very willing to obey the King in any thing to their power: when the Assembly meets, which will be in October next, your Lordship's letter shall be read to them. It came very seasonably to give us a true account of the rebellions in Scotland and the west of England; malicious and factious reports having pestered this place, which came every day by the way of Boston. In my opinion, the King cannot do better than with all expedition to send his Governor thither. It would certainly alter the way of that people very much for the better." * * * * "This place is composed most of strangers; and we have very few or none of ill principles among us that I know of. If any of the English be so, they have the wit to conceal it. A new seal of this Province is very much wanting, and the people extraordinary desirous to have the King's seal to their patents and other papers that concern them."†

26 June. 18 Septem. Dongan's letter to Sunderland. A new seal wanted.

The Assembly had adjourned in October, 1684, to meet again in September, 1685. But the question arose whether it was not dissolved by the demise of the crown. To prevent future trouble, the council, of which Captain Baxter had been sworn a member, thought that it was expedient to dissolve the Assembly and to call a new one. Dongan accordingly, by proclamation, dissolved the first Assembly; and writs were sent out for the election of new representatives, to meet at New York on the twentieth of October. On that day the new Assembly met, and chose William Pinhorne, formerly an alderman of the city, its speaker, and Robert Hammond was again made clerk.

Assembly. 3 June. 5 August. 13 August. 17 August. 20 October. Meeting of the New York Assembly.

* Min. of C. C., i., 285, 287; Dunlap, ii., App. cxxxiv.; Col. Doc., iii., 218; R. I. Rec., iii., 160; Shea's note to Miller, 103; *ante*, 410. The Jews were then, as they are now, classed with Turks, infidels, and heretics by the Roman Catholic, the Protestant Episcopal, and the Reformed Dutch Churches. In his Instructions to Dongan of 1682, James did not repeat the clause he had inserted in those of Andros in 1674: compare Col. Doc., iii., 218, 331-334; *ante*, 373. But he renewed it in 1686: Col. Doc., iii., 373. Saul Browne, the petitioner, afterward became Reader in the Jews' Synagogue in New York: Shea's note to Miller, 103.

† Col. Doc., iii., 364, 365; Council Min., v., 125; Col. Rec. Conn., iii., 345, 346; Mass. H. S. Coll., xxxv., 139; Hutch. Coll., i., 344; Chalmers, i., 378, 379; *ante*, 158, *note*.

CHAP. IX. 1685. 3 Novem. Six laws were enacted. Three bills passed the Assembly, but did not receive the governor's assent. One bill, which made a single witness sufficient in revenue cases, passed the council, but failed to receive the sanction of the representatives. At the close of its session the Assembly adjourned to the twenty-fifth of the following September. But, before that time came, such changes happened that it never met again.*

The second New York Assembly ended.

After the adjournment of the Assembly, a day of thanksgiving was proclaimed by the governor, according to the old Dutch custom, for the king's victory over the rebels under Argyll and Monmouth. Collector Santen, who had not given a satisfactory account, was ordered to produce his books of revenue before the council. Thomas Rudyard, formerly governor of East Jersey, whom Dongan had made attorney general of New York the year before, now made his will, and determined to emigrate to Barbadoes; and the governor commissioned the metropolitan recorder, James Graham, to be Rudyard's successor. This caused other official changes. Isaac Swinton was made a clerk in Chancery in Graham's place, and was installed, with his older colleague, John Knight. Nicholas Bayard, who had succeeded Minvielle as mayor of the city, was now sworn as a royal counselor. A Court of Exchequer, to determine all royal revenue cases—and which was composed of the governor and council—was also appointed to be held in the city of New York on the first Monday of each month. This tribunal was thought necessary, because it was found that when the king's revenue causes were tried in the "settled Courts," there was a "great hazard of venturing the matter on Country Jurors; who, over and above that they are generally ignorant enough, and for the most part linked together by affinity, are too much swayed by their particular humours and interests."†

20 Novem. Thanksgiving. 20 Novem. 7 Decem. 10 Decem. 16 Decem. 17 Decem. 17 Decem. 14 Decem. Court of Exchequer.

* MS. Laws, Secretary's Office; Council Min., v., 123; Col. MSS., xxxiii., 152, 153; Min. of C. C., i., 283; Dunlap, ii., App. cxxxiv.; Col. Doc., iii., 364, 716; Council Journ., i., Int., xiii.-xv.; Wood's L. I., 102; Thompson, i., 162; *ante*, 408. The note in N. Y. H. S. Coll., iii., 355, that there is "no evidence of any session of an Assembly" during the reign of James the Second is erroneous.

† Council Min., v., 131, 138-146; Col. MSS., xxxiii., 184, 185, 196, 200, 216; xxxiv., 93; Col. Doc., iii., 351, 390, 412, 657; iv., 847; ix., 293; Daly's Sketch, 32; *ante*, 409. Mr. Whitehead, in his "East Jersey," 99, 124, 125, and his "Contributions," 81, does not state that Rudyard became attorney general of New York; and he makes him die "abroad in 1692," at Jamaica.

CHAP. IX.

1685.

In his first letter to Secretary Blathwayt, Dongan reported that the French were "now quiet," and that the English trade would be "much better, if we take but the same care as the French, by putting a little fort on this side of the Great Lake [Ontario], as they have on the other. It is in the King's dominions, nearer to us than to them, and would be an obligation to the Indians to bring their beaver to us, which would be six for one at present. I put the arms of the Duke, now his Majesty, upon all the Indian Castles near the Great Lake, and that by their own consent who have submitted to this government. They are a considerable people, and ought to be encouraged, because they have a considerable influence over most of the Indians in America. The French quarrel only because they cannot obtain them, which, if they should, they would be troublesome to most of the King's subjects in these parts of America."*

11 August. Dongan's report to Blathwayt.

Before Dongan's arrival, Greenhalgh and his comrade were the only "Christians" under the New York government who had gone as far as the Seneca country. To carry out his policy of attracting their fur-trade to New York, the governor licensed a Canadian refugee, Abel Marion la Fontaine, with several others, to hunt beaver in the woods among the Western savages. A similar pass was given to Captain Johannes Rooseboom, of Albany. These adventurers went a three months' journey to the Ottawas and Miamis country, as far as Michilimackinac, whence they brought back many beaver-skins. They were very well received by those Indians, whom they found more inclined to trade with them than with the French; and Rooseboom and his party of young Dutchmen were "invited to come every year" by the Western savages, who desired that their enemies, the Senecas, "would open a path for them, that they might come to Albany."†

1 April.

12 August. Dongan gives passes to New Yorkers to hunt in the West.

Notwithstanding the treaty made the last year, some Cayugas had committed outrages on the frontiers of Virginia. Dongan, however, summoned the Five Nations to meet "Assarigoa" at Albany, and confirm the peace. But Lord

* Col. Doc., iii., 353, 363, 393–396; *ante*, 398, 399, 420.

† Col. Doc., iii., 250–252, 256, 395, 437, 438, 476; v., 76, 731; ix., 275, 297, 302, 1023; Doc. Hist., i., 133; Col. MSS., xxxiii., 106, 107, 142, 150; Charlevoix, ii., 332; La Hontan, i., 97; *ante*, 310.

CHAP. IX. 1685. 13 August.

Effingham's wife, "Philadelphia," having died in Virginia, he deputed one of his council, Colonel Bird, and his attorney, Edward Jennings, to represent him. Accompanied by chiefs of the Pamunkeys, Chickahominies, Mataponys, and Powhatans, the Virginia agents came to Albany; and

September. Conference with the Iroquois at Albany.

Bird sharply reproved the New York savages for having broken their covenant. The Senecas and Mohawks freed themselves from blame, and chid the other nations. The offending cantons apologized, and promised satisfaction. The orator for the Mohawks then declared that the path of friendship led to Albany, where was the "House of Peace." And then he sang "all the covenant chain over;" after which he admonished the Oneidas, Onondagas, and Cayugas, and sang another song in honor of the sachems who had come from Virginia. The younger Garakontié attended this conference as the Onondaga deputy. By

$\frac{1}{10}$ Sept. Lamberville's letter to Dongan.

him Lamberville, or "*Teiorensere*," wrote to Dongan, urging him, as well by his "zeal for the public peace, and especially for the Christians of this America," as by his devotion as a Romanist, to solicit the Senecas to be friendly with the French; of whose faith he declared the "sole object" was, "that the blood of Jesus Christ, shed for all men, may be useful to them." Lamberville's adroit letter did not deceive the straightforward Dongan.*

Effect of De la Barre's treaty on the Iroquois.

After De la Barre's treaty at the Salmon River, the Iroquois began to despise the French, whose "Onnontio" had proved himself a poltroon; and the Mahicans promised them twelve hundred warriors if they should be attacked by the Canadians. Dongan also offered them all needed aid of men and ammunition. The Senecas, accordingly, instead of paying the beavers which they had promised to De la Barre, carried more than ten thousand of those furs to Albany.†

7 Jan'y. Louis removes De la Barre, and appoints Denonville to govern Canada.

When Louis heard of De la Barre's submission to the Iroquois, and abandonment of the Illinois, he superseded his weak Canadian representative, and appointed in his place Jacques René de Brisay, Marquis de Denonville, a colonel of his dragoons, and a French nobleman, "equally estimable for his valor, his integrity, and his piety." De-

* Col. Doc., iii., 453, 454; ix., 259, 261, 274; Doc. Hist., i., 121, 122; Burk, ii., 291; Collins's Peerage, v., 25; Colden, i., 48, 58, 59, first ed., 61, 68, 69; *ante*, 398, 402.

† Charlevoix, ii., 321, 322, 323; *ante*, 405.

nonville was instructed to "humble the pride of the Iro- CHAP. IX.
quois," and to sustain the Illinois and other Western tribes
who had been abandoned by his predecessor. Notwith- 1685. 10 March.
standing Dongan's "unjust pretensions," a good under- Denonville's in-
standing must be maintained between the French and En- structions.
glish colonists; yet if the latter should "excite and aid the Indians, they must be treated as enemies, when found on Indian territory, without at the same time attempting any thing on territory under the obedience of the King of England." Barillon was also directed to complain that Don- 10 March.
gan had hoisted English flags on the Iroquois villages, and to demand "precise orders" from James to "confine himself within the limits of his government, and to observe a different line of conduct towards Sieur de Denonville." It does not appear that the "precise orders" which Louis asked of James were given.*

Early in August, Denonville landed at Quebec with a August.
large re-enforcement of troops, and went to Fort Frontenac, where he established a garrison. In his dispatches to 20 August.
Seignelay, he declared that a war with the Iroquois was in- 3 Septem.
evitable; that Englishmen, led by French deserters, were 12 Novem. 13 Novem.
trading with the Ottawas; and that it was necessary to Denonville to Seigne-
subdue the Senecas, and establish good French posts at Ni- lay.
agara and on Lake Erie, so as to check both the English and the Indians. The French king should make himself "absolute master" of Lake Ontario, which the English coveted; and "nothing, save the power alone of the Iroquois, prevents them having posts there, inasmuch as it is quite easy to go from Manatte and Orange to Lake Onta- French
rio on horseback — the distance being only one hundred policy proposed.
leagues through a beautiful country." Denonville also desired the Jesuits in Canada to send their Father Millet, lately of the Oneida mission in New York, to Fort Frontenac, to be interpreter there, and co-operate with Lamberville, who yet lingered among the Onondagas. This was accordingly done. But Denonville, adopting the suggestion of Duchesnau in 1681, urged that "the most certain safe-

* Col. Doc., ix., 269–272, 801; Charlevoix, ii., 323, 324; Garneau, i., 256; La Hontan, i., 68; Doc. Hist., i., 121. The French government was so mortified with De la Barre that the copy of his treaty at La Famine, now in the archives of the Marine at Paris, is indorsed by Seignelay, "*These are to be kept secret:*" Col. Doc., ix., 236; Doc. Hist., i., 77. As to the orders which Louis asked James to give to Dongan, nothing appears in Dalrymple, or Fox, or Clarke: compare Charlevoix, ii., 330, 336; Col. Doc., v., 731; Colden, i., 44, 250.

CHAP. IX. 1685. guard against the English of New York would be to buy it from the King of England, who, in the present state of his affairs, will doubtless stand in need of the king's money. We should thus be masters of the Iroquois without a war." In the light of Quebec, Denonville reasoned well.*

Denonville quickly notified his arrival to Dongan, and complained of the harboring of Canadian deserters in New York—alluding probably to La Fontaine and others. In his reply, Dongan charged De la Barre with having "meddled in an affair that might have created some indifference between the two crowns;" and that, as to the fugitives from Canada, they would be surrendered to the proper officers of that government whenever sent for.†

13 October. Dongan and Denonville.

New Jersey continued to prosper at the expense of New York, yet not to the degree expected by its proprietors. To arouse more interest in Scotland, George Scot, of Pitlochie, following John Reid, published in Edinburgh a pamphlet entitled "The Model of the Government of the Province of East New Jersey, in America," in which he attractively set forth its condition, and refuted objections to emigration. With a ship-load of colonists—many of whom were exiled by Perth and his Privy Council for having taken part in Argyll's rebellion — Scot embarked for the land which he had done so much to make so favorably known. The author died at sea, leaving his printed work immortal. Perth Amboy was now made the seat of government instead of Elizabethtown. Dyer, who had been appointed surveyor general of the king's customs in his American Plantations, was admitted by Governor Lawrie to discharge his duties in New Jersey. But he soon complained to the commissioners of the customs at London, "that when he prosecuted vessels, the juries found their verdicts against the most undoubted facts."‡

New Jersey, Reid, and Scot. August. April. Dyer. June.

By this time James the Second had settled the affairs of his kingdom greatly to his own satisfaction. Domestic rebellions, which menaced his throne, had been crushed; and

* Col. Doc., ix., 165, 265–268, 273–286, 297; Doc. Hist., i., 123–126; La Hontan, i., 68; Charlevoix, ii., 323–326, 335; Shea's Missions, 309; Quebec MSS., iv. (ii.), 420; *ante*, 401.

† Col. Doc., ix., 275, 290–293; Charlevoix, ii., 328; *ante*, 429.

‡ Wodrow, iv., 216, 220–223, 332, 333; Whitehead's East Jersey, 104–109, 115, 231–333; Contributions, 23–49; Leaming and Spicer, 175, 283; Chalmers's Ann., i., 621; Mass. Rec., v., 530; Penn. Col. Rec., i., 148, 197, 198, 209, 210, 211; Hist. Mag. (ii.), i., 87–95; N. Y. Col. Doc., iii., 354, 392, 493; *ante*, 369, 392, 412.

victims of the Scotch Privy Council, and the remnant who escaped the tender mercies of Kirke's "lambs" in the south-west of England, dangerously crowded the ships bound to the American Plantations. And now the king could think of the deferred affairs of his colonies. The most pressing of these seemed to be the establishment of a government in Massachusetts, where, for more than nine months since its charter had been canceled, local authority had been administered by doubtfully appointed officials. But the Plantation Committee moved slowly. They seem to have been aroused by the letters of the Corporation of New York, and of Dyer, the surveyor of the king's customs in East Jersey, complaining of the inconvenience of the existing arrangements there. Accordingly, they recommended that writs of Quo Warranto should be prosecuted against the proprietors of East and West New Jersey, and of Delaware, because it was growing prejudicial "that such independent governments be kept up and maintained without a nearer and more immediate dependence" on the crown. Quakers and Roman Catholics—Penn, and Perth, and Baltimore—were alike involved. They were all now the subjects of a new sovereign. Randolph having exhibited articles against the charter officers of Connecticut and Rhode Island, the Plantation Committee also recommended that similar writs should be issued against those corporations. James approved these recommendations, and directed Sir Robert Sawyer, his attorney general, to proceed against Connecticut and Rhode Island "forthwith," and against the several claimants of East and West Jersey and of Delaware, "if he shall find cause."*

James takes up colonial affairs.

15 July.

17 July. Connecticut, Rhode Island, Jersey, and Delaware.

Randolph now urged that "a temporary Government" should be established in Massachusetts, by the king's commission, "to the best disposed persons upon the place, until such time as his Majesty's Governor General shall be dispatched from hence to take upon him the government of all the Colonies in New England." He even named candidates for offices, and suggested a joint Assembly, in which the people of Massachusetts, Plymouth, Maine, and New

18 August. Randolph's advice.

2 Septem.

* Col. Doc., iii., 361, 362, 363; Chalmers, i., 278, 297, 301–304, 371, 621; Arnold, i., 481; Palfrey, iii., 482, 505, 508; R. I. Rec., iii., 175–177; Col. Rec. Conn., iii., 347–352; Dalrymple, ii., 53; Burnet, i., 647–651; Wodrow, iv., 216–223; Mackintosh, 14; Macaulay, i., 565, 628–630; *ante*, 426, 432.

CHAP. IX. 1685. 9 Septem. Hampshire should be represented. But, in spite of the opinions of Sawyer and Finch, his attorney and solicitor general, James expressly directed "that no mention of an Assembly be made in the Commission." This, however, was only following out the order of the late king in November, 1684. Joseph Dudley, for whose loyalty Dongan 27 Septem. vouched, was accordingly appointed president, and seven- 8 October. New England regulated. teen others counselors, of that part of New England including Massachusetts, New Hampshire, Maine, and the Narragansett Country, or the King's Province, to govern the same until the "chief Governor" should arrive. As his special reward, Randolph had his previous appointment 21 Septem. by Charles confirmed by James's commission to be "Secretary and sole Register" of this territory. Moreover, as the Duke of York's personal interest in the revenues of the post-office was now vested in his crown, Lord Treasurer 19 Novem. Randolph deputy postmaster in North America. Rochester appointed Randolph, whose attention had been awakened by Dongan's movement, to be deputy postmaster of New England—apparently the first instance of the kind in American colonial annals.*

Septem. Baptism of negroes in the English Plantations. While thus arranging a temporary government in New England, James took care to announce in his Privy Council his resolution "that the negroes in the Plantations should all be baptized; exceedingly declaiming against that impiety of their masters prohibiting it, out of a mistaken opinion that they would be, *ipso facto*, free." This determination of the king was afterward practically enforced in the Instructions to his colonial governors. It appears to have been suggested by the second article of the famous "*Code Noir*," which Louis had just published at Versailles, and which required all slaves in the French colonies to be baptized and taught in the Catholic religion.†

The King of France now took a step which moved both

* Col. Doc., iii., 350, 364, 365, 579; Chalmers, i., 417, 418, 419, 463; R. I. Rec., iii., 178, 195, 196, 200; Mass. H. S. Coll., v., 244; xxvii., 148, 149, 161, 162; Hutch. Mass., i., 341; Coll., 543, 557, 559, 560; Belknap, i., 185, 186; Douglas, i., 413; Palfrey, iii., 395, 482–485; Force's Tracts, iv., No. 8, p. 13, 14; *ante*, 419.

† Evelyn, ii., 245; Anderson's Col. Ch., ii., 303; Long's Hist. of Jamaica, iii., Appendix; Oldmixon, ii., 130; Burk, ii., 129, 130; Martin's Louis XIV., i., 489, 490; Hurd's Law of Freedom and Bondage, i., 165, 185, 186, 210, 281; Col. Doc., iii., 374, 547. In Valentine's Manual for 1861, 640–664, are numerous instances of the marriages of negroes with negresses by the Dutch ministers in New York, from 1642 to 1683; and several children of such marriages appear to have been baptized: Val. Man., 1863, 738–834. In 1667, Virginia enacted that baptism did not free slaves from bondage: Hening, ii., 260; Hurd, i., 232; Anderson's Col. Church, ii., 344.

Europe and America. His grandfather, Henry the Fourth, had made an edict at Nantes in 1598, which granted to Protestants full liberty of conscience, and many privileges they had not before enjoyed in the French kingdom. This edict had been respected by Louis the Thirteenth, by Richelieu, and by Mazarin. But, after the death of Colbert, and the secret marriage of Louis the Fourteenth with Frances de Maintenon, a great change happened. Roman ideas took the place of Protestant ideas. Huguenots, protected by Henry, were persecuted by Louis, who sent his dragoons to convert them to the Romish doctrine. At last the king revoked his predecessor's Edict of Nantes. The consequences of this act were immediate and immense. Brutal persecutions drove more than two hundred thousand of her million and a half of Protestants out of France. The refugees sought new homes in England, Holland, Prussia, and America, where they introduced unknown French arts and industry. Scorning thraldom, genius renounced allegiance; and Schomberg, Basnage, Rapin, with a host of others, under freer skies, gave their talents and their gallantry to help the retributive humiliation of the vainglorious persecutor of their faith.*

17 October. Louis revokes the Edict of Nantes.

William Penn had meanwhile been employed in helping himself at Whitehall. Penn was an uncommonly adroit and selfish Englishman. He knew where, when, and how to touch his sovereign's weaknesses. And he had the luck to touch James, to his own great gain. Yet, in his controversy with Lord Baltimore about the undefined boundaries of Maryland, William Penn had on his side the advantage of historical truth. When the case was brought to the king for decision, the rival claimants were politically equal. One was a Romanist, the other a Quaker. So James took up the question. As Duke of York he had, since 1669, denied Baltimore's claim to the Delaware territory; and in 1682 he had conveyed it to Penn. After patient hearings, the Plantation Committee reported that Lord Baltimore's patent granted "only land uncultivated and inhabited by Savages;" whereas the territory in dispute had

Penn successful with James in England.

8 Novem.

* Anderson on Commerce, ii., 568–571; Lavallée, iii., 257–263, 316; Martin's Louis XIV., i., 534–558; ii., 30–56; Anderson's Col. Ch., ii., 329–331; Wodrow, iv., 349–351; Burnet, i., 655; Macaulay, ii., 13–17; iii., 124; Evelyn, ii., 253, 254; Arnold, i., 496, 497; Palfrey, iii., 453; N. Y. Col. Doc., iii., 399, 426, 450, 650; ix., 309, 312, 425, 509, 540, 549.

1685.

been inhabited and planted by Christians before his grant. Delaware, therefore, did not form a part of Maryland. But, to end differences, the committee recommended that the land between the Chesapeake and the Delaware should be divided into two equal parts, of which the half nearest the Delaware should belong to the king (or to Penn), and that nearest the Chesapeake remain to Lord Baltimore.

13 Novem. Decision about the Delaware territory.

This report was approved by James in council, who ordered the division to be made accordingly. This decision established the original title of the Dutch as they maintained it in 1659; while it denied the rightfulness of the Duke of York's patent for New Netherland in 1664, and "invalidated the reasonings upon which England had always contended for American sovereignty."*

Perhaps the most important result of Penn's visit to England was the introduction of the art of printing into the middle colonies of British America. Up to this time the only printing-press in the English-American Plantations had been the one in Massachusetts, which had always been under Puritan censorship. A new act of Parliament had

2 July. Press censorship revived in England.

just revived the censorship of the English press, which had expired in 1679. Freedom of printing was not one of the ideas of that age. But the necessity of the printer's art was every where felt. That necessity had moved the council of Pennsylvania, when, in July, 1684, they "left to the Governor's discretion to have the laws and charter printed at London." So the proprietor, while there, engaged "a friend," William Bradford, to set up a printing-press in Philadelphia. Bradford was then twenty-two years old, born in Leicestershire, and said to have gone, as a stripling, to Pennsylvania with Penn in 1682. He was now married to a daughter of Andrew Sowle, a distinguished Quaker printer, of Grace Church Street, in London, to whom he had been an apprentice. George Fox

6 August.

therefore wrote to several eminent Quakers in America, that "a sober young man, whose name is William Brad-

* Col. Doc., ii., 88–100; iii., 186, 339, 340, 342-347, 362, 363; Chalm., i., 371, 650, 651, 663; Hazard's Reg. Penn., ii., 202, 203, 225; Proud, i., 290–295; ii., 208–211; Grahame, i., 327, 328, 521; Bancroft, ii., 308, 393, 394; Dixon, 222–227; Macaulay, i., 502–505, 650; *ante*, 150, 164, 367, 393; vol. i., 666–669. The boundary between Pennsylvania and Maryland was run from Delaware westward, between 1763 and 1768, by Charles Mason and Jeremiah Dixon, and is now popularly known as "Mason and Dixon's line:" see interesting papers on this subject in Hist. Mag., ii., 37–42; v., 199–202.

ford, comes to Pennsylvania, to set up the trade of printing Friends' books." On reaching Philadelphia, Bradford quickly started his press; the first work of which seems to have been an Almanac for the year 1686, compiled by Samuel Atkyns. This almost unique curiosity at this day was sharply censured by the critics of Pennsylvania. It stated, as a chronological fact, that at a certain day in 1682 was "The beginning of government here by the Lord Penn." These words provoked much Quaker wrath; and the temporary subordinate of the absent proprietor—without whose active friendship many probably would never have seen Philadelphia—ordered Atkyns "to blot out the words *Lord Penn*" from his Almanac, and charged Bradford "not to print any thing but what shall have license from the council."*

CHAP. IX. 1685. Bradford begins to print in Philadelphia. 1686. 9 Jan'y.

Meanwhile an order of the New York Council in March, 1684, requiring the several towns in the province to renew their patents, had caused much anxiety. Dongan had a double motive to enforce it; for the king's revenue from the new quit-rents would be increased, and he would himself gain a harvest of fees. The towns did not delay when they saw they must act. Hempstead and Flushing made large grants of land to the governor, and obtained advantageous patents. Flatbush also got a new charter. After a long negotiation about boundaries, Newtown likewise procured Attorney General Graham's approbation to a patent, which the council resolved should be the model after which all those for other townships should be drawn. Accordingly Brooklyn, and all the other towns on Long Island, with the exception of Huntington, in the course of this year obtained new patents from the governor. This result, however, was not gained without opposition. Easthampton was especially stubborn; and Mulford and others riotously protested against any interference with their old patents. James, the minister of the town, preached a stirring sermon against those who acted under the governor's order. The offenders were summoned to New York, where Attorney General Graham filed informations against

Dongan granted land by Hempstead and Flushing. 20 Febr'y. New patents for towns. May to December. 6 October. 17 October. 19 Novem. Easthampton.

* Penn. Col. Rec., i., 74, 82, 117, 165; Historical Mag., iv., 52; vii., 70, 71; viii., 274–276; Thomas's Hist. Print., ii., 7, 8, 91; Dixon, 208; Penn. H. S. Mem., i., 104, 105; Wallace's Address, 1863, 20–27; Statute 1 James II., cap. 17; Macaulay, i., 248, 579, 580; Lingard, xiii., 165, *note; ante*, 89, 145, 338.

CHAP. IX.

1686.

9 Decem.

them. They came accordingly, and humbly asked pardon for what they had done, which was granted; and, in the end, Easthampton was glad to take out "a more full and liberal" patent from Dongan.*

24 April.

The Corporation of New York had for some time desired a new charter from the king, confirming their old privileges, and granting to them all the vacant land in and about the city. As Bayard, its mayor, was one of the council, and Graham, its recorder, attorney general of the province, a draft of the desired patent was quickly submitted to the municipal authorities, who agreed to give Dongan three hundred pounds, and Secretary Spragg twenty-four pounds, as their official fees. The engrossed charter, having been read and allowed in council, was accordingly signed by the governor, who caused it to be sealed with the old provincial seal which the Duke of York had sent out to Lovelace in 1669, and which was yet the only one that could be used. The instrument itself is too familiar to need a particular description here.†

27 April. New charter for the city of New York.

May.

Soon after signing the metropolitan charter, the governor went up to "settle his Majesty's business" at Albany, the inhabitants of which were anxious to be incorporated. Dongan had granted a patent for Rensselaerwyck on the 4th of November, 1685, to its Dutch proprietors, for which they paid him two hundred pounds. But after their patent was sealed it was found inconvenient, because it included Albany, which, being the second town in the government, should not "be in the hands of any particular men." Through the influence of Graham, Palmer, and Van Cortlandt, the Van Rensselaers now released "their pretence to the town, and sixteen miles into the country for Commons to the King."‡

Rensselaerwyck patent.

20 July. Release of the Van Rensselaers.

The governor accordingly executed a charter agreed upon between himself and the magistrates at Albany, for

* Council Min., v., 63, 148, 161, 183, 188; Col. MSS., xxxi., 121; xxxii., 26; xxxiii., 66–80, 99; Doc. Hist., iii., 213–218; Wood, 41, 103, 104; Hedges' Address, 20, 88–95; Thompson, i., 315, 336, 414, 468; ii., 14–17, 82, 105, 185, 193, 223; Riker's Newtown, 106–113; Stiles's Brooklyn, i., 200–202; Hoffman, i., 95; Patents, vol. v.; Col. Doc., iii., 333, 401, 412.

† Col. Doc., iii., 360, 361, 365, 412, 425, 427, 495; iv., 812; v., 369; Council Min., v., 155; Min. of N. Y. Common Council, i., 272, 299, 300; Val. Man., 1844, 318; 1858, 13–24; Dunlap, ii., App. cxxxiv.; Hist. Mag., vi., 375; Doc. Hist., iv., 1*; Patents, v., 381–406; Hoffman's Treatise, i., 20; *ante*, 158, *note*, 409, 427.

‡ Patents, v., 228–235; Munsell's Annals, iv., 145; Barnard's Sketch, 130–135; Doc. Hist., iii., 552; Col. Doc., ii., 558; iii., 224, 225, 269, 270, 351, 401, 410, 411, 455, 495; *ante*, vol. i., 535; ii., 258, 287.

which they promised him three hundred pounds. By this instrument Dongan incorporated the "ancient town" of Beverwyck, or Willemstadt, or Albany, as a city, with large franchises, including the management of the Indian trade; and appointed Peter Schuyler to be its first mayor; Isaac Swinton, its recorder; Robert Livingston, its clerk; Dirck Wessels, Jan Jansen Bleecker, David Schuyler, Johannes Wendell, Levinus van Schaick, and Adrian Garritse, its aldermen; Joachim Staats, John Lansing, Isaac Verplanck, Lawrence van Ale, Albert Ryckman, and Melgert Winantse, its assistants; Jan Becker, its chamberlain; Richard Pretty, its sheriff; and James Parker, its marshal. The mayor and the sheriff were afterward to be appointed annually by the governor; the recorder and the town clerk to hold office during his pleasure; and the aldermen and assistants to be annually elected by the inhabitants on the Feast of Saint Michael, or the twenty-ninth day of September. The charter, being brought up to Albany, "was published with all the joy and acclamations imaginable;" and the officials named in it were duly sworn.*

CHAP. IX. 1686. 22 July. Albany incorporated as a city. 26 July. The Albany charter published.

Dongan also appointed Robert Livingston to be sub-collector and receiver of the king's revenues at Albany, which, with his place as town clerk, "might afford him a competent maintenance." Appointed by Andros to be secretary of his Indian Commissioners at Albany in 1675, Livingston secured colonial position by marrying, in 1683, Alida, widow of Domine Nicolaus van Rensselaer, and a sister of Peter Schuyler. Gifted with remarkable acquisitiveness, and enjoying peculiar official advantages, he learned that there were valuable lands on the east side of the Hudson, just below those of the Van Rensselaers, which had never been granted by the government of New York. So Livingston quietly secured the Indian title to all the territory from Roeloff Jansen's Kill, opposite Catskill, to a point opposite the Saugerties Kill, with all the lands further east-

12 July. Robert Livingston made comfortable.

* Patents, v., 446–478; Munsell's Annals, ii., 62–92; viii., 205–216; Col. Doc., iii., 401, 407, 411, 426, 494. As to the families of Bleecker, Van Schaick, and Livingston, see Holgate, 87–98, 141–200; and as to that of Schuyler, see Munsell, ii., 177; O'Call., ii., 177. Denonville, the governor of Canada, writing to Seignelay from Montreal, in August, 1687, reported that, by his charter to the city of Albany, Dongan had, "for money, divested himself of the finest right he possessed—that of nominating the magistrates and other officers, whereby he was enabled to execute the orders of the King of England. Thus he is no longer master of the merchants:" Col. Doc., ix., 337.

CHAP. IX. 1686. 22 July. Livingston's patent.

ward toward Massachusetts and Connecticut, called "Tachkanick." He then got Dongan to give him a patent for this vast region, with manorial privileges; and thus the shrewd Scotch clerk of Albany became one of the largest landowners in New York.*

8 May. Denonville's Canadian policy.

After his first winter's experience, the new governor of Canada informed Seignelay of Dongan's enterprise in trading with the Western savages by Albany parties, led by Canadian deserters. The only way to check this would be to establish a strong French post at Niagara. Moreover, Fort Frontenac, at Cataracouy, should be made a magazine to aid an attack on the Senecas, who must be humbled. The Iroquois, he declared, "maintain themselves only by
12 June. the assistance of the English." Again, Denonville insisted "that the English are the principal fomenters of the insolence and arrogance of the Iroquois, adroitly using them to extend their sovereignty," which they pretended covered Lakes Ontario and Erie, "and the whole territory towards the Miscissippi."†

15 April. The Five Nations summoned to Albany.

To counteract Denonville's policy, and to maintain his own, Dongan summoned the Five Nations to meet him at Albany. A new order had been made, forbidding all traffic with the Indians, unless the governor's license had been obtained. The commissaries there represented that its trade had been diminished by the intrigues of the French among the Indians, and asked to have the French priests removed from their castles, and to have them replaced by "English, capable to instruct and continue them in the knowledge of the Christian religion." Dongan accordingly promised to establish a church at "Serachtague," or Saratoga, for such Iroquois as should come back from Canada, and to ask King James to send over English priests as soon as possible. He also warned the Five Nations of Denonville's purpose to attack them; and, promising his friendship, advised retaliation. Lamberville, the elder French missionary at Onondaga, had endeavored to pre-
10 May. vent this meeting at Albany, and appealed to Dongan's re-

May. Dongan wishes English Jesuits to replace the French among the savages.

* Pat., v., 491-499; Doc. Hist., iii., 367-435; Col. Doc., iii., 401; iv., 251, 514, 791, 822; Col. MSS., xxxiii., 266; Council Min., v., 117; Ord., Warr., etc., xxxii½, 13, 14; Sedgwick's Liv.; Hunt's Liv.; *ante*, 287, 300.

† Col. Doc., ix., 287-296; Quebec MSS. (ii.), v., 189-252; Doc. Hist., i., 126-128; Charlevoix, ii., 327, 328, 332; *ante*, 405, 429, 432.

ligious sympathy. The governor replied that he would protect him from any danger he might apprehend from the Indians; the question as to the dominion over whom must be left to the kings of England and France. At the same time he invited the younger Lamberville to Albany, and even asked the Onondagas to send him there; but the missionary staid at his post. Dongan also wrote to Denonville that his preparations at Cataracouy had alarmed the Iroquois; and he warned him not to attack "the King of England's subjects," nor to build his intended fort "at a place called Ohniagero [Niagara], on this side of the Lake; —within my master's territories, without question." War would not begin on the side of New York; and the governor of Canada should "refer all questions home, as I have done."*

1686. 20 May. 22 May. Dongan warns Denonville.

Denonville now appealed to Dongan, as a Roman Catholic, for aid in converting the savages, and asked him to return deserters from Canada; promising reciprocity, and alleging that he had done all he could to find and send back two New York negroes, whom Tesschenmaeker, the Dutch clergyman at Schenectady, supposed to be harbored in Canada. A few days afterward, Denonville asserted that the supplies sent to Cataracouy should give no umbrage; that the Iroquois were treacherous; and that the pretensions of the English to their country were not as good as the actual possession by the French, who had long maintained establishments there, in regard to which "our masters will easily agree among themselves, seeing the union and good understanding that obtain between them." Dongan, in reply, complimented Denonville at the expense of De la Barre, and promised to do all he could to prevent the Iroquois harming the French missionaries, and also to surrender all refugees from Canada.†

5 June. Denonville to Dongan. 20 June. 26 July. Dongan's reply to Denonville.

Informed by the Minisinks of the designs of the French, Dongan summoned the Five Nations to send delegates to

7 August.

* Col. MSS., xxxiii., 234; Col. Doc., iii., 394, 395, 418, 419, 454, 455, 456, 464; ix., 296, 297, 311, 302; Doc. Hist., i., 128, 129; Charlevoix, ii., 329, 330, 331, 332; Shea's Missions, 314. Colden does not mention this meeting at Albany. The date of Dongan's reply to Lamberville's letter, in Col. Doc., iii., 464, and Doc. History, i., 143, 144, is wrongly given as 1687 instead of 1686: compare Col. Doc., ix., 311. Dongan was not at Albany in May, 1687: Col. MSS., xxxv., 64.

† Col. Doc., iii., 456–461; ix., 297, 312; Doc. Hist., i., 129, 130, 131; Charlevoix, ii., 329–334; Shea's Missions, 314; Warburton, i., 406; *ante*, 380, 432.

CHAP. IX. 1686. 30 August. Dongan's conference with the Iroquois at Fort James.

New York. A conference was accordingly held at Fort James, when the governor told the Iroquois that the King of England would be their "loving father;" that they should not meet the French at Cataracouy; that no Europeans would be allowed to go to the Susquehanna River and trade there without Corlaer's consent; that he was about sending other expeditions to the Western savages, and wished some from each Iroquois nation, especially the Senecas, to accompany them; that he would provide good land and an English Jesuit priest for all the Iroquois Christians at the Sault Saint Louis who would return to New York; that he would also establish English Jesuits among the Five Nations, who, he wished, would dismiss their French missionaries; that they should send to him all Frenchmen who should visit their country; and finally he said that if they were attacked by the Governor of Canada, "Let me know; I will come; it will be with me he shall have to settle." The next day the several nations answered in their turns. Although Albany was the "appointed place" to talk, they had cheerfully come to New York; and they were glad that they were to be "no more Brothers, but looked upon as children." As to trading on the Susquehanna, they avoided committing themselves; but the Mohawks—from whom most of the proselytes at the Sault Saint Louis had gone—earnestly desired that Dongan would "order that land and a Priest may be at Saraghtoge."*

English instead of French Jesuits.

1 Septem. Reply of the Five Nations.

An English priest wanted at Saratoga.

October. Lamberville deceived by Denonville.

Detecting this movement, Lamberville hastened to Denonville, who sent him back, with instructions "to assemble all the Iroquois nations, next spring, at Cataracouy, to talk over our affairs;" and also to dispatch his younger brother James to Canada, while he remained alone among the Onondagas. "The poor father knows nothing of our designs," wrote Denonville to Seignelay, "and I am sorry to see him exposed." And well might the marquis-governor feel "sorry;" for his purpose was to use the adroit but sincere missionary as the instrument to accomplish one of the vilest stratagems which ever marked the policy of France in North America.†

8 Novem.

* Council Min., v., 163, 165–170; Charlevoix, ii., 333, 334; Col. Doc., iii., 395, 489; ix., 302, 308, 310, 320, 802; Doc. Hist., i., 139, 141, 142, 265, 266. Colden does not give any account of this interview at New York.

† Col. Doc., iii., 453; ix., 298; Doc. Hist., i., 134; Charlevoix, ii., 334, 335; Shea, 315.

Denonville sent Dongan a caustic reply, charging him with duplicity in his transactions with the Iroquois; wrongfulness in sending English parties to Michilimackinac; and want of religion in furnishing the savages with "Eau de vie," which converted them into demons, and their cabins "into counterparts and theatres of hell." With Irish wit, Dongan retorted that he had "only permitted several of Albany to trade among the remotest Indians," and hoped that they would be civilly treated by the French, among whom they intruded; while as to furnishing liquors to the savages, "certainly our Rum doth as little hurt as your Brandy; and in the opinion of Christians, is much more wholesome."*

CHAP. IX. 1686. 1 October. Denonville to Dongan. 1 Decem. Dongan's retort.

Dongan did not fail to show that he was as bold as his French rival. The expedition he had sent from Albany the last year having been so successful, he again commissioned Captain Rooseboom to go with another party and trade with the Ottawas. Rooseboom's company was made up of active young men, chiefly Albanians, among whom were the sons of Arent Schuyler, and Jan Jansen Bleecker. The refugee La Fontaine accompanied them. From Schenectady they traveled westward in canoes, twenty of which, "freighted principally with rum," were reported by James de Lamberville as having passed "Galkonthiage," near the head of Oneida Lake. This party was to winter among the Senecas, and go on to Michilimackinac in the spring. It was accompanied by two savages from each of the Iroquois tribes, as Dongan had desired.†

13 Septem. Rooseboom and others again sent to the West. October.

Another party was organized to start from Albany early in the spring, under the command of Major Patrick MacGregorie, a Scotch officer, who had served in France, and whom Dongan had made ranger general of Staten Island, and muster master general of the militia of the province. MacGregorie was commissioned by the governor to

15 June. 16 Septem. 21 Septem. 4 Decem.

* Col. Doc., iii., 461-463; ix., 298, 312, 979, 1073; Doc. Hist., i., 131, 132, 139, 140; Wolley's Two Years, etc., 35, 47; *ante*, 146, 332.

† Col. Documents, iii., 436, 437, 463, 476, 489, 513; ix., 302, 308, 802, 816; Doc. Hist., i., 167; Col. MSS., xxxiii., 286, 292; *ante*, 409, 429, 432, 442. Johannes, the eldest son of Captain Jan Jansen Bleecker, was eighteen years old when he left Albany with Captain Rooseboom on the eleventh of September, 1686. He was taken prisoner by the Canadians in the following May, and did not return to Albany until "after the second sermon," on Sunday, the 23d of October, 1687. Johannes Bleecker became recorder of Albany in 1700, and mayor in 1701; and was member of the Provincial Assembly in 1701 and 1702: Holgate, 91; Munsell, iv., 119, 122, 142, 145, 153; *ante*, vol. i., 625, *note*.

CHAP. IX.

1686.

MacGregorie's party also sent westward.

be commander-in-chief not only of his own party, but of that of Rooseboom, which he was to overtake, and lead both to the Ottawas country and back again to Albany. Viele, the interpreter, accompanied MacGregorie, who was ordered "not to disturb or meddle with the French."*

13 October. 8 Novem. 10 Novem. 11 Novem. 16 Novem.

Population of Canada.

In his dispatches home, Denonville complained of Dongan's proceedings, and insisted that Canada would be lost to France if war were not made against the Iroquois the next year. The population of the colony was now a little over twelve thousand, and its military strength only eight hundred men. Troops must be sent from France, and the post at Chambly be strengthened, so as to hold the Mohawks in check, while the main attack should be made on the Senecas. A strong fort should be established at Niagara, and that at Detroit be maintained, so as to command the Western lakes. Fifty or sixty Huguenots from the French West Indies had lately settled themselves in New York, and some had come to Boston from France. These were "fresh material for banditti." Exasperated at Dongan's trading-parties to the West, Denonville asked the minister to send him specific orders, "for I am disposed to go straight to Orange, storm their fort, and burn the whole concern."†

Huguenots sheltered in New York and Boston.

Denonville wishes to burn Albany.

Pemaquid.

10 June.

19 June.

The affairs of Pemaquid had meanwhile fallen into confusion; but as Dongan was unable to go there, it was determined in council to send Judge Palmer thither with large powers. West was likewise deputed by Spragg to act for him as secretary at "Pemaquid, in the County of Cornwall." Dongan also licensed Spragg, Graham, and others to take up parcels of land in that country. On reaching Pemaquid, Palmer and West tore "all in pieces" the old grants and settlements of Andros. "They placed and displaced at pleasure, and were as arbitrary as the Great Turke." Extravagant grants of land were made, chiefly to Dongan's favorites. As they had been directed to claim all the territory eastward to the Saint Croix as

September.

Palmer and West arbitrary as "the Great Turke" in Maine.

* Col. Doc., iii., 395, 431, 437, 442, 473, 476, 483; ix., 308, 318; Doc. Hist., i., 100; Col. MSS., xxxiii., 137, 138, 236, 298; Council Min., v., 175; Licenses, etc., v.

† Col. Doc., ix., 296–318, 801, 802; Col. MSS., xxxiii., 219–298; Quebec MSS. (ii.), v., 259–345; Doc. Hist., i., 132–139; Charlevoix, ii., 333–336; Garneau, i., 259, 260. Dongan reported that the population of Canada, in 1685, was 17,000: Col. Doc., iii., 396; Chalmers, i., 609. This is an error of 5000 (17 for 12), as in 1686 Denonville reported a census of 12,373: Col. Doc., ix., 316.

belonging to New York, the commissioners seized from Saint Castin, at Penobscot, a quantity of wine and brandy belonging to John Nelson, of Piscataqua. This seizure was at first thought good; but, at the instance of Louis's ambassador at London, James ordered the "chearing comodity" to be restored. In the autumn Palmer and West returned to New York, and reported their proceedings at Pemaquid. Disgusted with the trouble and costliness of that distant dependency, Dongan prayed the king to annex it to Massachusetts, and, in its place, to add Connecticut and Rhode Island to the government of New York.*

CHAP. IX. 1686. 23 July. Saint Castin's liquors seized. Novem. Dongan disgusted with Pemaquid.

Randolph had meanwhile returned to Massachusetts in the Rose frigate, accompanied by Robert Ratcliffe, an Episcopal clergyman recommended by the Bishop of London. For the first time the Protestant service of the Church of England was celebrated in the Boston Town Hall, with Bibles and Prayer-books provided by James the Second. The king's commission was published; and President Dudley, with his associate counselors, quietly replaced the magistrates of the late corporation. Instead of Sewall, who had controlled the Puritan colonial press, Randolph was made its censor; and Massachusetts sullenly sunk into her condition as a part of her sovereign's territory of New England. While a baffled oligarchy mourned its loss of power, James's new government of his colonies assumed its duties, "with the generall consent and applause of the people."†

14 May. Randolph again at Boston, and the English Church service celebrated. 26 May. Dudley installed at Boston. Randolph censor of its press instead of Sewall.

Although sectarian tyranny was quelled in Massachusetts, the older colony of Plymouth had departed from the liberal maxims of its founders. Quakers were taxed for the support of its Puritan ministers. Randolph expressed to Governor Hinckley his regret that, while their king had made conscience free in Massachusetts, it was restrained in Plymouth, "without any particular directions from White-

22 June. Quakers unjustly taxed in Plymouth.

* Col. Doc., iii., 387, 391, 402; ix., 919; Council Min., v., 157, 186, 187, 188; Col. MSS., xxxi., 166; xxxiii., 47, 48, 249–253; Patents, vi.; Quebec MSS. (iii.), i., 134; Hutch. Mass., i., 370; Coll., 547, 548, 563–565; Mather's Magnalia, ii., 586, 589; Force's Tracts, iv. (9), 37; Maine H. S. Coll., v., 89–91, 107–130; Col. Rec. Conn., iii., 366, 367; Williamson, i., 581–584; Palfrey, iii., 533; *ante*, 394, 407.

† Col. Doc., iii., 368; Col. Rec. Conn., iii., 351, 352; Hutch. Mass., i., 341–343, 350–353, 355, 356; Coll., 544–550; Mass. Rec., v., 452, 515–517; Anderson's Col. Church, ii., 454, 455; Coit's Puritanism, 203; Dixon's Penn., 241; Palfrey's N. E., iii., 484–495, 500, 519; *ante*, 434. Why should Mr. Palfrey (iii., 519) say that Randolph "*assumed to be censor of the press*" in Massachusetts, when he only took the place of Sewall, who formerly controlled that press? See Hutch. Mass., i., 355; Mass. Rec., v., 452.

CHAP. IX. 1686. hall." With caustic logic he added: "It will be as reasonable to move that your colony should be rated to pay our minister of the Church of England, who now preaches in Boston, and you hear him not, as to make the Quakers pay in your Colony."*

27 May. Connecticut claimed by James. Without loss of time, Randolph wrote to Governor Treat, of Connecticut, that "his Majesty intends to bring all New England under One Government, and nothing is now remaining on your part but to think of an humble submission and a dutiful resignation of your Charter, which if you are so hardy as to offer to defend at law, whilst you are contending for a shadow you will in the first place lose all that part of your Colony from Connecticut to New York, and have it annexed to that Government; a thing you are too certainly informed of already." In tribula-
14 June. Treat appeals to Dongan. tion, Treat besought Dongan to recommend Connecticut to the king's favor; suggesting that, if that colony must fall, it might be as easy to slide westward to New York as eastward to Boston; and that nothing said by Randolph had "at all prejudiced us against your Honor or your Govern-
3 July. ment." Again Treat asked Dongan's "good advice."
6 July. The General Court at Hartford also begged the king to allow his colony to retain its charter, which would "be most for the profit" of the inhabitants; while the contrary would "be very prejudiciall to them." The Massachu-
1 June. setts rulers had meanwhile prayed James's Plantation Committee that Rhode Island and Connecticut might be annex-
21 July. Dudley and Treat against Dongan. ed to the old "Bay" colony. Jealous of Dongan, Dudley informed Treat that "the consideration of the new modelling and perfect settlement of all his Majesty's Provinces, from Pemaquid to New York, is now lying before his Majesty, and probable to have a sudden and lasting dispatch; and that your parts, as lying between the two seats of government, may be the more easily poised either way, if early solicited." Pynchon and Winthrop, of the Massa-
27 July. chusetts council, were dispatched to Hartford to urge this
28 July. view. But Connecticut instructed an agent at London to
24 August. defend the colony against her king's *Quo Warranto;* and put off Dudley with a sarcasm, while she sent a special mes-

* Hutch. Mass., i., 356, 357; R. I. Rec., iii., 199; Arnold's R. I., i., 484, 485, 501, 502; Palfrey, iii., 504, 522.

senger to New York to ask Dongan's "favorable aspect." The metropolitan governor replied, that "for subjects to stand upon terms with Princes, is not very proper;" that the best policy of Connecticut would be "a downright humble submission;" and that if that colony thought it convenient to be annexed to New York, every thing would be made pleasant. Quit-rents would be lightened; ports would be continued where they now were; there would be "no necessity of entering at New York, or coming hither for any, except such as shall be named to be of the Council and Assembly; and the Judges in their circuits shall bring the laws to your doors. I shall say nothing of Boston, or any other place. You know what this is; and I am sure we live as happily as any in America—if we did but know it. The condition of some of our neighbors will best commend us." Dongan wrote truly. He might have said more.*

CHAP. IX. 1686. 4 August. 13 August. Dongan's reply.

While James's colony of Connecticut was thus coquetting with her wooers in Boston and New York, her sovereign at Whitehall was arranging her affairs to suit himself. In the previous November James had prorogued his Parliament, and then virtually annulled the Test Act of 1673 by stretching his prerogative so as to dispense with a statute of his realm.† And now he thought of New England, which Dudley and his council were temporarily governing. The king's attention had been drawn to the encroachments of the French upon the territory claimed by England in North America, and especially to their interference with the New England fisheries, of which Preston, his ambassador at Paris, had complained, but had gotten no satisfaction. It was therefore determined in the Privy Council that Connecticut, New Plymouth, and Rhode Island should be united with Massachusetts, New Hampshire, Maine, and the Narragansett country, and be made "one entire government, the better to defend themselves against invasion." This was good policy for En-

Jan'y. James's action at Whitehall.

* Col. Doc., iii., 368, 385–387; Col. Rec. Conn., iii., 207–213, 352–375; Hutch. Coll., 544–549; Chalmers, i., 419; Palfrey, iii., 494–511.

† Burnet, i., 667–671; Rapin, ii., 753, 755; Macaulay, ii., 35, 76, 80–84, 146, 209, 270; Hargraves's State Trials, vii., 611–646; *ante*, 201. It may interest Americans to know that Sir Edward Hales—whom James used as his instrument to procure a judicial decision that he could dispense with statutes—was appointed governor of Barbadoes in March, 1686, which office Hales exercised through his Lieutenant Stede, preferring to stay in England: Ellis's Correspondence, i., 85, 122, 297; Oldmixon, ii., 42.

CHAP. IX. 1686. Consolidation the idea of James.

gland. It was the despotic idea of consolidation. It was opposed to the republican system of confederation, as exemplified by the Helvetians and Batavians of Europe, and by the British colonists of New England. It was the antagonism of sovereignty and subordination. Consolidation was indeed the best mode of establishing in his colonies the king's direct government which Charles had adopted in November, 1684, and which James was now to enforce. It was charged, and it appeared to be true, that in some of the New England colonies there was less real popular liberty than there was in Old England. There certainly was less religious freedom in most of them. The reasoning of James was, that if the people of New England were not to govern themselves on democratic principles of general representation, they would be more equitably governed directly by the crown than by subordinate corporations, which justified their local tyranny by appealing to the grants of the crown. If there must be despotism, that of the sovereign of all Englishmen would be better than that of colonial oligarchies which, under English charters, claimed to rule in their own way all their fellow-subjects within their corporate bounds. In spite of the opinions of the crown lawyers, "that the right did yet remain in the inhabitants to consent to such laws and taxes as should be made or imposed on them," James had directed that there should be no mention of an Assembly in Dudley's commission. He now went a step further, and determined that the legislative and executive authority throughout New England should be conjoined in the same persons; "whereby a tyranny was established."*

Royal in place of colonial despotism.

Who should be James's governor general to "regulate" New England was already settled. As Kirke could not be spared from commanding his "lambs" at home, the king chose Sir Edmund Andros as a more fitting instrument to do his will in America. This arrangement seems to have been known to Randolph when he brought over Dudley's temporary commission. There was every reason why Andros should be selected. James had chosen him, in 1674, to govern New York; and in 1678, as the duke's deputy,

Sir Edmund Andros appointed governor of New England by James.

* Col. Doc., iii., 579, 581; La Potherie, i., 145; Charlevoix, ii., 302; Arnold, i., 494; Chalmers's Ann., i., 419; Rev. Col., i., 178; Macaulay, ii., 12; Palfrey, iii., 483, 485, 563; *ante*, vol. i., 361, 362; ii., 419, 434, 445.

he had recommended a strong royal government should be established in New England. Although "misrepresented as a Papist, because he was fond of prelacy," Andros—from his long American experience, his administrative ability, his irreproachable private character, and, above all, his soldierly notions of prompt obedience to orders—was just the agent to execute his king's arbitrary designs. Sir Edmund's worst enemies said that he had "large indowments of mind." Since his recall from New York, Andros had lived quietly in Guernsey. Yet his faithful service had not been forgotten by James, who, soon after his accession, promoted him to be the colonel of his daughter's (the Princess Anne's) regiment of horse.*

For more than twenty years James had been trying his "'prentice hand" upon New York. The time had now come when he was to use his master hand on New England. The best English lawyers concurred in the opinion that the only way in which English authority could be exercised in English unchartered colonies was by their king's commission under his great seal. Indeed, there was no other mode of securing English supremacy beyond "the four seas." Without the king's great seal no English patent had life. With it came power. If that "mysterious" seal could quicken a royal charter, why could it not quicken a royal commission? If the king could delegate any of his prerogatives to any of his subjects, so as to make them proprietors or corporations, by charters under his great seal, he certainly could delegate similar authority to his governor by a commission under the same waxen symbol of his sovereignty. This logic seemed to be indisputable. So, by the advice of Sunderland, James commissioned Colonel Sir Edmund Andros to be captain general and governor-in-chief over his "Territory and Dominion of New England in America," which meant Massachusetts Bay, New Plymouth, New Hampshire, Maine, and the Narragansett country, or the King's Province. Andros's commission was drawn in the traditional form, settled by the Plantation Board for those of other royal governors in Virginia, Ja-

American policy of James the Second.

3 June. Andros's commission.

* Chalmers, i., 419, 423; Douglas, ii., 247; Hutch. Mass., i., 342, 353, 354; Coll., 542, 547, 548; Palfrey, iii., 499, 517; Burnet, i., 647, 648; Mackintosh, 14; Col. Doc., ii., 741; iii., 263; Hist. Mag., viii., 247; N. Y. H. S. Coll. (1868), 366; Whitmore's Andros, 22, 23; *ante*, 316, 370, 419, 433, 434.

CHAP. IX. 1686.

maica, and New Hampshire. Its substance, however, was much more despotic. Andros was authorized, with the consent of a council appointed by the crown, to make laws and levy taxes, and to govern the territory of New England in obedience to its sovereign's Instructions, and according to the laws then in force, or afterward to be established. Vice was to be discountenanced and virtue encouraged. "And for the greater ease and satisfaction of our loving subjects in matters of religion," added the king, "We do hereby will, require, and command that liberty of conscience be allowed to all persons, and that such especially as shall be conformable to the rites of the Church of England be particularly countenanced and encouraged."*

Liberty of conscience to "all persons."

James's Instructions to Andros.

The king's instructions to Andros, which were also prepared by the Plantation Committee, followed the form of those given by the crown to its American governors: to Berkeley, of Virginia, in 1661; Culpepper, in 1679; and Howard of Effingham, in 1683; to Cranfield, of New Hampshire, in 1682; and to Sir Thomas Lynch, and Sir Philip Howard, of Jamaica, in 1681 and 1685. But Andros's orders differed from those models in important details.† They exhibit a singular picture of the mind of James:—"humane and severe, tyrannous and conciliatory; affecting an attention to the rights of the governed, while, by the same stroke, he removed the fence which secured them." This "fence" was a popular, a democratic "Assembly." Yet James should not be charged with having "removed" that which never existed. "The people" of Massachusetts, before the abrogation of the charter which a sectarian oligarchy misused, never had the share in local government which their fellow-English subjects in Jamaica, Virginia, Maryland, Pennsylvania, New Jersey, and

No Assembly allowed in New England.

* Macaulay, ii., 523; Chalmers, i., 141, 142, 345, 419, 420, 464, 465, 493; Col. Doc., ii., 488; vii., 363; Force's Tracts, iv., No. 8, 1–14; Mass. H. S. Coll., xxvii., 139–149; R. I. Rec., iii., 212–218; Narrative of the Miseries of New England, 33; Mather's Magnalia, i., 175; Palfrey, iii., 512, 516.

† The Instructions of James the Second to Andros, in 1686, among the New England "Entries" in the British State Paper Office, *have never been published.* A synopsis of them is given in Chalmers's Ann., i., 420, 421, 463. Mr. Palfrey, in his third volume, page 515, erroneously states that they are in what he calls "*O'Callaghan Documents*" (apparently intending to refer to the "New York Colonial Documents" procured in Europe—1841–1844—by the agent of the state, and afterward printed by its order), iii., 543. This is too gross a blunder to be passed by. The instructions thus cited are dated 16 April, 1688, and are Andros's *second*, not his *first* general orders from the king, which Mr. Palfrey refers to in a note on page 562 of his third volume.

New York actually enjoyed. Although arbitrary in form, the Instructions of Andros were equitable in substance. Among other things, the governor was directed to allow no printing-press without his special license. But this was only extending to America the restrictive policy of the late act of Parliament. It was no colonial novelty; for the royal governors of Virginia had been similarly instructed—and the press in Massachusetts had almost always been under the restraint of spontaneous Puritan censorship.*

CHAP. IX. 1686. Press censorship no novelty in Massachusetts.

A salary of twelve hundred pounds sterling was assigned to Andros; and a peculiar local flag was devised for the territory under his government. At the same time, a great seal for New England was delivered to the governor, which bore "a remarkable motto" abstracted from Claudian: "NUNQUAM LIBERTAS GRATIOR EXTAT." The phrase was, just then, "the theme of every song, and, by the help of some perversion of Scripture, the text of every sermon" in England; and it has always been familiar to the friends of despotism—"*Liberty is never more agreeable than under a pious king.*"†

29 Septem. Great seal of New England.

To secure Andros in his government, two companies of regular soldiers, chiefly Irish Papists, were raised in London, and placed under his orders. One of these companies was commanded by Captain Francis Nicholson, who, although a Protestant, had not hesitated to gratify the king by kneeling during the celebration of the mass in the royal tent at the camp on Hounslow Heath. At the suggestion of the Plantation Committee, James also ordered that the fort and country of Pemaquid, "in regard of its distance from New York, be for the future annexed to and con-

Soldiers sent to Boston.

20 June. Pemaquid annexed to New England.

* Chalmers's Ann., i., 244, 245, 340, 345, 392, 420, 421, 463, 493; Rev. Col., i., 179; Col. Doc., vii., 362, 363; Anderson's Col. Ch., ii., 281, 288, 289, 341, 375, 380; Belknap, i., 139–187; Mass. Rec., iv. (ii.), 62, 73, 141, 211, 509; v., 4, 32, 323, 452; Hutch. Mass., i., 248, 257, 258, 355; Palfrey, ii., 530; iii., 519; Thomas, i., 207, 246, 247, 276, 278; Penn. Col. Rec., i., 165, 278; iii., 145; *ante*, 89, 145, 146, 338, 436, 445. The names of Andros's counselors are given in Palfrey, iii., 604.

† Chalmers, i., 463, 465; New England Entries (S. P. O.), iv., 223, 267, 282, 311; Hutch., i., 362; Arnold, i., 495, 496; Palfrey, iii., 516; Claudian, Stilic., iii., 114; Gibbon, iii., 111; Fox's James II., 57. An engraved copy of this great seal, of which original impressions are now very rare, is published in Valentine's Manual for 1862, 738, 739: see also Hist. Mag., vi., 105, 106; Index to New Jersey Doc., 13; Mass. H. S. Proceedings for 1862, 79–81. The lines of Claudian—

* * * * * * "Nunquam libertas gratior extat,
Quam sub rege pio." * * * * * * * * * *

are thus translated by Hawkins:

"Ne'er liberty displays a higher grace,
Than under one where piety we trace."

CHAP. IX. tinued under the government of New England." Dongan, who felt the inconvenience of that far-off dependency, was about recommending this measure, so obviously proper. The king accordingly directed him to surrender to the governor general of New England the "Fort and Country of Pemaquid." Andros was at the same time instructed to demand the surrender of the charter of Rhode Island, and to receive a surrender of that of Connecticut, against which writs of *Quo Warranto* had been issued, and to take both these colonies under his government.*

1686.

19 Septem. Dongan ordered to surrender it.

13 Septem.

According to the declared intention of James, just after his accession, the government of New York was now "assimilated" to that which had been agreed on for New England. A royal commission, very like that to Andros, was issued to Dongan, which, although he was an avowed Roman Catholic, appointed him to be the king's captain general and governor-in-chief over his "Province of New York, and the territories depending thereon, in North America." The Test Act, as we have seen, did not of its own force extend to the English Plantations; and, moreover, James had dispensed with it in England. Dongan was authorized by the king, like Andros, to suspend counselors and nominate others for approval, so that there should be always seven at least. With the advice of his council the governor could make laws as near as might be to those of England, which were to be approved or rejected by the king; and levy taxes, continue those already imposed, and erect courts of justice. He was also empowered to appoint judges, pardon offenders, "collate any person or persons in any churches" which might be vacant, levy and command the military force of the province, execute martial law, build forts, act as vice-admiral, grant lands, appoint fairs, and regulate ports, harbors, and custom-houses; and he was required "to take all possible care for the discountenance of vice, and encouragement of virtue and good living, that by such example the infidels may be invited and desire to partake of the Christian Religion."†

10 June. Dongan's royal commission.

Power to make laws.

Other powers.

* Chalmers, i., 421; Clarke's James II., ii., 71; Secret Services Ch. II. and Jac. II., 139; Dalrymple, ii., 55, 65, 103; Col. Doc., iii., 391; Doc. Hist., ii., 17; Deeds, viii., 75; Maine H. S. Coll., v., 131, 265; Mass. H. S. Coll., xxvii., 160, 162, 163; xxxii., 295, 296; R. I. Col. Rec., iii., 218; Col. Rec. Conn., iii., 377, 380; Arnold, i., 495; Palfrey, iii., 516, 517; *ante*, 445.

† Col. Doc., iii., 357, 360, 377–382; Col. MSS., xxxiv. (ii.), 6; Chalmers, i., 588; *ante*, 423, 447. The clause in Andros's commission relative to liberty of conscience and the encour-

1686.

29 May.

Dongan's Instructions.

The Instructions of James to Dongan resembled those to Andros, and to his other governors in America. Dongan was directed to administer oaths of allegiance and of office, but not the Test oath, to Anthony Brockholls, Frederick Phillipse, Stephanus van Cortlandt, Lucas Santen, John Spragg, Jervis Baxter, and John Younge, whom the king named as counselors of New York, and who were to enjoy "freedom of debate and vote in all things to be debated of in council." The governor was to nominate proper persons to be appointed counselors, and to take care that all civil officers were "men of estate and abilities, and not necessitous people or much in debt," and that they should all be "well affected" to the royal government. "And whereas," added the king, "we have been presented with a Bill or Charter passed in the late Assembly of New York, containing several franchises, privileges and immunities mentioned to be granted to the Inhabitants of our said Province, You are to declare our will and pleasure that the said Bill or Charter of Franchises be forthwith repealed and disallowed, as the same is hereby repealed, determined and made void:—But you are nevertheless, with our said Council, to continue the duties and impositions therein mentioned to be raised, until you shall, with the consent of the Council, settle such taxes and impositions as shall be sufficient for the support of our Government of New York. And our further will and pleasure is that all other laws, statutes and ordinances already made within our said Province of New York, shall continue and be in full force and vigor, so far forth as they doe not in any wise contradict, impeach, or derogate from this Commission, or the orders and instructions herewith given you, till you shall, with the advice of our Council, pass other laws in our name for the good Government of our said Province, which you are to doe with all convenient speed."* The style of all laws was to be "By the Governor and Council," and not otherwise; and transcripts of them and of the Council Journal were to

Counselors.

The Charter of Liberties repealed.

Taxes and laws continued.

agement of Episcopalians (*ante*, 450), was not inserted in Dongan's, because there was no necessity for it in New York, where conscience had always been free, and where Episcopacy was not opposed. Religious freedom, however, was enjoined in his Instructions: Col. Doc., iii., 375.

* Col. Doc., iii., 357–359, 369, 370; Council Journ., i., 45. It will be observed that, although the king declined to confirm the New York Charter in March, 1685, he did not repeal it until May, 1686: *ante*, 383, 384, 423, 449, 450.

CHAP. IX.

1686.

be regularly sent to England. "You shall take especial care," was the king's further direction, "that God Almighty be devoutly and duly served throughout your Government; the Book of Common Prayer, as it is now established, read each Sunday and holiday; and the blessed sacrament administered according to the rites of the Church of England;" and "that no minister be preferred by you to any ecclesiastical benefice in that our Province, without a certificate from the most Reverend the Lord Archbishop of Canterbury, of his being conformable to the doctrine and discipline of the Church of England, and of a good life and conversation."* The ecclesiastical jurisdiction of the English primate was ordered to prevail throughout New York in every thing but collating to benefices, granting licenses for marriage, and the probate of wills, which powers were reserved to the governor. James further directed "that no schoolmaster be henceforth permitted to come from England and to keep school within our Province of New York, without the license of the said Archbishop of Canterbury; and that noe other person now there, or that shall come from other parts, bee admitted to keep school, without your license first had."† And then James the Second—in the very words he had addressed to Andros in 1674, and which the New York charter of 1683 had limited to *Christians*—directed Dongan to "permit all persons, of what religion soever, quietly to inhabit within your government, without giving them any disturbance or disquiet whatsoever, for or by reason of their differing opinions in matters of religion; Provided they give noe disturbance to the public peace, nor doe molest or disquiet others in the free exercise of their religion."‡ The orders of August,

Church of England service established.

Church of England's preferments.

School-masters from England to be licensed.

Liberty of conscience in New York.

* Col. Doc., iii., 36, 372: compare the Instructions to Berkeley and Culpepper, of Virginia, and Lynch and Howard, of Jamaica: Col. Doc., vii., 362, 363; Anderson's Col. Ch., ii., 289, 341, 342; Mass. H. S. Coll., xxxvii., 153; Hist. Mag., v., 153. The "ministers" to be preferred to benefices here referred to were those of the "orthodox," or Episcopalian Church of England. Dongan was not instructed to interfere with those of the Dutch, or Lutheran, or other churches in New York. Why the Archbishop of Canterbury, rather than the Bishop of London, was to have ecclesiastical jurisdiction in the province, will be explained: *post*, 456.

† Col. Doc., iii., 372. This Instruction was the policy of the Church of England influencing the Plantation Committee, and not that of James the Second, who had never before interfered with school-masters in New York, of all denominations. The restriction seems to have been adopted by the committee, at the request of Bishop Compton, of London, on 15 April, 1685, and to have been first inserted in the Instructions to Sir Philip Howard, as governor of Jamaica, on 27 April, 1685: Col. Doc., vii., 362, 363; Ellis Correspondence, i., 36, 99, 105, 109; Hist. Mag., vii., 330.

‡ Col. Doc., iii., 218, 359, 373; *ante*, 264, 383.

1684, prohibiting "any innovation" on the trade of "the River of New York" by East Jerseymen or others, under "groundless pretences," were renewed; and all goods passing up the Hudson River were required to pay duties at New York.* Dongan was also instructed to encourage "the Indians, upon all occasions, that they may apply themselves to English trade and nation, rather than to any others of Europe. But you are alsoe to act soe prudently, in respect to your European neighbors, as to give them noe just cause for complaint against you." * * * "You are to give all due encouragement and invitation to merchants and others who shall bring trade into our said Province, or any way contribute to the advantage thereof; and in particular to the Royal African Company of England. And you are to take care that there be no trading from the Province of New York to any place in Africa, within the charter of the Royal African Company. And you are not to suffer any ships to be sent thither without their leave or authority."† Treaties with foreign powers were to be carefully observed; and New York was required to pass a law against pirates, according to a transmitted formula. "Inhuman severities," which bad masters might use against their Christian servants or slaves, were to be restrained by law, and the willful killing of Indians and negroes made punishable by death. The conversion of negroes and Indians to Christianity was to be encouraged. The governor's salary was fixed at six hundred pounds sterling a year, to be paid out of the provincial revenue. "And forasmuch as great inconvenience may arise by the liberty of printing within our Province of New York, you are to provide by all necessary orders, that no person keep any press for printing, nor that any book, pamphlet, or other matters whatsoever, bee printed, without your especial leave and license first obtained."‡ Such were the main features of

No innovation on the Hudson River.

Royal African Company.

Conversion of negroes and Indians in New York.

No unlicensed printing.

* Col. Doc., iii., 248, 249, 373; *ante*, 411.

† Col. Doc., iii., 245, 365, 374; Col. MSS., xxxv., 77. Of this Royal African Company—one of the purposes of which was to bring negro slaves to America—James, while Duke of York, had been governor; *ante*, 6. In September, 1681, Governor Lynch, of Jamaica, was instructed to encourage this Royal English Company's trade in "merchantable negroes:" Anderson's Col. Ch., ii., 281.

‡ Col. Doc., iii., 374, 375. This restriction of the press in New York was according to the precedents of the Plantation Committee, in their Instructions to the several colonial governors. As proprietor, James had given no such orders to Nicolls, or Lovelace, or Andros, or Dongan: see *ante*, 89, 145, 146, 338, 434, 436, 445, 451.

CHAP. IX. 1686. the Instructions of James the Second to Dongan. Thus "a real tyranny," like that in New England, was established in New York, which, deprived of its popular Assembly, was "reduced once more to the condition of a conquered Province."*

3 June. Orders of the Plantation Committee. The Plantation Committee likewise ordered Dongan to send them, every quarter, a particular account of all important matters concerning the province, with his opinion how its government might be improved. Secretary Spragg 10 June. was also directed to transmit official transcripts promptly and faithfully.†

By James the Second's Instructions to Dongan, the Episcopal Church of England was, for the first time, directed to be especially fostered, and the "ecclesiastical jurisdiction" of its primate to be established, "as far as conveniently may be," in New York. James the Second establishes the English Episcopal Church in New York. Some episcopal power in his colonies appears to have been delegated by Charles the Second to the Bishop of London. But, as late as 1675, the Plantation Committee were doubtful of its extent; and the prelate himself considered his duties as merely ministerial, "the Plantations being no part of his diocese, nor had he any authority to act there." After the accession of Bishop Compton. James the Second in April, 1685, Bishop Compton, of London, was, at his own special request, authorized by the king to exercise "all ecclesiastical jurisdiction" in the Plantations, including the licensing of school-masters going thither from England. The bishop's power was accordingly declared in colonial Instructions. But Compton, having offended James by opposing his abrogation of the Test Act, January. was removed from the Privy Council early in 1686. For this reason the king, in his Instructions to Dongan, ordered Archbishop Sancroft. that the Archbishop of Canterbury, and not the Bishop of London, should have ecclesiastical jurisdiction in New York.‡

* Col. Doc., iii., 369–375; Chalmers's Ann., i., 588; Rev. Col., i., 181.

† Col. Doc., iii., 375, 376; Council Min., v., 241.

‡ Col. Doc., iii., 253, 372; vii., 362, 363; Anderson's Col. Ch., i., 411, 412; ii., 284–291; Hist. Mag., v., 153; Miller's N. Y., 108; Hazard, i., 344; Burnet, i., 665; Reresby, 226; Evelyn, ii., 258; Mackintosh, 55; Macaulay, ii., 32, 35; Ellis Corr., i., 6; *ante*, vol. i., 257, 258. The authority under which Bishops Compton, Robinson, and Gibson, of London, successively exercised episcopal power in the Plantations, was the instructions of the English sovereign. But, as that sovereign could delegate his supreme ecclesiastical jurisdiction over the British colonies only by *his patent under the great seal*, the attorney and solicitor general reported their opinion, in 1725, "*that the authority by which the Bishops of London had acted in the Plantations was insufficient.*" A patent was accordingly granted to Bishop Gib-

Curiously enough, the "Defender of the Faith" of English Episcopalians was a notorious Roman Catholic. This was very queer to honest Protestants. James openly rejected the English communion, and partook of the Roman mass in his palace. Encouraged, perhaps, by the former subserviency of Oxford, the king resolved to maintain his ecclesiastical supremacy. Accordingly, in defiance of precedents, he commissioned Chancellor Jeffreys, with Archbishop Sancroft and others, to punish summarily all who should oppose his will in religious matters. This arbitrary commission suspended Compton from his episcopal function. James then appointed the Bishops of Durham, Rochester, and Peterborough to manage the diocese of London during the suspension of Compton. But Sancroft, the Archbishop of Canterbury, although a weak man, was honest enough not to approve these illegal acts of his sovereign. The king therefore ordered in council "that the ecclesiastical jurisdiction in the Plantations" should thenceforth be exercised by the commissioners whom he had appointed in place of the Bishop of London. Thus the colonial episcopacy of the English primate, Sancroft, under James the Second, was even more short-lived than that of his subordinate, Bishop Compton.*

CHAP. IX. 1686. 14 July. 3 August. 6 Septem. James's ecclesiastical commission suspends Bishop Compton. 27 October. English ecclesiastical jurisdiction in the colonies.

Yet English Episcopalianism did not gain much foothold in New York. The Reverend Alexander Innis was commissioned by James to succeed Josias Clarke as the "orthodox" chaplain of his garrison at Fort James. But while the King of England was a Roman Catholic, "the Church," of which he was the lawful head, could scarcely thrive among honest colonial Protestants outside of the citadel.†

20 April. 7 October. Chaplain Innis at Fort James.

Dongan's royal commission and Instructions reached him on the fourteenth of September, 1686, when "his Excellency did take an oath duly to execute the Office and trust of His Majesty's Captain General and Governor-in-

14 Septem. Dongan receives his royal commission.

son by George the First, in February, 1727, and another by George the Second in April, 1728: Col. Doc., v., 849-854; vii., 363.

* Clarke's James II., ii., 88-93; Dalrymple, ii., 77-79; Burnet, i., 674-678; Evelyn, ii., 267; Kennett, iii., 454-460; Rapin, ii., 755, 756; Lingard, xiv., 92-95; Mackintosh, 68-70; Ellis's Corr., i., 144-148, 160, 187; Hargraves's State Trials, iv., 247-254; Macaulay, ii., 92-97; Col. Doc., iii., 388; *ante*, 414.

† Deeds, viii., 13, 31, 39; Col. Mass., xxxiii., 304; Col. Doc., iii., 415; Doc. Hist., iii., 245, 265; *ante*, 407.

CHAP. IX. 1686. Dongan's counselors sworn. Chief in and over the Province of New York and the territories depending thereon." Brockholls, Phillipse, Van Cortlandt, Spragg, Baxter, and Younge, whom the king had named as his counselors, were also sworn; but Santen's oath was deferred, because he was a hypochondriac, subject to fits, and "wholly unfit for business."*

Population of New York. At this time the population of New York was about eighteen thousand; although it was "not possible to give an exact account." The provincial Assembly had adjourned to meet on the twenty-fifth of September, 1686. Dongan, 4 Septem. Assembly prorogued. however, had meanwhile thought fit, "for weighty and important reasons," to prorogue it until the twenty-fifth of March, 1687. This he did, just ten days before he received his new commission and Instructions from James the Second, which abolished an Assembly in New York, and vested all legislative power in the governor and council of the province. After pondering this grave matter, Dongan and 9 Decem. Dongan and his council take order. his council at length "ordered that all the branches of the revenue, and all other laws that have been made since the year 1683, except such as His Majesty has repealed, remaine and continue as they now are, till further considera- 13 Decem. Council-day. tion." They also directed that "every Monday be council-day for the consideration of the King's affairs, and every Thursday for the hearing of public business." The next 1687. 20 Jan'y. The New York Assembly dissolved. month Dongan issued his proclamation that the General Assembly of the Province of New York was "dissolved." By this formality all the legislative authority which the king could vest in them, as his provincial subordinates, and which Judge Palmer and Attorney General Graham pro- 13 Decem. nounced to be "sufficient," remained in the hands of Dongan and his council. It was an awful trust; yet it was not the less a legal delegation of the sovereign's power. It was the forerunner of revolution. In the fullness of God's time, English subjects in America were to maintain the truth that "only a State can tax itself," which Hollanders had taught to Europe in 1572, when they perilled every thing to stop the exaction of an arbitrary tithe.†

Dongan and his council did their first legislative duty,

* Council Min., v., 172, 173; Col. Doc., iii., 369, 404, 416; *ante*, 453.

† Council Min., v., 164, 172, 173, 188, 189; Col. MSS., xxxiii., 291; xxxiv., 81, 83; xxxv., 16; Col. Doc., iii., 398; Council Journ., i., Introd., xv., xvii.; Min. of N. Y. Common Council, i., 303; *ante*, vol. i., 442; ii., 428, 449.

under their new instructions from King James the Second, by re-enacting the former revenue law passed by the New York Assembly in October, 1683, in consideration of his expected "confirming" of their charter; and another against privateers, according to the model which had been furnished from England. During the following summer and autumn, other laws of more or less importance were enacted. Among them was one to prevent Boston merchants, who refused to pay New York duties, shipping oil from the east end of Long Island; they must now export from the metropolis, and pay honestly, as others did, and as the law required. A patent, with the usual privileges, was also granted to the town of Kingston, formerly known as Esopus, in Ulster County.*

CHAP. IX. — 1687. 24 Febr'y. First laws passed by Dongan and his council. — 19 May. Kingston patent.

The Quakers in New York now raised an interesting question. By the militia law, persons who refused to train were liable to have their goods seized if they did not pay their fines. This the Quakers did not like, because they scrupled to bear arms. Accordingly, they presented an address to Dongan, claiming that, by the Charter of Liberties, all peaceable persons professing faith in Christ should enjoy freedom of conscience in New York, and that the seizure of the property of Quakers for not training was "an infringement upon the liberty granted in the forecited act." The absurdity of this position was evident. The council accordingly, on examining the militia law, "unanimously gave it for their opinion that no man can be exempted from that obligation, and that such as make failure therein, let their pretents be what they will, must submit to the undergoing such penalties as by the said Act is provided."†

24 Febr'y. Quakers in New York not exempted from military service.

Anxious to have the northern boundary between New York and New Jersey settled, Dongan had agreed with Lawrie in April, 1684, to appoint surveyors to run the line from the Hudson River to the forks of the Delaware, now known as Port Jervis. George Keith was accordingly named surveyor for East Jersey, Andrew Robinson for West Jersey, and Philip Wells, the New York surveyor general, who had been Andros's steward, and one of the surveyors of the Connecticut boundary in 1684, on the part

Northern boundary between New York and New Jersey.

* Col. MSS., xxxv., 32–115; Doc. Hist., i., 429; Patents, vi., 300–308; Council Journ., i., Introd., xvii.–xxi.; *ante*, 157, 384, 415, 420.

† Col. MSS., xxxv., 35, 36, 169; Doc. Hist., iii., 607, 608, 609; *ante*, 383.

CHAP. IX. 1687.

of New York. The New Jersey boundary-line, however, was not run for several years.*

Perth Amboy having been made the capital of East Jersey, its nearness to the sea attracted commerce, which Dongan thought illicit. So he reported to the English Plantation Committee: "As for East Jersey, it being situate on the other side of Hudson's River, and between us and where the river disembogues itself into the sea; paying noe Custom and having likewise, the advantage of having better land and most of the Settlers there out of this Government, Wee are like to be deserted by a great many of our Merchants whoe intend to settle there if not annexed to this Government. Last year two or three ships came in there with goods and I am sure that that Country cannot, noe not with the help of West Jersey consume one thousand Lb. in goods in two years, soe that the rest of these Goods must have been run into this Government without paying his Majesty's Customs, and indeed there's no possibility of preventing it. And as for Beaver and Peltry, it is impossible to hinder its being carried thither;—the Indians value not the length of their journey soe as they can come to a good Market which those people can better afford them than wee, they paying noe Custom nor Excise inwards or outwards. An other inconveniency by the Governments remaining as it does is that privateers and others can come within Sandy Hook and take what Provisions and Goods they please from that Side. Alsoe very often shipps bound to this place break bulk there and run their Goods into that Colony with intent afterwards to import the same privately and at more leisure into this Province notwithstanding their Oath, they salving themselves with this evasion that that place is not in this Government—To-day an Interloper landed five Tun and one half of teeth there. To prevent all which inconveniences and for the securing of this place from enemys, I desire to have an order to make up a small Fort with twelve guns upon Sandy Hook, the Channell there being soe near the shore that noe vessel can goe in nor out but she must come soe near the Point that from on board one might toss a biscuit Cake on

Febr'y. Dongan complains of East Jersey.

Smuggling.

Beavers and peltry taken to East Jersey.

Interlopers land ivory in New Jersey.

Dongan wishes to build a fort on Sandy Hook.

* Council Min., v., 65, 159, 170, 171; N. Y. Assembly Journ., ii., 528–535; Col. Doc., iii., 302, 356, 406; iv., 630; Col. MSS., xxxii., 89; xxxiii., 4; N. J. H. S. Proc., viii., 162, 163; *ante*, 389, 392, 410, 412.

Shore. If the Proprietors would rightly consider it, they would find it their own Interest that that place should bee annexed to this Government for they are at a greater charge for maintaining the present Government than the whole Profits of the Province (which is by quit Rents) will amount unto; for they are at the whole Charge, the Country allowing nothing towards its support soe that had they not the charge of the Government they might put that Money into their own pockets. And indeed to make Amboy a port, will be no less inconvenient for the reasons afore mentioned, neighboring Colonys being not come to that perfection but that one Port may sufficiently serve us all. We in this Government look upon that Bay that runs into the Sea at Sandy Hook to bee Hudson's River; therefore there being a clause in my Instructions directing mee that I cause all vessels that come into Hudson's River to enter at New York, I desire to know whether his Majesty intends thereby those Vessels that come within Sandy-Hook, the people of East Jersey pretending a right to the River soe farr as their Province extends which is eighteen miles up the River to the Northward of this Place. West Jersey remaining as it does will be noe less inconvenient to this Government for the same reasons as East Jersey, they both making but one neck of Land and that soe near situate to us, that its more for their convenience to have commerce here than any where else, and under those circumstances that if there were a Warr, either with Christians or Indians they would not be able to defend themselves without the assistance of this Government. To bee short, there is an absolute necessity those Provinces and that of Connecticut be annexed."*

CHAP. IX. 1687. New Jersey should be reannexed to New York. The mouth of the Hudson River at Sandy Hook. Inconvenience of a port in New Jersey.

Collector Santen had meanwhile been admonished to behave better, but still continued to talk "scandalously and incivilly." Charges were then filed against him, and proofs made out. On his side, Santen prepared counter charges against Dongan. At length the governor and council suspended the collector, and ordered his arrest by the sheriff. Thinking him "fitter for a retired life than to be the King's Collector," Dongan ordered him to be sent a prison-

1686. Septem. Collector Santen Novem. 1687. suspended. 13 Jan'y. Arrested and sent to England.

* Col. Doc., iii., 363, 392, 408, 416, 493; Doc. Hist., i., 95–118; Leaming and Spicer, 285–295; Whitehead's E. J., 109–118; Chalmers, i., 621, 622; *ante*, 333, 369, 433, 452, 455.

CHAP. IX. 1687. er to England, in the ship which conveyed Secretary Spragg and Major Baxter with important dispatches to the home government. During Santen's suspension, Counselor Van Cortlandt and Attorney General Graham were appointed to manage the king's revenue. As Younge lived one hundred and fifty miles away from Fort James, at the east end of Long Island, was now very old, and had no estate of his own, and as the absence of Spragg and Baxter in England would leave the council without a sufficient quorum, the governor swore Judge John Palmer and Mayor Nicholas Bayard to serve as counselors until the royal pleasure should be made known; and he also nominated six others "of the fittest" in the province to supply vacancies. Dongan also asked the king to allow him to name a collector who lived in New York, as those who came from England expected "to run suddenly into a great estate, which this small place cannot afford them."*

27 Jan'y. 23 Febr'y. Van Cortlandt and Graham joint collectors. 28 Febr'y. Palmer and Bayard sworn counselors. 2 March.

Dongan's report on New York sent by Spragg and Baxter.

By Spragg and Baxter the governor sent to the Plantation Committee his replies to their official "Heads of Inquiry," with a map of New York and the adjoining governments, showing "the extent and inequality of them, and of Canada alsoe;" which was accomplished "with much labor and charge." Dongan's report, although encumbered by details very interesting to himself, but of little present importance, is one of the most careful, as well as most honest pictures of his provincial government which an American subordinate ever sent home to his English sovereign.

Militia. Fort James. Prolific woman.

The several courts and the laws of New York in force were described. There were about four thousand foot and three hundred horse, besides one company of dragoons. Fort James had been repaired, covering two acres, and "though this fortification be inconsiderable, I could wish," said Dongan, "that the king had several of them in these parts—In this Country there is a Woman yet alive from whose Loyns there are upwards of three hundred and sixty persons now living. The men that are here have generally lusty strong bodies. At Albany there is a Fort made of

* Council Min., v., 173, 174, 180, 181, 186–189, 192–194; Col. MSS., xxxiii., 283; xxxv., 10–15, 18–24, 32, 33, 37, 74; Col. Doc., iii., 401–414, 416, 417, 420–424, 493–500; iv., 418; Doc. Hist., i., 104–118; *ante*, 428, 458. Dongan's nominees for counselors were Judge Matthias Nicolls, Attorney General Graham, William Smith, Gabriel Minvielle, Francis Rombouts, and Nicholas de Meyer: Col. Doc., iii, 417.

Pine Trees fifteen foot high and foot over with Batterys and conveniences made for men to walk about, where are nine guns, small arms for forty men four Barils of Powder with great and small shott in proportion. The Timber and Boards being rotten were renewed this year. In my opinion it were better that Fort were built up of Stone and Lime which will not be double the charge of this years repair which yet will not last above six or seven years before it will require the like again whereas on the contrary were it built of Lime and Stone it may be far more easily maintained. And truly its very necessary to have a Fort there, it being a frontier place both of the Indians and French. At Pemaquid there is another Fort built after the same manner, as I am informed; A particular description whereof I am not capable of giving having never been there, however its a great charge to this Government without being anything of advantage to it, having officers there with twenty men always in pay. And which makes it yet more chargeable I am forced to send from time to time provisions and Stores thither altho' its near four hundred miles from this place. If his Majesty were pleased that I might draw off the men and arms from that place with the Guns being of light carriage and that I might have leave to put them further into the Country, I would place them where I will give your Lordships an account hereafter. And then if his Majesty were further pleased to annex that place to Boston, being very convenient for them in regard of its vicinity affording great Store of Fishery and Islands fit for that purpose lying all along to the eastward of them —And in lieu of that to add to this Government Connecticut and Rhode Island, Connecticut being so conveniently situate in its adjacing to us and soe inconvenient for the people of Boston by reason of its being upwards of two hundred miles distance from thence. Besides, Connecticut, as it now is, takes away from us almost all the land of Value that lyes adjoyning to Hudson's River, and the best part of the River itself. Besides, as wee find by experience if that place bee not annexed to that Government it will bee impossible to make any thing considerable of his Majesty's Customs and Revenue in Long Island; they carry away without entering all our Oyles which is the greatest part of

CHAP. IX.

1687.

Fort Albany.

Pemaquid.

Dongan advises the annexation of Pemaquid to Massachusetts, and of Connecticut to New York.

CHAP. IX. 1687.

Right of New York to Connecticut.

what wee have to make returns from this place: And from Albany and that way up the river our Beaver and Peltry. This Government too has an undoubted right to it by Charter which his late Majesty of blessed Memory granted to our present King. And indeed if the form of the Government bee altered, their people will rather choose to come under this than that Government of Boston, as your Lordships will perceive by their present Governor's letters directed to mee." * * * "I believe for these seven years last past, there has not come over into this Province twenty English, Scotch or Irish families. But on the contrary, on Long Island the people increase soe fast that they complain for want of land, and many remove from thence into the neighbouring province. But of French, there have, since my coming here, several families come both from St. Christophers and England, and a great many more are expected; as alsoe from Holland are come several Dutch families, which is another great argument of the necessity of adding to this government the neighbouring English Colonies, that a more equal ballance may bee kept here between his Majesty's naturall born subjects and Foreigners, which latter are the most prevailing part of this government."

English, Scotch, and Irish immigrants.

French.

Dutch.

Petition of French Protestants.

The governor at the same time forwarded a petition of "the new-come naturalized French" Protestants, thanking the king for the privileges he had granted them, and asking that they and those who followed them might be allowed to trade with all the British American colonies. In reply to the inquiry about religious persuasions in New York, Dongan reported: "Every town ought to have a minister. New York has, first, a Chaplain belonging to the Fort, of the Church of England; secondly, a Dutch Calvinist; thirdly, a French Calvinist; fourthly, a Dutch Lutheran. Here bee not many of the Church of England; few Roman Catholicks; abundance of Quakers preachers men and Women especially; Singing Quakers; Ranting Quakers; Sabbatarians; Anti Sabbatarians; some Anabaptists; some Independents; some Jews: in short, of all sorts of opinions there are some, and the most part of none at all. The Great Church which serves both the English and the Dutch, is within the Fort, which is found to bee very inconvenient. Therefore, I desire that there may bee

Religious persuasions.

The Dutch Church in New York.

CHAP. IX.

1687.

an order for their building another; ground being already layd out for that purpose, and they not wanting money in store wherewithall to build it. The most prevailing opinion is that of the Dutch Calvinists. It is the endeavor of all persons here to bring up their children and servants in that opinion which themselves profess; but this I observe, that they take no care of the conversion of their slaves. Every town and county are obliged to maintain their own poor, which makes them bee soe careful that noe vagabonds, beggars, nor idle persons are suffered to live here. But as for the King's natural-born subjects that live on Long Island and other parts of Government, I find it a hard task to make them pay their ministers."*

No beggars nor idlers.

13 Jan'y.

The Corporation of the metropolis, wishing a confirmation of their charter from Dongan under his royal commission, authorized Mayor Bayard and Recorder Graham "to procure the same." They also addressed the king, defending their charter, which no one was displeased with except Collector Santen, "the author of those clamors;" and urged "the absolute necessity there is that those adjacent parts of Connecticut, East and West Jersey, Pennsylvania, or at least soe far of Pennsylvania as extends from the Falls of Susquehannah should bee united to this your Majesty's Province; the effect whereof will not only secure your Majesty's Government, but will likewise make it formidable against all that may become your Majesty's enemies, ease your Majesty of the charge, and alsoe bring in considerable profit unto your Majesty's coffers."†

Address of the Corporation of New York to the king.

Among the domestic incidents was the case of Francis Stepney, a dancing-master, who, having been forced to leave Boston, and having no visible estate, was ordered not to teach dancing in New York, and to give security that he would not become a public charge, or else to quit the province. But, upon Stepney's petition, he was allowed an appeal to the king in person.‡

3 Jan'y.

Case of Stepney, a dancing-master.

6 Jan'y.

* Col. Doc., iii., 389–417, 419, 420; ix., 309, 312; Doc. Hist., i., 95–118; Val. Man., 1850, 456–486; Col. Rec. Conn., iii., 292–294; *ante*, 316, 331, 435, 445–447. The Rev. Alexander Innis succeeded Josias Clarke as chaplain to the garrison in October, 1686; Domine Henricus Selyns was the Dutch minister in New York, Daillé was pastor of the French Calvinists, and Arensius of the German Lutherans: Col. Doc., iii., 415, 651, 749; Doc. Hist., ii., 247; iii., 289, 707; Secret Ser., Ch. II. and Jac. II., 130; *ante*, 174, 273, 329, 380, 407, 457.

† Min. of C. C., i., 308; Val. Man., 1844–5, 318; Col. Doc., iii., 412, 424, 425; *ante*, 426, 438.

‡ Council Min., v., 191; Col. MSS., xxxv., 3, 7, 8.

CHAP. IX. 1687. 4 April. New York postmaster.

As the colonial post-office, established by Dongan in 1685, had been modified by the appointment of Randolph to be deputy postmaster of New England under Lord Treasurer Rochester, the governor appointed William Bogardus to be postmaster for the province of New York.*

11 April. William Nicolls attorney general of New York.

In place of Graham, who was now joint collector with Van Cortlandt, Dongan appointed William Nicolls, a son of Judge Matthias Nicolls, and a regularly educated lawyer, to be attorney general of the province.†

June. A New York ship pillaged by an Irish pirate.

Notwithstanding all the laws passed against pirates by order of James, the American waters were infested by freebooters. The pink Good Hope, or Hopewell, Captain George Heathcote, on her way from New York to England, was stopped between Long Island and Nantucket by a pirate from Youghal, in Ireland, who pillaged money from the master and men, and a sail, provisions, and a boat from the pink. By their speech, the pirates seemed to be "North countrymen."‡

The Iroquois the "bulwark" of New York against Canada.

In his report, Dongan described the Iroquois as the "bulwark" of New York against Canada. The metaphor was admirable. The Five Nations were the "most warlike" savages in North America; and Dongan, following the example of Andros, suffered "no Christians to converse with them any where, but at Albany," and then only with his license. His policy was "to keep them peaceable and annexed to this Government," so that upon any occasion he could have three or four thousand of their warriors at a call to aid New York. Dongan accordingly recommended that the boundary with Pennsylvania be run westward from latitude 41° 40′ on the Delaware River; that forts be built on that line, and also at Niagara; and that, to counteract the French Jesuits, the English priests, whom he had promised the savages, should be sent over as soon as possible. Above all, it was "very necessary for us to encourage our young men to go a beaver-hunting as the French do." But, while the king's governor of "the centre of all his Domin-

Dongan's advice to the king.

* Council Min., v., 106; Col. MSS., xxxv., 52; Col. Doc., iii., 349, 350, 356; *ante*, 413, 434.

† Licenses, Warr., etc., v.; Col. MSS., xxxiv. (ii.), 59; Col. Doc., iii., 412, 424, 429, 709; Wood, 144; Thompson, ii., 391; *ante*, 312, 462.

‡ Ellis Corr., i., 330; Col. Doc., iii., 288, 374, 387, 490, 496; C. Wolley, 61, 97; *ante*, 286, 287, 459.

ions in America" was giving this good advice, James the Second was meditating other arrangements.*

CHAP. IX.

1686.

19 Decem. Andros at Boston.

Colonel Sir Edmund Andros, governor general of the king's "Territory and Dominion of New England," had meanwhile reached Boston in the frigate Kingfisher, accompanied by Francis Nicholson, his lieutenant governor, and the Irish soldiers who were to maintain his authority. The next day Andros landed; and, after being received with "suitable demonstrations," quietly assumed the power which Dudley and his associates had temporarily administered. It is remarkable that this event happened about the very day on which "the Pilgrims" from Leyden and England landed on Plymouth beach, sixty-six years before. But the anniversary, now so ostentatiously celebrated, was then passed by in Massachusetts without observance. A council was held a few days afterward at Boston, which was attended by members from Plymouth and Rhode Island. The Records of Massachusetts, obtained with difficulty from Rawson, were intrusted to Secretary Randolph, in whose place Dudley was appointed licenser of the press, "according to previous colonial custom." Among the first of his acts, Andros was obliged to reprove Hinckley, the late governor of Plymouth, for his intolerance in distraining the property of Quakers to pay compulsory rates for the support of other sectarian ministers. The governor soon afterward organized the Royal New England judiciary, by appointing Dudley chief justice, and William Stoughton and Peter Bulkley associate judges of the Superior Court; while George Farewell, a lawyer who had just come from New York with West, was made attorney general of the dominion.†

20 Decem. Andros assumes the government of New England.

30 Decem.

1687.

28 Jan'y. Dudley licenser of the press.

5 March.

25 April. Judges of New England.

The assumption by Andros of the government of New

* Col. Doc., iii., 391–396, 402, 415, 416, 418, 423; Doc. Hist., i., 96–101; Val. Man., 1850, 458–464; *ante*, 306, 307, 309, 395, 429, 440, 442, 447, 452.

† Chalmers, i., 421, 422; Col. Rec. Conn., iii., 376; R. I. Rec., iii., 218–224, 257; Douglas, i., 413, 478; Mass. H. S. Coll., xxvii., 138, 156, 162, 166, 171; xxxv., 149, 190; Hutch. Mass., i., 353, 354, 355, 357, 359; Coll., 555, 557; Arnold, i., 499–502; Barry, i., 486–488; Palfrey, iii., 486, 511, 515, 517–522, 526; Force's Tracts, iv., No. 9, p. 16; Palmer's Impartial Account, 22; Adlard's Sutton Dudleys, 77; Val. Man., 1862, 741; Col. Doc., iii., 657, 663; Col. MSS., xxxiii., 308, 342; *ante*, i., 133; ii., 445, 446, 451. The Records of the Royal Government of New England, which Hutchinson, i., 354, states were "secreted or destroyed," are preserved, in the hand-writing of Secretary Randolph, or his clerk, in the British State Paper Office, and the Library of the Worcester Antiquarian Society: Chalmers, i., 463; Palfrey, iii., 487, 493, 518; Mass. H. S. Coll., xxix., 187. The private papers of Andros were probably "burnt, or otherwise made away with," in 1689: Hutch. Coll., 575; *post*, 553.

CHAP. IX.

1687.

England concerned New York both directly and incidentally. He had been her governor, and many of her people esteemed him as their friend or patron. Among these was John West, the clerk of the New York Common Council, who resigned that office and went to Boston, where, through the influence of Andros, he hired from Randolph his place of secretary of New England. As soon as Dongan received the king's orders of 19 September, 1686, he surrendered Pemaquid to Andros, who sent thither Ensign Joshua Pipon, with some of the newly-come soldiers, to receive possession and garrison Fort Charles. The transfer from New York of its distant county of "Cornwall" to the government of New England was cheerfully made by Dongan, who had recommended it as expedient. But James the Second did not see fit to annex Connecticut to his own old province, as the desired equivalent.*

3 May. West goes to Boston and becomes secretary. 24 Feb'y. March. Dongan surrenders Pemaquid, or "Cornwall," to Andros.

1686. 22 Decem.

As soon as he could, Andros notified Governor Treat, of Connecticut, that the king had authorized him to receive the surrender of the charter of that colony, if tendered, and to take charge of its government, as a part of New England. A few days afterward Randolph served another writ of Quo Warranto upon Treat, suggesting that the people of Connecticut had "no way to make themselves happy" but by an early application to Andros. In this crisis a General Court was convened at Hartford, which left the business of the charter in the hands of Treat and his council. An evasive answer was returned by them to Andros. But a very artful letter was sent to Lord Sunderland, stating that they were unable to make a "suitable return" to the Quo Warranto, and adding: "We are his Majesty's loyal subjects, and we are heartily desirous that we may continue in the same station that we are in, if it may consist with his princely wisdom to continue us so. But if his Majesty's royal purposes be otherwise to dispose of us, we shall, as in duty bound, submit to his royal commands; and if it be to conjoin us with the other Colonies and Provinces under Sir Edmund Andros, his Majesty's present Govern-

28 Decem.

1687. 26 Jan'y. Artful letter of Connecticut to Lord Sunderland.

* Maine H. S. Coll., v., 110, 130, 131, 264, 265, 266; Williamson, i., 582–586; R. I. Rec., iii., 223, 224; N. Y. Deeds, viii., 75; Col. Doc., iii., 391, 417, 513, 515, 657; ix., 919; Col. MSS., xxxv., 36; Hutch. Mass., i., 358, 359; Coll., 555, 557; Mass. H. S. Coll., xxvii., 178, 180, xxxv., 156, 176; Palfrey, iii., 523, 531; *ante*, 310, 445, 452, 463. On the 25th of July, 1687, Sheriff John Knight (*ante*, 428) was appointed clerk of the New York Common Council in place of West, resigned: Min. of C. C., i., 313.

or, it will be more pleasing than to be joined with any other province."*

A curious intercolonial intrigue now followed. Andros, who had just come from London, and was fully acquainted with the king's policy about New England, did all he could to induce Treat and the other chief men of Connecticut to submit with a good grace to his government. But Dongan was not equally well aware of the intentions of James in regard to that colony; at all events, he was not informed by Andros, who regarded his royal fellow-servant and successor in the government of New York with personal jealousy, and always acted toward him with extreme official reserve. Both governors coveted Connecticut. Andros, who, as the Duke of York's deputy, had thought it a part of New York, was now anxious that it should be a part of New England; while Dongan sturdily maintained that what would have been advantageous to James as duke, would be more advantageous to James as king. Accordingly, Dongan, with less light than Andros, sent Palmer and Graham as commissioners to induce the people of Connecticut to submit to the government of New York, and to insure them of the enjoyment of their estates, offices, and other advantages. Dongan also wrote earnestly to Treat in the same strain. But the New York effort did not succeed. Palmer and Graham, although commissioned by Dongan to represent his views, appear to have sympathized with the present designs of their earlier patron, Andros. They wrote to him from New Haven that they found the leading men in Connecticut "all united in one mind that it was their only interest to be joined to York, and they did expect that his Majesty would accordingly dispose of them that way; but they were so foolishly fond of their charter that they unanimously agreed to be passive and not active in the case; that is, they would never surrender, but if it were his Majesty's pleasure to take their charter from them, they would submit thereto." And then the New York agents told the governor of New England that Treat and most of his council were on his side, but that the king would be obliged to

Andros jealous of Dongan.

13 April. Dongan sends Palmer and Graham to Connecticut. 21 April.

5 May. The New York agents write to Andros.

* Col. Rec. Conn., iii., 222–226, 375–379; Mass. H. S. Coll., xviii., 182, 237, 238; xxvii., 163, 165, 166; xxxv., 147; Hutch. Mass., i., 339; Chalmers's Ann., i., 279, 298, 306, 307; Palfrey, iii., 537, 538; *ante*, 452.

CHAP. IX. 1687. Duplicity of Palmer and Graham. proceed to judgment against the Connecticut charter; and that as Whiting, the agent of the colony at London, had just written "that it was the discourse at Whitehall that all to the Westward of Connecticut" [probably meaning the Connecticut River] "will be joined to New York," and as "the rest is not worth desiring," it would be Andros's "interest to make Court at home for accomplishing the matter." This "matter" was the annexation of Connecticut to New England rather than to New York, which the trusted agents of Dongan thus furtively advised Andros to "accomplish." 12 May. The Connecticut Court left its "emergent occasions" in the hands of Treat and six others. Treat accordingly replied to Dongan 12 May. Treat's reply to Dongan. "that the matter is in his Majesty's hands;" but that, if a new disposition was to be made, "we do earnestly request that our whole Colony or Province may together be annexed to such government as his Majesty shall see fit; for a dividing of it will be very prejudicial." 23 May. Palmer and Graham's report to Dongan. On their return to New York, Palmer and Graham reported to the council "that the people of Connecticut are obstinate not to surrender to the king." 27 May. Dongan's report to Lord Sunderland. Dongan, however, informed Lord Sunderland that Palmer and Graham had told him that they had prevailed on the Connecticut Assembly to write him a letter, in which "they signified their submission," and asked him to get them "firmly annexed" to the government of New York; and that this letter was "ready to be signed, having the unanimous approbation of the whole. But before that could be done, some of their clergy came among them, and quite overthrew all they had done; telling them that to whatever government they should be joined it would be a grievous affliction. * * * With these, and such like contrary expressions, the Assembly was wrought upon to let sending that letter alone."*

13 June. Andros, on his side, again urged Connecticut to surrender its charter as a "duty to his Majesty." John Saffin, the last speaker of the late General Court of Massachusetts, 14 June. also wrote to Secretary Allyn that all British America be-

* Col. Doc., iii., 235, 236, 396, 415, 416; Col. MSS., xxxv., 58, 61, 64, 73; Hutch. Coll., 556; R. I. Rec., iii., 223, 224; Col. Rec. Conn., iii., 227–236, 368–370, 379–381, 384; Palfrey, iii., 539, 540, 541; *ante*, 280, 285, 464. The Connecticut Records do not allude to this mission of Palmer and Graham from New York. Mr. Palfrey (iii., 539) wondrously muddles history by intimating that Dongan's agents were *sent by Andros from Boston!*

tween Carolina and Canada would soon "be brought under a more immediate dependency and subjection to his Majesty" by the abrogation of all charters; that, whatever might happen in England, "matters will never be againe *in statu quo* here, in each respective colony;" and that if Connecticut adhered "to the West," or New York, "you are an undone people, for there you part with your best friends." But Allyn cautiously wrote back to Andros that the Connecticut Court had "resolved to continue in the Station they are in, 'till his Majesty's pleasure be made known to them for a change," which would "readily be submitted unto."*

Connecticut urged to submit to Andros.

18 June.

By a curious coincidence, Lord Sunderland, that same day, laid before the king a report of his Plantation Committee on the Connecticut letter of the 26th of January. This report—incautiously assuming that letter to express, by its promise to "submit" to the royal commands a surrender of the charter, and also a desire to be annexed to New England rather than to New York—recommended that Andros should be instructed to signify his majesty's acceptance of the "dutiful submission" of Connecticut; to take the colony under his government; and to swear Treat and Allyn in the council of New England. James at once approved his committee's report; and Lord Sunderland was ordered to give the proper directions to Andros. This action was taken in too great confidence. All further proceedings on the Quo Warranto were dropped, in spite of Randolph's advice that a legal judgment on the writ was "absolutely necessary," as much in the case of Connecticut as it had been in that of Massachusetts. It was an error—like that into which gentlemen sometimes fall when dealing with sharpers.†

18 June.

Error of the English government about the "submission" of Connecticut.

Randolph's advice unheeded.

Ignorant of this action at Whitehall, Dongan again urged Lord Sunderland to have Connecticut and the Jerseys joined to New York, because he thought that the addition of any part of Connecticut to Massachusetts would be "the most unproportionable thing in the world, they having already a hundred times more land, riches and people than this Province, and yet the charge of this government more than that,"

8 Septem.

Dongan again writes to Sunderland about Connecticut.

* Col. Rec. Conn., iii., 237, 381–383; Mass. Rec., v., 514; Mass. H. S. Coll., xxvii., 177; Hutch. Coll., 556; Dalrymple, ii., 90.

† Mass. H. S. Coll., xxxii., 297, 298; Chalmers's Ann., i., 298, 305–310; Col. Rec. Conn., iii., 377, 378, 384, 385, 470; Force's Tracts, iv., No. 9, p. 47; *ante*, 468.

CHAP. IX. 1687.

which had "a vast advantage" by the recent annexation of Pemaquid. The next month, on hearing that Treat and Allyn had written to London their wish that Connecticut

4 October. Dongan reproves the conduct of Treat and Allyn.

"might be added to Boston," Dongan bluntly expressed to the Hartford Court his "great surprise" at the weak or the deceitful conduct of their governor and their secretary; and—yet in the dark about what had been done in England—pressed the Connecticut legislators to join their colony to New York. When, at length, the whole truth was revealed, Dongan, with Celtic impulsiveness, told Lord Sunderland that Connecticut had been taken from "the bulwark to Boston," and been added to New England, "by the fraud" of Treat and Allyn, "unknown to the rest of the

The people of Connecticut wish it to be annexed to New York.

General Court; and, for one that wishes it as it is, there is a hundred in that colony that desires it were annexed to the Government of N. Yorke." Dongan wrote honestly; but he did not fully know the mind of his sovereign in England.*

As soon as he received his "effectual orders" from James,

22 October. Andros at Hartford.

Andros left Boston with several of his council, and some sixty grenadiers as his guard; and, traveling by way of Providence, New London, and Wethersfield, reached Hartford, "where he was received with all respect and welcome congratulation," and was "greeted and caressed" by the governor and assistants of Connecticut. A General Court

31 October.

of the colony, specially summoned by Treat, was in session, and there was "some treaty between his Excellency and them that evening." It is related, upon "tradition," that Treat remonstrated against the surrender of the charter;

Andros secures the Connecticut charter, and Wadsworth its "duplicate."

and it is said that after Andros had secured one of the copies of the instrument, the lights were "blown out," and that Lieutenant Joseph Wadsworth secretly carried off "the duplicate" from the table, and hid it in a large hollow oak tree. No contemporary writing, however, mentions this alleged occurrence. Andros himself does not appear to have observed it; and Secretary Allyn, in his own handwriting, closed the old records of the colony with the following entry: "His Excellency Sir Edmund Andros, Knight, Captain General and Governor of His Majesty's Territory

* Col. Doc., iii., 429, 511; Col. Rec. Conn., iii., 386, 387. New England writers seem to have shunned or obscured this detail: see Palfrey, iii., 541, 542.

1687. 31 October. Andros takes the government of Connecticut into his hands.

and Dominion in New England, by order from his Majesty James the Second, King of England, Scotland, France and Ireland, the 31st of October, 1687, took into his hands the Government of this Colony of Connecticut, it being by his Majesty annexed to the Massachusetts and other Colonys under His Excellency's Government. FINIS." Thus did Andros—according to Puritan notions—"commit a rape on a whole colony."*

1 Novem.

Andros's royal commission read publicly in Connecticut, and royal counselors sworn.

The next morning Andros was conducted by the officers of the late Corporation of Connecticut to its "public Court-house" at Hartford, attended by the royal counselors Stoughton, Mason, Winthrop, Usher, Pynchon, Gedney, and Tyng, who had accompanied him from Boston. Suspecting no duplicity respecting the actual surrender of the Connecticut charter, the governor general had his commission publicly read, and then swore the complacent Treat and Allyn into office as royal counselors of New England. After establishing royal courts in Connecticut without any opposition, Andros crossed from New London to Newport, where the old seal of Rhode Island was broken, and his unquestioned authority was acknowledged. At last the dominion of James the Second was supreme throughout New England. A post-route—which had been originally suggested by Lovelace and urged by Dongan—was soon afterward arranged by Andros between Boston and Stam-

23 Novem. Post-office in New England.

* Col. Rec. Conn., iii., 248, 249, 387–390, 450; Trumbull, i., 371, 372; Holmes, i., 421; Bancroft, ii., 430; Arnold, i., 504, 506; Palfrey, iii., 541–543, 545; Force's Tracts, iv., No. 9, p. 47, 48. Chalmers (writing in 1780, eleven years before Trumbull) states that the Connecticut charter was carefully concealed "in a venerable elm," *at the time that the "submission" letter of 26 January, 1687, was written:* Annals, i., 298, 306; *ante*, 468. The tree in which Trumbull (i., 371) says that Wadsworth hid the charter on 31 October, 1687, stood in front of the house of Samuel Willys, and was long known as "The Charter Oak," until it was blown down, in a great storm, on the morning of 21 August, 1856: Holmes, i., 422; Hist. Mag., i., 4, 5; Palfrey, iii., 542. In May, 1715, the Connecticut Court granted Wadsworth "the sum of Twenty shillings," in consideration of his good service, "especially *in securing the duplicate charter*, in a very troublesome season, when our constitution was struck at, *and in safely keeping and preserving the same ever since, unto this day:*" MS. Conn. Rec., quoted by Palfrey, iii., 543. According to Doctor Stiles, Nathaniel Stanley took one copy of the charter, and John Talcot the other, when the lights were "blown out" in the Hartford Meeting-house. One of these documents is now in the office of the Secretary of State of Connecticut; and a fragment of the other is in the Library of the Historical Society at Hartford, "having been obtained from a tailor to whom it had been given, or sold:" Palfrey, iii., 543. Considering that Wadsworth appears to have safely kept "*the duplicate*" in his possession until 1715, it looks as if he *secured* it in January, 1687 (at the time stated by Chalmers), and that *the original*, which was so ostentatiously "brought into the Court" on 15 June, 1687 (after Wadsworth had "secured" the duplicate), was the one of which it is supposed that Andros "obtained possession" in October of the same year: compare Col. Rec. Conn., iii., 238; Palfrey, iii., 539, 543. Chalmers and Palfrey—the earliest and the latest printed authorities—make me skeptical about the traditionary stories of Stiles or Trumbull, so reiterated in New England Common School books.

CHAP. IX. ford, on the border of New York, upon which John Perry was appointed to carry a monthly mail as the deputy of the provincial postmaster Randolph.*

1687.

Dongan a true "New Yorker."

Of all the British colonial governors of New York, Dongan was perhaps most truly a "New Yorker." He seemed to have identified himself with her hereditary catholicity in religion, and her comprehensiveness in secular affairs. Learning that Lamberville had urged the Onondagas to meet the governor of Canada at Cataracouy, he forbade them to go there, and ordered the Jesuit to come to New York. Not long afterward, it was further ordered in council that the French should not be allowed to hunt "toward Schuylkill and the Susquehanna." When it was ascertained that Denonville really meant to attack the New York Iroquois, the Senecas, warned by Dongan, recalled their war-parties from Ohio and Virginia, and sent delegates to Albany to ask help from "Corlaer." The Indian commissioners there made the savages large presents of ammunition, but declined to send European soldiers to aid them in repulsing the Canadians. As they went sadly home, the Seneca ambassadors replied, "Since we are to expect no other assistance from our Brethren, we must recommend our wives and our children to you, who will fly to you if any misfortune shall happen to us."†

7 April.

6 June.

The Senecas seek the protection of "Corlaer."

But while Dongan was thus striving to hinder the French from interfering with the Iroquois, whom he graphically described as "the bulwark" between New York and Canada, his sovereign at Whitehall was paralyzing his well-meant zeal. The politics of Europe again swayed the interests of America. Louis, troubled by the condition of affairs in Canada, sent the Count D'Avaux to London "on purpose" to settle the boundaries between it and Hudson's

James and Louis.

* Col. Rec. Conn., iii., 390, 391, 393, 397, 398, 438, 439, 446; Arnold, i., 505, 506; Palfrey, iii., 536, 543-548; Force's Tracts, iv., ix., 47, 48; Mass. H. S. Coll., xxvii., 178; Col. MSS., xxxiii., 261; Chalmers, i., 298, 463; *ante*, 196-198, 413, 434. There is much curious and novel information about Boston and its neighborhood, in the autumn and winter of 1687, in a pamphlet entitled "Report of a French Protestant Refugee," privately printed by Mr. J. Carson Brevoort, of Brooklyn, L. I., in 1868. Among other things, the writer says, "You may also own Negroes and Negresses; there is not a house in Boston, however small may be its means, that has not one or two." * * "Negroes cost from twenty to forty Pistoles, according as they are skillful or robust:" Report, etc., p. 20; compare *ante*, 337. A list of the inhabitants of Boston in 1687 has recently been published by the Prince Society as an appendix to John Dunton's Letters.

† Col. MSS., xxxv., 54, 55, 60, 66; Col. Doc., iii., 393, 440; ix., 325; Colden, i., 78, 86; Doc. Hist., i., 144; Charlevoix, ii., 348; Penn. Col. Rec., i., 202; *ante*, 442.

Bay on the north, and New York on the south. But this was found to be "a thing which it was not possible to decide." Yet, to make the union of James with Louis "more perfect," the British ministers proposed a Treaty of Neutrality, which should be observed by the subjects of both crowns in America. James therefore empowered his Chancellor Jeffreys and others to arrange the details with Barillon, the representative of Louis. A treaty was accordingly signed at Whitehall, by which it was agreed that there should be peace and good correspondence between the subjects of both kings in America; that those subjects should not assist the "wild Indians" with whom either king might be at war; that those of the one should not fish or trade in the territories of the other; that unlicensed privateers should be punished as pirates; and that, notwithstanding any breach between their sovereigns in Europe, a firm peace and neutrality should be maintained between English and French subjects in America. The ministers of Louis foresaw "that if the King of England should arm and commission his subjects in New England, the Frenchmen in those parts could not stand before them." It was not pretended, on the part of James, that the Iroquois were his subjects, "and not a single word was said about it." In this remarkable treaty the French king gained a great advantage over his English brother, who thus sacrificed to his "mistaken politics" those noblest of native American tribes who had so long been "a mighty wall against the irruptions of the Canadians." Copies of it, in English and Latin, were sent to Dongan by the Privy Council, with orders to cause it to be "duly observed and executed."*

CHAP. IX. 1687.

1686. 16/26 Novem. Whitehall Treaty of Neutrality in North America.

Effect of the Treaty of Neutrality.

As soon as it was received at New York the Neutrality Treaty was published. Dongan also dispatched Anthony L'Espinard, of Albany, with a copy of it to Denonville, whom he requested to avoid any correspondence with the New York Indians "of this side of the Great Lake;" and that, as he was "daily expecting religious men from England," whom he intended to put among the Five Na-

1687. 8 June. 10/20 June. Dongan notifies Denonville.

* Clarke's James II., ii., 93, 94; Charlevoix, iii., 340, 341; Shea's Charlevoix, iii., 273; Chalmers's Ann., i., 589; Col. Doc., iii., 388, 393, 476, 508; iv., 169, 210; ix., 322, 330, 914, 915; Sylvius, xxiv., 4; Corps Dip., vii. (ii.), 141; Anderson on Commerce, ii., 575, 576, 577; Holmes, i., 418; Grahame, i., 435; Bancroft, ii., 425; Force's Tracts, iv., No. 11, p. 9; *ante*, 466. Smith, i., 78, *note*, errs in stating that this treaty made the Indian trade in America "free to the English and French." It did just the reverse: Garneau, i., 262.

CHAP. IX. 1687. tions, he asked that Lamberville should be ordered, as long as he staid with those Indians, to "meddle only with the affairs belonging to his function."*

5 Feb'y. Louis had meanwhile sent a copy of the Whitehall Neutrality Treaty to Denonville, with orders to "execute it exactly." He also approved the proposed expedition against the Iroquois, and directed that all prisoners who might be taken from them, in obedience to his order to De la Barre of 31 July, 1684, should be sent to France, to serve "in the galleys." The English were not to be attacked; but if Dongan should not obey his instructions to execute "the Treaty of Neutrality," his conduct was to be reported, so that "his Majesty may demand his recall from the King of England."†

30 March. Louis again orders Iroquois captives to be sent to his "galleys."

May. Vaudreuil in Canada. With these dispatches came a re-enforcement of eight hundred French regulars, under the command of Philippe de Rigaud, Chevalier de Vaudreuil, an accomplished soldier, who had distinguished himself at Valenciennes. A camp had meanwhile been formed near Montreal, in which were assembled eighteen hundred regular soldiers and militia, one hundred voyageurs, and three hundred domiciled Iroquois, among whom were the Oneida Garonhiagué, and Kryn, "the Great Mohawk." Denonville took the chief command, assisted by Callières and Vaudreuil. The army, accompanied by the Jesuit fathers Bruyas and Vaillant, went up to Cataracouy, where Millet was now stationed as chaplain and interpreter. In the mean time a number of Iroquois chiefs had come there, at the invitation of Lamberville, to confer with the governor of Canada. These were seized by Champigny, the intendant, and bound fast to stakes in the fort; whence, with some others captured on the Saint Lawrence, making in all fifty "able-bodied men," they were sent down to Quebec and quickly embarked for France, in obedience to the king's reiterated orders. Among these American prisoners was Oreouaté or Tawerahet, the Cayuga chief who had driven the Father Carheil out of that canton three years before. The capture

8 June.

Denonville's expedition against the New York Senecas.

Iroquois seized at Cataracouy and sent to France.

* Col. MSS., xxxiii., 142; xxxv., 67; Col. Doc., iii., 465, 467–472, 487; ix., 336; Doc. Hist., i., 145; Munsell's Alb. Ann., ii., 100; *ante*, 442. By L'Espinard, Dongan sent to Denonville "some oranges, hearing they are a rarity in your partes;" but the marquis replied that "it was a great pity that they should have been all rotten" before they reached Montreal: Col. Doc., iii., 465, 472.

† Col. Doc., iii., 487; ix., 233, 312–323, 330; Charlevoix, ii., 320, 340, 341; *ante*, 376, 406.

CHAP. IX.

1687.

of these savages was the weakest treachery ever ventured by a governor of Canada. Its first effect was to jeopard the life of Lamberville, who remained at his post, unconscious of Denonville's perfidy. When the news from Cataracouy reached Onondaga, its "Ancients" summoned their "Dawning of the day" into their council, and, full of just indignation, told him what "Onnontio" had done. But, while "Tieorensere" awaited his death-stroke, which appeared inevitable, an old Onondaga, through the influence of Garakontie, thus addressed him: "We have every right to treat thee as an enemy; but we cannot resolve to do so. We know thee too well not to be assured that thy heart hath had no part in the treason thou hast done against us; and we are not unjust enough to punish thee for a crime of which we believe thee to be innocent, which thou dost, no doubt, detest as much as we, and for having been the instrument of which, we are convinced that thou art in despair. Yet it is not proper for thee to remain here. Others would not, perhaps, do thee the justice which we do: —and when once our young men shall have sung the war song, they will see in thee only a traitor, who hath betrayed our chiefs into a harsh and degrading slavery, and they will listen only to their fury, from which we shall not be able to save thee." With these words the great-hearted sachems of Onondaga dismissed the trembling Jesuit, and ordered trusty guides to conduct him "through by-paths" toward Cataracouy; who never quit "Tieorensere" until he was beyond all danger. Thus the French missions among the Iroquois were closed by an act of the Canadian governor, the insanity of which was hardly relieved by the self-denying virtues of those faithful devotees who had labored so long to spread Christianity through Western New York.*

Lamberville in danger.

The Jesuit spared and dismissed by the Iroquois.

Denonville, on reaching Cataracouy, where he was informed by Lamberville of the result of his folly, sent back 20/30 June.

* Col. Doc., iii., 431, 433, 453; ix., 284, 298, 324–334, 358–363, 402, 925; La Potherie, i., 332; iii., 57, 62; La Hontan, i., 90–95; Charlevoix, ii., 342–346, 350, 424; Shea's Charlevoix, iii., 275–278, 282, 283; N. Y. H. S. Coll., ii. (ii.), 153, 154, 165–172; Pinkerton, xiii., 290, 291; Colden, i., 78, 79; Shea's Colden, 97, 138; Garneau, i., 261; Shea's Missions, 309, 315, 317; Bancroft, ii., 423; Doc. Hist., i., 134, 146; *ante*, 236, 377, 402, 442, 474. There is an interesting account of the galleys to which Louis condemned the Iroquois in the London Quarterly Review of July, 1866, p. 39–64, and another in the Edinburgh Review of July, 1866, p. 86–120.

CHAP. IX.

1687.

24 June. / 4 July.

to Onondaga the imprisoned son and the brother of Grande-Gueule, or "Hotre-houati," whom it was important to conciliate. The French expedition then proceeded along the south shore of Lake Ontario, so as to keep the Iroquois doubtful which of their nations was to be attacked. After a week's coasting it landed at "Ganniag-atorontagouat,"

30 June. / 10 July. The French at Irondequoit, in New York.

or what is now called "Irondequoit Bay," in Monroe County; the literal meaning of which, in English, appears to be "an opening from the Lake." There Denonville was joined by the French and Indian auxiliaries under Tonty, La Durantaye, and Du Lhut, who had been ordered thither from the West.* While coming from Lake Huron, early in May, about twenty leagues below Michilimackinac, La Durantaye met Dongan's trading party, which had set out from Albany the previous September, under the command of Captain Rooseboom. It consisted of twenty-nine Chris-

English and Dutch taken prisoners by the French.

tians, three Mohawks, and two Mahicans, who were at once made prisoners, and their goods, which would have bought eight thousand beavers, were pillaged. Below Fort Saint Joseph, at "the Detroit of Lake Erie," Du Lhut, who had been joined by Tonty, soon afterward seized MacGregorie and his later company of twenty-nine Christians, six Indians, and eight prisoners. Both these captured New York expeditions were brought to Niagara, and then to Irondequoit Bay, where they were delivered to the French gov-

1/11 July. La Fontaine Marion shot by order of Denonville.

ernor. By Denonville's order, the young La Fontaine Marion, who had accompanied Captain Rooseboom's troop, was shot to death as a Canadian deserter, in conformity with the edicts of Louis, notwithstanding he had a pass from Dongan. The rest of the prisoners were sent to Cataracouy, and thence to Montreal.†

* Col. Doc., ix., 255, 261, 327, 362–364, 402; Barber and Howe's Coll., 265; N. Y. H. S. Coll. (ii.), ii., 176. After being appointed governor of Louisiana (*ante*, 406), La Salle sailed from Rochelle for the mouth of the Mississippi on 24 July, 1684, and on 20 March, 1687, was murdered by some of his followers not far from the present town of Washington, in Texas. In February, 1686, Tonty went down the Mississippi in search of La Salle; and, on his return to Montreal in July, was sent by Denonville to bring down the Illinois in the rear of the Iroquois, which he did: Col. Doc., ix., 300, 301, 315, 316, 323, 327, 331, 332, 339, 363, 364; Hist. Coll. Louisiana, i., 67–70, 85–144, 214–220; N. Y. H. S. Coll., ii., 288–333; Charlevoix, ii., 347, 348; La Potherie, ii., 193–198; Sparks's La Salle, 119–159, 204; Shea's Discovery, 185–213; Shea's Charlevoix, iii., 270–281; Bancroft, iii., 168–173.

† Col. Doc., iii., 430, 431, 434, 436, 437, 438, 476, 483, 489; v., 731; ix., 224, 275, 300, 336, 337, 339, 348, 362–364, 383, 1023; Hist. Coll. Lou., i., 69; N. Y. H. S. Coll., ii. (ii.), 172–176, 190; La Potherie, ii., 200–207; Charlevoix, ii., 352, 353; Shea's Charlevoix, iii., 284, 286; La Hontan, i., 95, 96, 97; Pinkerton, xiii., 292, 293; Colden, i., 80; Smith, i., 79; Garneau, i., 262; Holgate, 91; *ante*, 121, 406, 429, 432, 443, 444.

CHAP. IX.

1687.

2/12 July. Denonville invades the Seneca country of New York.

Having palisaded their encampment—which was appropriately named "The Fort of the Sands," and garrisoned by four hundred men under D'Orvilliers — the French pushed southward along the east shore of Irondequoit Bay, through the superb "oak openings" of Monroe and Ontario Counties, which allowed them to march in three columns. Wood-rangers and savages formed the van and rear guards, while the regulars and the Canadian militia were in the centre. After passing two defiles the expedition reached a third, near the Seneca village of "Kohoseraghe," or Gannagaro, or Saint James, not far from what is now Victor, in Ontario County. The Senecas had meanwhile sent away their women, children, and old men to Cayuga, and to a lake—probably the Canandaigua—"to the southward of their castles." About five hundred—among whom were several women who would not leave their husbands—remained in an ambuscade near Gannagaro, and, as the French came confidently on, received them with a warwhoop and a fire of musketry. The European regulars, unused to warfare with the American savages, were thrown into disorder until their Ottawa auxiliaries repulsed the Senecas, who left nearly thirty dead on the field. The invaders had eleven killed and as many wounded, among whom was the Father John Enjalran, who had come down from his Ottawa mission with La Durantaye's party. Among the slain was the famous Oneida chief Garonhiagué, or *La Cendre Chaude*, who had led the first Iroquois emigration to Canada, and became a catechist at the Sault Saint Louis. Instead of pushing on, as their Indian allies advised, the French halted on the battle-field. The next day they marched triumphantly into the deserted and burned village of Gannagaro. Two old Senecas, who had been left behind, were shrived by the Father Bruyas, and then cooked and eaten by the French savages. All the maize that could be found was destroyed. Gandagaraé, or Saint Michael, was next visited in the same manner. The invaders then moved their camp to the great Seneca village of "Theodehacto," or Totiakto, or Conception, on a bend of the Honeyoye Creek, near what is now West Mendon, in Monroe County. Here a pompous "Act of possession" of all the Senecas' lands "conquered in the name of his

3/13 July.

Battle near Gannagaro.

4/14 July.

Gandagaraé.

Totiakto.

CHAP. IX.

1687.

$\frac{9}{19}$ July. The French take possession of the Seneca country. $\frac{11}{21}$ July.

Majesty" was attested by the chief officers of the French expedition; while every body shouted "Vive le Roy." At the gate of the small village of Gannounata, or Gannondata, near East Avon, in Livingston County, were found the English arms, which Dongan had caused to be placed there in 1684, "ante-dated as of the year 1683." This greatly disgusted the French, who thought it "beyond question that they first discovered and took possession of that country, and for twenty consecutive years have had the Fathers Fremin, Garnier, etc., as stationary missionaries in all these villages." After destroying all the Indian corn they could find, being more than a million of bushels, and

$\frac{14}{24}$ July.

a "vast quantity" of hogs, Denonville's expedition returned to Irondequoit without meeting any more Iroquois warriors.* And so, having destroyed the stored grain, and the acorn-fed swine, and the frail bark cabins of the thrifty native New Yorkers whose territory he invaded, the French marquis stopped. He was but a weak imitation of Louvois.

Denonville only irritates the Iroquois.

Thus far Denonville had only irritated the Senecas. He had not humbled the brave red Americans who had fatally disordered his disciplined European troops; whose wooden villages could soon be rebuilt; and whose yellow maize would spring again in quick abundance throughout the beautiful and fertile valley of the Genesee. If he had been a general, Denonville would have pursued the retreating Senecas eastward among the Cayugas and the Onondagas, whereby he might have crushed the power of the Iroquois. Instead

$\frac{16}{26}$ July.

of this, he sent back a part of his force to Cataracouy, and went with the rest to the east bank of the Niagara River,

Denonville builds a fort at Niagara.

where he built a palisaded fort on the spot which La Salle had appropriated in the winter of 1678, and had named the "Fort de Conty." It was "the most beautiful, most pleasing, and most advantageous site on the whole of Lake Ontario." La Salle had chosen it nine years before, to the

* Col. Doc., iii., 251, 252, 431–435, 446, 447, 479; ix., 334, 337–339, 364–368; Doc. Hist., i., 149, 151–154; Col. MSS., xxxv., 160; Hist. Coll. Lou., i., 70; N. Y. H. S. Coll., ii. (ii.), 157–163, 176–182, 189–191; La Potherie, ii., 207, 208; La Hontan, i., 98–101; Charlevoix, ii., 353–355; Shea's Charlevoix, iii., 285–290; Colden, i., 80, 81; Shea's Missions, 298, 318, 371, 375; Pinkerton, xiii., 293, 294; *ante*, 179, 236, 324, 398, 400. I think that La Hontan exaggerated when he wrote, "We found in all these villages *horses, cattle, poultry, and* an abundance of hogs." At all events, Denonville speaks only of the "vast quantity of hogs" which the French destroyed: compare Col. Doc., ix., 338, 367; Charlevoix, ii., 355; La Hontan, i., 101; Pinkerton, xiii., 294; N. Y. H. S. Coll., ii. (ii.), 191; Col. Doc., iii., 432, "in one village they got some hogs and fowle."

1687.

great disgust of Andros; and now Denonville occupied it again to "circumvent" Dongan. A formal "Act" was drawn up, declaring that La Salle's previous possession was "reiterated anew," in the name of Louis the Fourteenth. The Fort at Niagara was mounted with some small cannon, and the Chevalier de la Troye, who had led the expedition to Hudson's Bay the year before, was left in command of the garrison of one hundred men, with the Sieur des Bergères as his lieutenant; and Lamberville was appointed chaplain. Denonville then returned to Montreal by way of Cataracouy, where he left another garrison of one hundred men in charge of D'Orvilliers.*

21/31 July.

24 July.

3 August. De la Troye, Bergères, and Lamberville at Niagara.

The Mohawks and Oneidas had meanwhile advised Dongan of Denonville's invasion of the Senecas. The New York Council determined at once to protect the Five Nations; and the governor, with Counselors Brockholls and Palmer, hastened to Albany. Under the late Treaty of Neutrality, Dongan assumed that the Iroquois were British subjects, although they had not yet been distinctly claimed as such by his king. It was thought, too, that the French might push on eastward; and Brockholls was therefore sent down to New York, with orders to Colonel Bayard there, and to Major Willett in Queen's County, to send up the river militiamen for the defense of the frontier of the province at Albany and Schenectady.†

12 June.

24 June. Dongan's precautions against the French.

19 July.

Soon afterward Dongan talked with the Iroquois, whom he had convened at Albany. He congratulated his "Brethren" that the French had done them so little harm, and told them that he would send Palmer to report to the King of England all that had happened. In the mean time he advised the Five Nations not to kill any Frenchmen whom they might take prisoners; to manage their own affairs by a secret council; to make peace with the Ottawas, Miamis, and further Indians, as well as with the Mahicans; and to draw home those Iroquois who had been Christianized

5 August. Dongan's conference with the Iroquois at Albany.

* Col. Doc., iii., 396, 432, 435, 476; ix., 335, 336, 339, 349, 368, 369, 386, 388; Doc. Hist., i., 149, 150, 158; Col. MSS., xxxv., 160; La Potherie, ii., 208; La Hontan, i., 101, 102; Pinkerton, xiii., 294, 295; Charlevoix, ii., 337, 356, 366, 369; Colden, i., 81, 82; Shea's Lou. H. S. Coll., i., 70; N. Y. H. S. Coll., ii., 182, 185; Shea's Charlevoix, iii., 290, 291; Shea's Missions, 318; Garneau, i., 264. I have already noticed the misdate in Denonville's "Act of Possession:" *ante*, 163, 164, 325.

† Col. MSS., xxxv., 70, 71; Council Min., v., 195, 200; Doc. Hist., i., 150, 157; Col. Doc., iii., 475; *ante*, 475.

CHAP. IX. 1687. No French, but only English priests, to be allowed among the Iroquois.

in Canada; to name the "most convenient" place on Lake Ontario where the English might build a fort; to refuse to receive Lamberville or any other French priests, "having sent for English priests, whom you can be supplied with, all to content;" and to be on their guard, and make no treaties without Corlaer's means, nor do any thing with the French without his knowledge; "for then you will be looked upon as the King of England's subjects." Dongan then referred to the recent outrages of the Oneidas, who had "killed a fine gentleman, with some others," at the head of the James River. These outrages had obliged Lord Howard of Effingham to come with Sir Robert Parker from Virginia to New York, where, while lamenting the governor's absence at Albany, the citizen-peer was otherwise "satisfied with his entertainment." The Five Nations were chidden for their breach of the treaty of 1684, and told that, if they did so again, New York and Virginia would dig up the buried axes, and "totally ruin" the breakers of the covenant chains. But the Senecas, who had never done any thing against Corlaer's orders, were freed from blame, "except the making of that unlucky peace with the French three years ago, which has been the cause of all these troubles."*

Lord Howard and Sir Robert Parker, of Virginia, at New York.

6 August. Reply of the Five Nations to Dongan.

The next day, *Sindacksegie*, a Mohawk sachem, answered for the Five Nations that the French had attacked them only because, "about six years ago," the Senecas had troubled La Salle at Niagara during the government of Andros, who had forbidden those French to trade there; and because those New York Iroquois had "submitted themselves to the King of England," when Lord Howard, of Virginia, was with Dongan at Albany in 1684. As to hunting beavers in the great West of America, what, asked the Mohawk, had "the Christians to do with that," to the prejudice of its aborigines? "O, Brethren!" he added, with the serene logic of truth, "you tell us the King of England is a very great King:—why should you not join with us in a just cause, when the French join with our enemies in an unjust cause? O, Brethren, we see the reason

* Col. Doc., iii., 426, 428, 438–441, 475; Doc. Hist., i., 151; iii., 73; Colden, i., 53, 82–87; Smith, i., 80–85; *ante*, 396, 398. Neither Beverley nor Burk mention this second visit of Lord Effingham to New York in July, 1687.

of this. The French would fain kill us all; and when that is done, they would carry all the beaver trade to Canada, and the Great King of England would lose the land likewise. Awake, therefore, O, Great Sachem beyond the Great Lake [the Atlantic], and suffer not those poor Indians who have given themselves and their lands under thy protection, to be destroyed by the French, without cause!" After this pathetic appeal the Iroquois agreed to Dongan's propositions, and promised not to receive Lamberville or any other French Jesuit; and, if possible, would draw the Christian Indians back from Canada. They suggested the Salmon River, in Oswego County, as the best place for an English fort; and engaged that they would do every thing to prevent further mischief toward Virginia, and also that they would make no peace with the French without permission of the Governor of New York. Several Seneca sachems, who had been in the engagement near Gannagaro on the third of July, then gave an account of what the French had done in their canton. Upon this, Dongan felt justified in interpreting the Treaty of Neutrality so that he might supply the Senecas with arms and ammunition, which he did; although he declined to assist them with soldiers, as the farmers in New York were then all busy with their harvest.*

The Iroquois appeal to James for protection.

6 August. Dongan supplies the Iroquois with arms and ammunition.

On his return to Montreal, Denonville, having received the letter which Dongan had sent him by L'Espinard the previous June, charged him with duplicity in sending New York traders to Michilimackinac, "where no Englishman had ever put a foot, and where our Frenchmen have been established over sixty years;" and reproached him for breaking the Treaty of Neutrality, by advising and protecting the Iroquois, and causing the French missionaries to leave the cantons. MacGregorie and the other prisoners would be retained until the Neutrality Treaty should be executed. In a later letter Denonville rejected the claim of the English, and maintained the right of the French to sovereignty over the Iroquois; adding, "I am astonished that you should be ignorant that before Manate belonged to the King, your master—being in possession of

$\frac{11}{21}$ Aug. Denonville's reply to Dongan.

$\frac{12}{22}$ Aug. The French sovereignty over the Iroquois maintained.

* Col. Doc., iii., 428, 441–447, 474; v., 76; Doc. Hist., i., 151, 152, 157, 164; Col. MSS., xxxv., 90, 91; Shea's Charlevoix, iii., 289; *ante*, 326, 397, 479.

CHAP. IX. 1687.

the heretic Dutch, as you are aware—our missionaries, persecuted and martyred, found there an asylum and protection!"*

August. Kryn, the "Great Mohawk," meets "Blue Stocking" at Lake Champlain.

As Denonville wished to know what was going on in the Mohawk country, Kryn, "the Great Mohawk" chief at the Sault Saint Louis, offered to go with five others and bring his countrymen in New York to treat with Onnontio. Most of the party were dressed by the French in "very nigh Christian habits." On reaching Lake Champlain by way of Chambly, they met sixty Mohawks, commanded by "Blue Stocking," who, with Dongan's assent, were going to make prisoners in Canada. Kryn addressed his old companions so eloquently that he persuaded four of them to go back with him to Canada. Instead of capturing the Canadian proselyte and his followers, the Mohawks returned to their country, accompanied only by Kakariall and Adandidaghko, whom they sent from Albany to New York as prisoners, and who were examined before Counselor Van Cortlandt. They had both been with the French expedition against the Senecas, of which they gave interesting accounts. Both expressed their shame at having left their own country, but declared that "if a priest would settle at Saragtoga," many would return; "for they have waited a long time for it."†

31 August. 1 Septem. The Iroquois want an English priest at Saratoga.

18 August. 19 August. 20 August. War tax levied by Dongan and his council in New York. 2 Septem.

Upon returning to the metropolis, Dongan and his council, considering the expenses caused by the French, enacted the levy of an additional penny in the pound upon the freeholders and inhabitants of Kings, Queens, Dukes, Dutchess, Richmond, Orange, Westchester, and Suffolk Counties. But only a halfpenny in the pound was levied on New York, Albany, and Ulster, "these three places being the only support of the Government."‡

8 Septem. Dongan's instructions to Palmer going to England.

As Palmer was now going to England, Dongan gave him full instructions to lay before James the condition of

* Col. Doc., iii., 466–472, 487; ix., 336; Doc. Hist., i., 159–162; *ante*, vol. i., 346, 373, 374, 402, 423; ii., 119, 121, 466.

† Col. Doc., iii., 431-438, 483, 487, 488, 512, 514, 530; ix., 352, 353; Col. MSS., xxxv., 95; Charlevoix, ii., 357, 358; Shea's Charlevoix, iii., 292; Shea's Missions, 299, 319, 320; *ante*, 442, 476. Isaac Swinton, the deputy secretary under Spragg, having died while Dongan was at Albany, the council ordered, on 6 July, 1687, that Counselor Van Cortlandt should take charge of the seal, and John Knight act as deputy secretary: Council Min., v., 195; Col. Doc., iii., 407, 426; Col. MSS., xxxv., 162.

‡ Council Min., v., 198, 199, 200; Council Journ., i., Int., xx.; Col. Doc., iii., 476, 477; Doc. Hist., i., 154, 155, 158.

CHAP. IX.

1687.

Forts proposed, and colonial boundary with Canada to be adjusted.

8 Septem. Dongan wishes Irish people to be sent to New York.

12 Septem.

New York, and the conduct of the French in Canada. In this interesting paper the governor again urged that Connecticut and New Jersey should be joined to New York, which could not alone "help our Indians," as its revenue had fallen off from some thirty-five thousand beavers exported every year, to about nine thousand. Forts should be built on Lake Champlain, at Salmon River, and at Niagara on Lake Ontario; and smaller posts between them and Schenectady. The boundary with Canada should be adjusted in England; but not until the country had been better explored by the English, in which matter "the French at present have much the advantage." Priests should also be sent from England to live among the Indians. Dongan likewise asked Sunderland that people should be sent to New York from Ireland, "who had pretences to estates there, and are of no advantage to the country, and may live here very happy." A few days afterward he informed the lord president that news from Albany would oblige him to spend the winter there; and that "it is a great misfortune for this government that there are so few of his Majesty's natural-born subjects;—the greater part being Dutch, who, if occasion were, I fear would not be very fitt for service."*

7 Septem. Dongan, by advice of his council, resolves to winter in Albany.

9 Septem. New York precautions in favor of the Iroquois against the French.

11 Septem.

On receiving the information brought by L'Espinard from Canada, it was ordered in council that Albany and Schenectady should be strengthened with palisades, a watch kept, and Indian scouts stationed near Lake Champlain. Word soon came that the French had provided fifteen hundred pairs of snow shoes, with the intention of destroying Albany during the winter, and threatened to send its inhabitants to Spain, Portugal, and the West Indies. The council therefore ordered that the Five Nations should send all their old men, women, and children to the neighborhood of Catskill, "Livingston's land," and elsewhere along the Hudson River, where they could be assisted in case of need. It was also determined that Dongan should spend the winter at Albany, which was in great consternation; and that every tenth militiaman in the province should be drafted to go thither, "except those that were out

* Council Min., v., 200; Col. Doc., iii., 421, 428–430, 476–478; Doc. Hist., i., 157–159, 165; *ante*, 471.

CHAP. IX. 1687.

the last year a whaling."* This exception affected only the east end of Long Island.

The mayor and aldermen of Albany also conferred with the Mohawks, who gave up a French prisoner to the family of Viele, still held a captive in Canada, "to wash the tears of his wife and children." Their war-chief, Tahajadoris, lamented that their party who had met Kryn on Lake Champlain had not seized him; but they would at once send out expeditions to attack the French. The Onondagas also asked succor for the Senecas and Cayugas, and suggested that Oswego would be a better place than Salmon River for the proposed fort. They were told that Dongan would spend the winter at Albany with a large force, and expected them to send him re-enforcements; upon which they joyfully promised to "acquaint all the nations."†

14 Septem. Action of the Albany officers. 15 Septem.

Before going to Albany, the governor appointed and swore Stephanus van Cortlandt mayor of the City of New York, as successor to Nicholas Bayard. John Younge, who was now "a very old" man, and lived at the east end of Long Island, one hundred and fifty miles from Fort James, was removed from the council because he detailed "many aged and sickly men, and others without arms or cloths," to make up the quota of Suffolk County for the expedition to Albany. In his stead, James Graham was appointed and sworn as a counselor. Peter Schuyler was reappointed mayor of Albany. It was also ordered in council that certain Spanish Indians who had been brought from Campeachy, in Mexico, and sold as slaves, should be set free. This was only confirming previous legislation in 1680. The New England Puritans ruthlessly enslaved both the long-haired native red American, and the curly-haired imported black African. But New York was more just toward the superior aboriginal races, who occupied North America ages before Europeans usurped their lands.‡

29 Septem. 14 October. Dongan's arrangements for the government of the province. 8 October. 11 October. Spanish Indian slaves again set free in New York.

Dongan's uncle, Tyrconnell, the lord lieutenant of Ire-

* Council Min., v., 202–205; Doc. Hist., i., 155, 156, 162, 163, 166; Col. Doc., iii., 477–482, 487; Col. MSS., xxxiv., 120.

† Col. Doc., iii., 483–488; Col. MSS., xxxv., 99; Council Min., v., 206; Col. Rec. Conn., iii., 387; *ante*, 483.

‡ Council Min., v., 207, 209, 210; Col. Doc., iii., 416; iv., 726, 847; Val. Man., 1853, 386, 389; Dunlap, ii., App. cxxxv.; Min. of Com. Council, i., 319; Col. MSS., xxix., 86; xxxiv., 77, 78; xxxv., 169; *ante*, 296, 331, 462.

land, now informed him that it was "requisite" for the king's service that he should go home. The governor at once wrote to James that he would cheerfully obey his commands; but that he was largely in debt on his majesty's account, "and no ways left to paying it if Connecticut be not joyned to this government, which your Majesty will otherwise be continually out of purse to maintain, and whoever comes after me will certainly run your Majesty more in debt."*

24 October. Dongan writes to James about his expected recall.

The governor being now ready to winter in Albany, it was ordered in council "that Major Brockholls sign all warrants, papers, and licenses, usually signed by his Excellency, and that all other public business be managed by him and the council, as if his Excellency were present."†

25 October. Brockholls in command at New York during Dongan's absence at Albany.

Had Dongan's advice been adopted by his sovereign, English Jesuits might have replaced French missionaries in English New York. But the English disciples of Loyola do not seem to have had the manly spirit of adventure among the savages which distinguished their order in France. At this time there were three Jesuit fathers in New York: Thomas Harvey, of London, who had accompanied the governor from England; Henry Harrison, of Ireland; and Charles Gage, of Norwich. One of them seems to have taken charge of the Latin school which Jamison had relinquished; and Dongan asked James to endow it with the "King's farm." To this school Graham, Palmer, and Tudor "did contribute their sones for some time; but nobody imitating them, the college vanished," although the Dutch Church bell was tolled every morning at eight o'clock to summon the students. The Father Harrison appears to have assisted Harvey as Dongan's chaplain; and one of them seems to have taken the name of John Smith. He had a small chapel adorned with images, which the governor arranged in Fort James; and this Smith was a very "good-humored" man.‡

English Jesuit priests in New York under Dongan.

Latin school or college in New York under Dongan.

* Col. Doc., iii., 406, 422, 423, 428, 475, 478, 487, 492; Burnet, i., 246; Council Journ., i., Int., xxiii.; Secret Services Charles II. and James II., 195.

† Council Min., v., 211. On the 20th of October, 1687, before he left New York, Dongan chartered the manor of Pelham: Patents, vi., 306; Bolton, i., 536-539.

‡ Col. Doc., iii., 394, 465, 527, 613, 747; iv., 398, 490; v., 478; ix., 266; Doc. Hist., i., 145; ii., 14, 147; iii., 73; Smith, i., 90; N. Y. H. S. Coll. (1868), 398; Bayley's Sketch, 19, 22; Shea's Charlevoix, iii., 266; Shea's Missions, 314; *ante*, 374, 408, 431, 440, 442. Sixty pounds a year were paid to "two Romish priests that attended on Governor Dongan:" Coun. Min., vi., 17; Col. MSS., xxxvii., 163; *post*, 641.

CHAP. IX. 1687. Novem. Andros's jealousy of Dongan. On reaching Albany, where he was attended by Chaplain Innis and Father Harrison, Dongan asked from Governor Treat, of Connecticut, the assistance of some of her infantry and cavalry. But Andros, having now superseded Treat, paid no attention to Dongan's "very inconvenient" request.*

9 Septem. Dongan protests against Denonville's invasion of New York. Meanwhile Dongan had protested to Denonville against his invasion of English territory, and demanded the release of MacGregorie and the other New York traders whom he had seized for going to the Ottawas, who, with "the Indians who wear pipes through their noses, traded with Albany long before the French settled at Montreal." Denonville soon afterward returned them safely to Albany, 12 October. The New York prisoners returned. and asked that the Canadian prisoners whom the Senecas had sent to Albany should be given up; praising the English king, "whose rare virtues have attached him to the hearts of all the French."†

24 October. 3 Novem. Fort Chambly besieged by Mohawks and Mahicans. Exasperated against the Canadians, a party of Mohawks and Mahicans besieged Fort Chambly, burned houses, and took several prisoners. August. French captured at Cataracouy. Another band, led by an Onondaga chief, captured, near Fort Frontenac, Mademoiselle D'Allonne, and three soldiers of its garrison. Lamberville, who was then there, came out with a white flag, and gave two wampum belts to the savages to prevent them from injuring their prisoners, and from taking part with the Senecas, against which nation only the French were at war. The prisoners were carried to Onondaga, and thence Lamberville's belts sent to Albany. to Albany; and Lamberville's belts were faithfully handed to Dongan. The governor dispatched MacGregorie with 25 October. letters, demanding Denonville's explanations of these belts; 31 October. maintaining that the Iroquois had been in "brotherly cor- 10/20 Novem. Dongan demands explanations. respondence" since the first settlement of Albany; had "submitted themselves, their Country, and Conquests to the Dutch in their time, and to the King of England since this Colony came under his Majesty's obedience;" and suggest-

* Col. Doc., iii., 527, 579; Col. Rec. Conn., iii., 398, 399, 400; Mass. H. S. Coll., xxiii., 167-169; *ante*, 457, 469. Colonel Talcot, writing from Hartford on 5 December, 1687, to Andros at Boston, about Dongan's call for aid from Connecticut, says that in King Philip's War "Your Excellency did very honourably and wisely prevent the barbarous heathen from drawing the sword against His Majesty's subjects in the territory of New York, and then under your government:" *ante*, 286-296.

† Council Min., v., 202, 204; Col. Doc., iii., 436, 437, 472-475, 510, 512, 513; ix., 330, 348, 355, 356; Doc. Hist., i., 163-167; Holgate, 91; Shea's Charlevoix, 291; *ante*, 443, 478.

CHAP. IX.

1687.

ing that a French agent should be sent to arrange all differences with the English governor at Albany.*

18/28 Decem. Denonville sends Vaillant and Dumont to Albany.

Denonville accordingly sent the Jesuit, Francis Vaillant, who had been the last French missionary to the Mohawks in 1683, as his representative to Albany, with the Father Elambert Dumont, who could speak English. Vaillant was instructed to make no propositions, but only to receive any that Dongan might offer. On his return to Canada the father was to visit his old Mohawk flock. So, on the last day of the year, the Canadian agents began their dreary journey from Montreal.† 21/31 Decem.

15/25 Aug.

17/27 Oct. Denonville complains of Dongan to Louis, and advises the gaining of New York.

In writing to Paris, Denonville put as good a face as he could on his miserable Seneca expedition; blamed Dongan heartily, and advised a new French campaign the next year against the Onondagas and Cayugas. But the best thing for France would be to get the Iroquois country from the English, "either by exchange or otherwise." Dongan had not asserted English sovereignty over these savages until 1684, and would never faithfully execute the Whitehall Treaty of Neutrality. The forts at Niagara and Detroit must be maintained by the French; and more soldiers should be sent to Canada. If Louis could gain from England "the entire coast of Manate, it would be a great advantage for religion and our country, which will, sooner or later, suffer from the vicinity of the English." This idea, broached by Duchesnau in 1681, Denonville now enforced. Callières also urged that Dongan should be recalled, as the surest means of ending the French and English strife about the Iroquois. The acquisition by Louis of New York, with its beautiful harbor of Manhattan, "would render his Majesty master of all North America."‡ November.

English domestic affairs had meanwhile grown more critical. Having dispensed with the Test Act of 1673, James determined to take another step, which, he thought, would put the Church of Rome in place of the Protestant denomination which had been established by law in England. By his commissions and instructions to Andros and to Dongan,

* Col. Doc., iii., 479, 480, 513–517, 527, 529, 535; ix., 362, 389, 390; Quebec MSS., v. (ii.), 427; Doc. Hist., i., 266; Charlevoix, ii., 365, 366, 367; Garneau, i., 267; Warburton, i., 411; Smith, i., 85, 86; *ante*, 441, 481, 483, 484.

† Col. Doc., iii., 517–519, 521; ix., 389, 762; Quebec MSS., v. (ii.), 429; Charlevoix, ii., 367; Smith, i., 86; *ante*, 377, 476.

‡ Col. Doc., ix., 165, 286, 336–354, 357–371, 373, 919, 920; *ante*, 364, 401, 431.

CHAP. IX.

1687.

the king had already ordained liberty of conscience to all his subjects in New England and New York. He now adopted the same policy in regard to those in Great Britain. Among his motives, as stated by himself, were "the example of several foreign countries, where trade flourished most, that nothing could be more beneficial to it than liberty of conscience; that it was the support of Holland; and that the want of it in England had not only crampt its trade, but had furnished the seeds of several rebellions, which had no other origin than one religion's lording it over the rest." James accordingly issued his royal declaration—which Penn is said to have helped to draft—that all laws against non-conformity to the English formula of religion should be suspended, and that all British subjects should have free leave "to meet and serve God after their own way and manner." This declaration was ordered to be published throughout the kingdom, and in the Plantations of England.*

4 April. Declaration of liberty of conscience by James.

The Protestants, who had been driven from France after the revocation of the Edict of Nantes, were now openly favored in England; the liberality of the nation was again appealed to in their favor, and they were chartered to build a new church in London. In answer to a petition of several of them in New York, Dongan was directed to give such French Protestants as might settle in the province "all fitting encouragement, so far forth as may be consistent with His Majesty's service;" and letters of denization were promised, "whereby they may become qualified to trade."†

21 April. French Protestant refugees favored by James.

19 July. Denization promised.

At the same time, James resolved to carry out his purpose of making the Plantations more immediately dependent on the crown. He accordingly ordered writs of Quo Warranto "to forfeit all the Charters of the Proprietors and Corporations in America." New Jersey, Maryland, and Carolina were the special objects of this fresh attack; for Connecticut was understood to have surrendered her charter. Pennsylvania was excepted by the express com-

28 May. Writs of Quo Warranto ordered against charters and corporations in America. Pennsylvania excepted.

* Clarke's James II., ii., 102–115; Ellis Corr., i., 269; Evelyn, ii., 273, 276; Dalrymple, ii., 85–88; Reresby, 243; Wodrow, iv., 424–426; Parl. Hist., iv., 1388; Kennett, iii., 463–465; Rapin, ii., 757, 758; Burnet, i., 714; Lingard, xiv., 121–124; Macaulay, ii., 204–213; Palfrey, iii., 460, 548; Col. Rec. Conn., iii., 393; N. Y. Council Minutes, v., 214; *ante*, 452–455.

† Col. Doc., 419, 420, 426, 427; Evelyn, ii., 253, 262, 277, 282, 284; Ellis Corr., ii., 157; Kennett, iii., 472; Macaulay, ii., 76–80, 215, 216; *ante*, 464.

mand of James, as her proprietor had purchased immunity by becoming "a tool of the King and the Jesuits."*

East Jersey, however, obtained a temporary boon. Her capital and sea-port was Perth Amboy, which was considered to be "within the River of New York," up which Dongan had been instructed to allow no goods to pass, unless the duties on them should have been paid at the metropolitan custom-house. This regulation having been enforced, the New Jersey proprietors complained to the king, and asked that "an officer might be appointed at Perth Amboy to collect the Customs, [and] to cause the acts of Navigation to be executed." Dongan was accordingly instructed to permit all vessels bound to New Perth, in East Jersey, to go thither directly, without touching at New York; provided that the person whom he or the receiver general at New York might appoint should be suffered by the East Jersey government "peaceably and quietly to receive and collect for His Majesty's use the same customs and imposts as are usually paid at New York for such ships and their lading as are entered there."†

30 May.

14 August. Perth Amboy made a port, subject to a New York officer.

James at the same time ordered that a new seal, which had been so long desired, should be sent to the governor of New York. It was made of silver, engraved on both sides, and bore the significant motto, "ALIUS Q: ET IDEM"—*other, yet the same.* This seal was to be "of the same force and validity as any former seal" within the province.‡

14 August. New royal seal for New York.

These dispatches reached New York while Dongan was at Albany. Andrew Hamilton, the acting governor of East Jersey, having produced before the council a duplicate of James's letter regarding Perth Amboy, measures to give it effect were ordered. The king's declaration of the previous April for liberty of conscience was also read and published in the metropolis.§

19 Novem.

21 Novem.

25 Novem. Action in New York.

Collector Santen's case having been considered in London, his commission was revoked. Although Dongan had recommended Graham, Matthew Plowman, an English Ro-

4 Novem. Santen removed and Plowman appointed collector of New York.

* Dalrymple, ii., 89, 90; Annual Reg., 1771, 247; Chalmers, i., 298, 371, 425, 549, 622, 654; Grahame, i., 485; Whitehead, 111, 112; Col. Rec. Conn., iii., 378, 384; Proud, i., 309–314; Dixon, 239, 259; Kennett, iii., 469; Macaulay, ii., 292, 295–297; *ante*, 433, 471.

† Col. Doc., iii., 349, 373, 392, 428, 502; Chalmers, i., 622; Whitehead's E. J., 111; Index to N. J. Col. Doc., 12, 13; N. Y. Council Min., v., 186, 212, 213; *ante*, 455, 460.

‡ Col. Doc., iii., 360, 365, 378, 427; iv., 812; v., 369; Doc. Hist., iv., 1, *; *ante*, 427, 438.

§ Council Minutes, v., 212, 213, 214; Whitehead's E. J., 118, 155.

CHAP. IX.

1687.

man Catholic, was appointed collector and receiver of New York, at a cost of five hundred pounds. Plowman's instructions were fuller than Santen's in 1683. Among oth-

13 Decem.

er things, he was directed to permit all vessels bound to East Jersey to go directly to Perth Amboy. At Dongan's

10 Novem.

request, Counselor Stephanus van Cortlandt was commissioned by Auditor General Blathwayt to be his deputy in New York.*

18 May. Negotiation at London about New York.

Negotiations for the settlement of all differences in America between the French and English governments had been going on in the mean time at London. Louis sent Bonrepos to assist his ambassador Barillon, and ordered them to represent to James that Dongan continued to "thwart" the French in Canada; had supplied the Iroquois with arms; and had broken the Treaty of Neutrality of November,

28 Oct./7 Novem.

1686. The French ambassadors accordingly requested the king to order Dongan "to put an end to the troubles" he had caused; and also to direct Andros not to disturb the French established in Acadia by virtue of the Treaty of Breda.†

At this moment Palmer reached London with Dongan's September dispatches. It was now perceived at Whitehall that "a treaty of neutrality in America was not for the interest of England." Denonville's invasion of the Seneca country, and the appeal of the Five Nations to their "Great sachem beyond the great Lake," brought to a crisis the question of European sovereignty over the Iroquois. As that sovereignty must be either French or English, James determined to maintain the claim asserted by Andros and Dongan, that the Five Nations were British subjects. Ac-

10 Novem. James's instructions to Dongan about the Iroquois.

cordingly, he instructed Dongan that those savages had, "from all times," submitted themselves to English government, and, "by their acknowledgments," had become his subjects; and he directed his governor of New York to demand from the Governor of Canada the release of all British prisoners, "as well Indians as others," with the restitution of their goods. "And as we are sensible," continued James, "of what great prejudice it may be to us and our subjects,

* Col. Doc., iii., 335, 336, 407–414, 420–424, 429, 493–503, 641, 650, 718, 719; Doc. Hist., i., 110–116; Commissions, i., 78; Council Min., v., 223; N. Y. H. S. Coll. (1868), 290; *ante*, 462.

† Col. Doc., iii., 506; ix., 314, 330, 345; Ellis Corr., i., 224, 289, 305; *ante*, 475.

if any incroachment be allowed on our Dominions, or the French permitted to invade our Territories or to annoy our subjects without a due care in us to preserve the peace of our government, and to give all due protection to such as have brought themselves under our subjection; We do, therefore, hereby charge and require you to give notice, at the same time, to the said Governor of Canada, that upon mature consideration We have thought fit to own the Five Nations or Cantons of Indians, namely, the Maquaes, Senecas, Cayougas, Oneydes, and Onondagues, as Our Subjects, and resolve to protect them as such." To make good this assertion, James farther ordered Dongan "to defend and protect" those Indians from the Canadians; to build necessary forts; to employ the militia of New York; and to call on all the neighboring English colonies for assistance. Royal orders were, at the same time, sent to Andros and the other English governors in North America to give New York "such help" as her governor might require.*

CHAP. IX. 1687.

10 Novem. Orders to other royal governors.

"Very much surprized" at the complaints of Louis against Dongan, James answered that it was "well known" that the Five Nations of New York had been British subjects, as proved, since the first settlement of their country by Europeans, "and now lately by their voluntary submission, made and confirmed by them in writing to the Crown of England, on the Thirtieth of July, 1684, before His Majesty's Governors of Virginia and New York." The English king was therefore obliged to protect those Indians, "as other his subjects;" but he would not suffer them to annoy the French Canadians if the latter did not injure them; and the limits between the dominions of France and England in North America might be adjusted by a treaty between the two European crowns. The French commissioners, not prepared to make such a treaty at once, signed an agreement that until the first day of January, 1689, and afterward, no English or French commander in America should "commit any act of hostility against," or invade the territories of either king; and that the necessary orders should be given by each sovereign. At the same time, the agents of Louis, in answer to the "entirely novel" preten-

16/26 Novem. Answer of James to Louis about the Iroquois.

1/11 Decem. Agreement to prevent colonial hostilities.

3/13 Decem.

* Col. Doc., iii., 428, 438, 475, 503, 504; Chalmers, i., 425, 466, 590; Col. Rec. Conn., iii., 438, 442; Penn. Arch., i., 104, 105; Burk, ii., 301, 302; *ante*, 483, 485.

CHAP. IX. 1687. The French deny the English and assert their own claim to sovereignty over the Iroquois.

sion of James, insisted that the Iroquois had acknowledged French sovereignty since Champlain "took possession" of their country; that, in 1665 and 1666, they had by treaty declared themselves French subjects; that in October, 1666, Tracy had again taken possession of their country, and that their alleged acknowledgment of British sovereignty in 1684 "cannot be admitted, to the prejudice of the ancient right and actual possession of the French." Moreover, when the Neutrality Treaty was made in November, 1686, the English had not pretended that "the Iroquois were subjects of His Brittanic Majesty; and not a word was said about it." Here the negotiations at London ended.

1688. 22 Jan. James's orders to Dongan.

In communicating their result to Dongan, James directed him to avoid "all occasions of misunderstanding" with the Canadians; "entertain a good correspondence" with them, and take care that no just complaints should be made against him. Similar letters were sent to Andros and to Penn.*

Vaillant and Dumont at Albany.

Meanwhile Vaillant and Dumont, whom Denonville had sent to Dongan, had reached Albany, under the escort of MacGregorie, after maltreatment on their winter's journey by a party of drunken Mahicans. Dongan promptly restored their effects and punished the offenders. A long negotiation followed between the representatives of New York and Canada, chiefly upon the proper construction of the Treaty of Neutrality. The king's letter of November having been sent to him by Andros at Boston, Dongan announced that he "must protect" the Five Nations as English subjects, and required the French to demolish the fort at Niagara, and restore all goods and prisoners they had taken. At the request of the Iroquois, he also demanded that the forts at Cataracouy and Tircksarondie, or Detroit, should be demolished. The French agents demurred, and were sent back directly to Canada with a letter to Denonville, under the escort of Dirck Wessels, of Albany, and some savages, who did not allow them to visit the Mohawk country.†

February. Negotiations with Dongan.

$\frac{17}{27}$ Feb.

$\frac{8}{18}$ Feb.

Dongan also had an interview with "the wisest men of

* Col. MSS., xxxv., 187; Col. Doc., iii., 121-127, 135, 417, 418, 504-510, 549; ix., 371; Chalmers's Ann., i., 466, 590; Penn. Arch., i., 103, 104; *ante*, 397, 475, 481.

† Col. Doc., iii., 519-532, 536; ix., 389, 762; Col. Rec. Conn., iii., 438, 442; Charlevoix, ii., 367, 368, 370; Quebec MSS., v. (ii.), 441; Council Min., v., 218; Smith, i., 86; *ante*, 478, 489.

CHAP. IX.

1688.

the Five Nations" at Albany, and told his "Brethren" that the King of England had adopted, and would protect them as his own "Children." The sachems expressed joy that James had taken them under his protection, and said that instead of the French having any right to their country, the Iroquois could better claim all Canada. Dongan replied that his king was "the greatest man that the sun shines upon:—he never told a lie in his life," and he would surely protect them. He therefore wished them to promise not to make peace or war without the consent of all. The sachems answered that they would refer themselves wholly to Dongan, who represented their "great King," and hoped that he would remove the French from Niagara, Cataracouy, and Detroit.*

13/23 Feb. Dongan's talk with the Iroquois.

16/26 Feb.

In writing from Albany to Sunderland, Dongan reported his doings with the Canadian agents and with the delegates of the Iroquois, who must be kept "fast" to the English, "for if they were otherwise, they are able to ruin all the King's Colonies in these parts of America." And, he added, "we must build forts in the country upon the Great Lake, as the French do, otherwise we lose the country, the beaver trade, and our Indians; and also there must be Missionaries sent amongst them; the French Priest [Vaillant] desired of me leave for their Missionaries to go and live amongst them again, by which I find they make religion a stalking-horse to their pretence." Again he urged that the Jerseys would be a "very convenient" addition to New York, which, in case of war with the French or Indians, "must be the bulwark to Boston, which is not at the fourth part the charge New York is, and has ten times the revenue." Connecticut should also be annexed to the government of New York.†

19 Feb. Dongan's report to Sunderland.

Baxter now came down to New York with instructions from the governor for the Council to consider ways and means to defray the extraordinary charges which the French movements had caused the province. These charges were more than eight thousand pounds; and the Council, finding

13 March. Baxter sent down to New York.

* Col. Doc., iii., 510, 533–536, 579. A different account of this interview is given in Col. Doc., ix., 389, 390, upon the report of an escaped Caghnawaga prisoner, from which Charlevoix (ii., 368) compiled his statement about Dongan's advising the Iroquois only to cover the hatchet "under the grass."

† Col. Doc., iii., 510, 511, 512; Col. Rec. Conn., iii., 387, 442; *ante*, 472, 482.

CHAP. IX. 1688. that New York "alone is no way able to bear so great a burthen," advised that the "neighboring colonies" should be invited to contribute. A few days afterward Dongan returned to the capital, and gave the Council a full account of his doings at Albany. Under the authority of the king's letter of November, 1687, he also called on the governments of Pennsylvania, Maryland, Virginia, and New Jersey to aid that of New York with money; as New England, "being to help us with six hundred men, any other assistance cannot be proposed from them."*

28 March.

30 March. Dongan calls on the neighboring colonies for help.

To fortify Dongan's appeal to Sunderland from Albany, it was also resolved in Council to address the king "that this government has been much diminished by taking away Pemaquid, the Jerseys, Pennsylvania, and the lower counties of Delaware; that this is the bulwark of all these parts of America; that the revenue is but small, yet the charges very great; that Connecticut in his Majesty's patent from Charles the Second, is added to Boston by the contrivance of the Governor of it and the Clerk of the Colony, and unknown to the major part of the Colony; that the French war has stop't the beaver trade; so that, without some speedy help, this place will be ruined."†

28 March. New York's address to the king.

* Council Min., v., 220, 221, 222; Col. Doc., 503, 504; Doc. Hist., i., 167; Penn. Arch., i., 104, 105; Col. Rec., i., 217; Chalmers, i., 466; *ante*, 493.

† Council Min., v., 221, 222; Col. Doc., iii., 511; Maine H. S. Coll., v., 132; *ante*, 472, 482.

CHAPTER X.

1688–1689.

CHAP. X.

1688.

While Dongan and his counselors, in the citadel of Manhattan, were thus urging their trans-Atlantic monarch to restore to New York some of her ancient territory, as a means of protecting her frontier against colonial enemies, King James the Second of England, near the Whitehall banqueting-house, where his father lost his head, was arranging American provincial affairs to suit his own royal purposes.

Of all the sovereigns of England, James the Second knew most about her colonies. Soon after the restoration of his brother he was made the proprietor of a large royal English-American province. In the details of its administration he took a lively personal interest, because the revenue of that province affected his pocket. So, with his own hand, the hard-working Stuart prince wrote many letters to his deputies in New York. Certainly his dispatches had the merit of directness and precision. Unconstrained by the conventional phrases which often beguile mere secretaries, the terse holographs of the Duke of York uttered his own imperious will.

With this long proprietary experience, James became the sovereign of England and her dependencies. Yet, while as king he could no longer correspond directly with his colonial subordinates, he retained some tranquil pleasure in guiding the action of his Plantation Committee. The diligent business habits of the Duke of York infused order and economy into every department of the government of James the Second. As far as mere administration was concerned, his short reign seems to have been more effective than that of any other English sovereign.

Colonial administration of James the Second.

But with orderly and frugal administration, Englishmen got a more despotic system of government. The personal

CHAP. X. 1688. Government of James.

character of their industrious king was stamped on all his measures. James was too active to drift; he always wanted to row and to steer. His ministers were less his advisers than his instruments. Governing at last without a Parliament, James of England became almost like Louis of France, himself "THE STATE."

James more a bigot than a tyrant.

Yet James was more a bigot than a tyrant. His chief object was to establish in England the Roman Catholic religion in place of the Protestant. To this end he claimed sovereign power to dispense with statutes, forfeited charters of corporations, and delayed summoning a Parliament until he felt sure that it would meekly obey him. The king did not attempt, and probably did not desire, to abolish what popular representation there was in England, but he wished to make the English Lords and Commons as subservient as were his temporary ministers. He would have rejoiced to see Parliament in London resemble the docile "Bed of Justice" which affirmed the decrees of his kingly brother in Paris. If his English subjects would but think as he did, James would have liked their representatives to gather about him at Westminster and sanction the laws he desired. So they would maintain his supremacy by becoming a breakwater to defend the crown's hoary prerogative against the advancing surges of democracy.

Popular representation not allowed in the English colonies.

Thus shunning popular representation in England, James denied it to the English colonies in America. These he insisted on governing by his royal prerogative as "dependencies" of the British crown, and not as constituencies of the British empire. So had his predecessors determined; so had English courts awarded; so were most Englishmen willing that those colonies should be treated. As its proprietor, James had conceded to New York a popular Assembly, which, as its sovereign, he had abolished. Dongan, with his Council in New York, and Andros, with his Council in New England, were now the only English makers, and the only English enforcers of laws throughout the territory between the Hudson and the Saint Croix. In New York, Dongan represented that imperial crown which first had delegated, and then had recalled British authority. So Andros, in New England, represented the same sovereign whose delegations of colonial power had been abused by his trans-Atlantic subjects near Cape Cod. James had already resolved that the vigor of direct monarchy would be better for them than the discords of substituted oligarchies, which damaged his American realm. At the worst, Andros was but one English ruler instead of several. Governor or oligarchs—commissioned by the crown or chartered—all were creatures of their British king. "The People" in New England had not given, and could not give, any authority to their colonial rulers. In truth, the American government of James the Second was more tolerant and just than that which it superseded. Certainly it provided for the prosperity and happiness of all classes of inhabitants, who, while not allowed colonial assemblies, were guaranteed equal rights in America, and as large religious liberty as Englishmen in England.

CHAP. X.

1688.

James the Second's colonial policy tolerant and just.

Bigot and tyrant, James had one characteristic which shone in vivid contrast. He was a more patriotic Englishman than his faithless brother. Anxious for the support of Louis, James scorned to betray England to France. Yet he had stretched courtesy by his treaty of colonial neutrality in the autumn of 1686. Scarcely had he remedied that error by his next year's agreement and his orders to prevent hostilities in North America, when James saw that Louis had gained an advantage. The American British colonies were at stake. New France, with its undefined territory, was governed by a viceroy, who executed his French king's orders. The neighboring British possessions had discordant local administrations of English authority. To the savages, Louis seemed a greater monarch than James. As long as Canada had the energy of union, while New England, New York, New Jersey, and Pennsylvania were distinct and inharmonious, so long France would be stronger in America than England.

22 Jan. James faithful to England.

Dongan's warnings now impressed Whitehall. James's recent arrangement with Louis about colonial hostilities offered British statesmanship a grand chance to establish the supremacy of England in the trans-Atlantic world. And so the king did the best thing he could, which was to unite, as far as convenient, all the North American British possessions under one vice-regal government. Seeing that Andros had brought the New England colonies into de-

CHAP. X. 1688. Policy of Consolidating the English colonies in America.

pendence on the crown, James resolved to carry out his policy of union or fusion. By this means he hoped to secure all his American territories against their neighboring Canadian adversary, and, at the same time, strengthen his own arbitrary rule over them. For colonial reasons, Dongan had urged that Connecticut and the Jerseys should be annexed to New York. The matter of the Jerseys had been already decided. Finding that the king had expedited writs of scire facias against them, Perth, with his co-proprietors, surrendered their powers of government to him. (March. April.) Connecticut, however, had just been quietly joined to the other New England colonies under the government of Andros. So, instead of annexing Connecticut to New York, as Dongan had asked, James resolved to add New York and the Jerseys to his "Dominion of New England." Thus all the territory which his grandfather's patent of 1620 had named "New England in America" would be brought, for the first time, under one royal English governor. Hitherto, New York had never really been a part of the titular "New England" of James the First. Her central geographical position, her vast territory, her extraordinary variety of interests, and her peculiar relations to Canada and the Iroquois, had demonstrated that a separate government was a necessity for her. These considerations did not deter James the Second from his purpose of consolidating all his American colonies north of the fortieth degree of latitude. Yet he made one solitary exception:—it was Pennsylvania. Her Quaker proprietor had long enjoyed the favor of James, who at this moment found him too useful an instrument to be offended. Protected by her astute owner's "interest" at court, Pennsylvania, alone in her immunity, escaped the forfeiture of her charter. But all the rest of British North America, between Delaware Bay and Passamaquoddy, and stretching across the continent from the Atlantic to the Pacific, was now to be made a political whole, under one colonial governor chosen by the king, to rule his "Dominion of New England."*

(Peculiar condition of New York.)

* Col. Doc., iii., 363, 391, 392, 397, 415, 416, 425, 429, 492; Hutch. Coll., 559; Leaming and Spicer, 604, 605; S. Smith, 204, 206, 211, 568; Gordon, 53; Grahame, ii., 299; Bancroft, ii., 46, 47; Whitehead's E. J., 112, 113; Index to N. J. Col. Doc., 13; Chalmers's Ann., i., 590, 622; Rev. Col., i., 183; Proud, i., 322, 341; Dalrymple, ii., 89, 90; Narcissus Luttrell, i., 461; Macaulay, ii., 292, 295; *ante*, vol. i., 96; ii., 448, 490.

CHAP. X. 1688.

Whom that viceroy should be was already determined. Either Dongan or Andros must be displaced. Both had been twice commissioned by James, first when duke, and afterward as king. Andros had the largest experience in government, and, perhaps, the best executive talent. He had already governed New York, and was now vigorously ruling New England to the satisfaction of his arbitrary sovereign. Although "fond of prelacy," Sir Edmund was not a Roman Catholic. But he had proved himself an uncompromising executer of all the royal commands. A thorough soldier, Andros made quick obedience his canon of duty. On the other hand, Dongan, also a soldier, yet more a patrician, was an Irish Roman Catholic, a nephew of Tyrconnell, and the presumptive heir of the intensely loyal Earl of Limerick. But, with equal affection and fidelity to his king, Dongan had more independence of character than Andros. He had not hesitated to foil and embitter Penn, nor to anger Perth and Melfort in his own master's service. He had been sharply censured by the King of France for maintaining the American interests of the King of England. In a word, Dongan had shown more official "zeal" than a cunning politician might think expedient in a subordinate. So the Roman Catholic governor of New York was superseded, and offered the command of a regiment, with the rank of major general of artillery in the British army, and a new commission was ordered, making the Protestant Sir Edmund Andros governor general of James the Second's whole "Territory and Dominion of New England in America."*

Andros. Dongan. 23 March. Andros made viceroy in the American "Dominion" of James.

By this step James appeared to have made a graceful concession to Louis. Seignelay hastened to notify Denonville that Dongan had been recalled, and that his successor was to live in harmony with the Canadian authorities. "His Majesty," it was triumphantly added, "could not believe that the King of England would countenance the chimerical pretension which that Colonel would fain claim for him over the Country of the Iroquois." But in this Louis erred. While James recalled Dongan, he adopted Dongan's Indian policy; and the "speculative wisdom" which directed colo-

8 March. Louis deceived.

* Col. Doc., iii., 348, 354, 422, 423, 487, 492; ix., 314, 322; Mass. H. S. Coll., xxxii., 298; N. Y. Council Journals, i., Int., xxiii.; Chalmers's Ann., i., 425, 628; *ante*, 449–456.

CHAP. X.

1688.

$\frac{10}{20}$ March.

nial union in British North America anticipated that it would "be terrible to the French, and make them proceed with more caution than they have lately done." At the same time that Andros was instructed to "entertain a good correspondence" with the French Canadian authorities, he was enjoined to "protect" the Five Nations of New York as British subjects. So far was James from giving up what Louis called the "chimerical pretension" of Dongan, or from surrendering an acre of his claimed American dominion to France, that he affirmed his sovereignty over the whole region lying between the Saint Croix, the Saint Lawrence, and the great lakes on the north, and the fortieth degree of latitude on the south, and stretching across the continent from sea to sea.*

James affirms his sovereignty in America.

7 April. The king's new commission to Andros.

The new commission which James now sent to Andros was similar to that which he had given him in 1686, with an additional clause annexing to his government the neighboring colonies of Rhode Island and Connecticut, the province of New York, and East and West Jersey, "with the territories thereunto belonging." By this instrument Andros was made King James's captain general and governor-in-chief of "all that tract of land, circuit, continent, precincts, "and limits in America, lying and being in breadth from "forty degrees of northern latitude from the Equinoctial "line, to the River of St. Croix eastward, and from thence "directly northward to the River of Canada, and in length "and longitude, by all the breadth aforesaid, throughout "the main land, from the Atlantick or Western Sea or "Ocean on the East part, to the South Sea on the West "part; with all the Islands, seas, Rivers, waters, rights, mem-"bers and appurtenances thereunto belonging:—(our Prov-"ince of Pennsylvania and Country of Delaware only ex-"cepted,) To be called and known, as formerly, by the name "and title of our Territory and Dominion of New England "in America." Thus, after sixty-eight years full of marvelous vicissitudes, nearly all the nominal "New England" of James the First was brought, by his grandson, under the rule of a sole vice-regal representative of the British crown.†

Extent of James the Second's "Territory and Dominion of New England in America."

* Col. Doc., iii., 504, 543, 548, 549; ix., 263, 372; Hutch. Mass. Coll., i., 371, 559; Chalmers's Ann., i., 425, 590; Rev. Col., i., 184; Charlevoix, ii., 376; *ante*, 405.

† Col. Doc., iii., 537–542; Chalmers's Ann., i., 425, 426, 590; Mass. H. S. Coll., xxvii., 139

CHAP. X.

1688.

16 April.

The king's instructions to Andros as his viceroy in New England.

James's instructions to Andros, like those he gave to him and to Dongan two years before, were minute and specific. Forty-two* of the principal inhabitants of his several colonies and provinces were named by the king to be members of the Council of his "Dominion of New England in America," to whom his governor general was to communicate such of the royal instructions as he should "find convenient." These counselors were to have freedom of debate, and seven of them were necessary to act as a quorum, except on "extraordinary emergencies." By the advice and consent of a majority of these counselors laws could be made and taxes imposed. The governor was authorized to suspend any counselor "for good and sufficient cause;" and he was required to nominate to the Plantation Committee "persons fit" to supply vacancies. In nominating counselors, as well as in choosing judges, sheriffs, and other legal officers, he was "always to take especial care that they be men of estate and abilities, and not necessitous people, or much in debt, and that they be persons well affected to the government." All laws within the "Dominion" were to remain in force until the governor and his Council should make others. The "new seal," which had been devised in 1686 for the king's "Colonies of New England," was now to be alone used throughout his present "Territory and Dominion in its largest extent." As a consequence, it was directed that the seal of the province of New York, which had been ordered in August, 1687, should be "broken and defaced." Liberty of conscience in matters of religion was to be allowed "to all persons, so they be contented with a quiet and peaceable enjoyment of it," pursuant to the king's declaration of the fourth of April, 1687, which was "to be

The seal of New York to be destroyed.

-149; xxxii., 298; Force's Tracts, iv., No. 8; Rhode Island Col. Rec., iii., 212-218; *ante*, vol. i., 96; vol. ii., 449, 450.

* The persons composing Andros's council were now Joseph Dudley, William Stoughton, John Pynchon, Peter Bulkley, Richard Wharton, John Usher, Bartholomew Gedney, Jonathan Tyng, Edward Tyng, Barnaby Lathrop, Samuel Shrimpton, Simon Lynde, and William Brown, of Massachusetts and Maine; Robert Mason and John Hincks, of New Hampshire; Thomas Hinckley, William Bradford, Daniel Smith, John Walley, and Nathaniel Clark, of Plymouth; Walter Clarke, John Sandford, John Coggeshall [Coxhill], Walter Newberry, John Greene, Richard Arnold, John Alborough, and Richard Smith, of Rhode Island; Robert Treat, Fitz John Winthrop, Wait Winthrop, and John Allyn, of Connecticut; Anthony Brockholls, Frederick Phillipse, Jervis Baxter, Stephen van Cortlandt, John Spragg, John Younge, Nicholas Bayard, and John Palmer, of New York; Francis Nicholson and Edward Randolph, at this time of Boston. Col. Doc., iii., 543; R. I. Rec., iii., 255; Hutch. Mass., i., 354; Mass. H. S. Coll., xviii., 182; Williamson, i., 584; Arnold, i., 508; Palfrey, iii., 553, 562, 604; Col. Rec. Conn., iii., 441, 442, 447.

CHAP. X. 1688.

duly observed and put in execution." But nothing was said about the ecclesiastical jurisdiction of the Bishop of London or the Archbishop of Canterbury in the English American possessions. This had been provided for in the king's Instructions of June, 1686; but James, her "Defender of the Faith," now thought chiefly of subverting the English Church establishment. Neither did he require any schoolmaster to be licensed by the Bishop of London or the Archbishop of Canterbury, as formerly. The injunction, however, was renewed, that no press be used, nor book be printed, without the governor's license. The English Royal African Company was to be encouraged, and "ill masters" were to be restrained from inhuman severity toward their slaves, while the conversion of negroes and Indians to Christianity was to be promoted. The recent Instructions to Dongan respecting the Iroquois were reiterated, and Andros was directed to inform the Governor of Canada that the King of England had resolved to own the Five Nations as his subjects, and "to protect them as such." At the same time, he was to observe the agreement for preventing hostilities in America, and "entertain a good correspondence" with the French officers there.*

The Church of England not regarded in Andros's instructions.

Negroes and Indians to be converted.

The Iroquois to be protected as English subjects.

Such were the prominent directions of James for the government of his New England dominion. As its territory was now so vast, it was necessary that some one should be appointed to act as chief executive officer under Andros in case of his absence, and to take his place in case of his death. Captain Francis Nicholson, who commanded one of the companies of regular soldiers at Boston, was accordingly commissioned to be the king's "Lieutenant Governor of New England, with directions to observe such orders as he shall receive" from its chief governor. To Andros's present salary of twelve hundred pounds, two hundred were added out of the six hundred allowed to Dongan, of which the remaining four hundred were assigned to Nicholson as lieutenant governor. No place was fixed by the king as the "Seat of Government" of his dominion. It was necessarily transitory. It might be at Boston, or New York, or elsewhere, at the discretion of Andros, who, with

20 April. Francis Nicholson lieutenant governor.

The New England seat of government transitory.

* Col. Doc., iii., 372, 375, 427, 503, 504, 543–549; Mass. H. S. Coll., xxvii., 148; *ante*, 450, 451, 453–456, 490–494.

a majority of his counselors, could make laws whenever and wherever they pleased.*

CHAP. X.

1688.

22 April.

The king notifies Dongan.

These arrangements were notified to Dongan by James, who signified his pleasure that, on the arrival of Andros at New York, the seal and the records of that province must be delivered to him, and that its colonial governor should return to England, and expect marks of royal "entire satisfaction" about his services in the most important British possession in America.†

Dongan pledges his estate for New York.

Ignorant of these sweeping changes which his sovereign was directing at Whitehall, Dongan had pledged his personal credit, and even mortgaged his farm on Staten Island, to secure upward of two thousand pounds which he had borrowed from Robert Livingston to meet the expenses of the Albany expedition. The provincial debt was so heavy that the governor had been obliged to call on Pennsylvania, Maryland, Virginia, and New Jersey to assist New York with ready money.‡

30 March.

Little aid to New York from the other colonies.

But little aid came from abroad. Andros was required by the king to assist New York with the men, but not the money, of New England. In answer to Dongan's appeal, Pennsylvania withheld and Maryland refused any help. Virginia was not disposed to contribute; but Lord Howard, of Effingham, her governor, who had witnessed Dongan's zeal in Indian affairs, sent him five hundred pounds. New Jersey, anxious to stand well with the king, voted a tax for the benefit of New York, which, however, does not appear to have been paid.§

14 May.

When the accounts of the Albany expedition were at last made up, it was found that the province was so much in debt that a new levy of money was necessary. Dongan and his Council accordingly passed an act to raise two thousand five hundred and fifty-six pounds and four shillings in the several counties, according to a fixed rate. This tax was directed to be paid to Matthew Plowman, the king's new

3 May.

17 May.

New tax levied by Dongan and his council.

* Col. Doc., iii., 374, 537, 542; iv., 263; Hutch. Mass., i., 362, Coll., 559; Palfrey, iii., 561, 562; *ante*, 451.

† Col. Doc., iii., 550; Council Min., v., 237; N. Y. H. S. Coll., iii., 353; Hutch. Coll., 564; Chalmers, i., 590.

‡ Col. Doc., iii., 511; iv., 133, 134, 137; Hist. Mag., v., 184; Doc. Hist., i., 167, 168; Council Min., v., 222, 229; Secret Services Ch. II. and James II., 195; *ante*, 487, 496.

§ Col. Doc., iii., 566, 619, 620; Doc. Hist., i., 167; ii., 25; Penn. Arch., i., 104, 105; Col. Rec., i., 217; Proud, i., 338; Burk, ii., 301, 302, 303; Leaming and Spicer, 306–309; Whitehead, 113, 120, 121; Chalmers's Ann., i., 466, 629; *ante*, 396.

CHAP. X.

1688.

collector, at the custom-house in New York before the next November.*

4 April.

Interesting local events had meanwhile occurred. The minister, elders, and deacons of the metropolitan ancient Dutch Church prayed Dongan that, as they wished to build their new church outside the fort, as had been contemplated in 1680, the governor would establish them as "a body corporate and ecclesiastic, and thereby qualified persons, capable in law to have, hold, and enjoy lands and tenements, &c., under the name and style of *the Minister or Ministers, Elders and Deacons of the Dutch Reformed Church in New York.*" But years rolled on before a successor of Dongan granted the desired patent to this venerable church of Dutch Reformed Christians in North America.†

The New York Reformed Dutch Church asks to be incorporated.

30 April. 6 May. 19 May. 30 May.

Word having come from Albany that the French were again troublesome, the Council resolved that the governor should hasten there again, and soldiers be sent up the river to observe their enemy. Dongan accordingly commissioned his counselors, Van Cortlandt, Phillipse, and Bayard, to manage provincial affairs during his absence from the metropolis, and gave them full instructions how to act as his temporary representatives.‡

Dongan goes again to Albany.

11 June.

Intelligence of the negotiations at London reached Dongan at Albany, who informed Denonville that the King of England's letter to him of 22d January ought to end their disputes. A pleasant correspondence followed. The Iroquois were directed by the Governor of New York to withdraw from Canada, and Mademoiselle D'Allonne, who had been taken prisoner at Cataracouy, was sent, with several

Dongan's correspondence with Denonville.

$\frac{17}{27}$ July.

* Council Min., v., 229, 230, 234; Doc. Hist., i., 167, 168; Council Journals, i., Int., xxi., xxii.; *ante*, 492.

† On the 12th of December, 1686, Domine Selyns and the elders and deacons of the Dutch Church of the city of New York represented to the mayor and aldermen that they were willing to build their new church as soon as a convenient place and necessary materials should be provided, and prayed that their worships would grant them "a certain vacant piece of ground, formerly designated for that purpose, lying within this city, or any other convenient place," and also intercede with the governor to give them "a parcel of clipstone from the old fortifications." The Dutch Church was built in Garden Street in 1693, and its officers were made the first religious corporation in New York by Governor Fletcher in 1696. *Ante*, 331, 464, 465; Col. Doc., iii., 315, 415, 717; Doc. Hist., iii., 249, 265, 305; Records of N. Y. R. D. C., Liber A., 40, 161, 169, 199; Patents, vii., 27–36; Smith, i., 301, 302; Murphy's Anthology, 125, 126; Note F., Appendix, p. 661, 662, *post*.

‡ Council Min., v., 229, 231, 235; Col. MSS., xxxv., 148–163, 171; Commissions, i., 76; *ante*, 487. In June, after Dongan went to Albany, John Knight, who was about to return to England, delivered the New York records in his possession, as deputy secretary, to Van Cortlandt, Phillipse, and Bayard. Col. Doc., iii., 407; Col. MSS., xxxv., 162; *ante*, 468, 484.

others, from Albany to Montreal. But the French were desired to evacuate Niagara.*

Niagara.

The French did evacuate Niagara not long afterward. Louis would not admit the pretension of James that the Iroquois were British subjects. Denonville was therefore directed to send all the information he could to Paris respecting the French claim to Hudson's Bay, the Iroquois country, and "the Southern portion of Acadia, from Penobscot to the River Kinnebec;" and Louis declared his intention of appropriating all the unoccupied American territory necessary for the maintenance of Canadian trade. Seignelay also wrote that the exchange or gaining of New York was not possible at present, yet its inhabitants must be prevented from "thwarting the trade of the French." As the king must "chastise the Iroquois," he would send fresh European soldiers to attack the Mohawks and Onondagas who should winter in their country. Forts Niagara and Frontenac must be maintained, and new posts established at Sodus Bay and Salmon River, on Lake Ontario, as well as at the southern end of Lake Champlain, "towards the Mohawks," which would be "at the head of the whole." More Iroquois prisoners should be sent to France, "as it is certain that those Indians, who are vigorous and accustomed to hardship, can serve usefully on board his Majesty's galleys."†

8 March.

8 March. New York, Canada, and the Iroquois.

This masterly European scheme of Louis was not to be accomplished. Irritated at the deportation of their brethren to France, the Iroquois harassed the Canadians all the winter. Denonville sent re-enforcements to Niagara, where Millet had succeeded Lamberville as chaplain, which were attacked by the New York Indians, who then besieged Fort Chambly. Some Onondaga captives were restored; and Lamberville, at Cataracouy, persuaded the Oneidas, Onondagas, and Cayugas to send deputies to Montreal. Six hundred warriors, headed by Haaskouan, or Outreouati, the Onondaga whom the French called "Grande-gueule," then descended the Saint Lawrence to the Lake Saint Francis, where they were joined by six hundred more. There the savage force halted, while Grande-gueule, with a few others, went

The Iroquois menace Montreal.

* Col. Doc., iii., 556, 563, 564; ix., 391; Col. MSS., xxxv., 160; Quebec MSS. (ii.), v., 445, 452, 455, 459, 460, 464, 502; Charlevoix, ii., 374; Garneau, i., 267, 268; *ante*, 488, 494.

† Col. Doc., ix., 371–377; *ante*, 501.

CHAP. X. 1688. Grandegueule and Denonville.

down to Montreal. Denonville gave them instant audience. Speaking for the Cayugas, Onondagas, and Oneidas, their orator set forth the weakness of the French, and the ease with which the Iroquois could drive them out of Canada. Learning, he said, "that our warriors had resolved to come and burn your forts, and houses, and granges, and corn, so that after famishing you, they could have you an easy prey, I begged so strongly in your favor, that I have got leave to warn Onnontio that he can escape this evil by accepting peace on the terms proposed by Corlaer."*

Montreal dismayed.

These haughty words from the glib Onondaga who had humbled De la Barre at La Famine four years before, and the twelve hundred Iroquois warriors at the Lake Saint Francis, dismayed all hearts at Montreal. News had meanwhile come that nearly all the French left at Niagara the year before had died. Fort Frontenac was invested by the Iroquois, while from the Sorel River to Montreal scarcely a Canadian could venture out of doors. So Denonville agreed to a peace, including the Western savages, and the Mohawks and Senecas, provided he could send supplies to Cataracouy. He also promised to solicit the return of their brethren now in the galleys at Marseilles. The truce was concluded "on the spot," and the Iroquois deputies left hostages to ratify it "at the wane of the August moon."†

8 June. Denonville makes peace with the Iroquois.

15 June. The Iroquois assert their independence of France and England.

At Montreal, the Oneidas, Onondagas, and Cayugas rejected Dongan's assumption that they were British subjects. They declared that his claim "was not true; that they had always resisted his pretensions, and wished only to be friends of the French and English equally, without either the one or the other being their masters; because they held their country directly of God, and had never been conquered in war, neither by the French nor the English; and that their intention was only to observe a perfect neutrality." Thus, while Louis and James were wrangling about American sovereignty, the Iroquois asserted their independence of both, and preserved Northern New York, as their own native land, from annexation to Canada.‡

* La Potherie, ii., 221–227; iii., 58; Col. Doc., iv., 348; ix., 243, 247, 386, 387, 388, 390, 402; Charlevoix, 369–371, 373; Bancroft, ii., 424; Garneau, i., 268; *ante*, 403, 404, 481.

† Col. Doc., ix., 339, 391, 395, 396; Charlevoix, ii., 364, 372–374; Colden, i., 88; Garneau, i., 268; *ante*, 405, 481. With truly British contempt for even French idioms, Smith, i., 87, twists the "*sur le champ*" of Charlevoix into "in the field!"

‡ Col. Doc., ix., 384–386; Bancroft, ii., 424.

Soon afterward, the French captives whom Dongan had sent from Albany reached Montreal. In acknowledging his courtesy, Denonville said that, as soon as he could, he would withdraw the garrison at Niagara, "in order to contribute to a permanent peace." CHAP. X. 1688. July. $\frac{10}{20}$ Aug.

When Denonville's orders tardily reached Des Bergères at Niagara, he assembled the officers and made a formal record of the condition of the fort. A large wooden cross, eighteen feet high, with an appropriate inscription, which Millet had solemnly blessed on the last Good Friday, was left standing in the middle of the square. The cabins and quarters were also preserved entire, "for the purpose of maintaining the possession his Majesty and the French have for a long time had in this Niagara district." The garrison then evacuated the fort, and came down Lake Ontario to Cataracouy in the bark "la Generale."* 6 July. The French fort at Niagara demolished. $\frac{5}{15}$ Sept.

This abandonment of Niagara by the French was chiefly owing to the policy and the firmness of Dongan.† But before the event was accomplished, his own authority over New York had ceased. On his return from Albany, Dongan received the king's letter of the 22d of April, requiring him to surrender the government of New York to Andros on his arrival there. The unwelcome missive was read in Council, and "ordered to be recorded amongst the records of the Province of New York." And now all was agog. The Long Island Quakers set forth to the expiring government all the losses they had suffered for not training and not paying town-rates according to law; but they got no redress. The act which, in obedience to the king's desire, had been ordered to be engrossed in May, for the education of Indian slaves and negroes in the Christian faith, was either forgotten or dropped. But it was resolved in Council "that all Indian Slaves within this Province, subjects to the King of Spain, that can give an account of their Christian faith, and say the Lord's prayer, be forthwith set at liberty, and sent home by the first conveyance, and likewise them that shall hereafter come to the Province." This was only confirming the Council's action in the previous October. 28 July. Dongan prepares to give up his government to Andros. Quakers. Negroes. July 30. Indian slaves.

* Col. Doc., iii., 556; ix., 386–388, 391, 396; Doc. Hist., i., 168, 169; Col. MSS., xxxv., 160; Quebec MSS., v. (ii.), 460, 464, 502; La Hontan, i., 131, 132; Charlevoix, ii., 357, 364, 372, 374.

† Palmer, in his Impartial Account, p. 21, erroneously attributes the demolition of Niagara to the action of Andros under his new commission. Compare Col. Doc., iii., 556, 557.

1688.
30 July.

Robert Allison, who had purchased an Indian slave at Honduras, and brought him to New York, asked that he might retain him in bondage there; but his petition was rejected. As the administration was soon to be in other hands, Dongan and his Council, "for the ease of this, his Majesty's Province, which it is his Majesty's pleasure should be an-

30 July.
Tax law suspended.

nexed to his Government of New England, Ordered that all further proceedings towards the levying the late tax and imposition of £2555, 6, to be paid by the first day of November next, do cease, and it is hereby suspended 'till further order, and that the sheriffs of the respective counties have notice given them accordingly." The last law passed by

2 August.
Shoemakers not to tan hides.

Dongan was "to prohibit shoemakers from using the mystery of tanning hides," when Counselors Brockholls, Baxter, Phillipse, Van Cortlandt, and Bayard were present. The

Huntington patent.

same day the last New York patent under her recent provincial seal from James the Second was issued by Dongan to the town of Huntington.*

In the mean time Andros had been afflicted by the death

22 Jan.

of his wife at Boston, where she was buried with great

10 Feb.

pomp. Soon afterward he went to New Hampshire and

April.
Andros at Pemaquid.

Maine, where his presence was required. At Pemaquid he refreshed himself "with sheep and soles," and then went, in the Rose frigate, to the French settlement at Penobscot. Learning his approach, Castin retired, leaving his house shut. Andros respected the baron's altar and emblems of his Roman faith, but he seized his other property, and sent it to Pemaquid for condemnation, on the charge of illegal trading within the British dominions, which were claimed to extend as far east as the Saint Croix River. On his return to Pemaquid, Andros was joined by Secretary Randolph, and a conference was held with the neighboring Indian sachems, who were told not to fear the French, and promised the protection of the English. The conduct of Palmer and West in 1686 was thought by Randolph to be "as arbitrary as the Great Turke." Perhaps Randolph's criticism was deserved, yet not so much because Dongan's

* Col. Doc., iii., 374, 427, 550; iv., 510, 511; Council Min., v., 222, 224, 237, 238, 239; Col. MSS., xxxiv., 77, 78; xxxv., 168, 169; Doc. Hist., i., 167, 168; iii., 608, 609; Council Jour., i., Int., xxi., xxii., xxiii.; N. Y. H. S. Coll., iii., 353; Patents, v., 338–349; Anderson's Col. Ch., ii., 303, 344; Evelyn, ii., 245; Wood's Long Island, 103, 104; Thompson, i., 468; *ante*, 330, 331, 434, 455, 486. There are no regular New York Council Minutes in the secretary's office at Albany between 2 August, 1688, and 19 March, 1691.

CHAP. X.

1688.

10 March.

21 June. Andros returns to Boston.

Graham and Jamison favored by Andros.

Palmer made a New England judge.

late agents had been "arbitrary," as because they had ventured "to tear all in pieces that was settled and granted at Pemaquid by Sir Edmund" in 1677, when he was Governor of New York. But the jealousy of Dongan, which Andros continually manifested, was soon appeased. News came from Boston that the king had determined to add New York and New Jersey to Andros's present government. Fort Charles, at Pemaquid, was ordered to be repaired, and its command was intrusted to Ensign Joshua Pipon. Andros then hastened back to Boston to receive his new commission, for the arrival of which he waited "in great expectation." Meanwhile James Graham, who had been his fellow-passenger from England in 1678, and seems to have preferred him to Dongan, had resigned his New York appointments and hurried eastward, where he was made Attorney General of New England in place of Farewell. Graham appears to have been assisted in his new office by David Jamison, the Scotch "sweet singer," who had given up his Latin school in New York, and desired advancement under the rising sun. John West was already at Boston as Randolph's deputy. John Palmer, one of the judges of New York, whom Dongan had sent to London with his dispatches in September, 1687, now returned to New England, of which he had been named a counselor by the king. As the dominion was enlarged by the annexation of New York, Andros appointed Palmer to be one of the judges of its Superior Court, along with Dudley, Stoughton, and Bulkley. And now the governor was "safe in his New York confidents, all others being strangers to his Councill." Yet so far from being, as stigmatized by coarse Boston partisans, "a crew of abject persons," the gentlemen who came from New York were "well known to have lived there for a long time in esteem and reputation—enough to merit a better Epethite of all good and honest men."*

19 July.

When Andros's vice-regal commission reached Boston, it was proclaimed from the town-house balcony, and Captain

* Col. Doc., iii., 428, 429, 430, 450, 513, 515, 551, 567, 571, 657, 662, 663; iv., 282, 476; v., 478; ix., 263, 265, 380, 396; Charlevoix, ii., 360, 387; Col. Rec. Conn., iii., 437–446; Hutch. Mass., i., 364, 370, 371, 381; Coll., 557–565; Adlard's Sutton Dudleys, 77; Palmer's Impartial Account, 22; Force's Tracts, iv., No. 9, p. 8, 9, 16, 18, 21, 22, 37, 40, 53, 58; No. 10, p. 8; Mather, Mag., ii., 586; Williamson, i., 586–588; Belknap, i., 196; Palfrey, iii., 526, 533, 549, 552, 558–560, 562; Mass. H. S. Coll., xxvii., 180; xxxv., 190; R. I. Rec., iii., 257; Andros Tracts (Prince Soc.) i., 13, 43, 114; *ante*, 310, 318, 407, 444, 445, 467, 468, 469, 484.

CHAP. X. 1688. 31 July. Andros goes to New York.

Francis Nicholson was installed as Lieutenant Governor of the dominion. A fortnight afterward the governor general set out for New York, attended by Mason, Dudley, Usher, Randolph, and Walley, of his Council, and deputy Secretary West. Nicholson accompanied his chief as far as New London, whence he was sent back to Boston, because the Indians were making trouble near Springfield. On his way Andros was joined by Counselors Clarke, Newberry, Smith, Winthrop, and Allyn.*

11 August. Andros in the metropolis.

On Saturday, the eleventh of August, the governor general reached the metropolis, where he was received by Colonel Bayard's regiment of foot and a troop of horse. The king's new commission was read in Fort James, and then published at the City Hall. Immediately afterward, Andros sent for and received from Dongan the almost virgin seal of the late government of New York, "which was defaced and broaken in Council," according to the king's Instructions. In its stead, the great seal of New England was thenceforth to be used. A proclamation was at once issued continuing all persons not removed by order of the king in their offices, and directing taxes to be continued. Thus Andros began his second government of New York. He had left it seven years before to be justified with the Duke of York. In the interval, the province had gained and had lost a popular assembly. Her old governor now revisited familiar scenes to assume almost imperial authority as the viceroy of James the Second.†

The seal of New York broken. 11 August.

A few days afterward the governor general went over to New Jersey, with several of his Council, and at Elizabethtown published his commission, as well as the proclamation for continuing officers and the revenue. Similar ceremonies were observed at Burlington. Andrew Hamilton and others were appointed justices of the peace by Andros under the great seal of the dominion. It was remarked that the "out places" of both East and West Jersey were "very thinly inhabited," but that "all shewed their great satisfaction in being under his Majestie's immediate government."‡

15 August. 18 August. 25 August. New Jersey reduced.

* Col. Doc., iii., 550, 557, 567, 568; ix., 392; Hutch. Mass., i., 371; Coll., 566; Col. Rec. Conn., iii., 447; Barry, i., 496; Bancroft, ii., 431; Charlevoix, ii., 382.

† Col. Doc., iii., 283, 286, 316, 427, 546, 550, 554, 567, 722; Min. of C. C., i., 329, 330; Dunlap, ii., App. cxxxv; *ante*, 345, 451, 491, 503.

‡ Col. Doc., iii., 553, 554, 567; Chalmers, i., 590, 622; Smith's N. J., 204, 206, 568; Gor-

If the people of New Jersey were satisfied with the change which brought them directly under the government of their king, the people of New York were not generally pleased that their province should lose its individuality, and be consolidated with New England. It was true that their old governor, Andros, whom many preferred to Dongan, had come back to them. But Andros's return was accompanied with disagreeable circumstances. Geographically, politically, and socially, New York was unlike any other British possession in North America. For half a century before her conquest she had remained a distinct territory of the Dutch Republic, lying between the Puritan colonies of England at the east, and the Episcopalian and Roman Catholic colonies of England at the south. For more than that period her relations with the French in Canada and the savages within her own borders had required peculiar skill in their management. Up to this time New York had always been differently governed from any other British American colony. She had never been a chartered or a corporate government under Dutch or English authority. Her eclectic people never wished to be ruled by incorporated oligarchies like those in New England. What they desired, and what, for a season, they had enjoyed, was a "Charter of Liberties," securing to every inhabitant a share in local legislation, freedom of conscience, and equality of all modes of Christianity. While a Dutch province, New York, with the comprehensive liberality of her fatherland, had invited strangers of every race and creed to nestle among her own early colonists. The invitation had been greedily accepted. For these and other reasons, her people—especially those of Batavian origin—cherished a magnanimous "State pride," not surpassed by that professed in any of the colonies by which she was surrounded. She had desired the annexation of Connecticut and the Jerseys because they had belonged to her ancient territory, and because their restoration would only make her what she was intended to be by the patent which Charles the Second had granted to the Duke of York. But New York did not wish

Situation of New York.

New York dislikes annexation to New England.

don, 53; Bancroft, ii., 413, 431; Whitehead's E. J., 113, 121. The original great seal to Hamilton's commission still exists; Index N. J. Col. Doc., 13. It is difficult to understand what Palfrey, iii., 562, means by saying that "*New York and New Jersey had never before had what might seem a stable government of any kind.*"

CHAP. X. 1688.

to be united with Massachusetts, which—although included within the Dutch "New Netherland" of 1614, six years before the "New England" of James the First—had never been in her actual possession, and, if now joined to her, might be "ruinous and destructive." It is not surprising that, under these circumstances, the people of New York felt themselves to be in an "unmerited state of degradation," which they contemplated with "just dissatisfaction." Their metropolitan city, knowing that it had become "the envy of its adjacent neighbors, who did not cease by all their little artifices to interrupt its trade," especially lamented "that unhappy annexation to New England."*

New Yorkers indignant.

Peculiar reasons against the annexation of New York to New England.

Besides these political considerations were some of another character. The colonists at the eastern end of Long Island, who had chiefly come from New England, and who wished to barter their oil and other commodities at Boston rather than New York, were perhaps gratified at the change which brought them back to old sympathies. But the ancient Dutch possessors of New Netherland and their descendants had no reason to like most of the New England colonists or their characteristics. If they liked any, they preferred the people of tolerant Rhode Island, whom almost all other New Englanders disliked. The genial Episcopalians of Virginia and the liberal Roman Catholics of Maryland were nearer the hearts of the New York Dutch-English Calvinists than were the sour Puritans of Massachusetts, whose predecessors would not be comforted in Holland by the calm pleasures of a Leyden Sunday. On the American side of the Atlantic these antipathies deepened. Rivals and antagonists from the start, New York and Massachusetts could not be sympathetic. The two colonies differed essentially. The oldest, Dutch one, was always grand, inviting, and magnanimous:—the later, English one, was ever sectional, narrow, and selfish. The cardinal principle of New York was comprehensive liberality:—that of Massachusetts, Procrustean rigor. Both erred in persecuting noisy Quakers. But the history of the old Dutch province in North America is not marred by the despotic self-righteousness which deforms the annals of the "Bay

New York and Massachusetts very different.

* Col. Doc., iii., 576, 722, 795, 799; Chalmers's Pol. Ann., i., 590; ii., 29; Rev. Col., i., 212; Min. of N. Y. C. C., ii., 93-96; Dunlap, ii., App. cxli.; *ante*, vol. i., 62-65, 95, 96; ii., 500.

State." So it was natural that genial New York did not like too intimate an association with her surly and grasping eastern neighbor. She had acquiesced in the conquest which reduced her, in 1664, under the dominion of Charles the Second and the Duke of York, but she could never have submitted to the selfish and arrogant colonists who so long and so vainly coveted her territory. It was inevitable that New York should consider her compulsory union with Massachusetts, by order of their common sovereign, "an abhorred connection."*

CHAP. X.

1688.

Yet, if the people of New York generally felt it a "degradation" for their province to be annexed to New England, there were some who at first enjoyed a vainglory. The resident counselors Brockholls, Phillipse, Bayard, and Van Cortlandt found their official importance rather increased than diminished by the change. If the New England counselors could now vote on the affairs of New York, the New York counselors could likewise vote on the affairs of New England. This they were soon called upon to do. At a Council held at New York, a law to regulate the carrying of passengers in ships and vessels, which Andros could not pass at Boston because so many counselors there "strenuously opposed" it, was readily enacted. It was also ordered that the New York revenue act of the seventh of May, which Dongan and his Council had suspended on the thirtieth of July, should "be fully and duly executed."†

29 August. Laws passed at New York.

29 August.

Some of the Protestants in New York, who had been troubled at observing Papists settling themselves in the province "under the smiles" of Dongan, appear to have rejoiced in the return of their old governor, Andros. The Dutch Domine Selyns informed the classis of Amsterdam that "Sir Edmund Andros, Governor at Boston and the like, and now stepped into this Government of New York and Jersey—as such having charge from Canada to Pennsylvania—is of the Church of England; and understanding and

10 Oct. Domine Selyns's opinion of Andros.

* Col. Doc., iii., 391, 402, 576, 797, 799; Chalmers's Rev. Col., i., 212.

† Col. Rec. Conn., iii., 447, 448; Doc. Hist., ii., 45; Col. Doc., iii., 567, 568; Rev. in N. E. Just, in Force's Tracts, iv., No. 9, 13, 55; Palfrey, iii., 551, 562; *ante*, 510. The counselors present on this occasion were Dudley, Usher, and Randolph, of Massachusetts; Mason, of New Hampshire; Walley, of Plymouth; Clarke, Newberry, and Smith, of Rhode Island; Winthrop and Allyn, of Connecticut; Brockholls, Phillipse, Baxter, Van Cortlandt, Younge, and Bayard, of New York; in all sixteen, besides the governor. John West acted as deputy secretary.

CHAP. X. 1688. speaking the Low Dutch and French, he attends mine and Mr. Daillé's preaching." Yet no danger could arise from the few Roman Catholics who assembled to worship their creator with Dongan and others in a small chamber in Fort James. Even the Puritan Hinckley, of Plymouth, testified that the late Governor of New York showed "himself of a noble, praiseworthy mind and spirit; taking care that all the people in each town do their duty in maintaining the minister of the place, though himself of a differing opinion from their way."*

Hinckley's opinion of Dongan.

An event had occurred, however, which gave uneasiness to the Dutch people of New York. For almost half a generation they had looked with hope to the time when the wife of the Prince of Orange—the stadtholder of their fatherland, and their own chief magistrate fourteen years before—would become the Queen of England. Joyfully would they have mingled cries of "ORANJE BOVEN" with "*Long live the Queen.*" But divine Providence bid them wait. James the Second had married a Roman Catholic second wife, who, after due proclamation of her condition, bore him a son on the tenth of June, 1688. That son was at once declared Prince of Wales, and, if all went regularly on, he would become King of England on the death of his father. The news came from the Privy Council to Boston, with directions for Andros "to appoint such days, as well for a solemn thanksgiving to Almighty God for this inestimable blessing, as for such other expressions of public rejoicings suitable to this great occasion," as he should judge fit. Nicholson sent "the happy news" by express to his chief at New York, where, the same evening, it "was solemnized with all demonstrations of joy and gladness for so great a blessing." The hilarity waxed so boisterous that the Dutch Mayor Van Cortlandt "sacrificed his hat, peruke, &c." This exuberant manifestation of loyalty was afterward objected against the genial magistrate when the reminiscence was very inconvenient. The next day, Andros, with the advice of his Council, issued his proclamation for a general thanksgiving, "to be observed within the City of New York

10 June. Birth of the Prince of Wales.

23 August. Rejoicings in New York.

24 August.

* Chalmers's Ann., i., 590; Smith, i., 90; Council Min., vi., 17; Doc. Hist., ii., 14, 17; iii., 73; Bayley's Sketch, 19–22; Mass. H. S. Coll., xxxv., 161, 180; MSS. letter of Selyns to Classis, 10 October, 1688; *ante*, 487.

and dependencies on Sunday the Second day of September next coming, and fourteen days after in all other parts of this Dominion." At this time New York was undoubtedly the "seat of Government" of James the Second's "Dominion of New England."*

Indian affairs now required the governor's careful attention. The day he reached New York, he announced his arrival to Denonville, and claiming the Five Nations as British subjects, in obedience to his Instructions, requested that they should not be injured by the French. Word soon afterward came "that all was not well" with the Iroquois, and it was resolved that Andros should go to Albany. This he did, accompanied by Counselors Baxter, Mason, Van Cortlandt, and others, in a sloop, which also conveyed fifty soldiers and ammunition to supply the fort. At Albany he was joined by Nicholson, whom he had summoned from Boston, and who came overland by way of Springfield.†

$\frac{11}{21}$ Aug.

30 August. Andros at Albany.

The Five Nations, warned by "Arie," or Viele, sent delegates, who had a stately interview with Andros in the town-house of Albany. Sindacksegie, the Mohawk orator, in the name of the Five Nations, welcomed their "Brother Corlaer" as "the same person which did us the kindness to be called Corlaer when you was Governor formerly." The next day Andros named the Iroquois "Children," as Dongan had, and told them that they "need have no other regard to the French, nor hearken to them, than, as they are our friends, to do them no harm." But they should be on their guard, and call back those of their nations who had gone to settle near Montreal; and "'twill be your own faults if you do not eat, drink, and sleep in safety." Another conference followed, when the Mohawks, dropping the "Brother," said, "Corlaer, we are exceeding glad to see you here, who was formerly in Tionondoge, our third Castle; and are assured of your good inclinations towards us, because we have experienced your goodness heretofore. For you was pleased to accept the name of a man that was of good dis-

18 Sept.

19 Sept. Andros calls the Iroquois "Children."

20 Sept.

* Col. Doc., iii., 554, 655; Council Min., v., 223; Min. of N. Y. Com. Council, i., 330; Dunlap, ii., App. cxxxvi.; N. Y. H. S. Coll., iii., 353 (1868), 399; Penn. Arch., i., 106; Col. Rec. Conn., iii., 443; Palfrey, iii., 561, 562; Kennett, iii., 484; *ante*, 203, 248, 315, 504.

† Col. Doc., iii., 548, 553, 554, 555, 556, 562, 563, 569, 722; ix., 394; Quebec MSS. (ii.), v., 502. Andros's letter of 11 August was carried to Canada by John Smith, "the quaker from Albany." Col. Doc., iii., 566; Force's Tracts, iv., No. 9, p. 59; Andros Tracts, i., 146; La Hontan, i. 125; Charlevoix, i., 386.

CHAP. X. positions and esteemed deare amongst us, to wit, *The old Corlaer.*" They promised to have no correspondence with

1688. The old Corlaer. the French, but would treat them as friends, as Andros had proposed. Dongan had asked them about places for forts,

Salmon River. and they had named Salmon River, or the Oswego, and they understood that he would build a fort "at the end of Cor-

Ticonderoga. laer's Lake [Champlain] at a place called Onjadarakté, [Ticonderoga] and put great guns in the same." But they did

The Mohawks wish to remain "Brethren." not insist on this being done. "Let the old covenant that was made with our ancestors be kept firm. Then we were called Brethren, and that was also well kept; therefore let that of Brethren continue, without any alteration." Some of the Iroquois warriors, "whose names are known like the Sun," had not yet been sent back from France; nevertheless, "we keep to that which was done by the two great Kings beyond the Seas." But a Cayuga, speaking for that nation and the Oneidas, Onondagas, and Senecas, address-

The Western Iroquois accept the name of "Children." ed Andros as "Father Corlaer," and accepted "the name of Children." Only they desired the return of their twenty-eight countrymen, prisoners in France. "The Governor of Canada," they said, "is pleasant with his eye, and speaks fair with his lips; but his heart is corrupt, and we find that the old covenant made with this government has been kept

Andros's answer. inviolated." Andros answered these several speeches adroitly:—"You take notice of the word Brethren, and Children;—But leave it to me:—They are both words of relation and friendship; but Children the nearer." On the following

21 Sept. day, the conference with the Five Nations was ended by Andros promising them to do all he could to get back their

19/29 Sept. "people that were carried beyond sea." He also wrote to Denonville, charging him with being the author of the late murders by the Canadian savages near Springfield and Northfield, and hoping that the French had evacuated Niagara. This last mentioned step, as has been seen, had already been taken, chiefly at Dongan's solicitation.*

* La Hontan, i., 125; Charlevoix, ii., 386; Col. Doc., iii., 443, 475, 485, 535, 557–562, 568, 775; ix., 392, 393, 402; Col. MSS., xxxv., 172–181; Colden, i., 105, 106, 132; Quebec MSS. (ii.), v., 507; Chalmers's Ann., i., 428; Col. Rec. Conn., iii., 448, 449; *ante*, vol. i., 18, 42, 55, 67, 88, 422; vol. ii., 287, 483, 495, 509. Some of the Massachusetts Puritans objected against Andros in 1691 that he did not keep the Iroquois in hostility to the French, because "it was very advantageous to the English interest to have it so;" and they charged that the peace which he made those savages promise at Albany strengthened the French and weakened the English: Rev. in N. E. Justified, in Force's Tracts, iv., No. 9, 40, 41; Andros Tracts, i., 118; ii., 207, 218; Col. Doc., iii., 650, 651.

Leaving Baxter in command of Fort Albany, with Thomas Sharpe as his lieutenant, and a company of soldiers, Andros returned to New York. On his way down the Hudson he had an interview with the Esopus and other savages, whom he admonished to be at peace with the neighboring Christians. At Kingston, Colonel Robert Mason, of New Hampshire, one of the Council who had accompanied Andros, died, and was buried, in his fifty-ninth year.* CHAP. X. 1688.

Denonville had meanwhile waited in vain at Montreal until after the August moon had waned for the promised return of the Iroquois delegates. These had been chosen at Onondaga, and were about setting out, when Viele summoned the Five Nations to meet Andros at Albany. This they did, as has been seen. But Dekanesora, or Teganissoren, the Onondaga chief, who seemed to have succeeded Garakontié as the most unwavering Iroquois friend of the French, went on with a small party to meet Denonville, according to promise, at Montreal. When they reached La Famine, or Salmon River, on Lake Ontario, they were surprised and captured by a band of Hurons, led by their chief Adario, or Kondiaronk, whom the French called "The Rat." He was the bravest, most subtile, and most accomplished savage they had ever known in Canada, and well deserved to be called "The Machiavel of the Forests." He had come down from Michilimackinac to join the French in their war against the Iroquois, upon condition that these common enemies should be exterminated. At Fort Frontenac Adario learned that Denonville had just made a peace with them, and was awaiting at Montreal the return of their ratifying deputies. Seeing that his own nation had been betrayed, the wily Huron concealed his chagrin, and pretended to return home. But from Cataracouy he quietly went across Lake Ontario to La Famine, by which route he knew that the Onondagas must go to Montreal. After lying in wait for several days, the Rat captured the astonished Iroquois ambassadors, and told them that he had done so by order of Denonville. The artifice was worthy of the most refined European policy in wickedness. Both parties protested against the supposed double treachery of Onnon-

Dekanesora on his way to Montreal.

The Rat.

The Iroquois delegates captured by Adario.

* Col. Doc., iii., 568, 593, 640; iv., 202; Doc. Hist., ii., 57, 244; Hutch., i., 365; Belknap, i., 191.

CHAP. X. 1668. tio. Addressing Dekanesora and his companions, Adario said, "Go, my brethren; I untie your hands, and send you home again, although our nation is at war with yours. It is the French governor who has made me commit an act so black that I shall never be consoled until the Five Nations have taken a just vengeance." The false Huron's words were uttered on the very spot where the Onondaga Grande-gueule had humbled De la Barre four years before. Like his then, they served their turn now. Each savage party returned to its own home; and, full of anxiety at the mysterious absence of the delegates he had chafed for so vainly, Denonville went down the chilly Saint Lawrence to Quebec.*

Denonville baffled.

$\frac{1}{10}$ Oct.

$\frac{13}{23}$ Oct. From Quebec the Canadian governor wrote to Andros, in reply to his letters from New York and Albany, alluding spitefully to Dongan; announcing the withdrawal of the French garrison at Niagara, and complaining of the recent violence offered by the English to Castin at Penobscot, for which satisfaction was required. But the birth of the Prince of Wales had been the signal for rejoicing throughout "the whole country of Canada." In his dispatches to Seignelay, Denonville attributed the safety of New France "to God alone." He therefore sent Callières to France, that he might explain matters more fully. A treaty should be made between England and France, by which the Iroquois should be "ceded" to one or the other European power. "But," Denonville added, "in order to make peace, it will be necessary to return to Canada the Iroquois who have been sent to the galleys;" and proposed that they should "be dressed somewhat decently."†

10 August.

Callières sent to France.

On his return from Albany and Kingston, Andros learned that the savages in Maine had been disorderly near Casco Bay, and that men had been raised in Boston and sent

Indian troubles.

* Col. Doc., ix., 178, 181, 183, 189, 192, 227, 391, 393, 394, 402, 404, 465; La Hontan, i., 117, 125, 189–192; Charlevoix, ii., 383–386; Colden, i., 88, 89, 90; Smith, i., 87, 88; Raynal, viii., 81, 82; Garneau, i., 269, 270; Shea's Missions, 326, 332; *ante*, 364, 508. La Hontan—whom Colden follows and Smith repeats, instead of trusting the more accurate Charlevoix—errs in placing the scene of Adario's exploit on the cascades of the Saint Lawrence instead of at the mouth of the Salmon River. Compare Col. Doc., ix., 391; Charlevoix, ii., 384.

† Col. Doc., iii., 555, 557, 569–571; ix., 393–398, 401; Quebec MSS. (ii.), v., 511–560; Chalmers's Ann., i., 428. Charlevoix, ii., 391, 392 (who is followed by Garneau, i., 271), supposes that Callières went to Paris with a scheme of his own for the conquest of New York by the French. But it seems to me that this idea did not occur to him until he reached France, and found that a revolution had happened in England. See Col. Doc., ix., 401–404.

1688. 1 October.

thither without his orders. This intelligence obliged the governor to decide on an immediate overland journey to Boston, by way of Hartford and Springfield, "to prevent a second Indian war."*

Nicholson left chief in New York.

Nicholson was accordingly directed to remain in New York, at the head of its affairs, to be assisted by the local counselors Phillipse, Bayard, Van Cortlandt, Younge, and Baxter, the latter of whom was stationed in command of the fort at Albany. As it was most convenient for the governor general to make Boston his head-quarters for the present, such of the New York records as were thought necessary to have at hand were taken there. Accompanied by Brockholls, Randolph, West, and others, Andros hastened eastward from New York, supposing that the revenue for the support of his government amounted to about twelve thousand pounds a year, and that "all places were well and quietly settled, and in good posture."†

9 October. Andros returns to Boston with New York records.

After the departure of Andros from New York, Dongan retired to his farm at Hempstead, on Long Island. Nicholson, with Van Cortlandt, Bayard, Plowman, Beekman, and Minvielle, under the governor's own warrant, made an examination of the city fortifications, and drew up a detailed report of their condition. The fort was found to be "extraordinarily out of repair," and carpenters were employed to make the barracks weather-tight until the spring, when every thing was intended to be put in good order. A deposition of one of these workmen, afterward taken, declared that there was "great joy" among some at New York when Andros came from Boston, because they were delivered from a "Papist Governor," and had Nicholson as deputy in the fort, "who would defend and establish the true religion." It was thought that all images erected by Dongan in Fort James would be taken away; but Nicholson order-

15 Novem. Condition of Fort James at New York.

* Col. Doc., iii., 568, 569; Col. Rec. Conn., iii., 449; Force's Tracts, iv., No. 9, p. 35, 58; No. 10, p. 10; Palmer's Impartial Account, 33, 34; Chalmers, Ann., ii., 50; Andros Tracts, i., 54.

† Col. Doc., iii., 568, 569, 590, 655, 656, 711, 722, 723, 761, 769; v., 83; Col. Rec. Conn., iii., 449-452; Doc. Hist., ii., 3, 15, 23, 103, 128, 244; Chalmers's Ann., i., 427, 590; Palfrey, iii., 563, 564. In N. Y. Pass Book, iv., there is a memorandum of the records taken to Boston by Randolph, some of which do not appear to have been restored. In 1785, Judge Samuel Jones, of New York, saw at Boston, "on the floor in an upper room of a public building, among a parcel of loose papers, several parchment rolls, containing copies of acts of the Legislature of New York," supposed to have been taken away by order of Andros, who was "a great lover of method and dispatch in all sorts of business." N. Y. H. S. Coll., iii., 362; Burk, ii., 316; Hutch. Mass., i., 354; Coll., 575.

CHAP. X. 1688. Priest John Smith. ed the workmen to assist the priest John Smith to remove to "a better room in the fort," and arrange every thing for him "according to his will." This gave great offense to the Protestants, and no doubt helped to injure Nicholson. During the winter the lieutenant governor directed Mayor Van Cortlandt to send orders to every county to exercise the militia and see them well equipped, which was generally done. In the city of New York "he did the same, and was well beloved amongst the people."*

On returning to Boston after an absence of eleven weeks, Andros, disapproving what his subordinates there had done, issued his proclamation requiring the Indians to release their captives, and surrender the murderers of the colonists. But this was not heeded by the savages; and the governor sent eastward most of the regular soldiers in garrison, with necessary stores and vessels to secure the coast. It was also ordered in Council that a considerable force of militia should be raised out of the several colonies, and Andros offered the command of the expedition, "upon very good terms," to Fitz John Winthrop, of Connecticut, one of his counselors. But Winthrop, pleading illness, declined the duty, and the governor's offer was repeated to others, who "absolutely refused the service." Indeed, the Connecticut and Massachusetts colonists did not wish to do hardy work in the wilds of Maine during the cold winter; and many of them, asserting that Brockholls was a "Popish commander," imagined that the expedition was a plot "to bring them low," and made it a pretext for poltroonery. Seeing that none in New England were willing to take the command, Andros, by the advice of his Council, determined to do it himself. "The Governor's proposal to the Council about his going to the eastward met with no opposition, lest some of the military men there should have been bound in honour to have taken that imployment upon themselves." After dispatching MacGregorie with another message to Denonville at Quebec, Andros, at the head of some eight hundred men levied in the New England colonies,† according-

20 October. Action of Andros at Boston.

1 Novem.

Winthrop and others decline service in Maine.

Andros goes to Maine himself as general.

* Col. Doc., iii., 390, 391, 590, 591, 613, 655, 716; iv., 197, 213; Doc. Hist., ii., 14, 17, 147; iii., 73; Bayley's Sketch, 19, 22; Smith, i., 90; N. Y. Hist. Soc. Coll. (1868), 87, 88; Col. Rec. Conn., iii., 454, 455; N. Y. Surrogate's Rec., Wills, iv., 1-15; Valentine's Manual, 1855, 551-553; *ante*, 408, *note*, 487.

† According to the return in New England Papers, v., 202, quoted by Chalmers, Ann., ii., 88; N. Y. H. S. Coll., 1868, the militia force of Massachusetts, New Hampshire, Maine, Plym-

ly went to Maine, in the depth of winter, sharing all the hardships of the troops. Many of them died from fatigue and exposure in marches "above one hundred miles into the desart, beyond any Christian Settlement." But the attempt to capture the savages was like a project to "hedge in the cuckoo." Many canoes were destroyed, and two Indian forts were burnt. The savages were driven into remote retreats, where they were reduced to great straits, and "were ready to submit at mercy," had not "some merchants in Boston," during the governor's absence, sent a vessel, meanly cleared for Bermuda, with supplies of ammunition and provisions, to trade with them and the French between Port Royal and Penobscot.

CHAP. X. 1688.

Traitorous Boston merchants.

As he could not capture nor destroy its natives, Andros established some eleven garrisons for the protection of Maine. At Fort Charles, in Pemaquid, thirty-six regulars and sixty militia were placed under the command of Captain Brockholls and Lieutenant Weems. MacGregorie and Lockhart, of New York, were stationed at other forts. By presents and good treatment, the governor endeavored to win the chiefs of the savages. But all he did was misconstrued at Boston, where it was reported that he had engaged the Mohawks to attack New England in concert with the French, with other equally absurd stories. During the winter he caused a sloop to be built at Pemaquid for government service; but before it was completed, unexpected events happened.*

Garrisons established in Maine by Andros.

Among James's instructions to Andros and to Dongan was one to suppress "all Pirates and Sea rovers." These depredators had become so bold that Sir Robert Holmes was sent with an English squadron to the West Indies, in the autumn of 1687, to quench them effectually. From the time of Cicero, all civilized nations had denounced pirates as "enemies of the human race." In 1630, these outlaws took possession of the island of Tortuga, near Hispaniola; and many of them having been originally engaged in the

outh, Rhode Island, and Connecticut was 13,529. That of New York was probably 2000. Col. Doc., iv., 29, 185, 197, 213; Chalmers, Rev. Col., i., 228; Arnold, i., 520.

* Col. Rec. Conn., iii., 449–453; Hutch., i., 365, 370, 371; Coll., 566; Col. Doc., iii., 551, 581, 711, 723, 724, 769; Chalmers's Annals, i., 428, 429; ii., 20, 50, 51; Force's Tracts, iv., No. 9, 28–31, 35, 58, 59; No. 10, 11; Palmer's Impartial Acc., 34, 35; Andros Tracts, i., 54, 55; ii., 193, 216; Mather's Mag., i., 178, 179; ii., 588; Maine H. S. Coll., i., 195, 196; v., 30, 268, 269, 271; Mass. H. S. Coll., xxi., 85–87; Williamson, i., 589, 590; Palfrey, iii., 567–569.

CHAP. X. honest business of "boucaning," or smoking fish and meat, after the manner of the Carib savages, they and their piratical comrades were generally known in Europe as "Buccaneers." By the Hollanders they were named "Zee Rovers;" by the French and Spaniards, "Flibustiers"—which word modern usage has corrupted into "Filibusters"—while the English generally called them "Adventurers" and "Free-booters." The sack of Panama by the Welsh Henry Morgan, in 1671, gave the command of the Pacific to the buccaneers, who enriched themselves with the spoils of captured Spanish towns and galleons. Charles the Second had vainly attempted to repress the outrages of these bold scoundrels. Unlawful private expeditions were continually fitted out in the British American plantations, where many buccaneers found refuge and encouragement. The Carolinas, Virginia, New York, Rhode Island, and Massachusetts all share the odium of the scandalous renown; and the peremptory commands of James were not issued too soon.*

1688. Buccaneers or pirates.

In obedience to these orders, Nicholson imprisoned at Boston several supposed pirates in the summer of 1688. They had been commanded by "one Petersen;" and they remained in the common jail of Boston until the next spring, when they were liberated by another authority. The efforts of Andros and his officers to suppress piracy met with little sympathy among the chief men of Massachusetts. "Since the vacating their charter," wrote Randolph from Boston, "they have been kept from the breach of the Acts for Trade and Navigation, encouraged by their former government;" and "they are restrained from setting out privateers who, for many years together, robbed the Spanish West Indies and brought great booties to Boston; and also, they durst not, during the Governor's time, harbour pirates. This place was the common receptacle of pirates of all nations." Palmer also—in answer to complaints that Andros had taken measures to "damp and spoil" the commerce of Massachusetts—declared that "their constant and profitable correspondence with Foreigners and

31 August. Pirates imprisoned by Nicholson at Boston.

* Col. Doc., iii., 374, 490, 491, 547, 582; ix., 120, 793; Chalmers's Annals, i., 546, 547; Cic. in Verr., v.; Coke's Institutes, iii., 113; Hunt's Merchant's Magazine, xiv., 39, 49; Valentine's Manual, 1857, 455–461.

1688.

Pirates" had been "diligently obstructed" by the governor, "which was very disagreeable to many persons who had even grown old in that way of trade." The chief attraction of the freebooters to Boston seems to have been the colonial mint, established in 1652, of which Samuel Sewall had been the last master. This "encouraged pirates to bring their plate hither, because it could be coined and conveyed in great parcells, undiscovered to be such." If the abrogation of the Massachusetts charter had so fatally affected these illicit commercial interests, it had still more gravely concerned the ministers of Puritanism and their sectarian flocks; and it is not surprising that all these combined interests should have earnestly worked together to obtain the restoration of an oligarchy under which they had enjoyed such valuable privileges.*

The old Boston mint coins piratical plate.

Restoration of religious oligarchy desired by some in Massachusetts.

The charter which Charles the First had granted to Massachusetts in 1629 had made a corporation "which knew no representative body." Almost its first act was to form a religious aristocracy. By its laws of 1631 and 1664, no person could be a "freeman" of the Massachusetts corporation unless he was a Puritan Church member, or was certified to be "orthodox in religion" by a Puritan minister. Most of the inhabitants of Massachusetts in 1684, when its charter was canceled, were not Puritanical communicants; yet this popular majority was utterly disfranchised. Thus the Bay corporation was perverted into a mere sectarian oligarchy. The majority of her inhabitants were not represented in her General Court; they could not act as magistrates; they were taxed without their consent and against their will; they were forced to pay rates to support Puritan ministers whose preaching they did not desire; they could not worship their Creator in any other way than that which the "freemen" of the corporation dictated; and they were thus the victims of a hideous spiritual despotism. Class-government can not be democracy. Before the Massachusetts charter was canceled the majority of inhabitants had no real political equality; and not until the abrogation of that charter did exclusive privilege give way to equal

Class-government not democracy.

* Col. Doc., iii., 552, 553, 571, 581, 582; ix., 120; Hutch. Mass., i., 177, 178; Coll., 573, 574; Val. Man., 1857, 461, 462; Chalmers's Annals, i., 421; Palmer's Impartial Account, 20; Mather's Magnalia, ii., 399; Barry, i., 344; Palfrey, ii., 403, 404; Andros Tracts, i., 41.

CHAP. X. — 1688.

rights, nor was any genuine democracy known in the boastful colony.*

When the English crown resumed the power which had ruled Massachusetts indirectly by the perversion of a royal charter, it was natural that her Puritan preachers should have keenly felt their altered condition, and have bitterly vented their griefs. They could no longer control their flocks in choosing officers of the corporation, who would make laws to suit them. Their political supremacy was gone. There was now popular equality near Boston, where sectarian privilege had flourished of old. The cry soon went forth that "wild beasts of the field" had entered through the broken "hedge," and were ravaging that sheepfold of which Puritanism had so long enjoyed the exclusive pasture.

The Massachusetts "hedge" broken by Episcopal "wild beasts."

There was truth in this metaphor of Cotton Mather. Most composers of American history have denounced Andros, as Governor of New England, in terms of coarse invective. They generally describe him as a mere bigot, and minion, and tyrant, with hardly a redeeming trait. The chief authority for such representations are early New England writers, whose partisan statements have been reiterated without question, to the exclusion of almost every thing recorded by others. Whether James the Second's commission and instructions to his governor were more or less "arbitrary" or "illegal" than the canceled charter which Charles "the martyr" had granted to Massachusetts, was certainly not a question for Andros to answer. He was not to blame because James had directed New England to be governed without an Assembly, by himself and his counselors. Andros's duty was to execute his sovereign's commands; and this he did with characteristic energy—faithfully, fearlessly, and sometimes harshly. In doing this duty, he greatly offended the "perverse people" with whom he had to deal, and who had so long been accustomed to order every thing in their own way. So they thought it a great wrong that deponents should be required to touch

New England misrepresentations of Andros.

Andros's administration not liked in Massachusetts.

* Hutch. Mass., i., 25, 26, 231, 423; ii., 1–5; Coll., 1–23, 418, 484; Mass. Rec., i., 87; iv. (ii.), 117, 118; Chalmers's Annals, i., 136–154; Rev. Col., i., 41, 42; Col. Doc., iii., 87, 111, 582; Mather's Magnalia, i., 200; Story's Misc. Writ., 64, 66; Bancroft, i., 342–345, 360; ii., 75–83; iii., 74; Barry, i., 159–162, 392; Hist. Mag., Jan., 1867, p. 6; Boston Transcript, 21 Feb., 1867; Palfrey, i., 290, 291, 345–348, 353, 373–378, 388, 432–434; ii., 587, 610; iii., 359–366; *ante*, vol. i., 189, 208.

the Bible instead of holding up their hands; a grievance that Quakers should be allowed "freedom to worship God" in their own fashion, and be excused from paying forced rates to support Puritan clergymen; an offense that the Episcopal Church service should be celebrated in Boston by Rector Samuel Myles. They liked their own censorship of the press, but they did not like that press to be muzzled by an agent of their royal governor. It was especially galling that West, and Farewell, and Graham, and Palmer, the chief subordinates and "confidents" of Andros, had come from New York. Many of the acts of these experienced officials were selfish and oppressive. Land titles were questioned, perhaps that fees might be exacted for new patents. Other official charges were avariciously increased. The judges administered the law strictly; and they were stupidly blamed for not allowing writs of habeas corpus under the English statute of 1679, which did not extend to the British colonies. For every thing done by each of his subordinates, the governor was held responsible. Most of his own acts were able and statesmanlike, while some of them were arbitrary and provoking. The real fault of Andros was that he administered his government too loyally to his sovereign, and too much like a brave soldier. What is called loyalty often depends on fashion or accident. Instead of conciliating, Andros wounded; and James, seeing the injury his viceroy was doing him in New England, was obliged to rebuke his excessive zeal.*

The New York confidents of the governor.

The king's declaration for liberty of conscience of April, 1687, which had been proclaimed at Boston and in New York the following November, was at first received with joy by the most sanguine of his New England subjects. Puritans thought it a deliverance from English prelacy; Quakers and Anabaptists felt that they could at last share in the liberty which Congregationalists had monopolized; and the small band of Episcopalians gathered in Boston re-

Liberty of conscience in Massachusetts.

* Force's Tracts, iv., No. 9, No. 10; Mather's Magnalia, i., 175–178; Historical Magazine, vi., 10, 11, 13; i. (ii.), 7; Holmes's Annals, i., 403, 420, 421; Chalmers's Annals, i., 74, 142, 421–429, 464–468; Rev. Col., i., 179–185; Palmer's Impartial Account, 13, 21, 25; Col. Doc., iii., 357, 582, 722: Hutch. Mass., i., 353–363; Coll., 555, 557; Bancroft, ii., 425–432; Grahame, i., 357–387; Barry, i., 486–498; Arnold, i., 485, 499, 501, 514–517; Palfrey, iii., 518–555; R. I. Rec., iii., 199, 223; Anderson's Col. Church, ii., 456; Mass. H. S. Coll., xxv., 149; *ante*, 338, 511. The first Episcopal service in Boston was in the South Meeting-house, on Good Friday, 1687. An Episcopal Church was soon afterward built, of which Samuel Myles became the rector: Palmer, 33; Andros Tracts, i., 53; Mass. H. S. Coll., xxvii., 192–195.

CHAP. X. 1688. joiced that they might now freely hear the beautiful liturgy of their denomination read by a surpliced clergyman. What in modern times has been called "Broad Church" seemed now to be established by James throughout British North America. But the Puritan clergymen of Massachusetts quickly caught an alarm. They were vexed because "a licentious people take the advantage of a liberty to withhold maintenance from them," and because Andros would not allow distresses to be levied for the compulsory taxes by which they had been comforted of old. Puritanism waxed wroth around Boston when it discovered that its own hatred of Protestant Episcopacy was surpassed by that of the Roman Catholic head of the Church of England; and the most discerning politicians of Massachusetts began to dread a royal toleration more than the enforcement of the suspended penal laws about religion — "the only wall against Popery." Addresses of thanks to James were nevertheless adopted by several congregations; but, at the same time, petitions were signed for relief from the imperious administration of Andros. These were intrusted to Increase Mather, the most eminent Puritan minister of Boston, who, escaping the vigilance of Randolph, by whom he had been sued for a libel, sailed for London, apparently hoping to obtain from the king a restoration of the canceled Massachusetts charter.*

Puritan hatred of Episcopacy.

7 April. Mather goes to London.

But the determination of James to maintain the government he had established in New England could not be shaken. Personal favorites, successful in other points, were foiled in this. William Phipps, a native of Pemaquid, where he had spent his youth in honest toil, had won the king's special regard, in 1687, by his success in recovering a large treasure from a Spanish wreck near Hispaniola. The humble ship-carpenter of Maine was made an English knight; and his sovereign, who claimed half the riches taken from the sea, offered him an opportunity to ask what he pleased. Sir William prayed "that New England might have its lost privileges restored." But James replied, "Any thing but

Sir William Phipps.

* Rapin, ii., 758; Hutch. Mass., i., 75, 76, 357, 358, 366; Coll., 555, 564, 565; Chalmers's Annals, i., 170, 423, 424, 426, 464–468; Mather's Magnalia, i., 197; Col. Doc., iii., 578; Col. Rec. Conn., iii., 392, 393; Force's Tracts, iv., No. 10, p. 10; Mass. H. S. Coll., xxxv., 153–186; Palmer's Account, 32; Andros Tracts, ii., x., xi.; Bancroft, ii., 426–432; Barry, i., 498, 499; Palfrey, iii., 460, 548–558; *ante*, 490, 491.

1688.

that." Phipps then, at a large expense for fees, obtained a royal patent making him high sheriff of New England, hoping that he might thereby be able to supply it with "consciencious juries." Thus appointed, Sir William came to Boston, by way of the West Indies, in the summer of 1688, some months after Mather had gone to England. But Andros, who was then "in the western parts" of the dominion, (August.) or in New York, having already commissioned James Sherlock to be sheriff of Massachusetts, "found a way wholly to put by the execution" of Phipps's costly patent from the king, and "a few weeks" afterward Sir William returned (September.) in his ship to London, with some merchandise obtained from the imprisoned pirates in the Boston jail, and "with some further designs then in his mind."*

30 May.

Mather received kindly by James.

1 June.

In the mean time, Mather had been kindly received by James, to whom he presented the addresses of thanks he had brought from New England, and afterward submitted complaints of the "enslaved and perishing estate" of the inhabitants, by reason of the misgovernment of Andros. In concert with Nowell and Hutchinson, former magistrates of Massachusetts, Mather also presented memorials for liberty of conscience, and for favor to the college at Cambridge. But these spoke of the Episcopal Church in such "very indecent language" that they disgusted the king's ministers, and the agents having been summoned before the Plantation Committee, "they withdrew their petition (19 June.) and did not appear." Having gained the favor of Father Edward Petre, the king's Jesuit confessor and counselor, the agents then petitioned for a confirmation of estates in New England, "and that no laws might be made, or monies raised, without an Assembly; with sundry other particulars." James referred this petition to his Plantation (10 August.) Committee, who directed Sir Thomas Powis, the attorney general, to make them a report. But in the copy of the petition sent to Powis, "the essential proposal of an Assembly was wholly left out" by Lord President Sunderland, (Sunderland.) who told "Mr. Brent, of the Temple," the solicitor of the

* Mather's Magnalia, i., 167–176, 178; Douglas, i., 475; Kennett, iii., 470; Hutch. Mass., i., 396, 397; Coll., 558, 573, 574; Force's Tracts, iv., No. 9, p. 23; Col. Doc., iii., 491, 552, 582, 720; Oldmixon, i., 129–132, 134, 138; Evelyn, ii., 278; Ellis Corr., i., 295–297, 325; ii., 30; Palfrey, iii., 390, 590, 591; *ante*, 524. Mr. Palfrey errs in supposing that Mather found Phipps in London when he reached there. In the summer of 1688 Phipps was in Boston, after a second visit to the Spanish wreck in the West Indies.

CHAP. X. 1688.

petitioners, "that it was by his advice that the King had given a commission to Sir Edmund Andros to raise moneys without an Assembly, and that he knew the king would never consent to an alteration, nor would he propose it to his Majesty." Powis, however, was "dexterously gained," and by the assistance of Brent, a report was obtained from him that the charter of Massachusetts had been "illegally vacated." A copy of Powis's opinion was dispatched to Boston, where it was used to excite hopes of a new charter "with larger power." Hinckley, of New Plymouth, had also asked relief for that colony through Richard Wharton, one of the royal counselors then in London. During the summer, in spite of the declared opinion of the king, the Massachusetts agents still hoped to be allowed an Assembly elected by the inhabitants, without which their condition was "little inferior to absolute slavery," and the mere change of the governor would not "ease any thing." Seeing at length that they could not obtain their desire, they asked the Plantation Committee to report "that until his Majesty shall be graciously pleased to grant an Assembly, the Council should consist of such persons as shall be considerable proprietors of lands within his Majesty's dominions; and that, the counties being continued as at present, each county may have one at least, of such of the inhabitants of the same, to be members thereof; and that no acts may pass for law but such as have or shall be voted by the manifest consent of the major part of the Council." The agents of Massachusetts at last perceived that they could expect neither a restoration of its old charter nor a separate colonial government. Looking upon the "Dominion of New England" as permanently established, they now asked that each county should have a counselor *who must be a large landowner*, and that no laws should be passed without the consent of a majority of these counselors. This detestable proposition, if accepted by the king, would have placed English colonial government in the hands of a local aristocracy of landowners. Yet such was the deliberate supplication of Massachusetts to James the Second.*

Powis.

October.

The Massachusetts agents ask King James to establish a landed aristocracy in their colony.

* Narcissus Luttrell, i., 443; Narrative of the Miseries, etc., 32, 33; Andros Tracts, ii., xi.-xv., 3-14, 206; Mather's Magnalia, i., 197; Parentator, 109, 110; Mass. H. S. Collections, xxxv., 169-189; Hutchinson's Massachusetts, i., 362, 366-369; Coll., 565, 571; Chalmers's Ann., i., 424-427, 466-468; Rev. Col., i., 179, 185; Colonial Documents, iii., 578; Historical

Whether James would have adopted the policy thus solicited is a problem. Extraordinary events were culminating in England which postponed definite action in colonial affairs. Yet William Penn retained the favor of his sovereign, who made him "Supervisor of Excise and hearth-money," and promised to enlarge Pennsylvania by "a grant under the Great Seal for the three counties on the Delaware." If this promise had been executed, there would have been one less North American State, and New York would now have had a rival sister, no less powerful in commerce than in agriculture. Yet, while James especially favored Penn, he promised Mather a "speedy redress" of many grievances in New England; and that, in the mean time, Andros "should be written unto, to forbear the measures that he was upon." No "such thing," however, was done. Without consulting his ministers, the king nevertheless declared in writing that he would grant his subjects there "a full and free liberty of conscience and exercise of religion, and their several properties and possessions of houses and lands, according to their ancient records; and also their college of Cambridge, to be governed by a President and Fellows, as formerly. All to be confirmed to them under the great seal of England."*

17 Septem. Penn favored by James.

26 Septem.

16 October. James's promises.

But none of these promises were performed by James. While he was making them, as he afterward informed Pope Innocent the Eleventh, "it was his full purpose to have set up [the] Roman Catholic Religion in the English Plantations of America." This idea seems to have been meditated as early as 1671, when it was suggested to Charles the Second that Irish Roman Catholics "may transport themselves into America, possibly near New England, to check the growing Independents of that country."†

James's real design.

A revolution in England prevented any attempt to execute such a design. The rash bigotry of James precipitated the event which observing men had foreseen. It alarmed the penetrating judgment of the Vatican. "We

Magazine, vi., 13; Force's Tracts, iv., No. 9, p. 10; London Gazette, 18 June, 1688; Palfrey, iii., 564-566.

* Narcissus Luttrell, i., 461; Ellis Corr., ii., 211; Chalmers's Ann., i., 427, 468; Parentator, 114, 115; Rev. Col., i., 299; Dixon, 325; Historical Mag., vi., 13; i. (ii.), 8, 9; Force's Tracts, iv., No. 9, p. 10; Palmer, 32; Andros Tracts, i., 52; ii., xv., xvi., 274; *ante*, 366.

† King's "State of the Protestants of Ireland," 292; Mather's Magnalia, i., 179; Parentator, 116; *ante*, 184, 185.

CHAP. X. 1688.

must," said the thoughtful cardinals of Innocent, "excommunicate this king, who will destroy the little of Catholicism which remains in England." But before Rome could apply her "brake," the English king had accomplished his fate. A few days after James commissioned Andros to be the governor general of his enlarged "Dominion of New
27 April. James's second declaration for liberty of conscience. England," he issued a second declaration for liberty of conscience, in which he renewed his abrogation of all test-oaths and laws against dissenters, and announced that none should serve him but such as would aid him in his own designs. To give this unconstitutional declaration greater
4 May. effect, James ordered it to be read in every church in his kingdom. But Archbishop Sancroft, of Canterbury, and
18 May. six other bishops, in a petition, refused to obey the king's
8 June. command. This petition James pronounced to be "a sedi-
29 June. tious libel," and the seven prelates were committed to the
30 June. Trial of the bishops. Their acquittal. Tower, and arraigned before the Court of King's Bench. Eminent counsel, among whom was John Somers, defended the prisoners, whom, after full trial, the jury acquitted. The verdict was joyfully received by most Englishmen as a fatal blow to the arrogated prerogative of their sovereign. The only consolation which James had now left him was
10 June. Birth of the Prince of Wales. the hope that the son whom his Italian queen had meanwhile produced would succeed him as a Roman Catholic king of England, to the exclusion of both his Protestant daughters by Anne Hyde.

But no Prince of Wales was to succeed James the Second on the English throne. God's field in Britain had now been harrowed enough. The crisis had come. English Protestants—Episcopal and dissenting—were aroused. Oxford Tories now adopted the Whig doctrine of resistance. Even the insular antipathies of Englishmen were subdued. Feeling that their sovereign should be a Protestant, many who had never before looked for good from Holland saw that their only "Deliverer" could be the husband of their Princess Mary, the Stadtholder of the Dutch Republic, the Calvinistic William of Orange. The very day that the
30 June. The Prince of Orange invited to England. bishops were acquitted, a secret invitation was sent to the Dutch prince, imploring him to come over to England, where he was assured multitudes would hasten to his standard.

CHAP. X.

1688.

If no Prince of Wales had been born, the Princess Mary of England and of Orange would, of course, as heiress, have succeeded to the British throne on the death or the abdication of her father. But the event which gave so much joy to James compelled William to become a party to measures which involved a fundamental change in the British Constitution. By that Constitution Mary of Orange could not take the crown of England as its presumptive heiress as long as her new-born half-brother lived. While a rebellion might drive her father from his throne, nothing but a revolution could prevent the succession of his son. But such a revolution could only be the work of Englishmen. The Dutch Stadtholder's position was embarrassing. William's policy. Yet his capacity and prudence surmounted complicated difficulties. Quietly, but skillfully, he organized in Holland a military and naval expedition. For a time, both Louis and James were ignorant of its object. A declaration explaining William's purposes in going over to En- $\frac{1}{10}$ Oct. gland was at length printed at the Hague, and published in London. The prince then took leave of the States General, and embarked at Helvoetsluys. Cornelis Evertsen, Evertsen. of Zealand, who had led an avenging Dutch fleet up to Manhattan in 1673, now assisted in conveying the Prince of Orange to England. William's expedition landed at Torbay on the day after his own birthday, and on the 5 Nov. William lands at Torbay. eighty-third anniversary of the "Gunpowder Plot" of Guy Fawkes in 1605. "JE MAINTIENDRAI"—*I will maintain*—was the ancient legend of the house of Nassau. As William stepped on shore in Devonshire, his banner dis- 5 Nov. played his own Batavian arms, quartered with those of his English wife, and his unambiguous motto now read, "I WILL His motto. MAINTAIN THE PROTESTANT RELIGION AND THE LIBERTIES OF ENGLAND."*

The reception which William met at first in England was cooler than had been promised him. Indeed, if James had acted with judgment, he might even now have saved his crown and prevented the coming revolution. When,

* Lavallée, iii., 272–276; Kennett, iii., 470–495; Burnet, i., 736–788; Clarke's James II., ii., 151–214; Parl. Hist., v, 1–15; Echard's Revolution, 158; Dalrymple, ii., 189; Rapin, ii., 762–776; Mackintosh, 239–358; Macaulay, ii., 340–479; Sylvius, xxvi., 44, 45, 144–147, 165, 166; Wagenaar, xv., 394–479; Davies, iii., 190–212; Campbell's Chancellors, i., 357; iii., 550–566; Hargrave's State Trials, iv., 303–325; *ante*, 205, 206, 4[illegible]0, 516.

CHAP. X.

1688.

28 Sept. James's proclamation.

at length, the daft king was convinced of his danger, he issued his proclamation "that a great and sudden invasion from Holland with an armed force of foreigners and strangers" would speedily be made upon his kingdom, and warned his subjects to be prepared to defend their country. To conciliate them, he took off the suspension of

2 October.

Bishop Compton, restored the charter of the city of London,

17 Oct.

and gave back the franchises of all English corporations which had been forfeited. As a farther precaution,

16 Oct. The king's letters to the American colonies.

he wrote to Andros and his other colonial governors, warning them "to take care that upon the approach of any fleet or foreign force, the militia of that our Plantation be in such readiness as to hinder any landing or invasion that may be intended to be made within the same."*

A few days after the dispatch of this last colonial instruction of James, he removed Sunderland, the wily minister who countersigned it, for treasonable correspondence with the enemy. But these time-serving measures of James were accompanied by so many acts which proved his bigotry that his subjects would trust him no longer. And so the last male Stuart British sovereign became his own destroyer.

Englishmen flock to William.

Englishmen of rank and influence now hastened to the Prince of Orange, who was attended from Holland by the historians Gilbert Burnet and Rapin de Thoyras, and by John Balfour of Burley, and "other Oliverians." Richard,

Coote, Lovelace, Wharton, Cornbury, Kirke, George of Denmark.

Lord Coote, afterward Earl of Bellomont, was already one of William's household. John, Lord Lovelace of Hurley, the nephew of the former Governor of New York—in the vaults under whose old mansion of Lady Place many machinations of the revolution had been arranged—rose in arms for the Dutch prince. Edward, Lord Cornbury, the king's own blood nephew, with Philip, Lord Wharton, and his turbulent son Thomas, who wrote "Lillibullero," the venal Churchill, and the cruel Protestant Kirke, and others, went

25 Novem.

to the invader at Exeter. A few days afterward, Prince

* Kennett, iii., 489–492, 496; Rapin, ii., 772; Sylvius, xxvi., 154; Clarke's James II., ii., 185; Ellis Correspondence, ii., 218, 223–291; Virginia Entries, iv., 229; New England Papers, v., 34; N. Y. H. S. Coll. (1868), 20, 33, 34; Mass. H. S. Coll., xxxviii., 713; Force's Tracts, iv., No. 9, p. 10; Valentine's Manual, 1859, 452; Historical Magazine, x., 144, *sup.* The king's letter of 16 October, 1688, was sent to Andros by a vessel which reached Boston in the beginning of January, 1689, while the governor was in Maine. By the same conveyance Mather and the other New England agents warned their friends to prepare "for an interesting change:" Chalmers's Annals, i., 469; ii., 20, 33, 34; Palfrey, iii., 571, *note.*

George of Denmark joined his brother-in-law; and the Princess Anne, escaping from Whitehall, abandoned her father, to follow her husband and William.

10 Decem. The queen sent to France.

James's cause was now desperate. He tried to negotiate with William, and meanwhile he secretly sent the queen and the Prince of Wales to France. As soon as he was assured of their safety, he arranged his own escape. The time had now come which Charles had predicted, and James prepared to go a second time "on his travels." His last orders were to disband the royal army. A little after midnight on the eleventh of December, he left his palace in disguise, threw his great seal into the Thames, and went down the river to follow his queen to France. Thus James abdicated his crown. Arrested in his flight, he returned to London and once more attempted to play monarch, while the Prince of Orange's Dutch soldiers were mounting guard at Whitehall. Again James left the splendid apartments he was never more to see, and fled unquestioned to France. A mimic British court was established at the airy and beautiful heights of Saint Germains, which Louis munificently assigned to his fugitive royal guest. But the reign of James the Second over England and her dependencies was ended.*

11 Decem. The great seal thrown in the Thames. Abdication.

23 Decem. James goes to France.

* Kennett, iii., 491-505; Clarke's James II., ii., 215-283; Burnet, i., 684, 765, 789-804; Rapin, ii., 772-783; Echard, 161-193; Ellis Correspondence, ii., 288-376; Dalrymple, ii., 172; Col. Doc., iv., 851; Narcissus Luttrell, i., 435, 461; Sylvius, xxvi., 154-190; Macaulay, ii., 428-588, 597-599; Knight, iv., 431; Martin's Louis XIV., ii., 85-87; *ante*, 143, 420, 435, 449.

CHAPTER XI.

1688–1689.

CHAP. XI. 1688. AT the English Christmas of sixteen hundred and eighty-eight there was no king nor regent in England. James the Second had fled from Whitehall to France, pitched his great seal into the river, disbanded his army, and left no force in his realm to oppose the advancing battalions of the Dutch Prince Stadtholder.

Sensible Englishmen considered such poltroonery of their anointed sovereign an abdication of his crown. And so it was. With James and his "essential" great seal had vanished the machinery by which Englishmen allowed themselves to be governed. Prompt action was necessary to prevent anarchy in the deserted kingdom. In this crisis, the Archbishops of Canterbury and York, with other British peers, met at the London Guildhall, assumed provisional direction of English affairs, and declared for the Prince of Orange. William soon afterward came from Windsor to Saint James's, where a great multitude of Protestant Englishmen, wearing Orange ribands—"the emblem of civil and religious freedom"—assembled to welcome their Dutch "Deliverer."*

11 Decem.

William in London. 18 Decem.

Some of William's advisers now urged him to seize the English crown, as Henry the Seventh had done, by right of conquest. But this William refused to do. He had come to England as her deliverer from evil: if Englishmen wished him to become their king, they must themselves invest him with the royal office, and place its diadem on his brow. The peers of the realm, the members of the House of Commons during the reign of Charles the Second, and the Corporation of the city of London were therefore summoned to meet the Dutch Stadtholder at Saint James's. They assembled accordingly, and requested William to take

23 Decem.

26 Decem.

* Ellis Correspondence, ii., 346-360; Kennett, iii., 500-504; Macaulay, 530, 549-581.

on himself the provisional government of England, and invite the Protestant peers, and the several constituencies of the kingdom, by their representatives, to assemble in a Convention at Westminster. In obedience to this request, the third William of Orange assumed the direction of English affairs. Having received the communion according to the Episcopal ritual of England, as his "first act" of administration the Dutch prince published a declaration authorizing all civil officers in the kingdom, "not being Papists," to act in their several places until further orders.*

CHAP. XI. 1688. William at the head of England. 30 Decem. 31 Decem.

The prince's attention was soon called to the English North American colonies, "for the happy state of which he professed a particular care." Mather was promptly introduced to him by the Cromwellian Philip Lord Wharton, and he was fully informed of the warning letter which King James had dispatched to his American governors the previous October. William thought it proper to communicate to them at once his own directions. Accordingly, he wrote an adroit circular letter to the various colonial governors, directing that all persons, "not being Papists," who lawfully held any offices in the several English plantations, should continue to execute their duties as formerly, and that "all orders and directions lately made or given by any legal authority shall be obeyed and performed by all persons," until further commands from England. This letter, countersigned by the prince's secretary, William Jephson, a cousin of Wharton, was dispatched to Virginia, and it was directed to be sent to New England and the other colonies. But the Massachusetts agents in London saw that if it should be received by Andros it would be "fatal to their schemes," by reducing their constituents to the dilemma of submission to his authority under the direction of the prince, or of rebellion. Accordingly, Mather, with Phipps, who had just returned from New England, made such effectual "application" to Jephson that William's letter to Andros "was stopped, and ordered not to be sent." From this Massachusetts "trick" with the prince's secretary sprang much future embarrassment.†

1689. 9 January. William's first colonial acts. 12 Jan. The prince's circular letter not sent to Boston.

* Ellis Correspondence, ii., 370–376; Kennett, iii., 505, 506, 507; Rapin, ii., 782, 783, 784; Macaulay, ii., 581–593.

† Macaulay, ii., 589; Virginia Entries (S. P. O.), iv., 233; New England Entries, iii., 43; Chalmers's Annals, ii., 12, 21, 22, 35, 36, 39; Hutch. Mass., i., 377, note, 389; Mass. H. S.

CHAP. XI. 1689. 22 Jan. Convention. 29 Jan. 7 Feb. The Convention called by William declared that the throne was vacant by the abdication of James. It was then considered how the vacancy should be filled. The Commons resolved that the "religion, laws, and liberties" of England should be first secured. Somers accordingly submitted a report, reciting the causes of the revolution, and contemplating, among other things, that the forfeited or surrendered charters of the Plantations should be restored. But the clause respecting the restoration of colonial charters was omitted from the Instrument adopted by the Convention. That famous state paper—chiefly the work of Somers—set forth the errors and crimes of James; reviewed his administration; asserted the rights of subjects and of Parliament; defined the authority of the sovereign, and then settled the English crown on William, Prince, and Mary, Princess of Orange, during their lives, and the life of the survivor of them, with the executive power in the prince; after them, on the posterity of Mary; then on the Princess Anne and her posterity; and then on the posterity of William. New oaths of allegiance and abjuration were ordained in place of the abrogated oaths of allegiance and supremacy. This instrument—the most important in English annals next to MAGNA CHARTA—is known as the "DECLARATION OF RIGHT."*

Somers and charters.

12 Feb.

The Declaration of Right.

More than a hundred years before, in 1581, the States General of the United Provinces had declared their independence of Spain in a manifesto which, the more it has been studied, the more it has been admired for its bold assertion of the rights of the people, and its clear exposition

Copied from the Dutch.

Coll., ix., 245; xxxviii., 258, 364, 705; Parentator, 118, 119; Mather's Magnalia, i., 176, 178; Palfrey, iii., 591, 593; *ante*, p. 534. It was about this time that Increase Mather drew up and published in London the "Narrative of the Miseries of New England," etc., which makes the tenth number in the "Sixth Collection of Papers," 1689. The first paragraph of the narrative informs the British public and William "that he that is Sovereign of New England may, by means thereof (when he pleaseth), be Emperor of America;" and the last paragraph expressed the "hope that England will send them speedy relief; especially considering that through the ill conduct of their present rulers, the French Indians are (as the last vessels from thence inform) beginning their cruel butcheries amongst the English in those parts; and many have fears that there is a design to deliver that country into the hands of the French king, except his Highness the Prince of Orange, whom a divine hand has raised up to deliver the oppressed, shall happily and speedily prevent it." This "Narrative," which doubtless influenced events affecting New England in the spring of 1689, is reprinted by the Prince Society in 1869: Andros Tracts, ii., xvii., xviii., 274.

* Commons' Journal, x., 17, 22, 23, 28; Parl. Hist., v., 23-113; Kennett, iii., 507-514; Rapin, ii., 784-794; Burnet, i., 797-826; Sylvius, xxviii., 19, 20; Chalmers's Rev. Col., i., 231; Macaulay, ii., 616-652; Campbell's Chancellors, iv., 94-97; Martin's Louis XIV., ii., 88, 89; Clarke's James II., ii., 285-307.

of the principles of political liberty. This venerable Batavian declaration must have been carefully studied by Somers—for an English translation of it is in the printed collection of his papers—and internal evidence demonstrates that it was the model of the later English manifesto. The first William of Orange, under their marvelous declaration of national rights, and by the spontaneous act of his countrymen, became the chief of the Dutch Republic. A century afterward, his great-grandson—called out of Holland by the voice of Protestant Englishmen—cordially affirmed the instrument of which his own fatherland had furnished the pattern; and WILLIAM AND MARY of Orange, accepting the offered diadem, were proclaimed KING AND QUEEN of England and of "all the dominions and territories thereunto belonging."*

13 Feb. William and Mary king and queen.

Thus was the English "Revolution" accomplished. The first act of the new sovereigns was a proclamation confirming all local officers, "being Protestants," in the places which they respectively held within the kingdom of England, on the 1st of December, 1688. This did not affect the English colonies. The same day William chose a new Privy Council, which was wholly composed of English "Whigs." Two days afterward, the king named a Committee of the Council "for Trade and Foreign Plantations." This committee was: the Earl of Danby, Lord President; the Marquis of Halifax, Lord Privy Seal; the Earl of Devonshire, Lord Steward; the Earls of Shrewsbury and of Nottingham, Secretaries of State; the Earl of Bath, Viscounts Fauconberg and Mordant, Bishop Henry Compton, of London, Sir Henry Capel, Mr. Henry Powle, and Mr. Edward Russell, "or any three of them." The committee was directed to meet on the next Monday, the 18th of February, and "prepare the drafts of Proclamations for Proclaiming their Majesties in the several Plantations, and also for continuing all persons in their employments and offices 'till further order." Proclamations were accordingly prepared, and letters forwarding them to the several colonial governors were signed by enough privy

14 Feb. All Protestants confirmed in offices in England.

16 Feb. William's Plantation Committee.

19 Feb.

* Lord Somers's Tracts, xiv., 417–424 (Sir Walter Scott, ed. i., 323); Kennett, iii., 514; Rapin, ii., 795; Tindal, iii., 30, 31, 99; Clarke's James II., 307, 308, 309; Sylvius, xxvii., 27; Macaulay, ii., 654, 655; *ante*, vol. i., 446, 761.

CHAP. XI. 1689. William's first royal orders to the English colonies.

counselors. These letters signified to those governors their majesties pleasure "that all men being in offices of Government shall so continue until their Majesties further pleasure be known," and that the new oaths of allegiance and abjuration should be taken by each of them. The difference between the original proclamation of William and Mary continuing in their places the local officers in England and that sent to the Plantations, is significantly clear. In England only "Protestants" were to be kept in office. But in the Plantations, "all men being in offices of Government" were to remain undisturbed.*

How the English revolution affected the colonies.

The revolution in England was thus held by her statesmen as in no way affecting her colonies otherwise than in transferring, without their consent, their allegiance from one English sovereign to another, by the act of an irregular English Convention. It was certain that the Protestant religion could not be jeoparded in the English colonies as it had been in the mother country. The Test Act of 1673 had never been in force in those colonies, where Brockholls, and Dongan, and other avowed Roman Catholics had acted under undeniably legal commissions. The Prince of Orange's Convention of January, 1689, therefore, did not extend that Test Act to the English colonies. It merely required "all persons" in office to take its own ordained oaths of allegiance to William and Mary, and of abjuration of the Pope's "authority, ecclesiastical or spiritual, within this Realm" of England.†

23 Feb. This convention, however, was transformed into an English Parliament, which went on to make laws as if it had unimpeachable authority. The House of Commons tried to repair the significant omission in the Declaration
5 March. of Right by resolving that the forfeiting of the charters of the Plantations was "illegal and a grievance." A bill was
16 March. English Corporation Bill. accordingly brought in to restore all corporations, at home and in New England, to the condition they were at the Restoration of King Charles the Second in 1660. This crude measure passed the House of Commons through the active

* Kennett, iii., 514, 515; Tindal, iii., 38–41; Sylvius, xxvii., 29, 31; Smollett, i., 4; Parl. Hist., v., 113; Macaulay, iii., 1–27; N. Y. Col. Doc., iii., 572, 596, 641; Board Journals, vi., 195; Virginia Entries, iv., 236; Chalmers's Annals, i., 373, 431, 469; ii., 12, 22, 37, 38; Rev. Col., i., 201; Penn. Col. Rec., i., 341; Appendix, Note G., p. 662, *post*.

† Kennett, iii., 514; Chalmers's Annals, ii., in N. Y. H. S. Coll. (1868), 13, 37; *ante*, 202, 264, 447, 452.

exertions of Mather, Phipps, and Sir Henry Ashurst. But William detected the embarrassment it would cause to his prerogative; and his courtiers delayed it in the Lords until the Convention Parliament was dissolved. Thus "the Sisyphæan labour of a whole year came to nothing."*

The key-note thus sounded in the English House of Commons was meant to influence the colonial policy of their Dutch sovereign and his wife. A few days before Mary left the Hague for London, she was "dexterously gained" to favor New England by the "eminent" Abraham Kick, of Amsterdam, who had long been a correspondent of Mather, and at whose house Shaftesbury had died. Thus encouraged, Phipps and Mather petitioned William that Andros should be removed from his government of New England; that Massachusetts, Plymouth, Rhode Island, and Connecticut might be "restored to their ancient privileges," and that their former governors might be reinstated. The king referred this petition to his Plantation Committee, and ordered the letter of the Privy Council to Andros, of 19th February, to be "postponed 'till the business of taking away the charters should be considered." The committee, having heard Phipps's and Mather's counsel, as well as Sir Robert Sawyer, the late attorney general—who reported the reasons for canceling the Massachusetts patent—agreed to report "that his Majesty be pleased to send forthwith a Governor to New England in the place of Sir Edmund Andros, with a Provisional Commission, and with Instructions to proclaim his Majesty in those colonies, and to take the present administration of the Government in those parts until further order; in which Commission and Instructions it may be expressed that no money shall be raised by the Governor and Council only. And their Lordships will likewise propose that His Majesty do thereupon give further order for preparing, as soon as may be, such a further establishment as may be lasting, and preserve the rights and

22 Jan./1 Feb. Mary gained to favor New England.

18 Feb. Phipps and Mather's petition to William.

20 Feb.

22 Feb.

Queer report of William's Plantation Committee.

* Commons Jour., x., 17, 41, 42, 51; Parl. Hist., v., 159, 508–516, 537; Kennett, iii., 516; Tindal, iii., 119; Macaulay, iii., 393, 498, 517, 522, 532, 534; Chalmers's Ann., i., 415; ii., 61, 62, 90; Rev. Col., i., 231; Douglas, i., 465; Hutch. Mass., i., 389, 390; Barry, i., 509; Mass. H. S. Coll., ix., 246, 247; xxxviii., 680; Mather's Magnalia, i., 197, 198; Parentator, 122, 123; Andros Tracts, ii., xx., 276. If the bill passed by the House of Commons had become a law, important questions must have come up about the condition of New York, New Jersey, Connecticut, Rhode Island, and other American colonies, to which Charles and James had granted patents after May, 1660.

CHAP. XI. 1689. privileges of the people of New England, and yet reserve such a dependence on the Crown of England as shall be thought requisite." But the sending another royal governor to New England in place of Andros was not what Phipps and Mather asked; and William was prevailed upon to disregard "the salutary advice of his ministers." Accordingly, when the report of his Plantation Committee was considered by the king in Council, he ordered "that it be referred back to the Committee to consider of and prepare the draught of a New Charter to be granted to the inhabitants of New England, and [which?] may preserve the rights and properties of those colonies, and reserve such a dependence on the Crown according to the Report; and that, instead of a Governor to be sent in the room of Sir Edmund Andros, there be appointed two Commissioners to take upon them the administration of the Government there, with directions immediately to proclaim the King and Queen."*

26 Feb. William dubious.

This order of William, while it settled the fate of Andros, showed that the king meant to give a new charter "to the inhabitants of New England" which would allow them a Colonial Assembly, and yet preserve their "dependence on the Crown" of England, first, through two royal English commissioners, and afterward by a royal governor. William at once adopted James's policy of consolidation, so as to keep the "Dominion of New England" an entirety, under a royal governor; but he wished to modify that policy so as to allow "the inhabitants" to choose their own Assembly. This scheme may have suited Phipps, whose enmity to Andros was personal; but it was fatal to the views of Mather, who desired the restoration of Puritan oligarchy in Massachusetts, of which he was a chief preacher. Mather therefore got Lord Wharton to present him again to the king, whom he implored "to favour New England." This William readily promised, but he cautiously remarked, "there have been irregularities in their government." Being farther pressed, he added, "I will forthwith give order that Sir Ed-

William wishes to preserve the dominion of New England whole.

14 March. Mather again sees the king.

* Plantation Journals, vi., 197, 198, 200–204; New England Entries, iii., 200, 201; Privy Council Min., Will. and Mary, i., 21; Chalmers's Ann., ii., 22, 23, 25, 39; Mass. H. S. Coll., xxxii., 298; xxxviii., 101, 105, 107, 528, 598, 705; Force's Tracts, iv., No. 11, 11–14; Andros Tracts, ii., xvi., xviii., 149–170; Palfrey, iii., 592, 593. Kick, who wrote to Mary at the Hague, was made English consul at Rotterdam in 1690: Wagenaar, xv., 305.

mund Andros shall be removed from the government of New England, and be called unto an account for his maladministration. And I will direct that the present King and Queen shall be proclaimed by their former Magistrates." What William really meant by "their former magistrates" is not clear. But he certainly did not intend to sever or disunite his royal dominion of New England into its former several colonies. In this Whitehall uncertainty, Phipps, thinking that "the best stage of action for him would now be New England itself," hastened thither. But, "before he left London, a messenger from the abdicated King tendered him the government of New England, if he would accept it." James, who had now come from France to Dublin, seems to have thought that by removing Andros and appointing Phipps, he might retain his authority over New England. Phipps of course declined this Irish offer by "the abdicated King" of a colonial "government without an Assembly;" and he soon afterward embarked for Boston, carrying the Council's delayed letters to Andros, "with certain instructions from none of the least considerable persons at Whitehall," that if the people of New England gave them "the trouble to hang Sir Edmund, they deserved noe friends."*

CHAP. XI. 1689. William's orders.

James offers the government of New England to Phipps.

April.

After Phipps left, the Privy Council directed Secretary Shrewsbury, "upon inquiry from those who have the most considerable interest in New England, New York, and the Jerseys, to present to the King the names of such as may be thought fit at this time to be Governor and Lieutenant Governor of those parts." A few days afterward, the Plantation Committee, seeing that a war with France was at hand, suggested to the king "the speedy settling of such a government in New England, New York, and the Jerseys, as, upon recalling Sir Edmund Andros, may enable your Majesty's subjects, who are very numerous in those parts, not only to oppose by their united forces the French of Canada and Nova Scotia, but to carry on such further designs as your majesty may find requisite for your service;

18 April.

26 April. Plantation Committee's suggestion.

* Mass. H. S. Coll., ix., 245, 246; xxxii., 238; xxxviii., 705; Andros Tracts, ii., xix; Mather's Magnalia, i., 178, 197, 198; Parentator, 120, 121; Hutch. Mass., i., 377, 389, 390, 397; Oldmixon, i., 138; Chalmers, Rev. Col., i., 201, 207, 208, 231; Pol. Ann., i., 373, 431, 469; ii., 23, 25; N. Y. Col. Doc., iii., 578, 583, 587, 588; Bancroft, iii., 78, 79; Barry, i., 508, 509; Palfrey, iii., 592, 593; Clarke's James II., ii., 327-330.

CHAP. XI. 1689. without which union and government the French may easily possess themselves of that Dominion, and trade of those parts which are so considerable to the crown." The committee also proposed "that, as Maryland, Pennsylvania, and Carolina are Proprieties of great extent in America, which do not hold themselves subjects to your Majesty's immediate government, nor render any account to your Majesty of their proceedings, your Majesty would please, in this conjuncture, to give such directions as may better secure your Majesty's interests in those parts, and put them in a condition of defence against the enemy." This advice pleased William, who ordered the Plantation Committee to consult the Admiralty about sending ships to America, and also to propose "the names of fit persons to be sent as Governors to the Plantations, and what may be fit to be done for his Majesty's service in the present conjuncture, as well for settling the government of New England, New York, and the Jerseys, as for securing His Majesty's interest in the several proprieties in America." The committee shortly afterward represented that "the present circumstances and relations they stand in to the government of England is a matter worthy of the consideration of Parliament for the bringing of those Proprieties and Dominions under a nearer dependence on the Crown, as his Majesty's revenue in the Plantations is very much Concerned herein." Thus the Dutch king who had succeeded James the Second was advised by his Whig English counselors, in the third month of his reign, to carry into vigorous effect some of the most decided colonial measures of his predecessor, because they were now selfishly considered to benefit England.*

2 May.

18 May. The Plantations to be made more dependent on the crown of England.

Meanwhile, James had come over to Ireland at the head of a large French expedition, hoping to recover his deserted throne. By William's command, Secretary Shrewsbury wrote a circular letter to the British American governors, informing them that, by reason of the assistance which Louis had given to the king's enemies in Ireland, "and by the invading His Majesty's territories in America, and disturbing the trade of his subjects in those parts for several years past," preparations were to be made for a speedy war

12 March. James in Ireland.

13 April.

* Mass. H. S. Coll., xxxii., 298; N. Y. Col. Doc., iii., 573, 574; Chalmers's Rev. Col., i., 223; Dixon's Penn, 269.

CHAP. XI.

1689.

with France, and ordering them, with all diligence, to "take effectual care for the opposing and resisting any attempt of the French." The king and queen also issued their proclamation granting an asylum in England, with their royal protection, to the Protestants who had been driven from France after the revocation of the Edict of Nantes. This was followed by a declaration of war against France, drawn by Solicitor General Somers, which set forth, among other causes of hostility, the invasion of the territory of New York by the Canadians as an act "not becoming even an enemy." The necessity of promptly securing the English-American colonies was obvious, for it was reported in London that Louis had ordered their seizure before news of the revolution in England could cross the Atlantic. But the embarrassments of William's situation, and the folly of his Whig ministers, caused him to neglect the best opportunity which England ever had to crush the power of France in North America. Thus Whitehall placemen, sacrificing the interests of their mother country, inflicted present miseries on her Plantations, and left them victims to domestic discords and protracted border wars.*

William's colonial orders. 25 April. French refugees protected. 17 May. War declared between England and France. 27 April. Error of English colonial policy.

The policy of Louis the Fourteenth glittered in contrast with that of William the Third. The French king had around him at Versailles devoted and accomplished men, who did not hesitate to give him, when he demanded it, their best advice. Louvois, his ablest minister next to the dead Colbert, was yet savagely vigorous; Seignelay was laborious to please; and about Canada, the displaced Frontenac was at hand to personally relate all his own experience there. And now Callières reached Paris with Denonville's dispatches of the previous autumn. These were promptly considered. Louis was of opinion that if James had remained King of England, he "would no doubt have recognized" the French right of sovereignty over the Iroquois. But, however this might have been, the condition of European politics was greatly changed. A Dutch Protestant prince—the unrelenting enemy of France—was now a

January. Colonial policy of Louis.

* Clarke's James II., ii., 319-331; Dalrymple, ii., 311-342; iii., 45-52; Macpherson, i., 174-186; Kennett, iii., 526, 527; Tindal, iii., 80, 89, 90, 91; Sylvius, xxvii., 118; Narcissus Luttrell, i., 524; Macaulay, iii., 128, 170; Chalmers's Rev. Col., i., 223, 227, 228; Annals, ii., 9, 10, 35, 42, 87; Virginia Entries, iv., 244-246; Penn. Col. Rec., i., 301, 302; Dixon, 263; N. Y. Col. Doc., iii., 699; Doc. Hist., ii., 26; iii., 560; Bolton's Church in Westchester, 392; *ante*, 435.

CHAP. XI. 1689. chosen sovereign of England. Her Jesuitical old king was a refugee in France, encouraged to attempt the regaining of his abdicated royalty. Notwithstanding all his faults, Louis was a chivalric gentleman. With James on his throne in London, he might have negotiated about sovereignty over the North American Iroquois. With James his own guest at Saint Germains, Louis could not chaffer. Louis therefore gave James French soldiers, with which the March. "abdicated king" went to Ireland to regain the crown he had so foolishly thrown away. What the result of this Irish campaign might be was uncertain; but, at all events, Louis could have no friendly dealings with the Dutch Prince of Orange, who, he considered, had usurped the British throne. While James was thus in Ireland, and while William in London was declaring war against France, Louis resolved to make peace with the New York savages 1 May. Iroquois prisoners sent home. at any rate; and to render this more easy, he ordered that all the Iroquois prisoners which Denonville had sent over to serve in the royal galleys at Marseilles should be returned to Canada, and supplied with gaudy clothes from the shops of Paris.*

January. Callières's project. But Callières, in an able memorial to Seignelay, expounded the advantage, and even the necessity, of now seizing New York, where Andros, who was a Protestant, would certainly acknowledge the Prince of Orange, and be sustained in doing so by the inhabitants, who were mostly Dutch, and generally Protestants.† In a separate memoir, Callières detailed his plan, which was to advance with two thousand men, in canoes and bateaux, from Montreal, through the Richelieu River, Lake Champlain, Wood Creek, and the Hudson River, to Albany, and thence to New York; while two ships of war were to blockade the metropolis, the condition of which was described with tolerable accuracy. February. May. Louis, however, hesitated; and Callières again and again urged prompt action, arguing in favor of the conquest of New York that, even if James should continue to be recognized as king there, "we can make use of the plausible pre-

* Col. Doc., ix., 393-398, 416-418; *ante*, 520.

† Col. Doc., ix., 403, 404, 422. It is clear that the French did not expect Andros to betray his government to them, as suggested in Mather's "Narrative," and afterward charged by the Puritans of Boston: Force's Tracts, iv., No. 9, p. 41; No. 10, p. 11; compare Palmer's Impartial Account, p. 36; Andros Tracts, i.

text of having seized it with a view to preserve it for himself against the attacks of the rebels, and to give it back to him after his restoration, or treat with him for it." While the king "thought well" of Callières's project, he put off its execution, and ordered Denonville to send a full report on the subject. The English declaration of war, however, forced Louis to act promptly. Disregarding the treaty of colonial neutrality, he approved the project of Callières; but he confided its execution to an abler general than him whose ineffectual campaign against the Senecas was esteemed only valuable "as material to be put in history, as if it were some glorious achievement." Denonville was accordingly recalled to serve in Europe, and the veteran Frontenac, who had been living in poverty at Paris since 1682, was again appointed Governor General of Canada.*

CHAP. XI.

1689.

1 May.

7/17 May.

Louis approves the project of Callières.

Denonville recalled and Frontenac reappointed. 21 May.

Frontenac's instructions, prepared with great care by Louvois, after conferences with the new governor himself and La Motte Cadillac, of Acadia, were more complex than the original plan submitted by Callières. It was now determined that the English were to be simultaneously attacked at Hudson's Bay and in New York. The expedition was to embark at Rochelle, and after Frontenac had reached Quebec and organized his forces, he was to direct Caffinière, the admiral commanding, to coast southward to Sandy Hook, and then co-operate with him as soon as he should have passed victoriously down the Hudson. After the conquest of New York, its Roman Catholic inhabitants might be suffered to remain; but all French refugees, especially those of the "Pretended Reformed Religion," were to be sent to France. Mechanics and laborers might be retained as prisoners to work and build; but all the other inhabitants were to be sent to New England, Pennsylvania, and elsewhere. These instructions certainly did not suggest any anticipated co-operation of the Protestant Andros, or any purpose of Louis to acquire New England, for which he did not care. What he desired was to obtain New York, and New York only. After its conquest, Callières was to remain Governor of New York, under the command of Frontenac, and "all the English settlements adjoining Manatte, and further

7 June. Frontenac's instructions.

What was to happen in New York.

* Col. Doc., iv., 478; ix., 401-408, 411-422, 427, 803; Charlevoix, ii., 392, 393, 394, 395; Doc. Hist., i., 179-182; Garneau, i., 271, 301, 355-357; La Hontan, i., 196, 197; *ante*, 490, 499.

CHAP. XI. off if necessary," were to be destroyed. These savage instructions were worthy of the iron-hearted Louvois, who

1689. had just before directed the devastation of the Palatinate. French frigates, the "Embuscade," the "Fourgon," and the "Saint Francis Xavier," were ordered to be prepared at Rochelle to convey and co-operate with the expedition meant to lay waste New York. But while Maintenon could plead with Louis against the inhuman atrocities he had authorized on the Rhine, she felt no sympathy for his meditated victims on the far off Hudson. The providence of God alone was their almighty protector.*

In those colonial days news from Europe came tardily and uncertainly across the Atlantic. James's monitory letter to Andros of October, 1688, did not reach Boston until

1 January. the beginning of January, 1689. By the same vessel which bore it, Mather and his fellow-workers in London conveyed to their friends in Massachusetts the result of their "solicitations" with the king, and "warned them to prepare the minds of the people for an interesting change." James's

James's letter of October sent to Andros in Maine.

letter was sent by express to Maine, where Andros then was, bravely guarding the New England frontier against the savages. In loyal obedience to his orders, the governor general promptly issued his proclamation, dated "at Fort Charles at Pemaquid," charging "all officers civil and military, and all other, his Majesty's loving subjects within this his Territory and Dominion aforesaid, to be vigilant and careful, in their respective places and stations; and that, upon the approach of any Fleet or Forreign force, they be in readiness, and use their utmost endeavour to hinder any landing or invasion that may be intended to be made within the same."†

10 Jan. Andros's Proclamation from Pemaquid.

Soon afterward, while Nicholson was busily putting New York in a better condition of defense against a "foreign force," news of the landing of the Prince of Orange at Tor-

* Col. Doc., ix., 422–431, 446, 659, 660, 671; Doc. Hist., i., 183–185; Charlevoix, ii., 395–401; Garneau, i., 302; Macaulay, iii., 122–126; Martin's Louis XIV.; Chalmers's Ann., ii., 68. In the light of Frontenac's instructions, it is amusing to read the hearsay twaddle about Andros which its compiler has stuffed into the "Revolution in New England Justified:" Force's Tracts, iv., No. 9, p. 31–43; compare Palmer's "Impartial Account," p. 36; Andros Tracts, i.

† Chalmers's Ann., i., 469; ii., 20, 21, 23, 39; Force's Tracts, iv., No. 9, p. 10; Mather's Mag., i., 179; Hutch. Mass., i., 373; Coll., 571; Barry, i., 504; Palfrey, iii., 569, 570, 571, 579; New England Papers, v., 34–94; *ante*, 534. An original of Andros's Proclamation of 10 January, 1688–9, printed by Richard Pierce, "at Boston in New England," is in the New York Society Library, and a lithograph fac-simile of it is in Valentine's Manual for 1859, p. 452, and a copy in Hist. Mag., x., 144, *sup.*: see also a copy *post*, Note H., p. 662, 663.

bay reached Virginia. A coasting vessel from there came to New York, and Andries Greveraet, her master, called on the lieutenant governor in Fort James. Astonished to hear of William's invasion of England, Nicholson compared him to Monmouth, and prophesied that "the very 'prentice boyes of London will drive him out againe;" and he strictly forbid Greveraet to divulge the news. A week afterward, Jacob Leisler, then engaged in importing liquors, and commissioned a captain in Colonel Bayard's city regiment, received a confirmation of the intelligence by way of Maryland. The news, which, "to hinder any tumult," was kept private at first, was dispatched by Nicholson to Andros in Maine by two separate expresses, on land and water.*

CHAP. XI. 1689. 5 Feb. News of William's invasion received at New York. 1 March. The news dispatched to Andros. 2 March.

Having put the garrisons in good condition, and placed Brockholls in command at Fort Charles, the governor, as soon as he received the intelligence, left Maine, accompanied by West, Graham, and Palmer, and hastened to Boston, which he reached "about the latter end of March." A few days afterward a ship came to Boston from Nevis in the West Indies, which brought as a passenger John Winslow, who had copies of the Prince of Orange's declaration of the previous October, and also confirmatory intelligence of "his happy proceedings in England, with his entrance there." Instead of promptly calling on the governor, as Greveraet had called on his subordinate in Fort James, Winslow sullenly remained at home, and Andros, hearing that he had important intelligence, required his attendance. Being asked for the prince's declarations, Winslow refused to produce them, telling the governor that he was "afraid to let him have them, because he would not let the people know any news." Winslow was then sent before a justice of the peace, and, remaining obstinately contumacious, he was committed to prison for not imparting to the Governor of New England important and unique public documents from the mother country, which, in default of their open production, were supposed to be "traiterous and treasonable libels."†

16 March. Andros returns to Boston. 4 April. Winslow imprisoned at Boston for contumacy.

* Col. Doc., iii., 591, 660; Hutch. Mass., i., 372; Penn. Col. Rec., i., 246; N. Y. H. S. Coll., 21 (1868), 241–243, 359; Chalmers's Annals, ii., 21; *ante*, 533. Mr. Palfrey does not refer to this New York intelligence.

† Palmer's Narrative, 35; Rev. in N. E. Justified, in Force's Tracts, iv., No. 9, 10–12, 18; N. Y. Col. Doc., iii., 581, 723; Chalmers's Ann., ii., 21; Hutch. Mass., i., 373; Palfrey, iii., 570–575; Mather's Magnalia, i., 179; Andros Tracts, i., ii.; *ante*, 533.

CHAP. XI. 1689. Mather's intrigue ripens.

Mather's intrigue in London, which prevented the transmission to Andros of the Prince of Orange's confirmatory letter of the 12th of January, now produced its intended result. That wandering divine had written from England that a "charter with larger power" for Massachusetts would be obtained from James the Second. It was plausibly argued by Bradstreet and other correspondents, whom Mather had encouraged, that if favor was to be expected from James, much more would surely come from William. The Dutch invading prince—although the stadtholder of that large-minded Continental nation of which insular Englishmen were always jealous—was nevertheless a Protestant and a disciple of Calvin, whom the English Puritans also followed. The success of William of Orange over their bigoted popish king was now the earnest prayer of most British subjects in Old and New England. Although it was well understood in France that Andros would declare for the Dutch prince if he should become the sovereign of England, the chief leaders of opinion in Massachusetts pronounced otherwise. It was accordingly rumored that, by his proclamation from Pemaquid to hinder the landing of any "foreign force" in New England, its governor general meant to oppose the lawful commands of the British sovereign, whoever that sovereign might be. Of such a political solecism, Andros was too good an English soldier and too faithful a colonial officer to be guilty. In truth, few English-American governors were more thoroughly "loyal" than the slandered, domineering, and exacting Sir Edmund. He was only a prototype of meaner pretenders. But by this time an unusual excitement prevailed in and around Boston. Hearing of it, the governor wrote to Brockholls at Pemaquid that "there's a general buzzing among the people, great with expectation of their old charter, or they know not what;" and he cautioned all officers there to be faithful in their trusts, and careful "to avoid surprise." By this order, Andros meant to guard his subordinates in frontier Pemaquid—not from any imaginary "surprise" by William or the Dutch, who, if they had any longings for American dominion, would surely not have made their first demonstration there, but—from the French savages, to whom "some merchants in Boston" had, as has been seen, traitor-

Falsehoods rumored in Boston.

16 April. Andros's letter to Brockholls.

ously, but very characteristically, conveyed supplies of ammunition while their own governor was absent fighting those savage enemies in Maine.*

"Buzzing" in Boston.

Andros sent Brockholls an expressive metaphor. The "buzzing" people were stirred up by their ministers to swarm on the "old charter" granted by "King Charles the Martyr," under which Congregational clergymen had long been used to control their flocks in Massachusetts. But the most discerning colonial minds saw that the fate of the British Plantations must follow that of the mother country, and they wished to await in quiet the event in England, about which a few more days would bring those authoritative orders that no English subject in America could loyally question. So the "principal gentlemen in Boston," after consultation, agreed that they would, if they could, "extinguish all essays in the people towards an insurrection." Yet, if an "ungoverned *mobile*" should push matters to an extremity, those "principal gentlemen" would themselves head the movement, and secure any official rewards that might follow the contemplated stroke of state. Cotton Mather accordingly prepared a prolix "Declaration of the Gentlemen, merchants and inhabitants of Boston and the Country adjacent," giving their reasons for a revolt against the government of Andros, and announcing their resolution to secure him and his officers, "for what justice Orders from his Highness with the English Parliament shall direct, lest, ere we are aware, we find (what we may fear, being on all sides in danger) ourselves to be by them given away to a Forreign power, before such orders can reach unto us." This "Declaration" was just such a writing as its penman, who was "more a clergyman than a lawyer," was likely to draft.†

Politics of the Boston "gentlemen."

Lies circulated.

The mine, thus carefully prepared, was adroitly exploded. It was rumored that Boston and its inhabitants were to be destroyed by the New York Mohawks, and by undermining the town; that the soldiers in Maine were poisoned with rum; and that there was a French fleet on the coast. These

* Col. Doc., iii., 578, 581; ix., 403, 404; Chalmers's Ann., i., 469; ii., 20, 21; Hutch. Mass., i., 372, 373; Williamson, i., 589, 590, 606–610; Bancroft, ii., 445; Palfrey, iii., 571–577; Andros Tracts, i., 54, 55; ii., 193, 216; *ante*, 522, 523, 537, 546.

† Palmer's Impartial Account, 13; Mather's Magnalia, i., 179, 180; ii., 588, 589; Hutch. Mass., i., 373, 381; Palfrey, iii., 576, 578, 579; Byfield, in Force's Tracts, iv., No. 10, 6–12; Col. Doc., iii., 582; Historical Magazine, vi., 10–14; Andros Tracts, i., ii.

CHAP. XI. 1689. 18 April. Insurrection of the populace in Boston.

and other absurd stories were so generally believed as to provoke insurrection. On Thursday morning, the eighteenth of April, "a sudden irruption of the people from all parts" awaked Boston, and the town rose in arms, "without the privity" of her most "substantial men." Captain George, of the royal frigate Rose, was seized as he came on shore; and with him Sherlock, Randolph, Farewell, and other obnoxious officials, were imprisoned. About noon, Bradstreet, the last Governor of Massachusetts under its canceled charter, with several clergymen and other prominent citizens of Boston, had assembled at the Council Chamber in the Town House, in front of which "all the companies were soon rallied." Mather's verbose "Declaration" was read from the balcony, and a message from the "gentlemen" in the Council Chamber, for themselves and "many others," who were "surprised with the people's sudden taking of arms," was sent to their governor at the fort. It urged him to "forthwith surrender and deliver up the Government and Fortification, to be preserved and disposed according to order and direction from the crown of England, which suddenly is expected may arrive; promising all security from violence to yourself or any of your gentlemen or soldiers, in person and estate." If the signers of this summons were "surprised" by the insurrection, the "strange and sudden" movement was, as he himself deliberately wrote, "wholly a surprise" to Andros, who knew "noe cause or occasion for the same." He sarcastically "admired" whence so many armed men came now, because when he wanted them "to go to the eastward, he found it difficult to have them procured." But the lieutenant of the Rose frigate, hearing that her captain had been seized, had meanwhile prepared the ship for action, and had sent a boat ashore to bring off the governor. As Andros and his attendants were going down to embark, they were met by an armed party, headed by John Nelson, which, having overpowered the boat's crew, delivered the summons from the Town House. Seeing that it was signed by "several of the Council," some of whom he had particularly "sent for from distant parts," the governor and those with him went at once to the Council Chamber. As they passed thither, "the streets were full of armed men, yett none offered him, or

Cotton Mather's "Declaration" read.

CHAP. XI.

1689.

Andros imprisoned by the insurgents in Boston.

those that were with him, the least rudeness or incivility, but, on the contrary, usual respect." In his Council Chamber, Andros was ordered by those present, "who had no suitable regard to him nor the peace and quiet of the country," to be imprisoned, as were also Graham, Palmer, West, and other subordinate officers of the "Dominion." The insurgents broke open the secretary's office, and took away all the records; but they missed finding "Sir Edmund's papers," which they were especially anxious to secure; and the great seal of New England seems to have disappeared.*

Solecism of Massachusetts.

A more unjustifiable rebellion of colonists, who professed allegiance to their mother country, never happened. Yet it has been praised as patriotism by many writers of American history. If Massachusetts had been an independent state at that time, she might have well done. But Massachusetts was only a subordinate colony of England, and a part of its royal "Dominion of New England in America." The colony at that very moment was beseeching royal favor. Loyalty should have kept her quiet. There was no reason why she should vex William. Yet, with the headstrong audacity which always marked her pretensions, she set herself up as superior to other English colonies in America, and demanded privileges greater than those of her coequals.

Was Nicholson to govern in place of Andros?

The governor being safely in prison, the question arose how the government of the royal dominion of New England was to be lawfully administered? If Andros had embarked in the Rose frigate, as he intended, he would probably have transferred his seat of government to New York, and thus have maintained his authority. This is the main reason why the insurgents were so anxious to secure his person. Under the king's commission, Lieutenant Governor Nicholson was to succeed his chief only in case of his death or absence from the territory. Forced incapacity of the governor had not been contemplated. Whether the imprisonment of Andros entitled Nicholson to assume the government of New England under a strict construction of the king's commission, is doubtful; yet no maladministration

* Mass. H. S. Coll., xxvi., 205, 206; xxxv., 190–198; Conn. H. S. Coll., i., 77, 78; N.Y. Col. Doc., iii., 578, 723, 724; R. I. Rec., iii., 281–285; Palmer's Impartial Account, p. 9, 34–37; Force's Tracts, iv., No. 9, p. 30–39, 40–43; No. 10, p. 3–5; Hutch. Mass., i., 374–381; Coll., 567–571, 575; Chalmers's Ann., i., 429, 430, 469, 470; ii., 23, 24; Barry, i., 502–504; Arnold, i., 515; Palfrey, iii., 577–587; Andros Tracts.

CHAP. XI. 1689. could be alleged against him, as it had been charged against his immediate superior. It was certain that, next to Andros, the only chief representative of the English crown in the dominion was its Lieutenant Governor Nicholson. But this was disregarded by the Boston mutineers, whose object was to break that dominion into its old pieces. Their imprisonment of Andros was really only a cloak for "Secession." Massachusetts did not like union, unless she could control that union, as she had done for many years after the old colonial confederacy of 1643. She pined for a separate local government, like that which she had enjoyed under her perverted and abrogated charter. It was very galling to her that, in common with other British American colonies, she should be subjected by her king to the authority of a governor general. Although but a subordinate English colony, not claiming sovereignty, but imploring royal charity, she determined to revolt:—and so she seceded.

Massachusetts the author of "secession."

20 April. A "Council of Safety" assumed the government of Massachusetts, and hastened to cashier the officers of the king's regular companies, and to withdraw the garrisons which Andros had established in Maine. Major Brockholls, Lieutenant Colonel MacGregorie, and Captain George Lockhart were sent to Boston from the Maine garrisons. They were all New York officers; and Peter Schuyler served as lieutenant of Captain Lockhart's troop of horse on duty at Albany the previous winter.* The Boston notion of "secession" quickly spread throughout the dominion of New England. Plymouth—as Wiswall wrote to Hinckley—did not like "to trot after the Bay horse." Rhode Island certainly had no sympathy with the persecutors of Anne Hutchinson and Roger Williams. Connecticut—which had so adroitly coquetted with Massachusetts and New York—did not wish to be joined with either. New York, always imperial, abhorred a political connection with the New England colonies. New Jersey followed placidly in the wake of New York. And so, in the spring of 1689, all the constituent colonies which formed their sovereign's dominion of New England were ripe to adopt the "most sanctified" Massachusetts idea of "secession."

27 April.

Plymouth does not like "to trot after the Bay horse."

Secession triumphs.

* Williamson, i., 590, 593; Col. Doc., iii., 618, 724; Maine H. S. Coll., v., 394, 395; N.Y. H. S. Coll. (1868), 266; Col. MSS., xlviii., 120, 121, 122; Andros Tracts, i., 149–173.

Chap. XI.

1689.

Plymouth boldly reinstated her former Governor Hinckley, and went on in her old system of administration. Chief
Justice Dudley, on his return from holding court at South- 22 April.
old, on Long Island, was arrested at Narragansett and tak- 21 April.
en a prisoner to Boston. Dudley arrested. The freemen of Rhode Island
resumed their old charter government, and replaced their 1 May.
former magistrates. Connecticut emboldened. One of the copies of the charter of
Connecticut was brought out of the hollow tree at Hartford, and Robert Treat, the former governor, with his associates, resumed the functions they had surrendered eighteen 9 May.
months before. A few weeks afterward a Convention met at Boston, which, instead of entering on "the full exercise"
of the old charter government, merely reinstated the mag- 24 May.
istrates chosen in 1686, provisionally, until orders should
come from England. A vessel now reached Boston with 26 May.
news of the accession of William and Mary; yet the British sovereigns were not proclaimed in Massachusetts. Three
days afterward Sir William Phipps arrived with the delay- 29 May.
ed dispatches from Whitehall directed to Andros. Finding that the governor, whom he had intended to "secure," was already in custody, Phipps, instead of sending them to Nich-
olson, Phipps's felony at Boston. feloniously opened the letters addressed to Andros and to Secretary Randolph on public business, which, among other things, contained the official proclamations. The same afternoon William and Mary were proclaimed at Boston king and queen, "with greater ceremony than had been known." Emboldened by the advice of Phipps, the usurping authorities of Massachusetts determined that Andros, 27 June.
with Dudley, Randolph, Palmer, West, Graham, Farewell, and Sherlock, his most obnoxious subordinates, should be kept close prisoners without bail. But Brockholls, MacGregorie, Jamison, and others, who were at first imprisoned, appear to have been discharged.*

* Col. Doc., iii., 574, 575, 578, 581, 582, 583, 587, 588, 618, 724; Col. Rec. Conn., iii., 248, 250, 255, 455–459, 463–466; R. I. Rec., iii., 257, 266–269; Arnold, i., 512, 513; Plymouth Rec., vi., 208, 209; N. Y. H. S. Coll. (1868); Mass. H. S. Coll., xxxv., 190–202, 301; Maine H. S. Coll., i., 196; v., 271; Williamson, i., 593; Mather, Mag., i., 180; ii., 588; Force's Tracts, No. 9, p. 9–12, 18; No. 10, p. 3, 4; Hist. Mag., vi., 9–14; Hutch. Mass., i., 371–388, 413; Coll., 568, 571, 575; Chalmers's Annals, i., 429–431, 469, 470; ii., 24–28, 51; Rev. Col., i., 209; Grahame, i., 388, 390; Bancroft, ii., 447–450; iii., 71, 72, 78; Barry, i., 501–507; Trumbull, i., 376, 377; Palfrey, iii., 581–598; *ante*, 543. It is remarkable that Mr. Palfrey suppresses the accounts given by Randolph and French (Col. Doc., iii., 582, 583, 587, 588) of the behavior of Phipps on board the "Prudent Sarah," in which he came from England, and afterward on shore in Boston.

CHAP. XI. 1689.

Thus, without the knowledge, and against the purpose of King William, his "Dominion of New England" was "disunited." That dominion had lasted just eight months after the annexation of New York and the Jerseys to New England. By the "secession" of Massachusetts, a loyal but perhaps reluctant union was dissolved, and the most pretentious English colony became the first practical exponent in North America of that doctrine of "State Rights" which afterward produced so much national disorder. Yet, in all the insurrectionary movements in New England, there was no intent to revolt from the mother country. The colonial subjects who deposed Andros did not claim the right to frame their own local governments. On the contrary, vehemently protesting their loyalty to the crown, they sought to obtain from their actual sovereign a restoration of the charters which former English kings had granted to them. Local corporate privilege under royal authority, and not universal popular freedom, was the object desired, and in the mutiny to regain it, the selfish lust of oligarchy was more apparent than devotion to the genuine principles of civil liberty.*

Inconsistency of the Boston revolt.

The insurrection in Boston was wholly owing to Phipps and Mather's intrigue in London, which prevented the dispatch to Andros of William's orders in January. Had those orders been sent to him at once, as intended, there would have been no revolt in Massachusetts. The Protestant Governor of New England was too loyal a colonial officer to hesitate in obeying the directions of the head of his home authority. William and Mary would have been dutifully proclaimed as soon as the English royal Council's dispatches reached Andros, and the dominion of New England would not have been broken up by rebellious secession. The orders of the Privy Council were duly forwarded to Virginia, where William and Mary were promptly proclaimed at Jamestown. The case of Maryland somewhat resembled that of New England. Lord Baltimore, being in London, received the Council's orders there, and instructed his deputies in Maryland to proclaim the new sovereigns. But his directions were delayed by accident or design, and in April John Coode headed a Protestant asso-

The whole affair very mean.

29 April. Virginia.

* Col. Doc., iii., 581, 725; Chalmers, Rev. Col., i., Int., x., xi., 209; Annals, ii., 25.

ciation, which soon overthrew the proprietor's government, and carried on a usurped authority for some time with "predatory tyranny." Penn, who was also in England, received similar orders, which, like Baltimore's, were not forwarded, and the government of Pennsylvania was administered in the name of King James until the following November, when William and Mary were proclaimed.* CHAP. XI. 1689. July. August. Maryland and Pennsylvania.

When the first news of the revolution in England reached New York, its provincial affairs were administered under Andros by Nicholson, the lieutenant governor, and the three royal resident counselors, Phillipse, Van Cortlandt, and Bayard. The other New York members of the Council were absent from the metropolis—Brockholls in Maine, Baxter in Albany, Younge at Southold, on Long Island, and Palmer near his chief in Massachusetts. Nicholson, the lieutenant governor of the dominion of New England, was a soldier and a martinet, quick and irascible, a good subordinate, but hardly equal to responsible command; naturally a sycophant; professing to be a Protestant English Episcopalian, yet not troubled by inconvenient sectarian scruples; cheerfully kneeling among a Roman Catholic crowd while the popish mass was celebrated in the tent of King James, in his camp on Hounslow Heath, in the summer of 1686. This outward conformity to a ritual, which no gentleman accidentally present would refuse to accord, did not prove Nicholson to be a Roman Catholic. But it showed him to be a courtly English Episcopalian; and his timely genuflection told against him now, when the most trivial circumstances were distorted by popular credulity. Over many a Delft-ware teacup in the little society of New York the rumor went from mouth to mouth; and the verdict of the burghers and their wives, who compared notes every Sunday after hearing Domine Selyns expound the Heidelburg Catechism in the Dutch church, was very damaging to the lieutenant governor's reputation as a good Protestant. February. Nicholson.

Frederick Phillipse, one of the royal counselors, with fourteen years' experience in the office, was only remarka- Phillipse.

* Chalmers's Ann., i., 373, 374, 381-384, 431, 654, 667; ii., 13-20, 37, 38; Rev. Col., i., 202-206; Burk, ii., 306, 307; Anderson's Col. Church, ii., 381, 382, 400, 401; Doc. Hist. N. Y., ii., 19, 25, 126, 140, 150; Davis's Day Star, 87-105; Penn. Col. Rec., i., 301-305, 341; Proud, i., 347; Dixon, 262, 266; Grahame, ii., 50, 51, 368-370; Bancroft, ii., 245; iii., 30, 31; Andros Tracts, ii., 275; *ante*, 537.

CHAP. XI. 1689. ble for being the richest and the dullest man in New York. Stephen van Cortlandt, another counselor, was the mayor of the metropolis, and a brother-in-law of Peter Schuyler, the mayor of Albany. Being a gentleman, he was reputed to be an aristocrat, and his genial sacrifice of hat and wig the last August at the city carouse for the birth of the Prince of Wales marked him as a very loyal Conservative.

Van Cortlandt.

Bayard.

Nicholas Bayard, the third resident royal counselor, was a nephew of Stuyvesant, and, like Phillipse and Van Cortlandt, was an opulent man, according to the modest standard of those days. He had long official experience, and, having served as mayor, was now colonel of the city regiment of train-bands, of which the captains were Abraham de Peyster, Johannes de Bruyn, Gabriel Minvielle, Charles Lodwyck, Nicholas W. Stuyvesant, and Jacob Leisler. For more than twenty years Bayard and Van Cortlandt had been elders and deacons of the Reformed Dutch Church, of which their more quiet colleague Phillipse was also a communicant. With Nicholson, these were the three Protestant citizens who governed New York in subordination to the governor general of the dominion of New England.*

Bayard's captains.

Seeing that the news of the landing of the Prince of Orange in England "troubled the Papists very much," Nicholson and his council, being "jealous" of Plowman, the Roman Catholic collector, ordered him to bring the public moneys in his hands, amounting to nearly twelve hundred pounds, into the fort, "in a strong chest made on purpose." The next month "the surprising news" of the insurrection at Boston, and the imprisonment of Andros, reached New York by Ensign Vesey, of Braintree. Had the governor succeeded in his attempt to embark in the Rose frigate, and come in her to the metropolis, the course of events would have been very different. His vigor and experience would certainly have prevented what followed in New York. But Nicholson and his three counselors, without instructions from their imprisoned chief, in great consternation directed Mayor Van Cortlandt to convene the Aldermen and Common Council of the city, "to advise together what best is to be done for his Majesty's service, and the quieting of

Action of Nicholson and his counselors.

26 April.

* Col. Doc., iii., 584, 588, 648, 670; Doc. Hist., ii., 4, 17, 244; Hutch. Mass., i., 385; N. Y. H. S. Coll. (1868), 295; *ante*, 451, 516, 549.

the inhabitants of this place, in this dangerous conjuncture and troublesome time." The next day it was reported that France was at war with England and Holland, and the militia officers were called into council. By this "General Convention for the Province of New York," it was resolved that the city should be fortified. As half the regular soldiers in the garrison had been sent to Maine, Nicholson, "to prevent all manner of doubt and jealousies," himself proposed that a part of the city militia should mount guard in the fort. The inhabitants accordingly took their turns in watching, under the command of Colonel Bayard. As there was no time to lay taxes, and as the merchants began "to dispute the customs," Nicholson also proposed that the revenue from the first of May should be applied to the city fortifications; and this "was thankfully accepted of." The person who showed the greatest dislike to this arrangement was Captain Leisler, who, having a cargo of wine on board a ship, the customs on which amounted to a hundred pounds, refused to pay any duty, alleging that Collector Plowman, "being a papist, was not qualified to receive it, denying the then power to be legal." The justices and military officers of Kings, Queens, Westchester, Richmond, and Bergen counties, and Colonel Andrew Hamilton, of New Jersey, having been summoned, all appeared, and "promised to do their endeavour to keep the people in peace." A watchman was stationed at Coney Island, to give an alarm if more than three ships together should come within Sandy Hook. Letters were also written to Albany and Ulster, recommending the officers there to keep the people in peace and exercise the militia. The nearest royal counselors of the dominion, Winthrop, Treat, Allyn, Younge, Pynchon, and others, were invited to come to New York and assist with their advice. But none came; and none wrote answers except Smith, Clarke, and Newberry, of Rhode Island.*

27 April. Convention of officers called.

28 April.

29 April. Fortifications.

Justices summoned.

30 April.

Royal counselors do not come from other colonies.

Nicholson and his three associate counselors now dispatched a letter of condolence to Andros at Boston, and asked him to send back the New York records. They also wrote to the "Gentlemen" in power there, hoping "that his

1 May. Nicholson's letter to the Boston rebels.

* Col. Doc., iii., 575, 576, 591, 592, 636, 637, 639, 640, 667, 668, 725; iv., 200; Doc. Hist., ii., 17, 18, 229, 244, 245; Whitehead's East Jersey, 122; Hutch. Mass., i., 384, *note;* N.Y. H. S. Coll. (1868), 243–248; *ante*, 552.

CHAP. XI. 1689. Excellency and the rest of the officers may be restored to their former stations, or at least have liberty to come hither. For this part of the Government, we find the people in general inclined to peace and quietness, and doubt not the people will remain in their duties." This was certainly a reasonable request of the lieutenant governor. Although Massachusetts insurgents had overthrown the government of Andros within the old borders of that colony, they had no right to prevent him from exercising his commission within the rest of the dominion of New England, and especially in New York, which desired his presence. But those insurgents well knew that if the governor general should resume his authority in Fort James, there would be an end to New England "secession." So Bradstreet and Winthrop, in behalf of the Massachusetts "Committee of Safety," wrote back to Lieutenant Governor Nicholson and his New York counselors that Sir Edmund would not be released, and they inclosed a printed copy of Mather's declaration of 18 April as the justification of their action.*

11 May. Boston rebels truculent.

This Boston "Declaration" had already excited the New York people at the eastern end of Long Island. The county of Suffolk displaced their civil and military officers and chose others. Queens and Westchester did the same. Word now came to them from Leisler that Nicholson meant to betray the fort at New York "to a foreign power." So delegates from Southampton, Easthampton, and Huntington were sent to New York, "to demand the Fort to be delivered into the hands of such persons as the country shall choose." The Long Island militia who had been with Dongan at Albany now became clamorous for their pay, and some eighty of them met in arms at Jamaica. The New York city men who had been drafted did the same, and the Council ordered all to be paid off, which quieted the uproar. The delegates from Suffolk were told that each county might send a man or two to join with the authorities in New York, and letters were accordingly dispatched to invite them; "but none came."†

8 May. Long Island troubled by Boston.

8 May. Action of Nicholson.

11 May.

The lieutenant governor and his associate counselors now

* Col. Doc., iii., 592, 640; Hutch. Mass., i., 383-386; Force's Tracts, iv., No. 10, 6-13; N. Y. H. S. Coll. (1868), 250, 251; Hist. Mag., vi., 10-14; *ante*, 551.

† Col. Doc., iii., 575, 577, 592, 668; Doc. Hist., ii., 227; Wood, 109, 110; Hutch. Mass., i., 385, *note*; N. Y. H. S. Coll. (1868), 252, 280; (1869), 247, 248.

wrote to the British secretary of state and the Plantation Committee, regretting the want of intelligence from England; describing the rebellious secession of Massachusetts, Rhode Island, and Connecticut from the king's dominion; and declaring that, although "the seed of sedition had been blown from thence to some of the outward skirts of this Province," and that "libels and falsehoods" had been propagated from Boston against Sir Edmund Andros, which would excite the Canadians to ruin "all the English settlements on this continent," yet that New York, although deprived of "its free course of justice" by the imprisonment of Judge Palmer at Boston, and deploring its fatal annexation to New England, was "inclined to rest at peace and quiet 'till orders do arrive." These letters were intrusted to John Riggs, "a servant of Sir Edmund Andros," who, coming from Boston to New York, was persuaded by Nicholson to convey them at once to England. Riggs was accompanied thither by the Jesuit Father John Smith, who had performed the service of his church under Dongan. But Innis, the Episcopalian chaplain at Fort James, not instructed by his bishop, continued to read the authorized prayers of his religious "denomination" for the Prince of Wales; and that the dethroned King of England might be victorious over his enemies.*

CHAP. XI.

1689.

15 May.

Nicholson's report to William.

Riggs and Smith go to England.

George Wedderborne now came from Boston to New York, with verbal instructions from the imprisoned governor general of New England, directing Lieutenant Governor Nicholson to intimate to the Council "the unjust proceedings of the people in Boston, by keeping his Excellency prisoner, and the other gentlemen, upon frivolous pretences of their own, without any shadow of reason;" and desiring that Councilors Hamilton, of New Jersey, and Smith, of Long Island, should be sent "to Boston, with commission to demand his Excellency and the other gentlemen to be at liberty, that they may come amongst you." But Hamilton and Smith both excused themselves from going to Boston on a fruitless journey, because "they did think it not advisable in these dangerous times to act any further, for fear it would bring" New York "in actual rebellion." So Nich-

18 May.

Andros's verbal orders to Nicholson.

22 May.

* Col. Doc., iii., 574–576, 585, 593, 655, 747; Doc. Hist., ii., 244; N. Y. H. S. Coll. (1868), 27, 29, 253–266; Andros Tracts; Chalmers's Ann., i., 591; ii., 27, 29; Palfrey, iii., 585, 586.

CHAP. XI.

1689.

olson and his council, "seeing the uproars in all parts of the Government," thought it "most safe to forbear acting in the premises till they see the minds of the people better satisfied and quieted." The citizens of New York continued meanwhile to work on her fortifications, under the direction of Colonel Bayard, until one Joost Stoll, an ensign

22 May.

of Captain Leisler's company, and some others, presented to their commanding officer an "unsigned and ill penned" petition demanding that all papists should be disarmed. It

Needless bother in New York.

was also noised about that Staten Island was full of roaming papists, who threatened to burn the metropolis; that discharged Irish soldiers were coming from Boston to garrison Fort James; and that Dongan had fitted out an armed brigantine "for some warlike design." No explanations would satisfy the aroused populace of New York. There were ridiculously few Roman Catholics living in the province; and only seven disbanded soldiers came from Boston, who, with the others in the citadel, made twenty-two in all, among whom were some "old cripples." But, to avoid all jealousies," Ensign Russell, of Fort James, and Major Baxter, who had come down from Albany, being

27 May. Baxter and Russell suspended.

avowed Roman Catholics, were suspended from their commands and allowed to leave the province. Baxter went at once to join Dongan, who was staying in the "Neversincks," at the house of Captain Andrew Bowne, of Monmouth, in East New Jersey, preparing to sail for England in his brigantine.*

The crisis was at hand in New York. Hitherto there had been little or no sectarian intolerance within the prov-

Protestantism not jeoparded in New York.

ince. Certainly its preponderating Protestantism was in no danger from the sparse Roman Catholics who shared with others its long-cherished freedom of conscience. Yet their presence in New York was made the excuse for the events which followed. The example of Massachusetts, in seceding from the royal government of New England, had doubtless some influence. But the leading idea in New York was intense devotion to its old stadtholder, the Prince of Orange, who had delivered England from her Roman Catholic king. There was no suggestion of misgovernment

* Col. Doc., iii., 593, 632, 637, 640; Doc. Hist., ii., 4, 16, 17, 18, 244; N. Y. H. S. Coll. (1868), 263-267, 284-287; Col. Rec. Conn., iii., 461; Whitehead's E. J., 133; *ante*, 557.

against Nicholson and his counselors in New York, as there had been against Andros and his counselors at Boston. New York did not want a sectarian oligarchy, as did Massachusetts. But her Dutch people were so honestly attached to William that they doubted the sincerity of the officials of the dethroned James, although those officials were all Protestants — Nicholson an Episcopalian, and Phillipse, Bayard, and Van Cortlandt members of the Dutch Church.

Excess of religious feeling.

In popular movements trifles become momentous. Henry Cuyler, the lieutenant of Captain De Peyster's militia company, whose turn it was to do duty at Fort James, ordered one of his men to stand as a sentinel at the sally-port. The sergeant of the regular soldiers in garrison objected that the lieutenant governor had given no such directions. Upon Nicholson's return, late at night, the incident was reported, and Cuyler was summoned to attend him in his bedchamber. Irritated at this breach of military discipline, the lieutenant governor demanded, "Who is commander in this Fort, you or I?" Cuyler answered that he had acted under Captain De Peyster's orders. In a passion, Nicholson replied, "I would rather see the town on fire than be commanded by you," and—seeing in his chamber a stalwart corporal, Henry Jacobsen, who had accompanied his lieutenant thither as interpreter, with a drawn sword—he seized a pistol, and ordered them both out. The next morning the story was buzzed all over town, with the usual vulgar exaggeration. It was reported and generally believed that the lieutenant governor had threatened to burn New York, and it was added that he meant to massacre those of its inhabitants who should come to worship in the Dutch church in the fort the next Sunday. The absurdity of this rumor seemed to give it greater currency. No contradiction could satisfy the people. They would have it that Nicholson and his Dutch counselors were all "Papists." The flight of James from England, it was argued, had destroyed "all manner of Government" in New York, and there were not wanting noisy demagogues to work up popular credulity with the scoundrel industry of political adventurers of their class.*

30 May.

Nicholson insulted.

31 May. The story misrepresented in New York.

* Col. Doc., iii., 593, 594, 640, 668; Doc. Hist., ii., 8, 232, 245; Hutch. Mass., i., 385, *note*; N. Y. H. S. Coll. (1868), 292.

CHAP. XI.

1689.

Jacob Leisler. A German—not a Dutchman.

Of the events which now strode on in New York, Jacob Leisler must be considered the chief mover. Although commonly called a Dutchman, Leisler was no Hollander except by association. He was a German, born at Frankfort-on-the-Maine, and he had first come to New Netherland as a stipendiary soldier of the Dutch West India Company. For nearly thirty years he had lived in New York, where, from his first condition as a mercenary private, he had grown to be a prosperous merchant. By marriage he had become connected with both Bayard and Van Cortlandt; but he had been involved in lawsuits with them and others whom he felt to be his superiors in education and in social position. A rankling envy of these New York gentlemen moved Leisler, as it always moves those brutal natures which count elbows and impudence better than refinement. Leisler was a fair sample of his class. His nature was coarse and vulgar; his mind vigorous, but narrow; his temper hot, stubborn, and vindictive; his prejudices ungovernable; his vanity inordinate; his education very defective; his deportment presumptuous and overbearing; his personal integrity as unquestionable as was his active benevolence toward poor Protestants, and his blazing zeal against popery. Wanting judgment and discretion, but supercharged with unscrupulous boldness and low cunning, Leisler had many of the characteristics of a successful demagogue, but few of the qualifications of a statesman.

Leisler's character.

Peculiar situation of New York.

The peculiar position of New York offered Leisler an admirable opportunity. The province had never liked its annexation to New England, yet its form of government had not been changed by James's arbitrary measure which destroyed its old identity. It had no charter, as had Massachusetts, and Rhode Island, and Connecticut. Its people were glad when the New England colonies seceded from the dominion established by their king, although they would never have revolted themselves. Every one of them felt that New York must follow the fate of England, and that the sovereign of that country must be their sovereign, unless the province was independent. But the absence of directions from England, and the imprisonment of Andros in Boston, could not fail to produce disorder in New York. The only wish of Nicholson and his counselors was to keep the old province in peace until orders should come from the actual sovereign of England. Such orders they would gladly have obeyed. But they were sworn royal officers, and they could not act without their sovereign's instructions, which of course would be communicated—as in fact they had been—to his imprisoned governor general at Boston. Their situation was certainly trying. If Nicholson was an English Episcopalian, Phillipse, Van Cortlandt, and Bayard, his counselors, were eminent Dutch Calvinists, and these New York gentlemen all had strong sympathies with William of Orange. Yet, as royal counselors, they could not recognize an English sovereign whose accession had not been officially notified to them. But there was always a powerful Dutch under-current in New York, which now ran very strong. William of Orange was known to be the actual King of England; why should he not be proclaimed king in New York? But if official forms restrained Nicholson and his Dutch counselors, no such reserve affected the people of New York. Of these, the German Leisler now took the lead. Leisler had never been in the royal council, nor had he ever held any important provincial office; but he supposed that if he should exhibit headlong zeal for the Prince of Orange, it would help him with William as king. His narrow logic argued that if the prompt adherence of Lovelace, and Cornbury, and others in Devonshire contributed to the success of William the Third in England, so the prompt adherence of Jacob Leisler to William in New York would, in some degree, affect the great result. And so Leisler forgot that a towed yawl must follow the tacking of her ship.*

Dutch influence in New York.

Near the Cape of Good Hope there is a growth of prickly briers which sorely trouble incautious visitors. Long before Portuguese or Dutch saw these ugly brambles, the natives of Africa carefully avoided them. When the Hollanders first encountered these thorns, and found that they hindered the bold wayfarer who would dash through, they gave them an expressive name, "Wacht een beetje," which in English means *Wait a little bit.* The Dutch were a proverbially cautious people. If Leisler and his confederates had profited by this suggestive hint from the Cape of Good

"Wacht een beetje."

* Chalmers's Annals, ii., 35; Palfrey, iii., 489; Col. MSS.; *ante*, 534, 540, 543.

CHAP. XI. 1689. Hope, they would have shown wisdom, and have avoided much misery which their precipitate folly inflicted on New York.

The design imputed to Nicholson, of making the next Sunday another Saint Bartholomew's Day in New York, was so generally reported by Leisler's friends, and so readily believed by the people, that on Friday, the last day of May, the metropolis was in a great commotion. The lieutenant governor came from Fort James to meet the Council and the militia captains, who were all present at the City Hall except Leisler. All were "Protestants and principal freeholders." Nicholson explained to them what had occurred at Fort James the night before, and denied the truth of Cuyler's story. But Cuyler maintaining his version, Nicholson told him, "Go, fetch your commission; I discharge you from being Lieutenant any more." Upon this, Captain De Peyster took his lieutenant's part, and retired in anger. The drums were soon beat, and groups of citizens appeared in arms. The first among them were those of Leisler's company, who mustered tumultuously before their captain's door. Leisler, however, declining to head them, left the command to his sergeant, Joost Stoll, the keeper of a dram-shop, who quickly led them into Fort James, shouting "we are sold, betrayed, and to be murdered; it is time to look for ourselves!" Leisler now girt on his sword, and joined his company in the fort. Colonel Bayard, his superior officer, at the desire of the Convention sitting at the Town Hall, went there to bring Leisler's mutineers to reason, but their drunken Sergeant Stoll answered that they "disowned all the authority of the government." As the evening came on, Captain Lodwyck's company took its turn in mounting guard, and the people insisted on having the keys of the fort, which Nicholson kept with him at the City Hall. Sergeant William Churcher, of Leisler's company, was sent with an armed force to demand them, and the lieutenant governor was obliged to give them up, which he did to Captain Lodwyck. The six captains now agreed that each would take his daily turn in commanding the fort until orders should come from England. A "Declaration," drafted by Leisler, was also signed by some of those who had seized the fort, in which, aft-

[Margin notes: 31 May. — Mutiny in New York. — 31 May. Leisler's "Declaration."]

er referring to Dongan's "Popish" government, and charging Nicholson with having threatened to "set the city on fire," they announced that they were "entirely and openly opposed to Papists and their religion, and therefore, expecting orders from England, we shall keep and guard, surely and faithfully, the said Fort, in behalf of the power that now governeth in England, to surrender to the person of the Protestant Religion that shall be nominated or sent by the power aforesaid."*

1 June.

The next day there was a reaction, and Bayard was asked to take the "sole command" against the lieutenant governor. Leisler, seeing that he was being deserted, started fresh rumors that Nicholson and his Dutch counselors were papists, rogues, and traitors, who intended to secure the government for the late King James. These and other "falceties" were circulated verbally, and by "Pamphlets in writing," throughout the city, which then enjoyed no printing-press. The following day was Sunday, on which it was Leisler's turn to guard the fort, and he determined "not to leave it until he had brought all the train-band fully to join with him." He caused to be noised around that the Protestant religion and the government were in immediate danger, and that the inhabitants would meet "to sign and prevent the same." The militia companies were warned to come to the fort the next morning at a certain signal, and not to obey their officers if they should attempt to prevent them. Accordingly, on Monday morning, a sloop from Barbadoes arrived near Coney Island, and a rumor was spread over New York that French ships were inside of Sandy Hook. Leisler gave the concerted signal from Fort James, and the parade-ground in front of it was quickly filled with train-bands. The falsity of the alarm being soon discovered, Colonel Bayard ordered the captain whose turn it was to go with his company to work on the city fortifications, and the others, to dismiss their men. Instead of obeying their colonel, the train-bands, instigated by Sergeants Stoll and Churcher, of Leisler's company, pressed

2 June. Leisler in Fort James.

3 June.

False alarm about the French.

* Col. Doc., iii., 585, 593, 594, 629, 634, 637, 639, 668, 669, 763; Doc. Hist., ii., 3, 7, 8, 245; Chalmers, i., 591, 610; Smith, i., 91; Hutch., i., 385, *note;* Hist. Mag., v., 154; N. Y. H. S. Coll. (1868), 268, 288, 345, 346. This declaration was printed several weeks afterward by Samuel Greene, at Boston. Bayard, in saying that it was "antedated," confounds it with a second paper, signed on the 3d of June: Thomas, Hist. Print., ii., 286; Col. Doc., iii., 629, 630, 639; *post*, p. 568.

CHAP. XI. 1689. into the fort, reluctantly followed by their captains, who were told that, unless they also went in, their houses would be pulled down, and their lives jeoparded. Shouts and huzzas welcomed them within the gates, and a paper which Leisler had prepared was offered for their signature. It was a proclamation, declaring that they held the fort "till the safe arrival of the ships that we expect every day from his Royal Highness the Prince of Orange, with orders for the government of this country, in the behalf of such person as the said Royal Highness had chosen and honored with the charge of a Governor, that as soon as the bearer of the said orders shall have let us see his power, then, and without any delay, we shall execute the said orders punctually." This ill-worded document was quickly signed by all the six New York captains, and by four hundred of their men. Few of them really knew that they had actually signed a declaration that they would obey only the orders of the Prince of Orange, and not those of the crown of England. It was, in truth, a thoroughly Dutch movement. Most of the signers were Hollanders, "a notion being put in many of their heads that, by a vote of Parliament, all charters and Privileges were to be restored to all places of the Dominions, and they be put in the same state as they were in the year 1660. And by consequence this government to be restored to the Dutch; and therefore no orders from the authority or crown of England, but only from his Royal Highness the Prince of Orange, would serve their terms." This absurd idea grew out of the inconsequential resolution of the English House of Commons in the previous March, of which some inkling had reached America.*

Fort James seized. 3 June.

Leisler's proclamation.

3 June. If this idea existed, it was quickly corrected. The same afternoon, copies of the London Gazette containing the proclamations of William and Mary of 14 February, for continuing all "Protestants" in office in England, was received in New York. It was not yet known there that, in obedience to the dispatches brought over by Phipps and addressed to Andros, those sovereigns had been proclaimed at Boston, and that the English Privy Council had directed

* Col. Doc., iii., 584, 586, 594, 595, 630, 637–639, 669, 670; Doc. Hist., ii., 3, 4, 9, 66; Col. Rec. Conn., iii., 466; Hutch., i., 385, *note;* N. Y. H. S. Coll. (1868), 269, 288; Smith, i., 92, 389; *ante,* 541.

that "all persons" in the colonies should retain their offices. Two days afterward, Philip French, who had come from England in the same ship with Phipps, reached New York, and Leisler, who was now really at the head of affairs, "made bold" to open and read publicly in the fort all the letters which he had brought addressed to Nicholson, Bayard, and Van Cortlandt.*

CHAP. XI.

1689.

5 June.

Letters opened by Leisler.

Had Nicholson been equal to his position, he might have saved New York and her Dutch king from much trouble. But the lieutenant governor was a regular parade soldier. Without the directing mind of Andros, he shrunk into insignificance. His resident counselors were provincial gentlemen, conservative, and disliking public broils. Such controversies generally benefit impudent officials, who, if their schemes turn out well, make fortunes out of the plunder of their fellow-citizens. Such antagonism Nicholson and his advisers wished to avoid; but they had not the energy and skill to cope with the occasion, and so, by mere imbecility, they lost their opportunity, and left a vulgar, vigorous, and despotic usurper master of the field.

Nicholson's weakness.

Leisler's proceedings at New York were quickly communicated to the leading insurgents in Connecticut, her next colonial neighbor. The German captain now in command of Fort James wrote to Major Nathan Gold, at Fairfield, that he wanted to have "one trusted man sent to procure in England some privileges," and, assuming to speak for New York, he added, "I wish we may have part in your charter, being, as I understand, in the latitude." This was just such a display of folly as an ignorant demagogue would exhibit. It was followed by an address of "the militia and other inhabitants" of New York to William and Mary, which gave "a tedious, incorrect, ill-drawn" narrative of recent provincial events, and promised entire submission to their majesties' pleasure. The address was signed by Captains Leisler, De Peyster, Lodwyck, De Bruyn, and Stuyvesant, their colleague Minvielle having declined to act further with them, and obtained his discharge from Nicholson. Copies of the address and other papers were sent to some

7 June.

Connecticut appealed to.

Leisler's address to William.

11 June.

* Col. Doc., iii., 583, 584, 586–588, 595, 720; iv., 396; Doc. Hist., ii., 4; Chalmers's Ann., i., 469; ii., 29, 37; N. Y. H. S. Coll. (1868), 29, 37, 269; Hutch., i., 387, 397; Wood, 110; *ante*, 539, 555.

CHAP. XI. 1689.

Dutch merchants in London, who were asked to deliver it to the king, and put in "a seasonable word" if they could.*

After Leisler and his adherents took possession of Fort James, the lieutenant governor lodged at the house of Counselor Phillipse, and kept up the show of his authority, which a little timely vigor would have secured. If, when he received the London Gazette announcing the accession of William and Mary, Nicholson had at once proclaimed them king and queen in New York, official forms might have been violated, but much provincial trouble would have been avoided. He knew that those sovereigns had been proclaimed at Boston on the arrival of Phipps with the Privy Council's dispatches for Andros. But Nicholson was a fair example of a straightforward English official bound by "red tape." He had no instructions from his immediate chief, and would not act without them. Subordinate to the imprisoned Andros, and hampered, perhaps, by his conservative provincial advisers, Nicholson did not dare to take the bold steps which the unfettered Leisler trod. Upon these steps the fortunes of New York were for some time to depend. The lieutenant governor unwisely determined to go to England, "to render an account of the present deplorable state of affairs here." In the mean time, he deputed Counselors Phillipse, Van Cortlandt, and Bayard "to preserve the peace during his absence, and until his Majesty's pleasure should be known." These three counselors wrote by him to Secretary Shrewsbury that news had come to New York from Barbadoes and Boston of the proclamation of William and Mary in England, and that they "were in daily hopes to be so happy as to receive the suitable orders for to observe the same solemnities here. But before we could be made partakers of those our happy desires, it has come to pass that, by the means and ill contrivances of some disaffected and dangerous persons, all manner of government is totally overthrown here, in like manner as to that of Boston." And they expressed their belief "that although orders from his now Majesty should arrive for the continuing of the persons formerly entrusted in the Government, that no such orders would be obeyed." Several confirma-

6 June. Nicholson resolves to leave New York.

10 June. Letter of the New York Council to the English government.

* Col. Doc., iii., 583, 584, 595, 600, 670; Doc. Hist., ii., 3, 4, 9; Col. Rec. Conn., iii., 466, 467; Smith, i., 92; N. Y. H. S. Coll. (1868), 270, 271, 290, 291.

tory documents accompanied this letter, among others a Latin certificate by Domine Selyns and his Consistory, of the good standing of Counselors Van Cortlandt and Bayard in the Reformed Dutch Church. Innis, the Episcopalian chaplain at Fort James, also provided himself with the attestation of the Dutch and French ministers at New York of his being a good Protestant, and accompanied Nicholson to England. But feeling ran so strong that they were refused a passage by the captains of the ships which carried out the papers sent by Leisler. Nicholson therefore bought a share in Dongan's brigantine, in which he had returned from sea, and after some delay set sail for London. Dongan, however, having suffered from sea-sickness, determined to remain for the present in New York.*

CHAP. XI. 1689. 11 June. Innis. 24 June.

Nicholson's desertion of his post gave Leisler an unexpected advantage. Assuming the lead, the bold German captain invited each of the counties and neighboring towns to send two delegates to New York on the 26th of June, to form "a Committee of Safety," as well as two men from each to guard the fort, the name of which was now changed again from "James" to "William," which it had borne in 1673. Leisler also tried to put out of office the Roman Catholic collector Plowman, to whom he was obliged to pay duties on his imported liquors, but his colleague-captains would not help him in this personal spite. Finding that Leisler answered all objections with "What, do you talk of law? the sword must now rule," and declared that all commissions under the authority of James the Second "were utterly void," the city magistrates prudently "resolved to be passive."†

12 June. Leisler assumes the command. 16 June.

Connecticut having now proclaimed William and Mary, appointed Gold and Fitch to go to New York and give such advice and promise such assistance as might be necessary. Secretary Allyn also advised that no Roman Catholic be allowed to enter the fort, or keep arms within the city or government of New York. Learning that the Connecticut messengers were expected, Van Cortlandt and Bayard, with others, went to meet them at Colonel Morris's house, in

13 June. Sympathy of Connecticut. 20 June.

* Col. Doc., iii., 382, 542, 585, 586, 588, 595, 599, 613, 615, 616, 618, 630, 637, 649, 655, 669, 675, 731; Doc. Hist., ii., 3, 18, 38; Hutch., i., 387; Chalmers, i., 431; N. Y. H. S. Coll. (1868), 270–272, 288–292; Smith, i., 93; Wood, 105; *ante*, 555.

† Col. Doc., iii., 600, 614, 641, 671; Doc. Hist., ii., 3, 4; Wood, 105, 110; *ante*, 559.

CHAP. XI. 1689. 21 June. 22 June.

Westchester; but Gold and Fitch went directly on to the fort, and gave Leisler a copy of the printed English proclamation of the accession of William and Mary. The next morning, Mayor Van Cortlandt and his fellow-counselors asked the Connecticut delegates for their papers, so that the king and queen might be proclaimed in the city "with such honor and splendor as the occasion required." But Gold and Fitch replied that they had come "to the persons that had the fort in custody," and that they had already conferred with Leisler. A little while afterward the drum was beaten, and the king and queen were proclaimed by the German captain in the fort "in the most meanest manner." In the afternoon, Leisler, with Lodwyck, De Bruyn, and De Peyster, and their companies, marched from the fort to the City Hall, where the proclamation was repeated "with all the demonstrations of joy and affection they were capable of." Mayor Van Cortlandt, and his associate counselors Bayard and Phillipse, all of them Dutch gentlemen of New York, and well disposed toward William and Mary of Orange, were thus made to appear more lukewarm than Leisler's followers. A fire, timely discovered in the turret of the church in the fort, under which the powder was stored, was charged by Leisler as "a papistical design," and added to the excitement of the eventful day.*

William and Mary proclaimed in New York.

And so Leisler prevented the royal counselors in New York, who represented English sovereignty, from proclaiming William and Mary as they desired. Yet he failed in one important point. He did not publish the royal proclamation of the fourteenth of February, which confirmed all Protestant English officers in their places. It was not then known in New York that on the nineteenth of February all persons were confirmed in their offices in the English colonies; but Mayor Van Cortlandt, having received a copy, convened the municipal authorities at the City Hall, and published the royal proclamation continuing "all Protestants" in office. This made Leisler very angry, for it confirmed the authority of Phillipse, Van Cortlandt, and Bayard, all of whom were members and some of them officers of the Reformed Protestant Dutch Church. So he charged

Leisler's error.

24 June.

* Col. Doc., iii., 589, 595, 601, 614–617, 641, 671, 738, 764; Doc. Hist., ii., 10, 19, 245; Col. Rec. Conn., iii., 253, 255, 467, 468; Trumbull, i., 377, 378.

that all magistrates who would not join with him were "Popishly affected." On the other hand, the Dutch royal counselors and their friends likened the German Leisler to the Italian Masaniello, and declared that "not one Papist, or popishly affected, throughout this their Majesty's Province, were in commission of the Peace, and that many whom he hath thus wickedly scandalized have always been of far greater reputation both in Church and State than himself." The next day the acting counselors removed the Roman 25 June. Catholic collector Plowman, and appointed Counselor Bayard, Alderman Richards, with Thomas Wenham and John Haynes, merchants, to act in his stead as "Commissioners of the Customs" until other orders from England. Leisler, Leisler's audacity. however, came with armed men and forcibly drove them out of the custom-house, in which he installed Peter de la Noy as collector. Bayard, the especial object of Leisler's rage, was obliged to escape secretly to Albany.* 28 June.

In the mean time, some of the counties and towns, in Leisler summons a Convention. compliance with Leisler's invitation, had chosen delegates to a Convention. Brooklyn, Flatbush, Flushing, Newtown, Staten Island, Orange, Westchester, and Essex in New Jersey, each sent two, while New York was represented by Peter de la Noy and Samuel Edsall. The delegates were "the greatest Oliverians in the Government," some of whom openly declared that "there had been no legal king in England since Oliver's days." Not a third of the inhabitants of the province "condescended" to vote. Most of the towns in Queens and New Jersey, and all in Suffolk, Ulster, and Albany, would "not meddle themselves." The 20 June. Suffolk, Ulster, and Albany will not meddle. people of Suffolk county not only refused, but asked Connecticut to take them under her jurisdiction, because, after observing Leisler's conduct in seizing the fort, they "distrusted the purity of his motives." Connecticut, however, resolved to keep safely within her charter boundary, and declined to exercise authority in Long Island.†

At the appointed day, Leisler's Convention met at the 26 June.

* Col. Doc., iii., 596, 598, 602, 603, 604, 608, 609, 617, 641, 642, 661, 668, 671, 672; Doc. Hist., ii., 245, 246; Sylvius, xxvii., 29; *ante*, 539, 540.

† Col. Doc., iii., 597, 617; Wood's Long Island, 105, 106, 110; Thompson, i., 164; Smith, i., 42, 68, 95. The towns in Suffolk county sent a "representation" to Connecticut at this time, of which Smith speaks with personal knowledge. I have endeavored to recover it, but neither Mr. Trumbull nor Mr. Hoadley, of Connecticut, to whom I applied, have been able to find a copy. Compare N. Y. H. S. Coll. (1868), 241–248.

1689. Leisler's Convention meets.

fort in New York. It had not, and could not have, any proper authority. The Connecticut agents, Gold and Fitch, in a pompous letter, offered their advice, and promised that the government at Hartford would assist Leisler and his friends, if necessary. Two of the delegates, of "a clearer discerning than the rest, perceiving that the main drift was to set up Leisler and make him commander in chief," withdrew after the first meeting. The remaining ten, Richard Denton, Teunis Roelofse, Jean de Marest, Daniel de Klercke, Johannes Vermilye, Samuel Edsall, Peter de Lanoy, Mathias Harvey, Thomas Williams, and William Lawrence, formed themselves into a "Committee of Safety." Abraham Gouverneur was chosen to be its clerk, and a record of its proceedings was begun. The next day the ten members of the committee signed a commission appointing Leisler to be "Captain of the Fort at New York 'till orders shall come from their Majesties, and that the said Captain Jacob Leisler shall have all aid and assistance, if need be and demanded by him, from city and county, to suppress any foreign enemy and prevent all disorders which evidently may appear."

27 June. Committee:—Gouverneur its clerk.

28 June. Leisler captain of the fort.

The parentage of this document is obvious. It is said to have been signed under a threat of Leisler that, "unless they had made him soo, he would have departed the place in one of his vessels, and turned privateering." Yet it served as a pretext for the fraudulent authority which Leisler now usurped. He cleared vessels as "Captain of the Fort." He seized the public money and organized a company of soldiers, of which he made Churcher lieutenant, and Stoll, the "Dram-man," ensign and commissary. To this band Connecticut contributed ten men; and she also sent two cannon from New Haven to strengthen the fort at New York. A new semicircular battery, for some time known as "Leisler's Half Moon," was soon afterward built "behind the Fort, upon the flat rock to the westward."*

Leisler usurps authority.

Half Moon.

Thus passed away a summer's month in tolerable quiet at New York. The city was now under a military despotism, "the people being overawed by the strength of the

* Col. Doc., iii., 589, 590, 596–598, 604, 608, 609, 615, 617, 620, 630, 643, 644, 670; iv., 621; Doc. Hist., ii., 5, 7, 10, 11, 13, 15, 18, 230, 246; Col. Rec. Conn., iii., 255, 467, 468; Coun. Minutes, ix., 171, 174; Wood, 105, 106, 110; Thompson, i., 164; Smith, i., 42, 68, 95; Miller's Map, 1695; Riker's Newtown, 117; N. Y. H. S. Coll. (1868), 293, 294.

Fort." An actual dictator, Leisler sent out his Sergeant Stoll "to disarm the papists;" and all were counted as "Papists" who would not recognize the German captain. Fearing that the populace "would hale the magistrates by the leggs from the Town Hall," the Mayor's Court of New York adjourned for a month. Bayard had already retired to Albany, and his two colleagues, Phillipse and Van Cortlandt, could do no more as royal counselors than to write to Blathwayte, the secretary of the Plantation Committee, that "all is in a confusion." As none of the city magistrates would administer the oaths of allegiance in the fort, Leisler was obliged to send for Gerardus Beekman, a Long Island justice, to perform that service. Word now came that Andros had escaped from his prison at Boston to Rhode Island, and that Dongan had landed at New London to join him there, "with a design to sell Martin's Vineyard." This made Leisler jealous of "a bad design," and MacGregorie, who had just returned to New York, "to requite Dongan for his favors," offered to go with a guard and bring him a prisoner to the fort. Andros, however, was soon retaken, and carried back to his prison near Boston. Meanwhile four Cambridge "scholars" came with Perry, the postman, across the Brooklyn ferry, and knowing only Brockholls and Lockhart, who had served in Maine, Leisler chose to suspect them as "Papists." They were accordingly arrested; their letters were seized and examined; the drums beat an alarm, and in a short time over four hundred of Leisler's adherents appeared "courageously in arms." Several prominent citizens, disaffected toward Leisler, were arrested and imprisoned without warrant; but the traveling students from Boston, being soon found to be "honest men," were released, and the train-bands were dismissed. The ten members of Leisler's "Committee of Safety," under his inspiration, seized the opportunity to take a bold step. They signed and sealed a commission declaring that, "it being uncertain whether the orders shall come from their Majesties, that Captain Jacob Leisler is hereby appointed to exercise and use the power and authority of a Commander in Chief of the said Province, to administer such oaths to the people, to issue out such warrants, and order such matters as shall be necessary and requisite to be done for the preser-

2 July. Leisler's despotism.

5 August.

2 August.

16 August. Boston "scholars" arrested.

16 August. Leisler commissioned commander-in-chief by his tools.

CHAP. XI. 1689.

vation and protection of the peace of the inhabitants, taking always seasonable advice with militia and civil authority, as occasion shall require."*

A more impudent document it would be difficult to find in the colonial annals of North America. By ten persons, assuming to represent a few of the towns near the metropolis, Leisler was invested with dictatorial power over the province of New York. This appointment has been pronounced to be "in its form open to censure." It was much more: it was totally unjustifiable. No adequate power had given authority to Leisler's "Committee of Safety," which assumed to make him the military dictator of New York.

20 August. Leisler writes to William.

But Leisler now wrote his own story of affairs to the king and queen, which, while stating that he had been chosen in June to be "Captain of the Fort" in the metropolis, avoided any allusion to his absurd commission as "Commander in Chief" of the whole province of New York. This letter, with other papers, was sent to London by Leisler's dram-shop ensign, Stoll, whom Matthew Clarkson, a brother-in-law of the German demagogue's former colleague, Captain Lodwyck, accompanied thither.†

25 August. Jacob Milborne.

A few days afterward Jacob Milborne returned to Manhattan from Holland, where he had been recently staying. Milborne had already been notorious in New York affairs, and in 1687 he had become a partner with the Catholic Brockholls in commercial ventures, which had obliged him to go back again to Europe. Milborne's elder brother, William, was a noisy Anabaptist minister in Boston, who had taken an active part in overthrowing the government of Andros. Milborne had an "affected, ambiguous way of expressing himself," and seeing that his old friend Leisler was now at the head of affairs in New York, Milborne at once

Milborne's bad advice.

entered cordially into his views. The English Revolution, Milborne suggested, was a full justification of all that had been done in New York. To all objectors it was now answered, "By what law, warrant or commission, did the Prince of Orange go into England, and act as he hath done?

* Col. Doc., iii., 596, 608–610, 613–618, 620, 672, 673, 764; iv., 213, 214; Doc. Hist., ii., 6, 14, 15, 16, 19; Hutch., i., 392, 393; Barry, i., 519; Bancroft, iii., 52; N. Y. H. S. Coll. (1868), 295, 296.

† Col. Doc., iii., 609–618, 629, 630; iv., 213, 214; Doc. Hist., ii., 16, 230; Smith, i., 92; Chalmers's Rev. Col., i., 213; Bancroft, iii., 52; N. Y. H. S. Coll. (1868), 297, 298.

And how do you think King William can take that amiss in us, who have only followed his example?" Abraham Gouverneur, the youthful clerk of the Committee of Safety, not to be outdone, declared that "Leisler had carried the Government of New York by the Sword, and had the same right to it as King William had to the Crown."*

If New York had then been an independent sovereignty, as England was, the comparison would have been fair. But colonial New York did not resemble sovereign England; nor was the German captain, Jacob Leisler, the counterpart of the Dutch William of Orange. Orders from England, which had been sent to, but withheld from, Andros at Boston, were anxiously expected in New York; and the absence of those orders gave a rare opportunity to a political mountebank, of which Leisler did not fail to take advantage.

Fallacy of Leisler.

Under the inspiration of Milborne—and ignorant that William had confirmed "all" colonial officials, Protestant or Catholic, in their places—Leisler now ordered the several counties in the province to elect civil and military officers. "Some counties accordingly did, by the appearance of small numbers, turn out the Justices of the Peace, and military officers, and chose new; a method never formerly allowed of." Most of the counties disregarded Leisler's order; and in those in which elections were held, none but his own partisans were chosen. A faction was thus represented—not the people of New York. It was indispensable to Leisler's success that the metropolitan city should be under his control. Dongan's charter had appointed the Feast of Saint Michael the Archangel, or Michael-mas, as the time to choose its aldermen and Common Council. On that day the city wards all voted, and Leisler succeeded, "right or wrong," in returning his son-in-law, Robert Walters, as an alderman. The charter, however, required that the mayor and sheriff of the city should be annually appointed by the governor and council, and the clerk by the governor, and that they were to remain in office until others should be duly appointed in their places. The Com-

September.

29 Sept. Michael-mas in New York.

* Col. MSS., xxxv., 170, 190–207; xxxvi., 28; Col. Doc., iii., 301, 582, 621, 674, 680, 727, 755; iv., 621; Doc. Hist., ii., 42; iii., 527–530; Dunlap, i., 156; *ante*, 196, *note*, 300, 321, 356. Milborne was not at this time "Leisler's son-in-law." He was not married to Mary Leisler until 3 February, 1691: Pass Book, iv., 71; *post*, 625, *note*.

CHAP. XI. 1689. October. Farcical charter election in New York. mittee of Safety, however, ordered "all the Protestant freeholders" in the city to elect these officers. An election was accordingly held, at which "none but about 70 or 80" persons voted; and Peter de la Noy was returned as mayor, Johannes Johnson sheriff, and Abraham Gouverneur clerk —all devoted to Leisler. If the franchise had not been restricted to "Protestant freeholders," this election by a very small minority might be said to have been the first choice of a mayor of the city of New York by its people. But Leisler's farce was not a popular election. On the birthday of James the Second, as required by Dongan's charter, Leisler issued a proclamation confirming the persons so elected in their several offices. It was a curious inconsistency that he should thus have scrupulously observed that charter in regard to its two marked days—the Catholic feast of Michaelmas and the birthday of James the Second—while he violated it otherwise. But Leisler's logic was very peculiar. His object was to gain power by any means. Accordingly, he endeavored to imprison Mayor Van Cortlandt, who was obliged to fly privately out of the city, while his wife, "the Mayoress," was insulted in her own house by Leisler's rude followers, who came to demand the municipal records and seal.*

14 October.

16 October.

Feeling himself secure in the metropolis, where he had strengthened Fort William with supplies of powder from Burlington and Philadelphia, Leisler burned to extend his sway over the other counties which had refused to recognize his assumed authority. Albany, the only other city in the province, and its neighborhood, had long been controlled by a few prominent persons who now held office under Dongan's charter of 1686. Schuyler, the mayor of Albany, and his brother-in-law, Livingston, its clerk, and Wessels, its recorder, were appointed by the governor; while its aldermen, Wendell, Bleecker, Van Schaick, and others, were elected by the citizens, as in New York. Most of the Albany officers were Hollanders; Livingston, the clerk, was a Scotchman, and Pretty, the sheriff, an Englishman. They were all Protestants, and most of them were members of

Leisler attempts Albany.

* Col. Doc., iii., 620, 645, 655, 657, 674, 675, 684; Doc. Hist., ii., 21; Minutes of N. Y. Common Council, i., 336, 344–347; Val. Man., 1850, 201, 239, 486; 1858, 19, 20; Dunlap, i., 156, 157; *ante*, 438, 540. Cornelius W. Lawrence was the first citizen who was elected mayor of the metropolis by its people in 1834.

the Reformed Dutch Church, of which Schaats and Delius were the collegiate domines. None of them were at all "popishly inclined." When the news of the landing of the Prince of Orange reached Albany, the inhabitants, being generally Dutch, were overjoyed at the prospect of his becoming king. But Livingston, who owed much of his estate to official emoluments, dreaded the idea of a change, and, like Nicholson at New York, openly declared that the prince was at the head of "a parcell of rebells," and would "come to the same end as Monmouth did."*

CHAP. XI. 1689. April.

Connecticut now sent Captain Jonathan Bull, of Hartford, "to enquire how matters stand between them of Albany and the Indians." Bull was invited to meet the officers and magistrates, who were all "inquisitive for news;" but as he did not wish to speak freely before Baxter, the commandant of the fort, who was an avowed papist, he showed his "printed papers," containing the prince's declarations, first to Captain Bleecker, who did not agree with Mayor Schuyler in keeping "all intelligence from the people." The next day being Sunday, the news was generally known, and Baxter went down to New York, leaving the fort in charge of the Albany city officers. Bull then visited Schenectady, where the people were "much rejoiced with the news." A few days afterward he was present in the Albany Court-house, at a conference with the Mohawks, who renewed the old covenant chain, and, on hearing the news of the revolution in England, promised "neither to speak with the French, nor hear the French speak to them." At the same time, they showed their preference for the Dutch over the English. Addressing the Albany officers, they said, "We hear a Dutch prince reigns now in England; why do you suffer the English soldiers to remain in the Fort? Put all the English out of the town. When the Dutch held this country long ago, we lay in their houses; but the English have always made us lie without doors." The next month the Senecas, Cayugas, Onondagas, and Oneidas came to Albany and renewed the "old covenant" which was first made many years ago with Jaques Eelkens, "who came with a ship into their river. Then we first be-

18 May. Bull, of Connecticut.

Bleecker and Schuyler.

19 May.

24 May.

27 June.

* Doc. Hist., ii., 23, 35, 114, 115, 116; Col. Doc., iii., 747; Munsell, ii., 72, 92, 100; N.Y. H. S. Proc., 1846, 104; Dunlap, i., 164; *ante*, 549.

The old Dutch "covenant" with the Iroquois.

came Brethren," they said, "and continued so 'till last fall, that Sir Edmund Andros came and made a new chain, by calling us Children. But let us stick to the old chain, which has continued from the first time it was made, by which we became Brethren, and have ever since always behaved as such. Virginia, Maryland, and New England have been taken into this silver chain, with which our friendship is locked fast. We are now come to make the chain clear and bright."*

The city of Albany.

At this time the city of Albany was not much more than a large stockaded village, of which the two chief streets crossed each other at right angles. The one, "Handelaer's Straat," or Market Street, ran nearly north and south, skirting the river, proverbially apt to overflow its banks in times of great flood. The other, running about east and west, a little way up a steep hill, was called "Yonkheer's Straat," now known as State Street. About half way up the hill stood the fort, just outside one of the city gates, of which there were six. Albany had no large foreign commerce like New York, but she was the centre of the great internal traffic of the province with the native savages. Her importance was only second to that of the metropolis, and her magistrates always maintained their official dignity. As soon as they received from New York a copy of the proclamation, they formed the citizens in a procession and marched up to the fort, where William and Mary "were proclaimed in solemn manner in English and Dutch," and the guns were joyfully fired. The ceremony was repeated at the City Hall, and "the night concluded with the ringing of the bell, bon fires, fire works, and all other demonstrations of joy."†

1 July.

5 July. Bayard at Albany.

A few days afterward Bayard arrived at Albany, and "found most part of the inhabitants inclined to peace and quietness, and to maintain their civil government 'till orders do arrive from their Majesties." Leisler had endeavored to gain over the people of Albany and Ulster, and threatened to bring some of their magistrates prisoners to

* Col. Doc., iii., 559, 560, 592, 593, 599, 645, 775; iv., 902; Colden, i., 100, 101, 105, 132; Col. Rec. Conn., iii., 460–463; Munsell, ii., 106, 107; *ante*, vol. i., 18, 42, 55, 67, 81, 88, 146, 152, 229–231, 246; vol. ii., 518, 562. Colden, being an inveterate Scotchman, could never get rid of acrimony when speaking of the Albany Dutch.

† Doc. Hist., ii., 5; Munsell, ii., 53, 108; iii., 39; iv., 200.

New York. But those counties disapproved of the "mutinous proceedings" at New York, and agreed to remain steady, and maintain their local governments pursuant to the king's proclamation of 14 February. The Albany magistrates declared "that they were not in any wise subordinate to the city of New York, nor the power then exercised therein."*

1 August. Albany Convention.

A convention of civil and military officers was now held at Albany, at which it was "Resolved that all public affairs for the preservation of their Majesties interest in this city be managed by the Mayor, Aldermen, Justices of the Peace, Commission Officers and Assistants of this city and county, until orders shall come from their most Sacred Majesties." In taking this position, Albany, under her regular officers, was surely as justifiable as was the metropolis under Leisler. It was also resolved that, as there was news of a war between England and France, "the gentlemen now met at this Convention do each bring a gun, with half a pound of powder, and ball equivalent, to be hung up in the Church, in the space of three days; and that the traders and other inhabitants be persuaded to do the same, to make up the number of Fifty, to be made use of upon occasion." As some of the citizens, alarmed at the rumor of a French attack, were preparing to leave Albany, by which "bad example of such timorous and cowardly people, others will be discouraged to stay and defend their Majesties interests in this frontier part of the Province, and forasmuch as there is no settled government for the present in this Province," the Convention ordered that no able-bodied inhabitant should leave the county for the next three months without a pass from a justice of the peace. News of what the French and Indians had just done in Pemaquid was now published, so that all might "be upon their guard." The Onondagas having sent an ambassador with an account of what had lately happened in Canada, the Convention advised their "Brethren" not to be "imposed on by the idle and nonsensical speeches of the Governor of Canada," and desired them to send to Albany some Iroquois sachems and warriors, "whose feet shall be well greased."†

7 August.

21 August. Onondagas soothed.

28 August.

* Col. Doc., iii., 590, 598, 599, 604, 620, 645, 748; Doc. Hist., ii., 38.

† Doc. Hist., ii., 11–13, 46–50; Dunlap, i., 158; Munsell, ii., 108, 109.

CHAP. XI.

1689.

The news from New England and Canada was, indeed, startling enough. Instigated by Denonville, the Abenaquis, or Onoganques, and the Panococks, or Ouragees, had surprised Dover, in New Hampshire, and afterward Pemaquid, in Maine, whence the garrisons established by the military prudence of Andros had been withdrawn by the selfish jealousy of Massachusetts insurgents. The New England colonies were filled with apprehension, which was increased when they learned that the Abenaquis had tried to persuade the New York Iroquois and Schagtacooks to "take up the axe with them against all the Christians on this Continent." It was the unconquerable desire of the native red American to avenge the injustice of white European invaders of his territory. Of this injustice New England was peculiarly guilty. New York had always treated her aborigines kindly. The Iroquois naturally swung toward their genial friends. By the same impulse they became the bitter enemies of the French Canadians, whose governor had sent some of their most stalwart warriors in chains to row with felons and long-suffering Huguenots in the galleys of Marseilles. And so they besieged Fort Frontenac, where Denonville had treacherously seized their countrymen. Father Millet, who had been recalled from Niagara, was chaplain of the French post. Lured outside of its walls, he was taken prisoner and carried to Oneida, where he had formerly ministered. Saved from death by a Christian squaw, he was named *Genherontatie*, or "the dead who walks," and adopted as a brother by Gannasatrion, or Tareha. Soon afterward Millet was naturalized as an Oneida Iroquois, and made a sachem in place of their deceased Otasseté.*

The Abenaquis and New York Indians.

Sympathies of the Iroquois.

Millet an Oneida sachem.

These events were followed by the severest blow that Canada had yet felt. During the spring and summer Denonville had remained ignorant of the purposes of the Iroquois, as well as of those of his king. Callières was in France, and there was a general want of vigilance and subordination among the Canadians. Unconscious of danger, Denonville had gone, with his wife, from Quebec to Montreal. In the gray of a summer morning, after a tem-

* Col. Doc., iii., 610, 611, 621, 714, 724, 783; iv., 349; ix., 387, 440, 665; Charlevoix, ii., 345, 415-419; Hutch., i., 396; Belknap, i., 198-206; La Potherie, iii., 248; Colden, i., 60, 101, 110, 119, 188; Shea's Missions, 277, 319, 325; Garneau, i., 305; Bell, i., 322; Williamson, i., 590-595; Millet's letter of 6 July, 1691, 9-49; *ante*, 401, 442.

1689. 26 July. 5 August. The Iroquois ravage Lachine.

pest of hail and rain, fifteen hundred Iroquois warriors, who had quietly traversed Lake Saint Francis, suddenly landed from their canoes at Lachine, the upper end of Montreal Island. Most of the inhabitants were asleep; the men were killed at once, the women and children with greater deliberation and cruelty. In an hour two hundred French colonists perished, and all the houses in Lachine were burned. Montreal, only three leagues off, in consternation awaited an attack. French parties were sent out, and defeated or captured. At length the Iroquois retired, after losing only thirteen warriors, and ravaging nearly all the island of Montreal, and killing a thousand French Canadians.*

Denonville orders Fort Frontenac to be demolished.

Denonville was almost stupefied by this terrible calamity. Most of the "praying Iroquois" at the Falls of Saint Louis and the Prairie de la Madeleine retreated to Montreal. The victorious warriors sent "very insolent propositions" to Denonville for the demolition of Fort Frontenac, and he accordingly ordered it to be evacuated and blown up. The order was obeyed; a slow match was put in a mine under the bastions; three French barks on Lake Ontario were burned; and Valrennes, with his garrison, went down the rapids of the Saint Lawrence to Montreal. But the match in the mine went out, and the Iroquois soon took possession of the deserted fort, where they found a great quantity of powder and other French property worth twenty thousand crowns.†

2 Sept. 4 Sept. Albany and the Iroquois.

The news from Canada caused great anxiety in Albany, where every effort was made to keep the Iroquois friendly. The near Mohawks asked and were granted assistance of men and horses to draw the heaviest logs for stockading their "new castle of Tionondage, which they removed an English mile higher up." An express was also "sent down to Captain Leisler and the rest of the militia officers of the City and County of New York" for help of men, money, and ammunition "for the securing of their Majesty's fort

* Col. Doc., ix., 429, 431, 432, 434, 435; Mass. H. S. Coll., xxxv., 212; La Hontan, i., 193, 194; La Potherie, ii., 229; iii., 58; Garneau, i., 272–274; Bell, i., 295–297; *ante*, 520. Charlevoix, ii., 403, errs in stating this attack on Lachine to have been made on the 25th (instead of the 5th) of August; and Colden, i., 91 (whom Smith follows, i., 88), blunders still more, antedating it in 1688.

† Col. Doc., ix., 436–438, 441, 443, 464; Charlevoix, ii., 406–409; La Hontan, i., 195; Quebec MSS. (ii.), v., 28; Colden, i., 92; Documentary History, ii., 77, 78; Millet's letter of 6 July, 1691, p. 45.

CHAP. XI. 1689. 17 Sept. and the out plantations of this County." But the German captain in New York would not recognize the Albany Convention. The messenger reported that Leisler said "he had nothing to do with the civil power; he was a soldier, and would write to a soldier." Accordingly, he addressed a letter to Captains Wendell and Bleecker, declining to send men or money to Albany, and desiring them to "induce the common people to send two men to assist them in their Committee." Finding that Leisler was playing demagogue, and would not assist them, the Albany Convention raised money, sent down to the Esopus Indians on the river, and also wrote to Massachusetts and Connecticut, asking each to send one hundred men "to be in garrison here this winter, to secure their Majesties Fort and the frontiers of this County against the French or their Praying Indians."*

Leisler, Wendell, and Bleecker.

23 Sept.

4 Sept. New England agents at Albany. Meanwhile Pynchon, with Savage, Belcher, and Bull, had visited Albany as agents of Plymouth, Massachusetts, and Connecticut, to engage the Iroquois against the Eastern savages, and were "kindly treated by the gentlemen there," who quickly summoned the Five Nations to a conference. 23 Sept. But the New England agents failed in their endeavor to commit the Iroquois delegates to a war with the Abenaquis and Panococks. The Mohawk orator Tahajadoris, in an 24 Sept. adroit speech, declined to attack the Eastern savages, who had done the Five Nations no harm, and desired their "Brethren of the three colonies" to send men for the security of Albany against the French, where "the Christians have victuals enough for their entertainment." The next 25 Sept. The action of the Iroquois. day, at a private conference, the Iroquois delegates assured the Albany officers that, "if the French shall attempt any thing this way, all the five nations will come to your assistance; for our Brethren and we are but one, and we will live and die together. We have desired a hundred men of our Brethren of Boston to assist us here, because this place is most exposed." And they all joined in singing, and crying out "Courage! courage!"†

On the return of the New England agents, Secretary Al-

* Doc. Hist., ii., 19, 20, 50–55, 88; Munsell, ii., 108; Dunlap, i., 158; Mass. H. S. Coll., xxxv., 212, 217, 218; *ante*, 287, 517.

† Doc. Hist., ii., 19, 51; Col. Doc., iii., 611, 621; Colden, i., 106–111; Smith, i., 99, 100; Plymouth Records, vi., 213; Mass. H. S. Coll., xxxv., 205, 212, 217, 218. Millet's letter of 6 July, 1691, 40–45, gives an interesting account of what happened at Oneida when the Albany messengers came to summon that nation to the conference.

lyn, of Connecticut, notified Leisler that the ten soldiers of that colony doing duty in New York would be transferred to Albany. Governor Treat also wrote to the Albany Convention that eighty Connecticut soldiers would be sent there, under Captain Bull, if the Convention would pay the wages of the commissioned officers. This was agreed to, "Provided they be under the command and obey such orders and instructions as they shall receive from time to time from the Convention of this City and County;" and Captains Van Rensselaer and Teunise were sent to return "hearty thanks" to Connecticut. But Massachusetts, pleading "their present circumstances of things," declined to assist Albany.*

CHAP. XI. 1689. 10 October. 15 October. 24 October. Connecticut in favor of Albany. 25 October.

On the day appointed in its charter, the city of Albany duly installed its aldermen and other municipal officers, at least as regularly as New York had done. Lieutenant Thomas Sharpe, the commandant of the fort, and all his soldiers, also took oaths of fidelity to William and Mary. To stop the "false aspersions" of Leisler and his friends, who called them "Jacobites," the civil and military officers and citizens of Albany also swore allegiance to their new sovereigns. Three out of the four militia captains at Esopus declared that they would help Albany in case of need.†

14 October. Albany officers installed. 19 October. 25 October. Esopus.

There were now two rival local governments within the province of New York. The one was as rightful as the other. But the independent attitude of Albany galled the ambitious German captain, whose few subservient instruments had undertaken, in August, to declare him "commander in chief" of the whole province. Leisler therefore prepared a force of fifty-one men, under the command of Milborne, to go to Albany and take possession of its fort for himself. Hearing of this, the Albany Convention, through Alderman Levinus van Schaick, notified him that they would willingly accept any re-enforcements he might send for the defense of the country, "Provided they be obedient to, and obey such orders and commands as they shall from time to time receive from the Convention; and that by no means will they be admitted to have the com-

Rival governments in New York. 26 October. The Albany ideas.

* Doc. Hist., ii., 20, 21, 55, 56; Trumbull, i., 379; Mass. H. S. Coll., xxxv., 217, 218; N.Y. H. S. Coll. (1868), 28, 29, 68.

† Doc. Hist., ii., 56, 57, 58; Munsell, ii., 100, 110; Dunlap, i., 159; *ante*, 439.

CHAP. XI. 1689. mand of their Majesties' Fort in this city, which we intend, by God's assistance, to keep and preserve for the behoof of their Majesties William and Mary." The logic of this paper was conclusive. By the same right that the "Committee of Safety" exercised local power in New York, the "Convention" exercised it in Albany. As to formal regularity, Albany was perhaps more rightful than New York. But this made no impression on the infatuated

28 October. Leisler and his followers. They wrote letters to Albany, Kinderhook, and Schenectady, urging submission to the captain in New York; and some of them were stupid

2 Novem. enough to try to persuade the Dutch freeholders that "all lands, plantations, houses and lots, which were escheated since the year 1660, are again restored, by act of Parlia-

29 October. Leisler's absurd despotism. ment." Leisler himself declared "that they of Albany should bring their charter here, if they have one;" and that Lieutenant Sharpe and Sergeant Rodgers, of its garrison, who had sworn allegiance to William and Mary, "were Papists." Milborne, who was well "acquainted with the place and people," where he had formerly lived, was accordingly dispatched to Albany with three sloops full of armed men and ammunition.*

4 Novem. When the Albany Convention learned from Alderman Van Schaick that the German demagogue at New York meant to turn the government of their city "up-side down," and get possession of their fort, they acted. The citizens of Albany were summoned "by bell-ringing," and

5 Novem. Albany acts. a declaration was signed that they would not, in this conjuncture, suffer "them of New York, or any person else," to rule over Albany, of which the Convention was the "only lawfull authority." "To prevent all jealousies and animosities," Mayor Peter Schuyler—as thorough a Dutch-

8 Novem. man as he was a gentleman—was appointed to the chief command of the fort, with the loyal Lieutenant Sharpe under him; and the principal burghers of Albany with great pomp led Schuyler up the hill to the little fortress, where he was "with all cheerfulness received by the officers and soldiers of their Majesties' garrison."†

* Doc. Hist., ii., 14, 15, 23, 57, 59, 60, 63–67; Col. Doc., iii., 645, 646, 655, 675; Smith, i., 95, 96, 97; Dunlap, i., 159, 161; *ante*, 300, 575, 576.

† Doc. Hist., ii., 60, 61, 62, 63; Smith, i., 96; Dunlap, i., 159, 160.

The next morning the three sloops sent up from New York, under the command of Milborne, were descried at Albany, anchored near "Martin Gerritsen's Island," a little below the city. Leisler's emissary demanded, and was refused, admission into the fort, of which Mayor Schuyler was in command. Milborne then came to the City Hall, where he harangued the people "in a long oration, with a high style and language," telling them that all that had been done in the reign of King James the Second was illegal—"yea, the charter of Albany was null and void." This exposition was characteristic of the demagogues who had just gained local power in the city of New York by a pretended observance of a similar charter granted by the same governor. Wessels, the recorder of Albany, quietly answered that "there was no arbitrary power here." The next day, which was Sunday, "after the second sermon" in the old Dutch church, Milborne appeared before the Convention and produced his commission, signed by Leisler and his Committee of Safety. Recorder Wessels replied "that such a commission granted by a company of private men" in New York was of no force in Albany, "but that if he could show a commission from his Majesty King William," he would be willingly obeyed. Milborne then "made a long oration to the common people which were got together in the City Hall," condemning all things which had been done in the reign of King James, especially Dongan's charter to Albany. He was answered "that if all things were null and void which were passed in King James's time, then the inhabitants were in a desolate condition," and their land titles good for nothing; that there had been "a free election according to the charter;" that his only aim was "to raise mutiny and sedition;" and that if things were carried on as he would have them, "all would run into confusion with the Indians, and all authority be turned upside down, as in many parts of the government was done, to which the Convention by no means could condescend." Milborne was therefore told "to desist from such discourse, for that they would dispute no more with him about it, leaving all 'till a lawful power came, not acknowledging him to have any."*

CHAP. XI.

1689.

9 Novem.

Milborne at Albany.

10 Novem.

Good reasoning of Albany.

* Doc. Hist., ii., 63-68, 72; Col. Doc., iii., 646, 647; Smith, i., 98; Dunlap, i., 160, 161.

CHAP. XI. — 1689. 11 Novem. Milborne attempts a mob at Albany.

Defeated in the Convention, Milborne plied the people out of doors, about one hundred of whom, chiefly youths and not freeholders, met tumultuously at the City Hall and chose Jochim Staats, a lieutenant in Captain Wendell's Albany company, to command the men whom Leisler had sent from New York. Milborne also wrote to the Convention that Leisler's New York committee had authorized him to "order the affairs at Albany." The next day the Convention met at Captain Jan Jansen Bleecker's house, and refused to accept the men from New York unless they should be under the command of the Convention. Mayor Schuyler also explained to the burghers at the City Hall the reasons why he had seized the fort, which were to defeat Leisler's design "to make an absolute change of government, to carry some persons prisoners to New York, and so to make a general disturbance among the people, and force us to comply with their new-fashioned government." These reasons were satisfactory to the burghers, who thought that their Convention had done rightly.

12 Novem.

14 Novem. Bleecker and Schuyler oppose Milborne.

Milborne now resolved on a bold step to get the mastery. Assembling his company in arms, he marched out of the city gate up to the fort, of which he demanded possession. Schuyler answered that he held it for their majesties, and ordered him away "with his seditious company." Milborne attempted to enter, and, "having one foot in, was thrust out." He then withdrew his company inside of the city gate, before which he put up the king's Jack, ordered his men to load, and then "read a paper." Upon this, a protest by Schuyler, on behalf of the Convention, was read "off one of the mounts" of the fort, directing Milborne and his seditious troops to withdraw at once. These movements were watched by a company of Mohawks standing on the hill near the fort, who charged their guns, and sent word to Schuyler that if the New York soldiers came out of the city gates "in a hostile manner to disturb their Brethren in the Fort," they would fire on them. At Schuyler's request, Domine Dellius and Recorder Wessels went to pacify the savages; but they insisted on sending the domine to tell Milborne that if he came out of the city gates

15 Novem.

Leisler's emissary baffled at Albany.

"Martin Gerritsen's Island," or the old "Castle Island," just below Albany, was so named after Martin Gerritsen van Bergen, to whom it was leased in 1668.

they would fire on him. Upon this, Leisler's baffled emissary "marched down the town and dismissed his men."* CHAP. XI. 1689.

Finding that he could do nothing at Albany, Milborne, after signing a contract with some "private but extreme active men" for the support of his soldiers, prevailed on them to accept Staats as their captain, and went back to New York, leaving his company in great confusion. On his way down the river he stopped at Esopus; but the people of Ulster county, being informed of his defeat at Albany, dispatched him quickly from there "for to give an account of his misfortune to his commander Leisler and the committee that sent him."† 16 Novem. Milborne at Esopus.

A few days afterward Captain Bull reached Albany with eighty-seven men from Connecticut, who were "extremely well accepted." As it was necessary to garrison Schenectady, Lieutenant Enos Talmage, of Captain Bull's company, was sent there with twenty-four men. Staats refused to assist with any of his New York soldiers, but went to Schenectady himself, to create faction. Considering "the lamentable condition" of Albany, the Convention ordered that Wednesday, the fourth of December, should be observed as "a day extraordinary for fasting and prayer."‡ 25 Novem. Bull at Albany. 29 Novem. 27 Novem. Fast-day at Albany.

Anxious to visit New York, where his only son was very ill, Bayard had meanwhile written to the justices of the peace there, offering to answer any complaint against him. They replied that "the sword now ruled in their city," and that they could not protect him against Leisler. Upon this, Bayard, as their colonel, wrote to De Peyster and De Bruyn, two of the captains in his regiment, declaring that Leisler and his associates, without "any the least shadow of Authority" from William and Mary, having "subverted all manner of Government by law established" in the city of New York, it was his duty, as a royal counselor and their own colonel, to require them to "desist from any ways counselling, aiding, assisting, or abetting the illegal proceedings of the said Jacob Leisler and his associates," because the commissions issued by Andros, who represented the crown of England, were "in full force, notwithstanding 20 Oct. Bayard's letter denouncing Leisler.

* Doc. Hist., ii., 69–73; Smith, i., 98; Dunlap, i., 162.
† Col. Doc., iii., 647, 675; Doc. Hist., ii., 74; Dunlap, i., 163.
‡ Doc. Hist., ii., 74, 75, 76; Col. Rec. Conn., iii., 463; Dunlap, i., 163.

CHAP. XI. 1689.

the imprisonment, yea death, of any Governor that granted the same, he being only an inferior officer of the crown, and the commissions being matters of record."*

This was certainly a true exposition of English law. It was just what William himself had declared to be his will when he directed all English colonial officers in America to remain in the places which they held under James. But the German demagogue in New York, to whom Bayard's letter was shown, saw at once that its logic, if followed, would defeat his own personal ambition. Leisler therefore assembled his adherents in New York, Bergen, and Kings counties, armed, in the fort, where he told them, with impudent falsehood, that their Lieutenant Governor Nicholson, who had been some time in London, was a "Popish dog," and "was turned a Privateer, and would never show his face in England; and that he [Leisler] had discovered a plot, in which Bayard, with about three hundred men, would attempt to retake the Fort for the late King James." Bayard's Albany letter had clearly asserted the supremacy of William and Mary. So Leisler caused his partisans "to make a new subscription, in substance for to be true and faithful to King William and Queen Mary, and to be obedient to the Committee of Safety, as the supreme authority, and to himself as their commander in chief." Dongan, who was now living quietly on his farm at Hempstead, was charged with holding "cabals at his house and other places adjacent, to make an attempt on the Fort;" and this induced many to subscribe Leisler's new association. Such as scrupled were denounced as creatures of King James; and as Captains De Peyster, Lodwyck, and Stuyvesant were dissatisfied, more pliant officers were put in their places. Phillipse, who quietly submitted to Leisler, was not disturbed; but his colleagues, Bayard and Van Cortlandt, were roughly searched for in their own houses, as well as in those of their friends, including that of Domine Selyns, and the two royal counselors were obliged to hide themselves from Leisler's rage "till relief from England." These violent doings caused many of the inhabitants of New York to fly to East Jersey and Pennsylvania, where the German captain charged that the Quakers encouraged his opponents.

Leisler can not withstand Bayard's logic.

Leisler's falsehood.

Phillipse submits to Leisler.

* Col. Doc., iii., 646, 647, 658; Doc. Hist., ii., 22; Dunlap, i., 163.

Chap. XI.

1689.

Yet, amid all their troubles, the people of New York joyously kept two new holidays. The birthday of King William was heartily observed in the metropolis with bonfires and the roasting of an ox. The next day—which doubly commemorated the "gunpowder treason" of Guy Fawkes and the landing of William at Torbay—was as earnestly celebrated "with bonfires and burning the Pope."*

4 Novem. William's birthday.

5 Novem. Guy Fawkes.

* Col. Doc., iii., 634, 646, 647, 648, 655, 656; Doc. Hist., ii., 24, 25, 38, 246; *ante*, 533.

CHAPTER XII.

1689–1691.

CHAP. XII. — 1689. July. Trouble in London about the colonies.

WHEN the reports which Nicholson and his counselors had dispatched from New York in May, and the other colonial intelligence brought by Riggs reached Whitehall, they showed that William and his ministers had been duped by Mather and Phipps into committing a great mistake in colonial administration. The intrigue which had withheld from Andros the directed notification of the accession of William and Mary, and of the continuance in their several places under them of all English colonial officers, had resulted in a mutiny in Massachusetts, the disruption of the royal "Dominion of New England," and great confusion in New York by reason of "secession." After the departure of Phipps to Boston in April, the most active notice which William's embarrassed government took of his American colonies was to send a packet-boat in June with orders to the colonial authorities in Virginia, Maryland, and Pennsylvania announcing his war with France, and promising that a squadron would be sent to protect the English Plantations.

3 July. By a letter of Randolph from "the common gaol" of Boston, the king's Plantation Committee learned that the revolt in Massachusetts was not so much against Andros as for restoring the old charter of that colony, under which its Puritan ministers might regain power, and gainful pri-

4 July. vateering and illicit trade be encouraged. The next day Mather hurried to Hampton Court, where he was received by the king in his bedchamber, who did "kindly accept" of what the Boston insurgents had done. Sir Henry Ashurst also presented the Plymouth address to the king, who assured him "that he would take care of the good of his colonies in New England." But William saw that an unexpected colonial mutiny had broken up his "dominion" there, and that it was necessary for him to re-establish his

direct authority in the several colonies and provinces into which that dominion had been reduced against his will. Mather's adroit suggestion that "by means of New England" he might become "the Emperor of America," had no weight with the new British sovereign, whose mind was occupied with Europe. A few days afterward, when Riggs told the Plantation Committee his story of what he had witnessed at Boston, the whole truth came out. It was clear that Andros had been imprisoned because he had executed the orders of his lawful English sovereign. Such orders it was not William's colonial policy to undervalue. A petition from Andros having been read before the king in council, it was ordered that Sir Edmund, and his fellow English subjects, "seized by some people in Boston, and detained under close confinement there," should be sent at once to London "to answer before his Majesty what may be objected against them." A royal letter was accordingly written to the acting authorities in Massachusetts, requiring them to send Andros, Randolph, Dudley, Palmer, West, Graham, Farewell, Trefrey, and Sherlock by the first ship to England. The existing government of the colony was also authorized by William to continue in administration until further directions.*

William occupied by European politics. 16 July. 22 July. 25 July. 30 July. William's letter to Massachusetts. 12 August.

A letter was at the same time addressed to Nicholson by the Privy Council, directing him, as lieutenant governor, "with the assistance of the principal freeholders and inhabitants of their Majesties' Province of New York," to proclaim William and Mary according to a form which was inclosed. The king also authorized Nicholson to take on himself the government of the province, calling to his assistance such of "the principal freeholders and inhabitants" as he should think fit; and requiring him, until further order, "to do and perform all things which to the place and office of our Lieutenant Governor and Commander in Chief of our Province of New York doth or may appertain." William's letter, like that of his Privy Council, was addressed to "Francis Nicholson, Esquire, Our Lieutenant Governor

29 July / 8 August. 30 July. William's letter to Nicholson.

* Col. Doc., iii., 574–576, 578–583, 593, 664; Doc. Hist., ii., 26; Penn. Col. Rec., i., 301, 302; Burk, ii., 307; Mass. H. S. Coll., ix., 246, 247; xxvii., 191; xxxii., 299; xxxv., 199–202, 206, 209, 210; Parentator, 122; R. I. Rec., iii., 256, 257; Hutch. Mass., i., 388, 390, 391; Narcissus Luttrell, i., 557; Macaulay, iii., 379–414; Chalmers's Annals, ii., 26, 27, 29; Sixth Collection of Papers, 29; Davis's Morton, 472; Bancroft, iii., 79; Barry, i., 509, 510; Palfrey, iii., 585, 586; Andros Tracts; *ante*, 543, 561.

CHAP. XII. 1689. and Commander in Chief of our Province of New York in America, and in his absence, to such as for the time being take care for preserving the peace and administering the laws in our said Province of New York in America."*

20 August. The royal dispatches for Massachusetts were delivered to Increase Mather, who, after losing the Corporation Bill by the adjournment of Parliament, embarked for Boston. But Mather was obliged to give them to another passenger, aft- 12 Sept. er landing at Deal, where his son Samuel had "fallen sick with the small-pox." Those for New York were intrusted to John Riggs, who had brought over the letter of Nicholson and his council of the previous May. Nicholson, however, reached London before Riggs set out; but as it was supposed that the dispatches to him as lieutenant governor would be opened and acted upon by Phillipse, Bayard, and Van Cortlandt, the royal counselors whom he had left in charge, no alteration was made, and the messenger went on with his letters to New York.†

Riggs returns to New York with the royal dispatches.

Informed by Nicholson in person of the actual condition 31 August. of the province, the Plantation Committee moved the king "that a Governor be forthwith sent to New York, with such a Commission and Instructions as are intended for the other Plantations, and that a ship of strength be appointed to carry the Governor;" also that presents be sent to the five Iroquois nations, who "may be very useful to the English against the French;" and that two new foot companies be sent to the province, in place of those dispersed "by the 2 Sept. late disorder." The king, in Council, approved these recommendations, and declared Colonel Henry Sloughter to be his Governor of New York. Nicholson strove to obtain the post, "but had not interest to carry it." The appointment of Sloughter was probably secured by some of the corrupt courtiers of William; for the colonel, although praised by London merchants trading to New York for his "integrity, courage, and conduct," has been deliberately pronounced "utterly destitute of every qualification for government, licentious in his morals, avaricious, and poor."‡

Henry Sloughter appointed Governor of New York.

* Col. Doc., iii., 605, 606, 648, 675; Smith, i., 94; Dunlap, i., 166; Chalmers's Annals, ii., 29, 30, 35; Palfrey, iii., 480, *note*.

† Col. Doc., iii., 633, 635, 648, 654, 656, 664, 675; Doc. Hist., ii., 38, 246; N. Y. H. S. Coll. (1868), 290–299; Andros Tracts; Mass. H. S. Coll., xxxv., 206, 210; Hutch., i., 392; Macaulay, iii., 414; *ante*, 575.

‡ Col. Doc., iii., 618, 619, 633, 651; Smith, i., 109; Colden, i., 128; Hutch., i., 395; Dunlap,

To strengthen his government, Sloughter proposed that New York, "so advantageously situate between the colony of New England and Virginia," should include Connecticut, the Jerseys, and Pennsylvania; but, as the Connecticut charter had not been legally surrendered or adjudged void, that colony escaped annexation. It was then proposed to add Plymouth to New York, and Secretary Blathwayt actually included it in the draft of Sloughter's commission. But Mather, who had returned to London, with "industry and discretion" persuaded the governor that the addition of Plymouth would be of "little service" and rather an "inconvenience" to New York, and so it was stricken out again. The providential illness of young Samuel Mather thus prevented the annexation of Plymouth to New York. At length the revised draft of Sloughter's commission was approved by the king and ordered to pass the great seal. The same day Nicholson was consoled by being appointed lieutenant governor of Virginia, under Lord Howard of Effingham, who had returned to London. Phipps, who knew the ways at Whitehall, afterward asserted that Nicholson "was recommended by some that were about their Majesties, who for money got in many that were not for the King's interest;" but his appointment by William to such an important colonial office was certainly an emphatic approval of his administration in New York.*

CHAP. XII.

1689.

14 Novem.

Nicholson lieutenant governor of Virginia.

There was every reason why Sloughter should go at once to his government. It was known that the French had a design upon New York, and, if successful, would "put to the torture" some two hundred Huguenot families then in the province. The Bishop of London was appealed to in their behalf, and urged to procure from the king authority for Leisler to secure New York until Sloughter should come, who would not be ready until the spring. But no such authority was given to Leisler. A number of London merchants trading to the American colonies earnestly petition-

30 Decem.

i., 196; Chalmers's Annals, i., 594; ii., 68; Rev. Col., i., 242; Tindal, iii., 92–99; Macaulay, iii., 60–62.

* Col. Doc., iii., 622–629, 651, 719; iv., 8, 9, 10; Doc. Hist., ii., 127; N. Y. H. S. Proc., 1849, 106; Coll., 1868, 298; Mass. H. S. Coll., xxxv., 210, 211, 226, 229, 231, 248, 276; Magnalia, i., 198; Hutch. Mass., i., 392, 395, 405–407; ii., 481; Coll., 576; Davis's Morton, 472–476; Plymouth Rec., vi., 259; Burk's Virginia, ii., 310; Chalmers's Ann., i., 298, 347, 359; ii., 44, 90; Rev. Col., 211, 243, 261; Trumbull, i., 386, 387, 537–540; Grahame, i., 108, 271; Bancroft, iii., 66; Andros Tracts. Sloughter's commission did not pass the great seal until 4 January, 1690: Commissions, ii., 3; Col. Doc., iii., 623; Smith, i., 109; *post*, p. 627.

CHAP. XII. 1689. William urged to protect New York.

ed the king to dispatch a large force at once to protect New York, which was "the center of all English Plantations in North America, and if lost, it will become a nest of French pirates." The campaign in Ireland, however, and the wretched condition of the English navy, prevented due attention being given to the situation of New York, which, of all William's American Plantations, most needed his promptest action.*

9 Novem. Stoll in London.

While Sloughter's commission and instructions were yet under consideration, Ensign Jacob Stoll reached London and presented Leisler's dispatches of August to the king, who referred them to Secretary Shrewsbury. In a pompous memorial Stoll burlesqued his own great services, while he asked the approval of all Leisler's proceedings and a suspension of the governor's commission. Stoll's exertions, however, were of no avail. The boastful New York "dram-man" was foiled by the presence in London of Nicholson and Innis, who exposed the true character of Leisler's transactions; and, as Sloughter was appointed governor, the affairs of the province must thenceforth pass through his hands. But Matthew Clarkson, who had come over with Stoll, fared much better. By a patent under the privy seal, the office of "Secretary of New York in America" was created and granted to Clarkson during the royal pleasure and his own residence in the province, with power to appoint deputies.†

16 Novem.

6 Decem. Clarkson appointed Secretary of New York.

8 Decem. Riggs returns to New York.

After a long voyage Riggs arrived in Boston, and hastened with his important dispatches to New York. On reaching there late on Sunday night, he called at Bayard's house, where Phillipse having come, Riggs exhibited his packets to them, and declared that, as in Nicholson's absence, they belonged to his council, being in answer to their letters of May, he would deliver them to the three counselors whenever Van Cortlandt should join his colleagues in town; adding that he did not believe that Leisler would receive and

* Col. Doc., iii., 650–653; Macaulay, iii., 432–435; Chalmers's Annals, ii., 68, 91; Hist. Mag., xi., 333.

† Col. Doc., iii., 597, 614, 616, 629–633, 731; viii., 324; Commissions, ii., 17, 18; Smith, i., 93; N. Y. H. S. Coll. (1868), 298; *ante*, 576. Secretary Clarkson came out to New York, as a young man, in 1686, probably at the suggestion of his brother-in-law, Captain Lodwyck. He was a son of the Reverend David Clarkson, of Yorkshire, England, an eminent nonconformist divine (Neal's Puritans, ii., 332). In January, 1692, Matthew Clarkson was married to Catherina, daughter of Captain Goosen Gerritsen van Schaick, deceased, of Albany, and became the ancestor of the very respectable New York family now bearing his name.

CHAP. XII.

1689.
9 Decem.

open them if they should be tendered to him. But before the three counselors could meet together the next morning, Leisler sent a lieutenant and two sergeants to convey Riggs to the fort. At Riggs's request, Van Cortlandt and Phillipse attended him thither. Leisler peremptorily demanded the English packets. Phillipse and Van Cortlandt, on the other hand, claimed them as addressed to them, being royal counselors deputed by the lieutenant governor "to preserve the peace during his absence and until his Majesty's pleasure should be known." Leisler then told Riggs that they had nothing to do with the government, that they were papists, and that the packets belonged to and were directed to him, who was commander-in-chief under the commission of the Council of Safety, which he exhibited. Upon this Riggs surrendered his dispatches to Leisler, who gave him a receipt, and, turning to the two counselors, called them "Popishly affected, Dogs and Rogues," and, with "many opprobrious words," ordered them out of the fort, "for they had no business there."*

The dispatches given to Leisler.

These dispatches from England which Leisler thus seized were certainly intended for Nicholson, or, in his absence, for the three counselors whom he had left in charge of the province. William's letter of 30 July meant Francis Nicholson, and no one else, as his "Lieutenant Governor and commander in chief" of New York, and authorized him to perform the duties of that office. In Nicholson's absence, those duties were to be executed by "such as for the time being take care for preserving the peace," etc., in the province; and this duty William expected would be done by his resident counselors Phillipse, Van Cortlandt, and Bayard, of whom the first named was to act as "president," according to the commissions given by his predecessor to Dongan and Andros, the words of which were followed in that which he himself gave to Sloughter. The king's letter, therefore, was intended for, and ought to have been delivered to, the oldest counselor, Frederick Phillipse, who should then have acted as President of New York.†

Intention of them.

* Col. Doc., iii., 633–635, 648, 649, 654, 656, 664, 675, 676, 759; Doc. Hist., ii., 28, 38, 228, 232, 246; Smith, i., 94; Dunlap, i., 166, 167; Wood, 106; N. Y. H. S. Coll. (1868), 299, 326, 360, 378.

† Col. Doc., iii., 382, 542, 595, 606, 628, 633, 649, 675, 685, 759; iv., 1018; *ante*, 570. Dunlap, i., 166, alters the address on the king's letter from *such as "take care,"* etc., to *such as "takes care,"* and argues that "*thus the person at the head of the Government,*" mean-

CHAP. XII. 1689. But Leisler had now gotten the king's letter in his hands. It was the first royal letter he had seen. It was a sort of Godsend, and he determined to use it for his own advantage. The train-band captain was in possession of the fort of New York; and in August, ten of his tools, calling themselves a "Committee of Safety," had signed a commission appointing him to be "commander in chief" of the whole province. This impudent assumption of authority had been rejected by all the counties of the province except those near the guns of Fort William. But the German demagogue, who had hitherto pretended that "the people" of New York had given him power, now changed his tactics. Leisler saw that the time had come when he might, with equal right, pretend that he was the royal instead of the democratic chief of New York, and he acted boldly, yet cunningly. He carefully concealed William's letter to Nicholson from all except his own adherents, because he knew that it had not been meant for him; but he audaciously declared that "he had received a commission to be their Majesties' Lieutenant Governor, and that all their actions were well approved of."* Finding that this falsehood was believed, Leisler unwarrantably "esteemed his own authority to have received the royal sanction." He at once assumed the station and the title of "Lieutenant Governor" of New York, and he caused William and Mary to be proclaimed anew, according to the form which the English Privy Council had directed Nicholson, or his counselors, to follow. The next day Leisler called together De la Noy, Edsall, Beekman, and others of his friends, to advise who should be his council. The king's directions to Nicholson were that these counselors should be "the principal freeholders and inhabitants." Among these were assuredly Phillipse, Van Cortlandt, Bayard, and Minvielle, of New York; Smith, Nicolls, and Younge, of Long Island; Schuyler, Wessels, Bleecker, Van Schaick, Van Rensselaer, and Livingston, of Albany—all of them good Protestants. But the devotees to himself whom Leisler selected as his advisers were Peter de la Noy, Samuel Staats, Hendrick

Leisler's errors.

10 Decem.

11 Decem.

ing Leisler, "was empowered to take the chief command" of the province, which was not the case. C. F. Hoffman reiterates Dunlap: Sparks's Am. Biog., xiii., 210.

* Col. Doc., iii., 606, 676, 764. William's letter to Nicholson "was not openly communicated" to the people during Leisler's rule: Doc. Hist., ii., 202, 221.

Jansen, and Johannes Vermilye, for New York; Gerardus Beekman, for Kings; Samuel Edsall, for Queens; Thomas Williams, for Westchester; and William Lawrence, for Orange. Most of these had been members of the late "Committee of Safety," and all of them were now chosen by Leisler to be his royal counselors, because he knew they were "for his turn." Jacob Milborne was appointed secretary of the province and clerk of the Council, and he, with De la Noy, Staats, and Edsall, formed Leisler's "root," or cabinet. On Sunday the German usurper took his seat in the governor's pew in the old Dutch church, "with a large carpet before him," while his new advisers sat in the Council's pew; and thus a vulgar vanity was gratified.*

CHAP. XII. 1689. Leisler's counselors.

As the king's provincial seal for New York of 1687 had been broken by Andros in 1688, another was manufactured by altering the Duke of York's coronet in his old seal of 1669, and placing the crown of England in its stead. Thus a royal prerogative was boldly, perhaps ignorantly, usurped by Leisler. It was also ordered and proclaimed that the customs and excise duties settled by the colonial act of 1683 remained in force, and should be collected. The act had been disallowed by King James, but the duties it levied had been continued by order of Dongan and his Council. Leisler himself had refused to pay duties under that order; but now he attempted to enforce, by his own arbitrary decree, an act of a "Popish Governor," which his inconsistent logic had, up to this time, argued to be "null and void."†

Leisler makes a seal for New York.

16 Decem.

Duties to be collected.

The people, however, objected to Leisler's proclamation, which was torn down from the door of the custom-house, and another paper affixed in its place showing its illegality. Upon this Leisler issued another proclamation, forbidding any person to deface or take away any paper affixed "by the authority of this Province or city." Several persons were soon arrested under this order, and imprisoned in the fort during Leisler's will and pleasure. Others were arrested, and bail was refused until they would petition the usurping captain for release under the title of "Lieutenant Governor."‡

20 Decem. The people object.

23 Decem.

* Col. Doc., iii., 605, 606, 636, 656, 676, 764; iv., 1111; Doc. Hist., ii., 26, 27, 28, 246; Chalmers's Ann., i., 592; Rev. Col., i., 213; Smith, i., 94; Bancroft, iii., 52; Dunlap, i., 166, 168.

† Col. Doc., iii., 357, 370, 676, 677, 678; iv., 1018; Doc. Hist., ii., 29, 30; iv., 1*, 2*; *ante*, 157, 512, 559.

‡ Doc. Hist., ii., 30; Col. Doc., iii., 678-681.

CHAP. XII. 1689. December. Leisler's new commissions. 30 Decem.

New commissions were quickly issued by Leisler, making his friends justices, sheriffs, and military officers in the various counties of New York. But as those issued by Dongan and Andros were generally esteemed to be in full force, an order was issued requiring all persons holding them to surrender them to the nearest magistrate, and all who refused were "to be deemed and esteemed as persons ill-affected to this government, and unfit for bearing office, or having any trust reposed in them whatsoever, and to be regarded as the case shall require."*

1690. 11 Jan. 18 Jan. 20 Jan. Leisler's courts.

Courts of Oyer and Terminer were also commissioned for New York and Queens county. Finding that the people would not obey his order establishing custom and excise duties, Leisler erected a Court of Exchequer. This tribunal quickly summoned the recusants, and compelled payment by distresses, notwithstanding Thomas Clarke, in behalf of the defendants, objected that no member of the pretended court had a commission from King William to be a baron of his exchequer.†

7 Jan. Leisler's letters to the king and Bishop Burnet.

Leisler now wrote to the king that he had acted on the royal letter addressed to Nicholson, "although two of Sir Edmund Andros's Council pretended thereunto;" and he declared that his conduct was "to the great satisfaction of the generality" of his majesty's liege subjects in the government. Another letter, signed by Leisler and some of his Council, was addressed to Bishop Burnet, of Salisbury, setting forth in greater detail what had just been done in New York. Both these letters were sent by way of Boston, and were evidently drawn up by Jacob Milborne, the secretary of the province under Leisler's appointment."‡

As it was known that the king had ordered that Andros, Randolph, West, Farewell, and the others whom the Boston insurgents had imprisoned should be sent to London, letters to some of them were written by Bayard, Van Cortlandt, Nicolls, and others, which were given by Colonel Lewis Morris to the post-rider, John Perry, as he passed his house in Westchester. Fearing that the truth would be made known

* Doc. Hist., ii., 32, 196–199.

† Col. Doc., iii., 613, 673, 683; Col. MSS., xxxvi., 142; Doc. Hist., ii., 36. The members of Leisler's Court of Exchequer were Samuel Edsall, Benjamin Blagge, Johannis Provoost, Hendrick Jansen, and John Couwenhoven.

‡ Col. Doc., iii., 653–657, 700, 731; Doc. Hist., ii., 36, 247.

1690. 3 Jan.

in England, Leisler declared that he had "detected a hellish conspiracy" to subvert the king's government in New York, and ordered Lieutenant Daniel Terneure to arrest the postman to Boston, and bring him, with his papers, to the fort. Perry was accordingly brought before Leisler, who opened and read the letters he carried, and put him in prison. As they reflected on him very severely, Leisler ordered their writers, Bayard, Van Cortlandt, Brockholls, Morris, Nicolls, and Reed, to be apprehended and brought before him for "writing execrable lies and pernicious falsehoods." Private correspondence, proverbially sacred, was thus violated to serve a partisan despotic power. Leisler now declared "that he was invested with such a power as in a little time he could command the head of any man in the Province, and it would be forthwith brought him." Bayard and Nicolls were soon arrested and imprisoned in the fort; but Van Cortlandt escaped. The low spite of the German demagogue was chiefly manifested against his old colonel, Bayard, whom, with brutal triumph, he caused to be carried in chains around the ramparts of Fort William. Ill in body, and dejected in spirit, Bayard was obliged to ask freedom from his upstart persecutor under his assumed style of "Lieutenant Governor" of New York. Even this submission produced no effect. Abundant bail was offered and refused, and for thirteen months Bayard and Nicolls were kept in close confinement, while their houses were pillaged to gratify the vulgar malice of Leisler and his followers.*

16 Jan. Perry's letters seized. 17 Jan. Their writers to be apprehended.

Bayard and Nicolls imprisoned.

24 Jan.

The usurper at New York had meanwhile been greatly troubled that Albany would not submit to him. Acquainted by Milborne with the characters of the principal men there, Leisler acted with prompt decision. He issued his own commission to Captain Jochim Staats to take possession of "the fort Orange," and command it until farther

1689.

28 Decem. Leisler's letters to Albany.

* Doc. Hist., ii., 32, 35, 36, 37, 38, 39, 101, 246, 247; N. Y. H. S. Coll. (1868), 379; Col. Doc., iii., 657, 661–663, 682–684, 709, 716, 721; Dunlap, i., 168, 169, 171, 172; *ante*, 593. An account of Leisler's proceedings to the 21st of January, 1690, was drawn up—probably by Bayard and Nicolls, and their friends—which they meant to have presented to the Mayor's Court of New York on the 25th of January. But the "fury and rage" of Leisler prevented this, and their paper, under the title of "*A modest and Impartial Narrative*," etc., was printed at Boston, and afterward reprinted at London: Col. Doc., iii., 665–684; Dunlap, i., 167, 169. It is written with acrimony, and perhaps is somewhat unjust; yet, without its help, a fair account of New York affairs at that time could not now be given. This pamphlet was not printed at New York, as its title-page states, for there was no press there in 1690.

CHAP. XII. 1689. orders. Leisler also wrote to the Albany magistrates and to Staats, directing "a free election" to be made for a mayor and aldermen; but he carefully named the persons he was "willing to have chosen, if the people will elect them."*

1690. 11 Jan. Convention assembled. When these letters reached Albany, Schuyler assembled the Convention, which called on Staats to produce his orders, and show that Leisler had been made lieutenant governor by the king, in which case they would cheerfully obey. Staats, however, only exhibited the orders sent him by Leisler, but not the king's letter to Nicholson. 12 Jan. The next day the officers of the county of Albany were convened to give their opinions whether Leisler should be acknowledged as lieutenant governor. Schuyler opposes Leisler's pretensions. Schuyler, the mayor, voted "that he can not acknowledge the said Captain Leisler to be Lieutenant Governor and Commander in Chief of this Province, nor obey his orders, 'till he hath shown that he hath lawful authority from his most sacred majesty, King William, so to be." This was plain good sense. The other officers were "of the same opinion with the mayor," except Captains Wendell and Bleecker, who could not "comprehend" the matter. Wendell and Bleecker do not "comprehend." The opinions of Captain Bull and Ensign Bennet, of the Connecticut forces, being asked, they said that for any thing that yet had been seen or heard, they had "no reason to conclude that Captain Jacob Leisler is either Lieutenant Governor or Commander in Chief of the Province of New York." Leisler's cunning in "not openly communicating" the king's letter to Nicholson thus served "his turn," but it was a sad calamity to the province.†

13 Jan. Albany Declaration. The Albany Convention now issued the ablest document which had been written in New York since the imprisonment of Andros. It declared that "Jacob Leisler, of the City of New York, merchant," with "restless and ambitious spirit," had assumed unlawful power and the title of lieutenant governor of the province, "without the least shadow of orders or authority so to do from his most sacred majesty King William," and that the king's letter to Nicholson was as much directed to them in Albany as it was to Leisler in New York. Moreover, in this juncture Leisler had

* Doc. Hist., ii., 30, 31, 81.

† Col. Doc., iii., 606, 676, 764; Doc. Hist., ii., 82, 83, 202, 221; Dunlap, i., 169, 170.

made "new confusion when peace and unity is most requi- CHAP. XII.
site," by sending his commissions and seditious letters, "so 1690.
that great part of the time must be spent to defeat the said Leisler's pernicious and malicious designs which otherwise could be employed to resist upon all occasions the common enemy." Staats was therefore prohibited from disturbing the peace, under Leisler's pretended authority, "upon pain of rebellion." This protest was published with great formality "in English and Dutch" before the church and at the fort. It was signed and sealed by all the county officers except Captains Wendell and Bleecker, who would "have nothing to doe with the Protest, when they heard it read."

The logic of this manifesto could not be confuted; but events were now at hand which subordinated all provincial jealousies. Suspecting that the French intended to invade
New York, the Convention employed the Mohawks to keep 20 Jan. Mohawk
scouts on Lake Champlain, and report any hostile move- scouts.
ment at once. This they faithfully promised to do; but 21 Jan.
they were not vigilant enough.*

Upon receiving his instructions, Frontenac, accompanied 1689.
by Callières, had set out from Paris full of hope, anticipat- June.
ing a rapid conquest of New York. But, owing to various
mischances, it was not until the middle of September that September. Frontenac
he reached Acadia, whence he went on to Quebec, after at Quebec.
ordering Caffinière, who commanded the ships, to cruise before New York until the tenth of December, when he was to return to France if no news reached him from the land
side. Crowds welcomed "the Redeemer of Canada" as he $\frac{2}{12}$ Oct.
landed at Quebec. The news of the late irruption of the
Iroquois at Montreal obliged him to hasten thither, where $\frac{17}{27}$ Oct. The con-
he found Denonville in great embarrassment. Frontenac quest of New York
at once saw that the projected conquest of New York must abandoned.
be abandoned. The Iroquois and the English were both on their guard, and the Canadians reduced to the defensive. Even his favorite fort at Cataracouy, which bore his own name, had been evacuated. Frontenac had reached Canada fully three months too late.†

* Doc. Hist., ii., 83-87; Dunlap, ii., 170.

† Col. Doc., iii., 621; ix., 419, 429, 430, 435-438, 462; La Potherie, ii., 233; iii., 59; La Hontan, i., 198-202; Charlevoix, ii., 400-409; Colden, i., 102, 103; Smith, i., 101; Garneau, i., 274, 304; Bell, i., 297, 320-322; Force's Tracts, iv., ix., 41-43; *ante*, 547, 583.

CHAP. XII. To conciliate the Iroquois, Frontenac dispatched a message to Onondaga inviting them to meet again at Cataracouy their "old Father," who was as much their friend as ever. This was conveyed by three of the savage prisoners who had been brought back from France, while Oreouaté, or Tawerahet, the Cayuga chief, in whose name it was sent, remained sumptuously entertained in the Castle of Saint Louis at Quebec. Lamberville also wrote to Millet at Oneida, and Le Moyne and Hertel sent wampum belts. When the messengers from Canada reached Onondaga, a general council was summoned, and a request was sent to Albany that Schuyler and others might be present and give their advice. The Convention, not thinking it "convenient at this juncture to send Christians," dispatched three "of the most prudent Mohawks" to Onondaga, to recommend the Iroquois Council not to hearken to the French; to inform them that a governor of New York was daily expected from England, who, it was hoped, would bring orders "that the English may unanimously go and root out Canada;" and to desire them to hold Millet as a hostage for their captured brethren, and send to Albany the letters he had received from Canada. A few days afterward, Tahajadoris, one of the chief Mohawk sachems, who was going to Onondaga, came to ask "the Brethren's advice how to act there." Upon this, the Albany officers directed Arnold Cornelissen Viele, the interpreter, to go thither, with Robert Sanders, and fully explain their message. Its purport was, that the Iroquois were "subjects of the great King of England," and should not hearken to the French, but send warriors to aid in protecting New York against their hostile designs, "since they have called all their garrisons together to Montreal."*

1689. French message to the Iroquois.

26 Decem.

27 Decem.

1690. 4 Jan.

5 Jan. Advice of New York.

6 Jan.

22 Jan. Grand Iroquois Council at Onondaga.

A grand Iroquois council now assembled at Onondaga, where eighty sachems were present. The Albany messengers were addressed by the Onondaga sachem Sadekanactie, who told them what the French had sent from Canada. Adarahta, the chief sachem of the "Praying Indians" near Montreal, then delivered the Canadian wampum belts. Tahajadoris, the Mohawk sachem, then gave the message he

* Col. Doc., iii., 733, 734; ix., 435, 436, 465; La Potherie, i., 333; iii., 62, 63, 70; Charlevoix, ii., 424, 425; Colden, i., 104, 112, 113, 114; Garneau, i., 304; Bell, i., 328; Smith, i., 102; Shea, 326, 332; Doc. Hist., ii., 76–80; Chalmers's Ann., ii., 69. Colden and Smith, ignorant of the real reasons why its officers could not leave Albany, unjustly reflect on their conduct.

had received at Albany "word for word." A Seneca sachem, Cannehoot, followed in a harangue about the peace his nation had made with the Western savages against the French, and gave the Council a calumet, and "a red-marble sun as large as a plate," as tokens of friendship. The wampum belts from Albany were hung up in the Council lodge, along with "the model of a fish," sent on behalf of "Kinshon," or New England, "as a token of their adhering to the general covenant." The superb salmon of Maine probably furnished the image; yet it may have been a Massachusetts cod.* CHAP. XII. 1690.

The Onondaga Sadekanactie then said, "Brethren, we must stick to our Brother *Quider*, and look upon Onnontio as our enemy, for he is a cheat."† All this passed in the presence of Millet, as an adopted sachem of the Oneidas. The letters to him from Canada were given to Viele, the Albany interpreter, who urged the Council not to hearken to the French. The Iroquois orator then announced the Albany message: "Brethren, our fire burns at Albany; we will not send Dekanesora to Cataracouy. We adhere to our old chain with Corlaer; we will prosecute the war with Onnontio, and will follow your advice in drawing off our men from Cataracouy. Brother Kinshon, we hear you design to send soldiers to the eastward, against the Indians there; but we advise you, now so many are united against the French, to fall immediately on them. Strike at the root:—when the trunk shall be cut down, the branches fall of course. Corlaer and Kinshon, courage! courage! In the spring to Quebec; take that place, and you will have your feet on the necks of the French and all their friends in America." In their reply to Frontenac, the Council refused to meet him at Cataracouy, and insisted on his sending back all the prisoners that had been taken to France. The Five Nations, however, were not unanimous. Millet's influence was strong enough to prevent the Oneidas and Cayugas from engaging themselves against the French. The two sachems who were sent to Albany to report the reply of the Council to On-

Stick to "Quider."

Kinshon.

Advice to attack Quebec.

* Colden, i., 113–116, 180; Doc. Hist., ii., 79, 80. The Iroquois allegorically called New England "*Kinshon*," after Pynchon, who had first covenanted with them in 1677: *ante*, 309; Millet's letter of 6 July, 1691, p. 48.

† "By *Quider* they meant *Peter Schuyler*, the Mayor of Albany, who had gained a considerable esteem among them; as they have no labeals in their language, they pronounce *Peter* by the sound of *Quider*:" Colden, i., 16, 116; *ante*, 309, 582.

CHAP. XII. 1690.

nontio, delivered a belt to *Quider*, or Peter Schuyler, in which only three axes were represented.*

But Frontenac had meanwhile seen that the only way in which the French could regain the respect of the Iroquois was to strike audacious blows against the English. After sending off his dispatches to France—among which was a fresh plan of Callières for the conquest of New York—the vigorous old governor organized three several expeditions against the English neighboring colonies—one at Montreal, to invade New York; another at Three Rivers, to attack New England, between Albany and Boston; and a third at Quebec, to ravage Maine. The party from Three Rivers, commanded by Hertel, destroyed the village of "Semenfels," or Salmon Falls, now Berwick, in New Hampshire, and joined that sent from Quebec under the command of Portneuf. The combined expedition then burnt "Kaskebe," or Casco Bay, now Portland, and alarmed the whole eastern frontier of New England.†

Frontenac organizes three expeditions.

28 Jan.

27 March.

Maine.

Frontenac's most important party from Montreal was directed against New York. It was composed of two hundred and ten men, of whom eighty were "Praying Indians" from Caghnawaga, opposite Montreal, on the Saint Lawrence, under their "Great Mohawk" chief Kryn; sixteen Algonquins, and the remainder Canadian traders, or "bush rangers." The expedition was commanded by Sainte Helène and Mantel, Canadian lieutenants, under whom were Iberville, Repentigny, Bonrepos, La Brosse, Montigny, and other officers, as volunteers. Early in February the party set out from Montreal, and, after marching several days, held a council to determine which was the best point to attack. The French officers wished to go directly to Albany; but the converted Mohawks, who knew the country well, opposed this, and it was decided to march on Schenectady. After a severe tramp over an intensely cold desert covered with snow, the expedition halted within two leagues of Schenectady about four o'clock on a Saturday afternoon.

Expedition against Schenectady.

February.

Near Schenectady. 8/18 Feb.

* Colden, i., 116–119, 188; Col. Doc., ix., 465, 466; La Potherie, iii., 63–67; Charlevoix, ii., 425–427; Smith, i., 102, 103; Chalmers, ii., 69; Millet's letter of 6 July, 1691, 41–46, 51; *ante*, 582, 584. The French wrote Schuyler's Indian name of *Quider*, "Kouiter."

† Col. Doc., iii., 708, 720; ix., 428–439, 464, 471–473; La Potherie, iii., 61, 76–79; Charlevoix, ii., 409, 410; iii., 63, 72–79; Maine H. S. Coll., i., 201–205; Mass. H. S. Coll., xxvi., 210–218; xxxv., 253; Belknap, i., 207, 208; Doc. Hist., ii., 146; Garneau, i., 306, 307, 308; Bell, i., 325.

The great Mohawk, Kryn, harangued his "praying" countrymen, and exhorted them to avenge the massacre of the French at Lachine. A reconnoitring party was sent out, which reported that Schenectady was unprepared for attack; and a little before midnight the exhausted Canadians, benumbed with cold, and ready to surrender themselves if they had been summoned, advanced on the devoted village.

Kryn harangues.

Condition of Schenectady.

Schenectady was indeed lamentably unready. Reliance had been placed on the vigilance of the Mohawk scouts whom the Albany authorities had dispatched toward Lake Champlain, but who had not seen the French expedition. Leisler's recent letters had excited bitter party spirit in the village; neighbor was set against neighbor, and no watch was kept, "notwithstanding several gentlemen of Albany, no longer than three days before, were up there to persuade them to it." The villagers thought that in that bitter weather no foe could march on them from Canada, forgetting that exactly twenty-four years before Courcelles had gallantly demonstrated the endurance of his countrymen.* Disregarding the warnings of Talmage and his guard, they gayly spent their Saturday evening within their warm houses, leaving open both the gates of their stockade, and, instead of living sentinels, placing in mockery images of snow.

Carelessness of the inhabitants.

The village of Schenectady, at that time the western frontier post of New York, contained upward of eighty well-built and well-furnished houses, and formed an oblong, surrounded by a palisade, which could be entered by only two gates. One of these, on the west side, commanded the road to the Mohawk country; the other, on the east side, that to Albany, and both were now left "wide open." At midnight the French, under Sainte Helène and Mantel, entered by the Mohawk gate through a driving snow. The villagers were all asleep in their houses, after their evening's revelry. The "small fort" where Talmage and his garrison kept watch was the only place "under arms." This was at once attacked by Mantel; "the gate was burst in after a good deal of difficulty, the whole set on fire, and all who defended the place slaughtered." The sack of the village at the same time began with a war-whoop "given Indian fashion." Few houses made any resistance. Adam

The French enter and burn Schenectady. 9/19 Feb.

* On the 9th of February, 1666; see *ante*, 103.

CHAP. XII. 1690.

Vrooman secured quarter by a brave defense, and another house, belonging to a widow, was saved because Montigny had been carried into it after being severely wounded. The house of the Dutch domine, Petrus Tesschenmaeker, had been "ordered to be saved, so as to take him alive to obtain information from him;" but, as it was not known, it was destroyed with the others, and the domine and his papers perished. His head was put on a pole and carried to Canada. The massacre lasted two hours, and then the assailants took "some rest." With barbaric ferocity, the Iroquois atrocities at Lachine were avenged by French "Praying Indians" at Schenectady. "No pen can write nor tongue express," were Schuyler's words, the terrors of that cruel night. Sixty persons, including Talmage and several of his Connecticut soldiers, were killed, and an equal number of old men, women, and children, who escaped the first fury of the attack, were made prisoners. Twenty-five almost naked survivors fled from their burning homes, and pushed their miserable way through the snow to Albany. Some thirty Iroquois, who were lodging in the village, were spared, "in order to show them that it was the English, and not they, against whom the grudge was entertained."

Domine Tesschenmaeker killed.

Killed and prisoners.

At daybreak a party was sent to the house of Captain Alexander Glen, at "Scotia," on the north side of the Mohawk River, about half a mile above Schenectady. Glen, who was the chief magistrate of the village, and supported the Albany Convention, had become so unpopular among the partisans of Leisler at Schenectady that they threatened "to burn him upon the fire" if he came on guard with them. The English called him "Captain Sander," and the French "Coudre." Seeing that he was on his guard, the French told him that they had resolved that he and all his relations, and all his property, should be safe, in consequence of the good treatment which their countrymen had received from his father, his brother, himself, and his wife. Glen, thus assured, accompanied the party to Schenectady, where the French officers were directing the conflagration. A few houses, which he said were his, were spared, and several women and children, who claimed affinity with him, were released from captivity. The Canadian savages, observing the number of their prisoners so greatly reduced,

Glen, or Sander, or Coudre.

complained that "every one seemed to be a relation of Coudre's." CHAP. XII. 1690.

It was well for the French that they listened to their Indian advisers, and did not attack Albany, where they would have been annihilated by the vigilance of Schuyler. The next day they hastily collected their twenty-seven prisoners and their plunder, among which were "fifty good horses," and set out on their return to Canada, having caused a loss in Schenectady of "more than four hundred thousand livres." The retreating Canadians suffered from hunger and disease; thirty-four of their fifty captured horses were eaten for food, and Mohawk war-parties cut off many stragglers. At length the remnant of Frontenac's New York expedition returned to Montreal with its surviving prisoners, hoping that it had "greatly retrieved, in the estimation of the barbarians, the reputation of the French arms."*

$\frac{10}{20}$ Feb. The French return to Canada.

$\frac{17}{27}$ March.

The terrible intelligence from Schenectady was brought to Albany about five o'clock on Sunday morning by Symon Schermerhorn, who, wounded himself, and on a lame horse, had tediously worked his path there by way of Niskayuna. Schuyler quickly fired the guns of the fort to summon the people; and an express was sent through the deep snow to Esopus, and to Kinderhook, and Claverack, for assistance to Albany, which it was supposed would be next attacked. The next day, however, Bull was sent with a party to Schenectady to bury the dead and pursue the enemy. Leisler's letters were "found all bloody" in the streets. The French were pursued as far as Crown Point, whence the Mohawks followed them to Canada, and killed and took twenty-five.†

9 Feb. The news at Albany.

10 Feb.

Remembering the advice of the sachems at Onondaga, the Convention quickly wrote to the governments of Massachusetts, Connecticut, Maryland, and Virginia, and to "the civil and military officers of New York," desiring them "to join together, that Quebec may be taken by water in the spring." Thus from Albany, in the midst of its distress,

15 Feb. Albany advises an attack on Canada.

* Col. Doc., iii., 700, 708, 716, 727; ix., 466–469; La Hontan, i., 204; La Potherie, iii., 67–70; Charlevoix, iii., 63–68; Colden, i., 121–123; Chalmers, ii., 69, 70; Doc. Hist., i., 186–195; N. Y. H. S. Proc., 1846, App., 101–123; Coll. (1868), 403; Mather, ii., 595; Smith, i., 103–105; Trumbull, i., 379, 380; Mass. H. S. Coll., xxxv., 230, 268; Garneau, i., 305, 307; Bell, i., 323, 324; Dankers and Sluyter, 315, 316; Dunlap, i., 175–179; *ante*, 329, 583. I refer with some diffidence to such a blundering "authority" as Dunlap, who persistently substitutes the name of "*Frontignac*," the wine, for that of "*Frontenac*," the governor.

† Doc. Hist., i., 188–193; ii., 87, 88; Col. Doc., iii., 708; Colden, i., 123.

CHAP. XII. came the first suggestion of a union of the English colonies to attack the French.*

1690. 25 Feb. The Mohawks at Albany. The sachems of the Mohawk castles now came to Albany to condole with its magistrates on the calamity at Schenectady, which they could not call a French victory, "for it is done by way of deceit." With many wampum belts, they desired to wipe away all tears, and urge those who wished to go to New York not to leave Albany. "If the enemy should hear that, it would much encourage them; we are of the race of the bear, and a bear does not yield as long as there is a drop of blood in its body. We must all be so." Three years before they would have humbled the French if they had not been prevented by Dongan, who was then "Corlaer;" but now, "let us go on briskly with the war." "Let us not be discouraged; the French are not so many as people talk of; if we but mind our business, they can be subdued by the assistance of our neighbors of New England, whose interest it is to drive on this war as much as ours, that it may be speedily ended." The Albany magistrates the next day answered their brethren, reproving the carelessness of the Mohawk scouts, who had given no notice of the French approach, and informing them that letters had already been sent to the English colonies to urge the capture of Quebec, and promising that special messengers should be sent to New York and New England "on purpose to lay open the case before them, and to move them to rig out vessels not only to hinder succor coming from France, but to take Quebec itself, as also to send more men hither, that we may then send men along with you to annoy the enemy in their country." Thus the Albany officers in February foreshadowed the campaign which was attempted the following summer. At the same time they explained that Dongan had acted under the orders of a king who "was a papist, and a great friend of the French; but our present Great King will pursue the war to the utmost."

26 Feb. Carelessness of Mohawk scouts blamed.

Request to send Millet to Albany. They also desired the Mohawks to persuade the Oneidas to send Millet to Albany; "for you have seen how dangerous it is to have such persons among you, who inform the enemy of all your doings, and discover all our designs." The Mohawk sachems shouted their approval, and replied, "We

* Doc. Hist., ii., 89, 93; Colden, i., 117; *ante*, 605.

will go with a whole army to ruin the French country; the business must be soon brought to a period; therefore send in all haste to New England, for we nor you cannot live long in this condition; we must order it so that the French be in a continual fear and alarm."*

27 Feb. Barentsen dispatched to New York.

The Albany Convention accordingly dispatched Barentsen to New York, with instructions to wait on Governor Sloughter "if he be arrived, otherwise on the authority there," and urge "that every one exert his power to crush the common enemy;" that men and supplies be sent to Albany; and that the people in the metropolis should "bring all their sea-force together, to unite with our neighbors of Boston to attack Canada." Livingston and Teunissen, of Albany, and Garton, of Ulster, were also commissioned to hasten to Connecticut and Massachusetts, and ask that Captain Bull and his company should be allowed to remain; that more men and supplies be sent to Albany; and that both those colonies should unite with New York in attacking Quebec by sea, which "was but meanly fortified and few men there, the strength of Canada being drawn up to Montreal, which the French have fortified."†

3 March. 4 March. Livingston, Teunissen, and Garton sent to Connecticut and Massachusetts.

The idea of a confederation of British North American Plantations originated in New England in 1643. The policy of consolidating his colonies, to make them "terrible to the French," was the thought of James the Second in 1688. The patriotic purpose of a union of all the English dependencies in North America, from Virginia to New England, against a common enemy, was inspired by the New York Iroquois, and formally propounded by the Albany Convention in February, 1690. From Schuyler and his associates just praise should not be withheld.

The union of all the British colonies against Canada an Albany idea.

When the news from Schenectady reached the provincial capital, Leisler "made an alarm," and disarmed and imprisoned about forty officers who held Andros's commissions. Warrants were also issued against Dongan, Willet, Hicks,

15 Feb. Leisler imprisons Andros's officers, and issues warrants against Dongan and others.

* Doc. Hist., ii., 91–95; Colden, i., 123–127; Smith, i., 105, 106; N. Y. H. S. Coll., ii., 105–109; Proc., 1846, 122, 123; Millet's letter of 6 July, 1691, 49. Colden paraphrases rather than copies Livingston's verbatim account, which I follow, and postdates the interview of 25 February on 25 March, 1690. Compare N. Y. H. S. Coll. (1869), 165–186.

† Doc. Hist, ii., 95–99; Col. Doc., iii., 692–698, 703–710. Captain Thomas Garton, of Ulster, had married Ann Tye, who, after the decease of her first husband, Captain Daniel Brodhead, in 1667, espoused his former subordinate, William Nottingham, and was left a second time a widow: N. Y. H. S. Coll. (1868), 185; Munsell's Alb. Coll., iii.; *ante*, 123, 157.

CHAP. XII. 1690.

and others, and the sheriffs of the neighboring counties were directed to secure "all such persons who are reputed Papists, or hold or maintain any commissions" from Dongan or Andros. Van Cortlandt, Brockholls, and Plowman were ordered to be arrested. Finding himself thus persecuted, Dongan left his house at Hempstead and went to New Jersey, whence he came to Boston to "be quiet." Van Cortlandt escaped to New England. Hamilton, Townley, Pinhorne, and other New Jersey gentlemen, dared not come to New York for fear of Leisler's despotic tastes. To such a degree did he gratify his appetite for imprisoning, that Alderman Kip, a deacon in the Dutch Church, was sent to jail "for going in the church to old Mr. Beekman to receive the alms before he went to young Henry the baker," who was one of the Council.*

21 Feb.

Dongan in New Jersey.

Wrongly blaming the Albany Convention for the calamity at Schenectady, which was owing to his own intrigues, Leisler dispatched Counselors Vermilye and Blagge, with Secretary Milborne, to New Haven, where they had a conference with Treat and Allyn, the governor and secretary of Connecticut. The New York agents desired that the Connecticut forces should not obey the Albany Convention, but Leisler. Allyn, in behalf of Connecticut, advised "hopeful and peaceable measures for a right understanding" between the rival authorities at New York and Albany, and thought that the latter would yield when they saw the king's letters to Nicholson. But this did not satisfy Leisler. He caused Milborne to charge Treat and the Connecticut magistrates with being upholders of "rebellion" in Albany, and demanded that Allyn especially should be prosecuted as a traitor. Allyn calmly rebuked Leisler's "angry letter, stuffed with unjust calumniating charges," and declared that the Connecticut government had advised the gentlemen of Albany "not to contend, but to submit to the present power in the Province of New York, and to unite as one man to oppose the common enemy."†

21 Feb.

24 Feb. Leisler's agents in Connecticut.

1 March.

5 March. Leisler rebuked by Connecticut.

Adopting the Albany suggestion of 15 February, Leisler wrote to Coode, of Maryland, asking him to assist New York "to destroy or take Canada," and to invite Virginia to join.

4 March. Letters to Maryland and Massachusetts.

* Doc. Hist., ii., 41, 43, 103; Col. Doc., iii., 636, 701, 716, 719, 721; Wood, 108.
† Doc. Hist., ii., 40, 43–46, 103; Dunlap, i., 180–182.

At the same time he asked Bradstreet what assistance Massachusetts would give, charging that Connecticut had "refused to advise" with New York. The next day, hearing that Livingston had gone on his mission to Boston, Leisler dispatched Blagge thither, and Terneure to Hartford, to apprehend him under a general warrant, which alleged that he had doubted the success of the Prince of Orange's invasion of England.*

CHAP. XII.

1690.

5 March. Warrant against Livingston.

On reaching Hartford, Livingston and his colleagues explained to Treat and his council the condition of affairs at Albany, and in a powerful memorial urged a union of all the English colonies "by sea and land to invade and subdue Canada." The Connecticut authorities, however, insisted on recalling Bull and his soldiers from Albany. At the same time, they informed Leisler that his warrant to apprehend Livingston was defective, and, promising to join "with all the rest of the Colonies and Provinces in this wilderness to do what we shall judge necessary to manage the design against the French," advised moderation and as little alteration as possible among the officers at Albany, so "that nothing be done to discourage the Five Nations in amity with us."†

11 March.

12 March. Action of Connecticut.

From Hartford the Albany agents hastened to Boston, where they earnestly pressed the capture of Quebec, which would be "the downfall of Anti-christ," and the plunder would "ten times pay the charge of the expedition." Lamenting the distractions in New York, where, by reason of Leisler's ambition, "there is neither pleasure nor satisfaction to be in office," they set forth the influence the French had gained over the Iroquois by their Jesuit missionaries, and urged that "young divines" should be sent from Massachusetts "to instruct the Indians, especially the Mohawks, in the true Protestant religion, since divers have an inclination to it, one being by the great pains and industry of our minister, Domine Dellius, brought so far that he made his public confession in the church at Albany." Massachusetts, however, received Livingston's propositions coldly. She was fitting out an expedition, under the command of Phipps, against Port Royal, where spoil was nearer. But

20 March.

Massachusetts treats the Albany agents coldly.

* Doc. Hist., ii., 35, 89, 95, 100–104, 114–117; Col. Doc., iii., 747; Dunlap, i., 182, 183; *ante*, 609.

† Col. Doc., iii., 692–694, 696; Doc. Hist., ii., 105, 106.

CHAP. XII. 1690. But refuses to let Livingston be apprehended. 1 April.

when Blagge demanded the apprehension of Livingston under Leisler's warrant, he was flatly "denied." The Albany idea of taking Canada, however, was not dropped, and a sloop which Andros had built in Maine was dispatched from Boston to England to beg a supply of powder. By that conveyance Ashurst was informed that, "there being now wars between Holland and France, some are fearful least the Hollanders should essay the possessing themselves of Canada," and that it was better that the English should have it rather than "the French, or Dutch either."*

4 March. Leisler sends De Bruyn, Provoost, and Milborne to Albany.

Meanwhile Leisler had gathered a force of one hundred and sixty men in New York and its neighborhood, and had commissioned De Bruyn, Provoost, and Milborne to go with it to Albany, and "superintend, direct, order and controul" every thing there, and obtain possession of Fort Orange. A similar commission authorized them to "order, settle, and establish" the county of Ulster. The commissioners hastened up the river, taking with them presents to gain the Iroquois, and clothing for the refugees of Schenectady.†

17 March. 20 March. Fort Orange surrendered to Leisler. 22 March. Mayor Schuyler confirmed. 26 March.

On reaching Albany, Leisler's commissioners found its Convention ready to act on the advice of Connecticut, and recognize the authority in New York. A joint meeting was held, and Bull was desired to remain; but this he could not do; and, as he left Albany, he and his company received "uncivil entreaty" from Milborne. Fort Orange was surrendered upon written conditions, which were soon violated, and most of the soldiers discharged, including Lieutenant Sharpe, who had been wounded by the bursting of a cannon in firing the alarm for Schenectady. To calm all animosities, it was ordered that no one should asperse or reproach another, under penalty of breach of the peace. Schuyler, the mayor, and the other city officers, were confirmed in their places, and all persons charged to respect and obey them. Arrangements were made for an expedition against the French, and a detachment was sent to keep watch at Crown Point.‡

* Col. Doc., iii., 695–699, 709, 769; Doc. Hist., ii., 104, 127, 151; Hutch., i., 396, 397, 398; Mather, i., 183; ii., 439, 596; Chalmers, ii., 52–55, 88, 89.

† Doc. Hist., ii., 41, 100, 101, 103, 111, 112; Col. Doc., iii., 702, 703, 717. The remainder of the money that was gathered for the redemption of the slaves in Turkey in 1678, which Andros had given to build a new church in N. York, had been laid out in Osnaburg linen, which Leisler seized and sent to Albany with Milborne: Col. Doc., iii., 315, 717; Doc. Hist., ii., 111; *ante*, 331, 506.

‡ Doc. Hist., ii., 107–113; Col. Doc., iii., 705, 708, 709, 710, 716, 727.

Leaving Provoost and De Bruyn at Albany, Milborne went down to Esopus, and then proceeded to New York, accompanied by two Mohawk sachems, who received "great satisfaction" from Leisler. The next day Milborne went back to Albany with additional forces, and a large quantity of maize was sent up from Kingston to supply the soldiers.*

CHAP. XII. 1690. 1 April. Mohawks at New York.

As money was indispensable, Leisler, assuming the charter of 1683 to be in force, had issued his writ to the several counties, requiring them to elect and send representatives to New York "to consult debate and conclude all such matters and things as shall be thought necessary for the supply of this Government, in this present conjuncture." But he found the people "very slack" in complying. Suffolk absolutely refused. Easthampton "could not comply" with Leisler's demand to be recognized as the king's lieutenant governor, and informed him that they would petition their majesties to be rejoined to Connecticut. They "distrusted the purity of his motives," and would not submit to him. New writs were accordingly issued of the same tenor, under which several of the counties chose representatives "by a few people" of Leisler's side. Albany elected Jan Jansen Bleecker and Ryer Schermerhorn. New York chose John Spratt, Cornelius Pluvier, Robert Walters, and William Beekman. The latter excused himself from attending. Pearson, of Queens, refused to sit. Ulster, Kings, and Westchester sent some "very weak men." The Assembly, thus constituted, met at the house of Walters, the son-in-law of Leisler, and, having chosen Spratt to be speaker, passed an act "to raise throughout the whole government three pence in every pound real and personal, to be paid the first of June; and that all towns and places should have equal freedom to boult and bake, and to transport where they please, directly to what place or country they think it fit, any thing their places afford, and that the one place should have no more privileges than the other." This was aimed against the bolting monopoly which New York had enjoyed under Andros and Dongan, of which Albany and Ulster were jealous. But petitions from the inhabitants coming in "for the prisoners to be set at liberty, and that their griev-

20 Feb. Suffolk disregards Leisler's authority. 15 March. 10 March. 8 April. Representatives elected. 24 April. Assembly meets.

* Doc. Hist., ii., 118, 119, 127, 132; Col. Doc., iii., 709, 716.

CHAP. XII. 1690. ances might be redressed," Leisler hastily prorogued his Assembly to September when he saw "they intended to work with the prisoners." The German tyrant justly feared a popular inquisition, and doubted the fidelity of his professed friends, some of whom were gentlemen.*

If Leisler was a despot and a usurper, he had more executive ability than most of the colonial governors in North America under British authority. In his youth he had struggled against his superiors in social position, while his talent and his mercantile training would have admirably fitted him to command if his education had equaled his experience in practical life. Like most men suddenly exalted, he was beguiled by vanity. He was as honest as he was vain; but his jealousy of gentlemen like Bayard and Van Cortlandt, his wife's own relatives, was so overpowering that he gratified it whenever he could. Nevertheless, Leisler was a true, though blundering colonial patriot. Sagaciously adopting the Albany idea jointly to attack Canada,

2 April. A colonial Congress called at New York. he urged Massachusetts, Plymouth, Connecticut, and Maryland to send delegates to New York to concert measures for that purpose. But, at Livingston's suggestion, Massachusetts had already called a New England meeting at Rhode Island. This, however, was abandoned; and the first North

1 May. American colonial Congress met at New York on the call of Jacob Leisler.†

To this New York Congress Massachusetts sent William Stoughton and Samuel Sewall; Plymouth, Major John Walley; and Connecticut, Nathan Gold and William Pitkin. New York was represented by Jacob Leisler and Peter de la Noy. Rhode Island sent no delegates, but voted that, as she could not give men, she would raise money in "reasonable proportion."

1 May. Action of the Congress. The Congress unanimously agreed that New York should provide four hundred men, Massachusetts one hundred and sixty, Connecticut one hundred and thirty-five, and Plymouth sixty, while Maryland promised one hundred; in all, eight hundred and fifty-five men. It was also agreed that Leisler should appoint the major, or

* Doc. Hist., ii., 42, 104, 114, 129, 131, 133, 151, 159; Col. Doc., iii., 702, 717; Wood, 106, 107, 110; Thompson, i., 163; Smith, i., 42, 68, 95; Chalmers, ii., 70; Council Journals, i., Int., xxiv; *ante*, 330, 391.

† Doc. Hist., ii., 89, 95, 97, 117, 125, 126, 130, 131, 132, 133, 134; Col. Doc., iii., 697, 698, 699, 709; Mass. H. S. Coll., xxxv., 232, 239, 244, 249, 250; Trumbull, i., 382; Hutchinson, i., 398; Bancroft, iii., 183; *ante*, 610.

"chief commander," and the other colonies the next captain. But, in Walley's judgment, "he is a man that carries on some matters too arbitrary." The Massachusetts delegates, however, "would not engage that their fleet should go in Canada River for Quebec; only if they had success at Port Royal, where they were bound they believed, being thereby encouraged, they should resolve then."*

CHAP. XII. 1690.

To stimulate Massachusetts, Leisler fitted out three vessels for the capture of Quebec—one a privateer of twenty guns, another a brigantine belonging to De Peyster, and the other a Bermudan sloop, commanded by Captains Mason, Goderis, and Bollen. They were commissioned to attack Canada and take French prizes at sea, and Mason was to act as admiral. Two sloops were also sent to cruise about Block Island and the Sound against the French. Thus Leisler zealously imitated the early energy of Nicolls in 1667.†

19 May. New York cruisers against the French.

Meanwhile the answer of the Iroquois at their January conference with the French had reached Montreal. Frontenac resolved to restore several of the prisoners, and sent back a reply, which he wished La Hontan to convey; but, as he declined, the Chevalier D'Eau, a "reduced" or half-pay captain, was chosen. D'Eau was accompanied by four Frenchmen, and carried full instructions from Frontenac and messages from Oreouaté, as well as a letter from Lamberville to the Oneida sachem, Father Millet.‡

9 March. Frontenac sends D'Eau to Onondaga. 6 May.

The authorities at Albany had not been negligent on their side. A conference was held with representatives of the Five Nations, whose speaker, "Diadorus," or Tahajadoris, accepted the metaphor of the Albanians that the French were like "a fox engendered by a wolf." At the same time, they desired their brethren to maintain peace among themselves, "and join together the several colonies of New England and Virginia, likewise those of Albany, who have always sat under the green tree; otherwise we shall destroy one another." They also recommended that Montreal

$\frac{3}{13}$ May. Iroquois Conference at Albany.

* Doc. Hist., ii., 133–135, 138, 143, 144; Col. Doc., iii., 717, 727, 732; R. I. Col. Rec., iii., 273; Mass. H. S. Coll., xxxv., 244, 245, 247, 249, 250, 251, 252; Hutch., i., 397; Trumbull, i., 382; Bancroft, iii., 183, 184; Arnold, i., 520; Chalmers, ii., 70, 71. In the Proceedings of the New York Historical Society for 1849, p. 104, 105, is an interesting extract from Sewall's Diary, giving an account of his journey to and from New York.

† Doc. Hist., ii., 132, 138, 141, 151, 152, 153, 165; Col. Doc., iii., 717, 727, 732, 751; Valentine's Man., 1857, 462; Dunlap, i., 185; N. Y. H. S. Coll. (1868), 321, 327; *ante*, 127.

‡ Col. Doc., iii., 714, 715, 733–736; ix., 465, 466, 469, 470; La Hontan, i., 205; La Potherie, iii., 63–67, 70–74; Charlevoix, ii., 425–429; Colden, i., 118, 129; *ante*, 605.

CHAP. XII. 1690. should be attacked by land, and Quebec by sea; that Schenectady should be fortified anew, as their own castles had been; and they promised that the Iroquois confederates would furnish eighteen hundred men to assist in conquering Canada.*

27 May. Orders were at the same time dispatched by Schuyler and others to apprehend the French agents on their arrival at Onondaga, and send them to Albany. They were accordingly seized, and despoiled of all their letters and presents. Four Frenchmen were given to the savages, who burned two of them. D'Eau, with his papers, was sent to Albany, and thence to New York. Among his papers was the Latin letter of Lamberville to Millet, which, containing some expressions of good-will toward Domine Dellius, of Albany, gave Leisler the opportunity to charge that clergyman with "treasonable correspondence" with the enemy.†

D'Eau seized at Onondaga and sent to New York.

18 May. Another expedition had meanwhile been dispatched from Montreal to act against the English. It was composed of "Praying" or Caghnawaga Indians, and commanded by Kryn, the great Mohawk, and was accompanied by some French officers who had been at the burning of Schenectady. Going by way of the Sorel River and Lake Champlain, the expedition took several Iroquois and eight English women prisoners. 4 June. On their return they were attacked at Salmon River by a party of Algonquins and Abenaquis, who, mistaking them for English, killed two and wounded ten. Among the slain was Kryn, the "Great Mohawk," whose death was the more deplored, because Frontenac and the Jesuits had hoped that through his influence all the New York Mohawks would eventually be drawn to Canada.‡

Kryn, the "Great Mohawk," slain.

20 May. Ensign Stoll now returned from London with galling news to Leisler. The king had taken no notice of him, but had appointed Sloughter governor of New York, and Nich-

Stoll returns with unpleasant news to Leisler.

* Doc. Hist., ii., 136, 139; Col. Doc., iii., 712–714, 783. Colden does not notice this conference. There is a remarkable difference in style between the minutes kept by Livingston and those which now seem to have been recorded by Milborne.

† Col. Doc., iii., 714, 715, 732–736, 753; iv., 214, 219; ix., 470; Doc. Hist., ii., 138, 144, 150, 151; La Potherie, iii., 74, 110; La Hontan, i., 206, 207; Charlevoix, iii., 83, 84; Colden, i., 129; Smith, i., 106; Millet's letter, 43, 52.

‡ Col. Doc., iii., 716, 727; ix., 473, 474; La Potherie, iii., 81–83; Charlevoix, iii., 69–72; Shea's Missions, 320; Doc. Hist., ii., 151.

olson lieutenant governor of Virginia, where the latter soon arrived. "The merchants, traders, and others, the principal inhabitants" of New York, accordingly drew up an address to William and Mary, complaining that for nearly a year they had been oppressed by the "arbitrary power" exercised by some "ill men," who, in spite of the king's proclamation, ruled New York "by the sword, at the sole will of an insolent alien [meaning Leisler, who was a German], assisted by some few, whom we can give no better name than a rabble, those who formerly were scarce thought fit to bear the meanest offices among us, several of whom also can be proved guilty of enormous crimes." These persons imprisoned at will, opened letters, seized estates, plundered houses, and abused the ministers of the Reformed Dutch Churches, so that "several of the best and most considerable inhabitants are forced to retire from their habitations to avoid their fury." This address was signed by Domines Varick, of Long Island, and Perret, of the French Church in New York, with several elders, and deacons, and other prominent persons.*

CHAP. XII. 1690. 19 May. Address of the principal inhabitants of New York to William and Mary.

The people of New York not in Leisler's interest now became restive. "In a most audacious manner" they demanded the release of their fellow-citizens, whom he had imprisoned and kept captive because they would not acknowledge his government; and many refused to pay the tax which his pretended Assembly had imposed. Leisler himself was assaulted in the street, but his opposers were quickly overpowered, some "twenty odd" of whom were put in prison, charged with being "Papists." There was probably more real despotism in New York at this moment than in any other government pretending to be "popular." To clinch his power, Leisler proclaimed that all who would not sign a declaration of fidelity to himself as representing King William "shall be deemed and esteemed enemies to his Majesty and country, and shall be treated accordingly." Dispatches to the king and Lord Shrewsbury were also prepared by Leisler and his council, which were intended to be sent to England by Milborne, but which were intrusted to

6 June. Leisler assaulted. 7 June. 23 June. 24 June. Letters to the king and Lord Shrewsbury sent by Blagge.

* Col. Doc., iii., 415, 719, 731, 748, 749, 762; Doc. Hist., ii., 247; Chalmers's Annals, i., 610; Bancroft, iii., 52. The very imperfect extract of this address by Chalmers has misled some later writers.

CHAP. XII.

1690.

Blagge, as Milborne could not well be spared from New York at this time.*

25 May. Milborne appointed general by Leisler. Objected to by Connecticut and Massachusetts.

Leisler had prevailed on the colonial Congress in May to allow him to name the commander of the expedition against Canada. Accordingly, he hastened to commission Milborne to lead the forces of New York, New England, and Maryland. This very unfit appointment was especially distasteful to Connecticut, where Winthrop was known to be the best general. Seeing that Massachusetts united with Connecticut in favor of Winthrop, with an "importunity that was irresistable," Leisler appointed him commander, and sent a blank commission for the purpose to Albany. But Massachusetts and Plymouth, which had agreed to contribute forces, recalled them, in consequence of the French attack on Casco Bay.†

20 June.

14 July. Winthrop, appointed general, marches to Albany.

Having received a commission from Governor Treat, of Connecticut, "to command the forces designed against Canada," Winthrop set out from Hartford, accompanied by Livingston. After a week's march "through the difficult and almost impasible parts of the wilderness," the Connecticut general reached Kinderhook, where some of the Albany officers hastened to meet him. On reaching Albany, Winthrop made Livingston's house his headquarters, and "found the design against Canada poorly contrived and little prosecuted, all things confused, and in no readiness or posture for marching." None of the quotas of men were equal to those promised at the New York Congress, and Milborne, as commissary, was inefficient and obnoxious. After several days spent in frivolous disputes, Winthrop accepted the commission which Leisler had sent up to be commander-in-chief of the combined expedition of New York, New England, and Maryland against Canada. The forces moved northward, through Stillwater and Saratoga, to Wood Creek, near the head of Lake Champlain, where a council of war was held. The savages advised the army to advance at once to Isle La Motte, at the foot of the lake, where the Western Iroquois were to meet the expedition. But word soon came

21 July.

31 July.

7 August. Council of war at Wood Creek.

* Col. Doc., iii., 732–748, 750, 764, 765; Doc. Hist., ii., 14, 147, 148, 151; N. Y. H. S. Coll. (1868), 326, 327. If Milborne had gone to England, he would have escaped the fate which befell him.

† Doc. Hist., ii., 135, 142–147, 149–152, 170; Col. Doc., iii., 703–707, 727–731, 752; Mass. H. S. Coll., xxxv., 258–260; *ante*, 606.

that Milborne could furnish no provisions from Albany, and that the Senecas were suffering from the epidemic small-pox, and "that the Great God had stopt their way." Attempts were nevertheless made to construct canoes of elm instead of birch; but it was so late in the season that the bark would not peel. The small-pox now broke out in the camp, and another council of war was called, at which "it was thought most advisable to return with the Army." This decision saved Canada from her threatened danger. But, by the advice of the savages, Captain John Schuyler, a younger brother of the Mayor of Albany, was detached, with forty Christians and one hundred and twenty Mohawks, Schatacooks, and River Indians, to attack the Prairie de la Madeleine, opposite Montreal. Disheartened by circumstances which he could not control, Winthrop led his army back, "many of the soldiers being sick and lame," and in a few days encamped it at Greenbush, opposite Albany.*

CHAP. XII. 1690. 9 August. Epidemic small-pox. 15 August. The army marches back to Albany. 20 August.

Meanwhile Phipps had sailed, with a large force, from Boston to attack Quebec. Knowing this, and furious at the return of Winthrop's army, Leisler hastened to Albany. Assuming supreme power, he "questioned" the Connecticut general and put him in prison, with other officers, whom he selected as "chief actors." This outrage excited the Mohawks and the Connecticut soldiers at Greenbush, and Leisler was obliged to set free his prisoners. Nevertheless, he insolently required Winthrop "to make his defence" before him at New York. The Connecticut government at once sharply rebuked the vanity of the German demagogue. "The army being confederate," it wrote, "if you be concerned, so are we, and the rest; and that you alone should judge upon the General's and Council of war's actions, will infringe our liberty." The wholesome reproof was added "that a prison is not a *catholicon* for all state maladies, though so much used by you."†

9 August. 27 August. Leisler, at Albany, imprisons Winthrop. 1 Sept.

The long-talked-of conquest of Canada had failed; yet one masterly achievement blunted the edge of disappointment in New York. Captain John Schuyler's expedition

* Col. Doc., iii., 752, 753; iv., 193–196; ix., 492, 495, 513, 514; Doc. Hist., ii., 149, 151, 152, 157, 158, 160, 169, 170; La Potherie, iii., 126, 127; Charlevoix, iii., 86–94; Trumbull, i., 382, 383; Millet's letter, 44, 46, 47; Chalmers, ii., 55, 56.

† Col. Doc., iii., 753; Doc. Hist., ii., 160, 162, 163; Hutch., i., 400; Trumbull, i., 384, 385, 540, 541; Millet's letter, 47; Chalmers, Rev. Col., i., 230; Annals, ii., 57; Dunlap, i., 191; Valentine's Man., 1861, 686.

CHAP. XII. was a brilliant success. Leaving their canoes at Chambly,
they marched to La Prairie, opposite Montreal. Frontenac
1690. had meanwhile gone up to Montreal from Quebec to oppose
the expected expedition, and a force of twelve hundred men
22 August. / 1 Sept. was reviewed; but no enemy appearing, vigilance was relaxed. Learning from his spies that the farmers and the
garrison were all cutting grain, Schuyler endeavored to gain
25 August. / 4 Sept. possession of the fort; but the eagerness of the young savages precipitated the attack, and enabled many of the French
Captain John Schuyler's expedition successful. to escape. Nineteen prisoners were taken and six killed;
all the houses and haystacks were burned, and one hundred
and fifty head of cattle destroyed. Schuyler then fell
30 August. back to Chambly and returned to Albany, having lost only
one European and six Iroquois. Thus Schenectady was
avenged.*

15 Sept. On his return to New York, Leisler wrote to Bradstreet,
at Boston, charging the failure of the Albany expedition
upon Winthrop's "treachery and cowardice," and Livingston's confederacy with the New England officers. His re-
30 Sept. ply to Connecticut was still more intemperate. Winthrop
Leisler's letters to Massachusetts and Connecticut. was charged with lax morality, and called upon to vindicate
himself; while the Hartford authorities were threatened
that, when "searched with candles," their nakedness would
be uncovered. This, however, did not affect the General
9 October. Court, who approved Winthrop's conduct, and thanked him
for his "fidelity, valor, and prudence."†

The Massachusetts naval expedition against Quebec had
9 August. meanwhile sailed under the command of Phipps, with Walley, of Plymouth, as general of the land forces. It consisted of thirty or forty vessels and two thousand men, and was
23 Sept. more than a month in reaching Tadoussac. Hearing of its
approach, Frontenac hastened with a large force from Mon-
$\frac{4}{14}$ Oct. treal to Quebec, which he quickly put in a state of defense.
Two days afterward Phipps anchored at Beauport, and sent
$\frac{6}{16}$ Oct. a pompous summons, which Frontenac was required to answer within an hour. The veteran refused to negotiate
with those who served the Prince of Orange, "a usurper,"

* Col. Doc., iii., 753; iv., 196; ix., 477–481; Doc. Hist., ii., 160–162, 169; New Jersey H. S. Proc., i., 72–74; La Hontan, i., 207, 208; La Potherie, iii., 98, 101, 102; Charlevoix, iii., 86–91; Chalmers, ii., 74.

† Hutch., i., 399, 400; Doc. Hist., ii., 169, 170; Trumbull, i., 385; Dunlap, i., 192, 193; N. Y. H. S. Proc., 1849, 107.

1690.

8/18 Oct. Phipps repulsed at Quebec.

Paper money.

and would answer only by his cannon. An ill-conducted attack was made and vigorously repulsed, and the discomfited expedition retreated. A church was dedicated at Quebec to "our Lady of the Victory," and Louis ordered a medal to be struck in honor of one of the most glorious deeds of his reign. Phipps returned humiliated and without spoil to Massachusetts, which was obliged to issue the first paper bills in America to pay its public creditors.*

22 July. / 1 August. New York cruisers take French prizes.

23 July.

17 Sept.

During the summer, however, the three vessels which Leisler had fitted out had been quite successful at Port Royal and Isle Percée. On one of the captured French vessels was a letter from Louis to Frontenac, intimating that he could afford no further assistance to Canada this year. Hearing that some French privateers were committing excesses at Nantucket and Block Island, Leisler commissioned four other vessels to cruise against them. Several French prizes were taken and brought in triumph to New York, which were condemned by a Court of Admiralty appointed by Leisler, of which De la Noy was president, while Milborne acted as attorney general.†

11 Sept.

18 Sept. Assembly at New York.

2 October.

4 October. Laws passed.

Owing to Leisler's absence in Albany, the Assembly, which he had prorogued to the first of September, did not meet, and new writs were issued summoning it for a later day. At its meeting the Assembly enacted a law requiring all persons who had left the province to return within three weeks after its publication, under pain of being "deemed and esteemed as persons disobedient to the government." Another law levied a new tax for the support of two hundred men as Leisler's garrison in the fort. A third law declared that any person refusing to accept a civil or military commission from Leisler should be fined seventy-five pounds; that any one leaving Albany or Ulster without his permission should be fined one hundred pounds; that no merchandise from those counties should be brought down the Hudson River without his license, under penalty of confiscation;

* Col. Doc., ix., 452, 455-462, 481-491, 495; La Potherie, iii., 111-123; La Hontan, 208-217; Charlevoix, iii., 94, 95, 110-128, 130, 134; v., 107; Hawkins's Quebec, 133, 137-140, 229, 314; Hutch. Mass., i., 399-402, 554-566; Mass. H. S. Coll., xxxv., 263-268; Plymouth Rec., vi., 248, 249; Humble Address, etc., by L. Hammond; Chalmers, ii., 56-58, 89; Andros Tracts; Smith, i., 107, 108. Colden, i., 137, 138, wrongly dates this expedition in 1691.

† Doc. Hist., ii., 141, 154-156, 164-168, 172, 176, 229, 230; Col. Doc., iii., 751, 752; ix., 452, 475, 477; La Potherie, iii, 89, 90; Charlevoix, iii., 101-106; Mass. H. S. Coll., xxvi., 263-274; Arnold, i., 521, 522; N. Y. H. S. Coll. (1868), 322, 327; Col. MSS., xxxvi.; *ante*, 617.

CHAP. XII. and that "all persons" who had left those counties must return within fourteen days after publication of the law, "at their utmost perils." In the annals of "popular" legislation, it would be difficult to find more despotic laws than these.*

1690.

Leisler now superseded his former commission to De Bruyn, Provoost, and Milborne, and appointed Staats, Wendell, Bleecker, Bogardus, and Schermerhorn "to superintend, direct, order and controul all matters and things relating to the city and county of Albany, and the safety and defense of the subjects therein, according to the laws of this Province, and the present establishment." Wendell was also commissioned to be mayor in place of Schuyler, and on King James's birthday aldermen and assistants were elected who all appear to have been Leisler's friends.†

10 October. Albany officers.

8 October.

14 October.

20 October. Letters were also written to the king and to Lord Shrewsbury, as it was not known that he had resigned his office of secretary of state. "New England's perfidy and disappointments" were set forth offensively, and the "Cocceian" Domine Dellius, of Albany, and others, denounced as traitors. These letters, which were the last that Leisler addressed to England, seem to have been written by Milborne.‡

Leisler quarrels with the Dutch and French ministers.

Among other quarrels, Leisler engaged in several with the Dutch and French ministers. Dellius at Albany, who was a favorite with the Indians, had opposed his authority, would pray only for the crown, and not for the King of England, and had been kindly spoken of by the Jesuit Lamberville. Leisler endeavored to imprison him in New York, but Dellius wisely escaped to Boston, whence he intended returning to Europe, and complain. Varick, of Flatbush, who had signed the address to the king and queen of the previous May, for uttering his sentiments too freely, was obliged to fly to Newcastle, and, on returning to his house, was arrested and imprisoned "for speaking treasonable words against Captain Leisler and the Fort." After a trial before De la Noy and others, under a special commission, he was sentenced "to be deprived from his ministerial function, amerced in a fine of eighty pounds, and to remain in

* Doc. Hist., ii., 133, 158, 159, 163, 181, 200, 201; Col. Doc., iii., 753; Col. MSS., xxxvi., 118; Council Journals, i., Int., xxv.; S. Wood, 108; *ante*, 616.

† Doc. Hist., ii., 100, 171, 199, 200; Munsell, ii., 112.

‡ Col. Doc., iii., 751–754; Mass. H. S. Coll., xxxv., 277.

close prison until that fine should be paid." Upon making his submission to Leisler, he was released. Selyns offered bail for Varick, but he was refused, and "grossly abused by Leisler himself in the church at the time of divine service, and threatened to be silenced." The French ministers, Perret and Daillé, were often menaced "because they would not approve of his power and disorderly proceedings."*

20 May. Huguenots at New Rochelle.

A colony of French Huguenots had meanwhile been founded at New Rochelle, upon ground sold to them by Leisler, who had bought it of Pell. Its first minister was the Reverend David Bonrepos, who, a few years afterward, removed to Staten Island. Small as it was, the new colony, greatly to its disgust, was called upon to raise the taxes imposed by Leisler's Assembly.†

26 October. Long Island against Leisler. 28 October. Milborne to subdue the refractory. 30 October.

Discontent was now spreading through the province. The people would not readily pay their taxes, especially as the Canada expedition had failed, for which Leisler was held responsible. In Queens County they declared against his government, and he suspended the session of the court "until the said rebells be suppressed, and the counties on Long Island reduced to their obedience." Milborne was also commissioned to raise what force he could, and, "with all violence and hostility," to subdue all "that are refractory to the established government." Another commission directed Edsall and Williams to assist Milborne, and examine vessels, search houses, and secure all "suspected persons." These orders were executed with such predatory violence that the inhabitants of Hempstead, Jamaica, Flushing, and Newtown met and directed Captain John Clapp to write a letter to the king's secretary of state explaining their miserable condition "by the severe oppressions and tyrannical usurpations of Jacob Leisler and his accomplices." The letter was telling and bitter. Leisler was styled a "bold

7 Novem. Captain John Clapp's letter to the secretary of state.

* Doc. Hist., ii., 247; Col. Doc., iii., 415, 646, 651, 672, 696, 715, 732, 749, 753, 771; iv., 219, 489, 533; Col. MSS., xxxvi., 142; Corr. Cl. Amst.; Murphy's Anthology, 103, 108, 113, 116, 118; N. Y. Christ. Int., 21 Sept., 1865; N. Y. H. S. Coll. (1868), 407, 409. Leisler appears to have been so hostile to Selyns, who had married his daughter Catharine to Walters in February, 1685, that he would not allow him to marry his daughter Mary to Milborne on 3 February, 1690–1: *ante*, 577. By whom the ceremony was performed does not appear: compare Val. Man., 1861, 652, 665; 1862, 604, 611, 646; 1863, 791, 830; Pass Book, iv., 71; New York Marriages (1860), 230, 262.

† Doc. Hist., ii., 171; iii., 560; Col. Doc., iii., 745, 746; Bolton's Westchester, i., 375–396, 414; Church in Westchester, 388–396; Selyns to Classis; Murphy's Anthology, 120, 127; Dr. De Witt, in N. Y. H. S. Proc. for 1848, p. 82.

CHAP. XII. 1690. usurper," and Milborne's former conviction for clipping coin had made him "famous for nothing but infamy." In a barbarous and inhuman manner houses had been plundered by them, women stripped of their apparel, and estates sequestered, "because we would not take commissions from the pretended Lieutenant Governor to be part executioners of his tyrannical will and exorbitant demands, and extort an illegal tax from the subjects." The crimes which Leisler had committed would force him to take shelter under Catiline's maxim, "The ills that I have done can not be safe but by attempting greater;" and the king was besought to "break this heavy yoke of worse than Egyptian bondage."

Adverse feeling in New York. Popular feeling could not be so openly expressed in New York, which was overawed by the fort, and where none were safe but Leisler's "faction." It was alleged, nevertheless, that much of the plunder which he obtained from houses, shops, cellars, and vessels was "sold to his friends in this city, and shipt off for the West Indies and elsewhere."*

Yet Leisler did not neglect the security of Albany against

16 Novem. the French. The Ulster officers were directed to send thither as many men as they could upon the first notice. Viele

20 Novem. Viele agent at Onondaga. was also appointed general agent of the province, to go to Onondaga and reside among the Iroquois, to act according to his best "knowledge, skill, and power."†

11 Decem. Leisler advised by Boston. Leisler was now advised from Boston that Governor Sloughter was "daily expected," and that it would be well for him, against whom many "strange reports" had been made, to temper "justice with moderation and mercy," especially when the king's own settlement of the matter was so near. But this good advice had little influence on one who clung to his usurped authority with the tenacious grasp of a despot. His last letter to Treat had not been answer-

1691. ed. Milborne therefore drafted for him a characteristical-

1 January. Leisler's abusive letter to Connecticut. ly abusive New Year's greeting to Connecticut, in which Saint James was cited as condemning "hypocrites," and the colony reviled for its "fig-leaf" righteousness and its "extent of treachery." This joint "effort" was a coarse and unsuccessful imitation of the usual Puritan style.‡

* Doc. Hist., ii., 173, 174, 175, 247; Col. Doc., iii., 754–756; Wood, 108, 109; Thompson, i., 167; Riker's Newtown, 119, 120; Onderdonk's Queens County, 12; N. Y. H. S. Coll. (1868), 381, 382.

† Doc. Hist., ii., 177, 178.

‡ Doc. Hist., ii., 178, 179, 180; Mass. H. S. Coll., xxxv., 277, 279.

Seeing that even the New York county militia were in disorder, Leisler ordered their major, De Bruyn, to "settle" them. A few days afterward he issued a proclamation requiring the appointment of assessors and collectors of his last tax in each town, at their "utmost peril." But before this spasmodic effort of waning despotism could be accomplished, Leisler's pernicious colonial authority was overthrown.*

CHAP. XII.

1691.

6 Jan.

25 Jan. Last acts of Leisler's despotism.

The revolution which shifted the crown of England from James the Second to William and Mary, at the same time transferred the allegiance of the English colonies from the old to the new sovereigns. Thenceforward Parliament assumed more immediate direction of colonial affairs than it had ever before taken. Nevertheless, the English crown remained the unquestioned sovereign of all British Plantations. But the crown was taught wisdom by experience.

Parliament and the crown.

Not less fond of power than James, William ordained for New York a government which continued substantially in operation for nearly a century. It consisted of a governor and council, appointed by the English sovereign, and an Assembly elected by a majority of the freeholders in the several counties of the province. In their mimic sphere these provincial authorities faintly shadowed the king, the lords, and the commons of England. Yet, supreme above miniature colonial legislation soared the undefined prerogative of the crown of England and the imperial arrogance of her Parliament.

1690.

William's New York government.

Sloughter's commission from William resembled in form, and in most particulars, those which James had given to Dongan and to Andros. Its chief difference was the authority intrusted to the royal governor and council to summon Assemblies of the freeholders of the province of New York. The governor, with the consent of the Council and a majority of the Assembly of the freeholders, could make local laws conformable to those of England, which colonial laws the king might approve or disallow at any time. The governor might negative all laws, and adjourn, prorogue, and dissolve such Assemblies. The new oaths enjoined by Parliament were to be sworn to by the councilors as "the

4 Jan. Sloughter's commission.

Assembly.

* Doc. Hist., ii., 181; Col. Doc., iii., 753; *ante*, 623.

CHAP. XII. 1690. Test" of 1673, which, not affecting America, James had waived. But William now required it to be taken, as well as that for the due execution of their places. Like Dongan and Andros, Sloughter was authorized to appoint judges, erect courts, pardon offenders, collate ministers in vacant benefices, command the militia, execute martial law, and act as vice-admiral. In case of his death or absence from the province, his duties were to be executed by the commander-in-chief, if the king should appoint one, and if not, by "the first counselor," who was to act as president, with the usual "powers and preheminences."*

Council.

31 Jan. Sloughter's instructions.

William's instructions to Sloughter were also modeled in most respects exactly after those which James had given to Dongan and Andros. Sloughter, however, was required to cause the Test of 1673 to be subscribed by all officers, besides their other oaths, and was directed to appoint an attorney general and call a Court of Exchequer. The former orders respecting the Church of England were renewed, by which the Bishop of London was to have ecclesiastical jurisdiction in New York, certifying ministers and licensing schoolmasters. The governor, however, could collate to benefices, grant marriage licenses, and have the probate of wills as surrogate. Liberty of conscience, which James had granted to all peaceable inhabitants, was restricted by William to all such persons "except Papists." The old instructions limiting the liberty of printing was repeated in the same words. The royal councilors in New York named by William were Frederick Phillipse, Stephen van Cortlandt, Nicholas Bayard, William Smith, Gabriel Minvielle, Chidley Brooke, William Nicolls, Nicholas de Meyer, Francis Rombouts, Thomas Willett, William Pinhorne, and John Haines. Of these, Phillipse, Van Cortlandt, and Bayard had been Andros's former counselors, and their reappointment by the Dutch king showed that he approved of their loyal conduct under Nicholson. But he left out Leisler, because he was a colonial demagogue, with brains and honesty, but blunderheaded, and Brockholls and Baxter, because they were

Councilors.

* Col. Doc., iii., 377–382, 537–542, 623–628; Commissions, ii., 3; Narcissus Luttrell, ii., 2; *ante*, 201, 202, 264, 452–455, 502–504, 564. It will be remembered that the English "Test Act" of 1673 required all officers in England to take oaths of allegiance and supremacy to the king, receive the Sacrament according to the English Episcopal form, and sign a declaration against the Romish doctrine of transubstantiation: *ante*, 201.

"Papists," while he appointed Smith, Minvielle, Rombouts, and De Meyer, nominated by Dongan.*

In the mean time the acting authorities in Massachusetts had sullenly obeyed the royal command to send to England, to answer "what may be objected against them," Andros, Dudley, Palmer, Randolph, West, Graham, Farewell, and Sherlock, whom they had kept in close confinement. The prisoners were meanly shipped on board the deeply-laden bark Mehitable, in which they "endured all the miseries of a troublesome winter voyage." But three days before the Mehitable sailed, Cooke and Oakes were dispatched in the Martin, as special agents of the insurgents, to assist Mather and Ashurst, on the part of Massachusetts. With them sailed Wiswall, of Plymouth, who was "an artist at sea." When Andros and his fellow-prisoners appeared before the Plantation Committee, they were ready to charge Massachusetts with "rebellion against lawful authority, and imprisoning the King's Governor." The agents of that colony were then required "to give the reasons of the opposition to Sir Edmund and his authority." This was done in an unsigned paper, which the committee, of course, disregarded. Upon their report the king ordered the prisoners to be discharged. A month afterward Andros submitted to the committee a full report of his administration, which was answered by the Massachusetts agents. But William, full of Irish affairs, took no further notice of this New England quarrel.†

Andros and others sent to England.

14 Feb.

11 Feb.

10 April.

14 April.

17 April.

24 April. Andros discharged.

27 May.

30 May.

Andros being thus absolved by his sovereign, Dudley and Graham, with their associates, shared the triumph of their chief. The question of a new charter for Massachusetts was left undecided, and meanwhile the king directed that Dudley should be added to the Council of New York as its

Dudley.

* Col. Doc., iii., 369-375, 417, 543-549, 685-691; Chalmers, ii., 91; N. Y. H. S. Coll. (1868), 392; Wood, i., 152.

† Doc. Hist., ii., 42; Chalmers's Annals, ii., 27, 28, 29, 61, 89; Mass. H. S. Coll., xxxii., 299, 300, 301; xxxv., 225-229; Col. Doc., iii., 722-726; Maine H. S. Coll., v., 393, 398; Hutch. Mass., i., 388, 391, 393-395; Coll., 568, 575; Barry, i., 510, 511; Arnold, i., 515; R. I. Rec., iii., 256, 257, 281-285; Narcissus Luttrell, ii., 32; Hist. Mag., i., 342; Palmer's Impartial Account, Preface; Rev. in N. E. Just., in Force's Tracts, iv., ix., 9, 10; Andros Tracts; Palfrey, iii., 582, *note; ante*, 593.

While imprisoned in Boston, Palmer drew up his "*Impartial Account*," which he could circulate there only in manuscript, it "being branded with the hard name of a Treasonable and seditious libel;" but, on reaching more liberal London, he had it printed "*for Edward Poole, at the Ship, over against the Royal Exchange, in Cornhill*, 1690." Palmer's "Account" has been reprinted in the Andros Tracts, together with an answer to it, entitled "*The Revolution in New England Justified*," which also makes No. 9 of Force's Tracts, iv.

CHAP. XII. 1690.

first member. Graham was also recommended to be made recorder and attorney general.*

Graham. 26 April.

The king in Council also ordered that one of the sloops built by Andros, together with the guns taken from Pemaquid, and the New York Records which had been carried to Boston, should be delivered to Sloughter; and a letter was accordingly written to the acting authorities of Massachusetts. A new seal was likewise appointed for New York, and delivered to Sloughter. It represented on one side the effigies of the king and queen, with two Indians kneeling and offering presents of beaver, and on the other the royal arms, with appropriate inscriptions.†

New York Records. 30 April. 31 May. New provincial seal.

It was more than ever important that Sloughter should hasten to his government; yet, after all the delays that had already occurred, his departure was again retarded. The frigate appointed to carry him to New York was detached as a convoy to Ireland, where William went to conduct the campaign in person. The defeat of James at the River Boyne enabled the king to return soon afterward triumphantly to London. The French, however, were still very strong at sea. It was so difficult to obtain convoys that English merchants were obliged to hire the protection of Dutch privateers. At length the frigate Archangel and three smaller vessels were assigned to convey Sloughter, with two companies of soldiers, from Spithead to New York. Of one of these companies Sloughter himself was made the captain. The other was commanded by Major Richard Ingoldesby, of "a worthy family," but "a rash, hot-headed man," who had formerly served in Holland, and had just returned from victorious service under William in Ireland. Ingoldesby probably owed his promotion to the friendship of the eccentric Marquis of Winchester, whom William had made Duke of Bolton. His commission required him to obey the royal "Governor of New York now and for the time being," but it did not authorize him to act as commander-in-chief in case of Sloughter's absence or death.‡

1 July. 7 October. Soldiers for New York. 10 Sept. Major Richard Ingoldesby's commission.

* Col. Doc., iii., 364, 721, 760, 761, 767, 768; iv., 551, 847; Council Min., vi., 2; Doc. Hist., ii., 202; Mass. H. S. Coll., xxxv., 277, 279; Hutch. Mass., i., 395; ii., 313. Although Dudley was made a New York counselor, he was not appointed its chief justice by the king, who had intrusted that power to Sloughter, who accordingly commissioned Dudley on 15 May, 1691: Col. Doc., iii., 625; Council Min., vi., 27; *post*, 639.

† Col. Doc., iii., 427. 546, 624, 710–712, 769; Doc. Hist., iv., 2*; Commissions, ii., 16.

‡ Chalmers's Annals, ii., 68, 73, 91; Rev. Col., i., 242; Burchett's Memoirs, 47, 58, 62, 103–

CHAP. XII.

1690.

Blagge in London.

Meanwhile Blagge had reached London with Leisler's dispatches of June, and submitted "a memorial of what has occurred in New York," with a petition to the king, praying that Leisler's proceedings might be approved, that the Assembly of New York might choose the members of the Council, and that the petitioner might be heard in person. Blagge, however, met with no more favor than his predecessor Stoll. So far from recognizing Leisler as lieutenant governor, or approving his conduct, the king did not even name him as one of Sloughter's counselors. The Privy Council referred all the papers received from "Captain Leisler and others calling themselves the Council of New York," as well as the address from its principal inhabitants, to Sloughter, with directions strictly and impartially to examine the several allegations on his arrival, and return "a true and perfect account of the state of that province."*

17 Oct. His papers referred to Sloughter.

At length Sloughter set sail from the Isle of Wight for Bermuda and New York in the Archangel frigate, Captain Jasper Hicks, which was to convoy the Beaver, the Canterbury, and the store-ship John and James. Ingoldesby, with his company of soldiers, and Counselor Brooke, who had also been appointed collector and receiver of New York, Secretary Clarkson, and others, embarked in the Beaver. The other soldiers were in the Canterbury. Dudley, the "first Counsellor" of New York, appears to have sailed directly to Boston. After keeping company for some time, the three ships separated at sea from the Archangel, "without any direction or allowance," and made the best of their way to New York, while the frigate steered for Bermuda.†

1 Decem. Sloughter sails for New York and is carried to Bermuda.

The Beaver and the store-ship arrived safely at New York, and presently after, Stephanus van Cortlandt and many others came on board, complaining against Leisler, and urging Ingoldesby to land his soldiers and take possession of the fort. As the Archangel, with Sloughter on board, had not yet arrived, Ingoldesby was the highest royal officer in the province. Accordingly, he sent Counselor

1691.

29 Jan. Ingoldesby at New York.

113; Narcissus Luttrell, ii., 127; Collins's Peerage, i., 229; Macaulay, iii., 128, 170, 435, 532, 579, 600–677; Doc. Hist., ii., 126, 140, 186; Col. Doc., iii., 618, 757, 791, 810, 845; iv., 214, 719, 760; Col. MSS., xxxvi., 119; N. Y. H. S. Coll. (1868), 299, 300.

* Col. Doc., iii., 631, 650, 731–750; Doc. Hist., ii., 33, 34, 151, 203, 220, 221; Mass. H. S. Coll., xxxv., 277; *ante*, 619, 620.

† Col. Doc., iii., 756, 757, 759, 766; iv., 321, 525; Wood, 152; Mass. H. S. Coll., xxxv., 277, 279.

CHAP. XII. 1691. Brooke, Lieutenant Shanks, and Ensign Simmes to demand from Leisler possession of the fort for the king's forces and their stores. The fort was certainly the proper place in which Ingoldesby and his soldiers should be quartered, and the king's commissioned officer naturally considered the German usurper no more than a "pretended Governor." Leisler was "very angry at the demand;" he was willing to receive the king's stores, but not the king's soldiers into the fort, and he asked Brooke "who were appointed of the Council in this Province?" When informed that William had named Phillipse, Van Cortlandt, and Bayard, among others, and not himself, Leisler fell into a passion, and cried out, "*What! those Popish Dogs, Rogues—Sacrement, if the King should send three thousand such, I would cut them all off.*" It was a crushing blow to the colonial demagogue who had thus been reproved by his king, and his taste of power had so infatuated him that he could not "bear the thoughts of a supersedeas," nor conceal his resentment toward those "harbengers, as he judged, of an authority to which he must submit."*

Leisler very angry.

Leisler's dilemma.

And now Leisler had to meet a serious dilemma. He had seized the fort, as he pretended that it would not otherwise be safely kept for William. He had usurped the government of New York by sheer impudence, and without the least authority from the English crown. The only person now in the province who held William's commission to command the king's forces there was Ingoldesby, and he was bound to obey Sloughter, and him only, as the royal governor of New York. As the proper place for the royal garrison was the royal fort, Leisler should have let Ingoldesby and his soldiers occupy it at once. If he had done so, much trouble would have been avoided.

Leisler obstinate.

Nevertheless, Leisler resolved to hold out against the change which he saw William intended. Sloughter had not arrived, and perhaps he might not come; while Ingoldesby was only commissioned to obey the king's governor of New York for the time being. Of this technical dilemma Leisler took advantage, and assumed that, in Sloughter's absence, he was himself the commander-in-chief of

* Col. Doc., iii., 757, 791; iv., 525; Doc. Hist., ii., 247, 248; Wood, i., 152; Thompson, i., 263; N. Y. H. S. Coll. (1868), 315, 318, 329, 392.

New York. He refused to give up the fort unless Ingoldesby had directions to that effect from King William or Governor Sloughter. So he sent De la Noy and Milborne to inspect Ingoldesby's orders, and offer all sorts of accommodations for himself, his officers, and soldiers. The absurdity of Leisler's position is obvious. To this proposition Ingoldesby and the king's counselors on board the Beaver could not assent. They knew that when Sloughter left England, William had never recognized Leisler's usurped authority. So Ingoldesby replied:—"I have seen the copy of his Majesty's letter directed to Lieut. Govr. Nicholson, etc., but cannot find how you may derive any authority to yourself from thence. I want not the accommodation you speciously offer to his Majesty's soldiers under my command. Possession of his Majesty's Fort is what I demand from you; and if you refuse that, I must esteem you no friend to their Majesties King William and Queen Mary." The same day Ingoldesby issued a mandate to Captain Samuel Moore, of Long Island, for aid against the "rebels" who opposed his Majesty. Leisler answered this by a protest, and a call of the neighboring militia to obey his own orders. Finding that malicious rumors had been spread against him, Ingoldesby declared that his purpose was not to disturb, but to protect the people. The next day Leisler announced that Sloughter had been appointed governor of the province, and that the fort at New York would be surrendered to him on his arrival; and meanwhile directed Ingoldesby and his soldiers to be entertained in the city. So he forbade all persons from aiding or comforting the major of William's forces, who had no orders from the governor. At length Ingoldesby, feeling that the "well affected" in the city would stand by him, landed his soldiers, with as much caution as if he had "made a descent into an enemies' country," and quartered them in the City Hall.*

[Margin notes: 30 Jan. — 30 Jan. — 31 Jan. — 2 Feb. — 3 Feb. — 4 Feb. Leisler opposes Ingoldesby. — 6 Feb.]

As Bayard and Nicolls, whom Leisler held close prisoners in the fort, had been named royal counselors by the king, Ingoldesby demanded their release. But Leisler replied that they must "remaine configned until his Majesties further orders arrive." For a while there was quiet in New

[Margin note: 14 Feb.]

* Doc. Hist., ii., 181–185, 219, 240; Col. Doc., iii., 757, 759, 791; iv., 214; Dunlap, i., 195–198; N. Y. H. S. Coll. (1868), 300, 301, 302, 315–320, 383, 384, 403; *ante*, 593, 597.

CHAP. XII. 1691. Leisler's fresh lies. York, Ingoldesby hoping for, and Leisler dreading the arrival of Sloughter. But as time wore on, and the governor did not come, Leisler and his friends circulated reports that William's officers and soldiers were "Papists and disaffected persons fled from England," and that they had "forged their commissions, and were enemies of King William and Queen Mary." Upon this, Dudley, who had come on from Boston, and the five other members of the royal Council, except Bayard and Nicolls, whom Leisler still kept confined

Action of the royal Council. in the fort, met in the city, and endeavored to "dispose the people to a better understanding." It was observed, however, that armed men from all parts of the province and from New Jersey were constantly brought, with large supplies of provisions, into the fort, the guns of which were taken from the river front and trained to bear on the city. The block-houses were likewise filled with the adherents of Leisler, who objected to the king's soldiers going the rounds, and threatened to beat the houses of the citizens "about

4 March. their ears." This obliged the counselors to call for the militia of the neighboring counties, and to desire "Major Richard Ingoldesby, the chief commander of their Majesties' forces sent thither, to take into his care and charge the defending their Majesties' subjects in this Province from any outrageous and hostile proceedings whatsoever, in such manner, and by such proper and just means as to him shall seem reasonable, 'till such time as his Excellency, Colonel Henry Sloughter, shall arrive, or their Majesties' pleasure shall be farther known." In the absence of the governor, this was evidently the only way in which the king's regu-

5 March. Leisler's proclamation. lar authority could be maintained. Leisler, however, issued another proclamation from Fort William, declaring that he was "constrained to take up arms in defence of their Maj-

10 March. esties' supremacy," and denouncing the "illegal, unwarrantable, and undue practices" of the king's own counselors and the second in command of the royal troops under Slough-

12 March. ter. He also wrote to the governor at Bermuda, hoping that his excellency might speedily arrive.*

By order of six of the king's counselors, Matthew Clark-

4 March. son, the royal secretary of New York, meanwhile wrote to

* Col. Doc., iii., 757, 758, 759, 760, 765; Doc. Hist., ii., 186, 187, 188, 189, 192, 193; Dunlap, ii., 199; N.Y. H. S. Coll. (1868), 304–310.

the government of Connecticut, giving an account of affairs in the province, and soliciting their advice. Secretary Allyn replied, advising the New York counselors "to avoid contest with Captain Leisler, and rather to bear any thing tolerable and redressible, 'till his Excellency's arrival." At the same time he wrote to Leisler that there was no doubt "but that the ships and gentlemen arrived, do come in subordination to his Excellency Colonel Sloughter, and that his Excellency, as Governor from their Majesties, is daily expected at New York; that therefore you so act and demean yourself as may no ways violate their Majesty's subjects peace and safety."*

Clarkson writes to Connecticut.

11 March. Allyn's advice to Leisler.

The advice of Connecticut was seconded by several of Leisler's own followers. Gerardus Beekman assembled the people of Kings and Queens at the ferry, "to write together a peace address." With this he came to the fort, "to persuade Leisler from such base and inhuman actions." But "the malice of a choleric man" could not be restrained. Seeing that he meant to hold out, and had already gathered three hundred men in the fort, the Council hastened the militia from the neighboring towns, and in a short time five hundred came into the city. Clarkson wrote again to Connecticut, asking for three or four hundred men to assist in maintaining the king's government. Captain William Kidd, a "blasphemous privateer," was also employed by the Council, and did "many good services" with his vessel.†

"Peace address" from Kings and Queens counties.

16 March.

William Kidd.

Leisler now prepared a long declaration against Ingoldesby and the royal counselors, requiring them to disband their forces; otherwise they would be pursued and destroyed as "impious and unreasonable men." This was sent the next day, and an answer required within two hours. A temperate reply was returned, that the counselors, officers, and soldiers were commissioned by King William, and wished to preserve the peace, and that those who should attack them would be "public enemies to the crown of England."‡

16 March. Leisler's declaration against Ingoldesby.

17 March. Reply of the Council.

Affairs were now coming to a crisis. Having usurped

* Doc. Hist., ii., 185, 188, 189; Dunlap, ii., 199, 200; *ante*, 596. It is marvelous how perversely Dunlap blunders in calling Clarkson the "Secretary of the pretended King's Council of New York."

† Doc. Hist., ii., 169, 190–192, 194, 209; Col. Doc., iii., 760; Col. MSS., xxxvi., 16; Council Min., vi., 6; Journals, i., 3; Assembly Journals, i., 6; Hunt's Merchants' Mag., xiv., 41.

‡ Doc. Hist., ii., 193–196; Col. Doc., iii., 758; Dunlap, i., 200–202.

CHAP. XII.

1691.

the authority of lieutenant governor by a false construction of the king's letter to Nicholson, Leisler determined to attack the king's own commissioned officers and soldiers. In the absence of the governor, William had expressly directed that the commander-in-chief, or the "first counsellor" appointed by himself, should take the administration. The Council held that Ingoldesby was such chief commander, and therefore Dudley, the first councilor, did not act as president. Certainly both were commissioned directly by William, which Leisler never had been.*

Ingoldesby chief commander.

Scarcely a quarter of an hour after he received the reply of the Council, Leisler, with his own hand, fired one of the guns of the fort at the king's troops as they stood on parade. This was followed by other shots at the house where they were lodged, and by volleys of musketry, which wounded several and killed two, one of whom was an old soldier, Josiah Browne, said to have been slain by Gouverneur. Balls were also heated in the furnace to fire the town. The guns of the fort were answered from the land side, and, in firing one of the cannon, six persons, among whom was MacGregorie, were killed. Leisler had meanwhile ordered the block-house on the Smith's Vlye, at the opposite side of the city, to support the fire from the fort. But Ensign Brasher, its commander, not willing to oppose Ingoldesby's soldiers, who were preparing to attack, went to the fort for farther orders, where he was imprisoned; and, in his absence, the burgher guard in the block-house laid down their arms and went to their houses.

17 March. Leisler fires on the troops.

Persons killed.

Block-house surrenders.

This defection greatly discouraged Leisler and his adherents, now closely invested in the fort. The next day, however, he fired a few more shots, which did no harm; while Ingoldesby refrained from attacking and held his men on the defensive, expecting a sally from the fort, or a battering down of the city. To distinguish his men from those of Leisler, Ingoldesby directed them to wear white bands on their left arms.†

18 March. Leisler fires more shots.

18 March. At this critical moment word came that the Archangel
19 March. had anchored below the Narrows. The next morning Dud-

* Col. Doc., iii., 606, 628, 791; Doc. Hist., ii., 192; N. Y. H. S. Coll. (1848), 404.

† Col. Doc., iii., 395, 758, 760, 765, 767; Doc. Hist., ii., 205, 206, 222, 227, 231, 233, 248; Mass. H. S. Coll., xxxv., 282–284; N. Y. H. S. Proc., 1849, 107; Coll. (1868), 384, 404. Neither Dunlap (i., 202) nor Hoffman (222) refer to the events of 17 and 18 March.

ley and the other councilors went down in a brigantine and met the long-expected governor. The frigate had been nearly lost upon the rocks at Bermuda, where she was detained three weeks; and six weeks more were consumed in coming from there to Sandy Hook. On learning the condition of affairs in New York, Sloughter hastened up to the city in the ship's pinnace, passing through the Buttermilk Channel, on the east side of Nutten Island. "The noise and shouting that followed upon the Governor's landing" made the hearts of Leisler's followers "to devide." Going at once to the City Hall, Sloughter caused the bell to be rung and his commission to be read, after which he took the required oaths and swore in Councilors Dudley, Phillipse, Van Cortlandt, Minvielle, Brooke, Willett, and Pinhorne, all who "were at liberty."* The governor directed Ingoldesby to go with his company and demand entrance into the fort. This was refused by Leisler, who sent Stoll with a letter to Sloughter requiring "orders under the King's own hand, directed to him." Sloughter told Stoll that he was glad he had seen him in England and now again at New York, and Ingoldesby was again directed to demand possession of the fort, the release of Councilors Bayard and Nicolls "to attend his Majesty's service," and the presence of "Leisler, Milborne, and such as are called his Council." To this second demand Leisler answered that the fort was not to be delivered "upon such easy terms;" and he sent Milborne and De la Noy, with Ingoldesby, back to the governor "to capitulate," as if he were an enemy; refusing to attend himself or to set free the royal councilors whom he held in prison. Upon this Sloughter committed Milborne and De la Noy to the guards, and ordered Ingoldesby a third time to demand the surrender of the fort, the enlargement of Bayard and Nicolls, and the attendance of Leisler; "all which was peremptorily and with contempt refused." As it was now nearly midnight, the governor directed the Council to meet the next morning, and so ended this eventful day.†

Arrival of Sloughter.

Councilors sworn.

Milborne and De la Noy imprisoned.

* Colonel William Smith, formerly Governor of Tangier, who had come from England to New York in 1686, and, having been recommended by Dongan as a fit councilor, was so named in Sloughter's commission, was sworn and took his seat on 25 March, 1691: Council Min., vi., 7; Col. Doc., iii., 417, 685, 760, 767; iv., 1137; Thompson's L. I., ii., 442.

† Col. Doc., iii., 756, 758, 759, 760, 765, 766, 767; ix., 507; Doc. Hist., ii., 202, 222, 240; Chalmers, Rev. Col., i., 243; Annals, i., 594, 611, 612; ii., 71; Council Min., vi., 1, 2; N. Y.

CHAP. XII.

1691.

20 March.

On Friday morning, the twentieth of March, the Council accordingly met the governor at the City Hall. Deprived of Milborne, "his oracle, and De la Noy, his great Minister of State," who were now in custody, Leisler wrote to Sloughter, "I see very well the stroke of my enemies, who are wishing to cause me some mistakes at the end of the loyalty I owe to my gracious King and Queen;" and he supplicated the governor to receive the fort, and treat him as a person who would give "an exact account of all his actions and conduct." But this letter was not noticed. The governor ordered Ingoldesby and his soldiers to require the men in the fort to ground their arms and march out, promising that all should be pardoned except Leisler and his council. Leisler's men "readily forsook" the fallen demagogue; who was brought before the governor at the City Hall, and the king's letter to Nicholson taken from him, while he, with his councilors, "being found in actual rebellion," were ordered to be committed to the guards. Bayard and Nicolls, freed from their long imprisonment, were sworn of the Council, "and Bayard's chain put on Leisler's legg."*

Leisler's submission to Sloughter.

Leisler's men surrender.

Leisler imprisoned, and Bayard and Nicolls set free.

Sloughter at once took possession of the fort, which he named "William Henry," after the king, and then issued writs for the election of representatives to an Assembly to meet on the ninth of April. John Lawrence was commissioned as mayor of New York, William Pinhorne recorder, and Thomas Clarke coroner. Sheriffs of the several counties were also appointed. Thomas Newton, of Boston, who was reputed to be the best lawyer in America, was appointed attorney general of New York by the governor, who did not know of Graham's "pretensions" for the place. On the first Sunday after Leisler's imprisonment, Domine Selyns, whom he had so coarsely insulted, preached, in the fullness of joy, before the new governor, from the text in the twenty-seventh Psalm, "I had fainted, unless I had be-

20 March. Writs for an Assembly.

21 March. Officers appointed.

22 March. Domine Selyns's sermon.

H. S. Coll. (1868), 384, 404. It is surprising how Dunlap, i., 202, 203, misrepresents these transactions, and how implicitly Hoffman (223, 224) follows his errors, which later writers have reiterated.

* Col. Doc., iii., 767, 789, 794; Doc. Hist., ii., 202, 203, 216, 217, 222, 240, 241, 248; Council Min., vi., 2, 3; N.Y.H.S. Proc., 1849, 107; Coll. (1868), 310, 311, 405; Mass. H. S. Coll., xxxv., 283; Chalmers's Annals, i., 612; Smith, i., 110; Dunlap, i., 203, 204, 205, 206. It is amusing to see how obstinately Dunlap insists that Leisler was a "Dutchman," and not "a German." Many in our own times maintain the same vulgar error.

lieved to see the goodness of the Lord in the land of the living."*

1691. 23 March.

Councilors Dudley, Van Cortlandt, and Brooke were appointed to examine the prisoners with a view to their committal for trial. The prisoners asked Sloughter for a hearing before himself, under the reference to him by the Privy Council of the previous October. But that order did not relate to the recent transactions, which the governor judged it proper should be tried by a court. A special commission of Oyer and Terminer was accordingly ordered, under the king's large authority to Sloughter. The court consisted of Joseph Dudley and Thomas Johnson, whom the governor forthwith appointed judges in admiralty, together with Sir Robert Robinson, formerly governor of Bermuda; Colonel William Smith, Recorder Pinhorne, and John Lawrence, of the Council; Captain Jasper Hicks, of the frigate Archangel; Major Ingoldesby; and Colonel John Younge, and Captain Isaac Arnold, of Long Island, or any six of them, "one of the Judges always being one." This court was composed of persons "most capable of discerning the truth, and the least prejudiced to those people; who indeed executed their commission with all the lenity and patience imaginable." The prisoners were committed to the custody of Sheriff Lyndall, of New York, for trial before this tribunal on a charge of traitorously levying war against the king and queen, counterfeiting their majesties' great seal, murdering Josiah Browne, and other high misdemeanors. Councilors Bayard, Van Cortlandt, and Pinhorne were directed to prepare the evidence, and Nicolls, Farewell, and Emott were assigned as king's counsel to assist Attorney General Newton.†

24 March. Special commission of Oyer and Terminer. 26 March.

26 March. The prisoners committed to the sheriff.

30 March.

When the trial came on, the indictment found by the grand jury charged the prisoners with treason and murder "for holding by force the King's fort against the King's Governor, after the publication of his Commission, and he had thereby become Chief Magistrate, and after demand had been made in the King's name, and in the reducing of

April. Their indictment by the grand jury.

* Council Min., vi., 3, 5, 6; Col. Doc., iii., 721, 756, 761, 767, 768; iv., 219, 551, 847; Min. of N. Y. Com. Council, i., 353; Smith, i., 112; Dunlap, i., 206; Murphy's Anthology, 114; N. Y. H. S. Coll. (1868), 406; *ante*, 630.

† Council Min., vi., 5, 6, 7, 8, 9; Doc. Hist., ii., 153, 204, 205; Col. Doc., iii., 625, 663, 701, 747, 760, 767, 794; Col. MSS., xxxiv., 80; xxxvi., 32; xxxvii., 93, 94; N. Y. Wills, iv., 336; Smith, i., 110; Dunlap, i., 206; N. Y. H. S. Coll. (1868), 311, 323, 364, 405; *ante*, 599, 631.

CHAP. XII. 1691. which lives had been lost." There was nothing alleged against them for any previous irregularities or usurpations of authority. The petit jury was "composed of youths and other bitter men." Eight of the prisoners pleaded not guilty. But Leisler and Milborne refused to plead "until the power be determined whereby such things have been acted," and they insisted that the court should first decide whether the king's letter to Nicholson of 30 July, 1689, "had not given Captain Leisler an authority to take upon him the Government." This was simply begging the question. The court, however, would give no answer until the prisoners had pleaded, which they refused to do. Upon this, the court thought it best to ask the governor and Council whether the king's letter, or any of the papers which had been referred to Sloughter by the Privy Council, "can be understood or interpreted to be and contain any power and direction to Captain Jacob Leisler to take the Government of the Province upon himself, or that the administration thereupon be to be holden good in law." Sloughter and his counselors accordingly declared their opinion "that the aforesaid letters to Captain Nicholson, nor any other papers in the packet directed to his Excellency for a report, contains any power or direction for the government to the said Captain Leisler." Announcing this decision as its own, the court again called on Leisler and Milborne to plead to the indictment. But this they obstinately refused to do, and, "after several hearings as mutes" during eight days, the jury found them guilty, along with Abraham Gouverneur, Gerardus Beekman, Johannes Vermilye, Thomas Williams, Myndert Coerten, and Abraham Brasher. The jury, however, acquitted De la Noy and Edsall. Sentence of death, according to the barbarous English law then in force, was at once pronounced by Dudley, the presiding judge, upon the eight condemned criminals. "By the advice of the Judges," the governor reprieved the prisoners, upon their petition, until the king's pleasure should be known, "unless any insurrection of the people necessitate their execution."*

Petit jury.

Leisler and Milborne refuse to plead.

13 April. Opinion of the governor and Council on the king's letter to Nicholson.

Eight of the prisoners convicted.

Two acquitted.

20 April. Prisoners sentenced and reprieved.

In obedience to the orders of the Privy Council, Slough-

* Col. Doc., iii., 606, 759, 760, 762, 766, 767, 780, 792, 794, 811; iv., 215; Doc. Hist., ii., 206, 207, 208, 209, 211, 213, 217, 222, 235, 241, 248; Council Min., vi., 14, 59; Chalmers's Annals, i., 594, 612; ii., 71, 72; Rev. Col., i., 249; Assembly Journals, i., 7; Smith, i., 110, 111; Dunlap, i., 206, 207; N. Y. H. S. Coll. (1868), 311-317, 323, 350-364, 385, 406; *ante*, 593, 594, 597.

ter promptly examined into the allegations in the address of the merchants and other inhabitants of New York to the king against Leisler, and found them "severally true, and that they have been very modest in their relation." The memorial of Blagge was reviewed and answered by Bayard and Nicolls, and the governor was "very well satisfied with the truth thereof." In his report to England, Sloughter remarked that, during his absence, Ingoldesby "did behave himself with much prudence and discretion, and make it his whole care to prevent bloodshed, and had he not been covered by the militia, this place had been too hot for him. I was joyfully received amongst them. I find those men against whom the depositions were sent, to be the principal and most loyal men of this place, whom Leisler and Milborne did fear, and therefore grievously oppress. Many that followed Leisler are well enough affected to their Majesties' Government, but through ignorance were put upon to do what they did; and I believe if the chief ring-leaders be made an example, the whole country may be quieted, which otherwise will be hard to do." In his letters to Secretary Nottingham and the Plantation Committee, Sloughter declared that "the loyal and best part of the country is very earnest" for the execution of the prisoners, but advised that, "if his Majesty shall please to grant his pardon for all except Jacob Leisler and Jacob Milborne, it will be a favour."* As Clarkson was the provincial secretary by royal patent, the governor and Council appointed David Jamison, the Scotch "Sweet Singer," who had come back from Boston, to be its clerk. The affairs of Albany and its neighborhood having been considered in Council, letters were ordered to be written to Virginia, Maryland, and the other adjoining colonies, asking assistance to New York against the French and Indians, "the common enemy of the English in America." Domine Dellius, who had hastened back to New York after the fall of Leisler, was now, in consideration of his services among the Mohawks, allowed the sixty pounds "formerly paid yearly to two Romish Priests that attended on Governor Dongan."†

CHAP. XII. 1691.

27 April. Blagge's memorial answered. 7 May. Sloughter's reports to England.

27 March. 6 May. 7 May.

15 April. Jamison clerk of the Council.

Letters to Virginia and other colonies.

18 April. Dellius returns and is rewarded.

* Council Min., vi., 20, 21; Col. Doc., iii., 731–750, 756–768; Doc. Hist., ii., 220–223; Chalmers's Annals, i., 610, 611; *ante*, 631.

† Council Min., vi., 15, 17, 18; Col. MSS., xxxvii., 163; Col. Doc., iii., 771, 772; iv., 489; *ante*, 407, 408, 487, 511, 555, 596, 624.

CHAP. XII.

1691.

9 April. Assembly meets.

On the appointed day the Assembly which Sloughter had summoned met in the city of New York. It was the first time that the popular representatives of the province had convened under the direct authority of the English crown. The metropolis elected James Graham, after a contest with Abraham de Peyster, and William Merrett, Jacobus van Cortlandt, and Johannes Kipp. Albany chose Dirck Wessells and Levinus van Schaick; Ulster and Dutchess, Henry Beekman and Thomas Garton; Westchester, John Pell; Richmond, Elias Duksberry and John Dally; Suffolk, Henry Pierson and Matthew Howell; Queens, John Bound and Nathaniel Pearsall; Kings, Nicholas Stillwell and John Poland. Rensselaerswyck afterward sent Killian van Rensselaer. All the elected burgesses took the appointed oaths, with the Test, except those from Queens county, who scrupled because they were Quakers; in whose places Daniel Whitehead and John Robinson were returned. William Demire was also chosen from Ulster in place of Garton, who "could not attend." The members, who were all opposed to Leisler, chose James Graham, of New York, for their speaker, and John Clapp, who had drawn up the Queens county letter of November, 1690, their clerk. For many years, in want of better accommodation, the Assembly "sat in a Tavern."*

Its members.

Speaker and clerk.

Speeches of Sloughter and Dudley to the Assembly.

The governor and "President" Dudley each made speeches to the Assembly, advising them to prepare an address to their majesties, as well as laws to establish courts of justice, to maintain ministers in every town, to quiet the troubles in the province, to support the garrison at Albany, and to continue the revenue. As its first work, the Assembly took up a petition "by several Freeholders, inhabitants within this Province, setting forth several oppressions and hardships executed upon their Majesties subjects in this Province by Jacob Leisler, Samuel Edsall, and others." Upon consideration, the House resolved unanimously that Leisler's acts had been tumultuous, illegal, arbitrary, destructive, and rebellious; and that the tragedy at Schenectady could only be "attributed to the disorders and disturbances

15 April.

17 April. Its resolutions against Leisler's arbitrary acts.

* Assembly Journals, i., 1–10, 177, 191; Council Journals, i., 1–6, 216, 220; Col. Doc., iii., 756, 761, 768, 789, 792, 795; iv., 215, 847, 1115; Doc. Hist., ii., 230; Smith, i, 112, 113; Dunlap, i., 207; ii., App. xlvii., xlviii.; *ante*, 625, 626.

of those who had usurped a power contrary to their Majesties authority, and the right of government over this Province." This expression of the popular voice of New York was agreed to by the governor and Council, and ordered to be published. In answer to Sloughter's request for their opinion concerning a reprieve to Leisler and Milborne, the Assembly resolved "that their Majesties have only intrusted that matter of reprieving with his Excellency alone, and they dare not give their opinion thereupon." At the same time they presented him an address, "That as in our hearts we do abhorr and detest all the rebellious arbitrary and illegal proceedings of the late usurpers of their Majesties' authority over this Province, so we do, from the bottom of our hearts, with all integrity, acknowledge and declare that there are none that can or ought to have to rule and govern their Majesties subjects here, but their Majesties' authority, which is now placed in your Excellency."*

CHAP. XII.

1691.

18 April.

20 April.

18 April. Rebellion abhorred by the Assembly.

A few days afterward, upon information "That the several laws made formerly by the General Assembly and his late Royal Highness, James, Duke of York, &c., and also the several ordinances or reputed laws made by the preceding governors and councils, for the rule of their Majesties' subjects within this Province, are reported amongst the people to be still in force," the House resolved unanimously, "That all the laws consented to by the General Assembly, under James, Duke of York, and the Liberties and Privileges therein contained, granted to the People, and declared to be their Rights, not being observed, and not ratified and approved by his Royal Highness, nor the late King, are null, void, and of none effect: And also the several ordinances made by the late Governors and Councils, being contrary to the Constitution of England, and the practice of the government of their Majesties other Plantations in America, are likewise null, void, and of none effect nor force within this Province." Whatever may have been the motive for this extraordinary resolution, the Assembly did not present it to the governor and Council for their concurrence, and therefore it never had any legal effect in

24 April.

The Assembly resolves that the colonial laws of James are void.

The Council does not concur in this resolution.

* Assembly Journals, i., 2–7; Council Journals, i., 2–4; Smith, i., 113, 114; Doct. Hist., ii., 207, 208.

CHAP. XII. New York. James's laws remained in force there until regularly repealed.*

1691. 6 May. Assembly's address to William and Mary.

A loyal address to the king and queen was now signed by the governor and Council, and the Assembly, and sent to England by way of Virginia. Its chief point was to define more clearly the "territories depending" on the province, mentioned in Sloughter's commission and instructions. The king was therefore prayed to annex again Connecticut, New Jersey, Pennsylvania, and Delaware to New York, and thus re-establish her ancient bounds, for her better defense and support.†

15 April. Bills to be drawn by attorney general. 16 April.

As the members of the House of Assembly were not experts in legislation, they asked the governor and Council that Attorney General Newton might "draw up such bills as are necessary for their Majesties' service, and the good of this government." This was ordered; but Newton at the same time told the Assembly that the governor had directed him to go to Boston, and bring back the provincial records. He was answered that "it was his duty and business to attend this House during the sessions." Newton, however, went to Boston, as Sloughter had ordered; and the difficulty was overcome by the appointment, first, of George Farewell, and then of Speaker Graham, to draft the Assembly bills.‡

6 May. Law to quiet disorders.

The first royal General Assembly of New York passed fourteen laws. Of these, the earliest was "for quieting and settling the disorders that have lately happened within this Province, and for the establishing and securing their Majesties' present government against the like disorders for the future." This law was thought "very necessary to remove the people's mistake they had been poisoned with from New England, that the Crown has nothing to do with the people here." It enacted "that there can be no power and authority held and exercised over their Majesties' subjects

* Assembly Journals, i., 8, 9; Smith, i., 114, 115; Chalmers's Annals, i., 585; Butler, 41; Daly, 34. Compare Journal of the Legislative Council of New York, i., 5–10, in which there is no record of the concurrence of the Council, nor of the assent of the governor. Smith ascribes this action of the Assembly to "art" rather than to "ignorance;" but I can not see how such transparent stupidity could deceive or sway even the weak Sloughter, much less his Council.

† Col. Doc., iii., 623, 685, 762, 768, 790, 795; Assembly Journals, i., 3, 11; Council Journals, i., 7; Col. MSS., xxxvii, 85, 86.

‡ Assembly Journals, i., 5, 7, 8, 10, 11, 12; Council Journals, i., 3, 7; Council Min., vi., 15, 51; Col. MSS., xxxvi., 91, 238; Col. Doc., iii., 721, 769; iv., 847.

in this their Province and Dominion, but what must be derived from their Majesties, their heirs and successors; * * * * and that none ought or can have power, upon any pretence whatsoever, to use or exercise any power over their subjects in this Province, but by their immediate authority under their Broad Seal of their realm of England as now established." As Bayard and others had suffered severely under Leisler, it was further enacted "that whatsoever person or persons shall by any manner of way, or upon any pretence whatsoever, endeavour by force of arms or otherways, to disturb the peace, good, and quiet of this their Majesty's government, as it is now established, shall be deemed and esteemed as rebels and traitors unto their Majesties, and incur the pains, penalties and forfeitures as the laws of England have for such offences made and provided."*

While the Assembly thus testified its loyalty to the English crown, it reasserted those popular rights which Dongan's first Assembly had proclaimed. An act was passed, "declaring what are the rights and privileges of their Majesties subjects inhabiting within this Province of New York," which followed, with little variation, the language of the repealed "Charter of Liberties" of October 30, 1683. It differed from its model in extending the Test Act of England to New York, and in omitting the clauses referring to the "privileged churches" and their ministers throughout the province. At the instance of the Council, a proviso was inserted that it was not "to give liberty for any persons of the Romish religion to exercise their manner of worship contrary to the laws and statutes of their Majesty's Kingdom of England." This was necessary, because William's instructions to Sloughter required him "to permit a liberty of conscience to all persons *except Papists*." Following the example of New York, Massachusetts the next year passed a similar law. But the government of William not long afterward disallowed both these laws, because, among other things, they contained "several large and doubtful expressions."†

13 May. Law declaring the rights of the people of New York.

* Bradford's Laws of New York, 1; Van Schaack, 1, 2; Col. Doc., iii., 790, 795; Assembly Journal, i., 8, 9, 10; Council Journal, i., 5, 6; Smith, i., 164, 165; Chalmers's Rev. Col., i., 291; Hargraves State Trials, v., 421. The latter clause of this act was repealed June 27, 1704, in consequence of the proceedings under it against Bayard himself: Council Journals, i., 208, 221; Col. Doc., iv., 1114, 1115.

† Bradford's Laws, 2-5 (ed. 1694, 15-19); Assembly Journal, i., 9, 12, 13, 14; Council

CHAP. XII. 1691. 6 May. Courts of judicature established.

Another important act was passed "for establishing Courts of Judicature." This the governor, with his Council, had the power to do by his commission and Instructions. But Sloughter recommended a law to be passed similar to that of Dongan's in 1683, which was "a forme found very agreeable to the Constitution of this Government." So it was enacted that, besides various local tribunals, there should be a Supreme Court, to sit in the city of New York, and be held by a chief justice, a second justice, and associate justices, to be appointed by the governor. The act was limited to two years, but it was afterward renewed from time to time.

15 May. Judges appointed.

Under this law Sloughter appointed Joseph Dudley chief, and Thomas Johnson second justice, and William Smith, Stephen van Cortlandt, and William Pinhorne associate justices. All the judges were members of the Council. The chief justice was allowed an annual salary of one hundred and thirty pounds, and the second justice one hundred pounds, "for riding the circuit;" but no pay was given to the other three "puisné," or inferior judges.*

16 May. Revenue Act.

"A revenue for defraying the public expense of the Province" was also granted by the Assembly. The moneys raised were to be paid to the receiver general, and issued under the governor's warrant. But the law was limited to two years; and this became a precedent, to the annoyance of the succeeding governors, who wished revenue to be granted for longer periods.

Limited.

At the same time, the Assembly asked the governor to order the receiver general to pay to Captain William Kidd one hundred and fifty pounds, "as a suitable reward for the many good services done to this Province," and also one hundred pounds to Major Ingoldesby for like "good services."†

Kidd rewarded.

Journal, i., 7, 8, 9; Smith, i., 117; Col. Doc., iii., 357, 370, 678, 689; iv., 263–265; Chalmers's Rev. Col., i., 235, 236, 244; Annals, ii., 31, 40, 72, 113; Hutch. Mass., ii., 64; Gordon's Amer. Rev., i., 97–99; Bancroft, iii., 56, 95; Butler, 35, 40, 41; N. Y. Laws of 1813, ii., App. iii.–vi.; *ante*, 383–385, 423; *post*, Appendix, Note E.

* Bradford's Laws (1694); Paine and Duer's Practice, ii., App., 715; Assembly Journal, i., 4, 5, 8, 9, 10; Council Journal, i., 3, 5, 6; Council Min., vi., 27; Col. Doc., iii., 364, 625, 687, 716, 756, 818, 848; iv., 25–28, 37, 1137; Wood, 140; Smith, i., 116, 370, 380; Butler, 44; Daly's Sketch, 34, 35, 36; Laws of 1813, ii., App. viii.–x.; *ante*, 386.

† Bradford's Laws, 27; Chalmers's Rev. Col., i., 244; Smith, i., 116; Butler, 43; Assembly Journal, i., 6, 7, 13, 14; Council Journal, i., 2, 3, 5, 9, 10; *ante*, 635. At the same time that Captain Kidd received the money voted him by the Assembly, he was married to Sarah, widow of the late John Oort, of New York: Val. Man., 1847, 350; Col. MSS., xxxvii., 112, 121; Doc. Hist., ii., 216; Hunt's Merchants' Mag., xiv., 41, 42.

1691.

The Assembly, however, did nothing in regard to Sloughter's recommendation for the establishment of ministers in each town. A bill was drafted by Farewell, but it was rejected, "not answering the intent of the House." The last law passed by the Assembly was "for pardoning such as have been active in the late disorders." It excepted, however, the most prominent actors, Jacob Leisler, Jacob Milborne, Gerardus Beekman, Abraham Gouverneur, Abraham Brasher, Thomas Williams, Myndert Coerten, and Johannes Vermilye, who had already been attainted of treason and murder; and also Nicholas Blank, Garret Duyckinck, Hendrick Jansen, John Coe, William Lawrence, Cornelis Pluvier, William Churchill, Joost Stoll, Samuel Staats, Jacob Maurits, Robert Leacock, Michael Hansen, Richard Parton, Joseph Smith, John Bailey, Roeloff Swartwout, Anthony Swartwout, Johannes Provoost, Jacob Melyn, Benjamin Blagge, Jochim Staats, and Richard Pretty, who had been Leisler's most obnoxious followers.*

1 May. No ministers' bill.

16 May. Amnesty law—certain exceptions.

All the laws were duly promulgated at the City Hall, and the Assembly was adjourned to the next September. At the same time, the governor issued his proclamation "for calling back such as through fears and jealousies have deserted their habitations, and to assure them of freedom and liberty from unlawful and vexatious suits."†

18 May. Sloughter's proclamation.

Meanwhile the conviction of Leisler and his accomplices had produced great excitement in the province. A petition for their pardon was largely signed, especially in Staten Island and in Westchester; for which Daillé was cited before the Assembly, and others imprisoned by order of the Council as promoters of "riots and disturbances." Word also came from Albany that the Mohawks, disgusted with Leisler's mismanagement, were in treaty with the French, and that it was indispensable that the governor should quickly conciliate the Five Nations. Those inhabitants who had suffered under the late administration bitterly complained of its tyranny, and demanded expiation. The Dutch ministers, Selyns, Varick, and Dellius, constantly preached and talked about Leisler's tyranny; and even the "wives of principal men" besought the governor "to

Petitions for Leisler's pardon.

His execution demanded.

* Assembly Journal, i., 7, 10, 11; Bradford's Laws (1694), 31–33; Doc. Hist., ii., 235; *ante*, 640.

† Assembly Journ., i., 14; Council Journ., i., 10; Col. MSS., xxxvii., 116.

CHAP. XII. 1691. 14 May. Resolution of the Council that sentence should be executed.

have compassion on them and the country" by executing the sentence of the court. "Upon the clamour of the People daily coming to his Excellency's ears," Sloughter asked the opinion of the Council; which unanimously resolved, "That, as well for the satisfaction of the Indians, as the asserting of the government and authority residing in his Excellency, and preventing insurrections and disorders for the future, it is absolutely necessary that the sentence pronounced against the principal offenders, be forthwith put in execution." The governor's first purpose had been to reprieve the condemned until the king's pleasure should be known; but the "clamour" of Leisler's and Milborne's victims could neither be restrained nor disregarded. Sloughter, said to have been induced by his wife, accordingly,

14 May. Sloughter signs the death-warrant of Leisler and Milborne.

with reluctance and sadness, signed a warrant for the execution of Leisler and Milborne, leaving the other convicts under reprieve. The same evening Domine Selyns was sent to announce to the prisoners their several fates, and exhort to preparation those who were to die. The resolution of the Council was communicated to the Assembly,

15 May.

which the next day answered "that this House, according to their opinion given, do approve of what his Excellency and Council have done." The judgment of the court was

16 May. Leisler and Milborne executed.

accordingly executed on Leisler and Milborne the following morning, which was Saturday. The governor "respited all the sentence saving the hanging and the separating their heads from their bodies." The gallows on which they were hung was near the old "Tammany Hall," in the city of New York, and their bodies were buried at its foot. Domine Selyns, in the midst of a drenching rain, offered the last consolations of religion to the sufferers. Leisler,

Their dying speeches.

in his dying speech, acknowledged "several enormities" committed against his will, and prayed for "pardon and forgiveness." Milborne, in a more theatrical vein, seeing Livingston in the crowd, impeached his recent Albany victim "before God's tribunal."*

* Council Min., vi., 22, 26, 28; Assembly Journal, i., 9, 10, 11, 13, 14; Doc. Hist., 211, 212–215, 217, 236, 247, 248; Col. Doc., iii., 762, 768, 789, 792, 794, 812, 826; iv., 219, 400, 620; Col. MSS., xxxvii., 56, 96; Val. Man., 1856, 441; 1860, 543; 1866, 597; N. Y. H. S. Proc., 1849, 108; Colden, i., 130, 131; Smith, i., 118, 119; Dunlap, i., 208, 209; Grahame, ii., 231; Bancroft, iii., 54, 55; New York H. S. Coll. (1868), 71, 72, 321, 406–409, 414. Upon "tradition," Smith (i., 113) asserts that Sloughter was invited to a feast, and that "when his Excellency's reason was drowned in his cups, the entreaties of the company prevailed with him to sign

CHAP. XII.

1691.

The execution of Leisler and Milborne a political mistake: its consequences in New York.

The execution of Leisler and Milborne, although perfectly lawful, was, nevertheless, a great political mistake. It at once made them martyrs instead of convicts, and gave rise to popular divisions, which for a long time injured the province. Concerning no prominent actor in New York colonial history has opinion more widely differed than in regard to Jacob Leisler. A German, and not a Dutchman, he has been generally held up as a champion of Dutch democracy against English aristocracy; of colonial liberty as opposed to the rule of the mother country; and of Protestantism against Romanism. His official career negatives these theories. His conduct proved him to be more a tyrant than a democrat, and as bitter an enemy of unquestionable Protestants as he was of avowed Roman Catholics. It was the selfish attempt of an upstart demagogue to obtain a local importance, which neither his own character nor the circumstances of the province warranted. Seizing colonial authority under false pretenses, he clutched it to the end with a firm hand, growing more confident, more despotic, and more obstinate as he gained lacking experience, and committing greater excesses in maintaining his impudent usurpation than any Governor of New York commissioned by the Duke of York or King James the Second. Leisler's assumption of provincial power did not benefit the English Revolution. If William's colonial government had remained in the hands of Nicholson or his counselors, the province would have been better protected against the French and the savages; the Canada expedition might have succeeded; and New York would not have suffered from the party enmities which long disturbed her peace.*

the death-warrant, and before he recovered his senses the prisoners were executed." The records of the Council and Assembly seem to disprove this "tradition," although it is affirmed in a letter of members of the Dutch Church in New York to the Classis of Amsterdam of 21 October, 1698. The address of the Assembly to Lord Bellomont of 15 May, 1699, attributes Sloughter's action chiefly to the "importunity" of Bayard, at whose house he was then lodging: MS. Journal, N. Y. H. S., 63, 64; Col. MSS., xliii., 12; N. Y. H. S. Coll. (1868), 406, 414.

* Col. Doc., iii., 827; Chalmers's Annals, ii., 71, 72; Wood's Long Island, 109, 110, 111; Miller's New York, 50, 51, 111, 112; Smith, i., 118, 119; Dunlap, i., 210, 211; Grahame, ii., 231; Bancroft, iii., 55, 56; Hoffman, in Sparks's Amer. Biog., xiii., 179–238. Ebeling is a German, and not a Dutch writer, as stated by Dunlap.

APPENDIX.

NOTE A, CHAPTER I., PAGE 17; CHAPTER VI., PAGE 261.

King Charles the Second's Grant of New Netherland, &c., to the Duke of York.

CHARLES the Second by the Grace of God King of England, Scotland, France and Ireland Defender of the Faith &c. To all to whom these presents shall come Greeting: Know ye that we for divers good Causes and Considerations us thereunto moving Have of our especial Grace, Certain knowledge and mere motion Given and Granted and by these presents for us Our heirs and Successors Do Give and Grant unto our Dearest Brother James Duke of York his Heirs and Assigns All that part of the maine Land of New England beginning at a certain place called or known by the name of St. Croix next adjoining to New Scotland in America and from thence extending along the Sea Coast unto a certain place called Petuaquine or Pemaquid and so up the River thereof to the furthest head of the same as it tendeth Northward; and extending from thence to the River Kinebequi and so Upwards by the Shortest course to the River Canada Northward. And also all that Island or Islands commonly called by the several name or names of Matowacks or Long Island situate lying and being towards the West of Cape Cod and the Narrow Higansetts abutting upon the main land between the two Rivers there called or known by the several names of Connecticut and Hudsons River, together also with the said River called Hudsons River and all the Land from the West side of Connecticut to the East side of Delaware Bay. And also all those several Islands called or known by the Names of Martin's Vineyard and Nantukes otherwise Nantuckett; Together with all the Lands, Islands, Soils, Rivers, Harbors, Mines, Minerals, Quarries, Woods, Marshes, Waters, Lakes, Fishings, Hawking, Hunting and Fowling and all other Royalties, Profits, Commodities and Hereditaments to the said several Islands, Lands and Premises belonging and appertaining with their and every of their appurtenances; And all our Estate, Right, Title, Interest, Benefit, Advantage, Claim and Demand of in or to the said Lands and Premises or any part or parcel thereof And the Reversion and Reversions Remainder and Remainders together with the yearly and other the Rents, Revenues and Profits of all and singular the said Premises and of every part and parcel thereof; To have and to hold all and singular the said Lands, Islands, Hereditaments and premises with their and every of their appurtenances hereby given and granted or hereinbefore mentioned to be given and granted unto our Dearest Brother James Duke of York his Heirs and Assigns forever, To the only proper use and behoof of the said James Duke of York his Heirs and Assigns forever, To be holden of Us our Heirs and Successors as of our Manor of East Greenwich and our County of Kent in free and common soccage and not in Capite nor by Knight service yielding and rendering. And the said James Duke of York doth for himself his Heirs and Assigns covenant and promise to yield and render unto us our Heirs and Successors of and for the same yearly and every year forty Beaver skins when they shall be demanded or within Ninety days after. And We do further of our special Grace certain knowledge and mere motion for us our Heirs and Successors Give and Grant unto our said Dearest Brother James Duke of York his Heirs, Deputies, Agents, Commissioners and Assigns by these presents full and absolute power and authority to correct, punish, pardon, govern and rule all such the subjects of us Our Heirs and Successors who may from time to time adventure themselves into any of the parts or places aforesaid or that shall or do at any time hereafter inhabit within the same according to such Laws, Orders, Ordinances, Directions and Instruments as by our said Dearest Brother or his Assigns shall be established; And in defect thereof in case of necessity, according to the good discretions of his Deputies, Commissioners, Officers or Assigns respectively; as well in all causes and matters Capital and Criminal as civil both marine and others; So always as the said Statutes Ordinances and proceedings be not contrary to but as near as conveniently may be agreeable to the Laws, Statutes & Government of this Our Realm of England, And saving and reserving to us Our Heirs and Successors the receiving, hearing and determining of the Appeal and Appeals of all or any Person or Persons of in or belonging to the territories or Islands aforesaid in or touching any Judgment or Sentence to be there made or given. And further that it shall and may be lawful to and for our said Dearest Brother his Heirs and Assigns by these presents from time to time to nominate, make, constitute, ordain and confirm by such name or name stile or stiles as to him or them shall seem good and likewise to revoke, discharge, change and alter as well all and singular Governors, Officers and Ministers which hereafter shall be by him or them thought fit and needful to be made or used within the aforesaid parts and Islands; And also to make, ordain and establish all manner of Orders, Laws, directions, instructions, forms and Ceremonies of Government and Magistracy fit and necessary for and Concerning the Government of the territories and Islands aforesaid, so always as the same be not contrary to the laws and statutes of this Our Realm of England but as near as may be agreeable thereunto: And the same at all times hereafter to put in execution or abrogate revoke or change not only within the precincts of the said Territories or Islands but also upon the Seas in going and coming to and from the same as he or they in their good discretions shall think to be fittest for the good of the Adventurers and Inhabitants there. And We do further of Our speciall Grace, certain knowledge and mere motion grant, ordain and declare that such Governors, Officers and Ministers as from time to time shall be authorized and appointed in manner and form aforesaid shall and may have full power and authority to use and exercise Martial Law in cases of Rebellion, Insurrection and Mutiny in as large and ample manner as Our Lieutenants in Our Counties within Our Realm of England have or ought to have by force of their Commission of Lieutenancy or any Law or Statute of this our Realm. And We do further by these presents for us Our Heirs and Successors Grant unto Our said Dearest Brother James Duke of York his Heirs and Assigns, That it shall and may be lawful to and for the said James Duke of York his heirs and Assigns in his or their discretions from time to time to admit such and so many Person and Persons to trade and traffic unto and within the Territories and Islands aforesaid and into every or any part and parcel thereof, and to have possess and enjoy any Lands or Hereditaments in the parts and places aforesaid as they shall think fit according to the Laws, Orders, Constitutions and Ordinances by Our said Brother his Heirs, Deputies, Commissioners and Assigns from time to time to be made and established by virtue of and according to the true intent and meaning of these presents and under such conditions, reservations and agreements as Our said Brother his Heirs or Assigns shall set down, order, direct and appoint, and not otherwise as aforesaid. And We do further of Our especial grace, certain knowledge and mere motion for us Our Heirs and Successors give and grant to Our said Dear Brother his Heirs and Assigns by these presents That it shall and may be lawful to and for him, them or any of them at all and every time and times hereafter out of any Our Realms or Dominions whatsoever to take lead, carry and transport in and into their Voyages and for and towards the Plantations of Our said Territories and Islands all such and so many of Our Loving subjects or any other strangers being not prohibited or under restraint that will become Our Loving subjects and live under Our Allegiance as shall willingly accompany them in the said voyages; together with all such clothing, implements, furniture and other things usually transported and not prohibited as shall be necessary for the inhabitants of the said Islands and Territories and for their use and defence thereof and managing and carrying on the trade with the People there and in passing and returning to and fro: Yielding and paying to us Our Heirs and Successors the Customs and Duties therefore due and payable according to the Laws and Customs of this Our Realm. And We do also for us Our Heirs and Successors, grant to Our said Dearest Brother James Duke of York his Heirs and Assigns and to all and every such Governor or Governors or other Officers or Ministers as by Our said Brother his Heirs or Assigns shall be appointed, to have power and authority of Government and Command in or over the Inhabitants of the said Territories or Islands that they and every of them shall and lawfully may from time to time and at all times hereafter forever for their several defence and safety encounter, expulse, repel and resist by force of Arms as well by sea as by land and all ways and means whatsoever all such Person and Persons as without the speciall Licence of Our said Dear Brother his Heirs or Assigns shall attempt to inhabit within the several precincts and limits of Our said territories and Islands: And also all and every such Person and Persons whatsoever as shall enterprize or attempt at any time hereafter the destruction, invasion, detriment or annoyance to the parts, places or Islands aforesaid or any part thereof. And lastly Our will and pleasure is and We do hereby declare and grant that these Our Letters Patents or the enrolment thereof shall be good and effectual in the Law to all intents and purposes whatsoever notwithstanding the not reciting or mentioning of the Premises or any part thereof or the meets or Bounds thereof or of any former or other Letters Patents or Grants heretofore made or granted of the Premises or of any part thereof by Us or of any of Our progenitors unto any other Person or Persons whatsoever, Bodies Politic or Corporate, or any Act, Law or other restraint incertainty or imperfection whatsoever to the contrary in any wise notwithstanding; although express mention of the true yearly value or certainty of the premises or any of them or of any other gifts or grants by Us or by any of Our progenitors or predecessors heretofore made to the said James Duke of York in these presents is not made or any statute, act, ordinance, provision, proclamation or restriction heretofore had, made, enacted, ordained or provided, or any other matter cause or thing whatsoever to the Contrary thereof in any wise Notwithstanding. In Witness whereof We have caused these Our Letters to be made Patents. Witness Ourself at Westminster the *twelfth* day of March in the *Sixteenth* Year of Our Reign. [1664]

By the King. HOWARD.

Original in State Library, Albany; Patents, i., 109–115; *Leaming and Spicer*, 3–8; *New York Colonial Documents*, ii., 295–298.

NOTE B, CHAPTER I., PAGE 18.

The Duke of York's Commission to Colonel Richard Nicolls.

JAMES, Duke of YORK and ALBANY, Earl of ULSTER, Lord High Admiral of ENGLAND and IRELAND, &c., Constable of Dover Castle, Lord Warden of the Cinque Ports, and Governor of Portsmouth, &c. WHEREAS it hath pleased the King's most Excellent Majesty, my Sovereign Lord and Brother, by His Majesty's Letters Patents, bearing date at Westminster the *Twelfth* day of *March* in the Sixteenth year of His Majesty's Reign, to give and grant unto me and to my Heirs and Assigns, All that part of the mainland of New England, Beginning at a certain place called or known by the name of *Saint Croix*, next adjoining to *New Scotland* in America, and from thence extending along the sea-coast, unto a certain place called *Petaquine* or *Pemaquid*, and so up the River thereof to the furthest head of the same, as it tendeth Northwards, and extending from thence to the River of *Kinebequi*, and so upwards by the shortest course to the River *Canada* northwards; And Also all that Island or Islands commonly called by the several name or names of *Matowacks* or *Long Island*, situate, lying, and being towards the west of Cape Cod and the Narrow-Higansets, abutting upon the mainland, between the two rivers there, called or known by the several names of *Connecticut* and *Hudson's* River; Together also with the said River called *Hudson's* River and all the land from the West side of *Connecticut* River to the East side of *Delaware* Bay; And Also all those several Islands called or known by the name of *Martin's Vineyard* and *Nantukes* otherwise *Nantucket;* Together with all the Lands, Islands, Soiles, Rivers, Harbours, Mines, Minerals, Quarries, Woods, Marshes, Waters, Lakes, Fishing, Hawking, Hunting, and Fowling, and all other Royalties, Profits, Commodities, Hereditaments, to the said several Islands, Lands, and Premises belonging and appertaining, with their and every of their Appurtenances; To Hold the same to my own proper use and behoof, With Power to correct, punish, pardon, govern, and rule the Inhabitants thereof, by Myself, or such Deputies, Commissioners, or Officers as I shall think fit to appoint; as by His Majesty's said Letters Patents may more fully appear: AND Whereas I have conceived a good opinion of the Integrity, Prudence, Ability and Fitness of RICHARD NICOLLS, Esquire, to be employed as my Deputy there, I have therefore thought fit to constitute and appoint, And I do hereby constitute and appoint him the said *Richard Nicolls*, Esquire, to be my Deputy-Governor within the Lands, Islands, and Places aforesaid, To perform and execute all and every the Powers which are by the said Letters Patents granted unto me, to be execute by my Deputy, Agent, or Assign. To HAVE AND TO HOLD the said place of Deputy-Governor unto the said *Richard Nicolls*, Esquire, during my will and pleasure only; Hereby willing and requiring all and every the Inhabitants of the said Lands, Islands, and Places to give obedience to him the said *Richard Nicolls* in all things, according to the tenor of His Majesty's said Letters Patents; And the said *Richard Nicolls*, Esquire, to observe, follow and execute such Orders and Instructions as he shall from time to time receive from myself. GIVEN, under my hand and seal, at *Whitehall*, this *Second* day of *April*, in the Sixteenth Year of the Reign of our Sovereign Lord *Charles* the Second, by the Grace of God King of England, Scotland, France, and Ireland, &c., *Annoque Domini*, 1664.
JAMES.

By Command of His Royal Highness,
W. COVENTRY.

Patents, i., 116–118; *Leaming and Spicer*, 665–667.

NOTE C, CHAPTER VI., PAGE 271.

Governor Colve to the Burgomasters &c of New Orange.

Burgomasters and Schepens being on the invitation of the H^r^. Govern^r^. assembled Collegialiter in the City Hall on the 15 Octr 1674:—

The H^r^. Governour General appearing at the meeting represents that he hath now received by the Government ship the *Muyll Tromp*, Letters & Absolute Orders from the Lords Majors and their High Mightinesses, for the Restitution of this Province of N. Netherland to his Majesty of Great Britain pursuant to the Treaty of peace concluded on the   February last; with further order for himself to return immediately with the Garrison, which His Honour thought fit to communicate to the meeting, further stating to them if they had any Representation to make to their High Mightinesses, and Honble Mightinesses that his Honour would willingly present the same.—*New Orange Records*, vii., 237.

Governor Andros to Governor Colve.

Being arrived to this Place with Orders to Receaue from you in the Behalf of his Matie of Great Britagny Pursuant to the Late Articles of Pease with the States Generall of the United Neatherlands, The New Netherlands and Dependances, now vnder your Command, I haue herewith, by Capt. Philipe Carterett: and Ens. Cæsar Knapton, sent you the Respective Orders from the said States Generall, the States of Zealand and Admirality of Amsterdam, to that Efect, and desire youl

Please to apoint some short time for it, Our Soldjers having [been] long abord, I pray your Answer by these Jentlemen and I shall bee Ready, to serve you in what may Lay in my Power, Being

Your Very Humble Servant.

From abord His Maties Ship
The Diamond, att Anker neare
Staten Island this 22nd of Octber
1674.

Superscription.

"For the Hble The Gouernor
Commander in Chief in The
New Netherlands, These." *Col. MSS.*, xxiii., 412.

Governor Andros to Governor Colve.

Sr.—I Receiued yours Last Night of the same date, by Capt Carell Episseyn & Lieut Charles Quirrynse which were I com in a private capasity or bound elsewhere, is very obligin to my superiors and Family. But I am suprized that being sent Authorized as I am for Receaving the Place which I length you severall Reteirated the States Generall, the States of Zealand & Admiralty of Amsterdam (which you also tell mee you had Already receaved before my Arival & itt being so long after the Tyme, itt should have been delivered if demanded) you have nott, so Much as Sett any Time for the Effecting itt, I doe nott Doubt the Freedom, & yr Kind Vsage of all Inglish, In generall wch is daylay practized betweene our Superiors, & Two Naçons in Vrope, & Elsewhere, but having no Orders to Land vpun a private acompt & The Ships sent wth mee by the King of Ingland, my Master, being nott onely att very great Expense, but designed for his Sarvice, elsewhere as soone as I am possesd of this Place; I againe desire you yt pursuant to the Articles of Peace, & the Severall Orders you haue Received, you will apoint a short Tyme for Effecting itt.

This is by Capne Philipe Carterett, Capne Mathias Nicolls & Ens: Cæsar Knapton who will tel you the same things verbally, and also ashure you as I now doe that if Mr Colve or any of yors or Ships should nott be Ready to goe on Bord, or Saile, that you shall not onely have all kindnesse as is dayly Practised att Home, butt myselfe, Ready to Sarve you upun all occacons to my Power: So nott Doubting yor Considering things as they your present Resolve, Conformable to friendship & orders of Superrrs & desiring yr Answer by these Jentlemen, I am in Reality

Yor Friend & Humble Servant,

Signed Edm Andros.

From Abord his Matys ship
The Diamond, at Anker neare
Staten Island; 23th Octber 1674.

Col. MSS., xxiii., 416.

Governor Andros to Governor Colve.

Sr.—I received yors yesterday in the Evening in answer to mine by the hands of Capt Philip Carteret Matthias Nicolls & Ensigne Cæsar Knapton.

You tell me That you hoped & did not doubt but within the space of eight days you would be ready pursuant to ye Articles of peace and Instructions to Surrender ye place now under yor Command.

If the Time for ye Surrender had beene certainly prefixt & by a Lesse space, I should not have had [the necessity of] giving you this farther Trouble. Now once againe by the same Gentleman I Desire you to lett me [know with certainty when] *I & my forces may pursuant both to your & my Orders [take possession of the] Fort and Government you now are [commanding] I alsoe wish you will take into your Co[nsideration to] pitch upon a shorter time then you have proposed:*

These Gentlemen I have now appointed to discourse with you about the [time] thereof that *nothing may further intervene to delay it & for the furthering of which if you thinke convenient & you may please to send some of yor Councell to mee* (or whom else you shall thinke fitt to authorize) that we may haue conference about the same.

I should bee very glad these matters may bee concluded in a Faire & amicable way I doe hope & will not doubt yor effectuall answer, desiring nothing more then a friendly Conference & the honor of seeing and serving you That I may not bee obleged pursuant as I think to my duty to justify my proceedings by a publick Protest. And if there yet shall remaine anything either publick or yor private Concernes, if you please to let me Know it by these Gentlemen or any of them I shall bee very ready & glad of all opportunitys to testify how much I am

Yor humble Servant.

From on board his Maties ship
The Diamond at Anchor
neare Staten Island Octob The 24th
1674. *Col. MSS.*, xxiii., 414.

Committee appointed to welcome Governor Andros.

$\frac{\text{24 October,}}{\text{3 November,}}$ A° 1674. Burgomasters and Schepens being met at the City Hall with the Burgher Council of war, they with the approbation of the H^r Governour, appointed and qualified, as they hereby appoint and qualify the H^r Cornelis Steenwyk, with the Heeren Burgomaster Johannes van Brugh & Willem Beekman to repair on board his Majesty's frigate now anchored under Staten Island, and there welcome the H^r Governour Andrews and to request together some privileges from him for the advantage of the commonalty.

The foregoing Commissioners returning this date reported that they welcomed the H^r Governor Major Andrews and requested from him to favor the Inhabitants with some privileges; Who answered them that they the Commissioners may assure the Inhabitants of the Dutch Nation that they should participate in the same privileges as those of the English Nation, and that his Honour would as far as possible promote their interests; referring himself further to the Instructions given him by his Royal Majesty & Highness the Duke of York.—*New Orange Records*, vii., 253.

Governor Andros to Governor Colve.

S^r—I rec^d yo^rs the last night by Mr Steenwyck & Capt Charles Eppisteyne together with the enclosed paper of severall particulars relating to the Towne; To which (did I think myselfe Authorized to Treat particularly of things of this nature afore my Landing) I should not scruple nor doubt to give you a particular and satisfactory Answ^r to most of them; which I hope you will have in the Gen^ll by my Assuring you as I now do againe, That I am not onely Commanded punctually to observe the Articles of Peace, But have also his Majesty's and Royall Highnesse particular Orders to do it in the best and most ffriendly manner with kindnesse to such Dutch as I shall finde upon the place; As to ye last relating to the Ship, I desire to do it as farre as reasonably they can expect (but It relates to some of our Acts of Parliam^t) I haue spoken to one of the Owners, and desire that they will amongst themselves and the Master advise together, how farre that may be with safety, particularly to themselves; Vpon which I shall bee willing to do the utmost in my Power accordingly. I have directed the Bearer, Captn Matthias Nicolls, Personally to conferre with you, more at large to this effect in any of these particulars, if you shall think fitt. I am sorry for the disorders you mençon, happened in the Towne, which I doubt not are now wholly remedyed by the Orders you have taken in commanding all the Souldyers to the Fort from rambling about the towne, as also enjoyning all others to repaire Home, which will (without doubt) quiet Peoples mindes; so that if you have not already released those Souldyers committed for som disorders in the street (being drunk) I againe now desire you to Pardon them, in which you will oblige mee; so hoping to heere from you to morrow, for sending p'sons on Shoare to see and take knowledge of such things as you shall leave in the ffort, for me to receive; with my thanks for yor last Civilityes, being ready to serve yo^u in what may ly in my Power, I remaine

S^r Yo^r most humble Servt

Signed E. Andros.

From on board his Ma^tys
Ship the Dyamond at
Anchor neare Staten Island,
Oct. 28th. 1674.

Col. MSS., xxiii., 415, 418.

Governor Andros to Governor Colve.

No: 2d 1674.

Sr.—This is to return you my acknowledgements and thanks for both yo^rs of the 10th and 11th ultimo upon the subject of my relieving you in this place, being also obliged to you for yor good opinion and Character of me here; & shall bee glad of all opportunity wherein I may testify yor Generosity in all yor proceedings since my arrivall to these parts.

I have upon yor desire wholly freed the two prison^rs you left mee here: I have also here enclosed sent you as you directed an answer in the Margent to the severall particulars in the s^d pap^r which I hope you will bee satisfyed is as full & ample as is any way in my power. But againe assure you that having his Maties & his R. H^s orders I shall endeauo^r all I may the good & welfare of ye Inhabitants of this place.

I haue now onely to adde my farther acknowledgements and thanks for ye present of the three horses & Coach, am onely confused that yor sudden departure for soe great a distance will deprive me of ye means of shewing how sensible I am of this particular obligacon to myselfe.

This is by Capt. Matthias Nicolls & E. Cæsar Knapton who will tell you the same verbally & wish you a good & prosperous voyage, also requesting you from mee to let mee know all opportunityes wherein I may serue you during yor longer stay in these parts. Remaining

Col. MSS., xxiii., 420.

Governor Andros's Answers.

Sr—I have upon yor desire for yor satisfaction given you the following Answer to yor severall Particulars:—

To the 1st. I shall bee ready upon all occasions to countenance and bee helpeful to any you shall think fitt to entrust in this place, as farre as may bee in my power pursuant to the Articles of Peace & Law.

To the 2nd. To continue pursuant to Law and the utmost of the Articles of Peace.

To the 3d. All Justice with friendship shall bee shewne, pursuant to the Articles of Peace.

To the 4th. The usuall discipline of their Church to bee continued to them as formerly, and the other of Inheritance, as farre as I may, & for those that shall desire it.

To the 5th. I have neither Orders nor directions for any pressing whatever and shall allwayes bee glad to favour the Inhabitants therein.

To the 6th. I shall allwayes bee ready to allow & favour so charitable a worke.

To the 7th. I shall take fitting Care in this particular to the satisfaction of all the good.

To the 8th. I have seene since my arrivall severall orders or Decrees upon Record, for the arresting & forfeiting the Effects of the West Indya Company in these parts, during the former Warre in 1664 & 1665, which I am also informed have since been accounted for at home, so not in my power.

To the 9th. I hope this will not bee expected from mee, which if due should have beene effected by my Predecessors & is not in my power.

To the 10th. This seemes to relate to the first, However I have his Royall Highnesse particular Orders & Regulacon for the Customes in every particular, from which I may not vary.

To the 11th. As to this particular, I shall continue all the favour and friendship I may pursuant to the Articles of Peace, and Acts of Parliamt & shall not take any advantage or tollerate it, but afford a reasonable Time.

Proposalls sent by Governor Colve *to Governor Andros previous to the Surrender of New Netherland, Oct.* 27 1674.

Myn Heer—Pursuant to my last I have considered it my duty to propose to your Honor herewith the following Articles, on the one side for the greater satisfaction of my Lords & Masters, and on the other for the greater tranquility of the good People of this Province, requesting I may receive your answer in the margin thereof—to wit:—

1st. As it is impossible to settle before my departure all the debts of the present government and to dispose of its effects consisting principally in the confiscated property of the late English Officers found here on the reduction of this Province, from which their personal debts must first be paid; and as it will be necessary for that end to leave authority here on behalf of my Lords Principals, I do therefore request that your Honor on being solicited, will be pleased to lend him a helping hand on all occurring occasions.

2. That all sentences and Judgments passed during my Administration may stand good.

3. That the present owners of the houses, lands and other effects of private persons confiscated during the war, may be maintained in their possession.

4. That the Inhabitants of the Dutch Nation may be allowed to retain their customary Church privileges in Divine Service and Church discipline besides their Fathers' laws & customs in the division of their Inheritances.

5. That they may be excused from Impressment, if not wholly at least against their own Nation.

6. That each Congregation whether Lutherans or others may support their own Poor.

7. That all Publick houses may continue according to the Customs now existing.

8. That the West India Company's creditors in this Country may be paid from their property and outstanding debts here.

9. That the City Tapsters Excise may remain for the benefit of the city until the debts of the City, contracted before my Administration, shall be paid, as was agreed unto by the Capitulation in the Year 1664.

10. Whereas the Inhabitants of this Province advanced some monies by form of a Loan for the fortification of this City, for the repayment of which money a small Impost was laid on exported Beavers and peltries and imported Indian goods, that the same Impost may stand good until the said expended monies shall be paid.

11. That the Ship the Beaver, Skipper Jacob Mauritz destined hence for Holland may be allowed to remain unmolested at anchor here to sell his goods, to receive his pay, to load his Ship here to depart with the same directly for Fatherland.

S^r Yo^r most humble Servt

For the Honble Governo^r Colve on board the States Ship the Surynam, These.

This is a true Copie of the Proposalls sent by Governo^r Colve to Gouerno^r Andros before the surrender of the Fort bearing date Octob^r 27th old stile with the Answer returned to the seuerall particulars therein afterwards; pursuant to the Assurance given by those employed.

MATTHIAS NICOLLS, Secr.

Endorsed
"Proposalls from the
Dutch Governo^r and the Governo^rs
Answer Nov. 2^d 1674."

Col. MSS., xxiii., 419, 421.

Governor Andros to Governor Colve.

S^r—I have rec^d yo^rs of the 13th new style, by Capt. Carel Epesseyn & Lieut Carel Quirinsen, together with the orders for the respective places of this Governm^t to bee delivered to mee pursuant to the Articles of Peace, And now have onely to adde my acknowledgm^ts and thankes for ye further kind Expressions to mee in yor letter.

As to yor Postcript concerning pressing I doe hope my former Answer will bee satisfactory for quieting ye minde of the Inhabitants; but for yor owne further satisfaction I doe further assure you, that I shall neither impose, nor desire their bearing Arms ag^st their Nation.

As to Mr Wm Dervalls molesting in words a person possest of a Confiscated house, As soone as I heard it, I did check the s^d Darvall for soe doeing, Letting him know, that all were to have the free benefit of ye law & Articles of Peace & did Assure the other of Right and Justice pursuant thereunto which in all Cases shall bee my Endeavo^r, as it is my Orders.

This is by Capt. Matthias Nicolls who will tell you the same verbally: & by whom (having had many addresses) I have sent you such demands as haue beene given mee in writings, for damages sustained from those under yor Comand, since the time limited for Peace in these Parts; vpon which I pray & will not doubt yor effectual Answer; If there bee any thing yet remaining wherein I may serve you before yor voyage, I shall bee ready to testify how much I am

Yo^r most humble Servt
Novemb^r 7th 1674.

Endorsed
"L re to Go. Colve
No. 7. 1674."

Col. MSS., xxiv., 7.

Governor Colve absolves the Dutch from their Allegiance.

At a Court; present the Heeren Burgomasters Schepens and Burgher Court Martial—holden and assembled by the Special Orders of the Heer Governour General ANTHONY COLVE, at the City Hall of the City *New Orange*, the 9th Novembr *stilo novo*, A^o 1674.

The H^r Governour General appearing in Court informed the same that he, pursuant to the orders of his Lords Principals, should on to-morrow Surrender the Fort and this Province of N. Netherland, conformably to the Articles of Peace, to the H^r Major Andros on the behalf of his Majisty of Great Britain. And hath thereupon thanked the Meeting for their past services and at the same time absolved and discharged them from the Oath of Allegiance taken to their High Mightinesses and his Serene Highness; further ordering that the 5 banners of the Out people together with the Cushions and Table Cloth now in the City Hall should be taken Charge of by the Bargomaster Johonnes van Brugh until they were demanded & removed by Superior Authority—taking thereupon, further, his farewell of the Assembly which I testify having occurred.

EPHRAIM HERMAN, Sec.
New Orange Records, vii., 254.

Governor Colve to the Sheriff of Esopus.

Honourable, Beloved, Faithful—Whereas I have received ample orders from my Lords Superiors their High Mightinesses the Lords States General of the United Netherlands, their Mightinesses the Lords delegated Councillors for the Province of Zealand, and their Mightinesses the Lords Commissioners in the Board of Admirality at Amsterdam, for delivering up the Province of New Netherland for the behoof of his Majesty of England, pursuant to the Treaty of Peace concluded between the two Nations dated the 19 February, to the Heer Major Edmond Andros who hath also arrived here from his Majesty of England for that purpose, with orders & qualifications to me exhibited, your Honour is therefore ordered & charged on receipt hereof to deliver up and hand over to the aforesaid Heer Major Andros or to whomsoever his Honour shall qualify thereunto, according to the tenor of said Treaty of Peace the Command, Right and Jurisdiction of the Places, situated under your Honors resort; further hoping and wishing at all times to hear of your future prosperity, happiness & welfare; finally assuring your Honour that my further services in Vropa if required shall not fail you, if demanded, to my uttermost power, to prove that

I am your affectionate friend

(was undersigned) A. COLVE.

Done, Fort Willem Hendrick
in N. Nethherland ady 10 Nov[r] 1674.

The superscription reads thus

Honourable Beloved Faithful
Sieur Isaacq Greveraedt Scout in the village
Swanenburg in the Esopus.

Agrees with the original
To my knowledge
W. DE LA MONTAGNE, Secret[y]. *Col. MSS.*, xxiii., 423.

Surrender of New Netherland to the English.

On the 10 November A° 1674, the Province of New Netherland was surrendered by Governor Colve to Governor Major Edmund Andross on behalf of his Britannick Majesty.

New Orange Records, vii., 255.

Compare Col. MSS., xxiii., 412–423; xxiv., 1–13; *New Orange Records*, vii., 237, 253–255; *Val. Man.*, 1850, 522; 1852, 415–421; 1853, 489, 498; *Doc. Hist.*, iii., 45–52.

NOTE D, CHAPTER VII., PAGE 354.

Petition of the Members of the Court of Assizes, to the Duke of York, for an Assembly.

To his Royal Highness, James, Duke of York and Albany:

The humble petition of the council of the province, the aldermen of New-York, and of the justices assembled at a special court of assize held at the city of New-York, June 29th, 1681,

Showeth—That we, your royal highness' most humble and obedient servants, assembled together by virtue of your royal highness' authority established in his colony, humbly craving the conjunction and assistance of this court to make a submissive address to your royal highness: therein representing the great pressure and lamentable condition of his majesty's subjects in this your royal highness' colony; and also presenting, for the only remedy and ease of those burdens, that an assembly of the people may be established by a free choice of the freeholders and inhabitants of this your royal highness' colony. The which request, we having maturely and deliberately weighed and considered, and having full assurance of your royal highness' good gracious and real intentions to encourage and advance the ease, benefit, and advantage of trade, and the merchants and inhabitants of this your said colony, and the removal of all things that might obstruct or hinder the same to us particularly, signified by your gracious commission given to John Lewin, your royal highness agent and servant here, bearing date the 24th of May, 1680, which with great joy and general satisfaction was received and published. Expecting and longing for the happy event of such your royal highness' grace and favour, the enjoyment of which we have not as yet attained, we find ourselves encouraged and obliged to concur with the said grand inquest; and in all submissive manner to prostrate ourselves at your royal highness' feet, and represent the miserable and deplorable condition of the inhabitants of this your royal highness' colony, who for many years past have groaned under inexpressible burdens by having an arbitrary and absolute power used and exercised over us, by which a yearly revenue is exacted from us against our wills, and trade grievously burdened with undue and unusual customs imposed on the merchandize without our consent—our liberty and freedom inthraled, and the inhabitants wholly shut out and deprived of any share, vote, or interest, in the government, to their great discouragement, and contrary to the laws, rights, liberties, and privileges, of the subject; so that we are esteemed as nothing, and have become a reproach to the neighbours in other his majesty's colonies, who flourish under the fruition and protection of his majesty's unparalleled form and method of government in his realm of England, the undoubted birthright of all his subjects. Which necessitates us, in behalf of this your royal highness' colony, to become humble suppliants and suitors to your royal highness; praying, and we do hereby humbly and submissively, with all obedience, pray and beseech your royal highness, that, for the redressing and removal of the said grievances, the government of this your colony may, for the future, be settled and established, ruled and governed, by a governor, council, and assembly: which assembly to be duly elected and chosen by the freeholders of this your royal highness' colony, as is usual and practicable with the realm of England, and other his majesty's plantations. Which will give great ease and satisfaction to all his majesty's subjects in this your royal highness' colony; who desire no greater happiness than the continuance of your royal highness' grace and favour, and to be and remain his majesty's loyal and free subjects. By order, &c., JOHN WEST, Clerk of Assize.

Wood's Long Island, pp. 178, 179.

NOTE E, CHAPTER VIII., PAGE 384, AND CHAPTER XII., PAGE 645.

"THE CHARTER *of Libertys and Privileges granted by his Royal Highness to the Inhabitants of New-York and its Dependencies.*

[Passed, Oct. 30, 1683.]

"For the better establishing the Government of this province of New-York, and thatt Justice and Right may bee equally done to all persons within the same: Bee it enacted by the Govern'r, Councell, and Representatives now in gen'all assembly, mett and assembled, and by the authority of the same,

"Thatt the Supreme legislative Authority under his Majesty and Royall Highnesse James, Duke of York, Albany, &c. Lord proprietor of the said province, shall forever bee and reside in a Governour, councell and the people, mett in a Generall assembly.

"That the Exercise of the Chiefe magistracy and administration of the government over the said Province, shall be in the said Govern'r; assisted by Councell, with whose advice and consent, or with att least four of them, hee is to rule and govern the same according to the laws thereof.

"Thatt in case the Governour shall dy or bee absent out of the province, and thatt there bee no person within the said province, commissionated by his Royall Highnesse his heyres or successors, to bee Governour or Commander in Chief there, thatt then the Councell for the time being, or so many of them as are in the said province, do take upon them the Administracon of the government, and the Execucon of the laws thereof, and powers and authoritys belonging to the Governour and councell. The first in nominacon, in which councell is to preside untill the said Governour shall returne and arrive in the said province againe, or the pleasure of his Royall Highnesse, his heyres or successors, bee further known—

"Thatt, according to the usage, costome, and practice of the Realm of England, a sessions of a generall assembly bee held in this province once in three yeares att least.

"That every ffreeholder within this province, and ffreeman in any corporacon, shall have his free choice and vote in the Electing of the representatives, without any manner of constraint or imposition, and that in all Elections the Majority of Voices shall carry itt, and by ffreeholders is understood every one who is so understood according to the laws of England.

"Thatt the persons to bee elected to sitt as representatives in the Generall assembly from time to time for the several Cittys, Towns, Countyes, Shires, or divisions of this province, and all places within the same shall bee according to the proporcon and number hereafter expressed—That is to say—For the city and county of New-York four—For the county of Suffolk two—For Queen's county two—For King's county two—For the county of Richmond one—For the county of Westchester one—For the county of Ulster two—For the county of Albany two—And for Schanectade, within the said county, one—For Duke's county one—For the county of Cornwall one.

"And as many more as his Royall Highness shall think fit to establish.

"Thatt all persons chosen and assembled in manner aforesaid, or the major part of them, shall be deemed and accounted the representatives of this province, which said representatives, together with the Governor and his councell, shall forever be the supream and only legislative power under his Roy'll Highnesse, of the said province—

"Thatt the said representatives may appoint their own times of meeting during their sessions, and may adjourne their house, from time to time, to such time as to them shall seem meet and convenient.

"Thatt the said representatives are the sole Judges of the Quallificacons of their own members, and likewise of all undue elections, and may, from time to time, purge their house as they shall see occasion dureing the said sessions.

"Thatt no Member of the Generall Assembly, or their servants, during the time of their sessions, whilest they shall be going to, and returning from the said assembly, shall be arrested, sued, imprisoned, or any wayes molested or troubled, nor bee compelled to make answer to any suite, bill, plaint, declaracon or otherwise, cases of High treason and felony only excepted—*provided* the number of the said servants shall not exceed three.

"Thatt all bills agreed upon by the said Representatives, or the major part of them, shall bee presented unto the Governour and his councell for their approbacon and consent, all and every which said bills so approved of and consented to by the Governor and his Councell, shall bee esteemed the Lawes of the province which said lawes shall continue and remaine in force until they shall bee repeeled by the Authority aforesaid; That is to say, The Governour, Councell, and Representatives in Generall Assembly, by and with the approbation of his Royal Highnesse, or expire by their own limitations.

"Thatt in all cases of death or removeall of any of the said Representatives, the Governour shall issue out summons by Writt to the respective Townes, Cittyes, Shires, Countyes or Divisions for which hee or they so removed or deceased were chosen, willing and requiring the ffreeholders of the same to elect others in their place and stead.

"Thatt no ffreeman shall bee taken and imprisoned, or bee disseized of his ffreehold or liberty, or free customes, or bee outlawed or exiled, or any other wayes destroyed, nor shall be passed upon, adjudged or condemned, butt by the lawfull judgment of his peers, and by the law of this province, justice nor right shall bee neither sold, denyed, or deferred to any man within this province.

"Thatt no aid, tax, tallage, assessment, custom, loane, benevolence, or imposition whattsoever, shall bee layed, assessed, imposed, or levyed on any of his Ma'ties subjects within this province, or their Estates uppon any Manner of colour or pretence, butt by the act and consent of the Governor, councell and representatives of the people in generall assembly mett and assembled.

"Thatt no Man, of whatt Estate or Condicon soever, shall be putt out of his lands or tenements, nor taken nor imprisoned nor disinherretted, nor banished, nor any wayes destroyed without being brought to answer by due course of law.

"Thatt a ffreeman shall not bee amerced for a small fault, butt after the manner of his fault, and for a great fault after the greatnesse thereof, saving to him his ffreehold, and a husbandman saving to him his wainage, and a merchant likewise saving to him his Merchandize, and none of the said amerciaments shall bee assessed butt by the oath of twelve honest and lawful men of the vicinage—*provided* the faults and misdemeanours be not in contempt of courts of Judicature.

"All tryalls shall bee by the Verdict of twelve men, and as near as may bee, Peers or Equalls of the Neighbourhood, and in the County, Shire, or Division where the fact shall arise or grow, whether the same bee by Indictment, Informacon, Declaracon, or otherwise, against the person, offender, or defendant.

"Thatt in all cases capitall or criminall, there shall be a grand Inquest, who shall first present the Offence, and then twelve Men of the Neighbourhood to try the Offender, who after his plea to the Indictment, shall be allowed his reasonable challenges.

"Thatt in all cases whatsoever Bayle, by sufficient suretys, shall be allowed and taken, unlesse for Treason or ffelony plainly and specially expressed and menconed in the Warrant of Commitment; *Provided alwayes*, thatt nothing herein conteyned shall extend to discharge out of prison, uppon Baile, any person taken in execucon for debts, or otherwise legally sentenced by the judgment of any of the Courts of Record within this province.

"Thatt no ffreeman shall be compelled to receive any marriners or souldiers into his house, and there suffer them to sojourne against their wills; *Provided always*, it be not in time of actuall war within this province.

"Thatt no commissions for proceeding by martiall law ag'st any of his Ma'ties subjects, within this province, shall issue forth to any person or persons whatsoever, least by colour of them any of his Ma'ties subjects bee destroyed or putt to death, except all such officers, persons and souldiers in pay throughout the Government.

"That from henceforward no lands within this province shall be esteemed or accounted a chattle or personall Estate, but an Estate of Inheritance according to the customes and practice of his Majestye's realme of England.

"Thatt no Court or Courts within this province have, or att any time hereafter shall have any Jurisdiccon, power or authority, to grant out any execucon or other writt, whereby any man's land may bee sold, or any other way disposed of, without the owner's consent; *Provided alwayes*, that the issues or meane proffitts of any man's land shall or may bee extended by execucon or otherwise, to sattisfy just debts, any thing to the contrary hereof in any wise nottwithstanding.

"Thatt no Estate of a ffeme covert shall be sold or conveyed butt by deed acknowledged by her in some Court of Record, the woman being secretly examined, if shee doth itt freely without threats or compulsion of her husband.

"Thatt all wills in Writing attested by two credible Witnesses, shall be of the same force to convey lands as other Conveyances being registered in the Secretarye's office within fforty days after the testator's death.

"Thatt a Widdow, after the death of her Husband, shall have her dower, and shall and may tarry in the chiefe house of her husband forty days after the death of her husband, within which forty days her dower shall bee assigned her, and for her dower shall bee assigned unto her the third part of all the lands of her husband during coverture, except shee were endowed of lesse before marriage.

"That all lands and heritages within this province and dependencyes, shall bee free from all ffines and lycences upon alienacons, and from all heriotts, wardships, liverys, primier seizins, year, day, and wast, escheats, and forfeittures upon the death of parents or ancestors, naturall, unnaturall, casuall or judiciall, and thatt for ever; cases of High Treason only excepted.

"Thatt no person or persons, which proffesse ffaith in God by Jesus Christ, shall, at any time, be any wayes molested, punished, disquieted, or called in question for any difference in opinion or matter of religious concernment, who do nott actually disturbe the civill peace of the province, butt thatt all and every such person or p'sons may, from time, and at all times freely have and fully enjoy, his or their judgments or consciences in matters of religion throughout all the province, they behaving themselves peaceably and quietly, and nott using this liberty to Lycenciousnesse, nor to the civill injury or outward disturbance of others; *Provided always*, Thatt this liberty, or any thing conteyned therein to the contrary, shall never be construed or improved to make void the settlement of any publique minister on Long Island, whether such settlement bee by two thirds of the voices in any Towne thereon, which shall alwayes include the minor part; or by subscriptions of perticular inhabitants in said townes; *Provided*, they are the two thirds thereof: *Butt* thatt all such agreements, covenants and subscriptions thatt are there already made and had, or thatt hereafter shall bee in this manner consented to, agreed and subscribed, shall att all time and times hereafter, bee firm and stable; and in confirmation hereof, it is enacted by the Governour, Councell, and Representatives, That all such summs of money so agreed on, consented to, or subscribed as aforesaid, for maintenance of said publique ministers, by the two thirds of any towne on Long Island, shall alwayes include the minor part, who shall bee regulated thereby: and also such subscriptions and agreements as are beforemenconed, are and shall bee alwayes ratifyd, performed and payd, and if any towne on said Island, in their publique capacity of agreement with any such minister or any perticular persons, by their private subscriptions as aforesaid, shall make default, deny, or withdraw from such payments so covenanted to, agreed upon, and subscribed, thatt in such case, upon complaint of any Collector appointed and chosen by two thirds of such towne upon Long Island, unto any Justice of thatt County, upon his hearing the same, he is hereby authorized, impowered, and required to issue out his warrant unto the constable or his deputy, or any other person appointed for the collection of said rates or agreement, to levy upon the goods and chattells of said delinquent or defaulter, all such summes of money so covenanted and agreed to be paid, by distresse, with costs and charges, without any further suit in law, any law, custome or usage to the contrary in any wise notwithstanding; *Provided always*, the said summe or summes bee under fforty shillings, otherwise to be recovered as the law directs.

"*And whereas* all the respective Christian Churches now in practice within the Citty of New-Yorke, and the other places of this province, do appear to bee priviledged Churches, and have been so established and confirmed by the former authority of this Government; *Bee it hereby enacted by this present Generall Assembly, and by the Authority thereof*, That all the said respective Christian Churches be hereby confirmed therein, and thatt they and every of them shall from henceforth, forever, be held and reputed as priviledged churches, and enjoy all their former freedomes of their religion in divine worship and church discipline; and thatt all former contracts made and agreed on for the maintenances of the several ministers of the said Churches, shall stand and continue in full force and vertue, and thatt all contracts for the future to bee made, shall be of the same power; and all p'sons that are unwilling to performe their part of the said contract, shall bee constrained thereunto by a warrant from any Justice of the Peace; *Provided* itt bee under forty shillings, or otherwise, as the law directs; *Provided allso*, That all other Christian Churches that shall hereafter come and settle within this province, shall have the same priviledges.

"*A continued* bill for defraying the requisite charges of the government.

[This *continued* bill grants certain duties on liquors, merchandizes, &c. to the Governor, for the support of government, and is on the same engrossed bill with the foregoing "charter of libertys," &c. and passed with it.]

"New-Yorke, Oct. 26, 1683.

"The Representatives have assented to this bill, and order it to bee sent up to the Governo'r and Councell for their assent. M. NICOLLS, Speaker."

"After three times reading, it is assented to by the Governour and Councell this thirtieth of October, 1683. THO. DONGAN.

"John Spragge, Clerk of the Assembly."

MSS. in Secretary's office, Albany; New York Revised Laws, 1813, ii., *Appendix*, iii.-vi.; *Colonial Documents*, iii., 357-359.

NOTE F, CHAPTER X., PAGE 506.

It would seem, from the printed minutes of "The Acts and Proceedings of the General Synod of the REFORMED PROTESTANT DUTCH CHURCH IN NORTH AMERICA" for the years 1866, 1867, 1868, and 1869, that that venerable body deliberately perpetrated one of the grossest outrages on American history ever done in this country. The Synod, after debate, and against the protest of some of the most devoted friends of the Church, resolved that the words "Dutch" and "Protestant" were not proper words to be retained in its title. Noisy and active members of the Synod denounced those words as "foreign," and not "American." Yet the oldest ecclesiastical body of Christians in our country is the one which has so persistently rejected these expressive designations. To say that the Church which Holland planted in America is not a "Dutch" Church, is to affirm a falsehood. To deny that that Dutch-American Church was a "Protestant" Church, is to reiterate an historical lie.

By this action of the venerable Synod of the Reformed Protestant Dutch Church in North America the history of our country has been belied. Ever since the surrender by the Dutch of New Netherland to the English, the Church which the Fatherland planted in New York was known and distinguished as a "Dutch" Church. Certainly it was a "Protestant" Church. How could it be otherwise? The blood of the martyrs in the "Dutch Republic" who resisted Alva must have been wretchedly diluted when any of their descendants in America could shrink from calling themselves "Dutch" and "Protestant."

In a vigorous memorial against the proposed change of this old "denomination," some members of it set forth their objections to the alteration of the name of the Church of their fathers. Their objections baffled, for a time, the synodical machinations of those who wished to destroy the identity of their ancient body. Its name was first officially given in the memorial which Domine Selyns, of New York, and his Consistory, offered to Governor Dongan in 1688. It was confirmed by a charter which Governor Fletcher granted to the metropolitan corporation in 1696, under the title of "The Minister, Elders, and Deacons of the Reformed Protestant Dutch Church in New York." This is the oldest religious corporation in our country. It still retains its honorable historical name. Yet, under foolish guidance, its superior ecclesiastical authority, in the full light of day, rejected the words "Dutch" and "Protestant" from the title of an act by which the Legislature of the State of New York, in 1819, authorized "*The General Synod of the Reformed Protestant Dutch Church*" in North America to hold estate.

The memorial to the Legislature of New York, referred to above, presented in its session of 1868, stated the history of the Dutch Church in this country, and showed, among other things, that the resolution of the Synod to change its corporate name to that of "*The Reformed Church in America*" was the impudent appropriation of an ecclesiastical designation which might rightfully be shared by those "Reformed" Churches which French and German Protestants planted here, after the Dutch established theirs. This memorial was met by scurrility from some who called themselves "Christian." Nevertheless, the Legislature would not sanction the proposed synodical change of name in 1868. But, as a preponderating majority of Dutch Churchmen chose to follow those leaders who insisted on the change, controversy was abandoned, and the Legislature, in 1869, passed the desired law.

The Acts and Proceedings of the Reformed Protestant Dutch Church, 1866–1869; *Historical Magazine for May*, 1868, pp. 268–270; *Hoffman's Ecclesiastical Law in the State of New York*, pp. 98–129.

Note G, Chapter XI., page 540.

The following is a copy of the Circular Letter of the English Privy Council to the several Colonial Governors:

After our very hearty commendations:—*Whereas*, William and Mary, Prince and Princess of Orange, have, with the consent and at the desire of the Lords Spiritual and Temporal, in Parliament Assembled at Westminster, been proclaimed King and Queen of England, France and Ireland, and of the Territories and Dominions thereunto appertaining; We have thought fit hereby to signify the same unto you, with directions that with the Council and other principal officers and inhabitants of [Virginia] you proclaim their most sacred Majestys, according to the form here inclosed [see N. Y. Col. Doc., iii., 605], with the solemnities and ceremonies requisite on the like occasion. And we do further transmit unto you their Majestys most gracious Proclamation, signifying their Majesty's pleasure that all men being in offices of Government shall so continue, until their Majesty's further pleasure be known. We do in like manner will and require you forthwith to cause to be proclaimed and published, as also that you do give order that the oaths herewith sent, be taken by all persons of whom the oaths of Supremacy and Allegiance might heretofore have been required; and that the said oaths of Allegiance and Supremacy be set aside and abrogated within your government. And so, &c. &c. &c.

From the Council Chamber, the 19th February, 1688–9.

Halifax, C. P. S.	Shrewsbury,	Macclesfield,
Bath,	H. Capel,	J. Boscawen,
Winchester,	Devonshire,	Delamere,
R° Howard,	R. Hampden.	

The foregoing dispatch was sent to, and acted on, in Virginia, and in Pennsylvania; and it would surely have been obeyed by Andros, if he had received it, in New England. Compare N. Y. Col. Doc., iii., 572, 583, 587, 588, 605; *Chalmers*, i., 431, 469; ii., *in N. Y. H. S. Coll.* (1868), 37; *Anderson's Colonial Church*, ii., 381, 382; *Penn. Col. Rec.*, i., 340, 341; *Historical Magazine, January*, 1867, p. 10.

Note H, Chapter XI., page 548.

The following is a copy of the Proclamation of Governor General Andros, dated at Fort Charles, at Pemaquid, on the 10th of January, 1688–9:

BY HIS EXCELLENCY

A

PROCLAMATION.

WHEREAS His MAJESTY hath been graciously pleased, by His Royal Letter, bearing Date the sixteenth day of October last past, to signifie that he hath received undoubted Advice that a great and sudden Invasion from *Holland*, with an armed Force of Forreigners and Strangers, will speedily be made in an hostile manner upon His Majesty's Kingdom of *ENGLAND;* and that altho' some *false* pretences relating to *Liberty, Property*, and *Religion*, (contrived or worded with Art and Subtilty) may be given out, (as shall be thought useful upon such an Attempt;) It is manifest however, (considering the great Preparations that are making) That no less matter by this *Invasion* is proposed and purposed, than an absolute Conquest of His Majesty's Kingdoms, and the utter Subduing and Subjecting His Majesty and all His People to a Forreign Power, which is promoted (as His Majesty understands) altho' it may seem almost incredible) by some of His Majesty's *Subjects*, being persons of wicked and restless Spirits, implacable Malice, and desperate Designs, who having no sence of former intestine Distractions, (the Memory and Misery whereof should endear and put a Value upon that Peace and Happiness which hath long been enjoyed) nor being moved by His Majesty's reiterated Acts of Grace and Mercy, (wherein His Majesty hath studied and delighted to abound towards all His Subjects, and even towards *those* who were once His Majesty's avowed and open *Enemies*) do again endeavour to embroil His Majesty's Kingdom in Blood and Ruin, to gratifie their own Ambition and Malice, proposing to themselves a Prey and Booty in such a publick Confusion:

And that although His Majesty had Notice that a forreign Force was preparing against Him, yet His Majesty hath alwaies declined any forreign Succour, but rather hath chosen (next under GOD) to rely upon the true and ancient Courage, Faith and Allegiance of His own People, with whom His Majesty hath often ventured His Life for the Honour of His Nation, and in whose Defence against all Enemies His Majesty is firmly resolved to live and dye; and therefore does solemnly *Conjure* His Subjects to lay aside all manner of Animosities, Jealousies, & Prejudices, and heartily & chearfully to *Unite together* in the Defence of His *MAJESTY* and their native Countrey, which thing alone, will (under GOD) defeat and frustrate the principal Hope and Design of His Majesty's Enemies, who expect to find His People divided; and by publishing (perhaps) some plausible Reasons of their Coming, as the specious (tho' *false*) Pretences of Maintaining the Protestant Religion, or Asserting the Liberties and Properties of His Majesty's People, do hope thereby to conquer that great and renowned Kingdom.

That albeit the Design hath been carried on with all imaginable Secresie & Endeavours to surprise and deceive His *MAJESTY*, HE hath not been wanting on His part to make such provision as did become Him, and, by GOD's great Blessing, His Majesty makes no doubt of being found in so good a Posture that His Enemies may have cause to repent such their rash and *unjust* Attempt. ALL WHICH, it is His Majesty's pleasure, should be made known in the most publick manner to His loving Subjects within this His Territory and Dominion of *NEW-ENGLAND*, that they may be the better prepared to resist any Attempts that may be made by His Majesties Enemies in these parts, and secured in their trade and Commerce with His Majesty's Kingdom of *England*.

I Do therefore, in pursuance of His *MAJESTYs* Commands, by these Presents *make known* and *Publish* the same accordingly: And hereby Charge and Command all Officers Civil & Military, and all other His Majesty's loving Subjects within this His Territory and Dominion aforesaid, to be *Vigilant* and *Careful* in their respective places and stations, and that, upon the Approach of any Fleet or Forreign Force, they be in Readiness, and use their utmost Endeavour to hinder any Landing or Invasion that may be intended to be made within the same.

Given at *Fort-Charles* at *Pemaquid*, the Tenth Day of *January*, in the Fourth year of the Reign of our Sovereign Lord *JAMES* the Second, of *England, Scotland, France* and *Ireland* KING, Defender of the Faith *&c.* Annoq; DOMINI 1688.

By, His EXCELLENCY's *Command.* E ANDROS.

JOHN WEST. d'y. Secr'.

GOD *SAVE THE* KING.

Printed at Boston in New-England by R. P.

INDEX.

THE END.

www.ingramcontent.com/pod-product-compliance
Lightning Source LLC
LaVergne TN
LVHW021047110826
845150LV00001B/4

* 9 7 8 1 4 2 5 5 6 8 5 5 9 *